The American Family

THE
AMERICAN
FAMILY

RUTH SHONLE CAVAN

Associate Professor of Sociology
on the Jane Addams Foundation
Rockford College

1955

THOMAS Y. CROWELL COMPANY - New York

MANUFACTURED IN THE UNITED STATES OF AMERICA
BY THE VAIL-BALLOU PRESS, INC., BINGHAMTON, N.Y.

Preface

This book supersedes the author's earlier text, *The Family*, published eleven years ago. Although it is written from the same sociopsychological point of view and in part follows the same organization, it is a successor to, rather than a revision of, the earlier text.

The basic thesis of the book is that the family has developed its ideals and forms in interaction with other parts of the social order. Hence, the book opens with a discussion of this relationship and of nine issues that have resulted from the unequal rates of change of the family and other institutions and from the inability of people to change their values as quickly as they change their behavior.

Part One in addition to presenting the unsolved issues also lays before the reader the general societal changes from which the issues emerged: the transition from an agrarian rural to an industrialized urban society, with the accompanying heavy migration of rural-reared people into individualized impersonal city life.

Part Two stresses the importance of social classes and ethnic groups for family life. The partial social isolation of these groups and the socialization of children in class and ethnic culture coupled with social mobility and intermarriage in adulthood create further conflicts between values and behavior patterns.

Parts One and Two form the backdrop for the portrayal of marital and family interaction, which is the subject of Part Three, The Cycle of Family Life. From adolescence to old age, subjects pertinent to marriage and family life are discussed. The material is organized chiefly around three concepts: changing concepts and values in the realms of heterosexual adjustment, love, sex, marriage, parenthood, divorce, and old age; roles and their coordination from the dating teen-age partners to the grandparents; and the satisfaction of personal needs, ranging from sex to psychological identification, in the family. The central figures in the discussion are husband and wife; since they are also parents, their roles in this capacity are included.

Two social situations—economic change and war—are so persistent in recurrence and have recently affected the family so severely that they have been given special attention.

In the final chapter the discussion comes again to the subject of Chapter 1—the issues resulting from rapid and uneven social change. An attempt is made to discover and evaluate the present degree of reintegration of the family into society. Amelioration is recognized as a stopgap rather than an indication of true social integration. Constructive aids are found in education, counseling, and the findings of research.

Selected bibliographies and questions follow each chapter. Topics for term papers and research projects, however, are contained in Appendix B without attempt to relate them to specific chapters.

Appreciation is extended to students at Rockford College and the 1951 summer session at the University of Michigan, whose reactions to various preliminary drafts of the book were of aid in revisions, to Mrs. Robert Foeller for the careful preparation of graphs, and to the many publishers who consented to the use of quotations.

RUTH SHONLE CAVAN

Rockford, Illinois
November 15, 1952

Contents

PART TWO

SOCIAL CONFIGURATIONS OF THE AMERICAN FAMILY

PART THREE

THE CYCLE OF FAMILY LIFE

Figures and Tables

FIGURES

TABLES

PART ONE

The Present Status of
the American Family

1

Issues in the American Family at the Mid-Century

The American family has two important aspects: as a social institution charged with important functions related to the public welfare; and as a mode of personal living for husband, wife, and children. As an institution the family is called upon to support some of the most fundamental traditional values of American society: legitimate birth of a sufficient number of children to ensure continuation of the society; the training and personality development of these children by their parents; regularization of sexual relations; and satisfaction of a great variety of emotional, social, and physical needs of adults and children. Support of these values has not been left to the good will of adults; laws establish the means by which they shall be accomplished. Typical are the laws that require physical examinations for venereal disease before marriage, stipulate the age of marriage, provide for a marriage license and ceremony and for public registration of the marriage and of the births of children, punish non-marital sex relations, and regulate divorce. The object of these laws is to place upon the family as an institution certain obligations that contribute to the integration of society. In addition, mores upheld by public opinion and social pressures supplement the laws. Every community and neighborhood has standards demanded of married couples and of parents. The laws and mores express the values concretely in definite expectations or social norms, and implement their accomplishment.

As a mode of personal living the family appeals to husband, wife, and children not as a formal institution but as an informal and intimate group supplying many of their personal needs. Institutionally, this group is held together by the legal technicalities and social obligations listed above; as an intimate group it is held together by affection, dependence of the

3

members on each other for the fulfillment of many emotional needs, satisfaction of utilitarian necessities, and often by habit.   When these needs are adequately met, the family members are happy, and it is now quite common for people to say that happiness is the chief thing they expect to get from marriage.

The institutional and personal aspects of marriage and family life are interrelated.   Social approval is denied to those who seek to grasp the personal privileges and intimate relationships of family life without entering into the institutional pattern.   Social disapproval and often legal penalties are directed against the unmarried person who assumes such marital privileges as sex relations or living with another as spouse.   Those who knowingly enter bigamous marriages are subject to the criminal law and usually suffer imprisonment.   Although conception of a child outside of marriage may not merit criminal punishment for the parents, it occasions extreme social disapproval.   Institutionally, marriage implies the acceptance of responsibilities toward the marital partner and children. The social norms decree that those who are unwilling to accept the responsibilities should be denied the privileges.   Most men and women fit their personal married lives within the basic confines of law and custom sufficiently well to avoid serious penalties.   Many, however, place personal happiness and convenience above the social values inherent in the family and thus create a situation of confusion and conflict.

The personal and the institutional aspects of marriage, found in all societies as far back as written records exist, do not always have the same relative importance in public opinion.   In the United States at the present time the personal aspect of marriage—personal happiness—challenges the importance of the institutional demands directed toward general social welfare.   Although the family in the United States has never been so highly institutionalized as in some societies, it was much more so in the past than at present.   In some other societies the family is so completely institutionalized that all arrangements for marriage are made by the parents (or even grandparents) with the betrothed couple perhaps not seeing each other until the hour of the ceremony.   This arrangement often occurs in societies where the family is of supreme strength, drawing to itself economic and political functions as well as biological and personal.   Selections of husband and wife are made in terms of appropriate family status, economic resources, and the health and character of the young person; less attention is given to beauty and virtually none to personal preferences of the young people themselves.   The bride and groom are expected to work out their personal relationships as best they can after marriage—a task not too difficult in a stable group where prescribed roles, attitudes, and conduct are the rule.   The traditional Chinese family provides an excellent example of the highly institutionalized family.   The early American family, as an outgrowth of English customs, was well institutionalized, but under the impact of a wilderness to be settled it developed a distinctive pattern of its own in which personal choices had a place.   In the course of time and social development, personal considerations have come to predominate over social considerations.

INTEGRATION OR CONFLICT

Ideally the three factors so far mentioned—the values, the social norms that embody the values, and the actual conduct of people—should be integrated.   Such a coordination reaches near-perfection in stable, homogeneous societies where there are little change of social conditions and no conflicting subcultures.   The United States does not now meet, and in fact never has met, these preconditions for coordination.   Variety of physical resources, change through inventions, and the constant introduction of ethnic groups with distinctive cultures have prevented complete integration of the three factors at any time with reference to the family or other institutions.   The past, however, was relatively stable and homogeneous as compared with the last 50 or 75 years and permitted greater agreement between the three factors than at present.   Moreover, changes have occurred so rapidly in the recent period that conflict at times flares up between traditional social norms and actual conduct.

In general, integration and conflict fall into an alternating sequence, correlated with social changes.   The sequence may be outlined as follows, with stability of marriage as the value that is in process of change.

1. Relatively stable social situation: The rural situation of 75 to 100 years ago was relatively stable.

2. Integration of values, norms, and social behavior, with strong social approval of conformity and disapproval of violations: The rural family was a strong, semi-institutionalized organization, formed through legal marriage, lasting a lifetime, and performing many functions.

3. Change of social situation from rural to urban: In cities, many institutions have taken over former functions of the family, thus weakening

it; neighborhood controls are weakened; the family is less necessary for survival or fulfillment of needs.

4. Nonsocialized or individualized behavior: When the old rural patterns and means of control break down, the way is opened for individualized behavior, sometimes of a bizarre nature. Unmarried couples may experiment with premarital intercourse or trial marriage; marriage partners choose each other on a personal basis with little regard for the responsibilities of married life; contraceptives are used to avoid or limit the births of children; divorces are sought for personal reasons with little regard to the effect on children. Among the more bizarre types of behavior that occasionally arise are the rare clubs of adolescents that demand intercourse as a requirement for membership, circles of married couples who exchange husbands and wives for a night or a week end, and acceptance by both husband and wife that each should have freedom for sexual affairs with other companions.

5. Clash of old norms and individualized behavior (No. 2 versus No. 4): There has been and still is wide disapproval of types of behavior stated under No. 4. Attempts are made to enforce a waiting period between application for a marriage license and marriage, to tighten application of divorce laws, and to make the laws themselves more restrictive. Families are blamed for juvenile delinquency and for adolescent freedom that may lead to premarital intercourse. Well-organized religious and other groups exhort the family to hold fast to the older values and norms.

6. Modification of values, norms, and behavior to fit the new social situation: Gradually, responsible groups begin to examine the entire situation and to think through the problem of adjustment of the family to urban life. Instead of berating the family for not following the older rural pattern, they seek to formulate a new standard for the family adapted to the urban situation. American society is now entering this stage in the sequence of change. Family functions are being redefined, and other agencies are modifying their programs to aid the family: for example, to assist young people to meet companionable friends, to prepare them for marriage through courses in school or informal discussion groups, and to counsel confused husbands and wives. The value of permanent marriage is being reasserted, but with a new standard for stability—to give lasting happiness for the couple and a secure environment for children.

7. Reintegration of the family into society: This stage has not been reached in American society, partly because the modifications given above

have not been uniformly accepted and partly because other institutions have not sufficiently modified their programs to give support to the new trend in the family.

At present the United States is in the throes of conflict between marital and family norms bred from the rural social conditions of the past century and new modes of conduct spawned by present industrial urbanization, which are not as yet well controlled by new social norms. The conflicts create issues of great social importance involving not only personal happiness but also social well-being. The need is great to understand these issues to the end that some rational control may aid and accelerate the slow natural processes of readjustment.

CONFLICT BETWEEN SOCIAL NORMS AND CONDUCT

Comparison of the present marital and family patterns with the social norms inherited from the past reveals where the current issues lie.

The basic meaning of marriage

Fundamental to marital practices is the basic conception or norm of marriage that is held by a society. In the United States in the past century a strong belief inhered in marriage as a sacred, divine, and holy institution entered into as a permanent relationship. Marriage was instituted by God and not to be tampered with by man, and its chief purposes were regulation of sex and the production and care of children; this view was upheld by both the Protestant and Catholic religions. Debate over this point of view was strong in the last quarter of the nineteenth century, primarily in connection with the increased rate of divorce, since divorce constituted a definite tampering by man with marriage. The clergy was generally forbidden to perform the marriage service for a divorced person. Although many denominations have altered their stand to the extent that the clergy may now marry divorced persons, the Catholic Church, with its 25 million adherents, still maintains the view that the family is regulated both by natural and divine laws and opposes divorce as a bold attempt by man to interfere with divine laws.

As the concept of marriage as sacred and inviolable yielded before contrary opinions, it tended to be replaced by the idea that marriage was a social obligation. The social functions attributed to marriage were similar to those supported by the earlier concept—regulation of sex and the production and rearing of children. It was asserted that security of persons, and of family life, demanded restrained sex activities and the strength of the nation depended upon maintenance or increase of the population. Social obligations related to family purposes as well as to the larger society; through marriage and children the family name was perpetuated and property, such as a family farm or business, might be passed on to succeeding generations.

Both the sacred and the social concepts placed emphasis upon the relation of marriage to the larger society and minimized the happiness of the individual members as the chief goal of marriage. Marriage and family life were end-values to society and not means by which individuals gained happiness for themselves. The sacred and social concepts were supported by some degree of necessity, for they were the outgrowth of a social situation in which the family was a strong institution with exclusive functions encompassing the production and preparation of food, the provision of shelter, care of the ill and old, the making and laundering of clothing, childbirth care, the rearing of children, the furnishing of physical protection, and many others. Since few institutions existed to supplement the family, not only social welfare but personal survival depended upon a strong and continuing family life.

However, the social concept of marriage, unlike the sacred, allowed room for a strong secondary motive of personal happiness. Without happiness, and especially with conflict, the family could not function for social betterment, the argument ran. Husband and wife would refuse to play their roles and achieve the desired functions, and children's lives would be warped or ruined if parental concord was absent.

As the necessity for the family to perform utilitarian functions declined, less was said about marriage as a social obligation. This concept, current from about 1880 to 1920, was challenged by a third concept and one strongly held at present: that marriage exists primarily for the personal happiness of husband and wife. If happiness is accomplished, the marriage is successful. Sacred values are left to the church; social values to a number of other agencies.

Thus, at the present time three concepts of marriage exist: the sacred, the social, and the personal. The sacred concept is usually limited to strongly organized groups, such as a religion, which through control of its members succeeds in bringing marital and family conduct into rather close coordination with the ideal norm. The social concept is supported by many religious groups, which, having abandoned the strictly sacred interpretation, uphold the social. As far as individuals are concerned, they now feel free to choose among the sacred, social, and personal interpretations and may even apply the social concept to one phase of married life and the personal concept to another. For example, the wife may insist upon the earlier-formulated social obligation that her husband should support her, simultaneously on the basis of personal preference rejecting care of the home, which was her complement to support, in favor of paid employment, the funds from which she uses for personal pleasure.

At present, therefore, there is no uniformity of opinion as to the basic meaning of marriage. Different institutions support conflicting views, and many unaffiliated people attempt to work out an individual concept, or simply try to solve each marital problem as it arises without a clear idea of the basic meaning of marriage to either society or themselves.

The issue is clear: What is the purpose of marriage? Is marriage primarily to accomplish certain religious values? Is it to support the social order? Is its main purpose personal happiness of husband and wife? Or should marriage and family life contribute to all three functions? If so, how may the three functions best be coordinated?

Should marriage be a permanent or a temporal relationship?

Lifelong permanence of marriage was a fixed corollary of the sacred concept of marriage and was strongly upheld by the social concept. At marriage a couple accepted sacred and social obligations for life, which they could not wantonly lay aside. If they found the relationship an unhappy one or if one spouse violated marital obligations, the one who suffered would be purified through pain but was not justified in terminating the marriage.

This attitude supporting the permanence of marriage began to break up after the Civil War, and divorce became a hotly debated issue about which there is not yet complete agreement. Although divorce laws have changed very little in this period of time (most of the minor changes have tightened the laws), their use as a means of terminating marriage has greatly increased. The consternation at present over the high divorce rate might imply that this increase is of recent origin. Actually, the increase began even prior to the Civil War, although it has been more spectacular in recent periods. Divorce was at first justified by the argument that the marriage contract was not sacred but civil: that its purpose was not to fulfill some divine plan and not solely for the social welfare, but also for the more limited well-being of husband, wife, and children. If the marriage did not work out happily, it could not fulfill its social functions with reference either to society or the family. It was immoral to continue a nonfunctioning marriage, and a divorce, far from being immoral, was actually moral.

Thus it was held that the primary purpose of marital termination was to rectify an intolerable social situation; it definitely was not for the purpose of freeing husband or wife and clearing the way for a second marriage. Some states provided for legal separation without terminating the marriage bond, an anomolous situation that prohibited full married life without freeing either party for a remarriage. Except for a limited period of time related to pioneer conditions, all state laws listed the violations of marital life for which a divorce might be obtained. The procedure of obtaining a divorce required one spouse to prove in court that the other had committed some act that fell within the stated violations or causes for divorce. The accused person was thus held up to public scorn as having failed in his obligations. (Although the same state laws are still in force, and the same formalities must be observed, the meaning of divorce proceedings has greatly changed.) Public opinion held that remarriage was a right only of the innocent party and that a proposal of marriage from a divorced man was an insult to the woman. The clergy generally refused to marry divorced persons, although a justice of the peace or judge would do so. In general divorce was widely disapproved, and even the innocent party often was subjected to social ostracism that might extend to the children of the divorced couple.

Gradually the opposition to divorce lessened, and new interpretations were voiced. From about 1900 to 1920 it was regarded as a necessary evil comparable to a surgical operation: avoided if possible, and always regretted, but in an intolerable situation regarded as justifiable.

Since the 1920's divorce has continued to increase except for temporary decreases related to the depression of the 1930's and the present postwar period, and with the increase another change in attitude has occurred. Many people now regard divorce as an individual "right" when one or both marital partners are dissatisfied with the marriage. It is not considered necessary that either partner shall have mistreated the other or violated the formal obligations of marriage by nonsupport or adultery;

it is sufficient that personal happiness has not resulted from the marriage. This is a conception of divorce related to the conception of marriage as for personal happiness.   Marriage as a civil contract has yielded to the conception of marriage as a personal contract to be entered into or broken at the will of the contracting parties without regard either to sacred or social obligations.   This conception of divorce also indicates a different attitude toward the permanence of marriage.   Whereas prior to 1920 permanent marriage was regarded as the norm, the preferred situation, present attitudes imply that in the future temporal marriage may come to be accepted as the norm, although it certainly has not yet reached such general approval.

The shift in attitude has been tremendous.   The family, formerly a unit strongly knit together, protecting, comforting, encouraging each member, forming a bulwark against the vicissitudes of life, and existing as long as its members lived, now tends to be thought of as a joining of two individuals, each of whom has, to be sure, a large stake in the undertaking but either of whom has tacit permission to withdraw if the marriage does not meet individual expectations.   Now, personal happiness and freedom from indignities and hardships take precedence over continuity of the family group.   Remarriages occur without prejudice.   Nor do those who remain married seriously disapprove of those who terminate their marriages.   Under other circumstances, might they not also have acted likewise?

The obvious result of the change in attitude toward the function of marriage and its lifelong permanence is the long-term trend of increase in the divorce rate.   Because divorces are a matter of public record and may be counted and compared year by year, they are often mistakenly seized upon as the primary cause of family instability, when they are actually only a result of changing attitudes toward family permanence, which rest in turn upon more fundamental changing conceptions of the values attached to family life.   Disapproval of divorce as such without appreciation of the attitudinal changes that underlie it leads only to fuzzy thinking, futile moralizing, and misguided attempts to tighten divorce laws.   These laws are no more lenient now than in times past; they do not determine family dissolution but merely recognize that such dissolution has occurred.   The significant factor is not increasing divorce but the change from a concept of the family as a permanent socially responsible unit to one of the family as an association of husband and wife for such a period of time as both believe the marriage contributes more to their personal happiness than would some other arrangement. Nevertheless, the trend in divorce rates points up the change in attitude as well as in behavior. Figure 1 shows the phenomenal increase since 1867, which is indicative of the growing opinion that marriage is for happiness rather than for life.

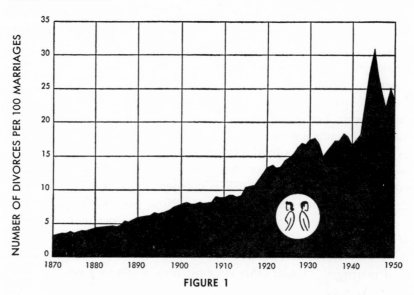

FIGURE 1

Divorces Granted per 100 Marriages Contracted in the Same Year

The ratio of divorces to marriages for the same year is a conventional way of expressing divorce rates. It means that for every 100 new marriages in a given year—say, 1950—a certain number of marriages were terminated by divorce—23 in 1950. The divorces in any year, however, rarely end marriages that occurred in the same year; the couples divorced in 1950 might have been married any number of years, with one third married less than five years. The decline in the rate after 1945 should not be interpreted as indicating a long-term trend; it is probably merely an adjustment to the more normal postwar conditions and in time will be followed by a slowly increasing rate. (Constructed from Appendix A, column IV.)

Concurrently with the development of a new attitude toward divorce, the aversion to divorced persons has changed to an attitude of acceptance, symbolized by the frequency with which divorced people remarry. One estimate places the proportion of divorced persons who remarry at more than 85 per cent.[1]   Another study shows that the rates of remarriage of divorced men and women are higher, age for age, than the rates of remarriage for the widowed, or the rates of first marriage for the single.[2]

At the same time, divorce still brings disapproval from some groups and much personal suffering.   The Catholic Church is still unalterably opposed to divorce, and certain Protestant denominations forbid their ministers to marry divorced persons.   Also, many persons suffer greatly from the experience of a divorce, and sometimes later regret it.

The issue again is clear: Should marriage be a temporal relationship; and, if so, under what conditions is divorce justified?

Should young people have a free hand in selecting a mate?

The choice of a mate has tended to shift from selection within a local community in-group to out-group selection.   In-group selection, which was a natural outcome of the rural community, is still characteristic of it. Before the 1920's and the advent of the automobile, each rural community tended to be socially self-contained.   Even now, when mobility has greatly increased, the movement is primarily away from the rural community toward the city, a movement that brings few new people into the small community but leaves a stable residue there.   In these rural areas mores developed that set standards for the preferred type of husband and wife, standards that tended to perpetuate the parental type.   To the extent that social classes existed in these small communities, each family taught its children to which class they belonged and who the other class members were.   Children were restricted in selecting their playmates, and adolescents in selecting their social group, to those who in the future would make acceptable spouses.   From the approved group in which membership had existed since the primary grade, each youth chose his mate.   Courtship tended to be brief and could safely be so, for the partners were already well known to each other and to the parental families.   The present long period of dating beginning in the early teens did not exist.   Girls who began to date early and to shift from boy to boy were regarded by the older generation as "flighty" and boys who sought out one girl after another as unsteady.   The social contacts of the teens were for the most

[1] Paul C. Glick, "First Marriages and Remarriages," *American Sociological Review*, 14 (1949), 730.

[2] "The Chances of Remarriage for the Widowed and Divorced," *Statistical Bulletin,* Metropolitan Life Insurance Company, 26 (May, 1945), 1–3.

part at church or school functions, often in affairs attended by entire families.   The adults watched at first hand the budding interests, curbing the undesirable ones and encouraging the desirable.   Only in drastically unsuitable alliances was the heavy parental hand laid upon the shoulder of the girl or youth.   The boy from a well-fixed family with a record of good behavior in school, an inclination to work steadily on the family farm or at Saturday and summer jobs, and the promise of work after leaving school in some store or on his father's or relative's farm was regarded as a desirable husband.   His wife needed the domestic skills that she learned from her mother, an interest in homemaking and children, an affiliation with the church and, if she belonged to the upper middle class, with the woman's club.   Falling in love grew gently out of the relationship.   Families and friends smiled on the couple, permitted a limited degree of love-making, provided the young couple with material goods in accordance with their means, and stood ready to assist if necessary in the early years of marriage.

As cities grew through the accretions of many young people from rural communities who were detached from family ties, family control and guidance necessarily declined.   Even families with long experience in urban life became less and less able to maintain supervision as cities grew and neighborhoods were replaced by widespread and impersonal contacts. When families stood in a position to influence the selection of the spouse, sober practical considerations of family status, potentiality of the girl for homemaking, future financial prospects of the young man, and steadiness of character of both were emphasized.   With the decline of in-group and family guidance, other factors have become dominant.   Personal attractiveness and appearance of the girl and attractiveness of the young man as well as his rating as a "good spender" often take precedence in young minds over practical considerations of stability and the ability to shoulder the responsibilities of marriage and children.

Those of widely different backgrounds may seem desirable on personal grounds or even because of the stimulating dissimilarity of conduct and attitudes.   Sometimes the marriage alienates the young couple completely from their families.   At other times, the young husband and wife find themselves unable to resolve their different cultural or religious outlooks even though they are strongly drawn to each other personally.   The adjustment that is finally made may involve each member of the family following his own beliefs, with resulting loss in family unity and failure to tie the children born to the new family firmly to the family or community institutions.

Some idea of the frequency of out-group marriages may be gained from statistics on interreligious and interethnic marriages. "During the decade 1940–1950," states one report, "mixed marriages sanctioned by Catholic nuptials approximated 30 per cent of all Catholic marriages in the United States"; [3] those not sanctioned by the Church would probably add another 10 per cent. Marriages between nationality or ethnic groups are to be expected as the groups become adjusted to American life and come into contact with each other. Nevertheless, noncompatible residual ethnic traits of husband and wife are thrown into sharp relief in the intimacy of family life and may lead to quarrels or to conflict over how the children shall be trained. Interethnic marriages account for 32 per cent of marriages involving ethnics in one rural Minnesota community.[4] Groups with long settlement in this country quite naturally have a higher percentage of interethnic marriages than do those more recently arrived.

Selection of the marital partner is now regarded as an individual right and often occurs on the basis of merely superficial acquaintance. Family, kinship, and community often stand aghast at these marriages. They feel that they dare not protest for fear their young people will turn against them and perhaps rush still more rapidly into marriage. A countermovement has been started by various social agencies that attempt to supervise social contacts of young people and to provide premarital education to help them in making wise selections.

Should sex relations be limited to marriage?

The social norms of the past sternly forbade sexual intimacies outside of marriage. Officially religion, law, and the popular mores allowed for no deviation. Unofficially there was partial recognition of a double standard whereby unmarried young men were condoned if they indulged in casual sex relations with women of uncertain morals. For these men sex had two connotations: especially in their youth, it was regarded as a right of virile young manhood and a source of physical pleasure; with marriage it assumed in addition social values in that children were desired and highly valued. For the girl of two generations ago, sex tended

[3] John L. Thomas, "The Factor of Religion in the Selection of Marriage Mates," *American Sociological Review*, 16 (1951), 488.
[4] Lowry Nelson, "Intermarriage among Nationality Groups in a Rural Area of Minnesota," *American Journal of Sociology*, 48 (1943), 589.

to have primarily the social value; many middle- and upper-class girls were reared with the idea that sex was "dirty," that a girl "submitted" because she owed this duty to her husband and also because it was the only means by which children might be attained.   Strict chastity for all women except a limited group of lower-class casuals and prostitutes was almost universal.   The girl who deviated from this code was pitied or reviled as a "fallen woman" who brought lasting shame and disgrace to herself and her family.

The trend has been away from these mores for some years.   Young women, seeking equality with men, have made the measure of that equality identity of privileges in a number of fields, including the same degree of freedom of sex expression accorded to men.

The increased sexual freedom between men and women of the same social status has led to a new conception of sex for both.   Now, young women look for personal satisfaction and pleasure in sex, similar to that long experienced by men.   In addition, for both men and women, sex has attained additional valuation as an expression of love and as a means of expanding the personality.   The social valuation related to children has not been lost, but it is no longer the only one for women, and often its aura has been dimmed by the decreased number of children in the modern family.   When the short period of childbearing has ended, other values than reproduction must be found for sex relations.

The separation of sex from childbearing in people's thinking and its accomplishment through the effective use of contraceptives implies the possible freeing of sex from marriage.   If sex has positive values in itself —if it is good and normal—why confine it to marriage?   Especially why is it not a justifiable part of courtship between two people in love with each other?   Many persons, who would regard it as reprehensible for a young unmarried couple to produce a child, are willing to condone premarital sexual relations and to regard them as the privilege of the two individuals involved.   Many others, concerned with family stability, fear the effect on the personalities of the young couple and the subsequent effect on the stability of their marriage.   Others condemn the act because it may result in conception.   Still others continue to hold the social code of the past: that sex outside of marriage is sinful and a highly immoral act.

Here then, is an unresolved issue of social, moral, and personal import with great emotional content: Are premarital sex relations ever justified and, if so, under what conditions?

Is it necessary for husband and wife to have complementary roles?

The family of our immediate past had developed roles for husband and wife that supplemented each other.   Children as they arrived also were immediately capped with ascribed roles, not only in relation to their parents but in relation to each other in terms of age, ordinal position, and sex.

The husband was the openly acknowledged head of the family, with well-defined duties: to earn or provide the living for his family, to provide the final but benevolent authority on matters of discipline and in decisions affecting the family as a whole, to maintain community contacts and to vote in community and national elections.   The wife was a junior partner, who contributed her opinions but accepted the decisions of her husband, who attended to the details of the household and the daily training of the young children, and who found her chief community outlets through the church and its attendant welfare activities.   On the farm and in the village her time was well filled with the necessities of family life.   In the cities some wives found it necessary to work to aid their husbands, but carried out this work in the same spirit that they did their housework, as a supplement to the husband's functions.   Sons were regarded with pride as the carriers of the family name and, if the husband owned a farm or business, as the future head of that venture.   Daughters were a source of satisfaction.   Well dressed and well mannered they proved the ability of the husband to care for his family and, in aiding their mother, added to his comfort.   Sons as future heads of families had higher status than daughters.   Even after college education for girls became an accepted fact, the family that could afford to send only one child to college sent a son, more or less regardless of the relative fitness of son or daughter for college achievement; likewise, inheritance might be unequally divided to favor the son.   Older children took precedence over younger, sometimes inheriting more and sharing with the parents the task of inducting the younger children into the social and family cultural heritage.   On the other hand, younger children were sometimes more indulged or received more educational privileges, as the financial pressure decreased with the adulthood and economic independence of the older children.

These roles were more or less predetermined, taught to the children by parents who had learned them from their parents, and therefore accepted by the children as final.   The community also upheld the roles, giving approval to adults and children who conformed, and reproving those who deviated. The stability of the coordinated pattern of roles gave to the family the attribute of dependability as a part of the social structure.

The trend has been away from fixed roles for all members of the family, but especially so for women. In fact during the period preceding World War I women became a storm center. With the more aggressive women organized into a militant feminist movement, a minority of women not

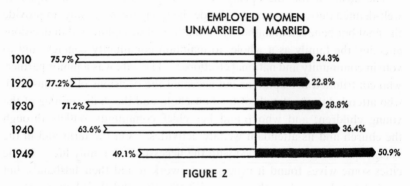

EMPLOYED WOMEN
UNMARRIED | MARRIED

1910   75.7% ⟩ ━━━━━━━━━━━━━━━━ ▶ 24.3%

1920   77.2% ⟩ ━━━━━━━━━━━━━━━ ▶ 22.8%

1930   71.2% ⟩ ━━━━━━━━━━━━━━━━ ▶ 28.8%

1940   63.6% ⟩ ━━━━━━━━━━━━━━ ▶ 36.4%

1949   49.1% ⟩ ━━━━━━━━━ ▶ 50.9%

FIGURE 2

Marital Status of Employed Women

Since 1910 the percentage of employed women who are married has more than doubled. (Source: "Marital Status of Women in the Labor Force, 1910–1949," chart published by Women's Bureau, U. S. Department of Labor.)

only adapted their roles to changed conditions but demanded new roles for themselves and sought to force those still content with the wife-and-mother role into roles previously the stronghold of men. Under the battle cry of equality, some women sought identity of activities with men, educationally, vocationally, politically, and in personal activities including minor and major vices. During the 1930's the situation tended to stabilize itself, but not around a new array of fixed roles. The stabilization was based on a choice of roles for women, with men more or less reluctantly conceding the right of a woman to make a choice, but not necessarily the obligation of man to accommodate himself if she chose other than the wife-and-mother role.

Men, therefore, have attempted to retain the older masculine role with its prerogatives of status and authority and its obligation of support and guidance of wife and children. Women, however, have been freed from complete necessity of following the traditional role, not only because of the liberating effects of the earlier feminist movement but also because the contemporaneous transfer of practical functions from the home to factory, school, hospital, retail store, and social agencies relieved her of many of her former tasks.   However, inasmuch as a unified new role common to all women did not develop, a woman today has a choice of roles, not only as between job or career and home, but among many types

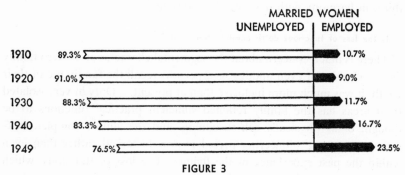

FIGURE 3

Employment Status of Married Women

This figure and the preceding one emphasize the growing tendency for women to acquire new nonfamily roles.   Since 1930 the increase in the proportion of married women who are employed has been spectacular.   At present one out of every four married women is employed.   Such employment changes the wife's relationship to her home duties and to each member of the family.   It calls for a new organization of the family and redefinition of the roles of other members.   (Source: "Married Women in Population and in Labor Force, 1910–1949," chart published by Women's Bureau, U. S. Department of Labor.)

of paid employment and many degrees of absorption in homemaking. Figures 2 and 3 show the shift in role so far as employment is concerned. In the 1950's the debate is loud over the kind of education that women should receive: to fit them vocationally for jobs with the development of aggressive, competitive personality traits; or to fit them for homemaking with stress upon cooperative, sympathetic attitudes.

When one role is provided and there is no alternative, when this role is generally approved by society, when the role fits into a pattern and provides satisfactions as well as demands responsibilities, the person to whom the role applies slips into it easily and without a feeling of frustration or of conflict.   On the other hand, when choices must be made and especially when, for many of the possible choices, coordinated roles are lacking for other members of society, there is both social confusion and personal anxiety and hostility.   The latter statement describes the present condition.   The significant feature of the issue regarding roles for husbands and wives is not that the old roles have been destroyed but that up to the present new roles have not evolved that are, first, complementary; second, definite and recognizable by the young men and women; and, third, in harmony with new social conditions.

Is the loss of functions detrimental to family life?

There is much concern about the segmental character of modern family life.   As older or even middle-aged persons recall the family life of their youth, it was much more inclusive than at present.   Only in very isolated rural areas has the family retained sufficient practical functions to be thought of as physically self-sustaining, and the almost complete self-sufficiency of the pioneering period is now historical rather than even within the past experience of the living.   The loss of functions, which began with the settled community, has accelerated with increasing urbanization.   Moreover, the process has reached out from the cities into the villages and rural areas.   The tangible crafts that have been lost are the ones most often referred to with a nostalgic tone of voice; the pans of browned bread on the kitchen table, the rows of canned fruit on the shelf, the party dress that the mother of the family sat up half the night to complete, are the things regretted by those who experienced them in their youth.   Interestingly enough, most of the lamented arts and crafts are those of women; either the activities of the father were less obvious to the children, or he had left the home and farm crafts behind him a generation earlier and it is now accepted that he should not do them.

More significant but less often mentioned than the abandonment of the tangible crafts and the practical physical activities is the loss of the social activities of the home.   The earlier family was not only physically but also socially self-sufficient.   The family as a whole more often than at present picnicked, attended the Chautauqua, explored the nearest city on a Sunday railway excursion, and visited or entertained other families. Also the fact that more work was done in the home created a social situation as parents and children of different ages joined in the tasks on a cooperative basis, with each doing work suited to his age and sex.   It is, in fact, the social inclusiveness of family life that is regretted, of which the physical crafts stand in memory as symbols.

In contrast to this inclusive family life of the past the family life of today seems to be composed of segments of experience, different for each member and often unintegrated within the experience of that individual. The parents do not know their children's friends, or meet them only casually without acquaintance with their parents.   Children of different ages and sex have each a private circle of friends.   Husband and wife plot their days along totally different lines that rarely intersect.   Only brief periods of time—early morning, a few hours in the evening, and perhaps a short time on Sunday—remain for the family to be together, and these periods often are given over to hurried practical details or represent merely the prelude to future separate departures from the home. Family life, therefore, seems to have become simply another segment in the general segmental pattern.

Undoubtedly, the enticing of adults and children alike into a variety of nonfamily associations changes the character of the family.   It loses unity, interdependence, common goals, and participation through which parents pass on to children the family and general culture.   On the other hand, through nonfamily agencies, each member acquires experience and knowledge beyond the scope of the family and relates himself to the larger community.   The question may well be asked: Is inclusive family life too limited, especially in the modern city?   Is it simply a relic from the rural past?   What contribution can the family make to fit its members to adjust to city life?

Can the family be economically independent?

A basic belief of the American people is that the family has the right to be economically independent.   This belief was nurtured by the ability of families to be self-sufficient when the country was primarily agrarian. Even if the standard of living was not always high, the ability to raise a major portion of its food gave the family a margin of safety even in years of poor cash crops or depressions.   The shock of the great depression of the 1930's undermined this belief and brought a realization of the insecurity both of the urban family that is dependent upon wages and of the present-day rural family whose farming is on a commercial rather than a sustenance basis.   In part, the disorganizing effect of the depression arose from the fear of this loss of self-sufficiency, of the rugged individualism of the expanding pioneering period when every family could acquire a farm or jobs for its adult members.   Consequently, many protests were raised against federal relief measures; the "dole" would create a nation of paupers.   With resumption of normal production and especially with the prosperity of the war years, the fear faded.   Nevertheless, family dependence is inherent in our economic system; family income is still linked with the business cycle, and another depression would again find thousands of families crowding the relief agencies.

TABLE 1

Federal Programs That Aid Families, 1950 *

Program	Number of beneficiaries	Comments
Unemployment insurance	7.0 million	Approximately one out of every seven persons with potential benefit rights received unemployment insurance.
Old age and survivor's insurance	2.9 million	Eighteen per cent of all persons aged 65 and over received benefits and in addition many younger dependents.
Old age assistance	2.8 million	Twenty-four per cent of all persons aged 65 and over received old age assistance.
Aid to dependent children	1.7 million	These children were in 654,000 families; of all families with children, one in 50 receives aid.
Aid to the blind	77 thousand	Between one third and two fifths of all blind persons receive aid.

* *Annual Report of the Federal Security Agency, 1950,* Social Security Administration (Government Printing Office, 1951), pp. 21, 23, 53, 56, 89, and 92.

Even in prosperous times, families are no longer completely self-sustaining; and the support of many old and young members, once entitled to family support, now rests in part upon public funds.   Table 1 summarizes the number of people receiving aid in 1950 from certain federal programs, and since that date the occupational groups covered by Old Age and Survivors Insurance have been greatly increased.   Financed by contributions from both employer and employee, this program is not strictly a relief measure; yet it does constitute a removal of initiative and responsibility for saving and providing for old age and dependents from the family to an official agency.   In addition to these federal programs of aid are many state and local forms of direct family aid and organized services financed both publicly and by private contributions.

Many arguments are advanced for and against this expanding program of public aid.   On the one hand, it gives an increased feeling of security, entitles certain classifications of families and individuals to aid without a personal appeal to charitable agencies, lifts the financial burden of dependents from families and relatives, and increases the standard of living. On the other, there is little provision for exceptional cases, some degree of "rugged individualism" is lost, and families have had loosened one tie that bound them together—economic interdependence of their members.

What constitutes an adequate number of children?

The conception of what constitutes an adequate number of children changes from time to time.   In the expanding agricultural period of the nineteenth century it was natural that large families should be highly valued.   In general many people were needed to settle the land and bring it to full fruition.   Large numbers of children and immigrants fulfilled this need.   In addition, what is natural tends to become what is right; in the years preceding popular acceptance of the use of contraceptives, unrestricted births were part of the folkways and in time part of the mores.   Any attempt to limit the number of children was condemned.

The desire to increase the population has now yielded to a desire to maintain it at its present level—a desire based in part upon the popular feeling that there is something decadent about a nation that does not replace itself generation by generation.   In addition, actual fear is engendered in some by comparison with the populations of nations that are increasing rapidly.   In the period preceding World War II the United States did not produce enough children to maintain the population level. This failure was part of a long-range decline in the birth rate (Figure 4). That the total population did not decline was owing to a declining death rate and a limited amount of immigration rather than to an adequate number of births.   The high birth rate in the recent postwar period is not regarded by population specialists as indicative of a reversal of trend but as a temporary phenomenon, hence, it is assumed that the birth rate will resume its decline.

On the personal side, married couples do not feel any social compulsion to have large families in order to increase the total population, nor indeed to have children at all.   Children have become a matter of choice.   In addition, in cities and to a lesser degree in rural areas children now are an economic luxury.   For many years they are an expense to their par-

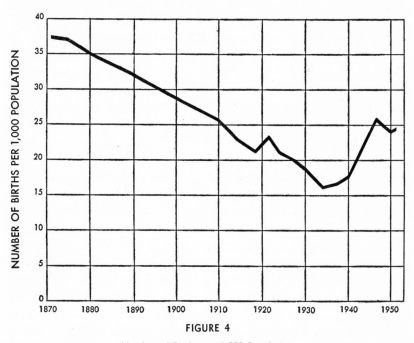

FIGURE 4

Number of Births per 1,000 Population

In the 80-year span the long-term trend has been down.   War's end and prosperous years temporarily send the birth rate up; depressions and war years tend to reduce it.   At present the future trend is somewhat uncertain. (Constructed from Appendix A, column II.)

ents; by the time that they are able to earn any considerable proportion of their expenses they have reached a marriageable age and divert their earnings from aid to their parents to the establishment of a home of their own.   Whereas married couples who like children continue to have them, controlling the number in terms of their standard of living, ambitions for the children, and personal preferences, couples who are not fond of children or who view them as an obstacle to other, more deeply desired objectives do not have them; nor do they feel guilty of any failure to fulfill social obligations.

A part of the controversy over the declining birth rate has centered on the decrease in population, a part on the effect of a childless marriage on husband and wife, a part on the plight of the only child, and a part on contraceptives as a separate issue.   Certain religious groups, the most outspoken of which is the Catholic, are opposed to all use of material contraceptives; the Catholics are not, however, absolutely opposed to control of births, since they advocate continence during certain periods when the woman is most likely to conceive.   Otherwise the attitude toward contraceptives has moved from attempts to suppress public information about them and to forbid their sale to a point where in most states information is easily obtainable and in some communities contraceptives may be bought freely even by young boys.   In fact, so complete has been the victory for information on birth control and distribution of contraceptives that a countermovement is now evident in some communities to bring both under control.   Another attempt at control is seen in the transformation of the Birth Control League, interested originally in limiting births, to the Planned Parenthood League whose object is to encourage married couples to have children, but at the same time aiding them to limit the total number and to space them according to some prearranged plan that fits into the total pattern of married life of the individual couple.

The issue with reference to number of children is reaching a settlement, with agreement between the actual practice of controlled births and the openly stated approval of this practice.   The question remains, however, of whether a general policy on children should be established.   Should any consideration beyond individual desires control the number of children born?   Is the childless marriage advantageous to society?   To the husband and wife?   In view of all that has been written about the personality problems of the only child, what size family is best for the children themselves?

What is the family's function in personality development of children?

Although many functions of the family with reference to the rearing of children have been transferred to other agencies, the family is still held responsible for the basic personality and character training of children.   At one time the family carried virtually all of the responsibilities.

The child was born at home, cared for there until he was six years old, spent after-school hours, Saturday, and most of Sunday at home, was nursed at home even through long and serious illnesses, carried on courtship under the watchful eye of the girl's mother, and was married in the parlor of the bride's home. The family then actually was almost completely responsible for the personalities and moral standards of its children.

As the family, especially under city conditions, became less and less able to provide for all the training needed, agency after agency was created to supplement the family. Not only formal and vocational education left the home, not only recreation left the living room for the park and commercial amusement place, but many agencies claimed for themselves the perogative of character-building. Families were widely blamed for juvenile delinquency, whereas community centers and group-work agencies claimed a right to philanthropic support on the basis that they prevented delinquency. Parents, unsure of themselves and fearful lest their children fail to develop as they wished, passively accepted this implicit condemnation of the family, sent their children to these agencies, and supported them with generous contributions. It is significant that many of these agencies did not work with children from disorganized city areas but with the children of middle-class families, which tacitly accepted the accusation of failure to build character into their children. Gradually, agencies working with children and youth have reformulated their objectives, with emphasis upon training in democratic and cooperative group interaction. Through this function, group-work agencies supplement rather than compete with the family.

Another type of agency that has assumed responsibilities once resting solely with the family is the child-guidance center. Children with emotional or mild behavior difficulties are referred to the experts in the guidance centers. The family thus is stigmatized as failing not only to inculcate moral standards in children but also to develop well-balanced and socially cooperative children. Schools must be included also, for the modern school visualizes its function as going far beyond teaching the general knowledge and skills needed for citizenship. The curriculum now includes skills formerly within the province of parents, recreation, and personality development.

Table 2 shows the membership among children and youth of a number of nationally organized agencies. The total membership of these agencies alone equals 99 per cent of the total number of boys and girls in the United States aged 7 to 17.   National agencies less well known than these as well as thousands of churches, community centers, settlement houses, and school recreation centers also claim a right to help train children.   Little children also are receiving more and more training away from home.   Figure 5 shows the increase in percentage of five-year-olds in school over a five-year period.

TABLE 2

Some National Agencies That Supplement the Family in Child Training *

Agency	Date organized	Number of members among children and youth
Young Men's Christian Association	1886	565,227 boys aged 17 and under
Young Women's Christian Association	1906	300,000 girls aged 12 to 18
Boys' Clubs of America	1906	275,000 boy members
Boy Scouts	1910	1,566,927 boys over age 9
Camp Fire Girls	1910	360,000 members (figure may include volunteer adults)
Girl Scouts	1912	1,213,958 girls aged 7–18
4-H Clubs	1914	1,750,000 rural young people
American Junior Red Cross	1917	19,000,000 boys and girls
National Jewish Welfare Board	——	454,000 boys and girls aged 14 to 18 in affiliated organizations

* Margaret B. Hodges, editor, *Social Work Yearbook, 1949* (Russell Sage Foundation, 1949), pp. 67–71.   National membership for Girl Scouts supplied by Rockford Council of Girl Scouts.

The replacement and supplementation of family functions by community agencies are recent phenomena.   Among the prominent national agencies listed in Table 2, only one antedates 1900.   Nursery schools and kindergartens also are of recent origin.   In 1900 there were 39 kindergartens, 10 nurseries, and 3 nursery schools; in 1942, 933 kindergartens and 965 nursery schools enrolled children under six years of age.[5]

Note should be made of the fact that many of the youth-training agencies depend upon volunteers for much of their leadership.   These volunteers often are parents.   The training that they give, however, is not of a parental type: it is based upon indoctrination by the professional

[5] Mary Dabney Davis, *Schools for Children Under Six,* Bulletin 1947, No. 5, Federal Security Agency, Office of Education (Government Printing Office, 1947), p. 33.

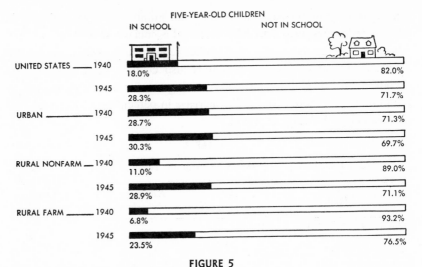

FIGURE 5

School Attendance of Children Aged Five

In addition to the increased percentage of five-year-olds in school, more and more younger children are being sent to nursery schools. Unfortunately, exact numbers are not available. (Source: Mary Dabney Davis, *Schools for Children under Six,* Bulletin 1947, No. 5, Federal Security Agency, Office of Education [Government Printing Office, 1947], pp. 21–22.)

staff of each agency. Volunteers typically attend training courses where they are taught the principles and techniques of the agency. Many become semiprofessionals, representing the agency rather than a parental or even an individual influence upon the children.

Children, whether many or few, have always been important in American culture. They are a source of pride and satisfaction to their parents. The condemnation of the family for the delinquency and personality maladjustments of children is perhaps the most serious threat of all to the values of family life. The aggressive eagerness of agencies to relieve the family of responsibility, and the lack of faith of these agencies in the ability of the family to rear its children properly, undermine one of the basic foundations of family life. So competent, so expert, have some of the agencies become that they no longer supplement the family but replace the family and tend to become in the minds of children and parents alike a supreme authority.

Is it for the good of children that the family become the weakest of the agencies that deal with children?

THE ISSUES AND THE CHANGING SOCIAL ORDER

Nine issues relating to marriage and the family have been discussed without attempts at solution. These issues have arisen because traditional social norms have increasingly failed to control the conduct of married couples and families, a situation that is indicative of a changing social order in which norms and values are still oriented to the past rather than to the present. Although readjustment is a slow process for any institution caught in the conflict between shifting social patterns, it is especially difficult for the family, which has no national organization—no central board of directors—to issue directives to individual families. Hence, families experiment, fail, try again; and eventually conduct is stabilized, norms are established, and new values accepted.

Comforting as it would be to think that such a new integration is developing, we cannot be complacent about stability. American society over many years has been constantly changing, with an increasing rate of innovations. The new form of the family must be flexible and adaptable to continued change, with norms based on principles rather than fixed rules of behavior. Values once centered in the family must be adjusted so that other agencies contribute to their accomplishment without depreciation of the worth of the family.

This book therefore does not look to the past for solutions to the issues. It attempts to present conditions objectively and to trace trends of attitudes and behavior, often with recognition that at present diversity exceeds unanimity. Nevertheless, an understanding of past and present social conditions is needed, for the issues are closely related to them. Chapters 2, 3, and 4, therefore, discuss the social backgrounds of the American family. Further analysis of the nine issues is woven into the remainder of the book.

QUESTIONS

1. Is the conception of the family as a social institution in conflict or in harmony with the conception of the family as a personal relationship whose main function is to provide personal happiness? Discuss.

2. Why is it difficult in the United States to achieve coordination between family values, norms that support the values, and actual conduct?

3. Does the present trend toward personal happiness as the chief end of marriage weaken or strengthen the family as a primary group?

4. Discuss the relationship between trends in the divorce rate and changing attitudes toward divorce.

5. What arguments are commonly given for and against premarital sex relations?   Which side has the stronger case?

6. Among well-adjusted couples that you know, how have the roles of husband and wife been coordinated?

7. Is it possible for the urban family to be socially and economically self-sufficient?   Discuss.

8. How can group work and recreational agencies benefit the child without alienating him from his family?

9. How can the issues discussed in Chapter 1 best be resolved?   Some possible ways would be by law; by religious condemnation of one side of an issue and support of another; by public discussions and consensus of attitudes; by scientific research and acceptance of the results; by doing nothing and assuming that issues will in time resolve themselves.

BIBLIOGRAPHY

The following references emphasize changing family functions, declining and emerging values, and problems of adjustment between family and society.

Brown, L. G., "The Family as a Universal Culture Pattern," *American Journal of Sociology,* 53 (1948), 460–463.

Burgess, E. W., "The Family in a Changing World," *American Journal of Sociology,* 53 (1948), 417–422.

Gruenberg, S. M., "Changing Conceptions of the Family," *The Annals* of the American Academy of Political and Social Science, 251 (1947), 128–136.

Hill, R., "The American Family: Problem or Solution," *American Journal of Sociology,* 53 (1947), 125–130.

Kolb, W. L., "Sociologically Established Family Norms and Democratic Values," *Social Forces,* 26 (1947–48), 451–456.

Mead, M., "What Is Happening to the American Family," *Proceedings of the National Conference of Social Work* (1947), 61–74.

Redfield, M. P., "The American Family: Consensus and Freedom," *American Journal of Sociology,* 52 (1946), 175–184.

Sirjamaki, J., "Culture Configurations in the American Family," *American Journal of Sociology,* 53 (1948), 464–470.

Tomars, A. S., *Human Relations in a Changing Society* (New York Society for Ethical Culture, 1949).

White, Lynn, Jr., *Educating Our Daughters, A Challenge to the Colleges* (Harper, 1950).

2

The Rural Family,
Past and Present

The issues and trends of the family of today can be fully understood only when the hidden heritage of the past is brought to light. The relationship of the family to both past and present is especially close because of two characteristics of the family: adaptiveness and conservatism.

The family at present is an adaptive institution; that is, it does not originate changes but constantly seeks to adjust to changes set in motion by the more powerful economic forces. If these forces do not function adequately (as in a pioneer situation or during a depression), the family demonstrates its adaptability by assuming more functions; if they are dominant, as in a period of prosperity, the family relinquishes functions and plays a lesser social role. To understand the family, it is therefore necessary to understand the situation in which it functions.

The social situation to which the family is now adjusting itself is dominated by four interrelated processes: mechanization, mobility, urbanism, and industrialization, all of which are still gaining rapidly. Beginning in the early nineteenth century, these processes were at first minor ripples in the agrarian hand economy that had begun to stabilize itself in one newly opened area of the West after another. After the Civil War, they began to overshadow the rural social organization, and by the 1920's had established a new social order to which the family, along with other social institutions, was forced to adjust. Rural society, on the decline since at least 1790, included less than half the population by 1920. With fewer persons needed upon the farms from year to year, industrial urbanism not only has spread into wider geographical regions but also affects the thinking of all people whether they live in cities or upon farms.

It is true, also, that in a developing country social change does not occur at an equal rate in all regions.   The East was well on its way to industrialization while the South was agonizing over the post–Civil War reorganization, the Middle West was a stable, primarily rural society, and the Far West was still in the frontier stage.   With our high mobility, people reared under one set of conditions, accepting one pattern of family life, found themselves in adulthood in an entirely different situation where their preconceived ideas of marriage and family often did not suit the realities of the society.

Since social changes rarely occur spontaneously but are of slow growth, the social norms of the past are always a factor in the present of any social institution.   This linkage to the past is especially true for the family, which tends to conserve values found important to orderly and effective living in the past, such as monogamy, permanence of marriage, and production and training of children.   It often adapts in utilitarian functions to a new situation (such as mechanized farms or city life) while pugnaciously defending the values of the past (in this case, a rural pioneer past). Many of the conflicts and confusing situations of today stem from this dual tendency, whereby the social norms or mores uphold one design (rural) for family life, whereas the actual situation (urban) seems to call for another.

In this chapter a foundation is built under the present family through a discussion of the heritage from the rural past and of the rural family today. The rural past set the pattern of family life that is still basic in the United States.   The present rural family, though more exemplary of the past than is the urban family, nevertheless is subject to many of the same influences as the urban family.   Change in the present rural family therefore will be emphasized rather than its linkage to the past.   In the following two chapters, the effects upon the family of mobility, urbanism, and industrialization are analyzed.

THE HERITAGE FROM THE RURAL PAST

The pioneer rural past

The rural past of the United States is peculiar in that in some regions its pioneer origin is so recent that it still affects many aspects of life.   Rural life in a pioneer region is vastly different from rural life in a long-settled area where the breaking of the land to the plow and the clearing of forests are no longer a memory even to the oldest inhabitant, often no longer even a legend in family histories.   Tremendous physical effort and privation over years of time attend the growing of the first successful crop, the building of a satisfactory house, the establishment of herds of cattle or droves of sheep.   Hardships were especially severe when the Middle West and Far West were settled, for work was done primarily by hand labor, supplemented where possible by animal power, but only occasionally by mechanical power and that chiefly the inflexible water power available solely at suitable streams.   Travel was by boat where feasible, otherwise by horse or oxen.   Typically, settlement preceded the railroads, although in many sections of the Middle West and Far West productive development of the land waited until improved waterways or railroads made it possible to ship farm products to the East.

Although in earlier years hunters, trappers, and Indian traders had traversed the land, permanent settlement was made not by these transient and nonfamily men who gathered the natural bounty of the land, but by permanent residents on farms where a living was made by cultivating the same plot of land productively year after year.   Migrants were induced to settle by the government policy of buying land from the Indians, surveying it, and selling it to settlers in plots of not less than 80 acres, for $1.25 per acre.   By 1850 the westernmost surveyed land covered Michigan, half of Iowa, most of Arkansas, and parts of Wisconsin.[1]   Settlers without the necessary cash to buy land moved further and settled on unsurveyed land which, when surveyed, they were allowed to buy.   Thus, as one area became settled, the pioneers pushed westward into the next unclaimed area.   The Homestead Act of 1862, granting land without cash payments, further stimulated westward migration.   Increases in population were fabulous.   In 1860, 300,000 people occupied Minnesota, Dakota, Nebraska, and Kansas; by 1870 the number had increased to almost a million and by 1880 to two and one half million.   Families that took up homesteads had almost no cash; they built sod or log huts and labored hard to make their farms productive.   One historian notes that never in the nineteenth century had so great a proportion of the farm population lived under pioneer or semipioneer conditions as in the post–Civil War period.[2]

[1] Carl Russell Fish, *The Rise of the Common Man, 1840–50* (Macmillan, 1927), pp. 152–155.

[2] Allan Nevins, *The Emergence of Modern America, 1865–78* (Macmillan, 1927), pp. 154–155.

Pioneer influence upon the family

What were the effects of the pioneering social situation upon the family, and especially what remains to the present?

The present popular American concept of the ideal family was established during the pioneer period, and many older people still cling to that ideal or remember it with nostalgia from their childhood.   This family was not only the rural family, but a special kind of rural family.   Contrary to most earlier practices, each pioneer family lived upon its own wide acres.   Before the development of widespread industry and commerce, most people of necessity raised their own food and made many of their own implements.   They were therefore rural in the sense of being self-sufficient.   The rural family of eastern United States, however, was often also a village family, participating in a communal life and at the same time cultivating outlying fields for their own use.   The pioneer sweep across the country preceded the building of villages and made the isolated farm with the operator living upon it the most common type in the North and West.   Moreover, the American farm ideally was owned by the man who lived upon it and worked it.   The belief in the goodness of ownership was in part a reaction to the peasant system of Europe that lay in the background experience or family history of many American families; and in part it was a result of the luxuriant expanse of land waiting for cultivation.   The federal government promoted ownership through its homestead laws, and many states enacted laws to protect the homestead.   Finally, the size of the farm was ample for the farmer to raise much of his own foodstuff as well as products to market for the cash that he needed to supply additional needs.   The standard of living anticipated was high—well above the line of necessity but not at the point of excess wealth or conspicuous display or consumption.   The ideal farm was not so large, however, that it could not be worked by the farmer, his wife, and growing children, with perhaps the aid of a hired man.   This was the ideal—the family-sized farm owned, occupied, and operated as a family enterprise to provide a good living for the family.   The farmer was comparable to the owner-artisan who owned his home and small business in the town or city, doing the work himself with perhaps the aid of an apprentice or two.   In both cases business merged with family life, and the objective was not thought of as amassing wealth or building a commercial enterprise so much as finding a satisfying and integrated mode of life that encompassed the entire family.

The family was the economic unit that moved into the opening West. Although husbands sometimes preceded their wives and young men sometimes bought land or took a homestead before marriage, soon wives, children, and sweethearts followed. Affection and desire for companionship were not the only motives at work, for each family unit had to be self-sustaining to a high degree; the skills of a woman were needed to supplement the work of a man, and the children soon grew to useful stature. The pioneer situation therefore encouraged early marriage and a high birth rate. Family life was highly valued.

Moreover, the communal unit was the family, for the principal pattern of settlement was farm by farm, with each owner living upon his own land, often definitely isolated in a period without good roads, telephones, rural free delivery of mail, or radios. A distance of even a few miles might isolate the family, as this description of a farm in Otsego County, New York, in 1848 emphasizes:

Our new home was in a comparative wilderness; not a house was in sight. The nearest neighbors on the south and east lived over a mile from us. On the west, the nearest lived three fourths of a mile, and on the north over one fourth of a mile; and a thick dark forest intervened.[3]

The family was therefore an interdependent social unit, with all lines of interaction turning inward.

The pioneer family, moreover, was the small-family unit of two generations. Never before had so many small-family groups been so completely dependent upon their own resources. This pioneer trend differed from the colonial type of settlement in which the family was subordinate to the village. New England was settled primarily by community groups made up of a number of families who established villages, with farms lying beyond the villages. Churches were quickly established and the community functioned as a unit in cooperative work and the control of deviant conduct.

Because the conditions of pioneering demanded family integration and organization, the family remained semipatriarchal; at the same time, how-

[3] H. C. Wright, *Human Life: Illustrated in My Individual Experience* (Boston, 1849), quoted in J. H. Kolb and E. de S. Brunner, *A Study of Rural Society* (Houghton Mifflin, 1946), p. 203.

ever, the need for labor gave the wife and children unusual importance and status.   Women were in great demand on the frontier, and men competed for each unmarried woman who appeared.   The seeds of equality were thus planted in the pioneer land as a result of the hard conditions of life, at a time when in the East certain women intellectuals were demanding equality with men as a matter of principle.

The necessity for coping with new conditions called for strength of character, ingenuity, and independence on the part of all.   Whereas in the East social classes had begun to develop and individuals found a definite social status based on family status, in the pioneer areas social classes scarcely existed and prestige accrued to the industrious, the planners, and the rational thinkers.   Abundance of productive land, easily acquired, also smoothed out potential class differences.   The leveling effect of the frontier was probably the most important factor in the development of the middle-class family, the present dominant type.   In the East, where an aristocracy had developed that looked to Europe for standards of taste and culture, the middle class was relatively weak, the lower class strong.   In the South, the distinction between upper and lower was even more sharply drawn.   By contrast, at the time that the middle class was growing in strength in the Middle and Far West, the upper limit to which it might climb was undetermined.   A sufficient number of pioneering families gained comfort and status in their lifetime, and achieved a social position above that of their parents to the East, to make any degree of upward social mobility seem a possibility.   The opportunity to try to improve one's position seemed open to any who were willing to move west and undertake the task of clearing the land or developing natural resources.   Liberty and equality were key words, born of the times, and had their effect on the family as on other institutions.

The settlement of the West by individual farms, the relative isolation of the families, and the delay in founding organized government and such regulatory institutions as courts, churches, and schools threw tremendous responsibility upon families.   Each family supplied its own protection, control of conduct of its members, care of the ill, religious services—even the marriage ceremony in the more remote areas until such time as the minister's circuit brought him to the neighborhood to validate the marriage.

Such a life of family self-reliance inculcated independence in each member.   As a result, when children grew to adulthood, they exercised great freedom of choice over selection of a spouse with only informal guidance by parents and were also free to decide upon their future occupations and places of residence. Families were large, and children who were not needed to operate the parental farm drained off to the newer land to the west or trickled into the newly founded cities.

The pioneering period thus made a number of contributions to the American family. It strengthened family unity and organization and broadened the scope of family functions at a time when, in the East, rural family functions had begun to decrease as dependence upon factory-made goods grew. The organization of the family, however, became more flexible, with greater equality between husband and wife. The self-reliance taught by pioneer conditions and the ever-beckoning opportunities of new areas freed younger adults from family ties in a process that was repeated again and again across the country.

In its adjustment to pioneer conditions the family demonstrated its adaptive qualities and changed in various ways from the village-bound family of the East. Nevertheless, the changes were of degree rather than kind; the essential family pattern remained the same, for the East in spite of its villages and small cities was essentially rural in economic base and dependent upon farms and the productive capacity of each family.

THE RURAL FAMILY OF TODAY

Today the rural family is a disappearing type. Decade by decade fewer people live on farms, and those who remain are rapidly losing their essentially rural characteristics and drawing near to the urban type of family. Nevertheless, the farm family, living in independence upon its own acres, is not only the prototype of the American family but is still accepted as the ideal family. It supplies the base from which changes in family life are measured, and these changes often are thought of as problems and threats to family life rather than as needed adjustments to non-farm social situations. However, a close examination reveals many types of farm family related to regional types of farming. It is clear, also, that methods of farming are changing rapidly, with corresponding changes in the rural family. In fact, a part at least of the popular conception of the farm family as secure, independent, and closely unified is a stereotype based on a past that is fast disappearing.

Farm families in the minority

At the present time, the most common habitat is not the farm but the village or city, and increasingly the urban area.   Even during the years of the great westward expansion and increase in number of farms, the population of towns and cities was expanding even more rapidly, so that with minor fluctuations the farm population as a proportion of the total population has been decreasing since 1790 and perhaps for longer.   Figures 6 and 7 show the trends clearly.

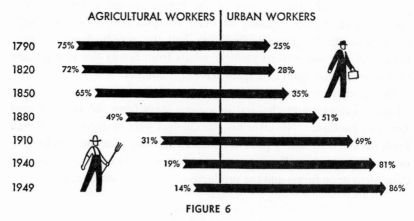

AGRICULTURAL WORKERS | URBAN WORKERS

1790	75%	25%
1820	72%	28%
1850	65%	35%
1880	49%	51%
1910	31%	69%
1940	19%	81%
1949	14%	86%

FIGURE 6

Increase in Urban Occupations

Since the earliest days of the Republic the percentage of agricultural workers has been declining; since the mid-nineteenth century the decline has been marked.   At present only 14 per cent of employed people perform agricultural work, producing enough to supply the entire nation with food and certain raw materials and to create large surpluses in some products.   The entire farm population, which would include housewives, old people, and children as well as workers, has similarly declined from 80 per cent of the total population in 1790 to 19 per cent in 1949.   (Source: Warren S. Thompson, *Plenty of People* [Ronald, 1948], pp. 136, 138; *Statistical Abstract of the United States, 1951* [Bureau of the Census, 1951], pp. 11, 174.)

This decline of the farming population has its explanation in changes in methods of farming that make it no longer necessary for most people to spend most of their time in raising food and other needed products to keep themselves alive.   In 1790 the most that one farm worker could raise was just enough to keep himself and 3.52 other persons alive.   With large families more than one worker per farm was needed simply for

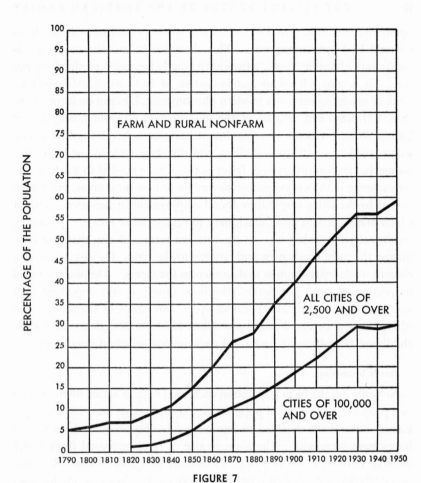

FIGURE 7

Increase in Urban Population

Population in cities of 2,500 and over has steadily increased from 5 per cent in 1790 to 59 per cent in 1950 of the entire population. Cities of 100,000 and over, nonexistent prior to 1820, now include 30 per cent of the population. Although the population of large cities has tended to remain stationary since 1930, urban influence has expanded to many of the smaller cities that cluster in the suburban and fringe areas. Farm, hamlet, and small-village population has declined from 95 per cent in 1790 to 41 per cent in 1950. (Source: *Statistical Abstract of the United States, 1950* [Bureau of the Census, 1950], p. 8; Noel P. Gist and L. A. Halbert, *Urban Society* [Crowell, 1948], p. 40; and preliminary reports of the 1950 Census.)

39

family maintenance. In 1945 one farm worker could provide for himself and 13.54 other persons.[4] This change is in part the result of scientific agricultural methods, which have greatly increased productivity per acre. It is also related to mechanization of farm work. Although we think of mechanization as a modern phenomenon, it began on farms more than 100 years ago, as part of the development of grain raising in the Middle West. Horse- or mule-drawn harvesters, horse rakes, tedders, balers, seeders, cultivators, shellers, and threshers were in use by 1850.[5] As mechanization progressed, fewer persons were needed to work on the farms; some of the excess people moved on to new rural areas, but others moved to the cities where they found employment in factories, some of which manufactured more machinery to release more farmers. Thus, a reciprocal relationship was set up between farm and city that still continues: the farm sends men and women to the cities; the city sends machinery made by these men and women to the farms. Despite the small proportion of rural population, the farm family is still important in a study of family trends and relationships. Our ideals of family life tend still to be rural-centered, and many urban residents struggle to adapt their childhood farm-training and rural experiences to urban conditions.

Trends in farming

Not only has the farm population decreased both in actual numbers and as a proportion of the total population, but the type of farm has changed. Family farms have declined in number while very small and very large farms have increased. The average size of farm increased from 138.1 acres in 1910 to 194.8 in 1945,[6] an increase that takes on added significance when it is related to type of farm operator. Much of the increase in acreage has gone into the large commercial farms, operated under professional management. In 1940, 34.4 per cent of all farm land was in farms of 1,000 or more acres, whereas only 16.2 per cent was in family-sized farms of 100–174 acres.

---

[4] M. R. Cooper, G. T. Barton, and A. P. Brodell, *Progress of Farm Mechanization,* Miscellaneous Publication No. 630 (United States Department of Agriculture, October, 1947), p. 5.

[5] Arthur Charles Cole, *The Irrepressible Conflict, 1850–1865* (Macmillan, 1934), pp. 106 ff.

[6] *Statistical Abstract of the United States, 1950* (Bureau of the Census, 1950), pp. 561, 569, 571, 573.

Types of farming

The interrelationships of farm size, tenure, and degree of mechanization produce several distinct types of farm:

1. The traditional family farm of 100–200 acres, operated by the owner or a tenant who often hopes to become an owner. This farm is especially typical of the north-central portion of the United States.

2. The small farm of less than 50 acres, found in mountainous areas and also abundant in industrialized areas. The operator and members of the family often have nonfarm employment, either during the off seasons or part time the year around.

3. The large-scale commercial farm, which may be operated by a number of tenants, by hired wage laborers, or by transient seasonal workers, under central control. These farms are most often located in the cotton region of the South and Southwest, the beef and wheat belts of the West, and fruit areas of the Far West.

Each type of farm is conducive to a different type of family life, and each shows also the impact of current trends of mechanization and urbanization as well as the influence of the past.

THE FAMILY FARM

The family-commercial farm

When the pattern of farming was set in the United States, farming was not primarily a business but a mode of life. The primary purpose of the family was to keep itself alive through raising grain, fruit, vegetables, meat for its own table, and wool, cotton, or other fibers for home manufacture of its own clothing and household textiles. Trees cut from the farm supplied logs or boards for house and barn as well as fuel for cooking and heating. Such complete dependence of the family upon its own production and home manufacturing is rarely found now, although it is approximated in a few isolated areas. More common is an adaptation of the subsistence farm to combined production for home use and commercial marketing. Vegetables and fruits are grown and canned on the farm; eggs are gathered fresh from the nests; a milch cow or two provides milk and butter; and a few meat animals are raised and butchered; but the major work of the farmer is the production of some one crop for sale. This specialty varies with the region and nearness to cities. In Michigan it may be fruit or sugar beets, in Illinois or Iowa corn, further west wheat, in the South cotton, and near large cities milk. Although the trend is toward large, highly commercialized and mechanized farms, most of these farms are still operated by family groups perhaps with the aid of a year-round hired man or a few seasonal workers where machinery cannot do the work. This farm, which may be called the family-commercial type, is the kind usually referred to in general discussions of the rural family. It is the type that is at present declining in numbers.

The family-commercial farm is unique among occupations in that home and work are merged both as to location and workers, a situation once true of many other occupations.[7] The farm family "lives in the midst of its occupation"; and, to the extent that it does diversified farming including animal care, it lives not by set hours of work but according to the seasonal or breeding demands of the farm. Each farm family is a unit, not only socially but economically. All members of the family contribute in some way to the work of the farm, all feel the pride of ownership, all are entitled to share in the proceeds. The fact that the yearly income may be secured at one time, after the harvest, prevents payment of wages and increases the family unity and interdependence. This family of necessity tends to be more highly organized than the urban family. There is no foreman or office manager to lay out the work and give instructions. The father usually is the head of the family, not merely in name but in fact; this means he is head both of intrafamily relationships and of work relationships. He directs the work, decides the timing of planting or harvesting and assigns the tasks to the various members of the family. He is not a patriarch in the sense that he rules absolutely over the destinies of his wife and children, but he brings order to the family functioning.

Children work closely with their parents, following a cultural pattern common to most farms—the little children and older girls working with the mother and the older boys with the father. Thus, through daily participation, children learn not only the skills of farming suitable to their sex roles but also the attitudes and standards of their parents through their continued informal contacts and observation of the ways in which their parents deal with many real-life situations.

Much of the leisure time is also spent by the farm family on the farm or elsewhere as a unit, since the family automobile is the usual means of

[7] J. H. Kolb and E. de S. Brunner, *A Study of Rural Society* (Houghton Mifflin, 1946), p. 204.

transportation and takes the entire family to church, picnic, shopping, and so forth.   The hours in school are almost the only ones that children consistently spend away from the farm and beyond family supervision. When the school is a rural or consolidated school serving a rural community, there tends to be consistency between school and home.

The farm family therefore tends to be a unit, and life for each member tends to be well coordinated, with few nonfamily contacts and few experiences not shared with other members.

Farm families tend to have a sense of continuity, for the farm typically passes from the father to a son.   In the East farms have often remained in the same family, following a direct line of descent from father to son, for more than 100 years, and some since colonial days.   Reared on the farm, accepting it as a way of life as well as a job, and anticipating inheritance of the property, one or more sons remain on the farm and keep it in the family from generation to generation.   A study of high school students in two counties in New York and a sample of Cornell University agricultural and liberal arts students shows the trend clearly.[8]   The study was limited to families in which the sons had already entered upon or selected an occupation.   Among two samples of farm families, represented by the high school students, 59 and 66 per cent contained sons who had chosen farming as a life occupation, whereas among the farm families with sons at Cornell 54 per cent had sons who became farmers. In contrast are the nonfarm families in the same samples, in which only 20 and 22 per cent, respectively, contained sons who had elected to follow the occupations of their fathers.   The transmission of farming is declining, however.   In the preceding generation (1885–1920) of the same New York families, three fourths of the farm families transmitted farming as an occupational choice to one or more sons as compared to approximately one fourth of the nonfarm families of the same period that had a son follow the father's occupation.   The decline in percentage of farm sons following the occupation of the father from the older to the younger generation is at least in part a reflection of the mechanization of farms, larger size of farms, and increased productivity due to scientific

[8] W. A. Anderson, *The Transmission of Farming as an Occupation*, Bulletin 768 (Cornell University Agricultural Experiment Station, October, 1941), pp. 6–7. It should be noted, however, that when sons, rather than families, are considered, only 31, 43, and 47 per cent of three groups became farmers.   Thus, although a high percentage of families had farmer-sons, they had almost twice as many sons who elected some other occupation.   The tradition of farming was transmitted to only about one third to two fifths of the sons.

agriculture, which reduce the number of farmers needed.   Another reason is the availability of other occupations.

The farm population continues to maintain itself in family units. The operation of the farm within the membership of the family gives the family unit great significance.   It is uncomfortable, although not impossible, for a single man or woman to operate a farm efficiently, and the addition of children is an advantage.

The farm family is imbedded within a rural community that has the advantage of occupational uniformity, and therefore uniformity of interests.   Although the automobile has freed the farm family from isolation, the distance from home that the farmer may go is still limited by daily demands of farm animals.   The limitation of contacts to the community is evident from the residential proximity of rural brides and grooms.   In Branch County, Michigan, 46 per cent of couples applying for marriage licenses between 1927 and 1937 gave the same post office address, and an additional 12 per cent had addresses within the county, a total of 58 per cent from the same local area.   In addition, 21 per cent lived within 50 miles of each other, leaving only 21 per cent who were more widely separated.[9]   In Scott and Carver Counties, Minnesota, during the 1930's, 41.4 per cent and 36.2 per cent of couples marrying, respectively, had the same post office address, and 23.5 and 23.4 per cent lived within the county.   Many who came from different counties were not far distant from each other, since 28.2 per cent and 33.5 per cent in the two counties lived not over 50 miles apart; only 6.9 per cent in each county lived more than 50 miles distant from each other.[10]   Marriage within the local community ensures a common background and the continuity of premarital social contacts and family relationships.

In time this tendency of farm youth to marry neighbors spins a web of family relationships that extends through an entire rural community and includes several generations.   The isolated self-sufficiency of the small pioneer family thus declines, and members of the larger family or great family exchange services at harvest time and when there is a new child, illness, or death.   Moreover, the larger family absorbs remnants of fam-

---

[9] Howard Y. McClusky and Alvin Zander, "Residential Propinquity and Marriage in Branch County, Michigan," *Social Forces*, 19 (1940), 79–81.   Persons securing licenses outside of the county are not included, but only those who received licenses in Branch County.

[10] Donald Mitchell, "Residential Propinquity and Marriage in Carver and Scott Counties, Minnesota," *Social Forces*, 20 (1941), 256–259.

ilies left by death, and exerts control over members young and old, with reference not only to conduct contrary to the social norms but also to family welfare. The selection of a mate becomes a matter of interested concern to all members of the kinship group, and the husband or wife who fails to play his expected family role is brought into line by pointed criticism.

The kinship family also is part of a larger rural neighborhood, with the several kinship groups that dominate a given area forming the backbone of the community life. Often one family in the past has donated the land for the rural school, another for the church, and a third for the cemetery, each institution bearing the name of its respective family-donor. The adult members of these kinship groups elect from their own circle the members of the school board and township and county officials, organize granges, raise money for churches, and in general control on a community level functions that in the pioneer family had been fulfilled by the family. The institutions in turn uphold and support family control in the considerable functions left to the family.

Community contacts beyond the kinship family develop from cooperative work, a formalization of earlier informal types of neighborliness whereby farm families helped each other with tasks beyond the capacity of a single family, and in so doing enjoyed the companionship of others. A description of cooperating groups in northern Michigan is illustrative.[11] Teams or companies are organized around joint ownership of an expensive piece of farm machinery that is needed on each farm for only a limited period of time and hence suitable for use on a number of farms in rotation. Other rings without ownership of machinery also form to aid each other with harvesting and threshing. The host farmer provides any extra labor needed, and his wife serves dinner to the entire group. If a member of a ring finds himself unable to work, he is obligated to find a substitute. These teams tie farmers into compact cooperative groups. As labor is shared, ideas are also exchanged, and social unity keeps pace with economic unity.

The family farm as a business

The trend of farming, however, is away from the family-farm pattern. The more prosperous farmer buys up a neighboring farm or two, installs

[11] Solon T. Kimball, "Rural Social Organization and Co-operative Labor," *American Journal of Sociology,* 55 (1949), 38–49.

his own machinery, and drops out of the cooperative ring.   He tends to place the actual operation of his enlarged farm in the hands of a tenant or a few men paid cash wages, so that farming becomes more of a business and less of a complete way of life.   The extent of this trend can be illustrated through the increased use of farm tractors.   Although machines have been used for farm work for many years, the introduction of the tractor is regarded as of special significance.   One rural sociologist states that "The most important single implement introduced into agriculture in this generation has been the gasoline tractor.   It has been improved over the years, reduced in cost, and adapted in size to farms of various sorts." [12]   The number of tractors has increased from 920,021 operating on 13.5 per cent of all farms in 1930 to 2,421,747 tractors in 1945 in use on 34 per cent of all farms.   By 1948 a further increase brought the number to 3,150,000.[13]   Detailed studies show that the introduction of tractors is accompanied by increase in the size of farms.   In Oklahoma during the period of 1920 to 1945 the number of tractors per 100 farms increased from 3 to 44; the average acreage of farms increased from 166 to 219, with the greatest gains in size occurring in the counties with the greatest degree of increased mechanization.[14]

Increased use of machines on the farm has been attended by decrease in the number of farmers needed to cultivate a given acreage.   According to the Oklahoma study referred to in the preceding paragraph, each tractor added was associated with the loss of three or four persons.   The decreased labor requirement might simply eliminate the necessity for farm laborers or might release sons of the farmer, or, when small farms were sold to create a larger farm for someone, entire farm families might leave the area.

With mechanization, the pattern of living for the owner's family changes, as does the relationship of the family to the rural community.   No longer is the family so closely tied either to the farm or to the rural neighborhood.   The owner's wife and children no longer have a direct part of the farm work; fresh vegetables, chickens, eggs, and the like are supplied to the family by the tenant.   Meat stored in the locker often comes from the neighbor who is still doing family farming.   The main

---

[12] Lowry Nelson, *Rural Sociology* (American Book, 1948), p. 103.

[13] *Statistical Abstract of the United States, 1950*, pp. 596–597.

[14] R. T. McMillan, *Social Aspects of Farm Mechanization in Oklahoma*, Bulletin No. B-339 (Oklahoma Agricultural Experiment Station, Oklahoma A. and M. College (November, 1949), pp. 6, 20.

crop of the farm tends to be more highly specialized, and the owner buys products that he formerly raised for himself. When the commercial farmer buys his own machinery and employs workers, he breaks his tie with his neighbors who are still operating on a cooperative basis. Often the center of interest shifts from the neighborhood to the more distant town or small city, not only for business purposes and shopping but for recreation and education. Such a family is further set apart by reason of its prosperity, for the farmer who has achieved success that for some reason is beyond the grasp of some of his neighbors associates with other commercial farmers in the area who form a rural upper class. Being freed from the daily tasks and sufficiently prosperous, he may take his family to Florida in the winter. Kimball, in discussing the development of commercial farming in Tuscola County, Michigan, states that a sufficient number of farmers from this one county winter in Florida to have formed a Tuscola County club there.[15]

THE FAMILY ON THE SMALL FARM

A deviation from the family farm is the small farm, often found on the borders of highly urbanized areas and sometimes operated on a part-time basis. This farm may be a subsistence farm whose products are for home use only, or it may be a truck farm upon which are raised vegetables for the urban market. Younger members of the family may have full-time employment or may leave the farm and migrate to the city; older members operate the farm and carry on some kind of part-time work. The nonfarm work may consist of a gas station on the highway, a fruit and vegetable stand in summer, or a hot-dog stand that is operated as a family project with the wife and such children as are at home aiding in the operation of the small business as they also aid in the operation of the farm. In other cases the nonfarm work is industrial and may be a feature of the winter months only. The pattern of seasonal work for wages to supplement farm income is not new, but its relation to the urban situation is. For example, in a 1930 study of Ohio, only 8 per cent of the heads of farm families in the most rural areas of the state had nonfarm employment, whereas in the most industrialized areas 27 per cent of heads were so employed.[16] For the United States as a whole, the percentage of farmers

[15] *Op. cit.*, p. 43.
[16] Kolb and Brunner, *op. cit.*, pp. 97–98.

with part-time nonfarm employment has varied little since the 1920's.[17] The percentage spending 100 or more days per year in such employment, however, has tended to increase: from 11 in 1929 to 15 in 1939 to 18 in 1944. These families are subject to both urban and rural folkways and mores. Under certain conditions they establish a stable and satisfying system of industrial-rural work.

Small-scale farming in the South

Many industrial workers in the South combine small-scale farming with working in textile mills, mining, lumbering, or collecting and distilling turpentine in the pine forests.[18] As these industries are all located in rural areas or villages, a family may easily live on a small farm or plant a few acres and be within a short distance of other work. Most of these combination rural-industrial workers (82 per cent) have been reared on farms or at some time farmed full time. Essentially rural in attitude and habit, they have successfully adjusted to industrial work in addition to farming. Their children, reared in the dual setting, will accept the pattern as normal.

The following description gives some idea of the family organization of a subsistence part-time farmer:

This man of 34 was a typical noncommercial part-time farmer who regularly worked full or part time in a textile mill. His wife worked approximately four months a year in the same mill. The family, which included four children from 7 to 15 years old, rented four and one-half acres of land with a five-room frame house. The house, unpainted, was unattractive in appearance and was not equipped with telephone, electricity, or running water. This little farm was seven and a half miles from the mill, to which the man commuted daily in a Ford.

The family did practically all the work on the farm, paying only for a small amount of machine work. The father worked Saturdays and evenings on the farm, while his wife milked the cows and fed the chickens. The livestock consisted of a cow which gave milk for ten months of the year, a pig which was butchered in the fall and the meat cured, and eight hens. Corn was raised for the livestock and a large variety of vegetables that the family

[17] In 1929, 30.2 per cent; 1939, 28.7 per cent; 1944, 26.8 per cent.—*Statistical Abstract of the United States, 1940* (Bureau of the Census, 1941), p. 659; *Statistical Abstract of the United States, 1950,* p. 581.

[18] R. H. Allen, L. S. Cottrell, Jr., W. W. Troxell, Harriet L. Herring, and A. D. Edwards, *Part-Time Farming in the Southeast,* Works Progress Administration, Division of Social Research, Research Monograph IX (Government Printing Office, 1937).

ate fresh or canned for later use.   Six pear and one fig tree yielded one and a half bushels of fruit per year.   The expense of this farm in the year studied was $70 per year, exclusive of rent, and the value of the food raised was estimated as $267.50.   The income from the mill for the family was $1,164 (in 1934).

The head of this family had had five years of farming experience before he moved to this location two years prior to the study.   He handled the work successfully and wished to find a larger farm.   The children were all in school and all members of the family attended Sunday School and church regularly.   There were no organized social activities in the neighborhood. The parents had completed grade school.[19]

The small farm in the urban area

Near large cities, the small farms tend to be commercial truck farms, in the North operated by foreign-born men with farming experience in Europe.   When the family is unable to supply all the labor required during the summer months, city people fill the need.   These city workers often are children and adolescents, unemployable in urban industries, who work on the truck farm by the day, returning home each evening.   In some cities, those desiring work congregate each morning at the end of the city carline, where they are picked up by the farmer who at the end of the day returns them to the same spot.[20]   The nearness to some large city, the competing possibilities of urban jobs for younger members of the farm family, and the marketing and labor interrelationships often create a disorganizing family situation.

A study of Landaff, New Hampshire, shows the way in which the family loses its unity under the impact of urban conditions.   Engulfed by the Boston milkshed, the community is subject to strong urban influences.   Younger family members, no longer prizing rural life, migrate to nearby cities, not because they could not make a living in Landaff but because they desire the sparkle of urban life and the use of regular wages. The parents, who accept the independence of their children as justified, are unable to exert sufficient family pressure or authority to keep them on the farms.   The unity of the family is therefore lost as each person strikes out for himself rather than sharing in the work and proceeds of the farm.   If, later, crises arise, each individual must make his own adjustment.   The role of the farm wife has lost value, and the daughters

[19] Allen *et al., op. cit.*, pp. 221–223.
[20] Katharine DuPre Lumpkin and Dorothy Wolff Douglas, *Child Workers in America* (New York: Robert M. McBride and Co., 1937), pp. 65–66.

do not want to become farmers' wives.   Sons also prefer the wages of city work to the independence of the farm.   The continuity of farm ownership from generation to generation therefore is weakened.   Wives often inherit the farm on the death of the husband, or the farm passes to a son-in-law if a daughter has married a farmer rather than to the son who has left for the city.[21]

THE FAMILY ON THE LARGE COMMERCIAL FARM

The commercial farm that is far beyond the capacity of one family to operate falls into another class.   Several types of family life have evolved, each an adjustment to a distinctive system of farming.

The cotton plantation

The Southern cotton plantation is a continuation of large-scale commercial farming that originated in colonial days.   First slaves and later, after the Civil War, tenants provided the labor.   Much has been written about the hard lot of the Southern sharecropper who is unable to rent his plot of land for cash and instead not only lives in a tenant house owned by the landlord but also is supplied with all farm equipment from the same source and is dependent upon the landlord for credit with which to buy clothing and food.   Whether white or Negro, the Southern sharecropper presents one of the least favorable pictures of the rural family in America. The standard of living and family organization are a survival of rural hand economy long since outgrown in the North and West.   Nevertheless, most of the rural population lives in the South—51.7 per cent as against 48.3 per cent in all other parts of the United States.[22]   Moreover, many urban families, North, West, and South, originated in the rural South.   As they move north and west they bring the vestigial attitudes and family organization suitable to an outmoded rural society into the urban situation to add to the complexities of urban family life.

The sharecropper's family life can be understood only in terms of the plantation system.[23]   The typical plantation, according to a study made

[21] Kenneth MacLeish and Kimball Young, *Landaff, New Hampshire, Culture of a Contemporary Rural Community*, Rural Life Studies, No. 3 (U. S. Department of Agriculture, Bureau of Agricultural Economics, 1942).

[22] *1950 Census of Population, Preliminary Reports, General Characteristics of the Population, by Regions: April 1, 1950*, Series PC-7, No. 3 (Bureau of the Census, April 30, 1951), p. 12.

[23] T. J. Woofter, *Landlord and Tenant on the Cotton Plantation*, Works Prog-

in 1936, consists of 900 acres operated by the owner or his manager. Except on newly mechanized farms, labor is performed by hand, either by tenant families or wage hands. The method of organization is to break the plantation up into plots or small "farms" with a sharecropper or other tenant on each, the wage hands being assigned also to specific plots. These plots, though comparable in size to small subsistence farms, are differently used, being planted to one commercial crop—cotton— which requires an inordinate amount of hand labor. Although each worker has his own distinct acreage, all tenants and farm workers are organized into a cooperative communal group, as Figure 8 shows. The community is not democratic, however, for it is managed by the owner or his representative toward whom all families and especially the share-croppers' families bear a dependent relationship.

The supervision of workers extends far beyond assigning a plot of land to be worked, and especially so for the cropper, with the extreme of control when the cropper is a Negro. The owner determines for the entire plantation such matters as fertilization, insect control, frequency and type of cultivation, and time for harvesting. Work animals (one mule per family) may be cared for in a central barn and assigned to workers as needed. Work hours are controlled, often with the ringing of a bell for starting and stopping work.

Furthermore, control extends into the personal lives of croppers. Since their income is low, they typically lack a reserve to tide them over from the time one crop is sold until another is harvested. The landlord therefore agrees to advance to each family a credit of $5 to $20 per month, the total amount plus interest being deducted from the cropper's share of the crop when it is marketed. A common practice is the operation of a store or commissary by the owner at which the cropper may—

---

ress Administration, Division of Social Research, Research Monograph V (Government Printing Office, 1936). In this study a plantation was defined as a tract of land with five or more resident families, including the landlord. Additional material is taken from Charles S. Johnson, *Shadow of the Plantation* (University of Chicago Press, 1934); Allison Davis, Burleigh B. Gardner, and Mary R. Gardner, *Deep South* (University of Chicago Press, 1941); L. W. Doob, "Poor Whites, A Frustrated Class," in John Dollard, *Caste and Class in a Southern Town* (New Haven: Yale University Press, 1937), pp. 445–484. Descriptions of white and of Negro sharecroppers from various sections of the South are almost identical as to living conditions, owner-sharecropper relationships, and family life. The Negroes have less education and worse housing and show less resentment toward domination by the owner or his agents, but the difference is merely one of degree; the pattern of living is the same.

or may be compelled to—make his purchases.   Of the plantations surveyed, 15 per cent had commissaries with compulsory buying and 11 per cent commissaries with optional buying.   The landlord thus controls the amount of spending that the cropper may do and often what he may purchase and the price he pays.

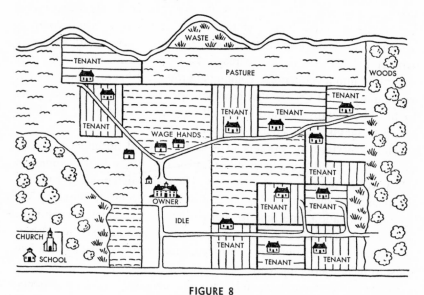

FIGURE 8

Layout of Southern Cotton Plantation

The typical cotton plantation in the South is a communal unit of families, ranked from the owner, through the wage hands, to the tenants and sharecroppers.   Large plantations may include a school, a church, and sometimes a commissary.   Houses are linked together by narrow roads and paths, and the lives of owner and workers by economic interests.   The average cotton plantation in the 1930's had 907 acres, most of which was in crops or pasture. (Source: T. J. Woofter, Jr., *Landlord and Tenant on the Cotton Plantation*, Research Monograph V, Division of Social Research, Works Progress Administration, 1936, p. xxxii.)

In this society, the landlord assumes a paternalistic role.   He is expected either to administer discipline or to help tenants who get into minor legal difficulties.   He is also expected to contribute to church projects and from time to time to provide a fish fry, dance, or barbecue. Sharecroppers, white or Negro, bring many personal problems to the landlord for his decision.   The landlord may become a "father surrogate" to the tenant families who surrender to him much of the authoritative role held by the father in the typical rural American family. The landlord's contribution to the plantation has been designated that of pocketbook and brain, the tenants' supervised brawn.[24]

The tenant's family is the economic unit on the plantation. By the time a boy is 9 or 10 years old, he knows how to hoe cotton so skillfully that he can cut out the grass without injuring the small plant. When he is 14 he begins to plow and at age 16 or 17 does a man's work. Since grass must be cut out every two weeks, many hands are needed. The larger the family, therefore, the more valuable the tenant is to the landlord, and fathers of large families or whose households include several relatives are in an advantageous bargaining position.

Men and women, old and young, and children of all ages past infancy work from dawn till dark. The owner or his representative puts great pressure upon all members of the family to work, sometimes reducing credit if there are idle members, or even resorting to the lash among Negro sharecroppers. The tenant or sharecropper family is not, however, simply a collection of individuals, each obedient to the will of the landlord or overseer, but is well organized within itself on a patriarchal basis—in fact, it is one of the few examples of the patriarchal family remaining in the United States. The landlord recognizes the father as head of the family and deals only with him, although the work and welfare of all members are at stake. Since individual wages are not paid and credit is on a family basis, the family functions as a genuine producing and consuming unit. If the father dies or is absent, the mother or some other older member assumes the authoritative headship. The family unity is based both on affection and necessity. Children are genuinely liked and welcomed as they come, without attempt at artificial restriction as to numbers. They are regarded also as economic assets and are reared in the philosophy of hard work; every attempt is made to keep them in the family group as long as possible.

The family is part of a larger kinship group, which recognizes relationships to the third cousin. These groups, in extreme cases, may number 40 to 75 people. Each family unit lives independently in its own house, but the household group may consist of persons of various degrees of relationship, such as half-brothers and half-sisters, a grandmother, or an illegitimate child (who is accepted without prejudice). Married sons

[24] Woofter, *op. cit.,* p. 32.

and daughters sometimes remain with the parental group, rearing a new family under the same roof with the parents' family and forming part of the same social and economic unit. Although they may not be employed on the same plantation, the families in the kinship group usually live in the same county and give each other informal aid, as well as provide contacts for visits and social life.

Not only is the tenant family a commercial producing unit but to some extent it forms a subsistence producing unit as well. Each family has a small vegetable garden; hunting and fishing on the plantation provide some meat and fish; and fuel is cut from the wooded areas.

The level of living is low. Unpainted frame houses, averaging 4.5 rooms, are typical, with a ratio of 1.2 white persons or 1.4 Negroes per room.[25] Unscreened windows, outside wells, outhouses, wood stoves, and absence of gas or electricity are the norm. Negroes have poorer quarters than whites. (Small-farm owners in the same areas often are able to provide themselves with only slightly better facilities than tenants on large plantations possess.) Tenant clothing is crude and coarse and may be so inadequate for the chilly months that children cannot attend school. Dietary standards are very low; and, during the summer months when gardens burn out in the sun, the family actually may not have enough to eat. Health is poor, and the death rate high. The lack of telephones, automobiles, radios, and reading material produces both physical and mental isolation. The educational level is low, both because of poor facilities and because it is not part of the traditional pattern of either the Negro or white tenant class. The work makes few mental demands, and isolation provides no stimulation to learn.

The plantation owner and his family live either on the plantation or in a nearby city, where they occupy an upper-class position in the social system of the South. Although operation of the plantation is a business for the owner, it goes far beyond an economic relationship. His close regulation of the lives of his tenants places human as well as economic responsibilities upon him and affords many types of satisfaction.

The cotton plantation of today represents a regional type of large commercial farm as it has developed in the "shadow of the plantation." A complete mode of family life for owner and tenants is worked out on the plantation, in part traceable to slavery traditions and in part an adaptation to the use of white tenants.

[25] Woofter, op. cit., pp. 91–106, 125–144.

The migratory farm family

Other types of commercial farms operate with different systems, a distinctive one being the employment of seasonal labor—men and women, or family groups, who come onto the farms only during the season of cultivation or harvest. Our chief interest is with the family that "follows the crops." The transient farm family's pattern of life is geared to the type of farming that it does. Chiefly, the transient family works on thoroughly commercialized farms run on an impersonal business basis with the primary object of making money.

The most thoroughly commercialized and hence least familial type of farm is that operated by a corporation. Some of these farms are found in the South; others are in the Middle West as a result of foreclosure of mortgage in the 1930's when ownership passed to an insurance company or bank. Most typical, however, is the large fruit or vegetable farm of the Far West operated by a corporation that has financed itself through the sale of stocks or bonds or by current loans from financial agencies. Although tenants may cultivate the land, more often a professional farm manager is employed with the actual work being done by hired wage laborers, many of them seasonal laborers and some with families. As the sole aim of the corporation is to operate the farm with economy in order to make as much profit as possible, the farm manager and laborers alike regard their work with the same businesslike, unsentimental attitude that the factory worker has toward his job. Nevertheless, so far as the transient family is concerned, the conditions of migratory farm labor have created a type of mobile family life adjusted to the work situation.

It is estimated that in 1949 one million migratory farm workers labored on farms at some time during the year, exclusive of Mexicans who illegally entered and then left the country after the completion of seasonal farm work.[26] Of recent years, since combines have displaced male migratory workers for grain harvesting, families have become more important in the migratory labor force, constituting a larger proportion than before.[27]

[26] Louis J. Ducoff, *Migratory Farm Workers in 1949,* Agriculture Information Bulletin No. 25 (U. S. Department of Agriculture, Bureau of Agricultural Economics, 1950), p. 1.

[27] Louis J. Ducoff, "Socioeconomic Backgrounds of the Migratory Agricultural Labor Situation," mimeographed copy of an address presented at the National Conference on the Church and Migratory Labor of the Home Missions Council of North America, Inc., September 27, 1949 (U. S. Department of Agriculture, Bureau of Agricultural Economics), p. 3.

An illustration may be found in the life of the migratory farm family of the Western states, as it passes in a regular circuit from crop to crop, beginning with berries in June and July and ending with apples in late autumn.   Some of the fruit harvests bring thousands of families, as well as detached workers, into one county for the harvesting of a particular kind of fruit.[28]   Usually a few idle months each winter are spent in some city where the family uses what little it has been able to save or appeals to a relief agency.   Each spring it starts on its trek, either following a customary circuit year after year or directing its route by company advertisements or word-of-mouth reports as to where workers are needed.   At each stop all able members of the family work: in the apple orchards men pick from ladders, while women pick from the ground or work in the sorting and packing sheds; on the berry farms men, women, and children pick, with children working alongside the mother under her supervision. But regardless of which members work, the entire family is packed into the automobile, surrounded by personal belongings and camping equipment, and travels together throughout the season.   In one area the family may find that the company provides small cabins or a room in a long barracks for its use, poorly furnished and with outdoor water and toilet facilities.   At another site, camp space only is provided, perhaps by the owner of the farm or by the city or county.   In other places, the families make use of the cabins in motor courts or rent space at an auto camp to pitch their tents.   At the worst, families may have to camp along the roadside or on a river bank.   Always the quarters are crowded, bare, near to the tents or shacks of other pickers, and lacking in indoor plumbing or water supply; often they are dirty and in poor repair.   In a succession of such quarters, the family lives, perhaps with residence in a flat or small house in some city for a few months of the year.   Some families make only three moves a year with longer residence in the city; others move from seven to twelve times.

Many of the families have young children and infants who prevent the mother from working or who are left in the care of a slightly older child while both parents work.   The family has a rather high degree of unity and feeling of identification.   Hiring and paying is by the family as a composite group, and the family moves as a unit from farm to farm,

---

[28] Marion Hathaway, *The Migratory Worker and His Family* (University of Chicago Press, 1934).   This report is based on a study of 100 families working at clam digging and fruit picking in Washington.

sharing crowded quarters.   The parents, while unable to give their children much care, nevertheless are often uneasily aware that the contacts
they make and experiences they have are not always advantageous to the
children, and often those with young children plan if possible to settle in
some city by the time the children are of school age.

Because of the short season for picking and the decreased value of the
fruit if it is not picked at its prime, pressure to work long hours is put
upon the family by their own economic necessity as well as by the foreman.
In the field by 4:30, the family works until dark with only brief stops for
food.   The poor cooking facilities and fatigue cause many families to rely
on cold food, and the necessity for beginning work at dawn drives the family to bed soon after dark.   Family life other than that found while at
work is therefore at a minimum.   The effort of the family is bent toward
making a living and if possible saving a little for the idle winter months.
Informal household participation of parents and children does not exist.

The family's relationship to the temporary community of pickers is
informal and friendly.   Week ends bring some relaxation, with families
crowding the highway in cars or attending a dance at some rented hall.
Employers and nearby communities make little or no effort to provide
recreation or to care for small children while the mothers work.   In fact,
they turn a cold shoulder toward any migrant workers who seek to participate in the established community activities and at the end of the
season make every effort to get them to move on somewhere—anywhere
—else as soon as possible.

In their winter quarters, the families have little more contact in the
community than they have in the summer communities.   Their level of
living is very low; and, as they stay only a few months, they are not welcomed into churches, clubs, or other organizations.   Children attend
school, it is true; but, known as members of migrant families, they are
shunned by the other children.   Since the children often enter a month
or more late in the fall and may move several times during the school year,
they are often retarded and their interest in school is almost nonexistent.
Consequently, they are not incorporated into the school socially, and drop
out as soon as possible.

Among the 100 families studied in Washington, 47 had at one time
followed agricultural work and 14 had never done anything else but follow
the crops, a few having been reared in migrant families.   During the
1930's, as a result of the depression and the Dust Bowl phenomenon,

many families abandoned or lost their farms or tenancy, and took to the road in automobiles, heading toward the Pacific Coast. Mechanization of farms in other areas has also released rural families, some of whom rove around seeking other agricultural work and eventually join the bands of migrant agricultural families on the Coast.

The migrant family has some of the characteristics of the traditional rural family—the unity of the family and its close cooperation in matters of work and family earning and spending. It differs greatly, however, in that it has no stable base of operations and no land upon which to establish itself. It is treated by the companies that operate fruit and vegetable farms or fish canneries as labor, provided with the minimum of living facilities, no accessory social life, and given an established rate of pay. The migrant family therefore is a corollary of commercialized farming; it has adapted itself to seasonable mobility while maintaining cohesion and unity.

MECHANIZATION AND TECHNOLOGICAL CHANGES

The trend is for large farms to move from cultivation by tenants, share-croppers, or migrant workers to complete mechanization with hired labor paid cash wages. The tractor is used with the gang plow, multiple-row cultivator, combine harvester, two-row corn picker, and many more machines that can perform work once requiring many workers and farm animals. A mechanical sugar-beet harvester lifts, tops, and loads beets in one operation. For the cotton plantation there are a four-row culti-vator and a mechanical picker said to reduce labor by 75 per cent. When these and other machines are in use, tenants must seek other land to cul-tivate, join the migrant farm laborers, or move to cities in the hope of finding unskilled work there. The reduction in number of workers needed is suggested by the following illustrations: [29] A cotton plantation in the Mississippi Delta gave employment to 160 sharecropper families; when the owner installed on his land 22 tractors and 13 four-row culti-vators, 130 families totaling about 700 people were displaced, and the plantation thereafter operated with but 30 families who were placed on a day-labor basis. On another plantation of smaller size, machines and a few men hired on a wage basis replaced the 35 families previously needed to cultivate the crops. The displacement by machinery of farm families

[29] Kolb and Brunner, *op. cit.*, pp. 99–100.

leads to much mobility and to the increase in urban population that is discussed in the following chapter.

Families that remain on farms are in the process of adjustment to increasing mechanization. Since the rate at which mechanization has proceeded has greatly increased since 1920 and will probably not reach its peak until about 1975, those changes in the rural family now observable as related to mechanization may be expected to continue at least through another generation.[30] The adjustments are more acute in the South than in the North. Large farm machines, drawn by great teams of horses, have been used in the corn and wheat belts for many years, so that the change to mechanized power displaces laborers but does not change the basic system of farming. In the South, on the other hand, the change is not one of degree of mechanization but a revolution in which hand labor performed on a family basis is being replaced by machines. This revolution entails a change in the basic system of farming and one that will increase the standard of living for owners of large plantations. Small farmers and those in the hills where hand labor is still necessary are at a disadvantage and will be increasingly so as they must compete more and more with the less expensive mechanized production. It is anticipated that in time half the tenants on plantations will be replaced by machine production.[31]

Technological changes greatly reduce the isolation of farm families and consequently destroy the typically rural folk culture. Automobiles not only increase the range of daily or weekly contacts, but facilitate long vacation trips during seasons of the year when the farm does not need daily attention and residual tasks may be left to a hired man. The hayseed, the hick, the hillbilly are being replaced by well-dressed and well-informed farm families. Local areas lose their piquant flavor of individuality. Of great importance also are motion pictures, radios, television, and the many magazines that are delivered at the farm mailbox. All these means of mass communication extend to all people, urban and rural, a uniform culture (Figure 9).

With the increased standard of living that mechanization brings, these facilities of communication and education are within the reach of more

[30] Robert T. McMillan, *Social Aspects of Farm Mechanization in Oklahoma*, Bulletin B-339 (Oklahoma Agricultural Experiment Station, Oklahoma A. and M. College, November, 1949).

[31] Arthur Raper, "The Role of Agricultural Technology in Southern Social Change," *Social Forces*, 25 (1946), 21–30.

and more families.   The higher living standard applies primarily to the owners of the mechanized farms, or to young tenants who aspire to become owners.   The shift from sharecropper or tenant who farms on shares to employment of farm labor for wages benefits the farm worker in various ways.   He has a more even income and therefore greater security in that he is less dependent upon the vicissitudes of the weather. At the same time, of course, he may not benefit from an especially fruitful year.   With wages the way is also open for a better control of rural child

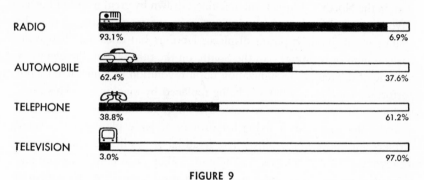

RADIO — 93.1% / 6.9%

AUTOMOBILE — 62.4% / 37.6%

TELEPHONE — 38.8% / 61.2%

TELEVISION — 3.0% / 97.0%

FIGURE 9

Means of Communication, Farm Families, 1950

This graph shows the percentage of farm families possessing each of the indicated communication facilities.   Not shown, however, is the unevenness of regional distribution.   The South is the least well equipped.   For example, approximately two thirds of Northern farms have telephones, one half of Western farms, but only one sixth of Southern.   (Source: *1950 Census of Housing, Preliminary Reports, Year Built, Household Equipment, and Cooking and Heating Fuel, for Dwelling Units in the United States: April 1, 1950,* Series HC-5, No 2 [Bureau of the Census, June 10, 1951], p. 7; and *1950 Census of Agriculture, Preliminary Estimate, 1950; With Comparisons, 1945 and 1940,* Series AC50–3, No. 00 [Bureau of the Census, November 25, 1951], p. 3.)

labor, organization of farm laborers into unions, and securing of benefits now available to the industrial worker.   On the other hand, study of some regions that have many very large farms with absentee and especially corporation ownership shows that schools and churches decline, recreational facilities are not provided, trade centers are not well supported, housing is poor, and the delinquency rate is somewhat higher than in rural communities with smaller farms operated by owners.[32]

[32] Kolb and Brunner, *op. cit.,* pp. 102–103.

Many household laborsaving devices have lightened the housewife's work as technology and especially rural electrification have brought electric washing machines, refrigerators, deep freezers, vacuum cleaners, stoves, and other modern equipment into the farm home (Figure 10).

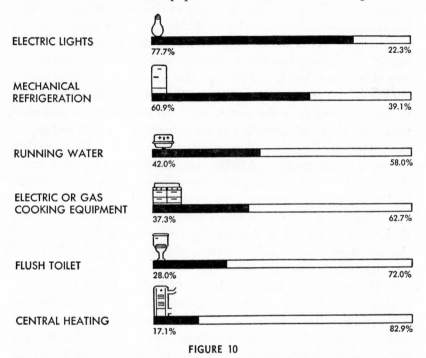

ELECTRIC LIGHTS — 77.7% | 22.3%

MECHANICAL REFRIGERATION — 60.9% | 39.1%

RUNNING WATER — 42.0% | 58.0%

ELECTRIC OR GAS COOKING EQUIPMENT — 37.3% | 62.7%

FLUSH TOILET — 28.0% | 72.0%

CENTRAL HEATING — 17.1% | 82.9%

FIGURE 10

Household Laborsaving Equipment on Farms, 1950

As shown by this graph, only electricity and mechanical refrigeration are owned by a majority of farm families in the United States. Moreover, regional distribution of these conveniences, like that of communication facilities, is uneven. New England farms are most thoroughly equipped and east south central farms least well equipped. (Source: *1950 Census of Housing, Preliminary Reports, Year Built, Household Equipment, and Cooking and Heating Fuel, for Dwelling Units in the United States: April 1, 1950,* Series HC-5, No. 2 [Bureau of the Census, June 10, 1951]; *Rural Family Living Charts* [U. S. Department of Agriculture, October 1951] pp. 44, 52.)

Women and children are freed by these household machines from much arduous labor, and the level of comfort is brought nearer to that of the city family. Thus, the distinctions between farm and city families based on different family functions and levels of culture are tending to lessen.

The farm family responds to technology as does the city family: it is set free from its geographical location and is exposed to many secondary and perhaps conflicting stimuli.

Mechanization also changes the meaning of the farm to the family. As the farm ceases to be a family project and becomes instead a business arrangement, sentimental attachment declines and some degree of family unity is lost.   As in the city, the husband tends to become the "chief earner" and the wife assumes the role of household manager and distributor of income.   She is still an important member of the farm family, but less a direct partner in production.   This change in functions and the variety of stimuli from the outside break up the traditional pattern of values and roles and open the way for rational adjustments and experimentation in family organization and interrelationships.   The home need no longer be the center of all family activities, for the automobile brings the city close.   The farm wife may join clubs and become a community leader.   Nor does the home necessarily shelter all its members.   The old person has less usefulness on the mechanized farm and is a hindrance to the freedom of younger members.   It is not surprising, therefore, to find that old people tend to "retire" to the nearby villages or cities, thus in old age making an adjustment from rural to city life.   Young people also leave the farm for jobs in nearby cities or for higher education.

Farming as a business widens the separation between farm families and helps to create rural social classes.   Large farms managed by owner-managers and worked by tenants or hired laborers always tend to create social classes.   Examples are the cotton plantations, with the owners set sharply aside from tenants, or the fruit farms of the West with the great social gulf between owners or managers and transient laborers.   As large mechanized farms increase, social stratification will also increase and families will become fixed in a certain social stratum.   It will become more difficult for the tenant to accumulate sufficient money to buy and equip a farm for himself, and a permanent class of farm tenants or farm laborers may develop, in which this status will pass from father to son.

RURAL CHANGE AND URBANIZATION

Overall figures on farm mechanization do not reveal the close relation of farm mechanization to urban influences.   A significant study published in 1949 classifies counties according to the percentage of the population that is rural-farm.[33] Counties range from less than 10 per cent rural to more than 90 per cent.   The percentage of the county that is rural is an index of urban influence, since in counties with a small proportion of rural people farmers are near to cities (2,500 population and over), whereas in the highly rural counties farmers have less contact with cities.

A glance at Table 3 shows the marked regularity with which household facilities decrease as rurality of counties increases.   For some facilities the table gives comparable percentages for 1930 and 1945.   In highly rural as in slightly rural counties, mechanical facilities on farms are increasing.   Mechanization appears as a definite process in all rural areas, but is most marked on farms near cities.

SIMILARITIES OF FARM FAMILIES

Traditional types of farming, whether carried on by the owners, tenants, or migrant families, tend to produce certain basic family characteristics.

1. Attachment to the land that tends to persist from one generation to another.

2. Limitation of social contacts to the rural neighborhood.

3. An inclusive type of family life encompassing all members and all phases of life and adjusted to the demands of farming.

4. Active daily participation of all members of the family in work and social life.

5. Well-organized family life with roles clearly defined, usually with the father as the head, but with all members functioning in useful ways.

6. Dependence of the family upon its own resources, those of the larger family, and, to some extent, those of the rural neighborhood.

From this rural situation arose the traditional values and social norms discussed in Chapter 1: social values of family life, permanence of marriage, family and neighborhood supervision of mate selection, limitation of sex relations to marriage, complementary roles of husband and wife, a wide array of family functions encouraging participation of all members, economic independence, large number of children, and rearing of the children by their parents.

But disturbing elements have intruded into this farm-adjusted family

[33] Grace L. Flagg and T. Wilson Longmore, *Trends in Rural and Urban Levels of Living,* Agriculture Information Bulletin, No. 11 (U. S. Department of Agriculture, Bureau of Agricultural Economics, December, 1949).

TABLE 3

Farms with Selected Household Facilities According to Degree of Rurality of Counties *

Facility	Total for United States	Counties having specified percentage of population living on farms									
		Under 10	10–19	20–29	30–39	40–49	50–59	60–69	70–79	80–89	90 and over
Running water in dwelling											
1945	24.0	53.0%	43.4%	35.0%	30.6%	23.4%	18.7%	12.9%	8.6%	6.9%	4.5%
1930	15.8	40.4	33.2	26.1	22.5	16.1	12.5	7.3	2.9	2.0	1.9
Electricity											
1945	44.5	72.4	65.4	59.0	53.6	47.3	40.4	29.4	23.3	19.2	16.6
1930	13.4	41.6	29.9	22.7	19.2	12.7	9.4	4.8	2.4	1.7	1.6
Mechanical refrigeration											
1940	14.6	36.5	28.4	21.3	19.2	14.4	10.5	6.7	5.5	4.7	5.2
Radio											
1945	68.0	76.7	74.6	74.1	72.1	70.6	70.1	64.5	54.8	48.6	52.0
1930	20.8	39.8	33.0	30.8	26.3	23.9	21.6	13.3	4.5	2.2	2.8
Telephone											
1945	29.8	45.4	40.1	38.5	34.7	34.9	32.9	22.1	9.6	5.5	5.7

* Grace L. Flagg and T. Wilson Longmore, *Trends in Rural and Urban Levels of Living*, Agriculture Information Bulletin, No. 11 (U. S. Department of Agriculture, Bureau of Agricultural Economics, December, 1949), p. 27.

pattern: an excess number of children who in early adulthood migrate to cities; displacement of farmers by machinery, again leading to migration; commercialization of farming with loss of sentiment toward it as a way of living; mechanization of the farm household as well as the farm plant with increased freedom of movement and participation in national and world affairs.

QUESTIONS

1. What evidences have you observed of the adaptability of the family to social conditions?

2. Discuss the origin of the present popular concept of the ideal family.

3. What did the pioneer period contribute to the American family?

4. Is it fair to say that the rural family is a disappearing type?

5. What changes has mechanization brought to the rural family? If you are a member of a rural family or know a rural family well, try to trace the changes that have occurred during the past generation because of mechanization.

6. How have farm families living near cities adjusted to the combination of urban and rural influences?

7. The two types of large-scale farming—the plantation and the Western commercial farm—contrast with each other in many ways. How do you account for the development of such different types of farming within one society?

8. Many people lament the passing of the family farm and the type of family life that it developed. Would it be possible to re-create the older type of farm family under present social conditions?

BIBLIOGRAPHY

Historical background

Adams, James Truslow, *The Epic of America* (Little, Brown, 1933).

Cole, Arthur Charles, *The Irrepressible Conflict, 1850–1865* (Macmillan, 1934).

Fish, Carl Russell, *The Rise of the Common Man, 1840–1850* (Macmillan, 1927).

Nevins, Allan, *The Emergence of Modern America, 1865–1878* (Macmillan, 1927).

History of the American family

Calhoun, Arthur W., *A Social History of the American Family from Colonial Times to the Present* (3 vols., Cleveland: Arthur H. Clark Co., 1919; also Barnes and Noble, 1945).

Background of rural life

Kolb, John H., and Brunner, Edmund de S., *A Study of Rural Society* (Houghton Mifflin, 1946, revised 1952).

Lively, C. E., and Taeuber, Conrad, *Rural Migration in the United States,* Research Monograph XVIII, Works Progress Administration, Division of Social Research (Government Printing Office, 1938).

Nelson, Lowry, *Rural Sociology* (American Book, 1948).

Shannon, Fred A., *The Farmer's Last Frontier—Agriculture 1860–1897,* Vol. V of the Economic History of the United States (Farrar and Rinehart, 1945).

United States Department of Agriculture, *Farmers in a Changing World,* Yearbook of Agriculture, 1940 (Government Printing Office, 1940).

Rural family life

Alexander, F. D., "Family Life in a Rural Community," *Social Forces,* 18 (1939–40), 392–402.

Beers, H. W., "A Portrait of the Farm Family in Central New York," *American Sociological Review,* 2 (1937), 591–600.

Davis, Allison, Gardner, B. B., and Gardner, M. R., *Deep South* (University of Chicago Press, 1941), Part II.

Hagood, Margaret, *Mothers of the South: Portraiture of the White Tenant Farm Family* (University of North Carolina Press, 1939).

Johnson, Charles S., *Shadow of the Plantation* (University of Chicago Press, 1934).

Loomis, Charles P., and Beegle, J. Allan, *Rural Social Systems* (Prentice-Hall, 1950), section on "Family and Informal Groups as Social Systems."

Miller, Nora, *The Girl in the Rural Family* (University of North Carolina Press, 1936).

Migration and the Family

Migration of families into and within the United States is not a new phenomenon. The colonies were settled by immigrants from Great Britain and Europe; the West was developed by migrants from the East. Early labor was supplied by slaves brought in from Africa; later, labor was drawn from the mass of immigrants from Europe and the Orient. However, these great movements of people had all passed or declined by the time of World War I.

SIGNIFICANCE OF PRESENT MIGRATION

Family mobility in America at present is primarily a result of internal movements. Compared with earlier years, few immigrants come in from other countries bringing with them major problems of cultural adjustment, whereas within the United States people move about with great freedom, sometimes as a temporary diversion from the usual life routine, sometimes in search of employment or a new way of life.

Ease of mobility

Mobility today is faster and more free-ranging than in earlier periods. Foot, horse, and boat—all slow and laborious means of travel—have been replaced successively by steam train, electric train, automobile, and airplane. The increase of distance that may be covered in a given length of time in the history of the United States is tremendous. Travel may now be accomplished with little discomfort and a minimum of loss of employment. In terms of local travel, the distance that can be covered in one hour is related to types of transportation as follows:

Foot	2½–3 miles
Horsecar	4–5 miles
Electric traction	7–8 miles
Rapid transit electric lines	17–18 miles
Automobile	50 miles or more

On cross-country travel the speed is still greater for trains, automobiles, and airplanes.[1]

In terms of the family the automobile is the most important means of transportation, since the individual family can afford to own and operate a car and to come and go at will on wide-flung highways that make all parts of the United States easily accessible. The family no longer needs to wait for the formation of a pack train to give security in crossing the Plains; to pack baskets of provisions; or to confine itself to the regions reached by railroads. At any hour of the day or night the family may bundle children, baggage, and pets into the car, secure in the knowledge that wayside motels and hot-dog stands will give them shelter and food as they speed over highways or jolt on side roads. Such ease of mobility has made Americans mobile-minded, and movements of many types are a part of the normal condition of life.

Types of mobility

Mobility is a very general term that may include the following types:

1. The daily pattern of movement between home and place of work or home and school. These movements become a customary part of life to which individuals and families adjust.

2. Repetitive movements of wider scope, as between winter and summer home; or the annual vacation trip, which tends to follow a definite pattern even though the destination may vary from year to year. These movements do not disrupt family life, since the entire family usually moves as a unit, thus maintaining habitual interactional relationships. In the alternation between winter and summer homes, the family also retains its community associations. On the vacation trip, no attempt is made at community adjustment on the trip, which becomes simply a mild interruption of community relationships at home. Often these repetitive moves by family units strengthen family unity by throwing the family into close association and by providing stimulating family projects.

[1] Amos H. Hawley, *Human Ecology, A Theory of Community Structure* (Ronald, 1950), pp. 405–406.

3. Change of residence within the community. Such movements are frequent, approximately 13 per cent of all people changing residence each year, though remaining within the same county (Table 4). Many of these moves are within the same village or city and might be no further

TABLE 4

Migration Status and Type of Migration *

	Total	Urban	Rural nonfarm	Rural farm
Nonmigrants	94.0%	94.4%	92.1%	95.3%
Same house	80.9	81.1	78.2	83.8
Different house in same				
county	13.1	13.3	13.8	11.6
Migrants	5.6	5.2	7.6	4.6
Within a state	3.0	2.5	4.0	3.4
Between contiguous				
states	1.1	1.0	1.8	0.6
Between noncontiguous				
states	1.5	1.7	1.7	0.6
Persons abroad,				
March 1, 1949	0.3	0.4	0.4	0.1

* Current Population Reports, Population Characteristics, Internal Migration and Mobility in the United States: March, 1949, to March, 1950, Series P-20, No. 36 (Bureau of the Census, December 9, 1951), p. 9.

than across the street. Some of these movements, of course, are linked with social mobility into higher or lower social-class levels, and in these cases involve some readjustment on the part of the family.

4. Movements over greater distance that carry people away from old kinship and community ties and often into new regions where cultural patterns are different. These longer moves, which are called migration, are the most significant for family adjustment; and it is with migration of families that this chapter is concerned.

Present migration differs from the earlier migration by which the West was settled, although much of the movement is still westward, in that the objective now is industrial production rather than agricultural development, and the destination is urban instead of rural. Therefore a different type of adjustment is needed. The pioneering settler's most difficult adjustment was to physical conditions—the land to be cleared; the river to be dammed for power; the droughts, blizzards, and tornadoes of the Western plains to be accepted as inevitable. Migrations today bring an impact not of man against nature but of migrant man as a socially formed human being against an already formed and functioning industrial culture, which may or may not be compatible with his own socially formed ideals and standards.

Industrial demands for migration

Employment opportunities are at the base of much internal migration. Fluctuation in employment seems to demand a fluid population, with families ready and willing at short notice to move to new locations.   At present opportunities are greatest in the urban areas in the North and West.   But even in these areas, available employment changes from one period to another.   Wars and preparation for defense call for thousands of additional factory workers, supervisory personnel, and administrative officers in specific industrial centers.   Peace closes some factories and, at least during a period of reconversion to peacetime production, releases thousands of workers; these unemployed people move on.   Depressions cause widespread unemployment; 30 per cent of the labor force was unemployed in 1933.   Some of the depression-unemployed try their luck in other places; some return temporarily to the farms where they were born.   Technological changes, whereby machines displace workers, also place families on the road.   This ebb and flow of opportunity, with first one area, then another, offering more security and higher incomes, demands a mobile population.

Not only do industrial realities call for mobility, but related agencies and developments support it.   Employment agencies, seeking to place the unemployed on the one hand and to satisfy the demands of industry on the other, encourage mobility, as do the automobile and trailer manufacturers who offer a mobile home equipped with bedrooms, bath, toilet, kitchen, and heat that requires only a space to park and connections with water, electricity, and drainage facilities.   In 1950, 63,000 trailers were manufactured, 93 per cent of which were sold for defense workers and military families.[2]   Such encouragement of mobility, although coordinated with our present economic development and production needs, nevertheless is contrary to our established ideal of a stable homestead and home ownership—an ideal toward which the mobile pioneer always strove.   Present mobility promises no such end.   Instead, it fosters a new mode of life

---

[2] News item in *Chicago Daily Tribune,* quoting president of the Trailer Coach Manufacturers Association, September 4, 1951.

for a segment of the working population—a mode to which neither families nor community institutions are well adapted at present, as the discussion of the transient rural family disclosed.

The birth rate and migration

Increased population is needed in urban areas not only because industries are expanding but also because the long-term trend in urban birth rates is low, so that, without in-migrants from some source, cities would actually decline in population. Figure 11 through comparison of the net

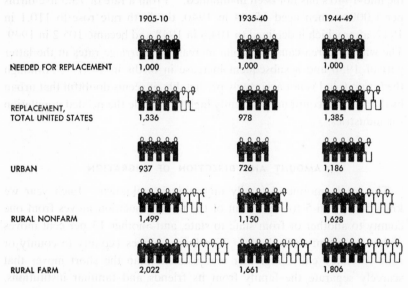

	1905-10	1935-40	1944-49
NEEDED FOR REPLACEMENT	1,000	1,000	1,000
REPLACEMENT, TOTAL UNITED STATES	1,336	978	1,385
URBAN	937	726	1,186
RURAL NONFARM	1,499	1,150	1,628
RURAL FARM	2,022	1,661	1,806

Each figure represents 200 people

FIGURE 11

Net Reproduction Rates

These rates indicate whether the population is replacing itself through a balancing of births and deaths. A rate of 1,000 signifies that the population is just replacing itself; a rate above 1,000 implies a potentially gaining population, a rate below 1,000 a potentially declining population. For many years prior to the 1940's urban population had not been replacing itself, depending upon an influx of excess rural population for maintenance of and increase in numbers. The prosperous, war-torn 1940's reversed the urban trend and increased the net reproduction rate of rural areas. The movement of excess rural people into industrial areas continues. (Source: *Statistical Abstract of the United States, 1950* [Bureau of the Census, 1950], p. 26.)

reproduction rates for urban and rural areas shows the great failure of urban areas prior to the 1940's to maintain their population through births alone. Conversely, rural areas produced more than enough children to maintain a stable population at the same time that fewer and fewer agricultural workers were needed. This lack of adjustment between number of people and number of jobs accounts for a large part of the flow of migration from rural to urban areas. Figure 11 also shows that in the mid-1940's urban as well as rural areas had birth rates sufficiently high to more than reproduce the population. However, the high birth rate of the mid-1940's has not been maintained. From a rate of 73.5 live births per 1,000 women aged 15–44 in 1940, the birth rate rose to 110.1 in 1947, after which it declined to 104.8 in 1948 and became 105.2 in 1949. The war in Korea caused a slight increase in marriage rates in the latter part of 1950 and a subsequent increase in births in 1951.[3] Although the future trend is not accurately predictable, it seems doubtful that urban birth rates will continue sufficiently high to provide the needed population for industries.

AMOUNT AND DIRECTION OF MIGRATION

The total amount of family migration is unknown. Each year we know that from 5 to 6 per cent of the total population moves from one county to another or from state to state, and another 13 per cent moves within the county (Table 4). The longer moves (county to county or state to state) call for greater readjustment than the short moves that scarcely separate the family from its friends and familiar institutions. With 5 or 6 per cent of the population migrating each year, the probability is very great that at least one significant move will be made within the marital lifetime of a couple. Many couples move often in response to employment changes: for example, during World War II families from nonindustrial areas flooded communities with war industries; at the end of the war, these families returned to their former homes or sought employment elsewhere. A few families, it may be assumed, become permanently migratory, following industrial employment as the rural migratory worker follows the crops.

The direction of migration calls for adjustment to new types of com-

[3] News release from Federal Security Agency, Public Health Service, Washington, D. C., dated August 3, 1951.

munities and new regional cultures. The trend for many years has been from rural to urban. Usually farmers move to nearby small cities, small-city people to larger cities, and so on, with the city people migrating longer distances than the rural.[4] The change in total population between 1940 and 1950 for different types of communities reflects the net migration (along with other types of mobility and the excess of births over deaths). The United States as a whole increased in population 14.3 per cent.[5] Cities of 50,000 and over increased 13.0 per cent, an increase above that gained from the urban excess of births over deaths and therefore indicative of either immigration from other countries or in-migration from small communities. The suburban areas around these cities increased 34.7 per cent, a gain showing a high degree of in-migration. Smaller cities and rural areas, with the highest birth rates, increased only 5.7 per cent. One phase of adjustment of the migrant family, therefore, is from rural to urban living.

Migration often carries the family from one cultural region to another. The usual lines of migration are from the South to the North and West and from the Middle West to the Far West, with minor reciprocal movements between Southeast and Northeast. The migration from the South includes both whites and Negroes. Normally migrating short distances, many Negroes were encouraged in the early 1940's to make long distance moves from the South to Northern industrial cities, such as Detroit and Chicago, where they were employed in war industries. The total westward movement during World War II was also wide-ranging. Although the average migrant to defense centers in 1940–1941 traveled 125 miles, those who entered the Los Angeles area averaged nearly 1,300 miles.[6]

The regional changes in population between 1940 and 1950 highlight the lines of migration.[7] As compared with an increase of 14.3 for the United States, the three Pacific states made a net gain of 47.6 per cent, the north-central region 13.6 per cent, the west-north-central only 3.6 per

[4] *Current Population Reports, Population Characteristics, Internal Migration in the United States: April, 1948, to April, 1949*, Series P-20, No. 28 (Bureau of the Census, March 17, 1950), p. 2.

[5] *1950 Census of Population, Preliminary Counts, Population of Standard Metropolitan Areas: April 1, 1950*, Series PC-3, No. 3 (Bureau of the Census, November 5, 1950), p. 1.

[6] Henry S. Shryock, "Wartime Shifts of the Civilian Population," *Milbank Memorial Fund Quarterly*, 25 (1947), 269–283.

[7] *1950 Census of Population, Preliminary Counts, Population of Continental United States by Regions, Divisions, and States: April 1, 1950*, Series PC-3, No. 1 (Bureau of the Census, October 15, 1950), p. 1.

cent with North Dakota losing population, and the northeast 9.0 per cent. The South, despite its high birth rate, showed a net gain of only 12.6 per cent, and three states (Arkansas, Mississippi, and Oklahoma) lost population. To the extent that different standards of living, types of family organization, and patterns of family interaction differentiate one region from another, families making long moves face problems of adjustment. They uproot themselves from among those of their own kind and for satisfactory fulfillment of needs must adapt themselves to the attitudes and mores of the new community.

THE UNBALANCED SEX RATIO

Rates of migration are not evenly distributed between both sexes or through all age periods; nor is the destination of migration the same for both sexes and all ages. The differentiation of migration by age and sex creates an imbalance of the sex ratio that affects the selection of marital partners.

TABLE 5

Percentage of Stated Age Groups Who Are Migrants *

Age	Males	Females
Under 18	5.7	5.7
18–24	9.8	10.5
25–34	9.1	7.8
35–44	4.9	4.1
45–64	3.6	2.4
65 and over	2.0	2.4

* Current Population Reports, Population Characteristics, Internal Migration and Mobility in the United States: March, 1949, to March, 1950, Series P-20, No. 36 (Bureau of the Census, December 9, 1951), p. 10.

Young adults migrate more frequently than do older people. The rate of migration is higher for those 18–24 than for any other age period, with the rate for the 25–34 age group only slightly lower (Table 5). Considered as a proportion of all migrants, men aged 18–34 constitute 42.1 per cent of all male migrants, and women of this age period 44.9 per cent of all female migrants.[8] Although the majority of migrants are

[8] Current Population Reports, Population Characteristics, Internal Migration and Mobility in the United States: March, 1949, to March, 1950, Series P-20, No. 36 (Bureau of the Census, December 9, 1951), p. 10.

married, many of marriageable age have never been married or are divorced or widowed and therefore often again interested in marriage. (Table 6).

TABLE 6

Marital Status of Migrants *

	Migrants aged 14–24	Migrants aged 25–34
Single	47.2%	11.4%
Divorced	1.1	3.2
Widowed	0.5	0.8
Married	51.2	84.6

* Based on *Current Population Reports, Population Characteristics, Internal Migration in the United States: April, 1947, to April, 1948,* Series P-20, No. 22 (Bureau of the Census, January 28, 1949), p. 8. Corresponding figures for the 1949–1950 migration are not available.

Since migration is an individual affair, uncontrolled by any national planning, young men and women neither migrate from their home communities in equal proportions, nor direct their migrations in accordance with the sex ratio at their destination. Unequal migration of young men and women from a community depletes that community of one sex and reduces the opportunities for marriage of the other. Similarly, unequal in-migration into a community disturbs the sex ratio and deprives the majority sex group of full opportunity for marriage.

Unequal migration is reflected in the sex ratio, which states the number of males per 100 females. In a natural community undisturbed by immigration, migration, or war the sex ratio tends to remain near 100, that is, equal numbers of males and females. In 1950 for the whole United States, the sex ratio was 98.1, which may be interpreted to mean a deficiency of 2 males for every 100 females. Migrations have greatly disturbed this sex ratio in many communities. Figure 12 shows the low urban sex ratio that has resulted from the migration of girls and women to cities. Men, remaining on farms or migrating to rural areas for farm work, cause a large excess of men in rural areas. It is not surprising, therefore, to find a higher percentage of rural women than of urban women married; for men, the reverse situation exists, with a larger proportion of urban than rural men married.

Interregional migrations also create shortages of marriage partners, as Table 7 shows. Women in Southern cities are the most handicapped of urban dwellers, either because of in-migration of women or out-

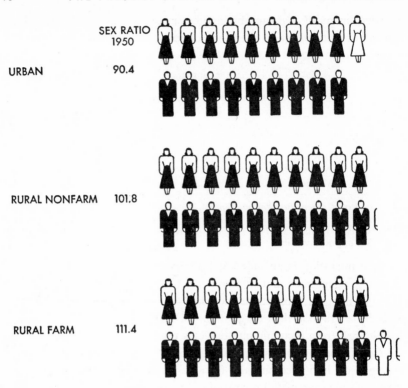

Each figure represents 10 persons.

FIGURE 12

Sex Ratio for Persons Aged 15–29

For every 100 females aged 15–29 in cities there were only 90.4 males in 1950; in rural nonfarm areas the sex distribution was almost equal; and on farms males exceeded females.   At these ages an unbalanced sex ratio disturbs dating and marriage.   Some members of the majority sex will be left without mates; on the other hand, members of the minority sex who lack some of the most desired qualities for mates will nevertheless be chosen for marriage.   (Source: *1950 Census of Population, Preliminary Reports, General Character of the Population of the United States: April 1, 1950,* Series PC-7, No. 1 [Bureau of the Census, February 25, 1951], pp. 6–7.)

migration of men, or both.   On farms in the north-central region and the West men greatly exceed women.   For Southern Negroes the pattern is somewhat different.   Of course, many local areas or individual cities have still greater imbalance of the sex ratio than is shown in Table 7; for example, areas with heavy industries attract men, whereas some commercial cities or others (such as Washington, D.C.) that offer attractive employment to young women may have a great excess of women.

TABLE 7

Sex Ratios for Regions, Urban and Rural, for Ages 15–29 Years *

	Northeast	North Central	South	West
Total population				
Urban	90.5	93.5	85.3	93.3
Rural nonfarm	116.2	93.4	99.5	105.2
Rural farm	108.6	117.6	106.4	124.7
Nonwhite population				
Urban	—	—	82.7	—
Rural nonfarm	—	—	112.4	—
Rural farm	—	—	90.4	—

* Based on *1950 Census of Population, Preliminary Reports, General Characteristics of the Population, by Regions: April 1, 1950,* Series PC-7, No. 3 (Bureau of the Census, April 30, 1951), pp. 12–13.

Migrations therefore create many problems related to mate selection and the marriage rate.

MIGRATION AND BREAKS IN FAMILY LIFE

At certain crucial periods, when adjustments are called for, migration becomes a means of facilitating the adjustment. The first year of marriage, when young people are establishing an independent family, is a time of migration: 21.4 per cent of young married people migrate, as compared with 6.5 per cent of all married people. Divorce also encourages migration, with 14.2 per cent of newly divorced people migrating, in comparison with 9.9 per cent of all divorced people. Newly widowed people also have a slightly higher rate of migration than those widowed for a longer time.[9] In all three cases, a general change in mode of living is occurring, which may be made easier with freedom from family and friendship ties and pressures. At the same time, if the migration carries the couple or person into a new type of cultural setting, adjustment to the new culture is necessary.

Other breaks in the life pattern, less closely related to family inter-

[9] *Current Population Reports, Population Characteristics, Internal Migration in the United States: April, 1947, to April, 1948,* Series P-20, No. 22 (Bureau of the Census, January 28, 1949), p. 8.

relationships, also foster migration.   Unemployment, for example, leads people to migrate.   The threat of unemployment implied by the growing mechanization of the rural South, together with the lure of greater freedom and higher wages in the North and West, has led Negroes into migrations that almost assume the proportions of a mass movement.

PATTERNS OF MIGRATION

Migration affects family life in the degree to which accustomed social and cultural contacts are modified.   Some types of migration carry the migrant into completely new social groups with an alien culture; he may completely lose his old contacts, and in a sense have to remake his personality in the mold of the new culture.   Other types of migration enable the migrant to retain his old social and cultural contacts or take him into a new community very similar to his old one.   Adjustment tends to be difficult or uncomplicated according to dissimilarity or similarity of the old and new settings.   The exception is found in the person or family not well adjusted to its social situation; migration then takes on the aspect of flight into a promised land.   In general, the relation of migrations to family adjustment may be analyzed under the following headings: (1) controlling body; (2) degree of cultural change involved; (3) recurrence of migration; (4) acceptance or rejection by the new community; and (5) personal and family satisfaction of needs.

1. The controlling body may be the entire community.   In the early days of settlement, a company of people from the same community in the East sometimes organized and made plans for a new settlement in the Middle West, usually duplicating their home community.   When the model was New England, the new settlement was laid out on paper complete with the village square, church, school, and orderly array of residential lots.   Agents were sent to the unsettled portion of the West to select a site, and when all arrangements were completed the entire company of family groups migrated, built their homes and public buildings, and continued almost without interruption their community and family life. The old mores continued to control, and the old habits sufficed.   Readjustment was at a minimum.   This type of migration has almost completely disappeared.

A second type of controlling body is the large family or kinship group.

When such a group migrates as a unit, personal interrelationships remain intact, although the exigencies of the migration may give members of the family new roles to play. For instance, the older members, in authority in the stable residence, may find themselves unable to adapt their attitudes to new conditions; the way is then open for control to pass to younger and more flexible members. An interesting fictional description of such a large-family migration is *The Grapes of Wrath,* in which John Steinbeck described the movement from Oklahoma to California of the Joad family after the destruction of their farm by draught and dust storms. With the furniture piled on a truck, the father, mother, grandparents, an uncle, adult and minor children, an itinerant preacher, and the husband of a daughter traveled as a unit, sharing both hardships and the earnings of any member of the family. Eventually, the adversities of the situation caused the family partially to disintegrate.

The small-family group more commonly is the migrating unit at the present time, often consisting of the newly married couple or the young family group with minor children. Again family interrelationships are maintained, and, since a high degree of interdependence in a physical sense also exists, the family has a high probability of maintaining its unity.

Finally, much of present-day migration is by individuals who leave the family unit. These individuals usually are young men or women who separate themselves from the parental family and strike out alone. Being unmarried, they face the problem of making satisfactory marital choices and adjustment outside the known community. Except as family training has instilled social codes in the form of personal standards and ideals, the individual is freed from family and community restraints.

2. The degree of cultural change may be so slight as to be insignificant. The farmer who moves from one county to another, or the urban family that changes residence within the same local urban area, makes a slight physical adjustment to new living quarters but has almost no cultural adjustment to make, as he tends to remain within his own ethnic and social-class group. Social adjustment also is at a minimum; he may still be able to trade at the same stores, to attend the same church, and to send his children to the same school. New institutional contacts are usually with institutions very similar to those relinquished by the move.

A somewhat greater degree of adjustment is necessary when the family or individual moves from one region of the United States to another. The

Negro or white who moves north from the Deep South finds a new set of mores controlling Negro-white relationships, which penetrates to neighborhood, school, and work contacts.   The Easterner who moves west may have to adjust his conceptions of friendliness, dress, or the function of divorce to the less restrained folkways and mores of the West.   Also, the rural family or person who moves to the city may find acceptable many types of behavior forbidden in the rural areas—Sunday dances, late hours, casual dating, or the peculiar combination of lack of neighborliness and lack of privacy of the apartment house.   Nevertheless, some preliminary preparation for the new culture has been gained from reading, motion pictures, conversations with returned travelers, or letters from friends. Often the move is stimulating rather than disorganizing, although it may be disorganizing if the family cannot modify its ideals to acceptance of the new values, or cannot make social contacts adequate to personal needs for friendship and recognition.

The most marked cultural change is experienced by the immigrant who leaves one culture and enters into another.   The adjustment is especially difficult if the immigrant comes individually rather than in a family group or into an already established ethnic colony.   This type of mobility and adjustment reached its peak in the period preceding World War I when in an occasional year more than a million European immigrants entered the United States; it has become of relatively minor importance since the 1920's when legal restrictions reduced immigration to a mere trickle and the 1930's when the depression sent back to Europe more people than newly entered.   Present ethnic family adjustment of an acute type is confined primarily to displaced European families and to Mexican and Puerto Rican families.

3. The recurrence of mobility also affects adjustment.   If only one move is made into a community where work may readily be found—or has been secured in advance—adjustment is facilitated by the knowledge that here is a new permanent home.   The family typically makes an effort to find a place in the cultural and social setting.

Adjustment also is made by the family that follows a pattern of repetitive or cyclical mobility.   The family with a winter and a summer home typically adjusts to both, and once the adjustment has been made simply shifts gears spring and fall, following one pattern of dress, family living, amusements, and social contacts in the summer and another in the winter.

Similarly, the transient family that follows the crops adjusts to the constant mobility with periods of a few weeks or, at most, months between moves.   These moves differ little from the daily mobility of the employed members of a family to their place of work or of children to and from school each day.   They are not disruptive but, on the contrary, are a means of securing daily satisfactions.   Families accept these repetitive movements and adjust to them.

Transiency without a pattern is apt to be disturbing.   The family does not accept transiency as the mode of life but retains the values and habits of fixed residence, although for some reason or other (such as inability to find satisfactory work) it is unable to establish fixed residence.   A common type of transiency in the 1940's and 1950's is that of the family of the man in military service, whose movements are not subject to his control and whose family follows him from place to place, setting up housekeeping in whatever quarters are available, making touch-and-go contacts with other families of servicemen but always unable to sink roots into the community.   Such a family is forced into dependence upon itself; when this breaks down during illness or inadequate income the family must turn either to strangers for types of aid usually given by relatives or neighbors, or must resort to public agencies.

4. The readiness of the new community to receive migrants is important.   Often migrants are encouraged to come by employment agencies, chambers of commerce, or newly opened or expanding factories without consideration of how these migrants are to meet even elemental physical needs.   The situation is especially acute when workers arrive with their families and personal belongings packed in the family car, assuming that the community has facilities waiting for them.   A heavy influx of workers into boom towns, such as occurred during World War II and again in the early 1950's, almost always finds the communities unprepared to house the newcomers.   If the workers are of a different race or cultural background, the community may be not only unprepared for, but resistant and antagonistic to, the migrants.   Shanty towns and unorganized trailer camps may grow overnight on the edges of the city, unsupplied with sanitary facilities, pure drinking water, or garbage collection.   Permanent residents may oppose the increases in taxes required to provide these services.   Local institutions may resent the newcomers, not only because they are inadequate to handle so many additional members but because

an influx of many strangers invariably disturbs established customs and roles.   The migrants, for their part, return hostility for antagonism, feeling that if they work in the community they are entitled to services and the use of local institutions.   Families often find that they receive no friendly help in making an adjustment.   Only when a complete breakdown in the family occurs is any assistance available, and then it is usually that of an organized agency—the relief agency in case of unemployment; the visiting nurse or clinic when there is illness; and the sheriff, police, and courts when some delinquency occurs.

Migrants who arrive in small numbers or come into a colony of friends find the community much more ready to accept them, for they do not disturb the community patterns, deprive permanent residents of accustomed privileges and services, or threaten established roles.

5. The degree of satisfaction of the family or individual depends upon the combination of the above factors.   If the family is able to supply its physical needs, retain some connection with its past in the way of standards and values, maintain satisfactory interfamily relationships, and relate itself to the new community culturally and socially, there need be no maladjustment.   But at any one of these points the family may fail.   The failure may affect only a few members, such as the adolescent boy or girl who is not accepted by his new school group.   The lack of adjustment may touch only one area of life; for example, the family may find adequate work with sufficient income and feel in harmony with cultural and social patterns, but some members may become so homesick for the old home community that they return there, perhaps at considerable financial sacrifice.   A case in point is the retired couple who sold home and furniture and moved from the Middle West to Florida, where earlier vacations had occasionally been spent.   But as the newness of the vacationland wore off, Florida seemed a lonely and strange place for daily living, and soon the couple was back in the city where they had spent many years, seeking a new house, buying new furniture, and eagerly announcing their return to their many friends.

In general, adjustment is good to the degree that the individual moves with a family or community group, that the cultural change is slight, the change permanent, the new community receptive, and personal needs still met.

Three groups typical of present-day migrations are rural whites, Southern Negroes, and the families of servicemen. The adjustment problems of these three groups are described in some detail.

The rural white family

Undoubtedly the most marked migratory adjustment that the rural white family makes occurs when the Southern rural family migrates to the Northern industrial city.

1. The migrating unit is the family or the individual. Unmarried men often crowd into new industrial areas. The rural family of the South has already been described on pages 50–54: remote from urban influences but with the men maintaining trading contacts in nearby small cities; semipatriarchal in organization; the women and children from an early age active in farm work; four or five years of schooling; early marriages; crude home equipment; low income. These migrants would find themselves in a foreign land when they migrate north were it not that a call for workers spreads through a community or among relatives and often families or individuals who know each other congregate in the same industrial town. In addition a feeling of camaraderie springs up among Southern migrants from different areas, who easily recognize each other's regional origin by mode of dress and speech. There is therefore a certain transfer of Southern culture to the urban area that tempers the impact of the city.

2. The degree of cultural change is much greater than would be true for a Northern rural family migrating into a Northern city. The standard of education for children is a case in point. The child who in the South is expected to drop out of school after grade school or perhaps after only a few years in school to work on the farm is required in the Northern city to attend until the age of 16 or 18, according to the state laws. Parents and children alike may fail to appreciate the necessity for the required education or the restrictions on child labor. Early marriage also runs counter to Northern standards. The rural white family maintains a close watch over its daughters until they marry, with marriage occurring soon after a girl begins to attract the attention of young men. In the city, such supervision is difficult to maintain, and of longer duration. Girls may be eager for the excitement of city life and lack the sophistication to control their contacts with strangers. Families, unaccustomed to electrical household equipment and indoor plumbing, often misuse these

facilities.   Many are the jokes regarding such misuse told by Northerners at the expense of Southern families.[10]

Southern rural families are not well prepared in advance for the change. The lure of the industrial North is largely economic, and little preliminary interest in cultural changes exists.   The low educational level, absence of reading habits, and absence of radios in the rural homes all militate against cultural preparation.

3. Recurrence of mobility is related to economic opportunities.   A lay-off, a depression, or a long-drawn-out strike sends a wave of Southerners back home for a prolonged visit until employment in the North improves.   Thus, longing for the old home competes with the economic lure of the North.

4. The city, North or South, permits the rural migrant to enter at the lower end of the social scale.   His lack of education and skills tends to place him there.   In his first search for housing, he usually finds himself crowding into the low-rent or slum areas.   In Lexington, Kentucky, rural migrants comprise 80 per cent of those paying less than $10 monthly rental and only 40 per cent of those paying $50 or more per month.[11] In Flint, only about half as many migrants as total population owned their homes, lived in homes with basements (implying central heating), or had running water in their homes.[12]

Vocationally, too, the rural migrant must change his ways.   Accustomed only to farming by hand methods or with the aid of a mule for power, he is not fitted for skilled urban labor.   In Flint, Michigan, 68 per cent of Southern white migrants who were employed were unskilled laborers, as opposed to 54 per cent of the total employed population who fell into this classification.

5. Lack of early adjustment is shown by the tendency, already mentioned, of migrants to return South whenever work is slack.   In Flint, later adjustment is indicated by their wide distribution throughout the city after they gain a foothold and the high percentage of marriages (48.5) made with Michigan-born persons.[13]   Later booms create a new

[10] E. D. Beynon, "The Southern White Laborer Migrates to Michigan," *American Sociological Review*, 3 (1938), 333–343.

[11] Howard Beers and Catherine Heflin, "The Urban Status of Rural Migrants," *Social Forces*, 23 (1944), 33–34.

[12] Beynon, *op. cit.*

[13] Mary Heaton Vorse, "The Child Reservoir of the South," *Harper's Magazine*, 203 (July, 1951), 55–61.

need for laborers, and new groups herd in who must repeat the process of adjustment.

The Southern Negro

The Southern Negro who migrates faces acute problems of adjustment.

1. Controlling body.   Negroes migrate individually or by small-family groups.   The low sex ratio of 90.4 for the rural South for ages 15–29 (Table 7) suggests that much of the migration is on the part of young unmarried men.   However, discussions of housing problems in specific cities show that many families also migrate.   The migrating Negro therefore breaks his kinship relationships and perhaps the small-family context. He comes into the new community without the group that usually exerts control over his behavior and that gives him help when he is ill or in trouble.   If he has come from a plantation he has also broken the tie of dependency upon the landlord.

2. The degree of cultural change depends upon the distance of migration.   Usually Negroes move short distances, that is, often from a rural Southern area into a Southern city.   Still within the same milieu, the Negro tends to find much the same attitude of dominance on the part of the whites to which he is accustomed.   He must adjust, however, to the lack of patronage from his landlord and to greater pressure from law-enforcing agencies.   His relationship with whites shifts from personal to impersonal.

During both World Wars Negroes migrated long rather than short distances, crowding into Northern industrial areas, such as New York, Philadelphia, Chicago, Detroit, and Western industrial areas.   Few settled on farms or in small villages.   In 1950, 47 per cent of the nonwhites in the South and 88 per cent of the nonwhites in the North were in urban areas, and of all urban nonwhites about one half lived outside the South.[14] These migrants to Northern cities have two adjustments to make—to the impersonal character of city life and to the changed attitudes of the North where Negroes participate with whites more freely, although by no means completely, in community institutions.   Negro migrants therefore have difficulties not faced by many other groups.

[14] *1950 Census of Population, Preliminary Reports, General Characteristics of the Population, by Regions: April 1, 1950,* Series PC-7, No. 3 (Bureau of the Census, April 30, 1951), p. 2.   The 1950 Census uses the terminology nonwhites to include Negroes, Indians, Japanese, Chinese, and other nonwhite races.   By far the greater number are Negroes.

The Negro must learn a new set of rules of race relationships, which are different from those of the South. In the South he is almost completely excluded from common usage of public as well as private facilities and institutions. In the North he may ride in any part of the streetcar or bus that he desires, does not need to yield the sidewalk to a passing white, and may attend churches, as well as movies and other amusements, patronized by whites. Technically he may eat freely in any restaurant. His children attend school with white children. Nevertheless, he finds opposition to his doing many of these things; the very fact that the opposition does not follow any set and known rules as in the South makes adjustment difficult, and his knowledge that he is legally entitled to equal participation arouses resentment when equality is denied. He also fails to find the leniency that often attends Negro-white relationships in the South, whereby the adult Negro is regarded as a child and not required to meet the standards of whites. In the North, he must punch a time clock at work, meet regular standards of production, and obey the laws. The Negro family earning cash regularly perhaps for the first time has to learn to handle this money, to budget sufficiently to be able to buy food and other necessities until the next pay check comes, to avoid luxuries offered in the many stores when necessities have not yet been provided for the family.

In the city the family organization also undergoes change. The rural Negro family worked as a unit with the children under the supervision of parents. Often when the Negro mother did domestic work she was able to have her children near her and to watch over them while she was at work. In the city parents are separated from children by their work, and, since many Negro mothers are employed in Northern cities, a serious problem arises. The parents, to whom city life is strange, often do not see the need to provide supervision for their children, who easily adapt themselves to the life of the streets and alleys.

Lacking both the kinship group of the South and the supervision of the landlord, the Negro family in the North has no one close to it to whom to turn when in trouble and must therefore seek aid from strangers or from impersonal relief agencies.

Even so simple a thing as the use of electrical devices, bathtubs, and flush toilets presents a problem of technique and sanitation. In a government-owned and -operated trailer camp near a Northern industrial city, Bendix washing machines were provided for the use of tenants, most of whom in the course of time were Southern Negroes employed in heavy industry. The task of teaching each incoming Negro family to operate the washing machines was in time abandoned, and the Negro mothers did their family laundries in the stationary tubs in the laundry, while the electric machines, out of order and unrepaired, stood idle.

Negro children from the South often have a difficult time when they find themselves attending schools for the first time with whites. They are not sure how to treat the white children nor what kind of treatment to expect from them. Coming from the inadequate rural schools of the South, they usually are retarded and find themselves in grades with Northern children, both Negro and white, who are younger and smaller than themselves. Often confused by the urban school system, the greater number of teachers to whom adjustment must be made, and the higher standards of attainment, they become "behavior problems."

3. Degree of recurrence of mobility. Most Negroes who migrated North or West between 1940 and 1947 remained there. Negroes who entered the North during World War I also tended to remain, until the 1930's when the unemployment fostered by the depression drove some of them South. Negroes may shift from place to place in the North and within one city may move their place of residence, but in general they do not return South except under the pressure of unemployment.

4. Northern communities, although able to absorb a small number of Negroes without opposition, usually are unprepared for the great influxes that attend an industrial boom. Industries encourage Negroes to migrate from the South, sometimes sending out recruiting agents or paying the fare north, but neither industries nor the local governments make provision for the housing of the Negroes or for the additional strain on schools, parks, and other recreational places. Inadequate housing often becomes the focal point of disturbances between Negroes and whites. Typically, incoming Negroes swarm into areas that are locally regarded as belonging to Negroes already settled in the community. In time, these areas are unable to accommodate all the Negroes, some of whom must of necessity push out at some point into neighborhoods held by whites. This invasion of white residential communities by Negro families is met with resistance, sometimes passive in the refusal to sell or rent to Negroes, sometimes through acts of vandalism against a house newly occupied by Negro families, stoning or shooting of Negroes, or beating of Negro children. Occasionally, a full-scale riot occurs. Often the housing situation is

coupled with resistance to Negroes' use of parks or bathing beaches formerly patronized exclusively by whites.   The race riot in Detroit in June, 1943, resulted partly from lack of prepartion for the thousands of Negro industrial workers who had flooded the Detroit area.   Housing and recreation facilities were totally inadequate.   In addition, white workers resented promotions of Negroes in factories.   In one plant 3,000 white workers had struck because three Negro workers were promoted.[15]   After World War I, for similar reasons, a riot occurred in Chicago.

Even though riots may be avoided, minor disturbances occur.   In Chicago in the 1940's the following incidents were reported, showing the rejection by whites of the growing Negro population: [16]

Two buildings, whose apartments were filled with Negro families, were burned, with severe injuries to several Negroes who were forced to jump from upper-story windows.   In other cases, Negroes lost their lives when residences were fired.

Rents were doubled when apartments were rented to Negroes.

So scarce was housing that families with as many as six members were forced to live in one room; as a consequence in warm weather much of the family life was carried on in the streets.

Many incidents occurred wherein Negroes were attacked on the streets.

Rarely is the community prepared to continue employment of Negroes when the boom period has ended.   In Chicago, for instance, during the 1930 depression three times as high a proportion of Negroes were on relief as of whites.[17]

5. Personal and family adjustment.   Evidences of personal and family disorganization and lack of adaptation to city life are many.   Sometimes the difficulty is simply the carrying over into city life of folkways that, even though they differed from those of white people, were controlled adequately under the family system of the South.   For example, common-law marriages sometimes of brief duration occur among lower-class Negroes in the South, often resulting in an illegitimate child.   Usually the young mother remains in her mother's family, and the baby is reared along with the mother's younger brothers and sisters.   Since in the rural South the family functions as a unit, there is no question of public

[15] Alfred McClung Lee, *Race Riot* (Dryden, 1943), p. 143.

[16] The Mayor's Commission on Human Relations, *Human Relations in Chicago, Report for the Year 1946,* pp. 63, 64, and newspaper reports and interviews.

[17] Mary-Jane Grunsfeld, *Negroes in Chicago* (Mayor's Committee on Race Relations, 1944), p. 32.

dependency or care of the pregnant mother. When a Negro girl who has migrated to the city attempts to continue this folkway, she finds herself in serious difficulty. Her contact is more likely to be made with another in-migrant Negro rather than with someone from the local community who may give her his protection for a time. She has no family or kinship group to whom to turn for care of herself and her child. Her baby therefore becomes a public charge, and she herself may be arrested and placed in a penal institution for a short period of time as a vagrant or prostitute. Studies in New York and Chicago show that most of the unmarried Negro mothers came from the South or the West Indies and had not lived for more than a few years in the cities where their children were born.[18] They were migrants who had failed to adjust economically or in personal behavior to the individualistic life of the Northern city.

The difficulty of supervising children when the mother works in kitchen or factory far removed from her city home instead of in the cotton fields with her children near her has already been mentioned. Here again, the mother is attempting to continue her role as supporter of her family, but in a social situation that affords no protection for the children.

Older children, finding Northern city schools unsuited to their needs and without skills for urban jobs, easily drift into minor delinquencies or become affiliated with rowdy gangs. The holdups and assaults in which they become involved are often aggressive reactions to slights from white people.

The family, held together by a strong family organization in the rural South and adapted to the work on a farm, tends to disintegrate under the impact of impersonal city conditions that place each member of the family in a different place during many hours of the day.

In time, of course, the families make some type of adjustment. Many of them succeed in establishing themselves economically and learn how to handle the problems of city life. They move from the slums into which they first came and form a middle-class Negro society with a minority in an upper-class position. As long as economic and cultural opportunities in the North are better than in the South, however, new Negroes will continue to migrate. The adjustment of rural Negroes to Northern urbanism is not a temporary problem but a continuing one.

The processes of adjustment are pointed out in the following discussion

[18] E. Franklin Frazier, *The Negro Family in the United States* (University of Chicago Press, 1939), ch. 16. Frazier cites numerous studies.

of three Negro families, each consisting of three generations, who migrated to the North.[19]

One family contained a grandmother who had been a field hand in the South and who imposed upon her daughter and granddaughter as well as she could the simple rural mores of her younger days.   But the rural mores were unsuited to the North, with the result that the family tended toward disintegration.   The grandmother was unable to change her personality and beliefs to meet Northern conditions; her daughter was torn between the Southern mores and the Northern demands and became uncertain and confused; while the grandchildren ran wild without the guidance of their mother.

Another family originally had been small landowners in the South. They had moved to a Southern town and from there to a Northern city. This middle-class family was conservative and religious, with strict morals.   The children married early, apparently in part to escape from the oppressive family mores, but without making a complete adjustment to the greater freedom of the Northern urban life.   In the North the adolescent granddaughter rebelled against restrictions and the crowded home. Finally she became pregnant, in violation of the respectable middle-class mores of her family.

The third family was sophisticated before its removal to the North. The grandmother had been a maid in a white family, where she had acquired tolerant attitudes and cultural ambitions.   She provided for the education of her children, and the Northern grandchildren were destined for college.   This family, already divorced from the typical rural attitudes of the Southern Negro, made the transition to Northern urban life without disorganization.

The author of this report summarizes the transitional process from the folk family of the rural South to the more sophisticated urban family of the North as follows:

The first generation was transplanted too late for fundamental changes to occur.   Habit patterns, thought patterns, and attitudes were long since fixed; new experiences were viewed in terms of the old.   Everything was comparative, and if the new or more recent clashed with the old, the fixed pattern in all probability remained intact.   If the new experiences did not involve an old emotion, a new attitude might be formed—but this was a very gradual process.

[19] Elizabeth G. Watkins, "Cultural Backgrounds and Attitudes among Negroes," *The Family*, 17 (1936–37), 52–58, 86–89, 118–122.

The second generation is truly on the fence; it understands both the first and the third—it is a part of both and its sympathies are divided. Ultimately, it seems, the second generation must make a choice, and a break; either it chooses to accept, on the whole, the cultural attitudes of the first generation and thereby causes a break between it and the third generation, or it rejects the old and adopts the new, thus causing a break with the past.

The third generation is the product of a complex social environment; it cannot accept blindly the attitudes of parents and grandparents—which, after all, are the products of a wholly different background of experiences. The younger generation sees no reason for being humbly appreciative of the cultural opportunities presented; it accepts them as a part of the environment; having known nothing else, comparisons are impossible. Why should there not be a natural acceptance of what the community offers? Their parents' eager thankfulness, whether expressed humbly or aggressively, creates conflict in their minds.[20]

The serviceman's family

A soldier's family during World War II offers another illustration of a type of migrancy that attends war and large-scale military training.

Mary was a girl of Finnish descent whose father had deserted her mother while Mary was still a child.[21] The mother had supported herself and her daughter in a Northern city by doing housework. Soon after graduation from high school, Mary met a young Southerner who recently had left the Civilian Conservation Corps to enlist in the army. Soon after he enlisted, the United States began its program of peacetime training in 1940. Joe was transferred to a smaller Northern city on the outskirts of which a training camp was being built. Within a few months, Mary also went to this city where she and Joe were married. Since the marriage occurred before the government had begun to grant allowances to the wives of soldiers, Mary found it necessary to obtain work. She secured a position as maid in a family of three. She and Joe rented a room about midway between the camp and her place of work, on a secondary business street. Shortly after the marriage Mary became pregnant, a condition that posed a serious housing problem in view of their low income and an overcrowded housing condition in the city. They found light-housekeep-

---

[20] Watkins, *op. cit.,* pp. 121–122. Additional material on the adjustment of Negro migrants to the North and to Southern cities may be found in Frazier, *op. cit.,* chs. 13–21; Frazier, *The Negro Family in Chicago* (University of Chicago Press, 1932); Frazier, *Negro Youth at the Crossways: Their Personality Development in the Middle States* (Washington, D.C., American Council on Education, 1940).

[21] Unpublished record.

ing rooms from which they were requested to move as soon as the landlady learned of the pregnancy.   Unable to find suitable quarters, Mary began to talk of returning to her mother.   The problem was solved by the family for whom Mary worked.   Mary and her husband were given a room in this home, where later they also brought the baby, which was born in a local hospital.   Adjustments were made in Mary's work and to a certain extent the family gave Mary the type of protection that her mother would have provided had Mary returned to live with her.   When the baby was about seven months old, the government granted family allowances, and Joe, Mary, and the baby moved into a federal trailer camp near the military camp where Joe was stationed.   Here they lived for approximately a year, during which Mary gave birth to a second child.   When Joe was transferred, Mary and her children returned to the Northern city where Mary's mother lived.   Her mother secured housework in a home where Mary and the babies were also allowed to live.   When Joe was transferred to a camp near his old home in the South, Mary and the two children traveled south and were established in a small house near the camp. Within a few months Joe was sent overseas.   Since Joe regarded the South as his permanent home, Mary remained where she was.   With Joe's release from the army he returned there and entered civilian work.

In this case the migrating unit was Mary alone, then Mary and her children, finally Mary, her husband, and children.   The occasion of her first move was her marriage.   Little change in culture was experienced, and a quick adjustment was made, the chief difficulties being financial.   Social contacts were very limited, however, as Joe was forced to spend most of his time at the camp, and Mary found herself with few avenues for contacts outside of the family where she worked.   When she moved south, Mary encountered cultural differences.   Joe, of lower-class origin, expected to have a large family (four children were born within about five years time), although his earning capacity was low both in and after he left the army.   Mary found herself living in poor quarters and struggling against insects and rodents that had not been a problem in the North. The migrancy was recurrent and made without planning.   Joe was subject to army regulations and had no choice as to where he was sent; Mary followed him as far as possible, but never regarded her residence as permanent until she reached the South.   She therefore made little effort to affiliate herself with local institutions and was lonely in her detachment from community life.   She found the neighborhood where she worked friendly and receptive toward her, in spite of the rejection by landlords of the family when children began to arrive. The marital adjustment of Mary and Joe was good; they satisfied each other's needs in many ways and were happy and proud over the birth of their first child. Financial insecurity and anxiety for Mary while Joe was overseas were inherent in the situation, as was the fluctuating residence during his period of service.

Community and neighborhood receptivity are not always part of the experience of the soldier's family. Exorbitant rents, high prices in stores, parking fines for soldiers' cars but not for civilians', discourtesies, and hostilities were reported from many communities during World War II and again in the 1950's. As with other migrant groups, servicemen's families disturb the community and often are both exploited and resented.

MOBILITY A CURRENT PHASE OF FAMILY LIFE

Migrations are not sporadic or episodic. They follow definite routes and are correlated with the economic cycle of depressions and prosperity. They are a necessary part of the American industrial economy. Therefore they form part of the social situation that shapes American family life. In their thinking American families need to substitute mobility for the homestead as the focal point of family adjustment. The transitions are severe from one subculture to another, from stable residence to repeated change, from the kinship family to the small family, from reliance on relatives and neighbors in time of need to a formal application at a welfare agency, from neighborliness based on long acquaintance to aloofness or hostility, from the familiar to the unfamiliar.

Until family life is placed upon a new basis of greater flexibility than at present, it is to be expected that many families will not be able to adjust to the uprooting and transplanting. Behavior often runs counter to social norms; some families disintegrate; individuals may become maladjusted or delinquent.

QUESTIONS

1. What type of migration is most disturbing to family life?
2. Contrast present migration with that of the pioneer period.
3. How is the birth rate related to migration?
4. Migration is not haphazard, but follows certain routes; account for these routes.

5. Discuss the relationships between migration, sex ratios, and marriage.

6. How could sex ratios be controlled in the interest of marriage?

7. From your own experience or observation, analyze one or more cases of family migration according to patterns of migration set forth in Chapter 3.

8. How could migration be guided or controlled in the interest of family stability and adjustment?

BIBLIOGRAPHY

Meaning and extent of migration

Freedman, Ronald, *Recent Migration to Chicago* (University of Chicago Press, 1950).

Hawley, Amos H., *Human Ecology, A Theory of Community Structure* (Ronald, 1950).

Research Memorandum on Population Redistribution within the United States, Bulletin 42 (New York, Social Science Research Council, 1938).

Effect of migration on family life

Beers, H. W., and Heflin, C., *Rural People in the City, A Study of the Socio-Economic Status of 297 Families in Lexington, Kentucky,* Bulletin 478, Kentucky Agricultural Experiment Station, July, 1945.

Beynon, E. D., "The Southern White Laborer Migrates to Michigan," *American Sociological Review,* 3 (1938), 333–343.

Leyburn, G., "Urban Adjustments of Migrants from the Southern Appalachian Plateau," *Social Forces,* 16 (1937), 238–246.

Watkins, E. G., "Cultural Backgrounds and Attitudes among Negroes," *The Family,* 17 (1936–37), 52–58, 86–89, 118–122.

Urbanism and the Family

Until farms became commercialized, farming was spoken of as a way of life. Urbanism also implies a way of life, sharply differentiated from the rural way. Just as the rural family at an earlier period molded itself to the exigencies of farming, so the urban family is in the process of adapting itself to the necessities of city life. The process is almost a continuous one, since city growth depends upon the influx of rural individuals and families who bring with them to the city the attitudes and personal habits of the rural family. Families that have lived in cities several generations have had a better chance to develop an urban family pattern they can transmit to succeeding generations, but even they are handicapped by the many innovations that change the urban environment from decade to decade.

CENTRIFUGAL GROWTH OF CITIES

Our usual conception of the large city is of tall apartment buildings, crowded with families whose children must play on the sidewalks or travel some distance to a park for play space. True, many families live in this way. The trends of urban growth, however, are toward an increase in the number of people living in suburbs and more remote fringe areas. Urbanism therefore is no longer limited to the official boundaries of cities but extends far beyond into communities of individual homes that are, nevertheless, bound economically and culturally to the city. Figure 13 indicates the widespread penetration of urbanism into the fringe areas around large cities.

Moreover, in urbanized areas, the rate of growth in fringe areas has

greatly exceeded the rate in the central cities.   Core cities have tended
to stabilize in population, while suburban areas have had tremendous
growth.   Core cities increased in population 13.0 per cent between 1940
and 1950, whereas outlying portions increased 34.7 per cent.   In contrast, areas lying beyond the influence of large cities have increased only

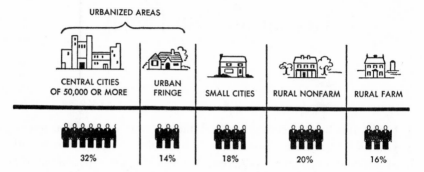

Each figure equals 5 per cent or about 7.5 million people

FIGURE 13

Distribution of Population by Type of Community, 1950

The Census staff recognized the growing influence of cities by creating the
term *urbanized area* to include one or more cities of 50,000 or more inhabitants, all nearby incorporated places of 2,500 or more, and nearby
closely settled smaller incorporated and unincorporated places.   In the
United States 157 urbanized areas contain 46 per cent of the population.
Fringe families, even though they may live in hamlets, are more urban than
rural in contacts and attitudes.   (Source: *1950 Census of Population, Preliminary Counts, Population of the United States, Urban and Rural, by
States: April 1, 1950,* Series PC-3, No. 10 [Bureau of the Census, February 16,
1951], p. 6; *1950 Census of Population, General Characteristics of the Population of the United States: April 1, 1950,* Series PC-7, No. 1 [Bureau of the
Census, February 25, 1951], p. 1.)

5.7 per cent.[1]   Within the outlying or suburban areas, growth tends to
occur not in the old established suburbs near the borders of the city but
in unincorporated communities or newly incorporated villages and small
cities beyond.   Sometimes these new communities are on good highways
or commuter's railways leading into the city to which the employed members of the families commute each day; sometimes they house the em-

[1] *1950 Census of Population, Preliminary Counts, Population of Standard Metropolitan Areas: April 1, 1950,* Series PC-3, No. 3 (Bureau of the Census, November
5, 1950), p. 1.

ployees of an outlying industry and form an independent industrial suburb. Cook County, Illinois, in which Chicago is located, will serve as an example.   Between 1940 and 1950 the state of Illinois increased 10.0 per cent in population, Chicago increased 6.2 per cent, but the remainder of Cook County increased 33.0 per cent.[2]   When smaller communities in Cook County are examined separately, the older suburbs show very low increases: Evanston, 11.7 per cent; Winnetka, 0.9 per cent; Wilmette, 5.6 per cent.   Oak Park, another established suburb, lost 4.3 per cent. In sharp contrast, smaller, more distant suburbs increased from 100 to 575 per cent in the decade.

Fringe families

Families living in the fringe areas are predominantly urban in origin; they come both from the central city and from other cities or in a minority of cases directly from rural areas.   A study of Milwaukee families living in the urban fringe showed that 60 per cent of the families had moved out from Milwaukee, 20 per cent from the large suburbs, 12 per cent from other fringe areas in the county, and 8 per cent from outside the county.[3] Most of the latter two groups were originally from an urban background. Of the fringe families around Madison, Wisconsin, 74.6 per cent had moved from a city, 17.6 per cent from villages or farms, whereas 7.8 per cent had made no moves since marriage.[4]   A few of the families had made two moves, rural→urban→fringe or urban→rural→fringe.   These studies do not show movement of families away from fringe areas, although some families undoubtedly leave the fringe area to move into the city or entirely away from the urbanized area.

The reasons for movement to the fringe and also the type of fringe community preferred show a desire to escape from some of the handicaps of the large city but not a desire to live under rural conditions.   Less congestion, more building space, and better conditions for rearing children motivated the centrifugal movement in Madison, Milwaukee, and Flint, Michigan (Figure 14 and Table 8).   Along with their greater freedom from density and city restrictions, the fringe residents wanted

[2] *1950 Census of Population, Preliminary Counts, Population of Illinois by Counties: April 1, 1950,* Series PC-2, No. 40 (Bureau of the Census, September 11, 1950), pp. 2–3.

[3] Richard Dewey, "Peripheral Expansion in Milwaukee County," *American Journal of Sociology,* 54 (1948), 119.

[4] Myles W. Rodehaver, "Fringe Settlement as a Two-Directional Movement," *Rural Sociology,* 12 (1947), 52.

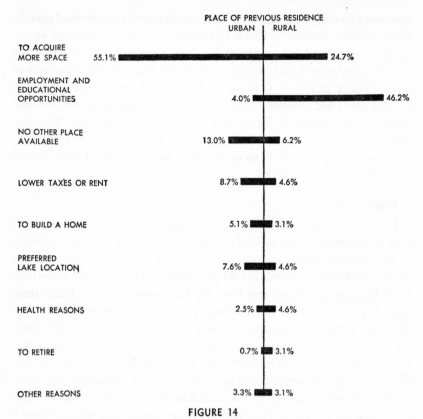

FIGURE 14

Reasons for Moving to Fringe Areas of Madison, Wisconsin

Families move from cities to suburbs for living space, and from farms to suburbs for work or schools. The figure, based on the replies of 276 former urban families and 65 former rural families, shows that more than half the former city residents gave desire for space as their reason for moving and almost half the former rural residents moved because of greater employment and educational opportunities in the fringe areas. (Source: M. W. Rode-haver, "Fringe Settlement as a Two-Dimensional Movement," *Rural Sociology,* 12 [1947], 53.)

urban services. The Milwaukee fringe families wanted to have a food market, grade school, and drugstore within walking distance.[5] Within a mile-and-a-half radius they wished to have beauty parlors, gas stations, a high school, churches, parks, and motion-picture theaters. Closeness

[5] Dewey, *op. cit.,* pp. 124–125.

to taverns was thought undesirable.   Among utilities listed as essential were electricity, telephone, public transportation, sewer, garbage collection, ash collection, gas connections, and street lights.   Highly desirable were a public water supply, sidewalks, and door-to-door mail service. Nearness to employment was less essential than proximity of services used by children or in the operation of the home.   Fringe families desire urban services and are content with separation of home from place of work; they dislike the congestion and density of the city itself.

TABLE 8

Reasons for Movement to Fringe Areas

Reason	Milwaukee *	Flint **
Better for children	32.0%	— †
Less congested area	18.0	34.8%
Cleaner	17.0	15.9
Larger lot	15.0	13.0
Lower taxes	10.5	23.0
Forced to move	5.0	15.9
Cheaper land, cheaper to build	4.0	5.8

* Richard Dewey, "Peripheral Expansion in Milwaukee County," *American Journal of Sociology*, 54 (1948), 121.

** Betty Tableman, "Intra-Community Migration in the Flint Metropolitan District," mimeographed, quoted by Hawley, *op. cit.*, p. 424.

† Data for the reason "better for children" is not included in the Flint study, but such a motive may be involved in the desire to move to a less congested area.

The fringe area as a whole is not homogeneous.   It breaks up into communities, some incorporated and some informal, varying in size from a dozen families clustered together with a few services to completely formed small cities.   Each of these communities has a high degree of homogeneity—more so than an independent community that is unrelated to a central city.   This greater homogeneity is possible because no one fringe community, large or small, is wholly independent and therefore is not forced to supply a full coterie of stores, schools, churches, and other services.   Communities may depend upon each other for some specialized services and all are within easy reach of the central city for other services. Therefore the occupational diversity within the fringe community may be narrow: many such communities have no doctor, dentist, newspaper, high school, motion-picture house, or retail stores that sell durable goods. Or the community may be served by a doctor who is a general practitioner but have no local specialists, or by a newspaper that emphasizes local events but does not subscribe to the services of a national press agency. The occupational homogeneity is related also to the economic level of the community.   Many fringe communities are promoted by one or two real estate companies that buy up plots of farm land and determine in advance the size of lots and quality of housing to be built, either building a quantity of houses for sale, or building a demonstration house that tends to set the pattern.   Lines of transportation, natural scenery or lack of it, nearness to factories, all help to increase the homogeneity of the fringe community.   Ordinarily, there is less diversity of occupation, income level, and social class in the suburban-fringe communities than in the independent city.   These communities fall into certain types, such as upper-class suburbs whose residents may be almost exclusively drawn from large-scale proprietors and successful professional men; middle-class suburbs whose employed members are clerical workers and in minor managerial positions; industrial suburbs that supply operatives to factories located within the suburb or on the edge of the city.

TABLE 9

Comparison of Cities, Fringe Areas, and Farm Areas, Michigan *

	Race and nativity			Sex ratio	Age			Fer-tility ratio
	Native-born white	Foreign-born	Ne-gro		Under 21	21–64	65 and over	
Urban	77.0%	16.4%	6.6%	102	33.6%	61.8%	4.8%	285
Fringe area	88.4	9.3	2.3	114	39.5	55.8	4.7	451
Adjacent farm-ing area	92.3	7.4	0.3	114	39.8	52.1	8.1	470

* J. Allan Beegle, "Characteristics of Michigan's Fringe Population," *Rural Sociology*, 12 (1947), 259.   The fertility ratio was computed by dividing the number of children under 5 years of age by the number of females aged 15–44 and multiplying by 1000.

Fringe areas may differ from central cities in population characteristics that are related to the family.   A study of Michigan farming, fringe, and city areas shows that the fringe population more nearly resembled the rural than the strictly urban (Table 9).   The fringe population, as compared with that of the city, has a lower proportion of foreign-born, fewer Negroes, a higher sex ratio (excess men), younger adults, and many more children.   Whether these relationships would hold also for other areas would depend in part upon the occupational structure.

The discussion so far has tended to emphasize some of the distinctive qualities of the fringe population and fringe family life.   Both fringe and central-city families are subjected to many of the same urban influences and face similar adjustments.

EFFECTS OF INDUSTRIALISM AND URBANISM ON THE FAMILY

Industrialism and urbanism, although not identical processes, are so intertwined that it is difficult to distinguish their separate effects on the family.   Industrialization is the broad term used to cover the transformation of an agrarian, household economy into a highly mechanized economy where machines perform much of the labor—and at a much greater speed—that formerly was done by hand.   Urbanization refers to the concentration in limited geographical areas of large numbers of people whose livelihoods come from manufacturing and trade rather than from the production of raw materials on farms, in forests, or in mines.   Some industries are built in small villages where they impose their influence upon an essentially rural society.   Likewise, some cities are not based upon industries, such as many capitals and university and resort cities; these cities exert a nonindustrial urban influence on family life.   But most typical of the United States is the combination of city and industry and the interplay of the two to form the milieu to which families must adjust.   Some of the typical urban and industrial conditions to which families are adjusting are discussed in the paragraphs that follow.

The family as the economic unit

For the majority of people the family in the city is not able to function adequately as the economic unit.   Work is not pooled in the city with a common fund coming into the family when crops are sold.   Each working member earns an individual wage and, having earned it individually, feels that he is privileged to use it individually.   On the farm, work belonged to the family, but in the city cash earnings do not.

The urban family is dependent upon wages that stop coming in when the worker is unable to work.   In spite of a general abundance of work, the individual worker can rarely be completely sure of his job.   Technological changes whereby machinery replaces workers, bankruptcy of businesses, changes in demand for a particular type of goods, all create uncertainty.   These are insecurities that attend normal production; when periodic depressions occur, unemployment becomes a crushing tragedy to many normally self-supporting families.   These periods of unemployment are unrelated to the desire or ability of the worker.   They are beyond his control.   They are an unavoidable factor in urban family living, creating insecurity and an inability to plan far into the future.

OCCUPATION	BIRTH RATE	
TOTAL POPULATION	83.2	
BUSINESS	73.3	
PROFESSIONAL	76.5	
SKILLED, SEMISKILLED	86.3	
UNSKILLED	104.0	

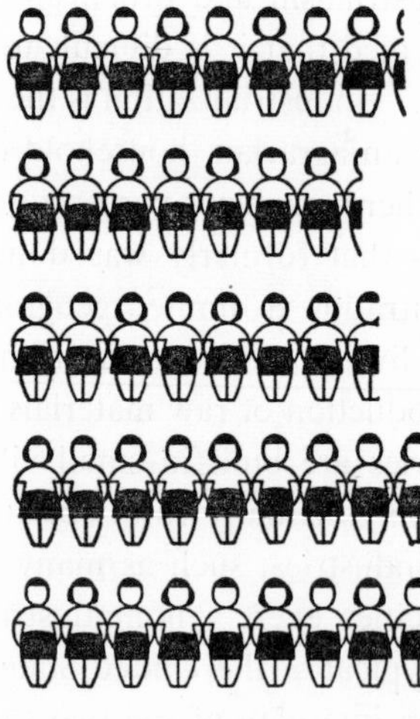

Each figure represents 10 babies.

FIGURE 15

Births per 1,000 Married Men, Aged 20–55 Years, by Occupation

The higher the occupational ranking, the lower becomes the birth rate. These rates are based upon approximately 30,000 married men in the 10 largest cities of the United States for the year 1935.   (Source: Christopher Tietze, "Differential Reproduction in the United States: Paternity Rates for Occupational Classes among Urban White Population," *American Journal of Sociology,* 49 [1943], 245.)

Even when employment is plentiful, the lower-paid worker has a difficult time making ends meet.   He has, moreover, adjusted least well to urban life in at least one respect—he tends to have a large number of children.   If he came—as many unskilled workers do come—from the rural South, his children were an asset, for they began to work at very early ages.   In the city they are an economic handicap, and especially so in states whose laws require school attendance and restrict employment until mid- or later adolescence.   Families that have had longer residence in the city tend to make several adjustments: their members, by acquiring more education and vocational training, lift themselves into a higher wage bracket; and they restrict the number of children.   Figures 15 and 16 show the decreasing number of children with increase in occupational level and income.   Children tend to be concentrated in the unskilled,

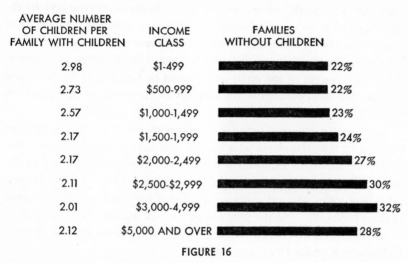

AVERAGE NUMBER OF CHILDREN PER FAMILY WITH CHILDREN	INCOME CLASS	FAMILIES WITHOUT CHILDREN	
2.98	$1-499		22%
2.73	$500-999		22%
2.57	$1,000-1,499		23%
2.17	$1,500-1,999		24%
2.17	$2,000-2,499		27%
2.11	$2,500-$2,999		30%
2.01	$3,000-4,999		32%
2.12	$5,000 AND OVER		28%

FIGURE 16

Childless Families and Average Number of Children per Family, by Income Class

The percentage of childless families increases with income up to the $5,000 level, above which childlessness decreases.   The same reversal in trend is shown for the average number of children.   The figure is based on data for families in which the head of the family is aged 35–44 years; children are limited to those under 18 years old.   (Source: T. J. Woofter, Jr., "Size of Family in Relation to Family Income and Age of Family Head," *American Sociological Review,* 9 [1944], 683.)

low-income class.   The differences are still more marked when the fathers are in their twenties and at the beginning of their earning power. Business and professional men marry later than skilled and unskilled workers and postpone the support of children until they have established themselves economically.   On the other hand, they support their children longer than does the skilled or unskilled worker.

Supporting a large number of children places a heavy burden on the urban family.   Since 1938, when the Fair Labor Standards Act set standards for establishments producing goods for interstate or foreign commerce, boys and girls have been forbidden to work in such establishments before the age of 16, with a minimum age of 18 for hazardous occupations. Children aged 14 and 15 may work only in a limited number of occupations and outside of school hours.   In addition, 20 states have a basic minimum age of 16 years for other types of employment.   The laws as a rule apply only to urban-type occupations.[6]   On the farm young children still may work, sometimes for many hours at a time and to the detriment of health and education.   They are, however, making their way and are not a financial burden.   Movement of rural families to the cities necessitates a change in attitude toward the function of children. When the concept of the child as a human personality to be developed replaces the rural concept of the child as an economic asset, restrictions on births tend to follow.

Another adjustment to urban insecurity comes through the employment of women: first, daughters who become self-supporting; then wives who help their husbands establish a home; and, finally, mothers under the pressure of needed support for children.   Figure 17 shows that the percentage of wives who are employed decreases with increase in the income of their husbands.   At the very lowest level of income, however, a third of all wives with no children under 10 years of age and one sixth of those with children under 10 are employed.

Although wives and older children aid the family, the lower-income groups are still at a disadvantage.   Unemployment beyond their control, illness, the birth of a new child may each constitute a financial crisis. With neither farm produce nor a kinship group to fall back upon, the family must turn to a relief agency or some form of public assistance. This step often violates the family's pride in its self-sufficiency; at the same time it restores a sense of security.   If long continued, it may lead to an attitude of dependency upon the agency.

At a slightly higher income level, families expect not only to make their own way but to improve their status over that of their parents; or, if they have newly come into the city, they must establish a status for themselves without reference to their parental status.   Women work neither from dire necessity nor because of an inner drive for a career.   They make a choice among several objectives, which may include ability to pay rent

[6] Margaret B. Hodges, editor, *Social Work Yearbook, 1949* (Russell Sage Foundation, 1949), pp. 92–98.

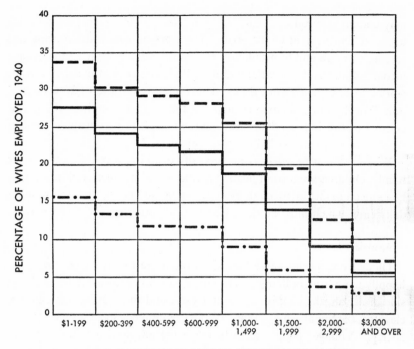

WAGE OR SALARY INCOME OF HUSBANDS IN 1939

— — — WIVES WITH NO CHILDREN UNDER TEN YEARS OF AGE
——————— ALL WIVES
•—•— WIVES WITH CHILDREN UNDER TEN YEARS OF AGE

FIGURE 17

Wives in the Labor Force, by Income Level of Husbands

The percentage of working wives decreases with increase in husbands' income; few wives work whose husbands' income is adequate for support of the family. And at all income levels the presence of young children tends to reduce the proportion of wives who work. Although data of the type shown here are not available for the postwar years, it is known that during World War II an abnormally high number of persons worked, many of whom left their employment with the end of the war. Women above age 35 tended to remain employed, whereas the number in the age range 20–34 fell below the expected figure because of the high marriage and birth rates following the war. (Source: *The American Family, A Factual Background* [Government Printing Office, 1949], p. 64.)

in a preferred section of the city, purchase of a car, or children.   Or they may compromise on one child and one of the other objectives, working to speed achievement of the goal.   The working makes the bearing and rearing of more children difficult; the family adjusts itself to the double income of husband and wife; and the wife becomes habituated to outside work and finds housework dull.   This family is still less of an economic unit than the lower-income family.   If there are no children, the family consists of two independent individuals who see fit to contribute some of their earnings to a joint living arrangement.

Whether the wife works from necessity or to improve the status of the family, children are a complicating factor.   The number of children may be reduced to one or two, but even this small number of children requires daily care, which must be delegated to some other person or an agency.

Apartment houses

Older women who move into cities often are totally unable to adjust happily to apartment living.   The consciousness of strangers on the other side of a wall, the lack of porch and yard, and the sharing of stairways, elevator, basement, and perhaps laundry equipment seem a restriction of liberty.   Younger people seem to make the adjustment readily and set the entrance to their private family life at the locked front door to their apartment rather than at the freely opened gate to a wide lawn.   Thoroughly urbanized people accept the apartment with the same attitude of naturalness that the rural-transplanted person has toward a house.   Some prefer the "elevator apartments" of five or more stories.   This preference is well expressed by a wealthy woman of 40 who lived with her husband and eight-year-old daughter on the thirteenth floor of a Chicago apartment building:

> I much prefer living in an elevator apartment because it is so much safer and cuts down the nuisance of having all sorts of people like salesmen and so on coming up.   My husband and I never lock our apartment because the elevator man always knows whether we are in or not.
>
> Karen [the daughter] is very friendly with the three elevator men. . . . They take her out to the drug store; give her birthday and Christmas gifts; and know all about her small affairs. There are quite a few children in the building but she doesn't know any of them at all. When I was a child we lived in a walk-up apartment.   I knew all the children in the building and mother was friendly with almost all of the women in the building.   In the elevator all of us say hello to each other but we never let it go further than

that. I consider the elevator men as part of my domestic household and at Christmas time tip each one $100.

Karen plays in the park with her nurse, goes to school, and makes dates with other children. She has her own room and many playthings. We don't associate with anyone in the building.[7]

In general, families with children avoid the larger apartment buildings when they are able. Interviews with families living in the Hyde Park area in Chicago (good residential area) show that families with children do not like elevator apartments and move from them when possible. Table 10 gives the average size of family in different types of housing in

TABLE 10

Median Size of Family in Chicago, and in Hyde Park, 1934 *

Type of dwelling	Median number in family
All dwellings in Chicago	2.97
All dwellings in Hyde Park	2.25
One-family and row dwellings	3.55
Two-family and double dwellings	3.14
Three-family dwellings	2.62
Multifamily dwellings	2.49
Hotels and apartment hotels	1.52
Elevator apartments over five stories	1.35

* J. B. Gittler, "Family in Skyscraper Dwellings," *Social Forces,* 21 (1942), 193.

Hyde Park. One-family and row dwellings had an average of 3.55 members in the family as contrasted with 1.35 members in elevator apartments. From pages 97–99 it will be recalled that suburban areas appeal to families with children.

In addition to the unsuitability of large apartment houses for children is the lack of play space in closely built-up areas. It has been estimated that a minimum of 100 square feet of space per child is needed for healthy play, with 1,000 square feet for running games.[8] Unless a park or playground is nearby, rarely does the city child find this quantity of space in the apartment-house districts. Children resort to alleys, streets, and vacant buildings, sometimes coming into conflict with the police in their search for play space. As they grow older, they may travel by streetcar, bus, or on foot miles from home to gain entrance to bathing beach or park.

[7] J. B. Gittler, "Family in Skyscraper Dwellings," *Social Forces,* 21 (1942), 209.
[8] Mabel A. Elliott and Francis E. Merrill, *Social Disorganization* (3rd ed., Harper, 1950), p. 508; estimate by Russell Sage Foundation.

The city is inhospitable to children in other ways also. The small size of apartments and the reluctance of many landlords to rent to families with children make children an unwanted part of the urban population. At an early age children must be taught to be quiet so that they will not disturb other families in the buildings, and their activities must be kept within the confines of the small units. Not only children but adults find apartments restrictive. There is little space for privacy or for the development of hobbies, indoors or out.

Loss of social functions

The urban family has lost many other functions besides the provision of primary necessities. The inability of the family to continue its rural functions is not due to lack of interest on the part of the family but because under urban conditions it has not been able to function. The small apartment does not provide the isolation and quiet needed by an ill person, and the victim of a contagious disease becomes a danger not only to his own family but often to other families. The lack of space for recreation has already been mentioned. The family, even in the rural area, is no longer adequate to assume responsibility for the education of children. The urban family is still less able to do so, for many urban occupations requires specialized training that goes beyond the capacities of parents to provide.

Family nonfunctioning in these areas has not led to neglect. Specialized agencies have developed to meet the need and often give a more efficient type of care than the nonspecialized family could supply. Nevertheless, certain dangers inhere in the situation. Some of the agencies are dedicated to the welfare of the family; but others, established on a purely commercial basis, are more interested in the profit to be made than in family welfare. Moreover, all the agencies contribute to a decrease in family unity at the same time that the better ones prevent personal demoralization by satisfying needs in an orderly manner. The agencies cannot be regarded as causing family disunity, however, for they arose to fill the needs left unsatisfied when the family was unable to function in the urban situation. In this relationship, therefore, they strengthen the family and add to its sense of security.

The transfer of functions can be measured through the increased use of nonfamily agencies. Care of the sick has become a hospital function, often with benefit to the health and preservation of the family (Figure 18).

Education is fast becoming an agency rather than a family function. The increasing number of young children in kindergartens has already been given in Figure 5. The proportion of adolescents attending secondary school has also increased tremendously (Figure 19). The span of years during which children are in school is therefore being extended to both younger and older ages. The family is losing its position of dominance in education when children are little more than babies, and never regains it. The result is both loss and gain to the family and the child.

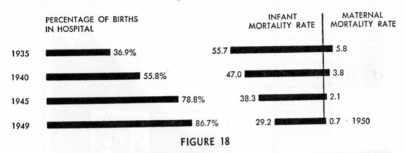

FIGURE 18

Hospital Births and Infant and Maternal Mortality Rates

Increased use of hospital facilities and medical care in childbirth has been accompanied by decreased rates of infant and maternal mortality. The infant mortality rate is the number of deaths among children under one year of age (exclusive of stillbirths) per 1,000 live births; the maternal mortality rate is the number of deaths from maternal causes among mothers per 1,000 live births. Although these figures are not limited to cities, they are more typical of the urban than the rural situation. The birth of children is one of the vital functions of the family that have benefited by specialized attention. (Source: National Office of Vital Statistics, Public Health Service, Federal Security Agency.)

Schools have gradually expanded their programs far beyond the elementary skills of "reading, writing, and arithmetic" to include social training, vocational courses, citizenship education, and personality adjustment. Counselors rather than parents help young people solve their personal problems and select their life vocations. Counselors are specialists in their respective fields and can bring to bear on the problem of the boy or girl a wealth of information and skilled techniques for which the average parent has not been trained. Such special training is needed to help the young person adjust to the complexities of urban life. Nevertheless, it undermines the interdependence of parents and children.

Recreation is the third function used to illustrate the passing of former family functions to community agencies and commercial organizations. Municipal provision for recreation is usually regarded as having its origin in a large sand pile placed in the yard of the Children's Mission in Boston in 1885.   So happy were the children who played in this sand pile that it was replenished year after year.   Playgrounds under leadership, num-

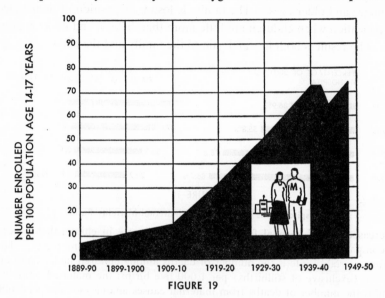

FIGURE 19

Enrollment in Secondary Schools

Enrollment has increased in the past 60 years from 7 to 74 per cent of boys and girls aged 14–17.   Adolescents, once closely associated with the family and contributing to family work and their own support, now organize many of their interests and activities around school life.   The high enrollment is conducive on the one hand to shrinkage of family life but on the other to preparation for urban occupations and responsibilities.   (Source: *Biennial Survey of Education in the United States, 1946–48*, ch. 1, "Statistical Summary of Education, 1947–48," Federal Security Agency [Government Printing Office, 1950], p. 25.)

bering less than 1,000 in 1907, totaled 11,000 in 1946.[9]   For the same year the *Recreation Year Book* reports organized recreation in 26,185 different centers in 1,743 communities.   These centers employed 31,000 leaders and expended some 54 million dollars on the projects.   In addition to municipal recreation projects are the many playgrounds and recre-

[9] George D. Butler, *Introduction to Community Recreation* (McGraw-Hill, 1948), pp. 33, 60, 75.

ational programs of community centers, settlement houses, churches, and schools.

Organized and supervised recreation is overshadowed by the huge number of competing commercial establishments, including motion-picture and other theaters, dance halls, taxi-dance halls, skating rinks, horse racing, various forms of gambling places, and night clubs. Various estimates place the number of motion-picture tickets sold per week at from 65 to 87 million, and the total amount spent for recreation at approximately four billion dollars per year.[10]

The family as the communal unit

The urban family is unable to function as an inclusive social or communal unit. For one thing, the number of people in the family has shrunk to the point where a diversified social group no longer exists. Husband and wife, or husband, wife, and one child, do not constitute a communal group with a rich variety of experiences based on interaction between old and young and siblings of different ages. Much of the small-group give and take of the larger rural family is assumed in the city by clubs and special interest groups, which differ from the family group in that each claims from its members only a small portion of their time and a limited range of interest. Each club, each association, supplies a fragmentary part of the needs of the person. The rural family or kinship group tended to mold and to fulfill the total personality. There was therefore more consistency in the rural social world. The associational contacts of the city person may not present a coordinated set of standards and customs; in fact, one person may belong to organizations that are opposed to each other, taking from each something that satisfies him and ignoring or rationalizing the conflicts. In this mosaic of contacts, the family is in danger of becoming simply another associational contact. True, the urban family cannot satisfy all needs, but the functions it does perform (loving response, and the bearing and rearing of children) are more fundamental both to the person and to society than the purposes served by other associations.

The associational contacts are adjusted to urban conditions. They are impersonal. Each member may join or resign at will. Interdepend-

---

[10] Martin H. and Esther S. Neumeyer, *Leisure and Recreation* (Barnes, 1949), p. 272, citing Gallup's Audience Research, Inc., for the estimate of 65 million. Elliott and Merrill, *op. cit.,* p. 516, citing *1948–49 International Motion Picture Almanac* for the estimate of 87 million; and the Chicago Recreation Survey for the total recreational expenditure.

ence among members is low.   This type of contact is typical of work and school relationships, shopping, riding on streetcars, audience behavior, and many other urban situations.   A child reared in the city solely within the close emotional circle of the family would be at a loss in adjusting to the impersonal contacts of the city that are based on superficial impressions and involve a high degree of self-interest.

THE URBAN FAMILY AS AN ASSOCIATION OF INDIVIDUALS

The pressures of urbanism have changed the center of gravity of the family.   Familism has been replaced by individualism.   The amount of time that each member spends away from the family forces each to think and act for himself; children carry into their outside contacts the attitudes and standards learned at home, but in the immediate situation they make decisions without family supervision or knowledge.   In extreme cases the family member may carry his individualism so far that he leads two entirely different lives, one at home where he adjusts to the family, and the other in some outside group.   Examples are the good son who also is a member of a delinquent gang; or the man who marries two women and maintains two independent households.

Individualism is fostered also by the ability of the wife and older children to support themselves independently.   It is also possible in the city (but not in the rural area) for an adult of either sex to live alone and find ways to meet many of his needs.   People no longer feel the need to marry for utilitarian purposes.   The small hotel, the restaurant, the laundry, and the hospital serve the individual.   Children are still dependent upon the family, although the family can find many agencies to relieve it of some or all the care of children, such as nursery schools, boarding homes, summer-long camps.   Such care releases the parents and furthers their individualism; it hampers the personality development of the children, however.

Individualism is increased also by the great diversity of urban conditions, the many opportunities for different types of residences, work, and recreation.   Each person is free to develop his peculiar talents and interests.   The nonconformer finds other nonconformers with whom he may form a congenial group.

Urban dating and courtship, flowering from chance acquaintance in office or factory, on the beach or bus, in a club or through a blind date, call for wariness as each takes the measure of the other.   Unprotected by the family, which has no way to provide or screen friends, each young person finds his own friends and makes his own selection of a mate.   They meet as individuals.

The urban family then comes to be an association of individuals.   The slender reeds that support the family are the personal attraction between two adults and the capacity of each to fulfill the needs of the other and receive in return fulfillment for his needs.   These needs are not utilitarian, but are the more subtle, evasive needs of personality itself—to love and be loved, to protect, to lean, to be praised, to admire, to confide, to receive sympathy and a host of other subjective needs that can be satisfied only in intimate personal association.   Marriage and the family constitute the ways provided in our society for the continuing satisfaction of these needs.   Personal happiness thus becomes the measure of a good marriage under urban conditions, and the temptation is strong to end the marriage if happiness does not come up to expectations.

One desire that most people have is to project themselves into the future through children.   The individualism that parents feel in their marriage they also grant to their children.   Except perhaps in the poorly educated groups, the child is a prized possession, upon whose personality development the parents focus much attention.   They search for hidden talents, attend child-study courses, and place the child in associations where they think his needs will be met.   They give the child the love and sympathy that impersonal associations cannot give.

Thus, if the family has become one of many segments of experience in the urban person's life, it is developing distinctive functions—the mutual meeting of personality needs of the husband and wife, and the personality development of children.

THE NINE ISSUES

The nine issues with which Part One began may now be reviewed. They have grown out of the rapid transition from an agrarian household economy, with families on isolated farms, to a highly industrialized and impersonal society, with families living in densely settled urban communities. The family, as an adaptive group, has not controlled the changes but merely attempts to adjust its organization, roles, and functions to the more powerful economic forces, at the same time keeping intact its primary functions of serving the personality needs of adults and children. Some of the old values of the family have changed; others have been transferred to specialized agencies where they often reach higher degrees of attainment than they formerly did through the family.

Although the issues are sometimes regarded as a conflict between urban and rural life, this conception is somewhat of an illusion, for farms are also becoming industrialized with the rapid introduction of mechanical equipment and the freeing of farmers from social isolation through better means of transportation and communication. The conflict is between the agrarian household economy of the past, which at one time permeated cities as well as rural areas, and the industrialization of the present, which originates in cities but rapidly expands to rural areas.

The beginning chapters of this book have sought to explore the unsettled state of the family. Little attention has been given to variations of families other than those closely related to the rural-urban transition. In any settled community, however, family types develop, based upon differences in socioeconomic status and ethnic backgrounds. An analysis of these types comprises Part Two of this book.

QUESTIONS

1. How do fringe families differ from those in central cities? From rural families? Is a new type of family in the process of development?

2. Compare the economic security of rural and urban families.

3. How do you account for the difference in number of children according to occupational and income levels? Which level seems best adjusted to urban conditions?

4. Employment of married women is sometimes viewed as a threat to family stability and unity; may it also be regarded as an adjustment to urban living that strengthens the family?

5. What reasonable changes could be made to make the city a more suitable place for rearing children?

6. The urban family is individualistic, in contrast to the older rural inclusive family in which most needs of all members were met through the family. Is the individualism beneficial or detrimental to the children?

7. Is the urban family in danger of disappearing as a primary group?

BIBLIOGRAPHY

The urban setting

Gist, Noel P., and Halbert, L. A., *Urban Society* (Crowell, 1948).
Hallenbeck, Wilbur C., *American Urban Communities* (Harper, 1951).

Hatt, Paul K., and Reiss, Albert J., Jr., *Reader in Urban Sociology* (Glencoe, Illinois: Free Press, 1951).

Hawley, Amos H., *Human Ecology, A Theory of Community Structure* (Ronald, 1950).

Smith, T. Lynn, and McMahan, C. A., editors, *The Sociology of Urban Life* (Dryden, 1951).

The fringe or suburban family

Beegle, J. A., "Characteristics of Michigan's Fringe Population," *Rural Sociology,* 12 (1947), 254–263.

Dewey, R., "Peripheral Expansion in Milwaukee County," *American Journal of Sociology,* 54 (1948), 118–125.

Rodehaver, M. W., "Fringe Settlement as a Two-Directional Movement," *Rural Sociology,* 12 (1947), 49–57.

Von Rhode, C., "The Suburban Mind," *Harper's Magazine,* 192 (April, 1946), 289–299.

The urban family

Gittler, J. B., "Family in Skyscraper-Dwellings," *Social Forces,* 21 (1942), 164, 193, 198, 209.

Hayner, Norman, *Hotel Life* (University of North Carolina Press, 1936).

Ogburn, W. F., *Recent Social Trends in the United States* (McGraw-Hill, 1931), Vol. II, ch. 13.

PART TWO

Social Configurations of the American Family

Upper-Class Families

The rural families described in Chapter 2 were found to be not all of one type; migrant, sharecropper, farm-owner, and commercial-farm families each have a distinctive pattern of family life into which children are inducted in infancy and that is therefore transmitted from generation to generation. Urban families also present definite distinctions; slums, apartment buildings, and suburbs differ vastly from each other in the quality of family life. True, certain uniformities tend to run through all, such as monogamy, family care of children, and various legal obligations. But the differences are many and marked. They are especially important in view of the mobility that brings families of different backgrounds together; intermarriage that occurs between members of different classes with attendant problems of adjustment; and the effect of the family culture on the personality of children. For these reasons, this and the next five chapters examine in detail family life in the major strata of American society.

SOCIAL CLASSES

Pertinent to the discussion of family life is a general description of social classes in America. The families listed above by descriptive terms fall into a heirarchy of social status. In common with all well-developed societies, American society differentiates between classes of people on the basis of certain attributes held to be of high value, the most important being socioeconomic leadership, source of wealth, amount of education, and occupational level. The length of time that the family has held the valued attributes helps to determine the solidity of its position in a certain social class.   The man whose forefathers during four or five generations have dominated the economic and social structure of a community finds it easier to assume such leadership than does the aspiring and capable man whose father was merely a salaried bookkeeper.   Likewise, the girl whose family for several generations has had a "bad name" finds it difficult to achieve a good name for herself; badness is expected.   The firmness of class placement is shaken, however, by several factors: we have a philosophy of equal opportunities for all and hence allow openings in the barriers between classes, whereby people may attempt to climb the social ladder if they so wish.   Some succeed in moving upward; others try and fail.   Our great amount of physical mobility also gives flexibility, since a person may move to a new community, leaving his family status behind, and attempt by his individual efforts to achieve a new status.   The typical picture, then, is one of families fairly well fixed in the social class of their ancestors but with a certain amount of social mobility based on family or individual effort and the breaking of old class ties.

The number of social classes varies from one community to another. Old communities tend to have a wider range than new communities, because families have tended to establish themselves at certain levels and the community has had an opportunity to classify them.   Large cities with extremes of wealth, education, and occupational skills have a wider range than small communities with a rather even level of educational and economic opportunities.   Six class levels, running from lower lower to upper upper, are typical of large, long-established cities, whereas two or three are more characteristic of small villages.

The population is unequally distributed into social-class levels, as Figure 20 shows.   The top levels, powerful in prestige and wealth, are small in proportion to the middle strata.   The proportion in each class differs also from one city to another, according to the economic base of the city.

UPPER-UPPER-CLASS FAMILIES

Although in small or newly established communities, the upper class may function as one unit, in larger cities it breaks down into a well-established upper upper class characterized by a position of social prestige and inherited wealth extending back many generations and a lower upper class whose status rests on more recently acquired wealth.

FIGURE 20

Estimated Distribution of Population in the
United States by Social Class

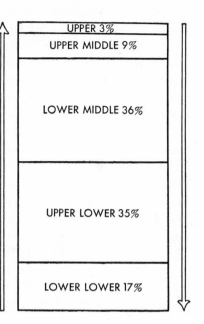

| UPPER 3% |
| UPPER MIDDLE 9% |
| LOWER MIDDLE 36% |
| UPPER LOWER 35% |
| LOWER LOWER 17% |

In older communities, the upper class may be divided into upper and lower upper. Locally, the distribution depends upon the type of community: heavy industry increases the proportion of the lower lower class; a state capital or a university city has few lower but more middle- and upper-class people. The social class in which a person is born and reared influences his personality and family life. In the American open-class system an individual's social-class placement may change either up or down (arrows). Such a change creates family tensions and schisms. (Source: Carson McGuire, "Social Stratification and Mobility Patterns," *American Sociological Review,* 15 [1950], 200.)

THE HISTORICAL FAMILY

The upper-upper-class family typically regards itself not as an independent unit but as a stage in the development of a historical family. It venerates the past generations whose accomplishments laid the foundation for the present family status. European ancestry of worth is respected, but real pride is felt for the ancestors who established themselves in the American community through individual energy and ability. Their early descendants consolidated the position won by the original American ancestors and passed on to their children an impregnable position of prestige, coupled with adequate stable income based on inherited wealth. The Lowells, Roosevelts, and Lees are examples of long-established upper-upper-class families.

The Lowell family is a recognized upper-upper-class family of Boston, best known at the present time for Abbot Lawrence Lowell, president of Harvard University from 1909 to 1933, and his poet-sister, Amy Lowell; and in the past for James Russell Lowell. A family that provided outstanding leadership in public affairs, education, the courts, the church, and the cotton industry, it had its roots in this country in Percival Lowle, classified as a gentleman in England, who emigrated to America in 1639.[1] The family required several generations to establish its prestige in America. Percival's great-grandson was the first of the family to be born in America (in Boston, since the stronghold of the family). His son, John, was graduated from Harvard in 1721, becoming a minister. John's generation set the family pattern, which still continues, of graduation of the men from Harvard and leadership in the professions and community affairs, supported (later) by wealth from the lucrative cotton manufacturing of New England. By 1800 the "high places of Boston were permeated with Lowell poets, manufacturers, diplomats, judges, historians, ministers, and educators," representing various branches of the family. Franklin Delano Roosevelt, an acknowledged member of the upper upper class, was a descendant on his mother's side of Philip De la Noye, who landed at Plymouth in 1621.[2] Philip had a grant of land at Fairhaven, Massachusetts, on part of which the family home still stands. Richard Lee, the founder of the Lee family of Virginia that early gained prominence in public affairs, which was maintained until the Civil War, came to America in 1640.[3]

Although in Eastern cities, eight and nine generations have helped to establish the upper-class family, in more recently settled regions, a lesser number of generations has similarly established an upper class, accepted as such in the local area. In the Middle West, for example, five generations of residence with perhaps four generations of leadership give the necessary prestige; in the Far West, the family history may be shorter. Often, these families of the Middle and Far West look with pride to connections with older established families of the East. But often, also, they owe their origin to persons of force and initiative who assumed leadership in a new community that they never could have demonstrated in an Eastern city where the social-class lines were firmly established with prestige and power fixed in a limited number of families.

Family continuity is emphasized by both material and nonmaterial symbols. Family names are important, as is a family crest if one exists.

[1] S. Foster Damon, *Amy Lowell, a Chronicle with Extracts from Her Correspondence* (Houghton Mifflin, 1935), p. 20.

[2] Rita Hall Kleeman, *Gracious Lady, The Life of Sara Delano Roosevelt* (D. Appleton–Century, 1935).

[3] Burton J. Hendrick, *The Lees of Virginia, Biography of a Family* (Little, Brown, 1935), p. 3.

The importance of names attaches both to the surname and to given names.   In the case of the late President, Franklin and Delano as well as Roosevelt are family names.   In the Saltonstall family in Boston, Nathaniel, Richard, and Leverett appear generation after generation, and the Quincy family had four generations of Josiahs.[4] Portraits also are symbols of family continuity, and give substance to the legends that arise of the beauty of the women and the bravery of the men of past generations. Certain professions or businesses are handed down from generation to generation, a son often being trained from earliest childhood for entrance upon the family occupation.   The medical profession may characterize one family, the ministry another, some specific business another.

THE KINSHIP FAMILY

The upper-upper-class family has not only historical continuity but also functioning lateral relationships.   It consists of small-family units closely interconnected by blood ties, marriage, the past history, and present joint ownership of property.   The great family thus includes uncles, aunts, and cousins of various degrees of closeness, organized into conventional small-family units but functioning also as a large kinship family. Moreover, the tendency of members of the small upper upper class to marry within the class—even within the larger family, as cousin with cousin—has created a complicated system of relationships, so that it often may be truthfully said that the entire upper upper class in a given community tends to be a related kinship group.   The family histories of the Lowells, the Lees, and the Roosevelts all include such marriages.[5]   More recently developed upper-class families also show the same tendency, according to Lundberg's popular study of America's 60 most wealthy families.[6]

The kinship is often held together, also, by joint property or by ownership of adjacent pieces of property by family members.   Fairhaven is an example of jointly held property.   The house at Fairhaven was built by Captain Warren Delano (great-grandfather of Franklin Delano Roosevelt) and at his death became the property of his children and their de-

[4] Cleveland Amory, *The Proper Bostonians* (Dutton, 1947), p. 19.

[5] Amory, *op. cit.,* pp. 20–21; Allison Davis, Burleigh B. Gardner, and Mary R. Gardner, *Deep South* (University of Chicago Press, 1941), pp. 87–90; Ferris Greenslet, *The Lowells and Their Seven Worlds* (Houghton Mifflin, 1946), p. 113; and numerous other references.

[6] Ferdinand Lundberg, *America's 60 Families* (Vanguard, 1937), pp. 9–22.

scendants, only one of whom (Warren Delano II) had children, one of whom was Sara Delano Roosevelt, mother of the President.   Eleanor Roosevelt in *This Is My Story* tells of visiting the Delano family assembled at Fairhaven for Thanksgiving in 1904, during the period of her engagement to Franklin Roosevelt.   The property was managed by Warren Delano III (uncle of Franklin Delano Roosevelt), and all members of the family were free to come and go.   In the latter part of her book, Mrs. Roosevelt speaks of taking her children in their turn to Fairhaven.   Such a gathering place, open to all through many generations, brought the family together from time to time.   Mrs. Roosevelt refers to the feeling of security within the family and the unity of the entire clan when it rallied to the support and protection of any member in time of misfortune.[7]

In the South the kinship group is held together partially by the joint ownership of plantations or by the operation under one management of plantations owned by branches of one family.[8]   Lundberg discusses the great industries and trust funds in which the accumulated assets of America's wealthiest families are concentrated and passed on intact—and, indeed, greatly augmented—from generation to generation, the numerous members of each generation receiving ample income but no one person individually owning the industry or the capital of the trust fund.[9]   The concentration of wealth is aided by the intermarriages that occur between close or remote cousins.

The smaller units of large families also acquire real estate that is held through the generations and becomes the gathering place for the subunits of the larger kinship group.   Thus Campobello, the summer place of the Roosevelts, was acquired by James Roosevelt (father of the President) in 1883; the property at Hyde Park, where Franklin Delano Roosevelt spent his childhood, was acquired by his great-grandfather and has been in the family ever since.[10]

CULTURAL UNITY

Since, in a given community, all upper-upper-class families tend to have established themselves at appoximately the same period of time, they rep-

[7] Eleanor Roosevelt, *This Is My Story* (Garden City Publishing Co., 1939), pp. 117–123.
[8] Davis, Gardner, and Gardner, *op. cit.,* p. 277.
[9] Lundberg, *op. cit.,* ch. 2.
[10] Kleeman, *op. cit.,* pp. 107, 148.

resent the same ethnic stock and cultural traditions. In New England and Virginia, the stock tends to be English. People of other ethnic stocks, more recently arrived, are not readily acceptable in the circles of the upper upper class, regardless of amount of education, cultural sophistication, or wealth. In Boston, for example, among 2,350,000 people in the 1940's, 8,000 were included in the *Social Register*.[11] Among these 8,000 was listed the name of only one Jewish man and less than a dozen Catholic families, although the population of Boston is 79 per cent Catholic. Ethnic groups that came after 1850—Irish, Italian, Jewish, and Polish as well as other European nationalities—are almost unrepresented. Among the upper classes represented by the 8,000 families in the *Social Register* is a smaller group, an ultra-upper class, called by Amory "the Proper Bostonians." This group has not only a uniform ethnic background but a high degree of similarity in the family histories. The general pattern includes entrance of the original members into the colonies, although they may not have been leaders in colonial life; establishment of a family fortune between the periods of the Revolutionary and the Civil wars through an international merchant prince; wise investment of the fortune to form the basis of inherited wealth; often, continued production of wealth through industry and railroading; education of the male members at Harvard; local community leadership including philanthropic operations, often supplemented by state, national, and international statesmanship; entrance of some members of the family into the professions of education, law, medicine, but with other members of the family continuing as astute business men; limited travel abroad primarily to England with development of cultural interests.

In the middle states of the Deep South, the families are of English or French ancestry. Emphasis, however, is not placed on this remote ancestry but on the status of the family prior to the Civil War.[12] The pre–Civil War cultural pattern included ownership of a large plantation and many slaves, extravagant living, and lavish entertainment of guests. Although wealth was diminished by the Civil War, the upper-upper-class families attempt to maintain the plantation home as well as the city house, and cling to both the material furnishings and the memories of the past. So immersed may the families become in the past that they fail to maintain

[11] Amory, *op. cit.*, pp. 12–13.
[12] Davis, Gardner, and Gardner, *op. cit.*, pp. 73–75.

political or community leadership in the present.   Status rests on membership in a family with a glorious past rather than upon present accomplishments.

Cultural unity is also maintained by the withdrawal of the upper upper class from the common public institutions.   The class tends to form an isolated social world, protecting its isolation by a system of exclusive social contacts.   Nurses, tutors, governesses, and maids stand as a bulwark, both physically and in the training they give, between the children of the upper upper class and children who might be met in a freer existence.[13]   Later the children attend private day or boarding schools, which admit only children of the upper social classes.   Colleges and universities are no longer so exclusive as formerly, although within the institution small exclusive clubs may exist (as at Harvard where some 15 per cent of the student body belong to 10 clubs whose members are chosen on the basis of the social standing of their families).   Clubs, large and small, to which membership may be gained only upon election, also support the social isolation.   In his discussion of the First Families of Boston, Amory emphasizes the function of upper-class clubs in maintaining the social status of their members.[14]   It is virtually impossible for any except the descendants of earlier members to gain election to membership.   The clubs thus are an adjunct of the families.

Upper-upper-class families are thus welded into community solidarity through their common ethnic and cultural background and present exclusive social experiences.

ECONOMIC BASIS

Three factors characterize the economic basis of upper-upper-class families: the income must be adequate to maintain the standards of the class; the income is based primarily on inherited rather than newly acquired or currently earned wealth; and in each locality certain sources of income give prestige.   Each point merits some discussion.

Although the upper upper class is not usually characterized by ostentatious display, the style of living rests upon a liberal expenditure of money.   The education of children through tutors, private schools, travel or study abroad, and in high-fee universities in the United States is expensive.   The operation of a city and one or more country homes, both

13 Roosevelt, *op. cit.*   This account has many references to the nurses and governesses who cared for Mrs. Roosevelt and later for her children.
14 Amory, *op. cit.*, pp. 354–359.

SOCIAL CLASS OCCUPATIONS

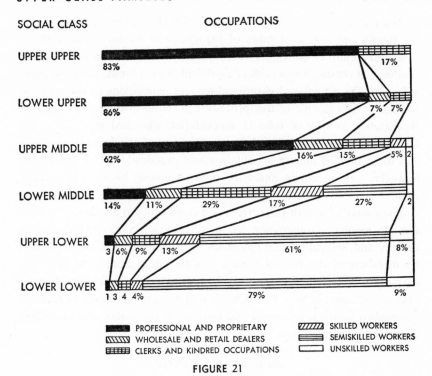

UPPER UPPER
83% 17%

LOWER UPPER
86% 7% 7%

UPPER MIDDLE
62% 16% 15% 5% 2

LOWER MIDDLE
14% 11% 29% 17% 27% 2

UPPER LOWER
3 6% 9% 13% 61% 8%

LOWER LOWER
1 3 4 4% 79% 9%

PROFESSIONAL AND PROPRIETARY   SKILLED WORKERS
WHOLESALE AND RETAIL DEALERS   SEMISKILLED WORKERS
CLERKS AND KINDRED OCCUPATIONS   UNSKILLED WORKERS

FIGURE 21

Occupations Typical of Different Social Classes in Yankee City

In this New England industrial city of 17,000 inhabitants the employed members of each social class except the lower middle are heavily concentrated in one occupational classification. Occupation is one influence on family life, affecting such things as hours of arising and going to bed, kind of clothing worn, affiliation with occupational and social organizations, family expectations for the children, and amount of income. As a result social classes predominantly of one occupational type have greater uniformity of family life than has the lower middle class with its varied occupations. (Source: W. Lloyd Warner and Paul S. Lunt, *Social Life of a Modern Community* [Yale University Press, 1941], p. 261.)

of which are perhaps open at the same time, again requires a large income for maintenance and servants. Support of philanthropies, an upper-upper-class community duty, calls for excess money. A family that spends lavishly and exceeds its income may hold its position for a generation but is disapproved by other families and soon loses its position of prestige, unless the next generation can recoup the losses or succeeds in marrying into a family of wealth.

The factor of inherited income is linked both to long establishment of the family and also to stability of the source of wealth.   Important in inherited wealth is the rather common practice on the part of the first producer of outstanding wealth of establishing trust funds, which securely safeguard the capital and permit subsequent generations to use only the income.   An example of this procedure is found in the will of William Rockefeller, brother of John D. Rockefeller, who died in 1922.[15]   He left a fortune of 50 million dollars, a portion of the income of which was to be divided among his children and grandchildren; the principal, however, was to remain intact for division among his great-grandchildren.

The source of wealth varies from one community to another.   In Boston, the acceptable sources are, first, merchandising in the early nineteenth century and, second, certain industries, such as the cotton mills operated by members of the Lowell family.   In the Deep South, the prestige-carrying source of family wealth is the large plantation established by an ancestral planter; in New York City, it is real estate; among more recently established families, industrial and railroad development and extraction of metal have ranked high.

RESIDENTIAL STABILITY

Since upper-upper-class prestige rests in part upon the length of time that the family has held a position of leadership in the community, residential stability is common to the families of this social class.   Frequent moving from one community to another causes a break in the family continuity.   Even though a family that has newly moved into a community is related to an upper-upper-class family elsewhere, it will not be fully accepted into the upper upper class of the new community.   Each kinship group has its own favorite central locale: the Lowells in Boston, the Roosevelts in New York City and Hyde Park; and the Du Ponts in Wilmington, where 24 Du Pont estates are located.[16]

KINSHIP ORGANIZATION AND ROLES

In the kinship family the ties of loyalty are very strong.   One is a member of the kinship family first, of the small-family unit second.   Family organization therefore tends to be on a kinship rather than a marital basis,

[15] Lundberg, *op. cit.,* p. 49.   Also see Amory, *op. cit.,* pp. 32–34.
[16] Lundberg, *op. cit.,* p. 420.

with the headship resting in the oldest person or in a group of collateral elders. Since women often survive their husbands, the head of the extended family may be a woman.

The elderly heads hold somewhat the same position in the kinship families that the elders hold in primitive societies. In their youth they knew members of at least two preceding generations whose lips repeated the legends of still earlier generations. Family victories are thus preserved—sometimes family defeats. Children are compared to earlier members of the family and expectations are established that these children will equal or surpass the feats of their ancestors. Admired personality traits of the ancestors are held before children in their impressionable years. The old men of the family hold the professional and business secrets that have spelled success in the past. Thus, as with primitives, the elders of the upper upper class are the repository of legend and wisdom for both the social class and the particular kinship group.

The elders wield great power over both adult and youthful descendants, often determining such matters as type and place of education, occupation, and selection of the spouse. If, as often happens, they hold the joint family property and wealth, they possess an enormous authority since they may control the amount of income of younger members. Thus middle-aged men who, in other social classes, would be independent heads of their small families and control their own social and economic destinies, in the upper upper class may still play the role of dependent sons to their old parents.

SMALL-FAMILY ORGANIZATION

The small-family units within the extended family tend to be patrilinear. The given names of the husband's ancestors take precedence in naming the children; the wife is expected to minimize the traditions of her family and to extol those of her husband's; sons are important to carry on the family name. Eleanor Roosevelt speaks of her great relief and joy that her second child was a son, for she knew the eagerness with which both her husband and his mother wished for a son to be named after her husband's father.[17] By the time the elderly wife becomes head of the family in her widowhood she usually is an excellent carrier of the culture of the husband's family. The husband, if he owns property individually, manages the finances of the family during his lifetime and sometimes

[17] Roosevelt, op. cit., p. 150.

creates a trust for their management after his death along lines laid down by him.

Socially, however, husband and wife tend to be on an equal basis. Friends are entertained at home with husband and wife as host and hostess. The two travel together, belong to some social clubs together, and attend concerts, opera, and the theater in each other's company. The men's clubs to which the husbands alone may belong are matched by women's clubs to which their wives belong, but the activities of these clubs tend to be subordinated to the joint activities of husband and wife.

MARRIAGE

In general, marriages occur at a later age than in other social classes. In Yankee City, an Eastern city of 17,000, the average age for upper-upper-class marriages is 27.9 years, higher than for any other social class and a full five years later than the average age in the lower lower class.[18]

Although in all social classes marriages tend to occur within the class, the tendency is most pronounced in the upper upper class. The social isolation and close supervision of the child and young adult limit his contacts, and hence possible choice of a spouse, to the small upper upper class. Moreover, the emphasis on family prestige and the quality of family stock makes it unthinkable for the young person to marry outside his class, for such a marriage would necessarily be into a lower social class. The debut also serves to promote the in-class marriage. It originated, apparently, during a period when girls were secluded during their adolescence and had few contacts with young men and sometimes few contacts with adults beyond the kinship circle. The debut served to introduce the girl to the friends of her parents and to their sons. It brought together the young people who were expected to marry each other and provided an opportunity for parents to survey each other's offspring. Although now young people of the two sexes are not segregated during adolescence to the same extent as formerly, the practice in upper-upper-class families of sending their sons and daughters to private schools organized on a one-sex basis implies a partial separation. The debut identifies for girls and young men alike the group within which marriage is suitable.

The young person who rebels and marries according to personal choice

[18] W. Lloyd Warner and Paul S. Lunt, *The Social Life of a Modern Community* (New Haven: Yale University Press, 1941), p. 423.

may find his mate barred from the more important social functions even though he may be included, or he as well as his mate may be ostracized or even rejected by the immediate family.   Sometimes personal attachments with those of a lower class develop but are summarily ended when the time for marriage comes; or occasionally they lead to irregular alliances.   The fictional story of Kitty Foyle concerns such an alliance between an upper-class youth of Philadelphia and a lower-class girl.[19]   Occasionally a mature adult of upper-class status, who has emancipated himself from the control of his kinship and class, marries someone from a lower social class.   So unusual is such an event, however, that it brings wider publicity in news magazines than does a marriage within the class.

CHILDREN

For several reasons, children are not only few in number but also few in proportion to the older people.   The birth rate has been declining for some years, thus creating a small childhood contingent.   In addition, the life expectancy has been increasing, wherefore the oldsters, born in a period of higher birth rate, are numerous.   A third factor operates in some cities to increase the proportion of older persons.   In Yankee City, for example, upper-upper-class families include a large number of unmarried women, left stranded in the old family homes when brothers and sisters married and moved elsewhere, and when marriageable young men of their social class left Yankee City to establish themselves in other communities.   The upper upper class in Yankee City, as a result of these factors, contains only 11 per cent of persons under 21 years of age and 39 per cent over 60 years of age.[20]

Children, though few, are important.   Sons are especially favored as they carry on the family name and provide for continued control of profession or business.   So important is this function of sons that when a childless couple consider adoption, they are often persuaded by the kinship group to adopt a daughter rather than a son so that only those of the true blood will carry the name through adulthood and pass it on to succeeding generations.[21]

Children belong to the kinship; they are links in the long chain of the

[19] For a sociological analysis of this story, see Milton Gordon, "*Kitty Foyle* and the Concept of Class as Culture," *American Journal of Sociology,* 53 (1947), 210–218.

[20] Warner and Lunt, *op. cit.,* p. 422.

[21] Amory, *op. cit.,* p. 21.

generations.   Their education includes a strong emphasis on the culture of the upper upper class and of the particular family.   The class culture comes not only through the family but also through the private schools, camps, clubs, and restricted social groups to which the children are sent. In Yankee City, at the time of the study made there, no upper-upper-class child attended the public high school.   The biographical and auto-biographical books on the Roosevelt family refer casually to the governesses and tutors who taught the children in their earlier years, and to the private local schools and eventually the private boarding schools to which the children of successive generations were sent.   The teachers and club leaders who serve the upper upper class are not themselves of this class; but, having familiarized themselves with the attitudes and standards of the class, they impose the class culture on the children.   In the South, a Negro mammy who has perhaps been associated with a particular family since childhood, may rear the children, impressing upon them the class and family culture.   As these adult intermediaries intrude between parents and children, the parent-child ties tend to weaken, and the children may feel not only great affection but emotional dependence upon some one nurse or governess who has become a parent-substitute.   Likewise, the resentment that children sometimes feel toward parents who both love and discipline them is directed toward the parent-substitute, while the parent-child relationship remains less intense but also more amicable.

The family culture is also impressed upon the child by the kinship group, of which the upper-upper-class child remains a member throughout his life unless he definitely wrenches himself loose.   Grandparents and elderly uncles and aunts impose on the child the standards of the family and feed to his listening ears the tales and legends of the ancestors.   The child becomes aware of a proud past that he must emulate in his own life and of the expectations of the family regarding his conduct and achievements.   Long before children are mature enough to think logically of their future the son knows what school and college he is destined to attend, what occupation the family has planned for him; the girl knows the kind of training she will receive and the type of young men she will meet at her debut, one of whom will become her husband.

Family gatherings at holidays when children and adults assemble under one roof are occasions for family reminiscing and account-taking. It is especially significant that these gatherings often are held in a home that has been in the family for generations, a repository for both the family portraits and the small mementoes that symbolize the personal history of past members of the family. Personal and family diaries of generations past often are open for younger members to read. On these occasions especially the child feels himself a member of the kinship group and of a historical family.[22]

Ritual, or prescribed formal procedures that acquire a sense of rightness, has more place in the upper-class family than in that of any other social class. Examples are acts of courtesy of children to all older people (rising when an older person of either sex enters the room); exclusion of children from the family dinner table except on special occasions; dressing for dinner; prescribed acts of deference of both children and adults to the oldest generation of the kinship group. These rituals emphasize the roles of the members of the family and place each in a hierarchical status with reference to the others, in terms of sex, age, and achievements. They also emphasize the kinship unity. In other words they both control and restrict behavior and at the same time incorporate each member firmly into the family.

Often the rituals center around the heirlooms and symbols of the past that have already been mentioned as important in inculcating a sense of family continuity and prestige. Cherished sets of fine china or silver may be used only on certain sacred family occasions. The christening dress or wedding jewels that pass from generation to generation for appropriate use emphasize to young and old alike the identity of a particular family.[23]

The effect on the child's personality is to give great personal and social security. The limitation of his contacts to his own social class with its unified culture eliminates comparison of his own class culture with that of other classes. He therefore does not suffer from cultural conflicts and develops a unified personality. Taught that he belongs to the class with greatest prestige, treated as superior by servants, salesmen, and teachers, he tends to accept his status without question. He becomes self-confident and assured of his own worth. College education, travel, attendance at

[22] Mrs. Roosevelt, for instance, speaks of her husband's interest in the old ship logs and diaries stored in the attic of the Delano family home at Fairhaven—*op. cit.*, p. 120. The President's great interest in the sea is easily accounted for in terms of the past history of the Delanos as ship captains and of the documents and mementoes that remained in the family.

[23] For a brief but interesting discussion of ritual in the different social classes, see J. H. S. Bossard and Eleanor S. Boll, "Ritual in Family Living," *American Sociological Review,* 14 (1949), 463–469.

the theater, concerts, and opera equip him for a place of leadership and give him a cultural background and degree of sophistication not found in less privileged classes. Since his family is already at the top of the social scale, he has no further heights to climb. As the child matures, however, he must put forth enough effort to maintain that position; if the family is mobile in a downward direction, he may of course suffer great insecurity and sense of inferiority.

Both economically and in terms of future life goals the upper-upper-class child is secure. Money comes from inherited sources as well as from the present efforts of the family. Often the child's plan of life is fixed before his birth. A place awaits the child in the family business, or in the professional firm of the elders. Informal family agreements may be made as to marriages between children. If the child is compliant to the family expectations, he faces a secure future without the anxiety of deciding for himself what his goals will be or of establishing himself.

The upper-upper-class child is secure also from influences or pressures outside his class, although he is heavily burdened with the expectations and pressures of his own class and family. In his study of Yankee City, Warner discovered that only one per cent of upper-upper-class people had had their names placed on the police record, as compared with 11 per cent of the lower lower class, and few indeed were the arrests of upper-upper-class juveniles. He states, however, that interviews revealed that upper-upper-class children had committed many of the same offenses as those for which lower-lower-class children had been arrested. The explanation lies in two factors: police are reluctant to arrest anyone with the prestige and known influence in the community of the upper upper class; in addition, the kinship group and intimate friends either tolerate depredations of their younger members or themselves take steps to punish and control juvenile rebels.[24] In another way, also, the upper-upper-class child is secure. Although the upper upper class is active in cultural and welfare agencies that are offered to or that impose their programs upon members of the lower classes, the upper upper class itself is free from such movements from the outside. Thus the upper-upper-class child must conform to his own class mores but he does not find it necessary, as do those of lower classes, to be aware of or conform to the mores of official agencies or of other social classes.

Exceptions exist, of course, to the general statement that the upper-

24 Warner and Lunt, *op. cit.*, pp. 427–428.

upper-class child tends to feel adequate, secure, and free from conflicts. Illnesses, deaths, loss of friends, or other disappointments may come. But even so, the upper-upper-class child often finds his situation less acute than that of a lower-class child.   He is rarely alone in his emotional stress.   The kinship group that surrounds him cushions his shock.

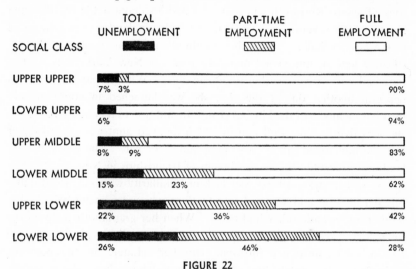

FIGURE 22

Unemployment by Social Class, Yankee City

The graph shows the percentage of unemployed among the working members of each social class at one period in the early 1930's during the depression. Unemployment and partial employment create family insecurity and loss of status for the unemployed persons.   Although relief agencies try to provide for basic needs, the necessity of applying for relief may bring a sense of degradation, especially to middle-class families.   The percentages of all persons on public relief were as follows: lower lower, 34; upper lower, 10; lower middle, 4; upper middle, less than 1.   No upper-class person received relief.   (Source: W. Lloyd Warner and Paul S. Lunt, *Social Life of a Modern Community* [Yale University Press, 1941], pp. 277–279.)

If the immediate family becomes disorganized or disintegrates or if the family is mobile downward, the growing child may become very insecure.   Eleanor Roosevelt in her childhood was a member of the former type—and perhaps of the latter.   In her autobiography she relates that when she was still a small child her father, perhaps because of ill health, began to drink.[25]   Hospitalization in various sanitariums followed; she,

[25] *Op. cit.*, pp. 1–165.

her mother, and two younger brothers then composed the small-family group. When she was eight her mother died, and her maternal grandmother assumed charge of the three children. Two years later her father died. By the time Eleanor was an adolescent the grandmother was secluding herself at her country home in the effort to stabilize one of her sons (Eleanor Roosevelt's uncle) who had also contracted the drinking habit. After several years spent in school in England, Eleanor returned to the United States. With the grandmother still at the country place, Eleanor and an unmarried aunt occupied the New York house. The time had now arrived for her to "come out." Without parents and with her grandmother out of the city, she was launched in young society by other members of the kinship group. In addition to the aunt with whom she was living, a married cousin and a married aunt accompanied her to important social functions or entertained for her. The years in England had prevented the establishment of friendships in New York. She speaks of her awkwardness, her lack of familiarity with American dancing, her chagrin and secret shame that she was not a social belle as her mother and grandmother had been. When her grandmother closed the town house because of the expense, she went to live with the married cousin, who entertained informally for her. Later, she accepted the invitation of an aunt to live in Washington, where she entered into the social life of that city. She speaks continually of her shyness, as she was passed from one relative to another. During all this period, the finances of the maternal grandmother were declining. Eleanor's marriage introduced her to a more stable and very well-organized family, where finances were handled efficiently. Not only her husband but her husband's mother took charge of her, planning her life and solving her problems for her. For a time she accepted this great security, only later developing the independent personality and great initiative for which she is now known.

The upper-upper-class child and young person may feel inadequate and personally insecure if he cannot meet the expectations of his kinship and class. The boy who lacks ability equal to the family tasks or the girl who lacks grace and beauty may suffer great agonies. Amy Lowell, heavy-set and awkward in her girlhood, suffered despondency and self-depreciation when she compared herself to other adolescent girls whose appeal to boys far surpassed her own.[26] Her diary contains many entries

[26] Damon, *op. cit.*, pp. 84–120.

to the effect that she was a fool, that no one cared for her, that she was rough, that she was a "dreadful pill." Eventually she established a reputation as a poet and also as an eccentric, but she did not achieve the marriage expected of girls of her class and generation. Individualistic as she became, she continued until her death to make her headquarters in the family home established by her father, apparently finding there security and a sense of continuity with her past.

Upper-class isolation is less complete today than formerly, and the break in the cultural wall permits contacts with those of other social classes. The trend now is for middle- and even aspiring and especially capable lower-class children to attend college and university. Although these young people may not belong to the same clubs or fraternities as upper-upper-class youths, nevertheless there is an exchange of ideas and information. Although the upper-upper-class children have more privileges than those of lower groups, they often have less freedom of individual choice. Some upper-upper-class children and young people therefore attempt to throw off the restraints of their kinship and class group and seek individual freedom outside the prescribed behavior of their class. This movement may be permanent, especially if the young person moves away from the stronghold of his family and establishes himself elsewhere as an individual rather than a member of his family. Marriage outside the class is probably the final sign of rebellion. Often, however, it is temporary with an eventual return to the family pattern. Amory lists by name various young Proper Bostonians (girls as well as young men) who sought individual careers in the motion pictures or journalism, or on the stage, but after a few months or years returned to the kinship fold.

The hold of the upper upper class on its younger members was also loosened as a result of the war, which in the 1940's affected not only young men but also girls, some of whom served in the WACS and the WAVES and others as volunteers to the Red Cross and similar agencies. In these groups they made contacts with many of other social classes and performed services at first hand for those of lower classes.

Many of the illustrations given of family life in the upper upper class have been drawn from published accounts of the family histories of the truly great. In order to coordinate the various phases of family life and to present the upper-upper-class family at a less exalted level, the following account is presented. Written by a younger member of an upper-

upper-class family in one of the older cities of the East, it mirrors both the objective aspects and some of the attitudes of the class.

THE UPPER UPPER CLASS IN AN OLD EASTERN CITY

River Boulevard is considered the most fashionable place to live in Eastern City.   As the years have gone by the suburbs furthest out along River Boulevard have become the most exclusive.   River Boulevard is made up mostly of the upper class, which is divided about equally between the lower upper and the upper upper.   Some of the suburbs have middle class people; Oak Grove is considered the worst suburb because so many "awful people" live there, "awful people" being middle class. Many times parents in an upper class family refuse to allow their daughters to go out with boys from Oak Grove, even though they know nothing other about them than this.

The newer houses which lie furthest from the city are larger than the old ones and each family seems to be trying to outdo the others.   The houses are large and rather formidable looking; they are surrounded by many acres of land, sometimes lawn and sometimes laid out in polo fields or as pasture for riding horses.

When a baby is born into an upper upper class family he is taught from the beginning never to forget it.   He is taught not to play with "those little children," but to play with these children.   Often a group of families know each other and their children play together.   Or sometimes different branches of one family live on one huge estate.   All the brothers and sisters and their respective families live in houses built around the "manor house."   The children on these large estates are inseparable and even after they go to school and make other friends, they remain extremely close to their cousins.   The upper class children rarely know any other children than those of their own class.   They have hardly any occasion to meet middle or lower class children.   The children usually have governesses up to the age of 12 and are carefully watched over.   The governess is sometimes French, so that the children may learn to speak French at an early age.   As the children become older, the governess gradually takes the role of personal maid to the girls.

There are three private girls' schools and two private boys' schools in the area.   The boy usually goes to the school that his father attended and the girl to her mother's school.   The friends that the child makes at these schools are all from the upper class and remain friends throughout the school years.   Every party, open house, or any kind of group gathering is made up of students from these five schools.   The students from the three public schools in the suburban community also stuck together.   The private schools and public schools did not have any activities in common.   They did not even compete in sports, except for practice games and then the two groups of students parted immediately after the game; they had nothing to say to each other. When the private schools played against each other, the game was always followed by a mixer when the host school would serve hot chocolate and the two teams would easily mix. The private schools are very particular about the children they accept. Children outside the recognized class are not accepted unless they have famous fathers and then the children often do not try to associate themselves with the upper class. When upper class families cannot afford to send their children to these schools, they are awarded scholarships.

After the girl is graduated from this school, she is given a debut by her parents. This function serves to introduce her to the adult friends of her family and also to an eligible group of young men, somewhat older than the boys with whom she had dated in school. She thus enters the upper upper class adult society under the guidance of her parents.[27]

Every family is proud of its heritage and talks freely about its ancestors. In almost every home on the wall in a prominent position is the family tree, appropriately framed. Many families have a crest, which is also framed, and which is used on stationery, rings, and so forth. The *Social Register,* a book containing only the names of people who are considered upper upper class, is used as the telephone directory. Very seldom does anyone in the family find it necessary to use the regular telephone directory. Only the people whose names are in the *Social Register* own the book. Outsiders are made to see that they are not wanted. Money has *nothing* to do with getting into the *Social Register.* The criterion used is the family background. If the family dates back for many generations, if the members belong to exclusive clubs, and the daughters have always made their debut, the family is considered upper upper class. "Outsiders" who suddenly make a lot of money are not readily accepted. The family background is what is important and you can't change that—you either have a good family background or you don't.

It is close to impossible to break into the upper upper class on River Boulevard. There are many institutions that help to keep the class untouchable. The exclusive private schools for children have already been mentioned. Many of the men belong to the City Guards, to which their fathers and grandfathers also belonged. A few newcomers, relatives and close friends, are admitted but only when they are acceptable to the Guard leaders. The Guards are determined to remain small and select. They go on maneuvers once a year and are the pride of the city. The men have another exclusive group—the Union League, which is in the city and provides a place for upper class men to meet, eat lunch, or give dinner parties. Sons and grandsons of members are readily accepted into the League; only a few "outsiders" are chosen each year from the long waiting list.

The women have similar exclusive clubs, such as the Junior League, to which new members are admitted only upon recommendation of an old member and approval by the board. Certain country clubs are considered "the"

[27] For a detailed account of the debut, dating, and courtship practices in this community, see pages 317–319.

clubs to belong to; prospective members are carefully screened. Informal parties are limited to members of the upper class.

The adults have many small parties, usually for members of both sexes. In addition, the women serve tea in the afternoon when women friends customarily drop in. Also, the women are together during much of the day, busy with such activities as charitable work or raising funds for some drive. The men in their leisure play golf, ride, or go to the club. The upper class is extremely interested in sports, mainly riding, hockey, tennis, squash, and football. Evening social affairs are for husband and wife together.

Manners are thought important in some families but not in others. In one leading family the daughter eats and dresses as though she were a manual laborer; in another the daughter would not be seen out of doors in her blue jeans.

The parents teach their children the manners of everyday life, but when big issues are to be decided the oldest member of the family is consulted. She (rarely he) is usually looked up to as a great figure and the children must be dressed perfectly and on their best behavior when with her. The family group usually is extremely close and large as there is a great deal of intermarriage. For example, during one year two sisters married cousins, all having the same surname.

The religion of this upper class community is predominantly Episcopalian, with Presbyterian next. There are a few upper upper class Catholic families, but no Jewish families. Occupationally, the men are usually professionals or business executives, while many are just "country gentlemen," who look after their investments, breed horses, and so on.

And so this is River Boulevard. Good, bad, prejudiced or what, to us who live there it is heaven on earth.[28]

LOWER-UPPER-CLASS FAMILIES

The family of the lower upper class treads upon the heels of the upper upper class, thus conforming to the general upward mobility of American families. In a newly developed country like the United States the general tendency is for families to move upward in the social scale. Generation by generation, education, income, and general cultural attainments have increased. Population has been fed not only by births but by a continuous stream of immigrants who enter at the lower-class level and begin the upward push against the class above them, motivating the members of that class to climb to higher levels by displacing them occupationally and in residential areas. Thus, except for the upper upper class, each social class has many members who deliberately aspire to enter the class

---

[28] Unpublished description.

above them.   This upward trend causes families to imitate the mode of
life of the next higher social class, which, because of its prestige and
privileges, seems desirable.

The lower-upper-class family, with the highest social status just one
step above, strives to become upper upper class in as many ways as possible.   In the older Eastern and Middle Western communities they may
never be admitted fully into the upper-upper-class group; but in the newer
communities of the Middle West and West, where the upper-upper-class
families are less securely entrenched, newcomers without a past history
in the community but with present income and cultural levels equal to
those of the upper upper class may be admitted into that class level within
one generation.   In Jonesville, for instance, an Illinois city of 6,000,
the old families and the new (upper-class) families join to form the top
social group, together constituting 3 per cent of the population, or about
50 families.[29]

THE FAMILY'S PAST

The lower-upper-class family can successfully imitate the upper-upper-
class family in everything except the age of the family stock after it
achieved prominence in the community.   Family *A* (upper upper class)
may have attained wealth and leadership in the 1750's; family *B* may now
have equal wealth and vigorous leadership, but have secured its position
in 1900.   Family *B* may have family portraits, but not of the great-
grandparents; it may have an adequately stocked library, but not one
with books carrying the inscriptions or notations of the grandparents;
it may have valuable antiques bought at the dealer's showrooms but not
acquired by the family at the time when the "antique" was the height of
current fashion.   Legends and tales of the family are limited to a generation, as the lowly past must be wiped out and forgotten.   Often the
family, having no accumulated record of the family history through documents and diaries, employs a genealogist to trace the family history, hoping
of course to find a link with some upper-upper-class family.   Whereas
the upper-upper-class family has acquired an honorable past and has
accumulated its material symbols of culture over four to six generations,
the newly arrived lower-upper-class family buys its past and surrounds
itself with the symbols of upper-upper-class status.

[29] W. Lloyd Warner and Associates, *Democracy in Jonesville* (Harper, 1949),
p. 24.

CULTURAL UNITY

There is less cultural unity among lower-upper-class families than among the upper-upper-class families.   For one thing, they represent more divergent backgrounds.   Some families have made wealth in the development of the West and then moved east to establish themselves and their children socially.   Others stem from groups that entered from different countries of Europe within the past 75 or 100 years and may retain some elements of their ancestral culture.   There is then somewhat more diversity of standards, attitudes, family traditions, and religious affiliation than among upper-upper-class families.   In addition, among families actively seeking a way up, a competitive situation develops.   These families do not stand together and consolidate their class position, but each seeks to remain in a fluid situation in order to identify itself when an opportunity offers with the class above.

ECONOMIC BASIS

The wealth of the lower-upper-class family is less likely to be inherited than is that of the upper-upper-class family; or, if inherited, it originated only a generation or two ago.   The wealth is "new money," acquired in the latter-day industrial developments rather than in the time-honored upper-upper-class occupations of shipping, cotton manufacturing, railroading, or plantation operation.

Often the amount of wealth of the lower-upper-class families exceeds that of the upper upper class.   Moreover, it is spent differently.   The study of Yankee City showed that the lower upper class spent more than the upper upper on food, house equipment and operation, rent and shelter, automobiles, vacations, club expenses; the upper-upper-class family exceeded in expenditures for clothing, taxes, formal education, gifts, and charity.[30]   The accounts of ostentatious expenditures made now or in the past by families of great wealth often refer to lower-upper-class families with newly acquired wealth unsupported by family standards of sobriety in expenditure.   The first generation of a family arisen from a lower-class level but with large amounts of excess money to spend has no family standards to control the spending of that money.   The first impulse seems to be toward extravagant and useless expenditures unrelated either to

[30] Warner and Lunt, *op. cit.*, pp. 290, 295, 296.

enhancing the culture and education of the family or to public welfare. Sometimes the period of a generation in a particular locality will be characterized by the extravagance of the new-wealthy.

As time passes and with the aid of public disapproval, the family develops standards that prohibit some of the ostentatious displays of wealth and passes the new standards on to the children. However, in families of great wealth that yields excess income, a permanent leisure group may develop, free to devote itself to whatever occupation it pleases. These leisure members may choose art, literature, or science, and contribute to art or knowledge; but in other families the leisure members focus their lives about themselves with personal pleasure as the dominating motive. Thus, breeding and racing of fine horses, near-professional polo, or boat racing may become the major occupations of some lower-upper-class individuals or families.

RESIDENTIAL STABILITY

Because of its late arrival at the upper part of the social scale, the lower-upper-class family usually has acquired a home suited to its status within the past generation, as compared with family homes in the upper upper class that may run back to the early development of the community, the exact number of years depending upon the length of time that has elapsed since the establishment of the community. Moreover, if the family is still mobile, occasional changes of residence will occur, as the family moves upward. In general the lower-upper-class family lives in a "new" part of the city or in a residential suburb, whereas at least the older generation of the upper-upper-class family is likely to live in an older part of the city, bulwarked by class solidarity against the encroachments of lower social classes as the city sweeps outward. In small communities, upper-upper- and lower-upper-class families may be intermixed geographically, but distinguishable because of the larger size and often greater age of the houses of the upper upper class.

The homes of the lower upper class are more likely to have modern equipment and hence to be more comfortable to live in than the old family residence of the upper-upper-class family; but of course they lack the aura of age and the implication of a family that has helped to found and develop the community.

FAMILY ORGANIZATION

The family unit of the lower upper class tends to be the husband and wife and their unmarried or minor children.   As the family gains status and becomes stabilized, three generations may function together; but rarely is there the large interconnected kinship group of the upper upper class.   Too often one branch of the family has pushed ahead, leaving collateral branches or parents in a lower social class.   It is both advantageous to the rising family and a means of avoiding jealousy and conflict for the small-family unit to retain its independence.   Also, the small family is characteristic of the middle class from which the lower-upper-class family has arisen.

The lower-upper-class family tends to be paternal in organization, with the husband functioning as head of the family as well as head of his business.   The wife is released by maids from too close household duties and finds time for active daytime participation in club life and philanthropic or community activities.   The husband has his luncheon clubs and business organizations.   The husband and wife also carry on joint social activities in the evenings and during vacations.   Husband and wife form a partnership with differentiated duties: the husband attends to the financial affairs, the wife to community duties and social life.   The wife profits by her husband's business acumen; he profits by the reputation she gives the family through charitable and community activities and association with socially desirable families.

MARRIAGE

Marriage occurs at only a slightly earlier age than in the upper upper class, according to the Yankee City study: an average age of 26.6 years as compared with 27.9 years for the upper upper class.[31]   In Elmtown, a small Midwestern city, marriage usually occurs in the middle twenties.[32] The age is markedly higher, however, than in the lower social classes. Marriage tends to be within the class or, preferably, upward.   The unusually attractive daughter or the brilliant son may make this move.   Or the son or daughter of a wealthy lower-upper family may be acceptable in marriage to a member of an impoverished upper-upper-class family. Marriage downward into the middle class is accepted by the family but

[31] Warner and Lunt, op. cit., p. 255.
[32] A. B. Hollingshead, "Selected Characteristics of Classes in a Middle Western Community," American Sociological Review, 12 (1947), 388.

without enthusiasm.   Marriage tends to be stable; divorce is frowned upon as a blight.

CHILDREN

Children are planned for, with a limited number desired.   In Elmtown, one or two children, or at most three, are considered sufficient.[33]

Since the family unit is small, children belong to the parents rather than to a kinship group.   Nursemaids, tutors, governesses, private schools, and private camps function in the rearing of children, although not to the same degree as in the upper-upper-class family.   The private camps and schools patronized by the lower-upper-class family tend to be the same institutions to which the children of upper-upper-class families go; they form an important avenue of communication and are the source of informal friendly relationships that later may lead to adult social relationships or intermarriage between families in the two social classes.

The children of the lower upper class have many of the same types of security as those of the upper upper class: economic, future life goals, freedom from police or charitable interference.   Socially, the child has less security unless his family has accepted its status and does not aspire to enter the upper upper class.   If the family is still upwardly mobile, the child may become insecure simply because of the pressure put upon him to conform to the standards of the upper class and to attempt to enter it socially, or through business or marriage.   If the family is slipping downward the child may be very insecure as a reflection of the family's anxiety.

Children are not an economic asset, as in some lower classes, but are an extension of the family into the future.   They are the bright hope of the parents that the family may enter into the upper upper class.   Children therefore are reared with this end in view.   Both boys and girls are given a good education; boys are assisted to establish themselves in business or a profession; and girls are shepherded into the proper groups for a desirable marriage.

[33] August Hollingshead, *Elmtown's Youth* (Wiley, 1949), p. 85; in this discussion the two divisions of the upper class are not distinguished from each other; therefore the estimate of number of children desired applies to the entire upper class.

Symbolic Importance of Upper-Class Families

Although the two upper classes include a very small proportion of American families, they are extremely important. They have been and still are responsible for much of the industrial development of the country; they are the custodians of great wealth and determine how that wealth shall be used, whether for themselves individually or for the benefit of science, art, or community welfare through the establishment of foundations that subsidize research, creative effort, schools for the underprivileged, pensions for the old, and many other welfare projects. Although some of this wealth and a portion of the services are now in the process of transfer to governmental agencies, industrial leadership is still linked to families.

In another way, too, the upper classes are significant. They are a symbol of accomplishment; their wealth and prestige are a reward for astuteness and industriousness. What these families have achieved by individual effort in the past, all ambitious individuals and families believe they can accomplish in the future: "there is always room at the top," "any boy can be President," "we are as good as they," are verbalizations of this belief. A sufficient number of families have been spectacularly successful to give credence to the belief that, though not all families could achieve similar success, any family has a chance. This belief has influenced the middle-class family in its choice of activities and especially in its goals of child training.

QUESTIONS

1. Why is it important to study social-class patterns of family life?
2. What are the characteristics of the upper-upper-class family?
3. How are children trained in the upper-class pattern?
4. How does the kinship group gain its power over individual family units?
5. In what ways is the upper-class child given security?
6. How does the lower-upper-class family differ from the upper-upper?
7. What differences are there in the roles of children in the upper-upper- and the lower-upper-class families?

BIBLIOGRAPHY

Theoretical framework for social class and the family

Warner, W. Lloyd, and Associates, *Democracy in Jonesville* (Harper, 1949).
Warner, W. Lloyd, and Lunt, Paul S., *The Social Life of a Modern Community* (Yale University Press, 1941).
Warner, W. Lloyd, Meeker, Marchia, and Eells, Kenneth, *Social Class in America* (Chicago: Science Research Associates, 1949).
West, James, *Plainville, U. S. A.* (Columbia University Press, 1945).

Upper-class family life

Adams, James Truslow, *The Adams Family* (Little, Brown, 1930).
Amory, Cleveland, *The Proper Bostonians* (Dutton, 1947).
———, *The Last Resorts* (Harper, 1952).
Davis, Allison, Gardner, B. B., and Gardner, M. R., *Deep South* (University of Chicago Press, 1941), ch. 4.
Lundberg, Ferdinand, *America's 60 Families* (Vanguard, 1937).

6

Middle-Class Families

The middle class, like the upper class, has a unique culture. Among some families, which in economic status, length of residence, and degree of influence, edge near the lower upper class, the family pattern consciously follows that of the upper class. Likewise, among middle-class families with low and insecure economic and social status, the family pattern may vary little from that of the lower class. But in general the middle class has developed its own culture, deeply rooted in the family and supported by the church and public school. Although the middle class is a feeder for the upper classes, the small proportion of families (3 per cent) in the upper classes indicates that the upward mobility at the top is limited. Within the middle class itself, however, there is ample range for mobility from lower to upper middle. Nevertheless the entire class has certain unifying features, including a belief in the goodness of middle-class status that prevents envy of the upper classes. The lower middle class is more mobile, seeking to achieve upper-middle-class status and using many precautions not to slip downward. Thus, faith in the middle class is accompanied in the lower ranks by an uneasy fear of downward mobility.

THE FAMILY UNIT

Unlike the kinship clan of the upper upper class, the middle-class family unit is the small or nuclear family composed of husband, wife, unmarried adult children, and minor children. The family begins with the marriage of a man and woman, who typically move into an independent house or apartment and become relatively autonomous and free from the control of parents or other relatives. The family ends with the death of husband and wife or sometimes with the death of one and the envelopment of the other by the family of a married son or daughter. Since the old widow or widower who abandons independent existence is considered no longer to constitute an independent family but at the same time often is not accepted as a fully accredited member of the offspring's family, he or she is a social isolate without family classification or family status. An unmarried son or daughter typically continues to live with the parents and is considered a member of the parental family, often contributing liberally to the support of the parents and sometimes (especially true of daughters) continuing in the status of a minor whose life is directed by the parents.

The relatives of the small family maintain a close relationship on a friendly basis. Married children exchange visits with their parents and with married brothers and sisters. Relations with cousins, uncles, and aunts are friendly but less close. The relationship circle may be considered a primary group but not a true kinship family with reciprocal familial responsibilities and controls. For instance, each marital unit owns and controls its own property; inherited property, usually limited in amount, is divided equally among the children who may then dispose of it as they wish. This procedure is true even of farm land, where division of the farm would create units too small for efficient farming. Although occasionally the farm is operated jointly by the heirs the usual procedure is either to sell the farm and divide the money among the heirs or for one heir who wishes to operate the farm personally to buy the interests of the other heirs. Each marital unit decides upon its place and type of residence and usually is responsible for financing it; a well-to-do brother would not be expected to aid a less able brother to buy a home. Even in case of severe hardship, relatives are not expected to go much beyond small gifts to tide over an emergency and often these are considered as loans. The exception is in the case of elderly parents who are still regarded as the financial responsibility of the middle-class family if they are unable to support themselves in old age. Likewise, parents aid if they are able in the higher education or business-launching of their children, but not of nieces or nephews. Any attempt on the part of collateral relatives to criticize or control the activities of the small-family unit would be resented, not only by the family in question but by other collateral members who would view this attempt at dominance as a threat to their own independence. Likewise, married children resent attempted dominance by their parents, and parents by their children. Each small-family unit regards itself as socially and financially independent and autonomous, but with friendship ties attaching it to related units.

The nearest semblance to kinship grouping occurs in times of crisis, especially illness or death.   Then relatives come with comforting sympathy, freely give assistance in household or business operations, and tide over a brief financial crisis.   Likewise, a wedding often brings the kin together to celebrate and often to help the young couple on their way with substantial gifts.   These kinship activities are temporary, however, and do not represent a continuing relationship of unity or responsibility. During the depression of the 1930's unemployment and resulting poverty sometimes brought kinship responsibility into play, but the pattern was not consistent.   In some instances, the deprived family was expected to apply for relief even though parents, brothers, or sisters had moderate means.   In other instances, the family that had exhausted its resources moved into the home of a relative or, in the case of some urban families, back to the parental farm.   The arrangement was considered temporary, however, and sometimes the newcomers were made to feel that they were unwelcome guests, who might easily overstay a reasonable visit.   Sometimes a portion of the home was set aside for the incoming family, which then was enabled to maintain a certain family independence.   With renewed employment, the secondary family was expected to move as soon as possible.   Similarly, during the housing shortage after World War II, many young married couples found it necessary to live with parents or other relatives.   Adjustment between these two family units often was difficult with a conflict of roles as parents sought to continue to direct their child, whereas the child sought to play the role of the independent married adult.   With increased building, the young couples moved as soon as possible into their own homes.

THE FAMILY'S PAST

The middle-class family has a brief past.   Personal contacts rarely extend over more than three generations, and if the family has been socially mobile or migratory they may be limited to two generations. Absorbed with earning a living and without education in the past to develop an interest in journals or diaries, middle-class families as a rule do not possess records written by past generations.   Family portraits and valuable heirlooms are lacking.   The past possessions of the family have been consumed with daily use or lack the beauty or pecuniary value of heirlooms. If the family has been upwardly mobile, the desire may have been to forget the past; all tangible articles have been sold, given away, or destroyed; sentimental attachments to the past, even the admission of knowing a foreign language native to the parents, are rejected. Family names may be changed slightly to rid them of foreign connotations, and reluctance may be shown to admit kinship with less mobile relatives. However, if the family has its roots in a status-giving European nationality (especially English), it may generate unusual interest in the past family history. Genealogies may be compiled in the effort to find a tie with a higher social class. The true middle-class family, however, is content with its independence, its freedom from the past and from collateral kinship groups, and an opportunity for upward mobility within the class.

CULTURAL UNITY

The cultural unity of the middle-class family in general is less marked than in the upper class. In cities that have grown through immigration, the middle class has a certain proportion of members whose parents or grandparents were European-born, thus creating diversity of religion, differing standards for family life, and differing conceptions of and interest in art, music, literature, and education. Threads of the ethnic patterns run through the general fabric of middle-class culture even when the family no longer consciously identifies itself with the ethnic group. Yankee City supplies an illustration.[1] In the upper upper class all families were Yankees for a number of generations back with no remnants of ethnic culture; in the lower upper class, less than 5 per cent were identifiable as ethnic, all being Irish in stock, but with several generations' residence in America; in the upper middle class, although only 6 per cent were born outside the United States, 17 per cent were identifiable as of non-Yankee stock, only a few being other than Irish; in the lower middle class 14 per cent were born outside the United States and 33 per cent represented some ethnic background, primarily Irish but including smaller proportions of French Canadians and Jews. Also, in the middle classes, fewer were born in Yankee City or its immediate vicinity than was true for the upper classes. In Jonesville, a smaller city in the Middle West with less ethnic diversity, Norwegians closely affiliated with the Lutheran Church form the chief ethnic group. None of the Norwegian-Lutherans

[1] W. Lloyd Warner and Paul S. Lunt, *The Social Life of a Modern Community* (New Haven: Yale University Press, 1941), pp. 422, 430–431, 435, 439.

are members of the upper class, and only 3 per cent of the ethnic group ranks as upper middle, but about a third are in the lower middle class.[2] (The remainder are chiefly in the upper lower class.)

There is also greater diversity of religious patterns in the middle class than in the upper class. In Yankee City, the upper upper class is represented in eight churches out of a possible eleven, but ranks high in affiliation with only one; the lower upper class has high affiliations with three and small affiliation with eight; the upper middle class, however, has high affiliations with six and some affiliation with five; the lower middle class has high affiliation with four and some affiliation with seven.[3] In Jonesville, the upper class attends six churches, but is predominantly in only one.[4] The upper middle class attends eight churches, with predominance in the same church that is patronized by the upper class. The lower middle class attends ten churches with attendance rather evenly divided among them.

The middle class, therefore, suffers from lack of cultural unity or tends to split up into unified subcultural groups on an ethnic or religious basis. The cultural differences are reflected in families, either through the social contacts with others of the same class but different ethnic or religious groups, or through intermarriage between the subcultural groups. Even when there is no family conflict, the culture transmitted by each family must be recognized as tending to have a dual aspect—partly middle class and partly ethnic-religious.

ECONOMIC BASIS

Unlike the wealth of the upper class, the income of the middle class is only to slight degree based on inherited wealth and that only in the upper middle class. As soon as a family accumulates any noticeable degree of inherited wealth, it tends to shift from the typical middle-class small-family pattern, interested mainly in its current affairs, into the kinship pattern of the upper class with a tendency to glorify the money-accumulating ancestors. The savings of the lower-middle-class family usually amount to only a few thousand dollars, sufficient to tide over the old-age period. Inherited by children, the amount when divided is negligible. If a business is inherited, usually it is small, and the active daily

---

[2] W. Lloyd Warner and Associates, *Democracy in Jonesville* (Harper, 1949), p. 177.

[3] Warner and Lunt, *op. cit.*, p. 360.

[4] Warner and Associates, *op. cit.*, p. 155.

work of the heirs is necessary for continued operation. At the lowest end of the middle-class scale, money is used as it is earned, often with almost no savings for old age.

Typical occupations for the upper-middle-class men are proprietorships of small businesses, the professions, and managerial positions in the large-scale business operations of the upper class. In the rural area the upper-middle-class farmer owns a large farm upon which he does some of the work but with the help of various hired hands whom he supervises. In the lower middle class are found clerical, skilled and semiskilled workers, artisan proprietors, and in the rural area men who operate their own farms without outside help or who are stable tenants.

Employment of women, rare in the upper classes, becomes apparent in the middle class. In the upper middle class the adult daughters often work before their marriage, not from actual necessity, but because of the middle-class reverence for industriousness and thrift and abhorrence of idleness. Young married women may also work in the first few years of marriage and middle-aged women after their children are married or in college. In the lower ranges, married women often work, especially before children are born and at times of emergency thereafter. Young children are not expected to work. For boys, however, Saturday or vacation jobs are regarded as praiseworthy attempts to establish the much-prized middle-class independence.

Within the range of occupations reserved for the middle class, each young person is free to choose the one he wishes to enter. Parents may bring gentle pressures to bear upon the son or daughter to guide them, but usually the parental concern is that the child may choose an occupation suited to his middle-class status rather than that the child should enter some particular occupation. Preferably the son should select an occupation of somewhat higher status than that of the father, although some sons follow the father's occupation—a doctor's son may become a doctor; a businessman's son may plan to enter his father's business. But it is conceded that each child has the right to select his own vocation, and in most instances the parents do not have a vocational opening waiting for the son or daughter.

The middle-class family cares for its own financial emergencies, and these, though more frequent and severe than in the upper class, happen less often than in the lower class. The 1933 depression, which seemed to sweep everything before it, was weathered without outside help by many middle-class families.   A study of 331 middle-class families surveyed in 1927 and again in 1933 shows the minor degree to which they were affected by a severe financial crisis, and the adjustments that they made.[5] The occupations of the husbands in this group place about two thirds of the families in the upper middle class, with one third in lower middle. Seventy-three per cent of the men held the same positions in 1933 as in 1927, and 10 per cent had positions of equal rank; only 1.8 per cent were unemployed at the time of the 1933 survey.   The increase in percentage of employed wives in 1933 over 1927 was negligible.   Although 11 per cent of the families had higher incomes in 1933 than in 1927, and 31 per cent had approximately the same incomes, 51 per cent had lower incomes (8 per cent are not accounted for), and the proportion with incomes below $1,200 had increased from 1 to 14 per cent.   None found it necessary to seek relief.   During this period some families were so far from need that they were able to increase expenditures and to assist relatives in distress.   Others, with decreased income, adjusted by borrowing on insurance policies, eliminating music and dancing lessons for their children, canceling magazine subscriptions, and delaying major expenditures such as the purchase of a home.   Another depression study of 100 families, about equally divided between middle- and lower-class families, shows the types of losses that occurred during the depression, in order of frequency: insurance lost or borrowed upon (30 families); savings or investments lost (23 families); borrowing (21 families); debts (20 families); loss of home, business, or other property (12 families).[6]   Of the 42 families that were definitely of middle-class status, only 7 sought relief, and most of these families were ones with a long history of disorganization prior to the depression.   In Yankee City, from 1930 to 1935 only 1 per cent of upper-middle-class and 4 per cent of lower-middle-class families found it necessary to receive relief.[7]   The middle-class family, therefore, appears as one able to handle all usual expenses and many severe financial setbacks without applying for relief; reduction of expenditures, postponement of plans involving a large amount of money, and borrowing or the use of savings enable the families to maintain their independence and family integrity.

[5] Winona L. Morgan, *The Family Meets the Depression* (Minneapolis: University of Minnesota Press, 1939).

[6] Ruth Shonle Cavan and Katherine Howland Ranck, *The Family and the Depression* (University of Chicago Press, 1938), pp. 44, 51.

[7] Warner and Lunt, *op. cit.*, p. 437.

RESIDENTIAL STABILITY

The middle-class family is more free to move its place of residence than the upper-class family, for it is not held in one place by the location of family property or family industry. Since each married couple starts life independently, they are free to remain in or to leave the city where their parents live. Even if they remain in the city of their childhood, they typically make several moves during the period of their married life. Each young couple, with some aid from parents, establishes itself and depends upon its own resources, which often are small during the early years of married life. The parents may live in a neat suburban district; but they may have started married life in a two-room furnished apartment. It is thought appropriate that their children, in turn, begin married life in a small and relatively inexpensive apartment, moving from one residential area to a better one as their resources increase until they also are able to live in the suburb. Middle-class children are not expected to begin married life "where the parents left off"; not only each generation but each child must prove its worth and establish itself anew in the middle-class status.

In small and medium-sized cities and in middle-class suburbs, the ambition is to own rather than rent. In Elmtown, 90 per cent of upper-middle- and 66 per cent of lower-middle-class families owned their homes; in Yankee City, a larger community, 17 per cent of the lower-middle-class families owned their homes.[8] (Upper-middle ownership is stated to be higher, but the percentage is not given.) In larger cities, the final residential goal is settlement in an area publicly esteemed as middle class, or home ownership in a middle-class suburb.

SMALL-FAMILY ORGANIZATION

The small-family organization is of prime importance in the middle-class family. It tends to be paternal (although scarcely patriarchal) in type with a trend toward an equal partnership in many areas. The husband is the economic head of the family. Usually he is the sole wage earner during the years when children are minors and often throughout the lifetime of the family. Even when other members of the family are employed, the husband typically earns by far the largest amount and is re-

[8] August Hollingshead, *Elmtown's Youth* (Wiley, 1949), pp. 91, 97; Warner and Lunt, *op. cit.*, p. 440.

garded as the producer of stable and dependable income.   His wife and his daughter may work if they wish, but are under no compulsion to do so; consequently, they may also stop working at will, whereas it is contrary to all middle-class expectations that the husband should stop working. In the family circle, also, the husband is regarded as the authoritarian head of the family, and major decisions are referred to him; or, in case of a family council, the final or the weighty vote comes from the husband. Nevertheless, his headship is benevolent.   He is deeply concerned for the welfare and happiness of his family and hence is swayed by their opinions and their reactions to him.   His decision, therefore, often is a nominal one, being merely the vocal expression of the joint opinion of the family.

Functionally, husband and wife have differentiated but strongly interlocking roles.   The husband, in addition to being the chief income producer, has many duties about the home, seen most clearly in the smaller city or suburb where families live in individual homes without the janitorial services found in large-city apartment buildings.   He mows the lawn in summer, tends the furnace in winter, and makes not only minor but often major repairs in, or remodels, the house.   He installs screens and storm windows with the seasons.   With the help of half-grown sons he frequently paints the house inside and out as needed, using week ends and long summer evenings over a period of two or three months.   At the lower end of the scale, where manual skills are part of the equipment of the male members of the family, it is not unusual for the family to build its own house from basement to chimney.   Other families have gardens, often renting land on the outskirts of town or securing the free use of vacant lots for this purpose.   Typically the husband and sons work the garden, while the mother and daughters can or deep freeze the extra food for winter use.   A few fruit trees in the back yard are prized by the middle-class family.   Thus the husband not only contributes the major money income but through his labor adds to the economic standing of the family.

The wife has a triple role: as wife and mother, as housekeeper, and as social arbiter.   The maternal aspect of her interpersonal role tends to supersede the wifely aspect—a reversal of the situation in the upper upper class.   Only during the first few and childless years of marriage do husband and wife place the sexual and social phases of their own relationship above the demands and welfare of their children.   The husband's interest in his home and children makes it possible for the wife to become more mother than wife during the years of her children's minority.

The mother personally rears the children, according to the wishes of both husband and wife. Plans for the children, standards of conduct, and methods of discipline are usually fairly well agreed upon by husband and wife, but it is the wife who most often administers the regulations and the discipline. Rarely does the middle-class mother have a nurse or governess for her children; at most she has a "baby-sitter," employed by the hour as needed. Her personal care of the children creates a strong emotional bond to which the mother as well as the children respond. She finds in them as well as in her husband a stimulus for emotional expression and a source of emotional response to her needs. To the extent that the father enters into child training, he tends to be more concerned personally with his son than his daughter, and with his older son coming into adolescence than with his infant son. The son represents an extension into the future of his own personality and he hopes intensely that the son will reach the ideal goal that he failed to reach. Many fathers place wide opportunities for development before their children but are reluctant to discipline them, feeling that the short periods of time that they are able to be with their children should be agreeable and pleasant. The mother thus often remains the disciplinarian, even when the husband assumes an active father role.

The middle-class wife is not only the manager of her home but its actual keeper, especially in regions where inexpensive domestic help is lacking. At the upper range of middle class, she may possibly have a full-time maid, but she more usually has a laundress or a "cleaning woman" who comes in one or two days a week or a school boy on Saturday to do rough work. In the lower-middle-class range, even such part-time assistance is unknown. Since the wife expends much time and energy on her home and carries out many of her own ideas of decoration and ornamentation in it, it becomes an extension of her personality. She receives much satisfaction from praise of her home from other women. The home, together with its furnishings, therefore become something to be preserved and cared for rather than something for the use and comfort of the family. She therefore makes many restrictions regarding the use of the home by her family. The children may play only in certain rooms (their bedrooms, the kitchen, the basement playroom). No one may put his feet on a chair or couch; cigarette ashes may not accidentally fall on the rug;

chair arms or table tops must not be marred by wet glass rings or hot cigarette butts.   Violation of these wife-made rules is an affront to the wife herself, an attack on her ego.

The social activities of the family rest largely in the hands of the wife. "My wife keeps the social calendar" is the stock reply of one husband when any question arises of social activity outside the family.   This manipulation of social participation relates not only to husband-wife activities but to those of the children as well and over as long a period as the mother is able to exert control over her children.   The middle-class woman tends to be very conscious of social position and exerts a deliberate effort to preserve or improve the position of the family.   She passes judgment on invitations and feels free to accept or reject in terms of their value to the family status, her husband's business opportunities, or the children's future.   She also makes the list of invited guests to her home, with the husband perhaps having a veto power.   She guides her children's choice of friends by all methods from subtle insinuations that a certain child is undesirable, through direct statements that one child is "dirty" and another child "good fun," to outright forbidding of certain contacts and deliberate inclusion of her child in desirable groups.

Her community activities often extend beyond the purely social role, especially as her children mature and leave her with free time.   Middle-class wives form the bulwark of the boards, committees, and volunteer groups that "run" civic and community ventures.   The origin and successful operation of many welfare groups, children's agencies, recreational programs, homes for old people and the like have rested in the hands of some small group of persistent middle-class women who have brought their husbands and other men into the picture financially and to solve legal problems but have never relinquished their essential control of the projects.

MARRIAGE

Marriage occurs within the subclass (or an adjacent class) at a slightly lower age than in the upper classes.   In Yankee City, for instance, the average age of marriage was 26.10 years in the upper middle and 25.10 years in the lower middle class.[9]   In Elmtown middle-class marriages occurred on the average a year earlier than in the lower upper class.[10]

[9] Warner and Lunt, op. cit., pp. 436, 440.
[10] A. B. Hollingshead, "Selected Characteristics of Classes in a Middle Western Community," American Sociological Review, 12 (1947), 390.

Although marriages tend to occur within the class, the range of choice is wider than in the upper classes. Middle-class children attend public schools where they meet children from all ranges of the middle class and the lower classes as well as such upper-class children as do not attend private schools. The number of middle-class children also is much greater than the number of upper-class children, thus providing a more

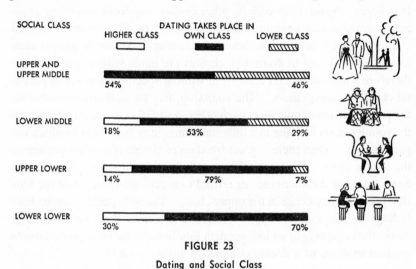

FIGURE 23

Dating and Social Class

In Elmtown (7,000 population), most teen-agers dated with members of their own social class. Previous friendships, control by parents, available spending money, and degree of familiarity with social-class customs are all factors in restricting dating to one's own social class. Dating activities also differ by social class, varying from the formal dances limited to country club members, through public school parties open to all pupils, to informal coke dates, and finally to the tavern and jalopy of the lower-lower-class youth. (Source: A. B. Hollingshead, *Elmtown's Youth* [Wiley, 1949], pp. 197–198.)

numerous group from which to choose. By the time high school is reached and dating begins, differentiation into class groups has been fairly well established. Some upper-class children have been sent to private secondary schools as preparation for both college and later class position; some lower-class children have dropped out of school. In the remaining group, primarily middle-class, many cliques form, identifying the various gradations in social status. These cliques solidify during the three or four years of high school, with dating becoming more and more confined to the members in a given clique. Although the cliques are formed primarily on the basis of class lines, they are not formed for middle-class children on the basis of parental friendships.   The boys and girls in a given clique may all be upper middle class, but their parents may be unknown to each other or know each other only by name, unless the community is a small one.   For those who attend college, the high school cliques tend to weaken, and new cliques, also largely class delimited, form in college.   Again, after college, other cliques may form, as college graduates scatter to new communities, or there may be a reforming of the old cliques if they return to the home community.   As young people tend to shift from dating to courtship, choices are made within the cliques—therefore within the social class—but without specific reference to parental choice or supervision.   The courtship may be well advanced before the parents of the couple meet each other, a situation especially true when the young person is living in a different community from that in which the parents live.   Thus there is great freedom of choice of marital partner in the middle class.   Parental pressure is informal and personal; there can be no threat of disinheritance or refusal to accept the spouse into the kinship group as may occur in the upper class.   The only penalty can be hurt feelings and displeasure—not too effective in a class where each marriage marks the beginning of an independent family and where the young couple are free to move to a distant community if they wish.[11]

CHILDREN

The middle-class family has more children than upper-class but less than lower-class families.   In Elmtown, for instance, the mean number of children was 2.3 per upper-middle family and 3.6 per lower-middle family, marked increases over the upper-class family.[12]

In the middle-class family the children "belong" to both parents, in contrast to the upper class where they belong to the kinship and are important as links in the historical family.   The family unit for the child consists of his parents, himself, and his brothers and sisters.   Next in importance are the grandparents, especially if they live in the same community and are seen often or if the children are left in the care of the grandparents when their parents go to some social affair or are on a vacation.   The tie to uncles, aunts, and cousins is less marked, and these relatives may be almost unknown if they live at a distance and are not

[11] For a detailed discussion of dating and courtship, see pages 307–316.
[12] Hollingshead, *Elmtown's Youth*, pp. 93, 99.

visited.   It is not uncommon for the middle-class child not to know the names of even first cousins if personal contacts have been allowed to lapse. This narrowing of the family circle to parents and children—and perhaps

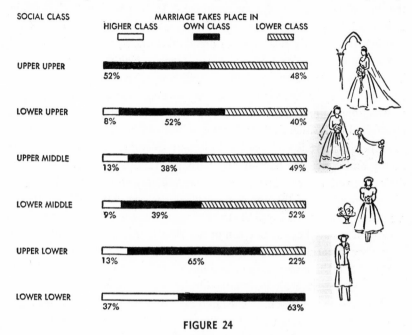

FIGURE 24

Marriage and Social Class, New Haven

Although the tendency is strong for men to select wives from their own social class, another tendency also appears—marriage with women of less social status than their own.   Only the lower lower class does not exhibit this trend.   Generally out-class marriages are between those of adjacent class status, rags to riches marriages being both unusual and socially disapproved. Marriages decline in formality and social control as social-class level declines. In the higher social classes, not only the family and kinship group tend to control the choice of mate, but the entire social class is interested in the preservation of class lines.   In the middle ranks marriage tends to be a family affair only, whereas in the lower classes marriage is treated as an individual concern of the man and woman alone.   (Source: A. B. Hollingshead, "Cultural Factors in the Selection of Marriage Mates," *American Sociological Review*, 15 [1950], Table 4, p. 625.)

grandparents—restricts emotional ties to a small group and consequently tends to intensify them.   The fact that children are relatively few in number and that the parents and especially the mother assumes personal care of the children also adds to the intensity.   Children often are taken by the parents on all vacation trips, and it is not unusual for the child never to have spent a night separated from the parents from infancy to the time of college entrance or marriage.   If the emotional relationship, as is usual, is one of love and dependence, the bond is very strong.   Conversely, if the family relationships breed resentment, anger, and a feeling of frustration, these emotions also are strong.   Neither child nor parent has a wide circle of less immediate family members from which to seek substitute satisfactions or upon whom to vent resentments.   Emotional satisfactions come from a small group, and emotional reactions, whether affectional or hostile, find their outlet within the narrow family circle.

Although there is no large kinship group to converge on the child with family ambitions, the parents and perhaps grandparents project on him their own ambitions.   The situation may become more intense than in the kinship grouping of the upper class, where, if one child fails, another— a cousin, perhaps—is available to carry on for the kinship.   In the small family there may be only one son or one daughter to satisfy family expectations or to carry out the unfulfilled ambitions of their parents.

When a crisis occurs—such as illness or death of a parent or, more recently, divorce—there is no large kinship group to which the child may turn to cushion the shock.   The child may be left to face the world alone except for remote relatives whom he scarcely knows and who feel only moderate responsibility for him.

The middle-class child is expected to fulfill not only family ambitions but also the social-class ambitions of his parents.   If they are firmly fixed in the middle class, he must see that he maintains their standard and does not slip downward.   The child of upper-middle-class parents must not permit himself to become lower middle class, and the child of the lower middle class must not disgrace his family by slipping down into the lower class.   And in many families, the child is expected to achieve greater success than did his parents, the son through entering a more highly preferred occupation, the daughter by marriage above her parents' social class.   Certain anxiety is established in the child by his parents' great need that he should bring credit to them.   He is exhorted by his parents not only to get as good grades in school as his father did, but also to equal or surpass the children of middle-class neighbors.   The boy must secure the quota of school honors, the type of job, and the amount of salary thought suitable to a middle-class child.   The girl must maintain the standard of dress, the fastidiousness of appearance, and the type of dating partner that other middle-class girls achieve.   Even though the children are "good" in a moral sense, the parents feel chagrin and even shame if they do not meet middle-class standards.[13]

Middle-class parents are self-consciously parents and follow the dictates of "scientific child care."   They strive to be intellectual about their parenthood, reading special magazines and articles in newspapers and women's magazines written for parents by educators, physicians, and child psychologists.   They compose child study groups, listening to specialists in child training; and they are the bulwark of the Parent-Teacher Associations.   Where preschool nurseries are available, they patronize them in order to give their children proper social contacts under trained supervision.   They attempt to follow not only what the specialist tells them is the correct way to feed or train their children; but also to understand some of the theories that underlie the advice.   Thus, they often attempt to curb their natural impulses to love and caress or to mete out swift punishment, in order to conform to the current theories of child training.[14]   Underlying the fetish-like devotion to rules is the isolation of the parents from a kinship group with established mores based on unified cultural antecedents that are passed from older members to young parents. In the middle class, each young couple in their independent isolation must learn anew what can be expected of children and how parents should react to the abilities and the deficiencies, the goodness or badness, of their children.   The general upward mobility of the middle class and, frequently, the ethnic characteristics of older family members cause the young parents to mistrust advice from the older generation.   They seek

[13] So marked is this emphasis on success that one writer at least has rephrased the social-class system in the United States as a success system with striving for success and upward mobility so dominant that class placement becomes only a temporary stepping stone to a higher placement.   The careful studies of class culture and measures of mobility indicate, however, that this point of view is distorted and emphasizes only one aspect of the middle class. See Margaret Mead, *And Keep Your Powder Dry* (Morrow, 1942), ch. 4.

[14] From decade to decade, as child psychological theories change, middle-class parents change their tactics.   In the 1920's, under the guidance of John B. Watson, they held their children to a strict regime of feeding, sleeping, and playing and refrained from fondling them, since following the natural inclination to do so would make the child too dependent.   Following Freudian concepts they permitted their children more or less to run wild, on the theory that repressions were bad for the child and any restriction might result in a repression.   In the late 1940's theories changed again, with major emphasis on a permissive attitude on the part of the parent toward minor infractions of social rules and an increase of fondling and caressing.

to reject the past, to grasp a better future.   Mobility from rural to urban also alienates the young parents from parental advice.   How can the farm grandparents know the problems of the young city family where children's food is suspect of germs and play space must be deliberately created and carefully supervised?

The middle class distrusts natural impulses, and the family early imposes upon children many repressive, regulative, and ritualistic routines. A firsthand study of the child-training practices of a small sample of middle- and lower-class families in Chicago revealed that middle-class infants and children are denied direct and complete satisfaction of natural impulses at an earlier age than lower-class children, whose parents feel less compulsion to conform to socially imposed standards.[15]   On the average, middle-class children, as compared with lower-class, are less often nursed by the mother; they are weaned from breast and bottle earlier; they are more often fed on schedule rather than whenever hungry, and held only during the feeding period.   Bowel and bladder training are begun earlier; half of the middle-class mothers began bowel training of their children at six months or earlier, as compared with only 23 per cent of lower-class mothers who attempted this inhibitive training at so early an age.   The middle-class children did not accomplish bowel and bladder control any earlier, however, than the lower-class children; they simply were subjected to the attempts of the mother to enforce control over a longer period of time.   In this connection it is significant that many more middle-class than lower-class children sucked their thumbs and masturbated, although middle-class parents abhor and try to eradicate both practices.   Both of these activities are often regarded as attempts of children to satisfy and comfort themselves when they feel socially frustrated or rejected, or suffer anxieties and fears.   It is pertinent at least to suggest that the repressive training at a very early age among middle-class children interferes with a warm and protective relationship between mother and child and arouses anxieties and frustrations in young children.

Other regulations are also imposed upon middle-class children, some of a protective nature, others to induce responsibilities.   Under the protective is the fact that 89 per cent of middle-class children as compared with 52 per cent of the lower-class children take daytime naps.[16]   Free-

[15] Allison Davis, *Social-Class Influences upon Learning* (Cambridge: Harvard University Press, 1949), pp. 12–22.
[16] *Ibid.*

dom of movement in the neighborhood is restricted. Middle-class boys as a rule have to be in the house by twilight or early dark and girls as a rule by five or six o'clock. Lower-class children are allowed greater freedom in the evening. Attendance alone at movies, although not disapproved by any middle-class parents in the sample studied, is not permitted to many middle-class children under the age of eight. In view of the restrictions on being out at night, this attendance would primarily be in the daytime. The implications of these findings are that the middle-class parent attempts to give security of health and supervised activities to his children and to protect them both from overfatigue and from miscellaneous social contacts.

Another prohibition imposed on middle-class children forbids an open expression of interest in sex. With larger homes and the privacy of separate bedrooms for parents, the middle-class child rarely sees sexual activities by accident, as the lower-class child may do. His restricted social activities, especially in the evenings, and the middle-class refusal to tolerate houses of prostitution or looseness of behavior in their communities further protect the child. Middle-class parents also are inhibited by their own early training from freely discussing matters of sex with their children. When they do give "sex education," it is often limited to biological facts and does not relate sex to the child's physical or emotional impulses. Thus the child is thrown back into his ignorance or projected into a state of anxiety. He seeks and finds information from slightly older children in his own group or secretively from talking with or observing lower-class children whose avenues of gaining knowledge and of sexual experimentation are wider.

The middle-class child is taught by his parents not to fight, or at most to fight only defensively. He is also taught not to annoy people, not to run over lawns or destroy flower beds, not to "swipe" fruit from orchards or back yards, not to "snitch" fruit in the grocery store, not to sneak into the movies without paying, and so on. All these activities, which employ physical and mental alertness and which give the satisfaction of victory over an opponent, are denied the middle-class child. He has certain substitutes in the nature of organized sports, playgrounds, play equipment at home, camping trips and youth organizations but always under adult supervision and within middle-class restrictive mores.

The impressing of habits and attitudes upon a child takes place primarily through the application of penalties and rewards. These may be physical in nature, such as a slap or a stick of candy, or psychological, such as a scolding or praise, or social, such as being isolated in a closet or allowed to accompany the parents to a picnic.   An unpleasant experience following some activity tends toward the inhibition of that act in the future; a pleasant result encourages repetition.   The relative frequency of penalties or rewards and the types used vary from one social class to another. In general, the middle-class parent tends to use rewards more than penalties; he especially uses physical penalties sparingly but may employ physical rewards.   Psychological and social penalties and rewards are both used.   In contrast, the lower-class parent tends to use physical penalties, swiftly applied with hand or strap, or physical rewards that often consist not of any specific object but of continued freedom of action on the part of the child.   The psychological and social penalties of the middle-class parent are longer lasting and often more devastating to the personality than the physically painful but quickly ended punishments of the lower-class parent.   The middle-class parent, by shaming the child, telling him the parent will not love him if he continues his disobedience, or shutting him in a room and thus refusing to associate with him, makes an attack on the child's personality and the child's conception of himself.   The experience makes a rift, however small, in the emotional relationship of the child with the parent and arouses fear and anxiety that the parent will not love and protect him, and give him security.   The lower-class parent does not raise the question of love.   He punishes the act, whereas the middle-class parent punishes the personality of the child.[17]

Many of the rules of behavior and training laid down for middle-class children are compulsive and ritualistic in nature.   They tend to become "right" in themselves.   Rituals with attitudinal content that tend to establish principles are less used.   The middle-class family does not have sufficient family history nor deep enough kinship connections to have many traditional rituals from past generations.   Upwardly mobile parents, perceiving the use of rituals by upper-class families, may somewhat self-consciously impose rituals upon themselves and their children.   Previous informal methods may be discarded in favor of formal methods that may not fit well into the total family pattern.   After-dinner coffee in the living room may convey satisfaction to the family that a step upward has

---

[17] W. Allison Davis and Robert J. Havighurst, *Father of the Man* (Houghton Mifflin, 1947); A. W. Green, "The Middle Class Male Child and Neurosis," *American Sociological Review*, 11 (1946), 31–41.

been gained, but may be at variance with breakfast in serial order in the kitchen as each member of the family snatches a bite to eat on the way to work or school at different hours of the morning. If not all members of the family accept the value of such rituals, they may become devisive rather than cohesive in the family life.

The effect of middle-class training on the child's personality is still a matter of speculation because careful studies have not been made. In certain areas the child has security; in others insecurity and anxiety. The family and the child have a reasonable amount of economic security, backed by college or specialized training of some sort. The child also has the security of the small-family group, but not of a larger kinship group—a lack that may not be apparent unless the family faces some major crisis in which it cannot meet its own problems. Crises are relatively uncommon in the middle class, however, as most middle-class families successfully adjust to depression, and family conflict and divorce are relatively infrequent. The family security is marred, however, by the attempts of the parent to train the child at an early age and to restrict many of his natural impulses and interests, as well as by the threat to exclude the child from the circle of the parents' love and companionship if he disobeys their injunctions. Anxieties and frustration focusing on sex and aggressiveness are especially common to the middle-class child— so common that one student in the field regards them as normal for middle-class children.[18]

CRISES

Except in periods of great social disorganization (depression or war), the crises of middle-class families tend to result from interpersonal relationships within the family. Other types of personal crises are infrequent. The isolation of each small family from parental or sibling families reduces the probability of conflict within the kinship group. Good breeding all but eliminates neighborhood conflicts and creates a tendency to overlook the breaches that occasionally occur. The economic resources are sufficient for such unusual demands as illness. The specialized training that places the middle-class man in a business or profession makes him of sufficient value that the risk of unemployment is low. Other members of the family, also trained in special vocations or with good general education, are able to supplement the income if neces-

[18] Davis, *op. cit.*, p. 37.

sary. Thus clashes with other families or disorganization because of economic strain are reduced to a minimum in the middle class. But the family is still subject to interpersonal crises dependent upon such factors as confusion in roles of husband and wife, failure of husband and wife to meet each other's personal needs, and numerous conflicts arising from incompatible expectations or interests. It is subject also to tensions between parents and children arising from misunderstandings, failures to meet needs, rebellions, and disagreements of many kinds.[19]

The middle-class family, whose expectations are high and mores for personal behavior fairly rigid, is sensitive to lack of harmony among its members and therefore experiences many interpersonal crises. It tends to recover quickly, however, and to make a readjustment that places the internal unity of the family upon a firmer basis. More consideration tends to be given to the individual needs of the members, and the family adapts itself to new ways in meeting these needs, thus demonstrating a certain flexibility and a yielding of family ways in order to preserve the family as a unit. Values may be shifted, but in all probability values are retained and ways of attaining them shifted.

The family tends to solve its problems within the family circle. Difficulties are hidden even from kinship families, and greatly reluctant is the family to seek the aid either of the old-time counselors, such as ministers or family physicians, or of newer facilities, such as the psychiatrist or marital counseling bureau. This tendency rests partly on the ability of the middle-class family to solve its own problems and partly on middle-class pride in successful family life that makes it all but impossible to admit failure.[20]

MIDDLE-CLASS FAMILIES AS THE BALANCE WHEEL

Middle-class families form a balance wheel between the small but financially powerful upper-class families and the laboring strength of the lower-class families. Although they include fewer people than lower-class families, their dominance in the professions places them in a position of leadership not only within their own group but in the lower class. Schoolteachers, who are primarily middle-class, teach the children of

[19] Earl L. Koos, "Middle-Class Family Crises," *Marriage and Family Living,* 10 (1948), 25, 40; "Class Differences in Family Reactions to Crisis," *Marriage and Family Living,* 12 (1950), 77–78, 99.

[20] Koos, "Middle-Class Family Crises," *loc. cit.,* pp. 25, 40; Koos, "Class Differences in Family Reactions to Crisis," *loc. cit.,* pp. 77–78, 99.

lower-class families.   Social workers, also primarily middle-class, guide the destinies of lower-class families in times of stress.   Related to the quality of this leadership is the degree of adjustment made by lower-class families to their problems.   Children are greatly affected by the attitudes of their middle-class teachers toward them.   Thus, the influence of the middle class spreads out to affect lower-class families and children.

Middle-class families, being more mobile than upper-class families, are more subject to the tensions of mobility.   They are less subject, however, than lower-class mobile families because usually they are better prepared for the move, less likely to move without some definite prospect of work, and better able financially to tide over a period of lowered income.

Of the three class levels, middle-class families are most involved in the issues of family life occasioned by social changes (discussed in Chapter 1).   The middle position, with the possibility of upward mobility and the threat of downward, makes the middle class very conscious of social values and also very conservative.   Moral injunctions are placed upon children early in life, and rigid standards are set for them.   Those who deviate (the career wife, the one-child family, the divorced couple, and so on) often feel emotionally guilty even though intellectually justified in their position.   The issues of family life consist very largely of the tensions that the middle-class family feels as it leaves the rural stronghold of the past and accepts the urbanism of the present.

QUESTIONS

1. Discuss the attitudes of middle-class families toward family histories.

2. In a given community why do middle-class families usually have less cultural unity than upper-class families?

3. What roles does the middle-class wife play?

4. What factors contribute to the intensity of emotional relationships between the middle-class mother and her children?

5. Why does the middle-class mother depend heavily upon specialists to guide her in child-rearing?

6. From your observation, are middle-class children inclined to be neurotic?

BIBLIOGRAPHY

Middle-class family life

Hollingshead, A. B., "Class Differences in Family Stability," *The Annals* of the American Academy of Political and Social Science, 272 (1950), 39–46.

Hollingshead, A. B., "Selected Characteristics of Classes in a Middle Western Community," *American Sociological Review,* 12 (1947), 385–395.

Koos, E. L., "Class Differences in Family Reactions to Crisis," *Marriage and Family Living,* 12 (1950), 77–78, 99.

——— "Middle-Class Family Crises," *Marriage and Family Living,* 10 (1948), 25, 40.

Davis, Allison, Gardner, B. B., and Gardner, M. R., *Deep South* (University of Chicago Press, 1941), ch. 5.

Useem, J., Tangent, P., and Useem, R., "Stratification in a Prairie Town," *American Sociological Review,* 7 (1942), 331–342.

The middle-class child and adolescent

Davis, Allison, *Social-Class Influence upon Learning* (Harvard University Press, 1949).

———, and Havighurst, R. J., "Social Class and Color Differences in Child-Rearing," *American Sociological Review,* 11 (1946), 698–710.

Ericson, M., "Child-Rearing and Social Status," *American Journal of Sociology,* 52 (1946), 190–193.

Green, A. W., "The Middle Class Male Child and Neurosis," *American Sociological Review,* 11 (1946), 31–41.

Hollingshead, August B., *Elmtown's Youth* (Wiley, 1949).

Neugarten, B., "Social Class and Friendship among School Children," *American Journal of Sociology,* 51 (1946), 305–314.

Lower-Class Families

Similar to the upper class and the middle class, the lower class also has two subdivisions—upper lower and lower lower.   The upper lower approaches the lower middle in culture, so much so that in some small communities the two are thought of in conjunction with each other under the vernacular term, the Common Man.[1]   The lower lower verges off into the ranks of the declassed—the vagrants, delinquents, and criminals who follow no class pattern but have their own small-group cultures.   In large industrial cities the lower lower class may be composed largely of people with definite non-American ethnic cultures brought with them from foreign shores.   Because these foreign-born or foreign-culture groups have special family situations, they are not specifically discussed in this chapter, in which the discussion of lower-lower-class families is general in nature.

The lower class is numerous in all communities, but especially so in the large industrial cities where unskilled and semiskilled labor predominates.   In such a situation the lower class far outnumbers the middle class.   Its contribution to community leadership usually is not marked, or, if marked, it is in the nature of retardation of community projects.   As officers of organizations, the middle class takes the lead in community planning and in enforcing the mores.

THE FAMILY'S PAST

Even more brief than the history of the middle-class family is that of the lower-class family.   The European origin a generation or two ago gives a finite beginning to the American phase of the family, often within

[1] W. Lloyd Warner and Associates, *Democracy in Jonesville* (Harper, 1949), p. 24.

the memory of the older members.   Dispersion of family members as they migrate from job to job breaks the connecting ties between related nuclear families.   Correspondence is irregular, and visits are made only at long intervals.   There are virtually no written family records.   For a minority at the lowest range, however, stability rather than mobility is common, for an impoverished and dependent class marks the lowest status in the social hierarchy.   This class is too dependent upon social institutions and too completely enmeshed in poverty even to migrate with the hope of finding work.   It has a history, not in its own family possessions, but in the records of social agencies and in the legends of the community that identify certain families as permanently worthless.   Some of these families have been in the active case load of social agencies off and on for two or three generations.

THE FAMILY UNIT

The family unit consists of the husband, wife, and their unmarried adult children and minor children.   In some respects, the stable and continuing family unit is the mother and minor children.   The death rate, especially of the men, is higher in the lower classes than in the middle or upper classes; therefore there are more widows.   In addition, the marriage bond is weak; desertions, separations, and divorces destroy the family unit. Almost without exception, the mother keeps the children, and the father is the one to withdraw.   New marriages—legal or common-law—bring a new man into the family as husband but rarely as a genuine replacement of the original father.   Occasionally, there may be a succession of husbands.   Thus, even in the event of a stepfather, the core of the family remains the mother and her children.

The ties with grandparents and collaterals are weak, although at a time of family crisis, usually with economic implications, they strengthen, and one branch of the family gives sanctuary to a stranded branch.   When the conditions change, the families separate.   Inasmuch as crises fraught with economic strain are more frequent in the lower-class family than in the family of any other class, these temporary mergings and withdrawals are fairly common.

CULTURAL UNITY

The lower class as a whole is a variegated group: families with a lengthy American background who somehow or other have failed to make the grade; newly arrived immigrant groups in the cities who, because of lack of vocational training and language difficulties, come into American society at the lower-class level; remnants of earlier ethnic groups who have failed to adjust to American culture at a higher level; groups that come into cities from other sections of the United States where they have been economically and culturally deprived (Southern Negroes and "poor whites" from the hills of the Southern border states).   When the ethnic groups are included, the variations of language, culture, and religion are great.   An illustration is found in the religious affiliations of the lower class.   In Jonesville, the upper lower class had affiliations with nine different churches with slightly over half the class having no church membership.[2]   In the lower lower class, membership in the same nine churches is represented, but only 28 per cent had church affiliations.   Diversity is also shown by birthplace of the class members.   In Yankee City, both upper lower and lower lower class contained 30 per cent who were foreign-born.[3]   The upper lower class had 28 per cent, and the lower lower class 38 per cent, who were born outside of Yankee City (although for the most part nearby or in other parts of New England).   No other social class in Yankee City included as few Yankee City–born members. The ethnic and racial groups, largely concentrated in the two lower classes, consisted of nine stocks, representing many different languages, cultural values, and religions: Irish, French Canadians, Jewish, Italian, Armenian, Greek, Polish, Russian, and Negro.

Confusion and conflicts are reduced by the tendency for families with the same cultural background to cluster together, living perhaps in distinct and separate communities.   Sometimes the majority of persons residing in one community work in the same industry, thus further reducing contacts.   The lower classes, then, somewhat resemble a mosaic of cultural groups, each with a distinctive and group-centered life of its own.   When groups meet, conflicts may arise; among adolescents and youths, especially male, physical conflicts may be sought, either in free-for-all or planned battles or on another level through competitive group sports. When marriages occur between members of different or opposed cultural groups, the conflict may be carried over into either an inter- or an intra-family conflict.

[2] Warner and Associates, *op. cit.,* pp. 154–155.
[3] W. Lloyd Warner and Paul S. Lunt, *The Social Life of a Modern Community* (New Haven: Yale University Press, 1941), pp. 209, 211.

Regardless of these differences, the general pattern of economic status and insecurity, the necessity for each member of the lower class to become self-sufficient, and the lack of community prestige and influence produce certain family similarities that characterize the lower classes.

ECONOMIC BASIS

Inherited wealth is unheard of in the lower classes. Income is primarily from wages earned through semiskilled and unskilled labor. These are the jobs that may be entered easily and that are easily refilled if the worker leaves. The workers are at the mercy of even slight changes in the market and may be laid off without ceremony because they are easily replaced. Much seasonal work is also done by lower-class workers. Income is not only low but uncertain; consequently, savings are small, and an accumulation of family wealth impossible.

The lower-class family is the one that experiences the economic life cycle observed by Rountree in his study of the English laborer.[4] In the life cycle of the family, early manhood and womanhood when courtship and marriage occur is a period of relatively adequate income; the youth is young and vigorous, the wife is able to work, and there are no children or one child. The second stage comes when the number of children increases and the wife drops out of employment, while expenses mount; this is a period of insecurity and perhaps downright poverty. As the children come into adolescence and begin to work, comes the third stage; the family income is larger and many home improvements are made, as the accumulated moderate incomes from several workers may make a respectable total. In the fourth stage, as children marry and leave home, income decreases but so also do expenses. With old age the cycle comes to a close with the old couple again facing the poverty and insecurity that they knew in their childhood. Savings are small or do not exist, and payments under Old Age Assistance or Old Age and Survivors' Insurance are often inadequate even for minimum essentials.

When savings are possible, as among the more thrifty upper-lower-class families, they may go into the purchase of a small home. In some cities this home is a small frame house with a basement flat and a second-floor flat, in one of which the family lives, the other being rented for additional income. In other cities, the upper-lower-class family buys a small plot in an unincorporated area beyond the city and there, unhampered by mu-

[4] B. S. Rountree, *Poverty—A Study of Town Life* (London: Longmans, 1922).

nicipal building ordinances, constructs a small house often of second-hand materials and without plumbing, electricity, or gas, although these may be added later.   But the proportion of lower-class families owning homes is small.   In Elmtown, 35 per cent of the upper-lower-class families and 19 per cent of the lower-lower-class families, as compared with 66 per cent of lower-middle-class families, owned their homes.[5]   In Yankee City, only 6 per cent of lower-lower-class families owned homes.[6]

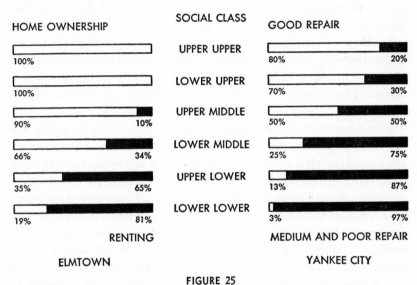

FIGURE 25

Homes According to Social Class

In Elmtown, a Midwestern city of 7,000, all upper-class people, but only one fifth of the lower lower class, own their homes.   In Yankee City, 80 per cent of the upper upper class, but only 2 per cent of the lower lower class, live in homes in good repair.   Ownership increases stability of family life and incorporation into community life.   (Source: A. B. Hollingshead, *Elmtown's Youth* [Wiley, 1949], ch. 5; W. Lloyd Warner and Paul S. Lunt, *Social Life of a Modern Community* [Yale University Press, 1941], pp. 425, 432, 437, 440, and 441.)

Only rarely are savings sufficient to tide the family over an emergency, such as a major operation of the chief wage earner or a long-continued period of unemployment.   A limited degree of security for as long as 26 weeks may be gained when the wage earner is eligible for unemploy-

[5] August Hollingshead, *Elmtown's Youth* (Wiley, 1949), pp. 97, 104, 116.
[6] Warner and Lunt, *op. cit.,* p. 448.

ment insurance.   Even the upper-lower-class family may have to apply for relief during an emergency, and the lower-lower-class family may be on and off relief as a permanent feature of life.   Relief, therefore, is accepted as a possibility or even a probability and is sought without the deep shame and loss of self-respect with which the occasional middle-class person reluctantly approaches a welfare office.   Moreover, it is sought before the family has lowered its standard of living or threatened its future security through the exhaustion of resources that typifies the middle-class family in economic distress.   The lower-class family has few resources to be exhausted, and life on relief often represents only a slight diminution of the customary standard of living.   The attitude of realistic acceptance of economic insecurity is expressed in these words by one lower-class father: "There's never been a time when I could be sure that I could care for my family.   And my father was that way before me, too." [7]

Regular or intermittent employment for all members of the family who can work is not only the common practice but is believed to be normal and necessary.   It is accepted by both husbands and wives, without shame or resentment, that wives should be employed a large part of the time, even when the children are small.   In Elmtown, 30 per cent of the upper-lower mothers and 55 per cent of the lower-lower mothers were gainfully employed.[8]   The necessity for women to work is increased also by the number of families in which the father is dead or has deserted either temporarily or permanently.   The mother, with whatever aid she can secure from social agencies or relatives, must pick up the economic responsibility for herself and her children.

Children also work without question.   Their work is not in support of an ideal of thrift and industry, as in the middle class, but from necessity. Since the educational ideals of the family usually are low, parents expect children to leave school and begin to work as soon as the law permits. Younger children are expected to secure after-school, Saturday, and vacation jobs.   Moreover, the children find it difficult to relate the training they receive in the average public school to the realities of their lives and are only too ready to find a legitimate excuse for ending their formal education.   Since they have neither a sound liberal education nor voca-

[7] Earl L. Koos, "Class Differences in Family Reactions to Crisis," *Marriage and Family Living*, 12 (1950), 77.   In contrast to the above is the attitude of the middle-class man, quoted by Koos: "I'd shoot myself before I'd go to the county welfare office and apply for help."

[8] Hollingshead, *op. cit.*, pp. 103, 112.

tional training, they enter unskilled or semiskilled work and thus repeat in their lives the cycle followed by their parents.   In securing work, the children answer newspaper ads or approach the employment office as the only contact between adolescent and employer.   Since the father's employment is on an impersonal and often impermanent basis, he is unable to provide an occupational opening for his children.

RESIDENTIAL STABILITY

Lower-class families have less residential stability than those in higher classes.   Many are newcomers seeking a better living than they had in some other community—for example, rural migrants.   Those who are able to build achieve a certain stability for a period of perhaps 10 to 20 years.   But the house may be lost through mortgage foreclosure, or sold if a job is lost and another found in some other community, or sold as old age approaches.   Those who rent move frequently, and those who do not own furniture but live in small furnished rooms or flats move most often of all.   Nevertheless, in each community some lower-class families have held that status over a period of generations without rising in the social scale.   In Elmtown, many lower-lower-class families have been residents of the community as long as the upper-class families, and, like the upper-class families, are linked in the public mind with the past behavior of their ancestors.[9]   The legends that cling to these permanent lower-lower families are notorious, however, rather than laudatory: a murder, chronic drunkenness, or family abuse on the part of the grandfather hangs over the present generation, giving a pattern for the children and lowering community expectation of achievement from them.

Although we think of homeownership and residential stability as adding to a family's prestige, for great numbers of the lower class such stability is a handicap.   For one thing, it fixes them in a class level that has little to offer them or their children.   For another, it reduces their economic opportunities.   The semiskilled or unskilled laborer must be a ready migrant if he is to have work all the time.   Tied to one locality, he may be unemployed a much higher percentage of the time than if he is mobile.

MARRIAGE

Young people in the lower classes marry at an earlier age than in other classes.   In Yankee City the average age in the upper lower class is 24

[9] Hollingshead, *op. cit.*, pp. 113–114.

years and in the lower lower 23, or four or five years younger than in the upper upper class.[10]   In Elmtown, where all the marital ages are lower than in Yankee City, men marry in their early twenties and girls in their late teens in the upper lower class and in very early twenties and middle teens in the lower lower class.[11]

SOCIAL CLASS	YANKEE CITY, MEDIAN AGE	ELMTOWN, USUAL AGE BRIDE	GROOM
UPPER UPPER	27.9		
LOWER UPPER	26.6	MID-TWENTIES	MID-TWENTIES
UPPER MIDDLE	26.1		
LOWER MIDDLE	25.1	EARLY TWENTIES	EARLY TWENTIES
UPPER LOWER	24.4	LATE TEENS	EARLY TWENTIES
LOWER LOWER	23.2	MID-TEENS	VERY EARLY TWENTIES

FIGURE 26

Age of Marriage by Social Class

In Yankee City the average ages of marriage of upper-upper- and lower-lower-class people differ by almost five years.   In Elmtown all classes tend to marry younger than corresponding groups in Yankee City.   The early age of marriage in the lower classes is related to less emphasis on education and the early economic establishment of the men.   These young people marry with less formal preparation than do those of the higher class levels.   Often, however, they have gained early independence and are more aware of the problems of family life than the more closely supervised and protected youth of the upper social classes.   The period of childbearing is longer, and the first child may be born while the mother is little more than a girl.   (Source: W. Lloyd Warner and Paul S. Lunt, *Social Life of a Modern Community* [Yale University Press, 1941], p. 255; A. B. Hollingshead, "Selected Characteristics of Classes in a Middle Western Community," *American Sociological Review,* 12 [1947], 388, 390, 392, and 394.)

Marriages tend to occur between members of the same class, but if there is out-class marriage it is upward, since there is no lower class into which marriage may be made.   Thus the attractive girl or the enterprising youth may marry into a family somewhat above his own in social status.   Since

[10] Warner and Lunt, *op. cit.,* p. 255.
[11] Hollingshead, *op. cit.,* pp. 106, 116.

each marriage starts a new and independent nuclear family, however, the decision is more or less in the hands of the couple as to whether the future family pattern follows that of the lower or the higher class.

Marriage occurs with less preliminary social contact and with less ritual as to ceremony than in the middle or upper classes.   Eligible girls and men do not meet in a debut as in the upper class, nor through supervised mixed-group activities as in the middle class; they do not even meet at school, for many have left school before mid- or late adolescence.   The street corner, the tavern, or the factory provides the locale, and individual initiative brings youths and girls together.   Courtship is short, often sexually exciting, and ends with a marriage that is announced to family and friends after it has occurred.   The economic status of the husband may be low, for the criterion of selection is personal and sexual attraction rather than economic and social suitability.[12]

FAMILY ORGANIZATION

In the normal family unit of husband, wife, and children, the father is the head of the family.   Lower-class families are more nearly patriarchal than families in any other class.   The husband asserts his authority more thoroughly and more harshly than in higher classes, keeping wife and children in submission by physical force if necessary.   He is the final authority and disciplinarian to whom the mother refers in her daily training of children; except in times of stress, he is the chief wage earner and controls the purse; he makes the final decisions for the family.

Nevertheless, it is the mother who rears the children, and it is with her that the children remain if the family disintegrates.   The father, however, may make rules for the rearing of the children, which the mother enforces in his absence.   The mother's role also is that of housekeeper, and the husband does not expect to participate in housekeeping tasks after he comes from work.   The roles of husband and wife are more sharply drawn than in the middle class where there is more sharing in planning and often in execution of the plans.

The husband and wife have a life of their own which takes precedence over the demands of their children.   The bond between them is personal and sexual in nature.   Having fewer interests, husband and wife have less of a companionship and friendship relationship than the middle-class husband and wife achieve.   Children, though important and welcome in

[12] For a detailed discussion of preparation for marriage, see Chapter 12.

the lower-class family, nevertheless have less family importance than in the middle-class family. They are definitely subordinate to the parents, who neither cater to them nor sacrifice for their education and cultural development as middle-class parents do. Moreover, the expectation is strong that children will leave school after fulfilling the minimum legal requirements in order to work and contribute to the family until the day of their marriage.

Although the obligations are more simple than in higher social classes, the roles of husband and wife are specific. The husband earns the living if he is able to do so, supports his family, is not cruel but may be strict, and is faithful to his wife (although discreet deviations are tolerated, especially in the lower-lower group). The wife bears and rears the children, keeps house, earns money if her husband is unable to earn all that is needed, and is faithful to her husband. If these obligations are broken, the offended party may and often does leave, opening the way for a possible divorce. As has already been stated, the children almost without exception remain with the mother. Since the husband may find work almost as readily in another city as in the one where his estranged or divorced wife lives, he often leaves, thus obstructing any attempts of the wife to secure support for herself or their children. The wife therefore finds herself facing the roles of both father and mother to her children. Sometimes she and the children are absorbed back into her parental family where she may serve a useful function if her parents are old; or collateral relatives may give her room and board for a time, although rarely are they able to give cash help if she lives elsewhere. The mother faces three possible solutions: to work for the support of herself and her children; to remain at home with them and apply for Aid to Dependent Children, a form of public relief; or to remarry.

The role of the second husband is a peculiar and unstable one. He is husband to his wife but not father to her children. He does not assume authority over them, nor do they recognize him as their father; however, he may be friendly with them and help support them. If he attempts to discipline his stepchildren, conflict may result, with the mother siding with her children in their rejection of his authority. Sometimes the solution is found by placing the children with relatives who are willing to accept them, or permitting very young children to be adopted. At other times, the second marriage breaks on the rocks of family conflict.

Family life in the lower class is less stable than in the middle or upper classes. Separations, often without divorce, are frequent. The very fact that after a separation the marriage may be resumed without formality adds to the instability. One separation may follow another, often being in the nature of desertion by the father who moves out leaving the mother and children without support. With longer periods of separation, but no legal termination of the marriage through divorce, temporary alliances or more permanent common-law marriages may replace legal marriage. The death rate is higher in the lower classes than where there are more economic security and better health practices; and it is higher for men than for women. Widows, often with young children, are frequent. Another disturbing factor is the presence in the lower classes of detached men who have come into this country from abroad or have moved into certain industrial areas seeking work in proportions that disturb the natural sex ratio by providing an excess of men. Some of these men have wives and children elsewhere; others are unmarried; some are non-Caucasian. Seeking not only sexual satisfaction but the practical home-making advantages that a woman can provide in the way of food, mending, laundry, and a homelike place to spend evenings and holidays, many of these men are willing to become partners to temporary or illicit household arrangements. As job opportunities change or the desire comes to return home, they leave with as little ceremony as they came. In many families, although illegal unions are unknown, divorce or death breaks the family leaving a parent and perhaps children. Remarriage may follow, with the usual difficulties of adjustment.

The instability of the lower-class family is reflected in the rate of broken homes. In the upper lower class in Elmtown, 33 per cent of the homes are broken, and in the lower lower class 56 per cent.[13]

One may question why separations and divorces are disproportionately frequent in the lower classes. One possible answer is that stresses and strains are more frequent. The family lives closer to the thin line that lies between sufficiency and poverty. Ill health and disease are of more common occurrence. Homes are small and allow little freedom of movement or privacy.

Another plausible reason lies in personality development. As will be discussed later in this chapter, lower-class children are encouraged and openly taught by their parents to be aggressive. They are expected by their families to fight for status in their play groups, to elbow others

[13] Hollingshead, *op. cit.*, pp. 106, 117.

aside in securing work, and to employ small trickery in shopping and entering movies. Life in the lower classes demands aggression for survival. These aggressive attitudes are vented not only toward the outside world but within the family circle. Brother competes with brother for clothing, food, and the most comfortable chair or bed; parents compete with children; and children with parents. Aggressive individualism, tempered by a certain practical kind of familism in time of crisis, becomes habitual. Cooperation, conciliation, and compromise, common in the middle- and upper-class family, are neither taught to the child nor demonstrated in his family. Any encroachment upon the individual or his rights as he conceives them brings an aggressive reaction inside the family as well as outside.

Another personality trait of the lower class is withdrawal when faced with overwhelming odds. The boy or girl who finds schoolwork difficult or unpleasant does not wait until the legal age to leave school, but truants and perhaps becomes adept at evading the attendance officer. Many adolescent lower-class boys and girls leave home to evade parental control, sleeping in hallways or, in the summer, in vacant lots, or securing work and renting a cheap room. Boys may tramp across the country, working and begging alternately as they go. When marriage becomes a trial, the husband tends to follow the same pattern and withdraws. The wife less often leaves as she feels emotional ties to and responsibility for her children.

CHILDREN

Children are expected and accepted in the lower-class family without planning or birth spacing. The birth rate is higher than in the middle or upper classes, with a mean of 4.3 children per upper-lower family and of 5.6 per lower-lower family.[14] This situation exposes an interesting paradox—the section of society least able to support children nevertheless has the largest number of children per family. Several explanations are pertinent. By the accident of national origin, many lower-class families are descendants of recent immigrants from Catholic countries; they adhere to the Catholic prohibition against artificial control of conception. In addition, the use of contraceptives presupposes a certain degree of sophistication, self-discipline, and sometimes expenditure that are contrary to the lower-class culture. Another factor contributing to the high birth

[14] Hollingshead, op. cit., pp. 106, 116.

rate is that children are regarded as assets to the family in that they begin to earn early in life.   Also, lower-class values do not demand the heavy expenditures of middle-class families for prenatal care, hospital delivery, pediatric supervision, dental work, special educational classes in child-hood, and college education.   These have become routine necessities of child rearing in the middle class; they are regarded as superfluities by the lower-class family.

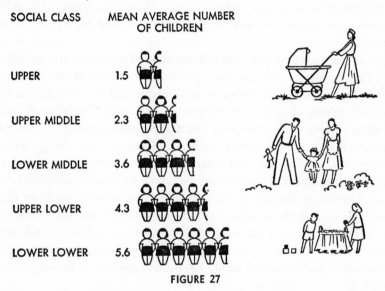

SOCIAL CLASS	MEAN AVERAGE NUMBER OF CHILDREN	
UPPER	1.5	
UPPER MIDDLE	2.3	
LOWER MIDDLE	3.6	
UPPER LOWER	4.3	
LOWER LOWER	5.6	

FIGURE 27

Number of Children by Social Class, Elmtown

Children have a different meaning in each social class: in the upper class children carry on the family name and keep the family inheritance intact; in the middle classes children are a projection of the parents' personalities into a brighter future; in the lower classes children are accepted as a natural consequence of marriage and a security against economic want.   The factor of security, however, is less important than formerly because of compulsory school attendance and restrictions on employment of children.   Care of chil-dren also differs with social-class placement, as the sketches at the right indicate.   (Source: A. B. Hollingshead, *Elmtown's Youth* [Wiley, 1949], ch. 5.)

Another factor is the early age of marriage, especially for girls, at a time when sex drives are strong and fertility high.   The early marriage also lengthens the total span for childbearing.

The training of lower-class children differs from that of middle- and upper-class children, both in objectives and methods.   The objective is to develop a tough-minded, hard-fisted individual, able to compete to the point of personal conflict in support of individual rights and privileges. When these rights are not challenged, the lower-class person is orderly and law-abiding.   The little boy is not taught, as is the middle-class boy, to wait until he is struck before he fights, nor to seek the protection of parent, teacher, or policeman.   He is expected to be able to take care of himself at an early age.   The little girl, likewise, is taught to be self-sufficient, to protect her virtue by a sharp tongue and her fists if necessary.[15]

At an early age both boys and girls are allowed to extend their activities into the community without the supervision of parents or other adults. They play in the neighborhood at night and attend movies alone at an age when middle-class children are carefully sequestered in house or yard by their parents.   They learn to ride the bus across the city, shop for their mothers, care for younger brothers and sisters, make change, avoid automobiles, earn money, and otherwise look after themselves and contribute to the utilitarian functions of the family while still well below teen age.   Conversely, they are not taught certain duties and aspirations that have high value in the middle-class family and that middle-class children are urged and coerced into learning—regularity of school attendance, ambition for at least high school graduation, excessive neatness and cleanliness both of person and the child's room, and avoidance of fighting unless attacked.

As stated in the discussion of the middle-class family, the methods of training differ between the two classes.   The lower-class mother rears her children with a combination of leniency and impulsive aggressiveness. One might say that she treats her children more naturally and more in accord with her own emotional needs than does the middle-class mother who trains her children with the child psychologist always peeping over her shoulder.   The lower-class child is nursed longer, toilet-trained later, fondled more, and spanked or slapped more than is the middle-class child. The mother responds to the personal relationship between herself and each child, whereas the middle-class mother tries to do what is "best for the child," often denying her own needs in the process.   The lower-class

[15] An excellent comparative statement of middle-class and lower-class child training is given in W. Allison Davis and Robert J. Havighurst, *Father of the Man* (Houghton Mifflin, 1947).

child is less likely to view himself as a person of special value for whom parental sacrifices are justified.   He plays a subordinate role in the family, gaining in status when he reaches an age to contribute financially.

Ritual is less used in the lower-class family than in the family of any other class.   Nevertheless, only in the very lowest levels is ritual non-existent.   The celebration of Christmas is a form of ritual if repeated year after year in characteristic fashion.   Catholic families tend to follow religious rituals that reinforce in the family the teachings of the Church. However, many of the rituals that reflect leisure (as the after-dinner coffee of the middle-class family) or that regulate relations between family members (as the standing of the child when an older person enters the room) are unknown.   Houses are crowded; duties crowd fast one upon another; tensions are often unresolved.   The members of the family may seek avoidance of each other through outside activities rather than find satisfaction in a closely integrated family pattern of rituals.

CRISES

That lower-class families are subject to many types of crisis has been implied in the preceding discussion.   Frequent unemployment, the higher illness rate than in other social classes, the higher birth rate that results in the more frequent introduction of a new member into the family circle, delinquency of younger members of the family, occasional or chronic alcoholism, and aggressiveness between neighbors or relatives as well as personal clashes within the family are some of the conditions that cause a breakdown of the orderly folkways of the lower-class family and require the family to readjust itself in some way.   The lower-class family is rarely equipped by education or training to resolve a personal crisis on the verbal level.   Verbal emotional explosions may relieve inner tensions but add to the disruption; and sometimes the verbal expression moves into physical aggressiveness against or between offending persons.   Thus, the husband may beat his wife, or the wife may throw china at her husband; children may be beaten; neighborhood fights may occur; and occasionally, in one of these personal clashes, someone is killed.   Such aggressions not only widen the breach but often serve to bring the crisis to the attention of the neighbors or the police.   Crises that emanate from lack of money are also frequent and difficult to resolve because the family lacks accumulated savings and finds it impossible, or nearly so, to establish credit.

Lower-class crises tend to be prolonged and often result in serious damage to family unity.   The family tends to disintegrate under the pressure of the crisis, although later it may re-form.   The husband may desert when a new baby threatens to upset the household routine or to impose extra expense; but he may return six months or a year later.   The adolescent boy or girl may run away but be sent home by some social agency or the police of another community.   At other times the disintegration is permanent, and the family may appeal to official agencies for help.   The wife may bring suit against her husband for nonsupport or obtain a divorce; she may ask for financial relief or aid in controlling rebellious children.

The official agency usually enters into the situation, however, after other efforts have been made to solve the problems.   The lower-class family does not keep its problems to itself.   Less reticent about its problems, less proud of its status than the middle-class family, the lower-class family tends to seek outside aid, but not of a professional nature in the first instance.   The druggist, the bartender, and relatives are approached for advice or financial assistance.   Only when they fail are the legal and social agencies approached.[16]

SPECIAL CHARACTERISTICS

The lower class as a whole abides by the common mores of our society and meets such expectations as family self-support (except, perhaps, in times of great crisis), legal monogamous marriages, conformity to laws, participation in community institutions (such as sending their children to school until the legal age limit), and affiliations with some type of church connection.

There is a small substratum, however, that deviates from the class and family mores.   These families might be illustrated by families of beggars, pauperized families that make no effort to break their dependency upon relief agencies, families that violate the sex mores through unofficial polygamy or the practice of incest or in which prostitute mothers teach their daughters to become prostitutes, and criminal families.   These families may belong to small groups that have developed mores of their own and a philosophy that cushions them against a feeling of guilt or rationalizes their conduct.   Other families are composed of demoralized individuals in the sense that they do not have a system of mores, have not developed

16 Earl L. Koos, "Middle-Class Family Crises," *Marriage and Family Living*, 10 (1948), 25, 40.

a conscience or superego, but live close to their natural needs and impulses.

THE LOWER CLASS AS A POPULATION POOL

The lower class forms a population pool from which higher strata—chiefly middle class—draw replacements necessitated by their lower reproductive rate. The excess members in lower-class families originate partly from the high birth rate and partly from immigrant groups, which usually enter the American social-class system as unskilled workers at the lower-class level.

Although the more aggressive lower-class families move upward, the lower class is never depleted. It remains the largest of the classes, with its distinctive culture and problems. It is less disturbed by the issues between rigid social standards and conduct than is the middle class, its problems being closely related to survival. It also includes many of the mobile and migratory families moving from depressed rural to urban areas and from region to region. A large segment is composed of ethnic families who are undergoing the dual process of establishing themselves economically and also fitting themselves into American culture.

QUESTIONS

1. What is the origin of lower-class families?
2. How does the lower-class family gain economic security?
3. What is the basic family unit in the lower class?
4. What role do children play in the lower-class family?
5. Does the training of children fit them for life in the lower class?
6. Contrast the families of the three social classes (upper, middle, and lower) on as many points as possible. Which class seems to have the most rigid type of family life? Which the most flexible? Is rigidity or flexibility most desirable under present social conditions?

BIBLIOGRAPHY

Almost all references for Chapter 6 include sections on lower-class families, children, and adolescents. In addition, see:

Koos, Earl L., *Families in Trouble* (King's Crown Press, 1946).

8

Ethnic Families

In each social class are some people whose mode of living is not thoroughly American but is derived from an alien culture. With only a few exceptions, these people are either foreign-born or the recent descendants of the foreign-born.[1] When such groups think of themselves as more closely affiliated with the nationality of their birth or of their recent ancestors than with American culture, they are called ethnic groups.

The period when the assimilation of foreign-born groups was one of the most serious of social problems and fascinating of social processes has passed. World War I stopped immigration temporarily; legislation of the 1920's placing quotas on the number of immigrants who would be admitted from almost all countries permanently lowered the immigration; and the depression of the 1930's and World War II reduced the once powerful stream of immigration to a mere trickle. The immigrants who crowded Northern industrial cities prior to 1914 are now either old people or have already died.

The children, and especially the grandchildren, of immigrants have been reared in the American culture with only traces of the older ethnic background. Nevertheless, loyalty to the ethnic group often remains, together with a tendency for many of the original families or their descendants to retain their residence in compact ethnic communities. These communities may not be the ones of original settlement, for the ethnic group as it finds new residential areas may still tend to remain together. This cohesion prolongs the period of time during which the ethnic culture is retained. Second- and third-generation families often

[1] American Indians are the chief example of non-foreign-born people who nevertheless have not accepted the American culture.

practice many of the culture traits and live by many of the traditional standards of the original immigrants. Family life still has distinctive features that may become sharpened in parent-child conflicts or when intermarriage between ethnic groups occurs.

Also, in a more limited degree than formerly, new ethnic groups arrive, either from non-quota countries, such as Mexico, or from certain parts of the United States where the culture is non-American. The Puerto Ricans who have recently come into New York are an illustration. These families, in limited areas where they concentrate, experience serious family problems.

Although ethnic groups have some characteristics in common, they do not merge into one common interacting social group. Each alien cultural group of the past has its own descendant ethnic group in the present. There is a Norwegian ethnic group, an Italian, a German, and so on. Not all descendants of foreign-born families can be classified as ethnic; only those that cling together with a certain degree of social isolation from other ethnic groups and from Americans can be termed ethnic. Individuals and families that have merged completely into the American pattern of culture and the American social world and who no longer think of themselves as Norwegian or Italian or German, as the case may be, are no longer ethnic.

Groups of non-Caucasian origin also fall into the classifications of ethnic or American. If they maintain a distinctive culture brought with them from their homeland—for example, Chinese who huddle into urban "Chinatowns"—they are ethnic. If they have exchanged their native culture for American culture, as the Negroes have, they are culturally American. The family life of non-Caucasians therefore is not discussed separately from the two basic divisions of ethnic and American. Nevertheless, racial affiliation may have a relationship to family life, either because the group is set apart through prejudice, or when intermarriage between races occurs.

CULTURAL AND SOCIAL ASSIMILATION

An analysis of ethnic families requires a distinction between cultural and social assimilation. The struggle toward cultural assimilation usually begins during the lifetime of the original immigrants. When large foreign-born groups formed indigestible masses in American cities, tremendous effort was made to induce them to give up their native culture and conform to American culture.   The Americanization programs of the first quarter of the twentieth century rested on an active and persistent effort to persuade, almost force, the immigrant to become an American.   Public schools and community centers located in foreign-born areas were especially active.   If they did not succeed with the foreign-born adults, they usually succeeded in giving to their children the rudiments of American culture—so much so that children often were alienated from their parents.   At the present time, unless the descendants of foreign-born groups have deliberately isolated themselves from American culture, it may safely be said that the descendants of immigrants who came prior to the restrictive laws are American in culture.

While the American culture was being impressed upon foreign-born families by organized institutions, social inclusion in American groups was neglected.   In fact, the pressure of informal American groups and families ran in the opposite direction—toward exclusion.   Foreign-born people and their descendants were not welcomed into close association with or as participants in American institutions.   They were neither elected to membership in American clubs nor invited as friends into American homes.   The exclusion was also discriminatory.   They were regarded by Americans as not only different but inferior.   Sought as factory workers or as maids, they were rejected as social equals.[2]

The newly arrived foreign-culture group may be distinguished from the ethnic group in this way: the foreign-culture group has not been adjusted either culturally or socially to American life; the ethnic group usually has adopted American culture, retaining only traces of the foreign culture, but has not been socially absorbed into American institutions or informal social life.   In a few instances, groups long removed in time from the original immigrant forebears retain a high degree of both cultural and social distinctiveness.   The Amish are an example: Although they have adopted many American culture traits, they cling to many of their original traits and form their own social world.   They are able to remain both culturally and socially withdrawn from American life only by forbidding contacts, assessing heavy penalties for violation of the rules of seclusion, and expelling from their community those who mingle with out-

[2] The distinction between cultural and social assimilation is interestingly stated in Peter A. Munch, "Social Adjustment among Wisconsin Norwegians," *American Sociological Review,* 14 (1949), 780–781.

siders.   The Amish therefore are an oddity in American life and do not represent the usual processes of adjustment.   The majority of foreign-culture groups, at least in the second generation, have been willing, even eager, to become a part of American life, but may fail when social pressures are opposed to their participation as equals in American institutions and informal groups.

Racial groups may also be fitted into the same conceptual framework. A newly arrived racial group, as the Negro Puerto Ricans who entered New York City in the 1940's, experience both cultural and social non-adjustment.   In contrast, American Negroes whose ancestors have lived in the United States for generations share American culture with white Americans, but continue to be excluded socially from all except formal participation in certain institutions and activities.   They are assimilated culturally but not socially.   The probability of social absorption of Negroes or other nonwhite racial groups is much less than that of eventual social absorption of the white ethnic groups.

The degree of cultural and social assimilation of an ethnic group affects the organization and interaction within the family as well as between the family and the community.

THE CULTURALLY AND SOCIALLY UNASSIMILATED FAMILY

Culturally, the basic problem of the foreign-culture family that comes to the United States to live is the same problem faced by the rural American family that migrates to the large city.[3]   A family that has adjusted itself to one type of physical and cultural environment through accepting the coordinated folkways and mores of that environment moves into a different environment where the old patterns of family life are not applicable.   However, the foreign-culture family has a much more difficult time than the rural family, which, after all, speaks the American language and shares with other Americans certain concepts and ideals both of family and community living.

The controlling unit in immigration

Immigrants come as individuals or small-family units.   Often the husband comes alone and later sends for his wife and children, using money earned and saved in this country.   Many young unmarried men immi-

[3] See pages 78–82.

grate and later send back to their native village or city for a girl already selected, or they ask their parents to select a wife for them; sometimes a fellow immigrant will arrange to send for a niece or sister who becomes the bride of his friend.   As men become adjusted they may marry the American-born girls whose parents are of their own nationality, or may marry outside their ethnic group.   Thus many of those who enter the United States as individuals soon establish families.

Although immigrants rarely come in as community groups, they tend to establish themselves in this country in areas limited to their own nationality.   Newly arrived immigrants are taken for a season into the home of a relative or family friend, who usually lives in a colony of his countrymen.   In large Northern cities these colonies are easily distinguishable, not by political boundaries or artificial barriers but by the physical characteristics, dress, spoken language, and names on stores that designate one block as belonging to, let us say, Italians, and the next to Greeks.

The individual and the family therefore are incorporated into a little community that perpetuates as much of the native culture as is possible in the changed environment.   The colony also provides social life, institutional participation, and an opportunity to choose a spouse of the same nationality.   The colony impedes both cultural and social assimilation, but it gives security and companionship and no doubt reduces personal and family disorganization, which, at best, often are concomitants of the process of readjustment.

Degree of cultural change

For all foreign-culture groups the degree of cultural change is great. The Englishman, educated and urban-adjusted, lives through a period of strangeness, in which he learns new meanings for old words, finds that the brashness of American children is normal and admired, and that Americans do not always share his national attitudes and ideals.   Foreign-language groups have a more difficult problem, although, nestled in their little urban colonies, they try to reproduce their native culture completely. In this project they never succeed, for the impact of American institutions and mores is immediately experienced.   The change in environment is greatest when the immigrant comes from a rural area in his native land to urban America, but even the urban-to-urban and the rural-to-rural immigrants find much that is strange.

Readiness of the community to receive immigrants

The deliberate attempt to make Americans out of foreign-culture people has already been mentioned. Too often only superficial American qualities have been adopted by the immigrants, without a corresponding change in attitudes. The result has often been family disorganization and violent conflicts between the parents who tend to retain the native culture and their American-educated children who have a muddled conception of both the native and the American standards. At present a new conception of adjustment is growing—that of cultural pluralism. A policy of pluralism involves readiness on the part of Americans to respect the culture of the foreign group and efforts by schools and community centers to give immigrants and their children pride in their own culture, at the same time helping them to incorporate American traditions into their native culture. The process of growth would be slow and no attempt would be made to coerce immigrants into rejecting their native culture and quickly accepting the American.

Degree of family adjustment

The processes of family adjustment are closely related to the preceding factors. Many of the immigrant groups entering the United States have two characteristics: patriarchal family organization and rural peasant background. This combination was true for the foreign-culture groups studied in Yankee City—Irish, Polish, Greek, and Armenian—as well as for other groups entering the East, Middle West, and Southwest, such as the Puerto Rican, Italian, Norwegian, Finnish, and Mexican.[4] The patriarchal organization and the rural background are related and reinforce each other. As in our own earlier history, when agriculture was carried on as a family project with a high degree of self-sufficiency, the family is a biological, social, and economic unit. All members work together, satisfy physical needs through the family life, and take much of their recreation as a family unit. The chief educational agency to transmit the culture as well as to train in skills is the parents and grandparents. The father or grandfather is not only head of the family but of the producing economic unit; he is family head and business head. Wife and children respect him as the authority in family matters and also as their work

[4] W. Lloyd Warner and Leo Srole, *The Social Systems of American Ethnic Groups* (New Haven: Yale University Press, 1945), ch. 6, "The Family."

manager.   With this close integration of functions and personnel and the hourly participation of all members of the family in the same activities, the family is a very stable unit.   There is no question in anyone's mind about his own role and status or about the role and status of each other member.

When such a family settles in an American city, the family organization is immediately broken.   The father finds work in a factory and therefore is absent from home all day.   Wife and children are freed from his personal supervision, although the wife may attempt to act as a surrogate for him.   Moreover, the father is no longer a free agent who can control his own time and activities in the interest of the family.   He is subject to the demands of his job and comes under the supervision of foreman or employer.   His status and prestige are therefore decreased.   As soon as the older children begin to learn American culture at school, they assume a new role in the family, as interpreters of the American culture to their parents and often as linguistic contacts between the parents, especially the mother, and outside agencies, such as stores or social agencies.   In their own eyes their status has increased, and often they compete with their parents for control of the family and in particular of the younger children.

When the children begin to earn money, the gap between status of father and children narrows.   The father often expects children to turn their pay over to him intact to be used for the family good, with the father making decisions as to expenditures.   An example is the Polish father in Yankee City who had been unemployed for several years without making an effort to find work.   His daughters, all over 18 years of age, gave him their earnings, which he accepted as his due.   He saved some of the money, bought what he thought the family needed, and gave or withheld small sums that the daughters might wish to have.   He saw nothing unjust in this procedure; in his native land the elderly father had lightened his work on the farm as children came to maturity but had still supervised their work and handled the family finances.[5]   Often the children object to such complete dominance by the father.   They wish to handle their own money.   Sometimes they pay a fixed amount to the parents but in other cases withdraw completely from the family, or remain in the family home but do not contribute and perhaps do not work regularly. Neither parents nor children are fully aware of adjustments made by American families whereby the children normally contribute an agreed-

[5] Warner and Srole, *op. cit.*, pp. 128–129.

upon sum to the parents and control the remainder of their earnings themselves, a procedure usually preceded by years of careful training by parents in the handling of small sums of money, budgeting, and saving. The immigrant family has no pattern in its background for the individual management of income by members of the family.

In other aspects, also, the immigrant family lacks behavior patterns for a family organized on any other than a patriarchal system.   When the authority of the father breaks down, as it almost always does in the urban situation, there is no alternative system of compromise, family counseling, and the like such as characterizes many American families.   The parents do not know how to strike that fine line between freedom and self-control for their children that marks the adolescent period of the American child.

Moreover, other agencies supplement or replace the family, assuming functions once the prerogative of the parents.   Recreational and educational agencies compete with the parents in supplying the needs of the children and often of the wife, sometimes with contrary teachings that tear down rather than give support to parental status.   Sometimes the parents find aid in ethnic institutions—clubs or church—provided that they do not simply try to re-establish the ethnic culture intact but recognize the necessity for adaptation to the new social situation.

The family therefore faces the problem of changing its old culture to meet the new social situation, a change that involves not merely external skills and a different physical environment but deeply seated traditions and highly valued ideals about which personality has been constructed.

New social contacts also give little help to the immigrant family. Each member of the family meets different social groups—the father at his place of employment, the children at school and settlement, the mother in her immediate neighborhood.   Unaccustomed to these divisive social contacts, unlearned in the skills of sharing them with each other, the family tends toward disintegration.   Sometimes, also, the social groups that are willing to accept the recent immigrant are ones that do not represent the best of American culture—the boys' gang, the street-corner boys, the unsupervised girls' clique.

The shifting of roles, the declining status of parents and increasing status of children, the inadequacy of the old family organization, and the need to change personal conceptions and standards of conduct all tend toward family disorganization and personal demoralization.   This phase of adjustment, however, is usually a transitory one, and in time increased familiarity with American culture and enlarged participation in American social groups bring about new family orientation.

Several illustrations are given of foreign-culture families still in the process of adjustment.   If repetition seems marked, it is only because a similarity of backgrounds and of present situations creates much the same process in different groups.   Each case, however, shows a somewhat different stage of adjustment.

The Mexican peasant family.   Mexican peasant-family life developed in a rural village, where families are held together by intermarriage and the sharing of a common body of traditions.   Roles are predetermined by custom, and public opinion is a potent force in the regulation of conduct. The family is organized on a bilateral basis, with both family names being borne by the children.   After marriage husband and wife remain members of their parental families, which are bound together through the marriage. In this larger kinship family the father or oldest wage earner is head; he controls finances, exercises authority over the younger members, and protects his wife and daughters from unwelcome attentions of other men. Respect for the mother gives her a status above her children but below her husband; the son outranks the daughter.   Marriages are made with the interest of the kinship family uppermost, and divorces are almost unknown.   The family is further extended and strengthened by the godparents, chosen as sponsors of the children.   The tie between godparents and children is strong, with the godparents assuming responsibility for the children if the parents die, and the children giving respect and love to the godparents.   Thus family life is controlled by the traditions of the village and large family group, and marriage is stable.

The roles of family members are well defined, with a definite separation between men and women.   Women work in the home and find their function in life through the care of home and children, whereas it is not seemly for the father to work in the home.   Young unmarried men and women do not associate freely with each other, their contacts being closely supervised by older members of the family.[6]

The migrant Mexican family in the Northern industrial city finds that the roles, family organization, and system of controls that worked very well in the Mexican village are not applicable.   Very serious indeed is the change in the role and status of the father.   As an unskilled laborer,

---

[6] R. C. Jones, "Ethnic Family Patterns: The Mexican Family in the United States," *American Journal of Sociology*, 53 (1948), 450–451.

the father often has temporary periods of unemployment when he is unable to provide for his family.   He loses status, both in the eyes of his family and in his conception of himself.   Sometimes he deserts temporarily either to seek work elsewhere or to escape the censure of wife and children.   As his status declines, his authority over his family also diminishes and family unity gives way to individualism.

If the wife remains in her secluded position in the home, she often does not learn that in America wives have a relatively high status; therefore she does not threaten her husband's position.   But if she has assimilated American attitudes and especially if she begins to work, she does threaten the status of her husband.   Likewise, if she extends her social life beyond the home, the husband feels that his exclusive possession of his wife is endangered.   He may object to his wife talking impersonally with another man or attending motion pictures with a woman friend.   Quarrels between husband and wife and with neighbors follow.

It is difficult for the father to fulfill his traditional role in other ways. He may not be able to care for aged parents as he did in Mexico; his daughters may resist and evade his protective supervision over them.

The children, and especially the oldest son, play different roles than in Mexico.   The oldest son, first to attend an American school, often is the first one in the family to learn American customs and accept American attitudes.   He directs and guides the younger children, thus assuming some of the traditional parental obligations.   When sons begin to work, they oppose the father's demand that their money should go into the family fund to be used for the family as a whole.   This withholding of money is an attack upon the unity and integration of the family and upon the headship of the father who in Mexico controlled the family finances. To the employed sons, such relinquishment of their earnings seems absurd; they wish to function as individuals rather than family members.   Daughters become restive under the prohibition upon mixed social affairs and are eager to follow the American custom of social activities between unmarried adolescent girls and boys.   Parties and dating are open to many misinterpretations by Mexican parents who believe their daughters to be either lewd or about to launch themselves into an unsuitable marriage disapproved by the family.

Gradually the roles of the family change.   The sons gain a position equal to that of the father and above that of the mother, while daughters secure a status equal to that of the home-staying mother.   The old family organization therefore breaks down, often before a stable organization on a more equalitarian basis has developed.

Kin and godparents usually are not present to support the old family organization. Mexican clubs and the Catholic Church provide some semblance of community control, but attendance is irregular, especially on the part of the older children.

Gradually individualism within the family and competition between families, fostered by the urban situation, replace the older close family unity and community integration of the Mexican rural community. In time, the family tends to become reorganized with greater freedom and higher status for the wife and children with less responsibility resting on the father; but this change usually does not affect the original migrating marital pair so much as their children.[7]

In summary, the process of cultural change in the Mexican family is slow and is attended by conflicts within the family. During the initial stages of the process the Mexican family usually lives in a community of other Mexican families, in which such institutions as Mexican clubs and the Catholic Church function. Mexicans are hindered in participating socially with Americans because of their non-American ways, and also because Americans often are prejudiced against their skin color inherited from Indian ancestors.

The Puerto Rican family. The Puerto Rican family in New York City is in the early stages of both acculturation and social acceptance. Since Puerto Rico is a part of the United States, its citizens are free to enter New York City without restriction. During the 1940's many Puerto Ricans entered New York, crowding into limited geographic areas.

Although Puerto Ricans are United States citizens, their language and culture are foreign to American ways. Originally inhabited by Indians, the island was settled by Spaniards in the sixteenth century and received an early influx of Negro slaves. The three races interbred, until now in lower-class families all degrees of hybrids are found, with little or no prejudice on the basis of color. Upper-class Puerto Ricans proudly proclaim their pure Spanish ancestry. Spanish is the native language, and Spanish culture is followed by the upper class and is a factor in lower-class mores. The migrants to New York are from the lower or working class, and range in color and physical characteristics from white to Negro; the

[7] N. D. Humphrey, "The Changing Structure of the Detroit Mexican Family: An Index of Acculturation," *American Sociological Review,* 9 (1944), 622–626.

Indian ancestry has been obscured.   In the Bronx settlement, about 75 per cent are white; in Manhattan, 43 per cent.[8]

Although Puerto Rico is primarily an agricultural island, most of the migrants have come from the cities with island occupations classified as manufacturing, trade and transportation, and services; only 9 per cent of the male migrants worked in agriculture.   Nevertheless, they were not fitted for the transfer to New York industry.   The island cities are small, work is done by hand rather than machines, there is no time clock to be punched, and no intricate transportation system to be mastered in going to and from work.   Although these immigrants have lived in poor areas of their native cities, they were not in overcrowded tenements, and the warm climate made it possible for them to spend much time out of doors. All in all, their way of life was more rural than urban.

The family in Puerto Rico reflects the Spanish influence; the dominant pattern of organization is patriarchal.   The father exercises strict control over wife and children, and especially over unmarried daughters.   The family of husband, wife, and children is part of an extended or kinship family, which sometimes includes a close relationship with the godparents of the children.   Orphan children and old people are cared for within the kinship unit, and in the small family children contribute their earnings to the family pool.

The migrant unit often is only a small segment of this family group. Contrary to most migrations, more Puerto Rican women than men entered New York.   In the island the sex ratio is 100 (equal numbers of men and women), but in the New York colonies there are only 63 males to 100 females, and among Negro Puerto Ricans only 30 males to 100 females. The percentage of divorced and widowed is higher than on the island, representing people already somewhat separated from the family before migrating.   Almost two thirds of the migrants are between the ages of 18 and 39, and came without the older relatives who control the kinship family.

[8] This discussion of Puerto Rican adjustment is based upon the following sources: *The Puerto Ricans of New York City* (Puerto Rican Department of Labor, New York Office, Employment and Migration Bureau, 1881 Broadway, New York City, mimeographed, undated); C. Wright Mills, Clarence Senior, and Rose Kohn Goldsen, *The Puerto Rican Journey* (Harper, 1950), which reports a study based upon interviews with 714 Puerto Ricans in Spanish Harlem and 399 in the Bronx, two areas of highly concentrated settlement; *Resumé of Dr. Clarence Senior's Study of the Puerto Ricans of New York City* (Welfare Council of New York City, 44 East 23rd Street, New York City, mimeographed, 1949); *Puerto Rican Children, Some Aspects of Their Needs and Related Services* (Welfare Council of New York City, 44 East 23rd Street, New York City, mimeographed, 1949).

The marriage rate is high among the migrants and the firstcomers often send for family members and relatives, all of whom may be hospitably received into the small tenement flat.   Thus in some cases the extended family appears in the New York colonies and unmarried people are included in loose family groups.

The first tendency of the migrant family is to carry over the family organization and roles of the island.   The father asserts his headship and finds a job, which usually is some form of unskilled labor regardless of the type of work he did on the island; he does not work around the home.   The mother remains in the home, limiting her contacts to other families in the tenement building.   Children are kept under close supervision.   All employed members contribute their earnings to a common family purse.   But this high development of familism is unsuited to the city and soon begins to break down.   The excess of women sets a new pattern of work outside the home; while the newly arrived husband's earnings are low and in periods of unemployment, wives begin to work, finding in New York many opportunities not available on the island.   The earning by women undermines the husband's position of authority and increases the status of the women.   Children also are soon evading or opposing their father's authority, either because they are earning their own money or because they come in contact with the greater freedom of American children in school or some local community center.   Girls especially have a difficult adjustment to make, being torn between habitual obedience to the father and the desire to share in mixed social activities of American adolescents.   Attendance at an evening party at the local center may be followed by a beating at the hands of the father, which is accepted by the daughter as justified.

New courtship and marriage practices beyond family control appeal to young people but dismay their parents.   In the lower class in Puerto Rico girls are not given the close chaperonage found in the middle and upper class.   They marry at a young age, often in a common-law union without the expense of a civil or religious ceremony.   In the compact island community such alliances are controlled by the extended families who usually know the man; therefore they tend to be as stable as legal marriages.   Fifty per cent of the unskilled class and 25 per cent of the skilled have contracted common-law marriages.   The children born are not considered illegitimate and have the usual care of both parents.   In New York such children are classed as illegitimate.   Without the stabilizing influence of the extended families and with many opportunities for chance meetings with strangers, nonlegal unions are unstable and afford little protection to the wife or children.

Courtship on the island is carried on with some degree of dignity. Adult Puerto Ricans are shocked by the open love-making of the American city and read into handholding and kissing immoral connotations. Their adolescent children are eager to enter into American life, but often have not learned the codes of control followed by American adolescents.

With the loss of integration of the large family and the inability of parents and older relatives to guide younger people in the strange urban ways, official agencies come onto the scene. Too often, however, they further undermine the family. Parents, brought into court on a charge of child beating, feel that the judge is upholding the child's rebellion. Accustomed to having dependents cared for within the kinship of the family, the family in need of help either leans too heavily upon the social agency as a substitute for the kinship group, or resents the authority exercised by the agency over family members and especially so when an attempt is made to place a child in a foster home. Schools and community centers, perhaps overly eager to Americanize the children, estrange them from their parents and inadvertently contribute to family disorganization.

Negro Puerto Ricans have an especially difficult adjustment to make. In the island, dark members of families are accepted as equals, whereas in New York, whites discriminate against the dark-skinned Puerto Ricans. These Negroes tend to withdraw into the Puerto Rican colony rather than yield to the discriminatory American treatment. Sometimes the white Puerto Ricans adopt the American attitude and reject them. They are then in a no man's land, both culturally and socially.

The Puerto Rican family, in its first decade of adjustment to a new culture and social world, is undergoing the family disorganization that attends the failure of old roles to fit the new situation, the clinging of older members of the family to their old position of status, duties, and privileges, and the eager rushing of younger members into the superficial patterns of American life without, however, a grasping of underlying ideals and codes. In time the Puerto Ricans, as other foreign-culture groups before them, will make an adjustment.

THE CULTURALLY ASSIMILATED BUT SOCIALLY UNASSIMILATED FAMILY

With the passage of time and continued exposure to American culture, the foreign-culture group becomes tolerant of or openly accepts some elements of American culture.   As rebelling children, marginal to both the native and the American cultures, marry and establish themselves creditably, parents have many of their fears eased.   The period of stress between the generations is followed by a decline in assertiveness of parents as they grow old and by an increase in dominance of the adult children. Sometimes the children pass quickly as individuals into the American community.   Often, however, they ally themselves with others of the same background to form the typical ethnic group—culturally more American than foreign but socially exclusive.   The family is one of the chief agencies through which ethnic affiliation is maintained.

The Italian family

Now in its third generation of American residence, the Italian family is rapidly passing from the culturally and socially unadjusted stage into the ethnic stage.[9]   It illustrates the later part of the process, the beginnings of which are found in such groups as the Mexicans and Puerto Ricans.

When the changes in the Italian family in America are traced over a period of 50 years and three generations, three stages appear as the immigrant family becomes the ethnic family.   (1) The original Italian families upon entering the United States attempt to continue the type of family life learned in the Italian rural village.   (2) Finding it unsuited to the American city and their growing children opposed to Italian ways and drawn to the American, the Italian parents gradually yield to the pressures but not according to a consistent plan.   The old coordination of roles and functions is disturbed, and family solidarity is weakened. (3) As the children become adult and in their turn marry and rear families, they are able to reorganize their family life on a pattern that is compatible with urban life and American social norms, but with definite ethnic

---

[9] The discussion of the Italian family is based primarily on Paul J. Campisi, "Ethnic Family Patterns: The Italian Family in the United States," *American Journal of Sociology*, 53 (1948), 443–449.

traces.   Table 11 summarizes the changes in significant areas of family life.

The relation of the Italian family to the community also changes with immigration.   In Italy the family owns its home and land and has little residential mobility.   It has become well integrated into the community, carrying on many community activities and sharing feasts and holidays with others in the community.   The family is fully developed and performs many functions usually carried out by institutions in America.   In the American city the family finds itself living in a rented flat, moving often, somewhat active in the Italian colony but not participating in American activities.   The family tries to transmit the Italian culture to its children but often finds its teachings in conflict with American culture taught by the public schools and other agencies with which the children make contact.   The Catholic Church, a dominant institution in Italy, remains relatively strong, but it also loses some of its influence.   In Italy, for instance, marriage is always a religious ceremony, but in America marriages increasingly occur outside the religion and marriage may involve simply a legal ceremony.   Divorce, forbidden by the Catholic religion and absent from the Italian family, now occurs although less frequently than among non-Catholics.

Residential migration

With increasing absorption of American culture, the Italian family moves also toward social assimilation into the American community.[10] It may Americanize the family name, move away from the Italian neighborhood into a completely American area, and have as few contacts as possible with the Italian-born parents.   This complete rejection of both Italian culture and social participation may aid the family to gain acceptance in an American community.   It is, however, of rare occurrence. Other families reject the Americans, culturally and socially, clinging in the second and third generations to the parental group, the old Italian colony, and Italian ways.   This tendency, also, is a minor one.   The most typical trend is for a slow migration to occur of second-generation families that have established themselves economically.   Leaving the original Italian colony, they do not disperse widely into the city but infiltrate into

[10] Campisi, *op. cit.*, p. 447; J. K. Myers, "Assimilation to the Ecological and Social Systems of a Community," *American Sociological Review*, 15 (1950), 370-372.

certain areas according to their economic standing and social aspirations. Thus the most successful may penetrate an upper-middle-class area, buying or building homes along one or two streets, and in time creating a

TABLE 11

The Italian-American Family Moves from Italian toward American Culture *

The family culture of the peasant immigrant from southern Italy	Adaptations made to American culture by immigrants and their children	American-Italian family culture of adult children in their marriages and with their children
	ORGANIZATION	
Large-family system including kin and godparents; 10 children not unusual.	Relation to kin close, but godparent bond is weakened; migration has broken the kinship pattern, although it is still the ideal; fewer children.	Small-family system, few children, godparents not considered in the kinship.
	MARRIAGE	
Parents select mate from same village and provide dowry; marriage in early teens.	Individual selects mate but with parental consent; parents urge marriage to someone from same province and oppose any marriage into another religion. No dowry. Marriage in late teens or early twenties.	Individual selects mate regardless of parental wishes; increasing number of unions with other nationality and religion. Marriage in early or middle twenties.
	ROLES AND STATUSES	
Father the patriarch with highest status; primogeniture gives eldest son high status; mother the center of the home and educated only for marriage. Individuals subordinate to the family with father enforcing his authority by force if necessary.	Father's status lowered or fictitiously maintained; mother relatively higher status and some outside activities; girls given wider education; sons less dominated by father; severe punishments avoided to prevent clashes with the law.	Trend toward equalitarian status of all members; education emphasizes personality; sons expected to do well in school but not to contribute to family finances. Family subordinate to individuals.

TABLE 11 (Continued)

The Italian-American Family Moves from Italian toward American Culture *

The family culture of the peasant immigrant from southern Italy	Adaptations made to American culture by immigrants and their children	American-Italian family culture of adult children in their marriages and with their children
	INTERPERSONAL RELATIONS	
Premarital kissing and petting not allowed; husband and wife show no demonstration of affection before the family or in public.	Husband and wife maintain old relationship but tolerate show of affection between married child and spouse; premarital love-making not openly allowed.	Husband and wife may show affection in family or public; premarital love-making openly practiced.
	DIVORCE AND SEPARATION	
Divorce not allowed and desertion rare.	Occasional divorces but contrary to belief; desertion rare.	Religion forbids divorce, but it occurs; desertion rare.

* Summarized from Paul J. Campisi, "Ethnic Family Patterns: The Italian Family in the United States," *American Journal of Sociology,* 53 (1948), 444–446.

little American-Italian colony.   They and their Italian parents and older relatives in the older colony visit back and forth, and no effort is made to conceal their Italian ancestry and allegiance.   Often they are regarded with curiosity or suspicion by their American neighbors and social acceptance is slow.   This group, culturally more American than Italian and socially tolerated but not accepted, becomes the ethnic group until such time as it becomes still more American and is accepted freely by the American group at which time it will break up and disperse into the American society as individuals or small-family groups, finally intermarrying with Americans and losing its ethnic identity entirely.[11]

This process of residential migration, illustrated by the Italians, is not peculiar to them.   Another example is the Norwegian colony that first settled in lower Manhattan in 1830.[12]   From the coastal district of Norway, the immigrants were adjusted to a combination of seafaring, fishing,

[11] Residential mobility and its relation to the transition from foreign-culture to ethnic status for Italians in Boston is analyzed in Walter Firey, "Sentiment and Symbolism as Ecological Variables," *American Sociological Review,* 10 (1945), 146–148.

[12] Christen T. Jonassen, "Cultural Variables in the Ecology of an Ethnic Group," *American Sociological Review,* 14 (1949), 32–41.

and agriculture, living in and loving the open green spaces of land.   Their first settlement in Manhattan was near the loading docks and drydocks for ship repairs.   As shipyards were opened in Brooklyn—and as Manhattan became more densely settled—families moved to Red Hook, the section of Brooklyn that lay across from the Battery.   Here from about 1850 to 1890 the colony was massed.   Again increasing density of population and the inroads of other ethnic groups pushed the Norwegians out further, until in succession three additional areas were occupied by them. Each move carried them to an area not closely built up and somewhat secluded from other ethnic groups.   New arrivals from Norway joined the older Norwegian ethnic group.   Churches and a foreign-language newspaper followed them.   Thus for more than 100 years, this ethnic group has maintained a distinctive group life through a process of residential migration.   During the process new increments of Norwegian population have been added and others have been left behind or have dispersed into the general population.

The residential migration of ethnic families as they merge into the culture and social life of the American city is not haphazard.   In general the first colonies established by immigrant families in American cities have been in lower-class areas.   Only as they become adjusted, earn more money, and accumulate some savings are they able to move away. Although in specific instances their movement may be to a remote area, in general a progressive migration occurs from the inner part of the city where they typically make their first settlement outward toward the edge of the city along some main line of transportation.   Thus, a certain amount of concentration of each ethnic group in one sector is characteristic.   Also, since a residue is left behind in each area of settlement, after a period of years members of the ethnic group representing several generations and several levels of success are found along the line from the center of the city to the suburbs.   They often also represent degrees of assimilation into American culture and social groupings, with the least assimilated in the interior areas, the most in the outer areas.   As the ethnic families infiltrate these outer areas, they come into contact with American families and along the edges with members of other advancing ethnic groups. These contacts decrease the ingrown character of each ethnic group and promote inclusion in the American social world.   In time the family no longer thinks of itself as belonging to some specific ethnic group and does not teach the children the old songs and legends, the old glory and pride of the ancestral group.   When the family thinks of itself as American and affiliates itself on a social-class basis with other families of whatever ethnic origin, the stage of ethnic affiliation has passed and the family is American.[13]

Religious affiliation

One phase of ethnic culture that is influential in family life clings after most other aspects have faded—religion.   So tenacious is religious affiliation that in the later stages of the transition from ethnic to American culture, religion may become the chief symbol of ethnic loyalty.   For example, in Viroqua, a small mixed Norwegian-American city in Wisconsin, in which the Norwegians have adopted the American culture but maintain an ethnic loyalty, Norwegian and Lutheran are almost synonymous.[14] When a Norwegian leaves the Lutheran Church to affiliate himself with some other church, he is no longer considered a Norwegian.   Lutheran women sometimes join the Ladies Aid in some other church, but non-Norwegians do not participate in Lutheran activities and indeed are not accepted socially in these activities unless they have married Norwegians. In Jonesville, another small Midwestern city, the Norwegian group, still holding itself aloof after 80 years, has taken on the characteristics of a Lutheran sect and is referred to locally as the Norwegian-Lutheran population.   The group no longer follows the Norwegian culture but adheres closely to the ideals, standards, and codes of conduct of the Lutheran Church and in so doing opposes itself to the American groups in the community.[15]

Religious affiliation shows strongly when marital partners are selected. In New Haven, Connecticut, when members of an ethnic group begin to marry outside the group, they show a strong tendency to marry into another ethnic group with the same religion.[16]   Irish, Italians, and Poles (all Catholic) tend to intermarry; British-Americans, Germans, and Scandinavians (all Protestant) likewise tend to intermarry; Jews are most

---

[13] For graphic illustrations of the outward advance of ethnic groups in Chicago from 1898 to 1940 see R. G. Ford, "Population Succession in Chicago," *American Journal of Sociology,* 54 (1950), 156–160.

[14] Munch, *op. cit.,* pp. 785–786.

[15] W. Lloyd Warner and Associates, *Democracy in Jonesville* (Harper, 1949), pp. 168–192.

[16] Ruby Jo Reeves Kennedy, "Single or Triple Melting-Pot? Intermarriage Trends in New Haven, 1870–1940," *American Journal of Sociology,* 49 (1944), 331–339.

likely to marry other Jews.   Thus, as general ethnic affiliation dies out, it is replaced by loyalty to the religion of the ethnic background.

Religious endogamy or exogamy is significant for family life, for each major religion has extended its ideals into a definite conception of marital relationships and family life.   Marriage within the religion assures unity of ideals to the family and their transmission to the children by both family and religious institutions.   Exogamy may mean that one religion is discarded, and the children are reared in the other; but it may also mean that both parents give up close allegiance to religion with the result that children are reared without the support that religious affiliation typically gives to family stability[17]

The family as the seedbed of ethnic culture

The disorganization of the family in the early adjustment period of the foreign-culture group has been discussed.   As the group passes beyond the conflict stage into the ethnic classification, the family becomes one of the strongest carriers of the ethnic culture, aided by the ethnic church or other religious institutions and perhaps by one or two ethnic clubs.   It is in the family that the correlation of the old and new cultures is made, and that children receive their first and much of their later ethnic training. Many of the European immigrants came from societies in which the family was the extended or kinship family.   That pattern is broken by the migration but remains in the memory of the immigrants and often is at least partially re-established as children and grandchildren are added to the original family.   The extended family with close ties of affection binding the foreign-born grandparents and the American-born parents and their children again functions, although not necessarily just as it did in Europe.   Perhaps the extended family is more characteristic of the rural ethnic settlements than of urban communities.   In Middle Western Norwegian settlements it helps to perpetuate the ethnic culture.   Among Wisconsin small-city Norwegians:

Another important focus of loyalty among the Norwegians . . . is the family, especially the extended family which is often referred to as the "clan." Here is where another important part of the social life of the Norwegian group takes place in the form of visiting, celebrations, and regular family reunions.   Of course, this is again a social activity from which the non-Norwegians are excluded although they are freely accepted in case they are

[17] For a further discussion of religious intermarriages, see pages 249–255.

married in the clan—which happens quite frequently—and assume a certain loyalty to the clan.[18]

Among Norwegians in western Iowa and South Dakota the family and the Lutheran Church are the two institutions that preserve the Norwegian culture into the third generation.   The ethnic culture is retained longer in the rural areas than in the small cities, for in the farm families Norwegian is spoken; daily customs, such as afternoon coffee, are preserved; and children and grandchildren alike have been taught the old Norwegian legends.[19]   It is the family expectation that children will marry within the Norwegian group and the Lutheran Church, thus automatically preserving much of the culture for the next generation.   Nevertheless, the culture thins out even in the rural areas, for careful study shows that fewer of the American-born children than of the foreign-born parents adhere to Norwegian customs and concepts.   In the small city deviation is more marked, although loyalty to the Norwegian culture is strong and is reinforced by ritualistic celebrations of outstanding events in Norwegian history.

It is significant to note that in many rural and semirural communities, where one ethnic group is relatively strong and the formal pressures toward Americanization found in cities are weak, the foreign-culture family passes into the ethnic family with a minimum of conflict and family disorganization.

FROM FOREIGN CULTURE TO ETHNIC TO AMERICAN—A FINNISH FAMILY

The account of a Finnish family written by a daughter shows the cultural and social adjustment of the foreign-born parents and their Americanized children.   It also shows the interpersonal tensions and conflicts not only between parents and children but also between husband and wife arising from cultural factors.

The rural family in Finland

Mary and John (to use American versions of their names) were born and reared on a farm in Finland.   Mary's father owned the land, which

---

[18] Munch, *op. cit.*, p. 785.
[19] Lieutenant John Useem, U.S.N.R., and Ruth Hill Useem, "Minority-Group Pattern in Prairie Society," *American Journal of Sociology*, 50 (1945), 377–385.

had been in the family for several generations, while John's father was a tenant. Economically interdependent, socially landowner and tenant lived in different worlds. The tenant was not, however, of the lowest class, for farm laborers occupied a still lower position.

With many lakes running through and between the large farms, each farm had a high degree of self-sufficiency, and the family was dependent upon its own members for utilitarian functions and social life. With a patriarchal organization, the eldest male, grandfather or father, was head both of his farm and his family. He supervised the work of tenants and laborers and carried out many duties himself. He arranged for the annual visit of cobbler, harnessmaker, tailor, and saddler to repair and replace worn equipment and clothing. He trained his sons, one of whom would inherit the farm. The mother's duties were also well fixed in the rural culture. She had charge of the household duties, training her daughters in them. She supervised and helped to carry out spinning, weaving, knitting, and dying cloth. Often, she made her own potato flour and candles. She also had farm tasks—the dairy, poultry, and vegetable garden were in her care. At times she aided in heavier work. The daughters—lowest in the family heirarchy—were assigned tasks according to their age and strength. The old and ill were cared for at home, a special bunk being constructed near the fireplace for their comfort. The farm home often housed three generations.

Social life was confined almost entirely to the family group, especially during the winter. The children had an outside contact in the school, rural children often attending for only four years between the ages of 9 and 13. The Lutheran Church also offered educational services and exerted strict control over the conduct of its members.

Marriage was arranged by the family with due regard to social status, property, and potential service to the family. Divorce, provided by law, was nevertheless a scandal. An illegitimate child was protected by law; he was entitled to the use of his father's name and to inheritance from both parents equal with that of legitimate children. Little social stigma attached to illegitimacy.

A special phase of family life was the steam bath with which the Finns purged their bodies prior to Sunday church services; these ritualistic and cleansing baths were carried out by both sexes simultaneously in a special bath house or souna. This was the only occasion when nudity was socially accepted.

Transition to America

From such a background John immigrated to the United States and settled in a small city, Milltown, where there was a Finnish colony. He left behind his status as farm tenant and was free to establish himself on whatever level he could; nevertheless, he brought with him some of the attitudes of a subordinate class. Mary rebelled against the marriage arranged by her family and against their wishes borrowed money and came to the United States with John's sister. Her plan was to save enough money to return to Finland and establish a small business. The two young women settled in the city where John was working. The remainder of the story is in the words of the daughter of John and Mary; statements in brackets call attention to crises and stages in the adjustment process.

[Employment was easy to find, with Mary using her household skills and John finding unskilled work.] My mother found a position in a household as cook, housekeeper, and nurse. From her small salary she was able to pay her debt in Finland. My father worked in a local steel mill.

[The Finnish colony provided social life; some American culture was learned in night school. The thrift and industry of early training are apparent in the home ownership.] Their culture conflicts in Milltown were minimal. They established friendships with other Finnish immigrants who had organized a self-sufficient neighborhood. About two years after my mother's arrival, she and my father were married. [This marriage was in violation of the Finnish mores. In Finland a marriage between the daughter of a landowner and the son of one of his tenants would have been socially impossible. Mary thus continues the rebellion toward her family that was evident in her rejection of their choice of a husband and in her migration to America. Later portions of the story suggest that her rebellion was against her family rather than the Finnish culture.]

Their combined earnings made it possible for them to buy a house in the Finnish neighborhood. Three children were born. The family organization was semipatriarchal. The greater part of social, religious, and political activities were confined to their ethnic group. My father went to night school and subsequently gained his citizenship.

[In the rural setting, the Finnish family patterns of their youth were more closely followed.] Eight years later my father's health began to fail. The house in Milltown was sold and a ten-acre farm seven miles from the city was purchased. During the years of the 1920 boom and the depression that followed the farm was relatively self-supporting; more land was rented. Three more children were born. The roles of family members followed closely the patterns learned by my father and mother in Finland. They did not conflict to any degree with the rural patterns of behavior practiced by the surrounding farm families. The semipatriarchal family organization continued. Father was the authority and administrator, but he found the role difficult as he had not learned it in Finland where he was a member of a tenant family. [The father was adjusting not only to a new culture but also to a new social-class position in America—an adjustment that he would not have been called upon to make in Finland.] He tended to cling to the old country methods of farming. The fields were plowed with a single horse and plow at a time when nearby farms were becoming mechanized and others were accepting federal subsidies that he refused as "charity."

Mother assumed the role she had learned in Finland. She made her own bread, canned, worked in the gardens and fields, and milked and cared for the cow [always the woman's task in Finland]. She later acquired a loom and made her own rugs. She frequently expressed a desire for a spinning wheel and some sheep.

The roles of the children were clearly defined. The boys enjoyed higher status than the girls. Early in life we learned that we were expected to carry out certain "duties." Earnings were pooled and thrift was emphasized.

The children were taught to be clean [the "souna" was frequented on Saturday night and on the eve of church holidays], religious, and thrifty, and to abstain from intoxicating drink, tobacco, and other "sinful" activities. We must work hard and love our parents above all except God. The aims of my parents were: to perpetuate the family name, to rear all of us so that we could support them in their old age, to teach us the moralistic attitudes and values of the Finns, to marry us into the ethnic group, and to provide us with better educations than they had. Their ultimate goal was to turn the farm over to the youngest son; they would build a house on the hill.

[The ethnic group provided social contacts. This circumstance was a limiting factor so far as ultimate social adjustment was concerned but gave support to the family ethnic pattern.] Religious, social, and business activities were confined to the ethnic group in Milltown. In the home, Finnish was spoken.

[As the children entered adolescence, when the American culture calls for mixed activities and considerable freedom from parental supervision, family unity was strained. The parents supported the Finnish folkways and mores, the children defended the American. It is significant that the tensions and conflicts did not result in open family disintegration; later the children dispersed and established individual small-family units as opposed to the Finnish extended family.]

From our schools we brought an increasing number of conflicting ideas and behavior patterns into the family. Also, the countryside was provided with a long-awaited public service—electricity. We had a radio, a car, and a telephone. My brothers and sister who had graduated from high school were employed in Milltown and brought friends into the home who were outside the Finnish circle of friends.

Quarrels took place between my father and brothers and my father beat the children for their defiance of his authority. The following are the most typical areas of conflict that contributed to the disorganization of the semi-patriarchal family that my parents had established in America: (1) language conflicts; we children spoke English and were embarrassed when the Finnish language was used in the presence of English-speaking guests; (2) dating, which was defined as courtship by our parents; we wanted to carry out the dating patterns of our schoolmates; (3) socially acceptable behavior; we wanted to drink and smoke if we chose; (4) sex education; we wanted to learn more about the facts of sex; (5) earnings; we wanted to keep our individual earnings for personal use instead of turning them over to our father for family use; (6) political attitudes; we could not understand why our relatives in Finland were fighting on the side of the Germans when we learned in civics classes that the Germans were "bad"; (7) class status; we were unaware of the class structure in Finland and could not understand the tension between our parents that grew from their difference in status there.

[As more of the children came to maturity, gained status in the non-Finnish community, and passed beyond the age where they could be beaten into sub-mission, the family reorganized on a compromise basis. Although the parents did not approve of their children's American behavior, they learned to tolerate it. The children either compromised in their turn or withdrew from the family either through marriage or by moving to another city. Such withdrawal is regarded as normal in American culture, although not in Finnish.]

Reorganization in some areas occurred even as disorganization began and often continued in other areas. Concessions were made on both sides. Eventually the family spoke only English when guests were present. Each child, down the age scale, found it easier to obtain greater freedom in her personal life. My parents learned that other patterns of behavior did not necessarily end in "sin." As a larger number of children found employment, the contribution that each needed to make to the family pool became smaller and was therefore less grudgingly given. Misunderstandings and grumbling continued and complete approval of the children's behavior has not been reached even to this day. Social drinking, even in minimal amounts, smok-ing, and irregular church attendance are consistently denounced by my father. He recognizes, however, that his position of authority is now merely nominal.

[The children in adulthood found it possible to enter fully into American life only by a decisive withdrawal from the family. There is a suggestion that the nonethnic marriages, the elopements, and the conversion to another religion may contain some element of revolt against the parents.]

Three children eventually moved away from the home area entirely in order to fulfill their individual ambitions. No child married into the ethnic group. Two children eloped since they knew their marriages would not be approved. One son—the potential heir—joined the Catholic Church prior to his marriage to a Catholic girl.   Another son was divorced and remarried.

[Eventually the father left the farm and became a contented member of the Americanized ethnic community in Milltown, a step made more acceptable to him by the increased personal status he secured in his second marriage which was not marred by the old-country concepts of social-class difference between husband and wife.]

After four children had left the farm and withdrawn from close affiliation with the patriarchal family, mother died after an illness of two years.   The farm was sold [symptomatic of the breakup of the patriarchal family], and father, my brother, and sister moved to Milltown.   For a time father tried living with one of his daughters whose home and family were completely Americanized.   But he was unhappy and there were many conflicts.   At the age of 64 he married a widow of 60, a woman who had been born in Finland but reared in America.   She has adjusted to both cultures but has her social activities in the Finnish community in Milltown [the true ethnic type].   She does not attach any social stigma to my father's status in Finland as a youth. She is cheerful, enjoys father's witticisms, admires his "good mind," is demonstrative in her affections, and takes a commonsense attitude toward his emotional and physical needs.   Father in turn is proud of her participation in social and religious activities.[20]

In summary, the family in its earlier years on the farm was able to maintain many elements of Finnish culture and to confine social contacts to the Finnish community and institutions; as the children grew to adulthood, the parents attempted to remain in this exclusive social world, whereas the children learned the American culture and expanded their contacts to the American social groups and institutions, living for a time in both the Finnish and the American culture and social worlds; their marriages and new places of residence, made on the basis of individual rather than family choice, marked the point of transition from the Finnish to American cultural and social adjustment.   The father, unable to follow them into the American world, made his adjustment to a Finnish ethnic community through his removal from the farm to the city and his second marriage to a woman in the ethnic community.

THE ETHNIC FAMILY AND SOCIAL MOBILITY

The transition of families from ethnic to American culture and social participation has been a common phase of family life in our society for several generations.   The presence of many families, always turning

20 Unpublished record.

away from and rejecting the culture of the past, has influenced our general patterns and values of family life. In these families, the parents and grandparents have been unable to serve as models or to pass on to their descendants values and customs compatible with the American situation. Individualism has been fostered, beyond that which urbanism normally produces. Young people have had to make their own decisions in courtship; they have experimented with new types of family organization; and child training has been learned from books and study groups. The integration of the original family stock (usually based on patriarchal kinship organization) has been lost, and the younger people have formed small nuclear families.

As families have made the cultural transition, they usually have also passed from one social-class level into another. Barriers of language, confusion of cultures, and lack of training in urban skills have handicapped the original immigrants. Their children and grandchildren, reared in American schools, have better economic opportunities. They move from the original, lower-class residential areas into neighborhoods with better housing and a higher standard of living. This movement from class to class is social mobility.

The following chapter analyzes in detail the passing of families from culture to culture.

QUESTIONS

1. Distinguish between foreign-culture, ethnic, and American families.

2. What is the difference between cultural assimilation and social assimilation?

3. Discuss the adjustment problems of the foreign-culture (immigrant) family in the United States. Would adjustment problems be less or greater if immigrants settled in rural areas instead of in cities?

4. Compare the adjustment problems of Mexican and Puerto Rican families.

5. Discuss the relation of residential migration to the process of social assimilation; of religious affiliation to assimilation.

6. From personal experience, observation, or original investigation trace the adjustment process of an individual family.

7. What might schools, churches, and other community agencies do to assist foreign-culture families to adjust with a minimum of family disorganization?

BIBLIOGRAPHY

The concept, ethnic

Firey, W., "Sentiment and Symbolism as Ecological Variables," *American Sociological Review,* 10 (1945), 146–148.

Ford, R. C., "Population Succession in Chicago," *American Journal of Sociology,* 56 (1950), 156–160.

Francis, E. K., "The Nature of the Ethnic Group," *American Journal of Sociology,* 52 (1947), 393–400.

Warner, W. Lloyd, and Srole, Leo, *The Social Systems of American Ethnic Groups* (Yale University Press, 1945), especially ch. 6, "The Family."

Ethnic family patterns and adjustment

References in Chapter footnotes to specific ethnic groups.

Hoffman, O. F., "Cultural Changes in a Rural Wisconsin Ethnic Island," *Rural Sociology,* 14 (1949), 39–50.

Thomas, W. I., and Znaniecki, F., *The Polish Peasant in Europe and America* (Knopf, 1927), Vol. II, Parts III and IV.

Thomas, J. L., "Marriage Prediction in *The Polish Peasant,*" with comment by Florian Znaniecki, *American Journal of Sociology,* 55 (1950), 572–578.

Wessel, B. B., "Ethnic Family Patterns: The American Jewish Family," *American Journal of Sociology,* 53 (1948), 439–442.

Young, Pauline V., *The Pilgrims of Russian-Town* (University of Chicago Press, 1932).

9

Social Mobility of Families

Under certain conditions a family may remain in the same social class over a period of generations. Other families change position, moving either up or down the social-class ladder. Closely allied with the shifting of social-class position is the training of ethnic families into the American culture. A special situation of mobility or stability is created by the ethnic family of different skin color, even after it has become completely Americanized. Religion, at first often a part of the ethnic culture, tends to have its own significance as ethnic culture declines. When families remain in one ethnic or racial group, in one social class, and in one major religion from generation to generation, they tend to have cultural as well as biological continuity and freedom from cultural conflicts. When the family, or some of its members, moves from one class or group to another, discontinuity of the family pattern is a necessary part of the transition. Usually it is accompanied by family tensions or open opposition and by personal insecurity and mental conflicts.

The coexistence in the United States of forces acting for and against stability is a situation to be expected in a diffuse and changing society. Therefore two trends operate simultaneously—toward continuity of family placement and toward discontinuity and change. Whether a family remains in one social position or is socially mobile depends largely upon whether it is exposed primarily to prostability or to antistability factors. When change occurs, it is primarily from ethnic to American and from lower to upper social class. When movement is made away from racial groups, it is usually toward placement in the race with lower prestige. Among religions, the more tolerant usually receives the mobile families.

FACTORS THAT FAVOR STABILITY OF FAMILY PLACEMENT

Generally speaking, stabilizing factors segregate families into groups where one culture is emphasized and isolate them from contacts with other groups.

Residential segregation

The most clear-cut examples of residential segregation are those in which some group is physically isolated and forms a small cultural island in the midst of the larger culture, even though it belongs to the same large cultural system.   Such segregation may result from mountains that prevent easy ingress and egress, so that the habitants of a series of valleys, or indeed of one valley, may form a self-contained community.   Few families or individuals leave the valley, few new people enter.   Trading contacts are impersonal and occur at long intervals.   The families often represent a uniform social class and their ways of living change little with the passage of time.   The Ozarks and the Appalachians contain such isolated valley communities, cut off from the main stream of culture and all sharing essentially the same class level.

A few groups in the United States segregate themselves physically by building impregnable social barriers to communication or contact.   In the past, utopian communities sometimes voluntarily withdrew from contacts in order to experiment with some form of family and community life radiating from a central ideal not held by the society at large.   Although the ideal usually permeated all aspects of social life, only the family type is mentioned here.   Examples are the Shakers, who denied sex relations and lived in large platonic "family" groups; Oneida Community with its group marriage and selective parenthood; the Mormons in the earlier decades of their history when polygyny was a part of their family life; and many smaller, less well-known, or short-lived groups. Many of these communities, finding their social systems unworkable, disbanded within a few years or decades.   Others, such as the Mormons, modified their practices toward conformity with the larger society and continue with only moderate physical but considerable social isolation, typified by their distinctive churches, colleges, and family mores (although these are no longer polygynous).   The Amish, too, have been able to retain the core of their beliefs and practices through self-imposed isolation in rural areas.

Such mountaineer and extremely self-segregated groups are, however, oddities. We are more concerned with the type of residential segregation that occurs in cities or rural areas, without complete economic isolation. Urban ecology has long since established the fact that areas of cities vary in many ways: desirability for business or residential purposes, land value, and rentals. In addition, physical features, such as lakes, rivers, mountains, and swamps, help to determine land usage. Finally, since families select their residences according to many motivations—the amount of money they can afford to pay for ownership or rent; nearness to place of work; interests, sometimes related to background culture, in art, music, the bright lights, gardening, hunting, fishing, and the like—the net result is that families sharing common economic, occupational, and cultural interests tend to cluster in the same area.

Although no one pattern of arrangement of residential areas applies to all cities, the lower income groups generally live in areas of low land value or low rental. Sometimes these areas are in a ring around the edge of the central business district in the oldest and least modern residences of the city; sometimes they are in unincorporated areas outside the city limits, beyond the reach of such public utilities as sewers, gas, and good transportation, or near swamps or other undesirable natural features. Foreign-culture and rural groups that enter the city at the level of unskilled labor tend to live in these areas, with each ethnic group huddling together for social companionship and the services of ethnic institutions. In general the middle class and the Americanized ethnic groups occupy a position beyond the central area of the city or in specialized white-collar suburbs, occupying homes of more modern construction with better equipment and more pleasant surroundings than those of the lower class. The upper class is found in several types of areas. If the city is not growing rapidly and developing a "ring of decay" around its center, upper-class families may be found near the center in homes built several generations ago, or newly developed areas along lake fronts or on high ground may attract them, whereas other upper-class families establish suburbs occupied almost exclusively by members of the one class.

Whatever the pattern of a given city, it tends to be a mosaic of residential areas, each given over to a special social-class, ethnic, or racial group. Within each area some type of communal life tends to develop that emphasizes the special culture of the group and provides for many of their needs. Children and unemployed wives especially find their lives circumscribed by the communal life.   Adolescents and employed members live to some extent a double life—partly in the community and partly in the wider contacts of the city.   As cities grow and change, the residents of one area move into another area, but they tend to retain a uniform class, ethnic, and racial pattern in the new areas as in the old.[1]   To the extent that these patterns of residential segregation are perpetuated, the culture of the group tends also to be perpetuated.

Institutions that serve one class or ethnic group

In the different communities institutions develop that are specifically designed to serve the local group.   These include special shopping centers that stock the goods desired by the group, parochial or foreign-language schools, churches with which the group is affiliated, and clubs and private schools with carefully selected membership.   These institutions, which preserve and transmit to their members and clients the in-group culture, are especially important when they serve the children of the community.

Family teaching of the class or ethnic culture

Segregation based on physical or social barriers is reinforced by the teaching of parents.   At birth each child automatically receives the social-class and ethnic status of his parents.   Whatever he may become in later life, the baby has no individual status but takes his status from his parents.   The family immediately begins to induct the child into the class or ethnic culture.

The teaching of class position is not carried on formally but through the daily supervision by parents of their young children's play contacts. The child is encouraged to invite certain children to his home and is called into the house when seen playing with some other, less desirable, child.   If children of several social-class levels are playing together in the home, the mother selects certain ones for attention and praise and ignores others, although she will not ask the children of lower-class level to leave the home.   Her own child, wishing to please his mother and responsive to her behavior and tone of voice, unthinkingly follows her lead in selecting his playmates.   Also, the visiting child who is ignored is equally responsive and soon feels that he is not wanted, whereas the child who is selected for favorable attention responds to the praise and

[1] Walter Firey, "Sentiment and Symbolism as Ecological Variables," *American Sociological Review*, 10 (1945), 140–148.

accepts the valuation placed upon him by his playmate's mother.   Thus the mother, by selecting her child's playmates, gives him his class identification of other children, which they in turn are receiving from their parents.   By the time children are in the fifth grade they are well aware of their own and other children's social-class placement.[2]

The family also is responsible for the first inculcation of class or ethnic culture.   The differences in family organization and standards in the various social classes have already been discussed.   The mother encourages, praises, punishes, as the child conforms to or rebels against the behavior that she demands of him.   In time, the child accepts not only the behavior but also the rationalizations that support the behavior.   He believes in the cultural peculiarities of his class or ethnic group.   The exception to this statement is found in situations in which the child's contacts are not confined to his own class or ethnic group; then other contacts compete with the family, and the child may come to identify himself wholly or partially with some other group.

Community expectations

The stability of family culture is bulwarked from without by the community expectations of how certain families will behave.   In Plainville, the little Missouri town studied by West, certain breaches of conventions and laws that would not have been tolerated if committed by middle-class families were regarded with tolerance when they occurred in the lower class.[3]   It was assumed that the lower-class families did not know any better.   Thus, when a man and woman lived together without marriage, the situation was regarded as amusing rather than immoral.   Lower-class men who stole chickens or corn were treated as though they were children, by scolding or scaring through a pretense of shooting.   Shiftlessness and lack of ambition are expected by the middle class of lower-class families. Likewise, the lower class looks to the classes above them for leadership in community activities and often for direct assistance in finances.   Sometimes a lower-class family will look to some particular upper-class family with whom there is a close tie, perhaps through years of employment, for assistance or protection in case of lawbreaking.   In general, however, delinquent and criminal behavior is regarded as typical and to be expected

[2] W. Lloyd Warner and Associates, *Democracy in Jonesville* (Harper, 1949), ch. 5.
[3] James West, *Plainville, U.S.A.* (New York: Columbia University Press, 1945), pp. 123–126.

of lower-class people, and the tendency is to allow the processes of the law to operate in order to teach the offender and his class what may be anticipated if such behavior continues. Similar behavior from members of the upper classes is regarded as more or less incidental and settlement is made outside of legal processes. Such differential attitudes toward and treatment of similar behavior help to set the limits of acceptable behavior for children growing up in any one of the classes.[4]

Thus, stability of family placement rests upon some type of segregation, whether enforced from the outside (as in some racial areas) or by the wish of the group itself. In this in-grown social situation the group culture is perpetuated and taught to the children by institutions, parents, and community expectations.

FORCES FOSTERING FAMILY MOBILITY

At the same time that the forces discussed above operate to give stability to families, other forces make for change and mobility into other cultural and social groups.

The expanding productivity of the United States

The development of the United States accounts for much upward mobility of families and individuals, including that of ethnic groups, which typically enter American life at a rather low status. The history of the United States has been a series of expanding economic opportunities. The vast expanse of land to be cultivated and the abundance of natural resources—timber to be cut, metals and coal to be mined, oil to be drained from the depths of the earth—offered opportunity for wealth and economic prestige to the capable of any social class. In point of numbers alone, the upper classes could not supply the need. Moreover, many of the upper-class families had become entrenched in their class position and a fixed mode of life before the greatest industrial development of the country began. Supervision of their inherited wealth, whether in investments or a family business, preoccupation with the arts, a family tradition of certain professions as appropriate for their sons, all deterred upper-class families from exploiting the resources of the expanding frontier.

4 Warner and Associates, *op. cit.*, ch. 6.

Although there is some indication that the making of great fortunes, which start families on the upward social trek, is a thing of the past, industrial booms (such as accompanied World War II), the opening of some new area for development, or a new invention may in the future pave the way for upward economic mobility that in time will eventuate in higher social-class placement.   The "shirtsleeve" millionaires in California are a case in point.[5]   In the course of 30 years laborers, peddlers, and small businessmen have become millionaires by hard work, the natural fertility of California land, irrigation, and scientific farming methods.   The families are not as yet upper class, although they own many of the material symbols—expensive cars, planes, swimming pools, and large houses. They have leisure for yachting, hunting, collecting and playing records, and growing rose gardens.   Succeeding generations will convert the economic values into social values and either enter or create for themselves an upper class.

Spatial mobility

The migrations already discussed, both in the pioneer period and more recently, are conducive to social mobility.   Freed from the ties to the home community, each family may make an individual effort to raise its social status.   Not all succeed: some remain at the same level; others move downward permanently or as a temporary stage in the process of readjustment.

Philosophy of the open-class system

The dictum that "all men are created free and equal," the right of all adult citizens to vote, the selection from any social level of a candidate for President and other positions of political leadership, the opportunities for individual wealth, the system of free education and, at the college level, low-cost education, all support the philosophy of the open-class system. Theoretically, any individual or family may climb as high in the socioeconomic scale as ability warrants.   There is no categorical selection of the families that are privileged to climb.   Actually, also, enough spectacular successes have occurred to give credence to the theory.   The fact that the proportion of any one class that reaches a higher level is small does not detract from the belief.

[5] "Shirtsleeve Millionaires," *Life,* 31 (September 3, 1951), 105–113.

Institutions that serve several or all classes and ethnic groups

Any institution that brings together people of different social classes or ethnic groups breaks down isolation and makes it possible for individuals from different cultural groups to become personally acquainted. They come to regard each other as individuals rather than as members of a stated class or ethnic group.   Each receives something of the culture of the other and in return gives some of his culture.   This cross transference of culture not only develops an appreciation of the other group but permits one who wishes to gain a toe hold on the social ladder to do so.

In the realm of the social heritage as well as the learning of skills, public schools may serve to bring individuals of different social classes and ethnic groups together.   The schools are free, open to everyone, and operate under state laws that require all children to attend until a stated age.   It is true that the schools are not completely free from class affiliation.   In a large city, all the children in the district may represent one class level or one ethnic group; then only the teachers may bring to the children the culture of another group.   In other schools, teachers, administrative officers, and the school board may represent the same culture group and may favor children of their own group.   Nevertheless, the persistent individual can continue in school, slowly absorbing the folkways and mores of other groups represented and making easier his eventual transition to another social class or from the ethnic group into the American culture.

Public libraries, art museums, public concerts are other such agencies that are open to all without restriction.   The exception is in the South where many such organizations are closed to Negroes.

Family mobility therefore is related to factors that destroy fixed social systems and encourage contacts, such as easy entrance into new occupations or new geographic areas or inclusion in institutions that cut across class and ethnic barriers.   Another factor is the abiding American faith in the right and potential ability of any person or family to improve in social position.

VERTICAL MOBILITY

Vertical mobility refers to changes up or down in social-class placement.   The lower-middle-class family that establishes itself or is able to establish a son in the upper class is upwardly mobile; the upper-class family that loses its position and in time becomes lower class is downwardly mobile.   Vertical mobility has been measured by the differential birth rate between social classes, change in occupational status between fathers and sons, and intermarriage between members of different social classes.

Differential birth rate by social classes

Differential birth rates by occupational groups are well known, with low rates among business proprietors and professionals—occupations typical of the upper classes—and higher rates as one progresses to less and less skilled occupations, until the highest rate is reached among the unskilled laborers.   Farm families also vary in fertility according to socioeconomic status.   Whether status is measured by tenure, relief, wealth, measurement scales, or education, the lower the status of the family, the greater the number of children.[6]

When the differential birth rate between social classes is examined in detail, it becomes apparent that the higher social classes are not reproducing themselves, whereas the lower classes produce more than enough children to replace themselves.   Assuming that the opportunities of the higher classes remain the same or increase, the decline in population at these levels opens the way for upward mobility from the social classes below.   Table 12 shows the estimated social-class distribution of the United States at present (column 1), and the future decline in the three higher classes that will occur if replacement rests upon birth rate alone (comparison of columns 1 and 2).   Our philosophy of the open-class system, however, makes it possible for members of lower classes to move upward. Column 4 shows the percentage of each social class from upper middle to lower lower that must move to the next higher class to maintain the present class structure.   The movement upward is limited, however; even the lower lower class, with most opportunity to move upward, will have less than a third of its members enter a higher class and in the upper strata the proportion with upward mobility is very small. Although there is not always "room at the top," some opportunity for upward mobility exists.

The theoretical presentation for the United States as given in Table 12 is corroborated by a study of 300 young adults in Jonesville, the small

---

[6] W. H. Sewell, "Differential Fertility in Completed Oklahoma Farm Families," *American Sociological Review,* 14 (1944), 427–434.

Midwestern city that has been thoroughly studied as to class distribution.[7] The comparison of the status of these adults with the status of their parents shows that 72.1 per cent have the same status as the parents, 23.4 per cent

TABLE 12

Social Mobility in American Society by Status *

Social class	Population distribution by status	Population by net rate of reproduction	Net social mobility required	Per cent of mobility from status below
Upper	3.0%	2.5%	+0.5%	+7.7%
Upper middle	9.0	6.5	+3.0	+10.7
Lower middle	36.0	28.0	+11.0	+28.2
Upper lower	35.0	39.0	+7.0	+29.1
Lower lower	17.0	24.0	—	—
TOTALS	100.0	100.0	+21.5	—

* "To comprehend the table, the figure +3.0 mobile to upper middle in the third column is the difference between 9.0 in column 1 and the 6.0 left in column 2 when +0.5 per cent of a generation move into upper class.   The fourth column indicates the per cent of young people in the social class just below (or others from farther down) who will have to move up in class status to maintain the composition of the American status-structure."—Carson McGuire, "Social Stratification and Mobility Patterns," *American Sociological Review*, 15 (1950), 200.

moved upward to higher class levels, and 4.6 fell to lower levels.   The lower social classes showed a much greater net upward mobility than did the higher classes.

These studies demonstrate that the chief trend of social mobility in the United States is upward, and that a minority of families is affected. For these families, the upward trend may occasion both pride and stress. One manifestation of upward mobility is the entrance of mobile sons into occupations requiring greater training and receiving larger incomes than the occupations of the fathers.

Occupational mobility of sons

Social mobility often occurs at junctures of family reorganization. One of these periods of reorientation comes when the son enters an occupation as an independent adult.   He then frees himself economically from the parental family.   At this time he may take the initial step toward changing his social-class position from that of his father.

[7] Carson McGuire, "Social Stratification and Mobility Patterns," *American Sociological Review*, 15 (1950), 202.

A study of 637 men in San Jose is illustrative, although it should not be assumed that the same degree of mobility would be found in all communities.   Table 13 shows that when occupations were loosely grouped according to status, from 58 to 76 per cent of fathers at different levels had at least one son who was in the same occupational stratum as the father.[8] These percentages indicate a low degree of social mobility.   With a

TABLE 13

Percentage of Fathers Having Sons with Similar Occupational Level *

Occupational stratum of father	Per cent	Categories included as relatively similar in each case
Large business	69	Large business and professional
Professional	64	Large business, professional, and small business
Small business	70	Professional, small business, white collar, and farm owners and managers
White collar	70	Small business, white collar, farm owners and managers, and skilled manual
Skilled manual	72	White collar, farm owners and managers, skilled, and semiskilled
Semiskilled	76	Skilled, semiskilled, unskilled, and farm tenants and laborers
Unskilled	58	Semiskilled, unskilled, and farm tenants and laborers
ALL STRATA	71	

* Table 2 in Richard Centers, "Occupational Mobility of Urban Occupational Strata," *American Sociological Review,* 13 (1948), 200.

more exact classification of occupations, greater mobility is apparent, with almost as much downward as upward (Figure 28).   The degree of mobility was slight, however, usually into the occupational level adjacent to that of the father.

In studies of this kind, some question may be raised regarding the relative status of different occupations.   Large business is conventionally ranked as higher than professions; therefore the sons of business magnates who enter the professions are classified as entering a lower occupational stratum.   The validity of this ranking is uncertain.   Likewise, small business is considered higher than white-collar jobs.   Again, a question

[8] The information was secured from the sons, who gave their fathers' occupations. Other sons might be in the same, lower, or higher strata as compared with the fathers.   Since no bias was used in selection of the sons included in the study, it is safe to assume that they represent a fair sample of all the sons.

might be raised.   In terms of social mobility, therefore, the looser group-ing of Table 13 may be more valid than the finer classifications of Figure 28.

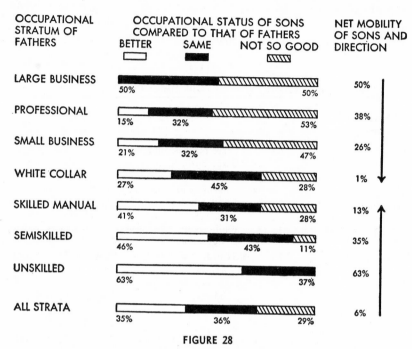

FIGURE 28

Occupational Mobility of Sons, Compared with Their Fathers

From 31 to 50 per cent of fathers in a study in San Jose had at least one son whose vocational choice was in the same occupational class as that of the father, indicating stability of class placement.   Downward and upward oc-cupational mobilities indicate at least slight change of class position.   Such mobility causes a division in the family, sometimes attended by tension or conflict.   The family may reject a downwardly mobile member, or an up-wardly mobile member may try to free himself from members who remain stable.   (Source: Richard Centers, "Occupational Mobility of Urban Occu-pational Strata," *American Sociological Review*, 13 [1948], 201.)

Vertical mobility through intermarriage

Occupational change involves one process of mobility; marriage be-tween members of different social classes is another method of transition, whereby one member to the marriage leaves his social class and com-pletely or imperfectly enters the social class of the other member.   Various studies, using different types of data, show dual trends—toward stability of social class through marriage within one's own class, and mobility through marriage into another class.

Measuring social class according to the previously classified areas in which the families of the marital couple lived, Hollingshead found that in New Haven 58.2 per cent of marriages occurred between people living

TABLE 14

Direction of Marriage of Men and Women in Different Social Classes,
New Haven, 1948 *

Social class of husband	Class position of wife			Total number	Per cent and direction of net mobility
	Higher	Same	Lower		
I	0	52.0	48.0	25	48.0 downward
II	7.6	53.3	39.1	105	31.5 downward
III	12.9	38.4	48.7	39	35.8 downward
IV	8.6	39.3	52.1	140	43.5 downward
V	12.8	64.8	22.4	389	9.6 downward
VI	36.8	63.2	0.0	310	36.8 upward
Social class of wife	Class position of husband				
I	0	59.1	40.9	22	40.9 downward
II	7.6	60.8	31.6	92	24.0 downward
III	20.0	33.3	46.7	45	26.7 downward
IV	12.0	38.7	49.3	142	37.3 downward
V	15.7	68.1	16.2	370	0.5 downward
VI	41.8	58.2	0.0	337	41.8 upward

* Based on Table 4 in August B. Hollingshead, "Cultural Factors in the Selection of Marriage Mates," *American Sociological Review,* 15 (1950), 625.

in areas of the same social stratum (not necessarily the same area), and an additional 24.6 per cent between those from areas of adjacent class level.[9]   Table 14 shows for each social class the percentage of both husbands and wives who married in the same, a higher, or a lower social class.   The amount and dominant direction of mobility vary from one class to another.

Elmtown, the small Midwestern city studied by Hollingshead, showed

[9] August B. Hollingshead, "Cultural Factors in the Selection of Marriage Mates," *American Sociological Review,* 15 (1950), 625, Table 4.   The study was based on all 1948 marriages in which the couple was still living in New Haven in February, 1949.

a marked tendency for people to marry within their own social class.[10]
Through a study of 489 adolescents and their relatives, Hollingshead determined that members of kinship groups tend to belong to identical social
classes or to the next adjacent social class.   For example, among 354
middle-class adolescents, 184 relatives were also in the middle class and
132 in the next class lower.   Only 38 relatives fell outside this narrow
range.   He concluded that in past generations marriages had occurred
within the social class, thus building up a kinship group that exemplified
the class culture and that not only trained the oncoming adolescent in the
class culture but guided him into marriage within that class by emphasizing such characteristics in a suitable partner as occupation, amount of
income, degree of education, religious affiliation, place of residence,
family background, ethnic origin, and reputation and friends—in all instances placing high value on the characteristics as found in the social
class of the kinship group and devaluing the characteristics of other social
classes.

Interclass mobility has also been measured by comparing marriages
between members of the same occupational class with marriages between
members of different occupational classes.   A cross-sectional study of
males, whose marriages occurred between 1885 and 1945, shows that
although many men marry women from their own occupational level, a
larger proportion marry outside their level (Figure 29).   The tendency
is strong in the higher occupational levels for men to marry into a lower
level, whereas lower-level men tend to marry into higher classes.   Both
stability and mobility are shown at each level.

In interclass marriages two people reared in somewhat different culture
patterns come together into an intimate daily association where adjustment rests in part upon consensus of ideals and similarity of behavior
patterns.   Although a thorough study of degree of adjustment in interclass marriages has not been made, some evidence exists that they less
often lead to satisfactory adjustment and more often to unsatisfactory
than do marriages between members of the same social class.   This statement rests upon a study that utilized the schedules of 428 husbands and
417 wives secured for an earlier study of prediction of degree of marital
adjustment.   From the original schedules Roth and Peck were able to
give a social-class placement to each husband and wife and then to com-

[10] A. B. Hollingshead, "Class and Kinship in a Middle Western Community,"
American Sociological Review, 14 (1949), 469–475.

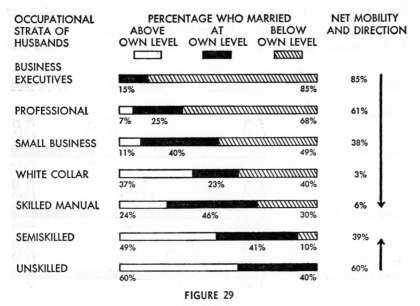

OCCUPATIONAL STRATA OF HUSBANDS	PERCENTAGE WHO MARRIED			NET MOBILITY AND DIRECTION
	ABOVE OWN LEVEL ☐	AT OWN LEVEL ■	BELOW OWN LEVEL ▧	
BUSINESS EXECUTIVES	15%		85%	85%
PROFESSIONAL	7%	25%	68%	61%
SMALL BUSINESS	11%	40%	49%	38%
WHITE COLLAR	37%	23%	40%	3%
SKILLED MANUAL	24%	46%	30%	6%
SEMISKILLED	49%	41%	10%	39%
UNSKILLED	60%		40%	60%

FIGURE 29

Marriages within and across Occupational Lines

The distribution of marriages by occupational strata shown here bears a striking similarity to the distribution by social classes in New Haven illustrated in Figure 24. Moreover, the interoccupational marriages classified here also tended to be among members of adjacent levels. The occupational classification of wives is based upon the occupations of their fathers. (Source: Richard Centers, "Marital Selection and Occupational Strata," *American Journal of Sociology,* 44 [1949], 533.) An earlier study of marriages by occupational levels (T. C. Hunt, "Occupational Status and Marriage Selection," *American Sociological Review,* 5 [1940], 494–504) used the woman's own occupational status rather than her father's and included a classification "at home." Since women follow somewhat different occupations than men, the correlation between men's and women's occupations is less clear than when the woman is classified according to her father's occupation. On the other hand, Hunt's method made allowance for cases in which the woman had a higher occupational status than her father had. He found very high percentages of intraoccupational marriages at some levels; for instance, 52 per cent of professional men married professional women, and 36 per cent of white collar workers married white collar workers.

pare marital adjustment by social class and by mobility. A direct relationship was found between social class and adjustment score, with better adjustment correlated with higher social-class placement. Our interest here, however, is with cross-class marriages. Figure 30 shows that

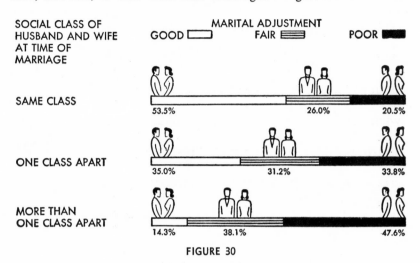

FIGURE 30

Marital Adjustment and Social Class

A striking decline in good marital adjustment is shown with increase in social-class dissimilarity. This graph is based upon an analysis of questionnaires from 428 husbands and 417 wives. The criteria of adjustment were agreements and disagreements between husband and wife, common interests and activities, demonstration of affection, confiding, expressions of satisfaction or dissatisfaction, and feelings of unhappiness and lonesomeness. These criteria were scored in such a way that a total score was secured indicating marital adjustment. (Source: Julius Roth and R. F. Peck, "Social Class and Social Mobility Factors Related to Marital Adjustment," *American Sociological Review,* 16 [1951], 481. Roth and Peck analyzed by social class and marital adjustment the schedules originally used by E. W. Burgess and L. S. Cottrell in *Predicting Success or Failure in Marriage* [Prentice-Hall, 1939].)

intraclass marriages are preponderantly characterized by fair or good adjustment; marriages with one class difference between husband and wife are about equally divided between good, fair, and poor adjustment; and marriages with husband and wife more widely separated in social-class placement have almost half showing poor adjustment and a very low percentage with good adjustment.

A slight difference was found according to whether husband or wife occupied the higher social position.   Marital adjustment was more often good, less often poor, if the husband occupied the higher status than when the wife had the higher position.   The difference is not marked, but it is in keeping with general trends whereby men tend to marry women with slightly less education or occupational status, whereas women prefer men superior to themselves in these respects.   The higher position of the wife is a violation of deep-seated traditions of husband-superiority and therefore may add to the difficulty of adjustment.

THE PROCESS OF UPWARD MOBILITY

When the family or some of its members are upwardly mobile, they must pass through a certain process with both sociological and psychological components.[11]

Rarely does an entire family achieve upward mobility.   Instead, one or two members may forge ahead and gradually establish themselves in a class one or, more rarely, two or more ranks ahead of the general family status.   The advancing individual often is a son or daughter, but sometimes husband or wife will move ahead while the spouse clings to the original class status.   The most frequent advances are made by those in the lower-middle and lower classes.   It will be recalled that in these classes the family unit tends to be the husband, wife, and their children. When the son or daughter marries, he or she tends to withdraw from close incorporation in the parental family and to establish an independent family unit with separate living quarters.   The movement of son or daughter into a higher social class therefore accentuates a process already accepted as normal.   Nevertheless upward mobility widens the breach between related family units, even when the parents have encouraged and financially aided the son or daughter to fit himself or herself for entrance into a higher class.   The desire of the middle-class parent to give his son or daughter the "advantages" he did not have in youth is linked with the pain of estrangement after the son or daughter has achieved the parent's goal.

[11] For a slightly different formulation of the mobility process, see Warner and Associates, *op. cit.*, 55–76.   An excellent case of a Negro family that was first upwardly mobile and then downwardly mobile, with the exception of one son, is given in Allison Davis and John Dollard, *Children of Bondage* (American Council on Education, 1940), pp. 99–126.

The process of upward mobility includes the following steps:

1. The person (or couple) must acquire some of the valued external characteristics of the higher class.

2. He must associate himself with the higher class.

3. Through this association he must absorb the subtle and intangible attitudes and values of the class.

4. Psychologically he must identify himself with the higher class and be able to destroy his identification with the class he is leaving.

5. He must be accepted by the higher class as a member. Since the person is probably well into adulthood before this final step occurs, acceptance of his spouse and children is also implied.

Each step merits further discussion in relation to family interaction.

Acquiring characteristics of a higher class

Certain external class characteristics can be acquired by those of a lower class without the direct aid or permission of individual members of the higher class. These external characteristics include amount of education, to some extent selection of schools attended, preparation for special occupations typical of the higher class, cultural attainments, manners, and style of dress. Preparation begins as a rule in childhood and may be initiated by parents or by a schoolteacher who is attracted by a child's mental ability or personal characteristics that seem to set him apart. Thus, the lower-class child who is being steered toward the middle class may be provided with a piano and given music lessons perhaps at some sacrifice to his parents and other members of the family. He will be provided with better clothing than other children of his class, and may be sent to the Sunday school of the middle class, although the parents may not be affiliated with the denomination. The community center that he attends may respond to his better appearance and achievements by making summer camp possible for him. The schoolteacher will single him out for inclusion in activities usually reserved for the middle-class children; he may appear in programs or serve on school committees to which other lower-class children are not appointed. Later, teachers will advise him to enroll for high school courses that lead into middle-class occupations and perhaps will help him to secure a scholarship, which makes some college or specialized training possible.

In like manner, the child of ambitious middle-class parents will be given some of the outer characteristics of the upper-class child. He will be enrolled in a dancing class patronized by the upper class, sent to a private summer camp, entered at the correct college, advised to prepare for some profession.   His social life will be guided away from those of his own class, and every opportunity will be seized to associate him with those of the next higher class.

The normal process by which parents pass on to their children the culture of their class is destroyed.   Slowly the child is alienated from his class and from his family as a part of that class.   He is no longer able to identify completely with his parents nor to take them for his models; rather, he must take as models the idealized conceptions of the higher class that the parents present to him by word of mouth, by story or legend, by the remote figure pointed out at public functions.   The more successful the parents are in preparing their child for advancement into the higher class, the greater is the alienation.

Association with the higher class

In all communities certain organizations cater to one special class; other associations, however, cut across class lines, at least to the inclusion of two or three adjacent classes.   Organizations based on a nonclass characteristic (such as the American Legion or the League of Women Voters), although they may be dominated by one social class, nevertheless are open to the aspiring climber from below.   Among children, the public school serves this purpose to some extent.   Junior and senior high schools, with larger districts than elementary schools, are more likely to include several social-class areas and thus bring together children of different classes. Freedom of entrance into cross-class organizations does not imply, however, that the child from the lower class is necessarily welcomed or made to feel at home.   He may be ignored, shunned, or ridiculed as the children of the higher class seek to preserve their own status by excluding a child of lower status.   Nevertheless, the persistent parent and child can find a few situations in which the child can be brought into contact with the children of the higher class.   In many organizations there are unwelcome tasks that may fall to the lot of the intruding child—the clean-up committee, the ticket sellers.   The willing child who accepts these tasks and is able to overlook personal rebuffs may gradually establish himself on the fringe of the higher group in institutional and organizational settings, although he probably will not be invited into the homes of the children. The following experience of a girl is pertinent.

One year when my middle-class parents found it necessary to spend the winter in the South, I attended a private school as my parents were unfamiliar with the different parts of the city or the quality of the public schools.   This school catered to upper-class children.   I made some friends at school and was invited by a little girl to spend Saturday at her home.   Her mother carefully led me to talk about my parents, where we lived, what my father's business was, and so on.   I was treated with courtesy but I was never invited to come again.

At a later period in life, the young man who has prepared himself for an occupation of a higher social class may find himself a valued member of a business or professional association; his wife may be prominent in civic groups; yet neither may be invited to the homes of their business or club associates.   Nevertheless, these nonpersonal contacts are a part of the preparation for the higher social class, for they permit absorption of the manners, speech, slang, jokes, attitudes, and values of the higher class. As these associations strengthen, the child or couple is drawn further and further away from the original class and family connections.   For a time the individual or couple may lead a very isolated existence in so far as personal contacts are concerned.   Secondary contacts may be many but those on a primary level lacking.

Absorption of attitudes and values

The process of changing classes is not that of socialization but rather of acculturation.   The socialization has gone on during childhood in the original family and in terms of the class culture of the parents.   Regardless of the efforts of parents to push their children into the culture of a higher class, they pass on to the child much of the culture of their own class.   It is necessarily so, for the parents are themselves steeped in that culture.   Later, as the child or young adult pushes his way into a higher class he must change some of his most deep-seated attitudes and convictions; he must abandon one culture and acquire another—the process of acculturation.   Mentally he probably faces many conflicts, for his affiliation is now to both classes.   If his original socialization has been in the lower class, he will have to abandon the idea of masculine superiority as well as acceptance of help from his wife's employment while children are small; he will have to remold his extramarital behavior with regard to sex; he will have to avoid dependence upon public agencies.   These attitudes and acts are frowned upon by the middle class.

Small and often subtle qualities that are class-marked have to be changed. The pronunciation of a word, the quality of laughter, the mode of greeting a stranger, the connotations of a joke must conform to the practices of the higher class.

Identification

Identification with the parents during childhood is a normal part of the process of maturing in our culture. Chapter 11 elaborates upon the value of such identification to the child in the development of feminine and masculine roles. Typically the parental identification is paralleled by social-class identification, exemplified first in the parents and, as the child widens his contacts, in playmates and neighbors. In freeing himself from parental identification, the adolescent often vacillates between burying himself deep in the security of parental identification and defying his parents in the attempt to free himself. He suffers from conflicting impulses and opposed needs. Eventually he succeeds in identifying himself not with any one person but with the mores of his own generation. In changing identification from one social class to another, the person undergoes similar difficulties. If the shift comes during adolescence, it may involve both the denial of parental and social-class identification. If it comes during young adulthood, after the parental identification has been broken, it will still be difficult and will also involve a still further withdrawal from the parental family.

In class identification, the individual accepts the values and responsibilities of his social class as his own. He tends to be somewhat ethnocentric about his class culture and to believe in it and rationalize deficiencies. He is aware of the errors and shortcomings of other social classes but regards his own social class as most adequate. In affiliating himself with the culture of another social class he must reverse his attitudes; he must accept the new social class as best and be able to accept and believe in the criticisms made by this class of his original class. Implied is criticism of his parents, siblings, and friends of the old class.

Before his new identification is complete, he will vacillate, as does the adolescent, between the two classes. At times he will feel that the old class is best, that he will never be accepted by the new class, that the prize of higher status is not worth the struggle and denial of family and friends necessary to attain it. At times he will feel guilty that his success is greater than theirs and perhaps will seek to assuage his guilt by buying a new home for his parents or financing a niece or nephew through school. He may try to pull his entire family up with him, moving parents or siblings to the residential area of the higher class.   But parents are usually too deeply imbedded in the old class culture to make the transition and only serve to impede him.   Gradually he will move toward a more secure position in the higher class.

The desire for full upper-class inclusion, which he may never attain, he will project upon his children, giving them full entrance into the higher class through their attendance at the proper schools and camps.

As he withdraws from his old social class, his family and friends, although proud of him and their early contacts with him ("I knew him when—"), also are secretly envious and often openly critical.   At best they recognize that he has grown away from them and is no longer one of them.   When more critical, they say that he is "high hat," or extravagant, or has a "swelled head."   Gently or ruthlessly, the social class and his own family reject him, and the ranks of his original class culture close behind him as the new class opens before him.

Acceptance by the higher class

The final step of acculturation into a higher class comes with acceptance of the aspiring individual and his family into the primary groups of the higher class.   He is elected to membership in exclusive clubs where a unanimous vote is necessary for membership; he is invited to the homes of his new friends; he is welcomed as a neighbor in the proper residential area.   He is accepted now not only because of his occupational standing, his willingness to serve on committees and contribute to the right causes, but as a person who understands the class connotations of words spoken as well as the dictionary definition and who laughs at a joke not because of its obvious humor but because of its subtle class meanings.   Sometimes the person who starts the upward climb is never fully accepted, this last reward going to his children or even grandchildren.   In small cities and the more recently developed regions acceptance requires less time than in the older cities of the East and South where the upper class counts its existence not in years but in generations.   The final mark of acceptance comes when he, or his child, is able to marry into the new class.

DOWNWARD MOBILITY

In general, downward mobility occurs when the individual or family is unable to meet some of the class expectations or has violated some of the mores of the class in which he was reared. He may not attain the expected amount of education or be unable to hold the kind of position typical of his class; the family may lose money through a depression or poor investments and be unable to afford the pattern of life characteristic of its class. In other cases the individual violates the class mores and slips into a lower class, perhaps pulling his family down with him.

The upper-class person who becomes alcoholic or a recognized philanderer, the middle-class man who refuses to support his family or who becomes a day laborer, the lower-class person who becomes a habitual criminal are all examples of those who repudiate their class mores. Many, although not all, of the residents of "homeless men" areas in cities once were members of the middle class or occasionally of the upper class. Not all downward mobility carries the individual or family to such low levels, however. The upper-class deviant may slip to middle class, the upper middle to lower middle, the upper lower to lower lower; the lower lower can move downward only a short distance but he may sink to the level of those who disregard all social rules.

Upper-class families often protect their deviants, their ne'er-do-wells, alcoholics, feeble-minded, and criminals through the power given by social prestige and wealth. A companion for the wayward girl, a bodyguard for the alcoholic, private sanitariums for the feeble-minded, a life abroad for the philanderer, financial restitution for crimes and other misdeeds all help prevent the downward journey of the upper-class person who fails to meet family and class expectations. In any other class the family would be unable to provide so impregnable a shield. In the upper class the coordinated family stands supreme, and only by a persistent effort can the individual escape from it.

The middle-class family, eager to protect the family's good name and unable to help the deviant, often repudiates the erring one, and thus saves the family name by denying responsibility for the deviant or even denying the relationship. Thus, a family may say of a related nonconforming family or person with the same name, "We don't claim them," or "They are very distantly related." The lower-class family may use the same device, especially if it is upwardly mobile and wishes to shake off entanglements with lower-lower-class members or relatives.   If the relationship cannot be wiped out by denial, the family may assume a fatalistic attitude— "Every family has one black sheep."   In the more religious families, the attitude is resignation over a trial sent to test their faith.

The person or family that is downwardly mobile often does not affiliate closely with any social class.   In occupation, place of residence, income, and education of children, the family may resemble a lower class than the class of origin.   But often the family holds itself aloof from the churches, clubs, and other organizations of the class.   It does not seek friendships in the lower class and may attempt to teach the children the attitudes and values of the class of origin.   If it succeeds in doing this and also in training the children for re-entrance into the higher-class occupations, the children may return to the higher social class.   But if it fails, the children in time will accept the lower-class placement.   Their attitude toward their relatives in the higher class may be one of pride, envy, or resentment, depending upon their parents' attitudes and the reception they have received in casual or planned contacts.

The attitude of the downwardly mobile person or family cannot be stated categorically.   He may feel guilty that he has not upheld the class standards; or relieved to be no longer subject to expectations and demands that he is not fitted to meet.

SOCIAL MOBILITY AND FAMILY DISUNITY

In earlier chapters the disorganizing effects of spatial mobility were discussed.   Social mobility likewise breaks down the unity of families as some members rise or fall, identifying themselves with a new class culture and rejecting the old.   Like migrations, social mobility is part of the fluid social and economic condition of our society—a part of the social background to which families must adjust.

QUESTIONS

1. How do families stabilize themselves at a certain social-class level?

2. How does the philosophy of the open-class system foster family disorganization?

3. The differential birth rate of social classes has been noted.   How does this factor affect social mobility?   Many people believe it would be beneficial to society if the higher classes increased their birth rates and the lower classes

decreased theirs.   How would such a change in birth rates affect family mobility?

4. The various measures of social mobility tend to show downward mobility in the higher levels, upward mobility in the lower levels, and very little mobility in the middle levels of class position.   Account for these differences in mobility.

5. From your own experience or observation analyze the adjustment problems of a marriage in which husband and wife come from different social classes.

6. How does upward social mobility destroy family identification?

BIBLIOGRAPHY

Types of mobility

Centers, R., "Marital Selection and Occupational Strata," *American Journal of Sociology,* 54 (1949), 530–535.
———, "Occupational Mobility of Urban Occupational Strata," *American Sociological Review,* 13 (1948), 197–203.
Hollingshead, A. B., "Cultural Factors in the Selection of Marriage Mates," *American Sociological Review,* 15 (1950), 619–627.
Hunt, T. C., "Occupational Status and Marriage Selection," *American Sociological Review,* 5 (1940), 495–504.
McGuire, C., "Social Stratification and Mobility Patterns," *American Sociological Review,* 15 (1950), 195–204.

Effect of mobility on marital adjustment

Roth, J., and Peck, R. F., "Social Class and Social Mobility Factors Related to Marital Adjustment," *American Sociological Review,* 16 (1951), 478–487.

10

Cross-Cultural Marriages

New alignment of families in the social structure takes place not only through vertical mobility but also through change in family affiliation from one race or ethnic group to another.   Such transitions are shown by interracial, interreligious, and interethnic marriages.

Such cross-cultural marriages occur in some degree between even the most rigidly segregated groups.   The problem, therefore, is not whether cross-cultural marriages exist, but the frequency with which they occur between different types of groups.   The tendency toward intermarriages in contrast to intramarriages (within one culture) is related both to the strength of the desire of members of the culture to maintain their indigenous culture through their marriages and to the mores of both groups. The mores tolerate some types of intermarriages but sternly oppose other types.   Studies indicate that the greatest opposition exists toward interracial marriages.   Lines between the major religious groups are next to race in rigidity, with a strong tendency for marriages to occur within the religious group.   Ethnic affiliations, often related to religion, rank third in determination of intermarriages.[1]   Each of these types of intermarriage is discussed as to frequency, related factors, and effect on family life.

INTERRACIAL MARRIAGES

The type of intramarriage most strictly adhered to is that within one race.   Not only do the laws of 29 states forbid certain types of interracial

[1] Ruby Jo Reeves Kennedy, "Single or Triple Melting-Pot?   Intermarriage Trends in New Haven, 1870–1940," *American Journal of Sociology,* 49 (1944), 331–339; August B. Hollingshead, "Cultural Factors in the Selection of Marriage Mates," *American Sociological Review,* 15 (1950), 619–627.

marriages,[2] but the mores of the entire United States oppose intermarriage along racial lines. All 29 of the states with opposing laws forbid intermarriage of whites and Negroes, variously defined, and 13 of these states also prohibit marriage with Orientals. Although most of the states with prohibitive legislation are concentrated in the South where the Negro population is relatively high in relation to white, other concentrations are found in the Far West where Orientals have settled, and in the west-north-central and mountain regions. In some of these states the proportion of nonwhites is less than 1 per cent. Penalties for violation are heavy: fines of $100 to $1,000 and one to five years' imprisonment are common, and in Kentucky the fine may run as high as $5,000. The classification of Negro is sometimes undefined, but some states define Negro as a person with one-fourth, one-eighth, or one-sixteenth Negro blood. The last designation would mean that among 16 great-great-grandparents 1 had been a Negro, while 15 had been white.[3]

Frequency

Even in the states that do not forbid Negro-white intermarriage, few such marriages occur relative to the total number of either Negro or white marriages.[4] A study of such marriages recorded in Boston from 1914 through 1938 shows that Negro-white marriages equalled from 3.1 to 5.2 per cent of all Negro marriages when the percentages were computed by five-year periods. The total percentage for the full period was 3.9 per cent. Since there are many more white marriages than Negro marriages in a Northern city, the percentage of white marriages in which one partner was a Negro was very low. For the five-year periods the percentages varied from 0.10 to 0.18 with a percentage of 0.12 for the entire period. For the period 1916 through 1937 Negro-white marriages in New York State exclusive of New York City varied from 1.7 to 4.8 per cent of all

[2] Alabama, Arizona, Arkansas, Colorado, Delaware, Florida, Georgia, Idaho, Indiana, Kentucky, Louisiana, Maryland, Mississippi, Missouri, Montana, Nebraska, Nevada, North Carolina, North Dakota, Oklahoma, Oregon, South Carolina, South Dakota, Tennessee, Texas, Utah, Virginia, West Virginia, and Wyoming.

[3] Otto Klineberg, editor, *Characteristics of the American Negro* (Harper, 1944), pp. 277–278. A detailed table is given, based upon a variety of sources, including C. S. Mangum, *The Legal Status of the Negro* (Chapel Hill: University of North Carolina Press, 1940), and Chester G. Vernier, *American Family Laws: A Comparative Study of the Family Law of the Forty-eight States, Alaska, The District of Columbia, and Hawaii to January 1, 1931* (Stanford University Press, 1938), five volumes.

[4] Klineberg, *op. cit.*, pp. 277–278. Earlier studies are summarized on p. 277.

marriages involving Negroes; the corresponding percentage of white marriages is not given but, as in Boston, would be very low.

In California, with its medley of races, various laws forbidding certain types of interracial marriages were repealed in 1948, thus opening the way for many types of interracial legal unions.[5]   An analysis of all marriage licenses issued in Los Angeles County in the 30 months following the repeal uncovered very few marriages between whites and those of other races.   Out of a total of 78,266 licenses, only 455, or 0.56 per cent, were issued to couples one of whom was white and the other of some other race.[6]

Degree of social integration

The study of Boston interracial marriages suggested that Negroes and whites entering into such marriages were not well integrated into racial social structures.   The whites of long American affiliation have a social-class structure, described in Chapters 5–7.   Ethnic groups usually have a social structure of their own, which may also include a class structure. Negroes likewise, because of their exclusion from American white social organization, have developed since the Civil War a class structure resembling that of the Americans with institutions and informal groups, business and recreation, churches and clubs, that meet the needs of their members.   The person, whether American white, ethnic, or Negro, who is well incorporated into his social structure is unlikely to intermarry, since his contacts tend to be within his own social unit where his needs are adequately met.   He marries within his social structure not because of any abstract belief that he should do so but because his contacts since childhood, his memories, his deepening adult friendships, and his dependencies and securities are within this structure.   It is natural for him to fall in love with a member of his cultural and social group.   An interracial marriage therefore indicates either that the person has not been thoroughly integrated into his social group or has withdrawn from it for

[5] Prior to the repeal, California laws forbade the marriage of whites to Negroes, Chinese, Japanese, and (after 1933) Filipinos.   Whites could marry Mexicans and American Indians.   Other racial groups than the whites could intermarry.   The laws were repealed following a suit brought by two Catholics, a Negro and a white, who argued that their religious freedom was denied by the laws: they were able to receive all religious sacraments except that of marriage, which was unconstitutionally denied to them.

[6] John H. Burma, "Research Note on the Measurement of Interracial Marriage," *American Journal of Sociology,* 57 (1952), 587–588.

some reason. His needs are not met there; he seeks elsewhere for contacts, friendship, and marriage. He tends to be either somewhat disorganized or a cosmopolitan person who makes friendships on a personal rather than cultural basis.

Such failure to find incorporation in the race structure may result from unbalanced sex ratios that prevent marriage of all members of a race within the race. Such a situation existed in California in the 1920's and 1930's, when there were approximately 2,400 Filipino males to each female. Between 1924 and 1933, out of every 100 marriages involving a Filipino, only 30 were within the Filipino group: the other 70 were with whites, Mexicans, or other Orientals.[7] So frequent did marriages between Filipino men and white women become that California passed a law in 1933 forbidding Filipino-white marriages. Since the repeal of the law in 1948, the most frequent type of intermarriage is between a Filipino man and a white woman, with the combination of Filipino man and Mexican woman ranking second.[8]

When nonwhites intermarry with whites, the white person often is foreign-born, a situation true in Negro-white marriages in Boston and elsewhere.[9] Foreign-born whites as a rule have less color prejudice than native-born Americans; moreover, the sex ratio of foreign-born groups often is unbalanced, usually with an excess of men. These men seek brides in other cultural and sometimes other racial groups, occasionally competing with the racial males even when the number of women is too few to supply wives for the men of the race. The status of a white person and perhaps a higher income may make the foreign-born white man attractive to the nonwhite woman.

Not all interracial marriages, however, occur between white men and nonwhite women. The Filipino-white marriages of California illustrate the reverse situation. New York and Boston studies show that Negro men married white women almost five times as often as white men acquired Negro wives; in New York State (exclusive of New York City) the Negro man–white woman marriage occurred almost three times as frequently as the reverse combination.[10] These Negro grooms tend to come from higher occupational strata than Negro men in general; when

[7] Constantine Panunzio, "Intermarriage in Los Angeles, 1924–1933," *American Journal of Sociology*, 47 (1942), 690–701.

[8] Burma, *op. cit.*, pp. 587–588.

[9] Klineberg, *op. cit.*, pp. 283–300.

[10] *Ibid.*

they do not marry white women of their own approximate occupational strata, they turn to unskilled white women who perhaps find satisfaction in the comforts that the Negro husband can provide, while the husband values his wife for her race.   The white brides, unlike the white grooms, do not, however, include an overproportion of foreign-born.   Both Negro grooms and white brides include a higher proportion of divorced persons than does the general population.

Often the initial contacts that lead to interracial marriages are made in the course of work.[11]   Negro brides, for instance, have a higher than expected representation of servants.   Accustomed to working for white families, these women are not closely integrated into the Negro community and have become adjusted to association with whites.   Negro grooms in interracial marriages also have a disproportionately high number whose work provides contacts with whites, as chauffeurs, porters, waiters, and cooks.   They are to some extent members of the white community.

The choice of spouse in an interracial marriage is controlled in part by laws and in part by the mores.   In California, during the 1930's, laws forbade whites to marry Negroes, Chinese, Japanese, and (after 1933) Filipinos.   Whites could, however, marry Mexicans and American Indians.   The mores, however, frowned upon all types of marriages between whites and nonwhites.   The infrequency of Negro-white marriages in the North is not related in most states to laws but to the mores of both races.

Adjustment in interracial marriages

Because of the social disapproval, and sometimes cultural differences as well, marital adjustment often is difficult.   Since Negro-white marriages have been more thoroughly studied than other types of interracial marriages, the discussion that follows applies specifically to them.

In entering into an interracial marriage—or even friendship—both the man and the woman must defy their racial mores and meet the disapproval and perhaps ostracism of their friends.   Flirtations and romances between Negroes and whites who work together, of a type that within one race would naturally lead on to marriage, are stopped at a casual level or, if they lead to more intimacy, are kept secret.   When deep affection develops, marriage often is not the outcome, or a secret marriage is consummated.   For an open courtship and married life the couple must be

[11] *Ibid.*

well withdrawn from dependence upon the approval of their respective racial groups and prepared to stand as an isolated couple withdrawn from both racial social structures.

A summarization made by Drake and Cayton of types of Chicago Negroes who intermarry with whites includes intellectuals and Bohemians, who are not responsive to social controls, or members of certain cults that include disregard of racial differences as part of their social philosophy.[12] Lower-class Negroes, without pride of race, also intermarried. Well-established upper-class and middle-class Negroes and the respectable lower class did not intermarry, although at an earlier period in Chicago relatively stable working-class Negroes did intermarry.

The degree to which the couple tends to be isolated is indicated by the following restrictions laid upon them:

They often lose their jobs if the intermarriage becomes known.

They have difficulty in finding a place to live and usually must find it within the Negro community; even here there is difficulty, as it is often assumed that they are not married and hence not "respectable."

The families, especially the family of the white partner, almost always disapprove; the couple therefore keep the marriage secret or "lose" themselves in the Negro community and break off all contacts with the white family.

Friends usually refuse to accept the partner of the other race, although they may continue to meet the partner of the same race.

Family and friends cannot be counted upon to help the couple in time of crisis.

The white partner (who usually is the wife) is branded by both whites and Negroes as not respectable no matter how circumspect her behavior.

The couple must continuously defend and rationalize their marriage.[13]

As a consequence, mixed couples tend to band together for social contacts and practical assistance. At one time in Chicago such couples organized a club, called the Manasseh club, which was both a fraternal benefit society owning a cemetery plot and also a social organization that met for dances and picnics. The club no longer exists, but mixed couples

---

[12] See St. Clair Drake and Horace R. Cayton, *Black Metropolis* (Harcourt, Brace, 1945), pp. 137–139.

[13] Drake and Cayton, *op. cit.,* pp. 140–153. Accounts of specific marriages sometimes reveal the attitudes of the couple and their relatives; see, for example, "My Daughter Married a Negro," *Harper's Magazine*, 203 (July, 1951), 36–40; R. L. Williams, "He Wouldn't Cross the Color Line," *Life*, 31 (September 3, 1951), 81–94.

still tend to associate with each other or with other tolerant groups.   To the extent that the couple can withdraw from both racial groups into a mixed racial group they are saved many strains upon their relationship and are given needed primary-group contacts and secondary-group associations that tend to support the marriage, give security, and provide justifications.

Interracial marriages of Americans in the armed forces

Service in foreign lands and especially the residence of occupation troops after active warfare has ceased have had, as a by-product, many marriages between American servicemen and local women.   From time to time, the United States government has made arrangements for the entrance of wives from other nations into the United States.   When the wives are Australian or European, the adjustment that they make is cultural and social; they meet a minimum of prejudice.   The Oriental wife, however, faces not only the cultural and social adjustment but also the barrier of racial prejudice.   The parents, brothers, sisters, and friends of the husband often are unprepared for the marriage and psychologically unable to accept an Oriental into the family and friendship circles.   The wife, also, is unprepared, since she usually is unfamiliar with American culture and unaware of the prejudice that will greet her.   Often she is the only Oriental in the community to which her husband has brought her and hence cannot turn to others of her own race for sympathy and friendship.   This type of interracial marriage is of too recent origin to have been thoroughly studied, and generalizations therefore cannot be made about the ultimate outcome.

Children

Children of white-nonwhite marriages usually resemble the nonwhite parent in skin color and therefore popularly are classified as nonwhite. Often, also, they are legally designated as nonwhite and subject to any restrictions placed upon the nonwhite group.   Nevertheless, with one white parent, the child may not have the same status as a child with both parents of the same race.   As more is known about Negro-white children than children from other racial mixtures, their situation alone is discussed.

Since the interracial couple lives as a rule in the Negro community and since the tendency is to classify all hybrids as Negroes, the interracial character of the family is a transitory affair lasting only one generation.

Children of the marriage, usually showing their Negro inheritance, are accepted by both Negroes and whites as Negroes. Their contacts are with other Negroes, and they are readily accepted into Negro social groups. Only occasionally and to slight degree does the fact of a white parent reflect upon them. Since light-colored Negroes have the opportunity to achieve a high personal status in the community because light color is esteemed more than dark, the children of interracial marriages have a certain advantage. Reared in the Negro community they become psychologically and socially Negroes; the process is furthered by the fact that the white parent often does not inform her parents or relatives of the birth of a child and the child therefore does not have contacts with or emotional disturbances over disapproving and emotionally disturbed grandparents, uncles, and aunts. When the white parent attempts to force her colored children into contacts with whites, she helps to create emotional conflicts for them. Perhaps the most trying situation arises when the child is very light and in a position to identify with either race. He has emotional ties through his parents with both races, but eventually tends to identify with one or the other. If very light, he may "pass" into the white group and sever contacts with his parents and childhood associates. In some cases the child is unable to identify with either race and is torn between the two, sometimes isolating himself from both. He may wish to identify himself with the whites, but his color or the knowledge that he is colored may cause the whites to reject him. Toward the Negroes who would accept him he develops a feeling of aversion or hostility. Most children, however, adjust successfully in the Negro group.[14]

RELIGIOUS INTERMARRIAGE

In some communities, the tendency is strong for individuals to marry within their own religious group, with Jews showing the greatest tendency toward intramarriage, Catholics next, and Protestants the least tendency.

Frequency

In New Haven, where marital selection has been carefully studied by several sociologists, 91 per cent of all marriages in 1948 were between affiliates of the same religious group.[15] The Jews ranked highest, with

---

[14] Drake and Cayton, *op. cit.,* pp. 154–159.
[15] Hollingshead, *op. cit.,* p. 623.

97.1 per cent of marriages involving a Jew being between members of the Jewish faith.   Among Catholics, 93.8 per cent of the marriages united two Catholics, and among Protestants, 74.4 per cent were endogamous. It is significant that when exogamous marriages occur, Catholics and Protestants tend to be the participants; few intermarriages involve Jews.

Other studies show a greater proportion of mixed religious marriages. Using records of the Catholic Church, Thomas found a much higher percentage of mixed marriages.   For Connecticut in 1949, mixed marriages sanctioned by the Catholic Church equalled 40.2 per cent of all Catholic marriages; with the addition of mixed marriages not sanctioned by the church, the percentage would probably approximate 50 per cent.[16] New Haven, therefore, seems to have a much lower proportion of Catholic mixed marriages than does the state in which it is located.   Catholic mixed-marriage rates vary greatly from one part of the country to another, with as many as 70 per cent of the sanctioned marriages in the dioceses of Raleigh, Charleston, and Savannah-Atlanta being mixed but less than 10 per cent of those in the dioceses of El Paso, Corpus Christi, and Santa Fe. For the United States as a whole, mixed marriages for the two decades 1930–1950 equal 30 per cent of all Catholic marriages.   Again, the addition of those not sanctioned by the Catholic Church would swell the percentage.   In 132 parishes distributed through the East and Middle West as many as a third of the mixed marriages were not so sanctioned.

All studies of Jewish intermarriage in the United States report low percentages.[17]   Pressure for in-group marriages comes from both within and without.   According to Orthodox principles, the Jew who marries outside the faith is considered dead; the death ceremony is held, and he is no longer accepted by family or synagogue.   Although this extreme measure of social annihilation is not followed in most American Jewish communities, the attitude is still definitely opposed to marriage outside the Jewish religion.   The vigilance of the parents extends to heterosexual friendships between boys and girls, since these might lead into dating and courtship.   The situation in a Connecticut city of 10,000 is described as follows:

. . . although it is quite common for a Jewish boy in Derby to have friends of his own sex among gentiles, it is only rarely that he will have

[16] John L. Thomas, "The Factor of Religion in the Selection of Marriage Mates," *American Sociological Review*, 16 (1951), 487–491.

[17] M. L. Barron, "The Incidence of Jewish Intermarriage in Europe and America," *American Sociological Review*, 11 (1946), 7.   A summary of studies is given.

a gentile "girl friend." One or two "dates" of this sort are sufficient for the relationship to become a topic of gossip in the community. In such cases, word usually reaches Jewish parents quite rapidly and they plead with their wayward sons to "stop bothering with 'Shikses' because there are plenty of fine Jewish girls in town."

More or less the same is true of Jewish girls. In fact, it is even more difficult for them than for unmarried Jewish males to cross the religious line heterosexually. The male friends of Jewish girls are very carefully checked, more so than in the case of gentile girls.[18]

Conditions influencing interreligious marriages

Certain social conditions affect the proportion of interreligious marriages. For example, when one religious group has few representatives in a community, many exogamous marriages occur. Rates of mixed Catholic-Protestant marriages are high in areas where there is a low proportion of Catholics in the population, thus reducing the number of persons from which individual selection of a spouse may be made.[19] One factor in the low rate of intermarriage of Derby Jews is that the young people of this small city have contacts with the larger Jewish communities in nearby New Haven and Bridgeport. The area of choice is thus greatly widened so that someone of compatible personality as well as Jewish religion is more likely to be found than if selection of the spouse were limited to the smaller community.[20]

Mixed marriages of Catholics also occur more frequently in upper social classes than lower, as measured by rental areas in one city. Among 51,671 families in one large city, the percentages of families living in different areas that were based on mixed marriages increased regularly from 8.5 per cent in the lowest-rental area to 17.9 in the highest, with 19.3 per cent among suburban families.[21] Although the study in question did not venture an explanation, it seems probable that persons in the higher-rental areas were also those with less ethnic affiliation and with higher education. Both of these factors would tend to increase their contacts in both number and variety with persons of other religious faiths and to free them from strict compliance with religious rules. Right of individual selection of the spouse would tend to direct the choice.

A social situation that reduces out-marriages is the coincidence of

[18] Barron, *op. cit.*, p. 8.
[19] Thomas, *op. cit.*, p. 489.
[20] Barron, *op. cit.*, p. 8.
[21] Thomas, *op. cit.*, p. 490.

religious faith and ethnic culture.[22]   As long as the ethnic culture is strong, marriages tend to occur within the ethnic group.   When the ethnic group represents only one religion, marriages are automatically within the religion as well.   Ethnic and religious affiliation strongly reinforce each other in determining marital selection.

Effect on family adjustment

The outcome of interreligious marriages has not been thoroughly studied.   Sociologists well recognize that incorporation from childhood in any of the religious faiths means more than a difference in theological beliefs, for religion reaches far beyond formal creeds into the very fiber of personal ideals and habits.   The difficulties of adjustment are not wiped away by tolerance toward interreligious marriages on the part of many Protestant sects or the willingness of the Catholic Church to sanctify a Catholic–non-Catholic marriage upon agreement by the non-Catholic member that the marriage will be broken only by death, that all children shall be baptized and educated in the Catholic faith, and that he will respect the religious principles regarding birth control.   It is difficult for either partner to the marriage to foresee the feelings of frustration that they will have if they are unable to carry out religious rituals in the home or to have prescribed foods because of the disbelief or lack of cooperation of the partner of the other faith.   Few young people are so thoroughly independent of their parents and relatives that their disapproval will not mar the marriage relationship.   And many husbands and wives find a new source of disagreement when children are born, even though they have agreed before the marriage into which religion the child is to be inducted.   Religious beliefs are deeply ingrained and are supported by many auxiliary beliefs and customs as to the relationship of husband and wife, the functions of the family, and the relation of the family to the church.   Even those who are "indifferent" to religion find under stress of some crisis that belief in their own religion and dislike or actual scorn of the religion of the spouse come into overt expression.[23]

Extremely significant, therefore, is a study by Judson T. Landis of 4,108 families (upper-middle-class families with children), which makes it possible to compare those in which husband and wife followed the same

---

[22] *Ibid.*, pp. 489–490.
[23] Ray Baber, "A Study of 325 Mixed Marriages," *American Sociological Review*, 2 (1937), 705–716.

religion with those in which two religions were represented.[24]   The information for this study was secured from college students through the use of a questionnaire in which each student was asked to estimate the degree to which religious differences had been a source of difficulty in his parents' marriage.   The results are shown in Figure 31.   When the parents were of the same religion (both Protestant or both Catholic), religious differences were negligible.   Although more than half of the marriages with Protestant husband and Catholic wife and 45 per cent of those with Catholic husband and Protestant wife had no difficulties, the percentages in each of the categories showing some degree of difficulty were greater than in the marriages representing only one religion.

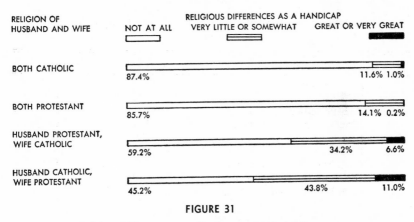

RELIGION OF
HUSBAND AND WIFE

RELIGIOUS DIFFERENCES AS A HANDICAP

NOT AT ALL   VERY LITTLE OR SOMEWHAT   GREAT OR VERY GREAT

BOTH CATHOLIC
87.4%   11.6% 1.0%

BOTH PROTESTANT
85.7%   14.1% 0.2%

HUSBAND PROTESTANT,
WIFE CATHOLIC
59.2%   34.2%   6.6%

HUSBAND CATHOLIC,
WIFE PROTESTANT
45.2%   43.8%   11.0%

FIGURE 31

Religious Differences as a Handicap to Marital Adjustment

When husband and wife are affiliated with the same faith, differences over religious matters are rarely a problem.   (Source: Judson T. Landis, "Marriages of Mixed and Non-Mixed Religious Faith," *American Sociological Review*, 14 [1949], 405.)

Equally striking is the difference in divorce and separation rates according to mixed and unmixed marriages, although the study does not indicate the degree to which religious differences may have been a factor in the marital disintegration.   It may be that some who had withdrawn sufficiently from affiliation with their religious faith to marry someone of another faith also had given up traditional attitudes opposed to divorce and therefore found divorce a simple solution to marital conflicts of

[24] "Marriages of Mixed and Non-Mixed Religious Faith," *American Sociological Review*, 14 (1949), 401–407.

whatever origin.   Table 15 shows several different patterns.   Marriages
with husband and wife adhering to the same religion have the smallest
percentage of divorces, with the three religions standing in the order of
Catholic least, Jewish next, and Protestant most.   Marriages with a
Catholic wife and a Protestant husband had only slightly more divorces
than the intrareligious marriages.   Other marriages with mixtures of
various sorts or with neither spouse claiming any religion have much
higher rates.   In general, Landis' findings corroborate earlier studies that
show mixed marriages or nonreligious marriages to have two to six times
as many divorces and separations as intrareligious marriages.[25]

TABLE 15

Marriages of Mixed and Nonmixed Religious Faiths Ending in Divorce
or Separation *

Religious categories	Number	Per cent
Both Catholic	573	4.4
Both Jewish	96	5.2
Both Protestant	2,794	6.0
Mixed, Catholic-Protestant	192	14.1
Both none	39	17.9
Protestant changed to Catholic	56	10.7
Catholic changed to Protestant	57	10.6
Protestant husband, Catholic wife	90	6.7
Catholic husband, Protestant wife	102	20.6
Husband none, wife Catholic	41	9.8
Husband none, wife Protestant	84	19.0

* J. T. Landis, "Marriages of Mixed and Non-Mixed Religious Faith," *American
Sociological Review,* 14 (1949), 403.

Children

What of the children of mixed marriages?   Landis' study shows that
the children were reared in the mother's faith from two to three times as
often as in the father's faith, regardless of whether the mother was Catholic
or Protestant.   (Too few Jewish mixed marriages were found to make
possible a similar comparison for them.)   This finding is in line with
our general knowledge that the mother in the middle class takes more

[25] Earlier studies include H. Ashley Weeks, "Differential Divorce Rates by Occupation," *Social Forces,* 21 (1943), 336, in which an analysis is made for 6,548
families of children in parochial and public schools in Spokane; and Howard M. Bell,
Youth Tell Their Story (American Council on Education, 1938), p. 21, based on
13,538 interviews in Maryland.

responsibility for rearing the children than does the father.   Regardless of agreements made before marriage, she wishes to rear her children in her own faith.   In some instances the parents solved the dilemma by acquainting the children with both faiths and permitting them to choose for themselves; in others some children attended the father's church and some the mother's; in only a small percentage of cases were the children reared without religious affiliation.   Children also sometimes fanned the flame of antagonism on the part of relatives who had reconciled themselves to the out-religious marriage of their sons or daughters but opposed the training of grandchildren in any except their own religious faith.   So potent a cause of quarrelling and tension is the question of the religious training of children that Landis concludes that in childless mixed marriages there would be small cause for conflict, but that the birth of a child revives old religious loyalties and pits husband against wife.[26]   In other families, and especially if one parent is more or less indifferent to religion, amicable agreements are reached as to the training of children.

ETHNIC ENDOGAMY

Ethnic endogamy is related to religion.   Each major religious group includes several ethnic groups.   Among ethnic groups represented in the United States, Catholics include Irish, Italian, Polish, French, and French-Canadian; Protestants include British, Scandinavian, and German; Jews include German, Russian, Spanish, and Portuguese.   In marriages there is a strong tendency toward endogamous ethnic marriages.   As the ethnics with continued residence in the United States lose some of their distinguishing characteristics (such as language, native clothing, and political ideals) and become more alike in culture, the tendency toward ethnic exogamy begins, but religious endogamy tends to continue.   For example, Irish tend to marry Irish, but among those Irish who marry outside the ethnic group the tendency is strong to marry into another Catholic ethnic group rather than into a Protestant ethnic group.

The first trend, toward ethnic intramarriage, is shown for New Haven in Table 16.   The decreasing percentages of endogamy from 1870 through 1900 to 1940 are due to increasing loss of divisive characteristics and increasing uniformity of culture among the once foreign-culture groups.   The Jews are included in this table, although they are not strictly

[26] Landis, *op. cit.,* pp. 403–405.

speaking an ethnic group in the same sense that the nationality groups
are; they are in reality a religious group originating from several national
backgrounds and with mixed religious-ethnic characteristics.   In the
purely ethnic groups, the Italians have shown the greatest persistence of
endogamy, whereas Germans and Scandinavians marry more often outside
the ethnic group than within it.   The Italian trend may be related to the
recency of arrival of the Italian group and its relatively low social prestige

TABLE 16

Intramarriage by National-Origin Groups, New Haven *

	1870	1900	1940
Jewish	100.0 %	98.92%	93.70%
Italian	— **	97.71	81.89
British-American	92.31	72.00	54.56
Irish	93.05	74.75	45.06
Polish	— **	100.00	52.78
German	86.67	55.26	27.19
Scandinavian	40.00	82.76	18.46
ALL NATIONALITIES	91.20	75.93	63.64

* Ruby Jo Kennedy, "Single or Triple Melting-Pot?   Intermarriage Trends in
New Haven, 1870–1940," *American Journal of Sociology*, 49 (1944), 333.
** In 1870 almost no Italians or Poles resided in New Haven.

as compared with ethnic groups that have become better adjusted to
American life.   Germans and Scandinavians have a longer history in
New Haven and are less clearly marked as an ethnic group.   In earlier
sections of this book the pressure toward ethnic endogamy in groups not
represented in New Haven has been discussed—for example, among the
Norwegians and the Finns.

Although religious endogamy tends to preserve certain family ideals
and institutional associations in exogamous ethnic marriages, other issues
may arise based on differences in culture.   These may concern such simple things as food habits and manners or vital ideals and relationships, such
as the relative status of husband and wife, ideals of educational level for
children, and moral standards.

TREND TOWARD STABILITY

Each of the measures of social mobility and transition shows a fairly
high degree of mobility, but they also show that stability is more common

than mobility.   From the point of view of the family the significant fact seems to be that our ideals and patterns of training the young tend primarily to maintain stability of individual and family placement.   Only among some socially ambitious families do we find definite attempts to train children for entrance into a higher social class, through family training and provision for education beyond that of their parents.   The desire of families, ethnic groups, and religious organizations is to perpetuate themselves in essentially the patterns of the past or at least of the present. Change is deplored, and eyes are closed to the fact that a high proportion of children will move away from the family pattern in some respect, either through entering a different occupational and social-class level or by intermarriage into another racial, ethnic, or religious group.   The young people who make the change often have little preparation for it, and when, as in intermarriage, each comes from a distinctive background of culture that has been taught to him as right, the probability is high that tensions and conflict will occur, on the one hand with the parental group and on the other between husband and wife.

Nevertheless, not all social mobility and transition end in disaster to the personality or to marriage.   The probability is increased, but in most instances adjustment is achieved.   The successful cases are the ones in which the change helps the person to fulfill his needs.   Upward social mobility gives prestige and certain types of security; marriage between the ethnic and American may aid the ethnic to learn and accept the American culture.

QUESTIONS

1. Our present philosophy of mate selection gives complete freedom to the individual to select his mate.   How can this philosophy be reconciled with laws forbidding interracial marriages?

2. Why are there so few interracial marriages in states that do not have prohibitive laws?

3. What special adjustment problems confront the children of interracial marriages?

4. From observation or investigation discuss the marital adjustment of white veterans who have married nonwhites abroad.

5. Compare the policies of Protestants, Jews, and Catholics with reference to interreligious marriages.   Is the member of the out-group rejected or accepted?   What is the status of children of the mixed marriage?

6. How could the handicaps of interreligious marriages be reduced?

7. How is ethnic endogamy related to religion?

BIBLIOGRAPHY

Theoretical concepts related to intermarriage

Marcson, S., "A Theory of Intermarriage and Assimilation," *Social Forces,* 29 (1950), 75–78.
Merton, R. K., "Intermarriage and the Social Structure," *Psychiatry,* 4 (1941), 371–374.
Stonequist, Everett V., *The Marginal Man* (Scribner's, 1931).

Interracial marriage

Adams, Romanzo, *Interracial Marriage in Hawaii* (Macmillan, 1937).
Drake, St. Clair, and Cayton, H. R., *Black Metropolis* (Harcourt, Brace, 1945), chapter 7.
Karpf, M. J., "Marriage Counseling and Psychotherapy: A Case," *Marriage and Family Living,* 13 (1951), 169–178.
Klineberg, Otto, editor, *Characteristics of the American Negro* (Harper, 1944), Part V.

Interreligious marriage

Barron, M. L., "The Incidence of Jewish Intermarriage in Europe and America," *American Sociological Review,* 11 (1946), 6–13.
———, *People who Intermarry* (Syracuse University Press, 1946).
Karpf, M. J., "Premarital Counseling and Psychotherapy: Two Cases," *Marriage and Family Living,* 14 (1952), 56–75.
Landis, J. T., "Marriages of Mixed and Non-Mixed Religious Faiths," *American Sociological Review,* 14 (1949), 401–415.
Slotkin, J. S., "Jewish-Gentile Intermarriage in Chicago," *American Sociological Review,* 7 (1942), 34–39.
———, "Social Factors in Amalgamation; Based on a Study of Jewish-Gentile Intermarriage in Chicago," *Sociology and Social Research,* 26 (1942), 346–351.
Thomas, J. L., "The Factor of Religion in the Selection of Marriage Mates," *American Sociological Review,* 16 (1951), 487–491.

Interethnic marriage

Hollingshead, A. B., "Cultural Factors in the Selection of Marriage Mates," *American Sociological Review,* 15 (1950), 619–627.
Kennedy, R. J. R., "Premarital Residential Propinquity and Ethnic Endogamy," *American Journal of Sociology,* 48 (1943), 580–584.
———, "Single or Triple Melting Pot? Intermarriage Trends in New Haven, 1870–1940," *American Journal of Sociology,* 49 (1944), 331–339.

PART THREE

The Cycle of Family Life

The Adolescent Personality

Legally, marriage begins with the wedding ceremony. It is preceded, however, by many years of preparation, including personality growth from infancy on and, during adolescence, more specific adjustments between boys and girls and the development of adult roles. Also, the reading of the marriage service does not guarantee that the couple will "live happily ever after." The wedding simply marks an important step in a process that begins in infancy and ends with death. In order to place each stage of the process in proper relationship to other stages, the entire cycle of family life is briefly reviewed.

THE CYCLE OF FAMILY LIFE

The family-life cycle can be separated into seven stages, the first three of which are premarital. It has been said that preparation for marriage begins at birth—a statement that recognizes the early origin of personality development and the importance of personal interaction in our present-day individualistic marriages. Attitudes and habits related to sex, as well as conceptions of marital and parental roles, begin to form in childhood. The first stage in the family cycle therefore is the one of close child-parent relationships.

This childhood development receives more specific significance for marriage at adolescence when, in our culture, three forces merge into one stream of personal experience for the boy or girl: biological maturity, acceptance of masculinity or femininity, and establishment of social heterosexual relationships. The span of years between the ages of approximately 13 and 20 forms the second period in the cycle.

Casual dating is followed by exclusive pair dating and engagement, which constitute a short, intensively emotional stage—the third. Engagement ends with marriage, which occurs on the average at age 24 for men and 21 for women.[1]

The early period of married life—stage four—is recognized by referring to the new wife as a bride during the entire first year of marriage and by smilingly calling the first year the honeymoon, although the actual honeymoon may have lasted only a few days or weeks. This early period of adjustment to marriage ends for the typical pair about a year after marriage when the first child is born.

The fifth stage covers the expansion of the family to include children. The average family has three children, spaced two years apart. Thus the honeymoon is followed by a period of intensive childbearing and adjustment to the roles of parenthood. This phase of married life typically finds the husband between the ages of 25 and 30 and the wife between 22 and 27. It overlaps and merges into the child-dependency period, highlighted first by the personality development of the little child and later by the releasing of the child from the family to enter adulthood. At this time there begins for a new generation the early training for family life already classified as stage one for the parents. The period definitely ends when the last child marries and leaves home, the parents then being in their early fifties.

After children attain independence, husband and wife are again alone for a quieter period (stage six) of lessened responsibility lasting for some eleven years, at which time in the average family either husband or wife dies. The median age at which wives are widowed is 61, that at which husbands become widowers, 64.

The seventh and last stage is old age, significant not because of the added years but because of changes in family life. Widows and widowers increase in proportion to married people; income declines; and the leisure of retirement replaces employment. The family ends with the death of the surviving spouse, which occurs in the median case at age 70 for the husband or 74 for the wife.

The family cycle is significant in that with each stage changes occur in the family membership and consequently in family organization, roles,

[1] *The American Family, A Factual Background,* prepared by an interagency committee of the federal government for the National Conference on Family Life, May, 1948 (Government Printing Office, 1949), p. 32; all medians and averages are from this source, pp. 32–33.

and interpersonal relationships. Income increases and then decreases; the employment of wives and mothers follows its own cycle, related in the case of mothers to the age of the children; contacts with relatives change, inasmuch as elderly and widowed grandparents often live with their middle-aged married children.

The medians give the average pattern. A finer analysis by social classes would show variations: Lower-class youth marry earlier and have more children; the upper class later and have fewer children. Childless families do not fit the pattern in all respects. In a minority of families divorce rather than death breaks the marital union and may be followed by another marriage that starts the cycle over again with different ages for marriage, the births of children, and the departure of children from home.

EARLY PERSONALITY DEVELOPMENT

The early experiences of the child, especially in his relation to his parents, set fundamental attitudes and habits that, years later, affect his adjustment in dating, courtship, marriage, and parenthood. The brief review of personality development given in this chapter is limited to the relation of the early years to later premarital and marital adjustment.

Motivations

Personality is the composite of inborn drives and capacities as these are molded and expressed through social relationships and cultural conditioning. The original motivations for behavior are the inborn ones existent in the child at birth. Within a few hours, however, these motivations are being modified by the other two components of personality— social relationships and cultural conditioning. The social relationships comprise all interaction between the infant and his nurse, mother, father, and other human beings who stimulate him in some way. The manner of their behavior to him, whether gentle or harsh, begins to affect his responses and to set attitudes and patterns of behavior. Cultural conditioning is found in the impress of societal customs upon the baby. The type of clothing, bed, food, and manner of handling and carrying the child are examples of the cultural element.[2]

[2] Comprehensive discussions of child development and personality are contained in the following: R. G. Barker, J. S. Kounin, and H. F. Wright, editors, *Child Behavior and Development* (McGraw-Hill, 1943); W. A. Davis and R. J. Havighurst,

The child's original motivations seem to be physical: the needs for food and liquid; rest and sleep; freedom from pain, cold, and other discomfort; and elimination. Soon, however, other motivations arise; as the child grows, he demands social responses as well as physical ones: he wants to be loved and praised, to feel equal to or superior to his playmates, to have his own way, to dominate people, and to be protected and encouraged. Before long he has acquired persistent habits that set definite patterns for his life. His socially formed attitudes are expressed in likes and dislikes for specific people, types of food, games, toys, and the like. The personality consists of a complex but related web of physical, social, habitual, and attitudinal motivations.[3]

Motivations lead to behavior. We may say, therefore, that conduct is purposive; that is, a person acts in order to satisfy some motivation or need. The restless, milling person is one whose motivations are not clearly defined so that he does not know in what direction to proceed, or one who, having failed to find satisfactory outlets, restlessly seeks some new means of expression. The well-adjusted person proceeds more directly to satisfaction of needs, either through well-established habits or as a result of rational deliberation. The exact form of his satisfying activities depends upon the culture of his society and the impact of his family. The later discussion of adolescent behavior shows some of the undirected and deviant efforts of adolescents to satisfy needs when new biological capacities of sex and wider social fields are opened to them.

Conception of oneself

A part of personality that develops through social contacts is the many attitudes that the person has—the valuations given to people, objects, types of conduct, and especially to himself.

The person's conception of himself has two main aspects. First, he tends to place himself in a heirarchy of values. What the dominant values are will depend upon the culture of a person's society or, more specifically, of the groups within the society with which the person is affiliated. The high value may be given to honesty or to chicanery; sub-

---

Father of the Man (Houghton Mifflin, 1947); J. McV. Hunt, editor, *Personality and the Behavior Disorders* (Ronald, 1944), I, ch. 3, II, chs. 20, 21; Gardner Murphy, *Personality, A Biosocial Approach to Origins and Structure* (Harper, 1947); Percival M. Symonds, *The Dynamics of Human Adjustment* (D. Appleton–Century, 1946).

[3] A more complete discussion of love in the young child is included in Chapter 15, "Love and Marriage."

missiveness or aggressiveness; cooperativeness or competitiveness. Each person finds his place in the heirarchy by the way in which he is treated by those around him, and the initial and perhaps the most lasting evaluation comes from the family circle. The child, dependent for care of all kinds upon his parents and with his contacts limited to the family, is very responsive to their evaluation of him. For example, if he is treated as though he were obedient and hears himself described in that way, he will tend to think of himself as obedient and to carry this conception of himself out in action. If, later, he is described and treated in the same way at school and in other social situations, his conception of himself as obedient will be strengthened. So with reference to many other facets of the personality.

Since different groups may have different standards of value, the child may develop several conceptions of himself, each related to a different group. He may have the conception of obedient-boy-at-home and at the same time the conception of tough-boy-in-the-gang. Although some people carry such conflicting conceptions of themselves throughout life, never bringing their different conceptions into one integrated self, normally the integration of conceptions takes place during adolescence when the boy or girl, eagerly or under pressure, decides what some of his future roles are to be: how much education; what occupation; early or delayed marriage; and others. The fact that our complex society has many acceptable roles increases the difficulty of integration. The girl, especially, may be torn between desire for a career and an urge toward marriage and homemaking.

Ways of reacting to other people and social situations

Each person has a wide range of possible reactions to other people and to social situations. These mechanisms of reaction include use of intelligence, imagination, emotions, and physical movement. Which ones are used depends in part upon the quality of innate factors, such as physical make-up or degree of intelligence, and in part upon the social relationship that the person has had, as in the case of a physically weak boy who tends to be submissive because he has learned through painful experience that he cannot be successfully aggressive with stronger boys of his own age.

Social relationships have a dual effect upon the personality. First, if the situations are satisfying, the reactions are cooperative and pleasant;

if they are frustrating or painful, then aggressive, withdrawing, or rational reactions tend to occur. Second, the reactions, as aggressiveness, may elicit a new social response that causes the person either to inhibit or continue his reaction. For example, the child may be forced to give up monopoly of a swing; he may become angry and start fighting the other children or the parent; he may then be shut in a room by himself. The next time, he may reluctantly give up the swing but not fight. Instead he may turn to fantasy as a reaction and go through the motions of swinging while standing on the ground.

The reactions learned in childhood tend to become habitual and are carried over into the new social situations of adolescence.

Personality subject to changes

We have the assertion of some psychologists that basic personality patterns are set by the fourth or fifth year of life. Nevertheless, personality may be modified when social relationships change. If the child lived out his life in one social group, such changes would be minor, although they would still occur, because others in the group would change in age and physical condition, thus calling forth different reactions. When contacts with social groups change often, as in our society, the person may find that he must suppress certain traits and develop new ones in order to adapt himself to the new group.

Any given society also has different roles for different age levels, occupations, and social classes. As the person passes from one age level to another, as he enters an occupation, if—as may happen—he changes his social class, new roles and hence new conceptions of the self are demanded. If they are not accepted by the person, he becomes a misfit.

There are certain periods of life when social relationships and cultural roles tend to change. With reference to marital adjustment, adolescence is a period of critical change. Other changes occur at the times of marriage; the birth of a child, especially the first child; divorce; death; and departure of grown children from the home. At each such period of change the person has to modify his conception of himself, his role with relation to others, and often his customary modes of reaction.

THE PARENTS' RELATION TO PERSONALITY DEVELOPMENT

Three phases of the parent-child relationship

That dependence of the baby upon the parent is a necessity of physical survival has long been recognized. Such dependence is also at the basis of a secure child who gradually gains the self-reliance to become an independent personality as he comes into adolescence. Dependence therefore is not limited to provision of physical needs but also includes love from the parent. From this relationship the child develops a conception of himself as worthy of love, as approved, as meeting the standards of his little society. When he enters the larger society of the adolescent, he confidently expects approval.

Closely related to the child's dependence upon the parent is his identification with the parent. Seeking the love and approval of the parent, the child comes to admire the parent and to seek to be like him. Most obvious is the imitative play of the child—the little girl who keeps house with her dolls, the boy who wants a doctor's case if his father is a physician or a baseball bat if his father is an ardent sports fan. Less obvious but perhaps more important is the acceptance by the child of the parent's standard of right and wrong, methods of meeting problems, and attitudes toward hundreds of situations. In fact, the parent's personality is the model for the child's own personality. This identification with the parent is the basis for the child's conception of himself and of his role. In attitudinal form, it provides his personal ideals or conscience, and in behavior it gives him the patterns of conduct for certain roles that he will play in adult life. By the time adolescence is reached, the child should be well on his way to being able to accept responsibility for his own decisions and conduct.

The basis for the parent's love and approval is also important in preparing the child for independence. If the parent lavishes love and approval without merit on the part of the child, a weak personality will develop. The child will continue to be dependent upon someone who will protect and praise him without effort on his part to earn these rewards. But if the parent has given love and approval in relation to the child's attempts to control and modify his conduct to meet parental standards, then the child will not expect approval in the larger society unless he makes some effort to earn it. This transition from the unearned love given the helpless baby to love and approval based upon contributing to the happiness and welfare of others is necessary before the adolescent can free himself from dependence upon his parents.[4]

Thus the child ideally should come into adolescence after passing through three phases in his relation to his parents: an early dependence that has given him security and self-confidence with which to meet the larger world; identification with the parents that has provided him with generalized principles of conduct; and the acceptance of social and personal ideals as the basis for love and approval.

The parent of the opposite sex

The parent with whom the child has most closely identified himself may also affect his capacity to free himself. Usually, boys and girls make their earliest close identifications with the mother, who has the major care of both in the typical American family. If the mother's conception of her own self and role are harmonious with the demands of her society, she provides a clear model for her daughter. But she also presents the same feminine role to her son. The boy therefore needs another model, an adult male, typically the father, to provide the masculine self and role that complement the feminine self and role.[5]

In rural areas or in the working-class group where the son early begins to share in the father's work as an apprentice, the son's identification with the father is more easily accomplished than in the upper social classes in cities, where absence of the father from home for nine or ten hours a day and his absorption in complex professional work make identification

---

[4] For a discussion of effects of extreme maternal dominance or indulgence see David M. Levy, *Maternal Overprotection* (New York: Columbia University Press, 1943).

[5] The relation of the boy or girl to the parent of the opposite sex has engaged attention of psychologists and sociologists since Freud developed his theory of the Oedipus complex, which assumed that all children go through a stage of sexual attraction to the parent of the opposite sex. Objective studies fail to show a universal trend in this direction. Cultural patterns and personal relationships between parents and children are ample to account for the usual situation in the United States: most small children prefer the mother who is the one who takes care of them; some but not all studies show a slight preponderance of girls over boys who prefer the father, with the reverse relationship to the mother. Case studies show that some of these preferences are related to the parent's initial attitude toward the child and often his relation to the spouse. The unhappy wife may give unusual attention to her son; the father without a son may select one daughter as a son-substitute and lavish attention on her. There seems to be no universal pattern that automatically occurs. See L. M. Terman, "Psychological Sex Differences," in Leonard Carmichael, editor, *Manual of Child Psychology* (Wiley, 1946), p. 983; Meyer Nimkoff, "The Child's Preference for Father or Mother," *American Sociological Review,* 7 (1942), 517–525.

by the son difficult.   The son may then tend to identify with his mother, acquiring admirable personality traits perhaps, but ones not necessarily suited to the masculine role.   The fact that teachers, even in high school, often are female adds to the boy's difficulty.   The adolescent boy often is catapulted from adult feminine models into a peer society of adolescent boys without having made an adequate identification with any adult male.[6]

The girl less often has a similar problem; in some cases, however, the girl identifies herself with her father rather than her mother.   The mother for some reason may have rejected the girl; or the father may have encouraged her identification with him, as sometimes happens when the father who desired a son attempts to convert his daughter into one.

Although close identification with the parent of the opposite sex is a hindrance to the child as he matures, this parent has the important function of teaching the child the complement to his own role.

The father through his daily contacts with his daughter gives her an idea of how a man may be expected to treat her as a girl and woman.   The father who is too exclusively only a parent to his daughter fails to give her a standard by which to measure boys and men.   The father who admires his daughter's appearance, who shows her the small courtesies of opening a door or holding her coat, who respects her opinions, in short who treats her like a young woman as well as a daughter, gives her both a conception of herself as a woman and also a model against which to measure boys and men whom she meets.   Likewise, the mother provides for her son his first experience with a woman, and from her the son will learn what his own role is with reference to women and also what to expect of women.   The mother, therefore, who encourages her son to be attentive to her, to hold her coat and to give her a seat, is helping him to learn his role as a young man.   Her respect for his judgment and her willingness to help and encourage him in his hobbies will teach him what to expect of the girls and young women whom he meets.

[6] Certain writers have overemphasized the baleful effects of mother love when it has prevented the son from breaking his early attachment to his mother.   Edward A. Strecker in *Their Mother's Sons* (Lippincott, 1946) used the term "momism" to signify the relationship in which "Mom" dominated her adult son.   Geoffrey Gorer, an English anthropologist, abhors the American situation whereby the mother provides most of the moral training of both sons and daughters.   He says the adult male carries within him an "encapsulated mother," or conscience developed on feminine lines.   See *The American People, a Study in National Character* (1948), ch. 2.   For a more scientific study, see Levy, *op. cit.*

Difficulties of emancipation from the parent

After the loving, dependent childhood, the adolescent in our society is expected to free himself from his dependence upon his parents.   The way is often made difficult for him.

The small number of children and the separation of the small family from the kinship group concentrate all close emotional ties within a very small number of people.   The child's dependency needs are met almost exclusively by the mother.   The one or two brothers or sisters are too near the child's own age to serve him; in fact, they may be competitors for the mother's attention.   The father is not in the home and grandparents live at a distance.   The mother-child ties therefore become intense.

Parents and child may be reluctant to break their mutually satisfying emotional relationship.   Parents may cherish the identification of the child and indeed may identify themselves with the child, responding as intensely as the child to every joy and sorrow.   Parents receive many satisfactions: pride if the child is clever or mannerly or handsome; compensation for early deprivations if the parents are able to give the child privileges that they did not have at an early age; love and affection. Parents may see nothing with which to replace the satisfactions, especially if the child is the only one in the family, the last child, or the only child of the parent's own sex.

The child, on his part, may wish with part of his personality to become more independent but at the same time feel insecure and inadequate in the face of the new demands made upon him by other adolescents and adults alike.   In a contest between parental standards and those of his own age-sex group, the parents' standards are followed, even though they may be less appropriate to the situation than those of the adolescent group or may involve alienation from the peer group.   The parents continue to be the chief source of love and approval.

The adolescent who has been unable to free himself from his parents faces two difficulties.   First, he may continue to conceive of himself as a child and therefore be unable to make satisfactory relationships with members of the opposite sex.   This is especially true if the adolescent is dependent upon the parent of his own sex.   Second, other dependent adolescents seek friends of the opposite sex but only those who remind them of the parent with whom they remain identified.   Thus, the boy who is closely attached to his mother may enjoy dating only girls who in some way resemble her; girls who still idealize the father may look for a minor image of the father in every boy.   Parents sometimes are flattered by this tendency or are made to feel secure in their child's choice of friends since in the friends they recognize some of their own qualities. They overlook the fact that the entire relationship may be colored by an effort on the part of the son or daughter to play a dependent-child role to the girl friend or boy friend rather than the masculine or feminine role of equality.

The process of emancipation

As has been stated, in the process of identification the child comes in time to internalize the precepts of his parents and to have a set of abstract principles to guide his behavior.   These principles have been formed, however, in a particular milieu, that of the parental family and immediate neighborhood of the child.   As the adolescent's milieu widens with en- trance into high school, these principles must be tested against the stan- dards of new groups.   The adolescent usually has not acquired a suffi- ciently firm set to his personality to be able to discard his identification and dependence upon personal approval.   Therefore he tends to seek new models, either to replace the parents or to supplement them.

Ideally, the transition is not accomplished by breaking the ties with the parent and then finding new ties, but by a gradual replacement of parental identification with other types.   The parent may be replaced by a teacher or adult friend, who for a time may be openly imitated by the adolescent in manner and dress and invited to share his problems and exultations.   Or the adolescent may retain his allegiance to the parent in some respects but emulate new traits in other models.   Another variant is identification not with an adult but with some friend or small group of the same age and sex, which usually is a step toward adulthood in that the age-sex group is the one in which the adolescent must eventually form his closest attachments.   So long, however, as the adolescent feels that he must attach himself to specific persons who form his models and from whom he receives approval, he has not achieved full independence.

If the parent-child identification has been too complete, the adolescent may be unable to free himself gradually.   In that case he may wrench himself free with a violent show of rebellion.   His attitude toward his parents may be one of marked hostility with rejection of their every suggestion or wish.   Or he may vacillate between rebellion and dependence. The rebellious boy or girl usually has no substitute models for the parents and has not achieved independent principles.   Therefore he flounders, confused and insecure, following first this chance group and then that, and often feeling guilty over violations of his parents' standards.   Therefore, from time to time, when insecurity or guilt overcome him, he returns to the status of dependent child seeking protection from the parents or from parent-substitutes.

Importance of parent-child identification

Identification with the parents as well as the achievement of freedom from that identification during adolescence are important in preparation for marriage.   Since the parents do offer the basic models, the roles that the parents fill as husband and wife and as father and mother are extremely important in determining the conception that sons or daughters will have of their future roles.   The most advantageous situation exists when the parents are consonant with the social situations that the child faces; then the modifications that the adolescent inevitably must make will not destroy the basic conceptions gained from the parents.   Parents who are elderly and therefore far removed from their own adolescence, or who were reared under different social conditions, often present to their children models that cannot be fitted into the current social situation.   Similar difficulty besets the parents in a socially mobile family, whose conceptions of family roles, learned in their childhood in a different social class, are not suitable for their children.   Parents of foreign culture or rural origin in urban settings also are handicapped in setting models for their children.[7]   The prevalence of this situation has led one writer to assert that all Americans are "third generation" and hence unable to find in their foreign-culture (or rural or lower-class) parents a clear model for their own adult behavior.[8]

In one important phase of adolescent life, almost all parents are unable to supply their children with a suitable pattern of conduct.   Adolescents invariably see their parents only as parents and mature married people. The parents, long past their own dating and courtship experience, cannot provide their children with an adequate model for dating and courtship. In fact, so firmly fixed in the adolescent's mind is the picture of the father

[7] See Chapters 9 and 10 on difficulties in ethnic and social-class mobility.
[8] Margaret Mead, *And Keep Your Powder Dry* (Morrow, 1942), p. 37.

and mother as settled middle-aged parents that he often cannot conceive of his parents as having moments of passion or as enjoying a movie hand in hand; much less can he visualize his parents as young and in love.   If the parents insist that they too have lived through the emotional ups and downs of dating and courtship and understand the problems of that period, the children are incredulous and believe that times have changed, even that human nature has changed.   Nevertheless, present-day parents were the "lost youth" of the 1920's or the early depression days who cast aside many of the restraining mores of an earlier generation.   Because of the inability of parents to provide a model for dating and courtship, adolescents necessarily turn to those of their own age or recently married youths for their models.

Sex education

The great importance of early sex education, preferably given by parents, is agreed upon by educators, psychologists, and sociologists.   Children secure sex information of some type at an early age, usually before parents regard sex as a suitable subject for discussion with their children. A study of middle-class boys in a city of 100,000 showed that 14 per cent had gained some sex information before the age of 6 and by age 11, 68 per cent had their initial information.   The origin of babies was usually the first information, followed by knowledge of masturbation (14 per cent by age 7) and intercourse (17 per cent by age 7).   Table 17 shows the percentage of boys who by age 11 had some information on sex-related subjects.   Knowledge was often rudimentary and not carried over into experimentation or practice.[9]

As sources of sex information, parents show up very poorly in the study.   Sixty per cent of the mothers and 82 per cent of the fathers had given no sex information to their sons.   Other studies confirm the failure of parents in this important area of education: in five studies made during the 1920's and 1930's from 40 to 50 per cent of parents provided no information.[10]   Parents were very lax about teaching their children about

[9] G. V. Ramsey, "The Sex Information of Younger Boys," *American Journal of Orthopsychiatry,* 13 (1943), 348.   The study is based on information from 291 boys between the ages of 10 and 20 of whom 85 per cent were aged 12–16, and all but 5 of whom were white.

[10] W. Hughes, "Sex Experiences of Boyhood," *Social Hygiene,* 12 (1926), 262–273; G. V. Hamilton, *A Research in Marriage* (A. and C. Boni, 1929); D. D. Bromley and F. H. Britten, *Youth and Sex* (Harper, 1938); O. M. Butterfield, *Love Problems of Adolescence* (Emerson Books, 1939).

anything except the origin of babies and menstruation.   Male companions, however, readily passed on to younger or less well-informed boys
what they knew about contraceptives, intercourse, and prostitution.
Other adults than the parents, schools, movies, and radio were of almost
no help to the curious boy.

The inadequacy of sex education is attested to by the curiosity and ig-
norence that continue into young adulthood.   A traveling lecture team
on "Sex: Fallacies, Facts, and Problems," which visited the occupation
forces in Europe, secured 1,127 questions from 20,000 troops (about

TABLE 17

Boys Who by Age 11 Had Stated Types of Sex Information *

Type of information	Per cent of boys
Origin of babies	85
Intercourse	80
Masturbation	63
Prostitution	43
Contraceptives	35
Ejaculation	34
Nocturnal emission	24
Menstruation	14
Venereal disease	10

* G. V. Ramsey, "The Sex Information of Younger Boys," *American Journal of
Orthopsychiatry,* 13 (1943), 348.

one question for every 20 men) that revealed great ignorance and many
unsound folk beliefs.[11]   A similar situation exists among young women.
The director of a mental hygiene clinic in discussions with senior nursing
students collected 1,908 questions, 31 per cent of which related directly
to sexual topics.[12]

Parents are often handicapped in giving sex education by their own
inadequate knowledge and personal inhibitions.   The unauthoritative
sources of information listed by boys show also that parents do not arrange
for their sons to receive education in a field in which they feel unprepared.

An important advantage of parental sex education is the relationship

[11] Fred Brown, "What American Men Want to Know about Sex," *Journal of
Social Psychology,* 27 (1948), 119–125.   A book containing the questions and
answers to them has been published: Fred Brown and Rudolf T. Kempton, *Sex
Questions and Answers, A Guide to Happy Marriage* (McGraw-Hill, 1950).
[12] Albert Ellis and Earl W. Fuller, "The Sex, Love, and Marriage Questions of
Senior Nursing Students," *Journal of Social Psychology,* 31 (1950), 209–216.

of confidence that is set up between the parent who gives information in a straightforward and sympathetic manner and the child who receives it.   Refusals and evasions give the child a feeling of rejection.   If the child has secured his first information from other and secret sources he may feel guilty, especially if the parent has made him feel that sex is a subject about which he should remain ignorant.   In either case the child is thereafter reluctant to ask questions of the parent.   Identification of parent and child in an important area of experience has failed to occur. If this confidential contact is not established when the child is young, it is almost impossible to establish later.   Once developed, however, it may be continued as long as the adolescent feels the need for adult guidance.

When sex information comes from other children or salacious literature, the emphasis usually is on the physical aspects alone.   In contrast, parents who function in this area tend to place sex in a setting of marriage and family life where it is coordinated with other activities, love relationships, and mutual responsibilities.

The failure of fathers to enlighten their sons leads to a hazardous situation.   Mothers who attempt to give their sons information speak from ignorance of the actual situations in which their sons will be placed when other and perhaps older boys confront them with sex information or practices in their crudest forms.   The fathers, having been through similar experiences as boys, could help their sons but are prevented by feelings of guilt or embarrassment.

THE ADOLESCENT PERSONALITY

At the beginning of adolescence, the personality is simply that of the child confronted by new situations.   We are able to speak of an adolescent personality primarily because in our culture the adolescent typically is faced with fairly uniform new situations and new cultural demands to which he must adjust without adequate preparation or support from adult groups.   The physical changes that occur at puberty also have an effect, but their effect is partly due to the way in which the changes are defined by the culture.   The degree of success that the adolescent has in meeting his adolescent situations helps to determine his adult personality and also his adult marital and family adjustment.

Physical changes

Obvious physical changes make it impossible for the adolescent to take his body for granted as does the child and adult. The appearance of hair on various parts of the body arouses anxiety if the adolescent is shrinking from maturity, or pride as a symbol of maturity; in either case, it almost certainly brings self-consciousness. Rapid growth in unequal rates for different parts of the body causes the awkward and clumsy adolescent to stumble over chairs and upset cups and tumblers. The actual physical awareness by the child is emphasized by the reaction of family and friends to the changes. Outgrown clothes become the occasion for comment and perhaps argument in the family. Kindly friends of the parents comment on how much the adolescent has grown since last seen. Mothers become concerned if puberty comes too early—or too late. Friends ridicule in envy the boy or girl who matures earliest, and condole with the ones who lag in the race toward maturity. Thus the adolescent is made conscious of his physical condition both by his inner awareness of change and by the reactions of other people.

Physical defects assume a new meaning. Some unusual facial formation, extreme but not abnormal height, or smallness of size creates a bitter problem. Very minor and sometimes temporary defects, such as birthmarks, moles, uneven teeth, or acne, are only less worrisome to the adolescent. Especially difficult for the adolescent to accept are features that cause a boy to appear feminine (curly hair or lack of a beard) or a girl to seem masculine (muscular physique or a deep voice). These defects not only affect the social acceptability of the adolescent but help to shape his personality and perhaps contribute to traits incompatible with later marital happiness.

The age of sexual maturity is important. For instance, the girl who experiences the menarche at the age of 10 may become extremely self-conscious and feel herself set apart in some discriminatory way from other girls of her age. Failure to develop secondary sex characteristics at the proper time—the girl's flat chest, the boy's treble voice—may cause extreme self-consciousness and anxiety.[13]

These physical features affect the adolescent in several ways, related to marital adjustments.

[13] "Physical and Physiological Changes in Adolescence," *The 43rd Yearbook of the National Society for the Study of Education,* Part I, "Adolescence" (University of Chicago Press, 1944), sec. 1.

1. Social participation. Although activities for adolescents are varied, certain ones are highly valued. Athletics for boys are of extreme value, not only for the boy's standing among boys but for the girl's evaluation of the boy. The girl who dates the football or basketball star, the fastest man in track, or the swimming champion has the envy of her girl friends. And almost any boy who makes the varsity team has higher status than the boy who tries out and fails, unless the latter achieves in another field. Although girls may gain status among girls through athletic ability, their standing is not so important to boys, perhaps because it is not customary for girls to play in public or before a mixed school group of spectators. The girl desires ability to dance; engage in mixed outdoor activities, such as hiking, picnics, and swimming; and participate in club and social activities.

Any physical condition that prevents social participation is a serious handicap in that it shuts off the normal contacts with those of the other sex.

2. Meeting ideal conceptions of group or self. Young people carry in their minds an idealized conception of the marriageable person of the opposite sex.[14] Although this conception is not limited to physical traits, it includes identity or similarity of race, good health, freedom from physical defect, and attractive appearance. In a study of 200 women and 173 men, all of whom were either engaged or recently married, 49.7 per cent of the men and 65.5 per cent of the women would not marry someone of another race; 27.2 per cent of the men and 26.5 per cent of the women would not marry anyone with a physical defect; and 22.0 per cent of the men and 13.5 per cent of the women would not marry a person who was not handsome or good-looking.[15] Nor are such ideals idle imaginings of adolescence, for 59.2 per cent of the young people believed that their chosen mates met the physical requirements of the ideal. (Personality traits, however, were more important than physical traits in selection of a mate.) In addition to these generalizations, specific groups of young people may have their own definitions of the desirable physical type of girl or boy and of the ideal wife or husband. Girls who fail to meet the specifications of boys are not sought for dates; boys who fall below the requirements of the girls are not accepted for dates.

[14] W. G. Mather, "The Courtship Ideals of High-School Youth," *Sociology and Social Research,* 19 (1934–35), 169.

[15] Anselm Strauss, "The Ideal and the Chosen Mate," *American Journal of Sociology,* 52 (1946), 204–208.

3. Effects on personality.   More important than the lack of social contacts occasioned by physical shortcomings is the effect of such defects upon the personality.   The boy who cannot meet the ideal physical standard of masculine attractiveness or the girl who fails to approximate the feminine ideal often develops a feeling of inadequacy and tends to withdraw from social contacts.   Withdrawal tends further to decrease social contacts.   The young person attributes his isolation solely to the physical shortcoming, failing to see that much of the difficulty may arise from his own self-attitude.   Thus he may come into maturity and the period for marriage with inadequate social experience and with a conception of himself as unattractive to the opposite sex.   His expectation of marriage is affected, as well as his standard for a mate, since he may be willing to lower his standard in the belief that he cannot otherwise secure a mate.

The rate of growth also has sociological and psychological effects. The boy or girl who grows to full adult size in the early teens may be expected by those who do not know his true age to conduct himself as an older adolescent.   The tall young girl may be sought for dates by mature young men, at a time when she is not prepared either by knowledge or acceptance of the adult feminine role to control the social interaction of dating on an adult level.   Both flattered and frightened, she may easily fall into a pattern of dating and sexual behavior that is unrelated to her little-girl personality.   Among her own age-group such a girl may feel awkward and conspicuous.   The tall boy faces somewhat similar problems.   The small girl, who finds herself still resembling a junior high school girl when in the last year of high school, may continue to play a childish role, seeking indulgence and protection from her larger companions.   The undersized boy, on the other hand, often hesitates to approach girls for dates for fear they will laugh at him or summarily refuse his request.

These peculiarities also have more lasting effects.   The boy or girl who does not date during adolescence comes into young adulthood without the normal experience of adjusting to varied personalities, of verbal fencing, or sorting out the "line" from the frank expressions of friendship. He then either goes through a delayed period of dating or enters marriage without the dating experience that has come to be an expected part of the marital process in the United States.   Also, the conception of personality built up during adolescence carries on into the more mature years.   The little girl, the athletic girl, or the prematurely tall sophisticated girl continues into adulthood to act childish, athletic, or sophisticated, even though growth and circumstances indicate the greater appropriateness of other roles.

Sexual development

Although it is now known that sexual drives are operative to some extent from early childhood, perhaps from infancy, the actual maturing of the sex organs and our cultural definition of sex make this drive one of the special problems of adolescence.

Early childhood manifestations of sex are physical in nature and are related to the little child's general interest in pleasant physical sensations and curiosity about his body. Sucking, being cuddled or patted, and playing with toes or fingers are examples of this hedonistic interest and curiosity just as much as is the more obviously sexual manipulation of the sex organs and inspection of the sex organs of children of the opposite sex. These tendencies of the young child seem to be as natural and untaught as the tendency to eat, play with toys, or explore. The reaction of adults to interest in or curiosity about the sex organs is entirely different, however, from their reaction to other pleasure-seeking or curiosity-satisfying activities. The child is placed in a sleeping position that makes touching the sex organs difficult or impossible; a hand that strays toward the sex organs in the daytime is pulled away with a scolding or a slap; clothing is designed to prevent a view of sex organs; at an early age most children are prevented from bathing, toileting, or undressing before those of the opposite sex, even siblings.[16] The good child, who meets the mother's approval, is the sexless child. The child therefore learns habits that prevent sexual exploration, and he learns to repress much of his curiosity about sex. When his questions are answered, he recognizes a reluctance or self-consciousness on the part of his parents. Rarely do parents voluntarily give information on sex, although they instruct the child on other subjects whether or not he is interested in receiving the

---

[16] The protection of sex organs is especially dominant in the American middle class, whereas some ethnic groups follow other practices. For example, in the souna or bath house, all members of Finnish families bathe together. In some Mexican families children up to the age of five play around the house in the nude. American lower-class little girls in the warmer parts of the United States may not wear underclothing; their bodies are freely exposed when they play. Lower-class children and often adults in large cities freely urinate in alleys or at the curb of streets without causing comment.

information.   The entire attitude and habit training with reference to sex tends to be repressive and to assume that the child has no sexual impulses or needs.   His need for physical pleasure is diverted into other channels, and his need for love is satisfied through nonsexual contacts.   His curiosity is met with evasive or partial answers.

Many studies show, however, that children are not the sexless creatures that their parents assume.   Children who are restrained at home because of disapproval of the parents exhibit considerable curiosity in a more permissive situation.   Writing of a school that provided a free environment, Augusta Alpert says that the six-year-olds exhibited more curiosity about sex than the preschool age, evidenced by questions about body structure and mating and attempts at mutual exploration of each other's bodies.[17] By the age of seven home repressions were beginning to affect their behavior, even in a free environment, and curiosity was expressed more secretively.   Bodily explorations, peeping, obscene language, smutty jokes, lifting of girls' dresses by the boys, and some masturbation carried the children to puberty, when interest centered on the opposite sex in a more personal and social manner.

Kinsey, in his mammoth report on sexual activities of males, states that 57 per cent of older boys and adults recall some sort of preadolescent sex play, while 70 per cent of preadolescent boys admitted such play.[18] Sex play includes kissing and caressing but not intercourse.   The sex play, which might be limited to a single experience, usually occurred between the ages of 8 and 13 and was with a companion of the boy's own age or a girl slightly older who served as teacher.   With the advent of adolescence about half of the boys gave up sex play, whereas the other half continued it until complete sex relations replaced it.

Although Kinsey states that sex play and, later, intercourse were more frequently practiced by lower-class than middle-class boys, an intensive study of 291 middle-class boys in a city of 100,000 shows that 66 per cent had experienced some sort of sexual play with girls before the age of 13 and half had attempted intercourse.[19]   In most cases the partner

---

[17] "The Latency Period," *American Journal of Orthopsychiatry*, 11 (1941), 126–133.   Alpert's conclusion was that there is no latency period, or period between age five and puberty, when organic and functional sex development is arrested. Seeming latency is due to adult disapproval that drives sex interests into hidden channels.

[18] A. C. Kinsey, W. B. Pomeroy, and C. E. Martin, *Sexual Behavior in the Human Male* (Saunders, 1948), pp. 165–166.

[19] G. V. Ramsey, "The Sexual Development of Boys," *American Journal of Psychology*, 56 (1943), 217–234.

was a neighborhood girl whose age was within a year of that of the boy. Eighty-five per cent of this same group of boys either practiced masturbation at age 13 or at some time in the past had practiced it. Sex interest may be assumed to be universal in boys.

Although the Kinsey and Ramsey studies report on males, the fact that the companions of boys usually are girls near their own age shows that sexual interests are not confined to boys. The sex play is in most cases sporadic rather than habitual, and secretive in order to avoid punishment.

With the advent of puberty, sex can no longer be ignored. It is thrust into the life of the child, not as a matter of curiosity or fumbling secretive sex play, but with the potentiality of intercourse and possibility of pregnancy for the girl. It must be controlled and integrated into the heterosexual social life expected of American adolescents.[20]

HETEROSEXUAL ADJUSTMENT

Superficially, heterosexual adjustment refers to the social adjustment between teen-aged boys and girls—joint participation in organizations and informal social affairs and the development of boy-girl etiquette. Basically, however, heterosexual adjustment involves the acceptance by each adolescent of his own sex-role and adjustment to the sex-role of the opposite sex.

Preadolescent differentiation of sexes

Prior to adolescence, differentiation of boys and girls is made within the family. Boys are more often encouraged to disregard minor injuries than are girls, to be more venturesome and unafraid, and to compete with other boys by earning money or in sports. Roughness and crudities are overlooked as the prerogatives or natural tendencies of the "real boy." Girls are encouraged to remain more closely under parental supervision and hence to retain dependence longer; they are praised for having nice manners and scolded for roughness that would merely bring an indulgent smile if performed by their brothers. Fathers may take their young sons fishing or hunting; mothers take their daughters to teas and on shopping expeditions for clothing or household supplies. Thus, early in life boys

[20] See Chapter 14 for a discussion of premarital sex relations.

and girls are given a realization of expected differences in masculine and feminine ideals and conduct—or conceptions of the self and role.

Nevertheless, barriers are erected by adults and accepted by children that hinder early development of the adult masculine and feminine conception of the self, especially in the middle and upper classes. The father and mother have a separate and private life into which children are not admitted. Not only sex but the more intimate forms of caressing are hidden from the children, who see their parents as rather unemotional and settled adults, unmoved by sexual or social stimulation from the opposite sex. In other ways, too, children are shielded from full observation of or participation in adult roles. Serious family problems of finance, change of the father's occupation, change of residence, and so forth often are settled by the father and mother and the final result announced to the children. Children are expected to be children, untroubled by adult problems. Lower-class children, living under more crowded conditions that prevent great privacy, often have from infancy on knowledge of many phases of adult life, sexual as well as family crises.

Children are also prevented from making preliminary adjustment to those of the other sex. Although the separation of the sexes is not so complete as formerly, in many ways children's activities are deliberately organized on a one-sex basis. Parochial and some public schools, Scouts, Sunday school classes, children's parties, and physical education classes in coeducational schools tend to cater to boys or girls but not to both. Adult leaders of these activities give several reasons for the separation, chiefly that the needs of boys and girls differ and separation makes possible specialization and that discipline is easier in the one-sex group. The first reason emphasizes a tendency to prepare the boys and girls for masculine or feminine roles; the second implicitly recognizes an early interest between the sexes, which is met by avoidance or repression rather than by acceptance and guidance.

As a result of this situation, children tend to build their closest associations with those of their own sex. The repressed natural interest in the other sex is expressed through antagonism and hostility as well as through the occasional sex play already described. Boys chase girls home from school, throw snowballs at them, and otherwise express their interest and hostility. Girls scream and call names, run from the boys, or maintain a scornful silence. Boys linger on the edge of the back-yard play group of girls, while the girls giggle and whisper secrets. Each sex believes strongly in its own superiority and devalues the opposite sex.

Within their own groups, both boys and girls may express initiative, leadership, and acceptable aggressive activities through competition—personality traits that are considered masculine in our society. Thus, the separation of boys and girls tends to develop in girls masculine traits that later interfere with their heterosexual adjustment.

When boys and girls are included in the same groups, they are encouraged to share equally in initiative and activities. Coeducational schools pride themselves on making no discrimination. Also, in such situations, stimulation and response based on sex differences are discouraged. The boy who teases a girl in the classroom is punished; the girl who flirts with the boy seated behind her has her seat changed. Openly expressed interest in the opposite sex is reduced to a minimum.

With the approach of adolescence, however, adults tend to face in the opposite direction and expect boys and girls also to make a right-about-face in attitude and associations. Just as separation of boys and girls prior to adolescence is defended, so heterosexual adjustment during adolescence is accepted as right and necessary. The statement by Frankwood E. Williams, made in 1930 and still widely quoted, expresses the seriousness with which adults view the situation.

If heterosexuality is not accomplished in these four or five years [of adolescence] it never will be accomplished in a normal way. It may be accomplished later by some technical interference, but then only after much conflict, failure, and illness. These four or five years hold the only chance the average boy or girl will have to establish their heterosexuality. Once prevented, it can never come naturally and normally again. It is a real problem, therefore, that faces the child.[21]

Abruptly, instead of enforced separation and tolerance of aggressive antagonism, adults place before the young adolescent a wide array of mixed activities and are worried if boys and girls do not eagerly enter into them. High schools, in contrast to junior high schools or grade schools, plan many mixed activities; churches invite attendance at mixed young people's meetings; parents plan mixed parties. Everything is done to bring boys and girls together. Children do not always accept these offerings quickly, for they call for readjustments of the one-sex attitudes and habits established in preadolescence.

[21] Frankwood E. Williams, *Adolescence, Studies in Mental Hygiene* (Farrar and Rinehart, 1930), pp. 112–113.

The masculine self and role

The adolescent boy faces the task of coordinating his earlier conceptions of himself and relating them to his relationship to girls of his own age and social class.

Although the boy has been allowed and even encouraged to be aggressive in his own age and sex group, at the same time he has been taught to be compliant and obedient to his parents and to accept their leadership and authority. It is necessary for him to bring together these two conceptions of himself with respect to the adolescent and the adult worlds. In general, the adult masculine role demands aggressiveness from the adult male, directed, however, in certain channels and modified by considerations of fair play and sympathy for others. Obedience sinks to secondary importance, but functions in certain situations, for instance, in obedience to laws, and to occupational superiors. The coordination of the two conceptions of aggressiveness and submission is usually accomplished by the boy without serious difficulty.

More serious is the fact that childhood obedience has been primarily to women—to his mother and to women teachers. The adolescent boy therefore has a conception of himself as docile where older women are concerned. In achieving adulthood, he must change his attitude toward older women in order to become the aggressive dominant male of our culture. Although some boys go through a period of expressing rebellion, ridicule, and scorn for older women, in time most accept the approved attitude of kindly deference to them—a kind of lip service of obedience combined with actual aggressiveness and protectiveness.

The submission to women creates a conflict in early adolescence in the boy's relationships with girls. Girls mature some two or three years earlier than boys, and often are taller than boys of the same age. They have experienced the menarche, and their interest is directed toward boys as different from themselves and the source of new and exciting emotional and social experiences. If they have received attention from older boys, they have a sophistication unknown to the boys of their own age. In early social relationships, girls often are the aggressors, with boys behaving in a shy and feminine way. At school mixers, the boys stand in little clusters while the girls approach them, forcing conversation and sometimes openly inviting boys to dance with them. A girl may make tentative physical approaches—patting the boy's cheek or leaning her shoulder against his in an automobile—before the boy is bold enough to do so. Boys, unsure of themselves and accustomed to feminine dominance, accept this situation for a period of time. It increases the difficulty of adjustment between boys and girls, for the girl thus reinforces her dominance tendencies nourished in her childhood group, and the boy reinforces his dependence and obedience tendencies learned in his relationship to mother and teachers.

When the boy becomes pubescent, shoots ahead of the girl in height, surpasses her in muscular strength, exhibits such secondary sex characteristics as a beard and deepened voice, a struggle follows between boy and girl. This struggle exhibits itself in quarrels over which movie a couple will attend, in futile arguments over facts or opinions, in betting who is right about some inconsequential fact, and among younger adolescents sometimes in physical tussles of strength. Gradually, the boy asserts his dominance, both physically and in his control of social situations. The mores give assistance: for instance, boys are encouraged to display their physical strength publicly in sports that demand a degree of endurance that girls in time recognize they could not equal. Also the mores decree that the boy shall invite the girl on dates, pay for the entertainment, provide and drive the automobile, and lead in dancing. He is in a superior position with reference to his choice of a girl and where he wishes to take her. He may drop a dominative girl after one date.

At the same time that the boy succeeds in establishing his dominance over his girl friends, he learns to curb that dominance and to confine it to certain types of relationship. After the tussles of early adolescence have been outgrown, physical struggles are frowned upon and are given a connotation of sex by adults. Sexual dominance is forbidden by the mores, and a willingness to refrain from such dominance is a part of the masculine conception. Undue pressure and rape definitely are beyond acceptance of the mores.

Masculine acceptance of sex

The masculine role also includes the acceptance of sex as such. The boy accepts sex as a natural function more readily than does the girl. As he comes into adolescence, he cannot avoid consciousness of sexual tensions and their natural release through involuntary nocturnal emissions. This experience is so closely related to the actual role of the male in sex relations that the boy is literally forced to accept the fact of his physical masculinity. Moreover, as we have already seen, before adolescence, most boys have acquired a varied knowledge of sex and perhaps some type of experience through masturbation or sex play.

Because of the dual sources of sex information for the boy (adults on one hand, boys on the other), sex often comes to have two connotations for him. From adults he learns that sex is a responsibility, something to be conserved until marriage, and that it is related to the birth and up-bringing of children. From his own age group he learns of sex as pleasurable, exciting, and stimulating, with possibilities for experimentation in the present. The second interpretation often is more acceptable to the boy, not only because it promises immediate gratification but because it is compatible with other traits of the adolescent personality. The adolescent is still essentially self-centered, seeking satisfaction for his inner needs and unable to accept altruistic obligations to other people. The adult conception of sex as related to marriage and children contains a large element of altruism, of giving and compromise, as well as an element of personal pleasure. The adolescent finds it difficult to accept this conception of sex inasmuch as his personality as a whole has not developed to an altruistic stage.

Even when the boy accepts an adult interpretation of sex, he may find it difficult to apply it to his own conduct during adolescence. A gap of five to ten years intervenes between the onset of puberty and the time when the boy may expect to be sufficiently well established socially and economically to marry. Although postponement of immediate pleasures for the achievement of future goals is part of the growing-up process, the long delay combined with the self-centered aspect of the young adolescent's personality poses an almost insuperable problem for many boys. This situation gives rise to a tendency for boys to separate sex as a pleasurable, physical reaction from sex as a responsible part of marriage. They accept marital sex for the future, physical sex for the present. Whether a boy represses, expresses directly, or sublimates sex during adolescence depends upon the individual boy and his background of training and experience.

The boy whose early training has been very restrictive and repressive, who associates sex with sinfulness or disgust, may continue to repress sex—to deny its existence in himself as a motivating force.

Direct expression of sex does not necessarily mean sex relations with women. Many adolescents indulge in masturbation and contain their sexual pleasures within their own activities.   Psychiatrists now concede the widespread tendency and recognize that the evils of the practice are not directly related to the physical practice but stem from the attitudes toward masturbation instilled in little children by anxious parents, who punish, shame, and disapprove the practice.   The practice, however, is simply a stopgap—a temporary adjustment on the way to a completely adult adjustment.

Another, and socially disapproved, method of direct expression for the adolescent is intensive petting or sex relations with girls or women, either frankly on the physical level (prostitutes) or rationalized as an expression of friendship or love (girl friends).   Few adolescents have the temerity frankly to accept sex on a physical basis and to seek a prostitute.   Their tendency is to establish ardent petting or sex relations on a temporary basis with some girl of their own or lower social status.   Unlike mature sex relations, these activities carry no commitments of responsibility to the girl.

Adolescents may pass from one to another mode of sex expression or may follow several simultaneously.   It is important to note that none of these modes is approved by the adult society and that most parents would be deeply disturbed and horrified if they thought their sons were following any of the practices and would in fact deny the possibility of such conduct. As a result of this situation, such sexual experimentation is carried out as an individual project or with the knowledge and approval only of other adolescents.   In this rather crucial area of maturing the adolescent is abandoned by parents and most other adults to work out his own solution without guidance and often against the approval of the mores.

The solution offered by adults is sublimation of sex impulses through a continuation of one-sex activities—for instance, athletics, hobbies, and special talents as art or music, and continued friendships with other boys. A more direct sublimation is through mixed social activities, such as adult-sponsored dances, sports parties, tours, clubs, and church activities.

As the boy gains maturity he tends to coordinate the various conceptions of sex that he has and to merge his different attempts to find expression for sexual impulses.   The adult conception of sex centers the social and the physical interaction in the same person, reduces the number of sociosexual partners to one, and leads to a culmination in the permanence of marriage.   Thus, ideally, with maturity all methods of direct sex satisfaction except intercourse with an adult female would be discarded; all prospective sexual partners except those with whom social interaction could be maintained would be abandoned; a selective process would designate one person as the chosen one; and marriage would create a permanent union.   That this ideal often is not reached by the time of chronological adulthood, and may not be maintained even though it is at some time attained, is evident from many cases of personal and marital maladjustment.

The feminine self and role

The adolescent girl enters a process that parallels and complements that of the boy—she redefines her conception of herself and relates her new conception and role to boys of her own age.

One of the earliest readjustments of the adolescent girl is the harmonizing of aggressive and docile roles.   Obedience of the girl is taught at home and is emphasized for the girl more than for the boy.   This attitude is compatible with the later subordinate role that she will be expected to play with reference to boys.   However, the role is not clear-cut for the modern girl.   In her own sex-group as a child she may express leadership and initiative; in other girls' groups, such as a school that enrolls only girls, Girl Scouts, girls' clubs, and Sunday school classes, she is encouraged to be socially aggressive.   Although feminism with its overevaluation of aggressiveness in women is less active than formerly, many girls at some time are brought under the influence of middle-aged women who as adolescents were drawn into the feminist movement and who retain their overevaluation of women and underevaluation of men.   The fact that many girls are employed between graduation and marriage and may compete with men again emphasizes aggressiveness in girls.   Thus, the girl finds two conflicting but socially approved patterns—aggressiveness and docility.   Whereas the mature woman in our society retains both elements but directs each to selected relationships and activities, the adolescent girl finds herself exercising one, then the other, tendency in identical situations, sometimes with unpleasant results.

The situation is further complicated by the uneven maturing of boys and girls, already discussed with reference to boys.   The girl in her early adolescence regards boys of her own age as backward, clumsy, and lacking in initiative; she therefore tends to prod them into mixed activities by direct and aggressive methods.   She may be helped to gain social compliance by association with older boys whom she admires and whose leadership she will follow. Otherwise, she becomes involved in a long struggle with boys of her own age but of less maturity. As boys come into dominance through physical growth and social prerogatives, she may withdraw from contacts with boys (as a few "man-haters" do), or she may comply. Often she does not so much change her evaluation of herself and her sex as find new ways of exhibiting her initiative and desire to dominate. Glamor, charm, and flattery are methods by which girls continue to dominate boys. Often the girl identifies herself with an outstanding boy and in her imagination shares some of the satisfaction of his initiative and aggressiveness. She is enabled to do this more satisfactorily if the boy meets the adolescent standards for outstanding ability so that she, as the boy's chosen girl friend, receives the admiration and envy of her girl friends and the attention of boys who admire the outstanding youth. Again, she may exhibit a docile attitude toward boys but become aggressive in her relationships with her family or girl friends.

The girl learns that compliance to boys is limited to certain areas of experience. She is expected to assume initiative and resistance with reference to sex. This area of feminine control includes personal talk about sex, sex jokes, ardent petting, and direct sex experience. Girls are taught and early accept for themselves the dictum that the girl is responsible for setting the limit to verbal or physical sexual experience. In this area alone the contest for dominance between boys and girls may continue after the girl has adjusted herself to a subordinate role in school and social activities.

Feminine acceptance of sex

Acceptance of the role of female is difficult for some girls. Since sex interests have been repressed in childhood, the girl has had little preparation for conceiving of herself as a potential woman. Whereas the boy's first introduction to sexual changes in himself is with a function directly connected with future intercourse that gives a pleasurable anticipation, the girl's first personal experience usually is with menstruation. If the girl is unprepared for the menarche or if she associates it with elimination, her emotional reactions may be of a negative nature. Fear, a feeling of guilt (this is some strange punishment), consternation, or disgust are common reactions. She may be embarrassed by the extra sanitary measures that are necessary or resent restrictions on her activities. Pain may further antagonize her. The young girl's knowledge of the relation of menstruation to maternity tends to remain purely on the intellectual level. She cannot conceive of herself as a mother, and the time of marriage is in the dim future.   Nature, she often feels, was very stupid in its construction of women and menstruation is regarded as a nuisance, in fact as a "curse."   Thus, whereas the boy's early association with puberty includes the idea of pleasure, the girl's attitude at best is neutral and often is distinctly negative.[22]

Occasionally the girl's inability to accept approaching adulthood is so great that she develops severe personality disorders, evidenced by extreme anxieties over physical changes, depression, or mild attitudes of persecution.   Or the reaction may take the form of withdrawal into fantasy or an intellectual withdrawal into philosophy.   Sometimes the reactions suggest schizophrenia, but differ in that they are an outward expression of a conflict that the girl cannot resolve, rather than indicative of the abnormal symbolic thinking of the schizophrenic.[23]

To the extent that the young adolescent girl feels sexual impulses, they are diffuse and unlocalized.   She may define them simply as general well-being, restlessness, or pleasure in the presence of certain boys.   She does not identify them as sex, and indeed they are not sex in a narrow physical sense.   Until she has had actual physical stimulation of the erogenous areas through caressing or manipulation, she is very unlikely to feel specific physical sexual responses.

The girl's conception of sexual experience therefore does not come directly by way of maturing of her sex organs but through verbalization. She is partially informed and warned by her mother, she reads about sex experience, or she listens to more knowing girls repeat hearsay events or jokes.   Intercourse is something that can and does happen to girls and women, but she may have difficulty believing that it can ever happen to her, much less that she can secure enjoyment from it.

Nevertheless, the girl shows indirect interest in sex.   She spends much time on her personal appearance; she copies alluring gestures and tricks of speech from older girls or motion-picture actresses and tries them out

[22] An extensive discussion from the psychoanalytic point of view is contained in Helene Deutsch, *The Psychology of Women, a Psychoanalytic Interpretation,* I, "Girlhood" (Grune and Stratton, 1944).   Contrasting attitudes among ethnic groups are described in Theodora Abel and Natalie F. Joffe, "Cultural Backgrounds of Female Puberty," *American Journal of Psychotherapy,* 4 (1950), 90–113.

[23] Sylvan Keiser, "Severe Reactive States and Schizophrenia in Adolescent Girls," *Nervous Child,* 4 (1944–1945), 17–25.

on boys of her social group. She is greatly interested in romanticized love —in love movies, in an endless succession of popular love songs played on victrolas or broadcast on radio programs, in newspaper accounts of weddings and photographs of brides. For the future she has a somewhat more realistic interest in love and marriage. She may select a silver pattern and begin a collection of silver even before she has a specific boy friend; she may embroider linens, collect house plans, and take courses in home economics or child care. In her daydreams she may vision herself using these articles and techniques, or she may imagine herself in love situations more ardent than any she has experienced directly. But in her present consideration of herself as a member of the female sex, she sets between herself and her admission of sex impulses in herself a high barrier of prudery, denial of sex interest, and disgust at the mention of sex. Expression of her active but unrecognized sexual interests tends to be indirect rather than in the more direct ways of the adolescent boy. For instance, only slightly more than half as many girls as boys masturbate.[24] Girls also often have crushes that they define as platonic and do not relate to sex but rather to a deep friendship. The crush may be with another girl, in which case the girls would furiously deny any sexual components; or with a boy but again without recognition by the girl of sexual drives.

With the entrance into dating, the girl recognizes that her interest in boys has a distinctive quality. She may still, however, avoid a realistic admission of sex in herself. She may think of love-making as a symbol of friendship and without sexual implications, at the same time that the boy of her own age recognizes clearly the relationship between kissing and embracing and his own sexual impulses. She may think of sex as something that she will assume at marriage along with the wedding ring.

As the girl slowly brings together her knowledge of sex and her own impulses and admits that she has sexual interests and drives, she faces many of the same problems as the maturing boy. She, as the boy, tends to be self-centered in her attitude toward herself and others. Thus she may have a self-seeking and exploitative attitude toward the boy, to match his attitude toward her. But whereas the boy may tend toward sex relations, the girl is held back by the strict teaching she has had and by her fears and feelings of guilt. Thus, the girl tends to exploit the boy socially.

[24] Georgene H. Seward, *Sex and the Social Order* (McGraw-Hill, 1946), pp. 171–174.

When she indulges in love-making she is also self-centered in that she has little consideration for (perhaps little knowledge of) the more pointed and sharp reaction of the boy. She disregards the fact that the degree of love-making that gives her a diffused feeling of excitement may make the boy acutely uncomfortable.

In the process of maturing normally the girl comes to recognize her own sexual impulses, to reconcile her conflicting aggressive and docile conceptions of herself, to shift from exploitative to cooperative attitudes, and to focus her love on one person.

THE HETEROSEXUAL GROUP

Although the family and the one-sex group are never entirely lost, the heterosexual group tends to replace them during adolescence. As the adolescent seeks freedom from family control, he finds himself in an anomalous position. He desires complete independence but is not yet ready for it. He still needs support from others, approval, advice, and joint participation in new ventures. The heterosexual group as well as the group of his own sex supplies these needs. He comes to feel better understood and more at ease in his own age group; he finds new satisfactions in a heterosexual group; and his own sex group provides him with an admirable sounding board for discussion of his new heterosexual group experiences. More and more the heterosexual group (and finally the heterosexual pair) replaces the earlier group affiliations. It supplies the authority for the actions of its members, sometimes in opposition to family rules. It also supplies security, for if all members of a group pursue a line of action or hold an opinion, each member feels self-confident enough to express the opinion or follow the line of action. Criticism from others is offset by approval of the group.

In seeking independence, adolescents sometimes repudiate not only the authority of parents but also their protective love. Yet they still need love and a feeling of close identification with a small group. The group of the same sex has supplemented the family in prepuberty days; in adolescence the heterosexual group tends not merely to supplement but to supplant the earlier family ties. The culmination of this shift is found in early adulthood in marriage, but along with it normally comes a recurrence of a friendly equalitarian love for the parents, as distinct from parent-child or dominant-submissive love.

Extreme dependence upon the peer group for approval and friendship is a passing phase of adolescence. As maturity approaches and the boy (or girl) gains a feeling of self-adequacy, he tends to free himself from this dependence just as at an earlier period he freed himself from too dependent an inclusion in the family. If the processes of family life and of peer-group life have on the one hand satisfied the current needs of the boy or girl and on the other added to his self-confidence, he will emerge into a competent, self-reliant adulthood, with ability to manage his own life realistically, to accept his responsibilities, and to find types of relationship with parents, husband or wife, and friends that meet both his and their normal needs in a mutually sympathetic and responsible relationship.[25]

Failure to make heterosexual adjustment

That some adolescents fail to make an easy heterosexual adjustment is clear from the behavior of certain young people. The excessively shy boy or girl fails at the social level. The hoydenish girl and the "sissy" among boys have failed to find clear conceptions of their feminine or masculine selves and roles. The boy or girl eager to fling himself into early sex relations has stopped at the self-centered stage and is not developing the cooperative attitude of the adult. The boy or girl whose sexual interests are turned in upon himself or are diverted explosively to others of the same sex has also failed to make a heterosexual adjustment. Many of these phases of personality are typical of certain stages of development, but long continuance means a fixation at a level that is immature and that may prevent growth toward maturity. Since our society encourages heterosexual activities during adolescence and holds out the bright goal of marriage with beginning adulthood, explanations must be found for failure to follow the accepted path.

Heterosexual adjustment implies entering new groups and gaining approval and status for oneself not only among new people but with the opposite sex. Therefore it creates tension and anxiety. As with any new venture, the secure person makes the adjustment more easily and quickly than the insecure person. The boy or girl who enters adolescence feeling more insecure, inferior, or inadequate than the average adolescent is handicapped. Such insecurity may result from various causes, such as the following:

[25] Caroline M. Tryon, "The Adolescent Peer Culture," *The 43rd Yearbook of the National Society for the Study of Education,* Part I, "Adolescence," (University of Chicago Press, 1944), Sec. 3, ch. 12.

Often when the adolescent enters high school he also enters a new social group.   In some areas, for instance, the rural or suburban schools carry the student only through the eighth grade, whereafter the student commutes to some nearby urban high school.   The patterns of social life change from rural to urban with an increased degree of sophistication, symbolized by later evening hours for social events, the substitution of formal for informal parties, and availability of public dances.   The rural student may have to modify his ideals of social usage and perhaps some of his moral concepts.   Otherwise, he may find himself without many friends or ill at ease in social groups.   Also, city students may be able to identify the rural students by mannerisms of speech or style of dress and may exclude them from social activities.

Somewhat similar is the situation of the student of foreign background. He may have attended elementary and junior high school in an ethnic community, where all his friends were reared in families like his own, with a foreign language perhaps spoken at home, and distinctive cultural traits. Schools in these communities, even though they are not staffed with members of the ethnic group, nevertheless often are forced to adapt the school program to the ethnic cultural ideas.   If the ethnic community is not large enough to support a high school, students may commute to another community where they may represent a minority group distinguishable by appearance, name, mannerisms, and ideals from the majority group. If they are not actively excluded from social groups, they may nevertheless feel ill at ease and may segregate themselves.

Although both rural and ethnic students may form their own social groups, often they fail to do so, but yearn for inclusion in the dominant group with its greater prestige and perhaps control of social events.   Thus they may go through adolescence on the fringe of a group that they are too insecure to enter.

Insecurity also may be the result of an insecure childhood.   If a child has been unwanted and unloved at home or if for some reason early friendship groups have ostracized him, the child grows up feeling rejected or socially "lost."   Some children resent such exclusion and make aggressive attacks either on those who have excluded them or displace their hostility on other social groups.   Sometimes this displacement is directly related to later difficult heterosexual adjustment.   Thus the girl who feels that her father does not love her may turn her resentment from her father to all men, or to all males.   She may be aggressive and bitter against all boys, showing her feeling in sarcasm, scorn, and belittling remarks.[26] Similarly, the boy who feels that his mother has failed him may despise or doubt the sincerity of all girls and women.

In other cases, rejection by the parents breeds a general feeling of doubt and insecurity.   The child may come to believe that he is unlovable, that something within his own personality or his appearance makes it impossible for others to like him.   Some of these children turn in upon themselves and, never having received love, are never able to give love. If friendship is offered to them they fear to accept it.   They do not know how to respond, and their early experience makes them fearful of even tentative response for fear the friendship will be withdrawn and they will be hurt further.   Such insecurity may manifest itself in friendships with those of the adolescent's own sex, but is perhaps even more likely to occur in connection with the opposite sex, since here the relationships are new and uncertain and greater show of friendliness is necessary to appeal to the would-be friend.   Heterosexual adjustment may therefore be delayed until the adolescent overcomes his insecurity through a series of mild or tentative friendships or through personal achievements that give self-confidence and a feeling of adequacy.

The adolescent may repudiate close friendships of all types, both with the same sex and with the opposite, because of an unwillingness to accept the responsibility of a steady relationship in which something must be given as well as something received.   This attitude of continued casualness and unwillingness to accept strong personal bonds may result from an earlier family situation in which the parents have placed on the child too much responsibility.   In the absence of the father, the son may have been expected to act the role of the husband and father before he was ready for an adult role.   Or parents may have held the child to standards beyond his possibility of attainment.   With the greater freedom of adolescence, the boy or girl may shake off responsibilities and seek complete freedom.   He then may continue into later adolescence the status of exploitative, self-centered personality that may be normal for the young adolescent but not for the one who is approaching maturity.

Too great dependence on parents may also unfit the adolescent for deeper emotional bonds with those of his own age.   Parents necessarily give young children unstinted love and physical care without receiving

[26] J. L. Despart, "Resistance to Change in the Adolescent Girl," *Nervous Child,* 4 (1944–1945), 8–16.

anything in return.   As the child develops the parents may continue to cater to the child's selfish wishes rather than to encourage a cooperative relationship where child and parent exchange tasks and obligations as well as love.   If the parents continue the infantile relationship, the child continues to be dependent upon the parents for all manner of tasks that he is able to perform for himself (as care of clothing, preparation of food, orderliness of room) and also fails to develop an attitude of self-reliance. Such a child enters adolescence with the expectation that others, even those of his own age, will cater to him as his parents have done.   He expects friends to help him with school work, to carry the burden of club projects from which he hopes to benefit, or to provide the refreshment at joint gatherings.   This attitude may carry over to heterosexual relationships.   If the mother has been the one to pamper the son, the boy expects other women and girl friends to do likewise.   If the father has been the indulgent one toward his daughter, the girl will expect her boy friends to carry the burden of their friendship.   The boy or girl who has been too greatly indulged by his parents finds it impossible to develop the give-and-take attitude and withdraws from deepening friendships.   Normally, however, the self-centered attitude yields to a mutual give-and-take.

Occasionally, a child has been reared in a family where all show of emotion has been suppressed.   The family may have an underlying loyalty and unity, but tender words and caresses even of the mildest sort may never be exchanged between members of the family.   The situation may extend to the point where giving of presents except on conventional occasions or doing small favors may be avoided as displaying some weakness of personality or sentimentality.   Such a child finds it difficult to make friendships outside the family.   His repressed behavior is interpreted by boys and girls alike as unfriendliness, and he is ignored or his tentative approaches are repulsed.

THE MATURE PERSONALITY

Failure to mature poses a serious problem for the person and society. Adult in years, prodded by social expectations of adult achievement, the immature adult is in reality an adolescent trying to live in an adult world. Adolescence is therefore a period of personality maturing.

Although all the traits of the mature well-adjusted person are important in marriage, certain of these traits may be emphasized in relation to the emerging personality of the adolescent.

Integration of attitudes and desires

The preceding discussion has mentioned the ambivalent attitudes and tendencies of the adolescent: his desire to remain under the protective wing of his parents and at the same time his desire for freedom; his self-centeredness and his desire for friendships; his fear of sex and his pride in maturity; his drive for physical sexual satisfaction and his desire for social approval. During adolescence these incompatible and often conflicting tendencies are slowly brought into an integrated pattern. Certain tendencies carried over from childhood disappear as the boy or girl finds new ways of securing satisfactions; for instance, he no longer needs to demand favors from his parents to prove that he is worthy of adult consideration; he receives his friendly approval by actual accomplishments in school or in the community. Other drives are redirected into channels that do not conflict with the basic personality pattern.

The many digressive interests that seem to pull the adolescent first into this immediate activity and then into that are screened through a selective process whereby some are dropped and others become the basis for continuing hobbies or vocational interest, often with a distant and planned goal to be attained in the future. Discordant attitudes also undergo a pruning and training process whereby consistency and dependability develop so that the person's actions may be more or less predicted regardless of the situation.

Selection in heterosexual friendships

This integrating process whereby balance is achieved and conflicts eliminated applies to heterosexual relationships as well as to other phases of life. The adolescent gradually finds the type of person to whom he is most closely attracted—and eventually the one person. His activities with those of the opposite sex also tend to stabilize. Many boys who have had one girl for secret sex relationships and another girl for more conventional social activities are able to modify and control their drives sufficiently to find all their satisfactions in one girl.

Development of self-reliance

Not only integration of traits but development of self-reliance is usually achieved during adolescence. The adult culture pattern expects self-reliance—that the person will be able to support himself, accept normal frustrations without permanent maladjustment of the personality, make his own decisions and hold them over a period of time, and control his own behavior in conformity with the mores.   The minimum requirement of this sort is acceptance of responsibility for oneself; the normal requirement in addition calls for partial responsibility for husband or wife and complete responsibility for children.   Self-reliance not only makes the person a functioning member of society but it also frees the person from preoccupation with self-centered attitudes.   Since he has met the expectations of society sufficiently well that he feels secure and able to meet his normal problems, his energies are released from the effort that occupies so much of the attention of the young adolescent—to offset his feeling of inadequacy and inferiority.   He accepts himself for what he is, with all his limitations but also with all his capacities.

Mature selection of friends

The integrated, self-reliant person is able to turn his energies outward toward building satisfactory relationships with other people.   One such relationship is with the opposite sex.   Early friends of the opposite sex were sometimes chosen because they resembled the protective parent and catered to the adolescent's need for someone to lean on or because in some way they bolstered the adolescent's self-esteem.   With the self-reliant older adolescent or adult, the person seeks only moderately to satisfy his personal needs; he also seeks the more unselfish satisfaction of making another person happy.   Thus, the love that once was turned in upon himself may now be turned outward to become focused upon another person.   Through this process the individualistic exploitative love of two adolescents becomes the mutually supportive love of two adults.

QUESTIONS

1. Describe the process whereby the child's conception of himself is formed.
2. How can the parent of the opposite sex assist the child to define his roles?
3. What is the normal process by which the American child emancipates himself from his parents?
4. Discuss the idea that young children have no interest in sex.
5. Criticize Frankwood E. Williams' statement, quoted in this chapter, regarding heterosexual adjustment.

6. In what ways does the boy find it necessary to redefine his role during adolescence? The girl?

7. What conflicting attitudes toward sex does the adolescent boy have? The adolescent girl?

8. Devise practical plans whereby adolescent adjustment problems could be eased or avoided.

BIBLIOGRAPHY

Theory of personality development and adjustment

Murphy, Gardner, *Personality, a Biosocial Approach to Origins and Structure* (Harper, 1947).

Symonds, Percival M., *The Dynamics of Human Adjustment* (Appleton-Century, 1946).

Child development

Barker, Roger G., Kounin, J. S., and Wright, H. F., editors, *Child Behavior and Development* (McGraw-Hill, 1943).

Bossard, James H. S., *Family Situations, Introduction to the Study of Child Behavior* (University of Pennsylvania Press, 1943).

———, *The Sociology of Child Development* (Harper, 1947).

Davis, W. A., and Havighurst, R. J., *The Father of the Man, How Your Child Gets His Personality* (Houghton, Mifflin, 1947).

Hunt, Joseph McV., editor, *Personality and the Behavior Disorders* (Ronald, 1944), especially Vol. I, ch. 3, and Vol. II, chs. 20, 21, and 22.

Levy, David M., *Maternal Overprotection* (Columbia University Press, 1943).

Ross, H. and Johnson, A. M., "Psychiatric Interpretation of the Growth Process," *Journal of Social Casework*, 30 (1949), Part I, 87–92; Part II, 148–154.

Adolescence

Carmichael, Leonard, editor, *Manual of Child Psychology* (Wiley, 1946), chs. 12 and 19.

Davis, K., "The Sociology of Parent-Youth Conflict," *American Sociological Review*, 5 (1940), 523–535.

Deutsch, Helene, *The Psychology of Women, A Psychoanalytic Interpretation* (Grune and Stratton, 1944), Vol. I.

Ellsworth, Dorothy, Mitchell, Margaret, and Little, Ruby, *Precocious Adolescence in Wartime*, reprinted from *The Family*, March, May, July, 1944 (Family Welfare Association of America, 122 East 22nd Street, New York 10).

Farnham, Marynia, *The Adolescent* (Harper, 1951).

Havighurst, Robert J., and Taba, Hilda, *Adolescent Character and Personality* (Wiley, 1949).

Horrocks, John E., *The Psychology of Adolescence, Behavior and Development* (Houghton Mifflin, 1951).

Watson, Goodwin, *Youth After Conflict* (Association Press, 1947).

12

Social Relationships
Preparatory to Marriage

The social preparation for marriage falls into two main divisions: dating without commitments; and courtship, including engagement. Much of the heterosexual adjustment discussed in the preceding chapter is accomplished through dating, whereas the selection of a spouse and direct premarital adjustment are functions of courtship and the engagement period.

DATING AN AMERICAN CUSTOM

So firmly is dating entrenched in the thinking and activities of young people, so completely is it accepted as a normal youth activity by adults, that it is difficult to realize it is a recent American innovation and not a traditional or universal custom.

Before dating became the common pattern for heterosexual social activities, a different set of customs prevailed. One-sex activities were prolonged through most of the teens; mixed parties were given, often by a girl's mother in her home; pairing of boy with girl in social activities that carried the couple beyond adult supervision was avoided until near the age for marriage. Pairing off was the beginning of serious courtship and presaged an early announcement of marriage plans. This procedure was essentially the rural and small-town method of courtship. Marital choices were based on years of acquaintance among families and young people, which made selection of a husband or wife possible without preliminary mixed-group recreation designed to throw young people together.

The specific antecedents of dating—the social conditions from which dating has developed—include the following:

301

1. The employment of young girls in factories and stores, as well as their entrance into coeducational colleges and universities, which became commonplace around the beginning of this century, removed girls from the watchful eyes of their parents. Girls became acquainted with many young men who were strangers to their parents. They were able to carry on an active social life incidental to employment or college, and away from home. By the time the parents met the men friends of their daughters, the friendships might be well advanced.

2. The movement from rural areas to urban centers accentuated the process started by the employment of women. In addition, it pushed the process to younger age levels. School children met and made friends with those of the opposite sex whose families were unknown to their parents. Children as well as young people of necessity judged and selected their own friends.

3. Commercial recreation, such as attendance at motion-picture theaters, public dance spots, cocktail bars open to women, and spectator sports, has had its major development within the last 30 years. Prior to this period there was literally little amusement other than that planned or carried out by families, churches, or schools. An occasional stock show or concert in the smaller communities provided some diversion. At present, even in the medium-sized community, a different form of entertainment outside the home may fill every night in the week. Hence, the present pattern of recreation of adolescents is away from the home and family supervision.

4. The automobile's significance in modern heterosexual social activities cannot be overemphasized. It is a definite part of the equipment of modern dating. In community after community, dating does not get under way until the age when young people may receive driving licenses. The car increases the range of mobility of young people and thus opens still more possibilities of recreation. It also carries young people completely away from the home community and places the full responsibility for conduct upon them. The parked car provides a degree of privacy almost impossible to obtain elsewhere.

5. The decrease in size of homes, found most clearly in the contrast of the urban efficiency apartment with the roomy rural or village home, gives less opportunity for privacy from the observation of the entire family or opportunity to talk, sing, dance, laugh without disturbing the family. The tendency is for young people to seek their recreation elsewhere.

FUNCTIONS OF DATING

Although dating is usually thought of solely in social terms, it is also one of the means by which adolescents establish their masculine or feminine roles.   Boys learn through dating what their own reactions are to girls, as well as the traits and types of behavior that are pleasing to them.   The horseplay and crudities typical of the boys' clique usually are not tolerated by girls.   The reaction to a member of the other sex—whether shyness, desire to have some physical contact, or a comradely feeling—is worked through in a relationship that does not entail great or lasting responsibilities and that may be repeated endlessly as the boy learns the range and control of his reactions to girls of different types.   The girl goes through a similar experience of adjustment.   She learns to control her aggressiveness or shyness, as the case may be, and to replace competitiveness with other girls by solidarity with a girls' clique that helps her set and maintain standards of dating.   She explores her reactions to mild physical contacts, and she finds out the type of boy who repels and the type who appeals to her.   In a period when great emphasis is placed on the personal relationship in marriage, dating no doubt serves a useful purpose in this respect.   At any rate, in American society it is the approved testing ground for the maturing masculine and feminine traits, both physical and psychological.

On the social side, dating gives experience in adjusting to the etiquette of social interaction between the sexes.   Because the adolescent's ego is involved in dating, the social standards set both for self and the dating partner are high.   The girl is more concerned than ever before to make a pleasing appearance; she also demands of the boy a higher degree of meticulous dress and nicety of manners than she would expect of her father or brother.   The boy is equally critical of the girl.

Dating also provides an opportunity to meet many members of the opposite sex and is often justified by adolescents and adults alike on this basis alone.   With abandonment of parental selection of friends, parents concede that wide opportunities are necessary to give the adolescent a chance to find unaided the type of friend he needs.

Nevertheless, as is pointed out later, dating creates many difficulties for adolescents and sometimes establishes attitudes and habits that are not compatible with the mores of marriage to which the adolescent, grown to young adulthood, is expected to conform.

CHARACTERISTICS OF DATING

One of the chief characteristics of dating is the emphasis upon individual ego-satisfactions rather than upon mutuality of experience. Especially during early adolescence, the establishment of status in the peer group is of prime importance. Dating has become a vehicle for status-building. So significant is this feature that one sociologist, Willard Waller, used the phrase "rating and dating complex" to describe the phenomenon.[1] Only those who rate high by the standards of the peer group are sought in dating. The objective of dating a high-rating person is the enhancement of the ego of the dater. The high school boy who appears at a dance with the most popular girl by his side is admired by all other boys; the girl invited by the outstanding athlete is envied by all girls. In other groups, other standards of rating may prevail—among out-of-school youth, the boy with the best-paying job and the girl with the smartest clothes rate high. Among college students membership in prestige-fraternities is an item.

The emphasis upon ego-satisfaction leads to another characteristic—the noncommittal and transient quality of dating. Unlike most other pair relationships (friendship, courtship, marriage, teacher-pupil, social worker–client, or employer-employee), dating does not imply continuity or more than temporary responsibility. Each date is a little unit of social experience, complete in itself. Neither party to the date is under any obligations to repeat the date, and even though one may very much wish another date, he (or she) does not feel mistreated or slighted if a second or third date is not forthcoming. The limited obligations of "going steady" are discussed later. The purpose of the date is solely recreational; even when, as sometimes happens, love-making is indulged in, that also is regarded as recreational and void of obligations. Conversation on a date is superficial and sometimes conventionalized into a "line." Deeper aspects of the personality are not revealed; problems are not discussed; primary-group relations are not assumed. "Dating doesn't count" beyond the hour of the date.

A third quality of dating, related also to ego-satisfaction, is its exploitative aspect. Each person tries to gain as much satisfaction as possible,

[1] Willard Waller, "The Rating and Dating Complex," *American Sociological Review*, 2 (1937), 727–734. This point of view is also emphasized in Geoffrey Gorer, *The American People, A Study in National Character* (Norton, 1948), ch. 4.

often ignoring the needs of the dating partner.   The girl is flattered by the boy who spends freely, regardless of her knowledge that his parents cannot afford to have their son become extravagant.   The boy may urge the girl to accompany him to a popular tavern, although he knows that her parents have forbidden it.   Dating often becomes a game of fencing in which each seeks both to protect himself and at the same time to gain an advantage over the other.   Victory brings a mild glow of success but also a doubt as to the quality of the partner chosen, and hence a lowering of ego-satisfaction.   The most satisfaction to both comes when neither breaks through the defenses of the other—when the one chosen for the date is equal in fencing ability to oneself.

A fourth characteristic is that dating is largely controlled by a peer-group code.   Parents, teachers, and youth leaders eagerly arrange and carefully supervise mixed-group parties and dances, but they are unable to follow the boy and girl into the date that follows the dance.   The folk-ways and mores of dating, therefore, represent two types of group influences—adult and the peer group.   In general the adult folkways and mores are in control of social affairs sponsored by churches, schools, clubs, or carried out in the adolescent's home with some form of chap-eronage.   Whereas the personal relationship between the boy and girl and conduct on affairs carried out by adolescents themselves (movie dates, car dates, picnics, dates in lunch rooms and taverns) represent the peer culture.   The peer culture is relatively independent of the adult control, but never completely so.   Although adolescents may adopt types of conduct not learned from their parents, they must always reconcile this conduct in some way with the earlier teaching of the parents.   Many go through a period of conflict and confusion, with feelings of guilt until a pattern that is acceptable to the adolescent's standards is attained.   In a changing society with new social conditions to adjust to that are unlike those of the parent's youth, the peer culture is never quite the same as the adult culture.   Moreover, the peer culture also is influenced by the need of the adolescent to achieve independence; thus, for a time, disregard or even defiance of adult standards may have a positive meaning to the ad-olescent and contribute to his feeling of independence and self-reliance.

Only in the case of rebellious youth, however, does the boy or girl follow his own impulses in the conduct of the date.   Peer culture implies group-accepted patterns of behavior.   In informal "bull sessions" a code is achieved.   These sessions are not as a rule heterosexual.   Girls develop their code; boys, theirs.   But the codes are always being tried out on dates and hence are coordinated.   Also the code of the opposite sex, as revealed on dates, is discussed, and those who violate the code of their sex or refuse to respect the code of the other are ruled out as desirable dating partners.   It is, for instance, usually part of the code that the girl sets the limits to the degree of "necking" and "petting"; [2] the boy, with no feeling of personal responsibility, is privileged to go as far as the girl will allow, but his code requires that he respect the girl's wish as to the intensiveness of physical contact to be attained.   The violator of the code is also censored by his own sex group as a traitor to his sex.

The fact that the code is derived by adolescents from their own experience and only indirectly reflects parental or other adult norms opens the way for codes that diverge widely from adult standards, hence the occasional discovery in some communities of a mixed group of middle-class adolescents who include sex intercourse as a part of their group dating. In these instances, the approval of the peer group overrides the inhibitions of middle-class training.   The peer-group code has the advantage, however, of throwing responsibility on young people, a responsibility that in a mobile, urban society they must learn.   The danger lies in too complete a separation at too young an age from adult culture; a disintegrating schism sometimes results with personal demoralization for the adolescents caught in such situations. [3]

As a new activity, dating has no precedent in our culture.   Adolescents, thrown by adults into heterosexual freedom, look to the next older age group for a model.   The relationship that they find between young men and women is the intensive, exclusive dating of courtship.   Overlooking the deeper implications of courtship, they have seized upon some of the superficial overt characteristics and incorporated them into dating. A relationship that is casual and transitory—dating—therefore has acquired many of the folkways of a more mature relationship that is based on mutual affection and responsibility.   For instance, dating has borrowed from courtship the dictum that the male pays the expenses, at a

[2] For want of better terms, the folk words necking and petting are used.   Necking implies light caresses that include kissing but avoid other erogeneous zones— "nothing below the neck" as some adolescents phrase it; petting implies more intense caresses that include definite stimulation of erogeneous zones and hence arousal of sexual reactions, but does not include intercourse, which has its own folk terms, such as "going the limit," "going all the way," "making" the girl, and many others.

[3] Marynia F. Farnham discusses this problem interestingly in ch. 8, "Adolescent Sex Behavior," of her book *The Adolescent* (Harper, 1951).

time when many boys are earning nothing or only small amounts of money.   Another illustration relates to kissing and caressing.   Adolescents, newly come into sexual maturity and curious about this new aspect of their lives, eagerly adapt the overt love-making of courtship to their more casual relationship.   Caressing becomes a technique of dating, unrelated to love, and expressive of physical stimulation and ego-enhancement.   Being fearful of sex, however, they attempt to control its expression through such simple rules as "no kiss until the third date," "necking but not petting" (or, in some groups, "petting but not intercourse"), "no parking in automobiles," "the double date gives safety," and the like.

Finally, dating develops some attitudes that are opposed to those needed in marriage.   The grasping after individual ego-satisfaction, the exploitation, the noncommittal attitude that takes little or no responsibility for the welfare of the partner, and the constant playing with sex on a superficial basis are all contrary to the relationship that underlies a harmonious marriage.

The foregoing gives the general characteristics of dating.   Each social class and ethnic group has its own variations, its own folkways and mores of dating, which will now be discussed.

MIDDLE-CLASS DATING

Dating is probably more highly developed among middle-class youths than in any other social class.   Upper-class youths date, but their contacts, at least before the college level, are to a high degree prearranged within their small social class.   The middle class is more numerous, and family contacts are less extensive and prohibitive; hence the middle-class youth finds in dating a useful activity by which he selects his friends and makes his own way socially.

Mixed-group activities

Middle-class parents, teachers, and church workers open the way for dating by arranging and encouraging mixed-group activities.   Although many of the activities in theory are open to all young people in the community, actually they "belong" to the middle class.   Upper-class young people date within the limited circle of their own class, through privately sponsored events held in exclusive clubs or in their parents' homes. Lower-class boys and girls are unable to meet the expense of many parties or dances.   They tend to leave school in mid-adolescence and enter upon a social life of their own.

In communities with a junior high school, the activities often are related to the school program.

In our city of 60,000, junior high school prepared us for three exciting senior high years by introducing dating on a small scale.   I returned from my first mixer thrilled right down to the toes of my very tired feet.   By the time we were in ninth grade we arrived at mixers fully confident that we would dance every record with a different boy.   If the fellows had just received their allowances the crowd would walk down to the Apex Ice Cream Shop for malts and potato chips.   It rarely would be even couples, but somehow, as the odd girls disappeared alone, the fellows chose the girls they would honor by escorting home.[4]

Mixed parties began in junior high school and were arranged for the afternoon.   They included simple school parties or afternoon movies, the bus providing the transportation.   Boys and girls attended, with or without dates. Girls could come unescorted, although that practice was not common, unless they came in groups.   During the winter, records were played at lunch time in a section partitioned off of the boys' gym, and couples danced during the noon hour.   Only couples attended; it was a friendly gathering to hear the latest records and try the newest steps.   The more athletic crowd did not dance but played basketball.   Saturday afternoon movie dates were also popular.

The dating age

The typical age for beginning to date is middle adolescence.   The prolongation of adolescence during college, based on economic dependence upon parents, tends to carry dating into the chronological age of young adulthood among college students.

A study of 489 men and women students in an eastern college led to the conclusion that among young people who were socially and emotionally well adjusted, dating tended to begin in junior high school, al-

---

[4] The characteristics of middle-class dating are illustrated by excerpts chosen from 50 descriptions of high school dating prepared by college students.   The students came from large and small communities scattered over the United States.   With some variations, based on size of community and a few original local twists, a surprising uniformity exists not only with reference to the meaning of dating to adolescents but also with reference to activities.   Discussion of college and other non–high school dating is based on a few descriptions by students and published reports, such as the following: Waller, *op. cit.;* John F. Cuber, "Changing Courtship and Marriage Customs," *The Annals* of the American Academy of Political and Social Science, 229 (1943), 30–34.

though going steady was postponed until the college years; of the total groups studied, only 1 per cent had not dated at any time.[5]   A canvas of 314 students at the University of Washington placed the peak age for first dating at 16 for boys and 14 for girls—a phrasing that implies earlier dating for a minority of the group.[6]

Dating becomes a fully recognized activity with entrance into senior high school.   The social situation is keyed to dating.   Although mixed-group activities, to which groups of boys and girls may come, continue, the outstanding social events of both school and community are limited to couples.   The pattern of social life is set by the seniors, who not only date but often are going steady, a special type of high school dating. First-year students, seeking to identify themselves with the much-admired seniors, emulate not only dress, manners, and speech, but also activities. Nevertheless, the beginning of dating is also related to the adolescent's own stage of maturity.   That girls in general desire to date at a younger age than boys may be related in part to earlier biological maturity, but it is also related to the difference in prestige-giving activities of boys and girls.   The outstanding boys are the athletes; therefore the freshman boy gives his time and energy to becoming an athlete.   The outstanding girl tends to be the one who attracts either the greatest number of boys or, if she goes steady, an outstanding boy.   The freshman girl, therefore, directs her activities toward attracting the attention of boys.   The motivation is the same for boys and girls—to secure prestige by identification with the type of boy or girl held in greatest esteem by the high school group.   This process leads the younger boy away from dating and the younger girl into dating.

The later social maturing of boys helps to establish the pattern of age differential that continues into marriage.   In many high schools the general pattern is for girls to date boys in the class ahead and for senior girls to date boys who have been graduated or, if there is a college nearby, college men.

The ritual of making a date

Because of their social insecurity, both boys and girls in the early high school period use many tentative, noncommittal approaches in making

[5] Meyer Nimkoff and Arthur Wood, "Courtship and Personality," *American Journal of Sociology,* 53 (1948), 266, 269.
[6] Rayanne D. Cupps and Norman S. Hayner, "Dating at the University of Washington," *Marriage and Family Living,* 9 (1947), 30.

dates.   Notes passed in class may precede a personal contact.   Seemingly accidental meetings in the corridors, actually planned, however, by both boy and girl, may follow.   Telephone calls regarding school work may fill in several weeks of time before the boy finally asks the girl for a date.   Sometimes friends act as intermediaries: the boy will discuss his interest in a special girl with his boy friend; this boy will approach a girl friend of the girl in question, who will relay the boy's interest to the girl. Then the girl's reaction is relayed back to the first boy.   The intermediaries often have not themselves reached the stage of dating and vicariously receive a thrill from this near approach to someone else's date.   As the first intermittent dates merge into regular dating, both boys and girls gain confidence and the ritual of feeling each other out goes on directly.

Dates in the middle class are prearranged.   Loitering on street corners or picking up casual acquaintances or strangers for impromptu dates are taboo.   Blind dates are permissible, inasmuch as the intermediary vouches for the attractiveness and good character of the two for whom the date is arranged.   In many adolescent circles a certain period of time must elapse between the time when the boy asks for a date and the date itself, perhaps three days for a movie date but two weeks for a formal dance.   Otherwise, the girl suspects that she is not the boy's first choice and her self-esteem is injured.

Through these rituals and techniques that are learned from older adolescents, boys and girls are inducted into dating.

Boy and girl initiative

As dating settles down into an accustomed activity, both boys and girls have appointed areas of initiative.   The boy in general controls the time and type of date.   He issues the invitation—although only when previous maneuvers have indicated that the girl will accept.   He usually proposes the destination, with the girl retaining a veto power.   He decides upon the transportation, whether the date will be single or double, and the amount of money to be spent.   If the couple doubles with another couple—much high school dating is carried on in this way—it is usually the boy and his friends who form the nucleus of the group.

The girl takes the initiative in determining the personal conduct on a date; she permits or refuses kissing, necking, and petting.   The assumption among girls is that most boys will go as far in caressing as the girl will permit.

Girls, perhaps in order to increase the number of dates with more prestige than movie dates, are aided by adults to sponsor dances and informal parties.   The girl then invites the boy, paying for the admission ticket; the boy retains the responsibility for transportation, corsage, and after-party refreshments.   In one city a student estimated that half the dances open to high school students were sponsored by girls' groups. The girl may also give parties at her home to which she invites other girls, who in turn invite their special boy friends.

Since dating is a new custom, and also no doubt because of a general movement toward equal status of the sexes, patterns of initiative are not always clear-cut.   Among 277 men students at the University of Minnesota, almost two thirds said they paid all the expenses of dating, and a third claimed to pay most but not all of the expenses.[7]   Women students were apparently reluctant to admit any part in expenses, for 78 per cent said that the men took care of all expenses.   The same students were asked the question, "Did the girl take the initiative in telephoning, visiting, and so forth?"   Seventy per cent of the men said the girls they had dated occasionally or often took the initiative; but only 44 per cent of the girls admitted such initiative.   Although these young men and women were not necessarily dating each other, it might be assumed that their reports would correspond.   Perhaps women dislike the implications of admitting initiative in a field in which they have traditionally been the sought-after rather than the seekers.

Routine of days, hours, and places

Friday and Saturday are date nights, Friday for the school football or basketball game followed by a mixer, and Saturday for the movie or dance date.   The Saturday date outranks the Friday date, and the formal dance outranks all other types of dates.   Sunday afternoon and evening less often are dating periods.   During the week, dating is replaced by informal loitering and talking around school, walking home from school together, meeting at coke bar or corner drugstore, and long telephone conversations.   During vacations other activities replace the school-sponsored ones—sleighrides, tobogganing, and private parties in the winter; picnics, hikes, and beach parties in the summer.   Many of the dances sponsored by community organizations come during the holidays (Christmas,

[7] Clifford Kirkpatrick and Theodore Caplow, "Courtship in a Group of Minnesota Students," *American Journal of Sociology,* 51 (1945), 122.

Thanksgiving, and Easter dances).   The routine gives a certain orderliness to the social life, makes it possible to correlate social and school activities, and provides an opportunity for a measure of control both by adults and by adolescents themselves.   It is possible to anticipate and to plan for activities well in advance.

Although hours may vary from one social clique to another, within a clique hours for ending a date are fairly well established.   They are usually determined by a compromise between parents who favor early hours and those adolescents who have the latest hour privilege.   By a process of jockeying and bargaining, adolescents and their parents arrive at some acceptable hour between the early and the late limits.   The pressure to do what the group does is very strong: as one informant stated, the boy or girl who had to leave a party earlier than the majority is regarded as a "dud."   More important than the exact hour for reaching home is the fact that it is always from one to two hours later than the time when a school or club party officially ends.   An interval of complete freedom follows the party, during which groups of young people are at liberty to do as they please at a time when most adults are in bed.   This time may be spent at the home of one member of a group, but more often it is spent in a restaurant, in driving around, or in a parked car.   It is primarily during this interval that the peer mores control personal conduct.

The hangout is an important part of dating.   This is a drugstore, confectionery, restaurant, or cold-drink counter where boys and girls gather, singly, in pairs, or in groups.   It is used after school and after the more formal part of a date.   At the hours that students assemble, few other people use the facilities, which then in a sense become the private property of the students, where they may sing, dance, "clown," or play practical jokes on each other.   Some communities have capitalized on this tendency by establishing special recreational rooms for young people, complete with juke box and coke bar, in the attempt to give some supervision to these activities.

Prestige symbols

Prestige is important in the dating system, and relates to groups, individuals, and techniques.   In some high schools, certain groups control the social life, especially when fraternities and sororities sponsor dances; the high school often finds itself unable to finance parties because the school parties lack prestige, being attended only by those who have lost hope of being included in the fraternity or sorority dances.   Although the social-class system is not prominent in some high schools, it may be reflected in that a group of upper-class students sets the pattern in dress, conduct, and choice of social activities, which other students, even though they may not be included in the select group, attempt to imitate.   Individuals also have high prestige, girls with dash and striking clothes and boys with athletic ability ranking high; class officers also have high rating. Scholarly achievement is less admired.

Going steady

Dating tends to have two phases, playing the field and going steady or dating only one person.   When dating first begins, most boys and girls play the field; that is, they seek dates with a number of persons, sometimes deliberately refraining from dating one person more than two or three times in succession.   Particularly those who plan to attend college may avoid dating only one person, although during college years they may go steady.

When a couple find themselves happy in their dating, with common interests and attitudes, they may tend to date only each other.   Group expectations and group pressure encourage the arrangement.

There are few boys and girls in high school who do not conform to the going steady formula.   If they do not conform they are regarded as queer and are left out of social gatherings and functions—not because of unpopularity but because couples are essential to the gatherings.

You just weren't accepted by the majority if you didn't have someone to give your undivided attention to.   It didn't matter really how often you switched from one person to another; the only essential was that at all times you had to have a "steady."

When a girl and a boy are seen together about five times people begin talking about the fact that they are going steady.   They then are expected to be seen together.   If they aren't, it is a mild scandal all over school.

Gradually, and it is almost inevitable, a certain couple are often seen together at high school functions.   Whether they like it or not they are looked upon as going steady and it is taboo to date another fellow's steady.   The girl is stuck.   However, there is compensation.   It is big moment to be asked to go steady; wearing the boy's class ring and his letters gives the girl a great deal of prestige.   Going steady is one of the most highly accepted statuses of the high school student.

Going steady becomes official when the boy asks the girl to go steady with him.   The term as used in connection with adolescent dating has a different connotation from its older usage, which indicated the beginning of courtship.   Going steady means simply that for a limited period of time neither boy nor girl will date anyone else.   It is assumed that for the time being they are more interested personally in each other than in anyone else.   But there are no future commitments as to permanence of the arrangement, love on the adult level, engagement, or marriage.   The mores of going steady are well established and include the following, at both high school and college levels:

1. No boy other than the chosen one will ask the girl for a date; this rule is highly respected and rigidly followed.   The girl, for her part, may not entice any other boy or show him favors.

2. The couple are always invited together to social functions; if one cannot attend, the other may not attend.   They have become a social unit.

3. Symbols are exchanged, such as rings, class pins, club pins, bracelets with the owner's name inscribed, or sweaters.   These symbols are not gifts; ownership remains with the original owner, the symbols being returned when the arrangement of going steady breaks up.   In fact, the absence of the pin or ring signifies to the high school crowd that the two are no longer going steady.

4. Nonmaterial symbols are cultivated between the two.   They may have a favorite song, a favorite seat in the motion-picture house, or a favorite place to park.   They thrill to the sound of "our song," and resent the innocent intrusion of another couple who happen to occupy the favorite seat or parking spot.

5. More intimacy is permissible and expected than with a casual date.

The motives of going steady are partly personal and partly social.   On the personal side is a greater enjoyment in the other's companionship than in that of any other—for the time being.   Often a high degree of emotional fervor wells up, and the two believe themselves in love, destined for each other.   This crush, infatuation, or "puppy love" is powerful while it lasts.   It is a natural phase of the process of maturing and of the inability of the adolescent to integrate or counterbalance his emotional reactions with other considerations.   All of his reactions tend to be strong.   He hates some things, can't stand others, just loves still others. His feelings toward people are strong and unrestrained by other considerations.   Therefore his interest in one of the opposite sex also tends to be strong and one-sided.   During college going steady may assume new meaning and become the beginning of courtship.

Going steady also gives a sense of security to both boy and girl.   The girl is assured of an escort and the boy is saved the painful procedure of approaching a new girl or one who plays the field, with the risk of being turned down.

There is prestige in going steady and especially so if the partner is admired by the friends of one's own sex.   Many girls maneuver boys into asking them to go steady so that they may display the boys' rings or pins.   Going steady therefore contributes greatly to the boy's or girl's sense of self-esteem and self-confidence.   The arrangement is proof of desirability of the person.

Socially, new avenues are opened to the couple going steady.   On one hand, parental anxiety relaxes a little if the partnership is approved.   It is possible to establish general rules with the couple and to know what to expect in the way of compliance with the rules.

At the same time, going steady creates new tensions.   Parents, glad of the greater stability of the relationship, at the same time are opposed on the basis that the boy or girl is limiting his social experiences, and also that the dating may (as it occasionally does at the high school level) lead into an early courtship.   The boy and girl, who eagerly leap into the intensity of going steady, soon find it a burden and long for greater freedom in companionship with a variety of persons.   The girl, especially, may feel uneasy over the expectation of more petting than she has previously permitted.

It is not surprising, therefore, that agreements to go steady are of short duration.   If the prestige motive is uppermost, every few weeks may find a new pairing off, with the girl wearing the pin or ring of a new boy.   This frequent shifting is accepted as proof of the girl's popularity.   The boy, in his turn, may desire to move from girl to girl, seeking ever more glamorous partners.   If the boy or girl is not sure of securing another partner, security may be the dominant motive and the arrangement may last longer —in fact it may become worn out so far as mutual enjoyment is concerned but continue because each dreads the necessity of making other contacts.

Even at the college level, dating that has reached the stage of "serious love affairs" follows much the same course as steady dating in high school. University of Minnesota students reported an average of 2.2 serious affairs each.   Of the total number reported by men, 73.0 per cent had broken up; of those reported by women, 71.0 per cent.[8]

According to Figure 32, breaking up usually follows mutual loss of interest.   The old, impassioned friendship sinks to the level of indifference, relief, or occasionally avoidance and dislike.   The Minnesota college students also stated their subsequent emotional reactions.[9]   Approx-

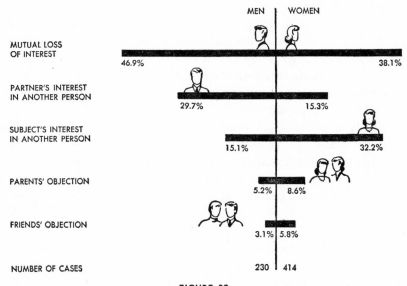

FIGURE 32

Breakup of College Love Affairs

College students, like high school students, are unstable in their love affairs; interest soon wanders to a new person.   The graph shows the distribution of the reasons for broken love affairs given by a group of Minnesota students. Interestingly, the percentages by sexes do not correspond.   (Source: Clifford Kirkpatrick and Theodore Caplow, "Courtship in a Group of Minnesota Students," *American Journal of Sociology*, 51 [1945], 123.)

imately one fourth of the boys and one third of the girls had severe emotional reactions; one fifth of each sex felt mingled regret and relief, whereas half of the boys and almost as high a proportion of girls were indifferent, relieved, or satisfied with the ending of the affair.   For the most part emotional involvement is not deep or, if deep for a time, is relinquished with relief.

[8] Kirkpatrick and Caplow, *op. cit.,* p. 114.
[9] Kirkpatrick and Caplow, *op. cit.,* p. 124.

UPPER-CLASS DATING

The contrast of middle-class dating with dating in well-established upper-class groups reveals the prevalence in upper-class groups of a formal, adult-controlled pattern within which the boy and girl work out their personal relationships.   The following account refers to an Eastern city in which the upper class has its roots in past centuries.

Dating begins at the age of 14 years and consists of Friday night movie dates, a quick trip to the favorite coke bar, and home by 11:30 o'clock.   This age also means the beginning of dances every other Saturday night at the country club.   These dances are a step higher than dancing schools, as nothing is taught and it is conducted like a regular dance.   Only certain people are invited to these dances, namely, students from the boys' and girls' private schools.   The boys and girls who meet at these dances become dating partners until the senior year in high school.

The cut-in system is used and a girl is a downright flop if she is not cut in on at least twice during one number.   This type of dancing is used at all the dances of this group of people—the system of a couple dancing only with each other is not used.   The cut-in system shows the preference for not going steady.   I should say that not one per cent of the private school students go steady.   In fact the very word is thought "common" among the group.   The idea is for a girl to go out with just as many boys as she can, and being seen with one boy more than three times in succession is embarrassing rather than being in a girl's favor.

At the age of 16 years young people graduate into dances at the country club that are for the older group and alternate with the dances for the younger boys and girls.   A boy takes a girl to the dance and takes her home, but during the evening they scarcely see each other.

Sex begins to play a small part in the relationship.   Dates for dances, movies, and so forth are usually terminated by a kiss and occasionally a necking session.   However, since the clique is relatively small, a bad reputation spreads like fire and so the girl hesitates before even kissing a boy goodnight.   Falling in love at this age is popular, but even if it is mutual the two rarely go steady.   They may go a little farther in their love-making but since they are in love it is kept pretty quiet.

When girls reach their senior year at high school they feel too old for the country club dances and also the senior boys.   Dating college men becomes frequent.   Week ends at the Eastern men's colleges are a must.   It is at this time that the girls narrow their field down to two or three boys, but they are usually conveniently scattered at different colleges to make the girl appear more popular.   These two or three boys very rarely include the one the girl eventually marries.

One of the nicest traditions of the upper class is the girl's debut, which occurs after she graduates from school. Since many derogatory remarks are made about coming-out parties, I will try to explain the debut. The debut is a beautiful tradition in these families, as the girl is following the pattern set by her mother and grandmother. The idea of a debut is to give the girl a chance to meet the friends of the family. Some she has known all her life, but others she has scarcely met, especially if they are from out of town. The debutante has become of age and is now considered a grownup. The parents are giving the party to celebrate this fact and to launch their daughter into the new group. Life is very different for the girl after her debut. The grownups that she meets will ask her to be on committees for charitable purposes or to join certain clubs. They have come to the party to welcome her into the adult group. Another purpose of the debut is to introduce the girl to a group of young men considered eligible as husbands. Up until the girl makes her debut she has usually dated only boys of her own age from the private schools. If she has attended boarding school she has scarcely dated at all. At the debut young men of 25–35 years old are invited. The parents explain to their daughter that she does not have to marry, but if she does here is a group of men that the parents consider acceptable. The young men have grown up in the same social class as the girl, they have mutual friends, likes and dislikes, and so, invariably, the girl does marry one of them. She wouldn't be happy marrying out of her class. She has been taught from childhood the values of her class position and the average girl wouldn't be able to accommodate herself to anything below at least an upper-middle-class position. The upper-class families do not regard the debut as a waste of money. They derive pleasure from the party and satisfaction in knowing that, according to their standards, they are doing what is right for their daughters, by introducing them to the people they will live and associate with for the rest of their lives. After the debut, couples tend to pair off. This pairing off does not mean that the couple remove themselves from the group, but means that they are pretty sure of each other. Two or three couples usually form groups within the larger social group and go almost everywhere together. Practically all the debutantes are married at least four years after they come out.

Families have a great deal to do with selection of a husband or wife by the daughter or son. Name and social position are very important and are usually determining factors. It would be almost impossible to fall in love with someone who isn't "accepted." If a boy or girl does fall in love with someone of this type, pressure from the family is usually successful in breaking it up. These relationships often develop while the boy or girl is at college. The outsiders don't know your families or social group at home and so won't tell of indiscretions. The student is away from the pressure of home and may be inclined to go wild. This tendency is true of girls as well as boys. However, the influence of home is always in the back of one's mind and few students think of marriage to these outsiders. After college the boys and girls return home, marry an old flame, and get back into their old clique.

LOWER-CLASS DATING

Lower-class dating is carried on primarily through commercial places of recreation, such as dance halls, drugstore or restaurant with a juke box, or taverns.   Lower-middle- and lower-class children from families with a strong church affiliation may find much of their recreation through the church or church mission.   In cities a certain proportion regularly attend club and mixed-group activities at settlements and community centers.

The failure of lower-class boys and girls to patronize school affairs is partly for financial and partly for social reasons.   Although many school recreational occasions may not entail any great expense, the outstanding events—the formal dances—necessitate an evening dress for the girl, a presentable suit (usually not a tuxedo or formal at the high school level) for the boy, money to buy the girl a corsage and provide refreshments after the dance, and some provision for a car or taxi.   Even when lower-class boys and girls are able to provide these necessary trappings for the formal school dance, they are often cold-shouldered by the middle-class students and made to feel unwanted; or they feel embarrassed and conspicuous because they are not familiar with the rituals and manners of the middle-class students.   They tend, therefore, to turn to less expensive and less exacting forms of entertainment.

Lower-class dating in a small city, Elmtown

Dating in the lower class has several distinguishing characteristics.[10] It is limited within the social class, except as some girls sporadically date boys one or two class levels above themselves; there is little playing the field during the teen-age period and much concentration upon a few dating partners, symptomatic no doubt of the early age of marriage in this class; and there is great freedom of the individual in choice of partner and place of the date.   These characteristics are related to the early age at which lower-class youth leave school.

Among Elmtown youth of high school age it was estimated that, whereas no upper- and only 7.6 per cent of the middle-class boys and

[10] Based on A. B. Hollingshead, *Elmtown's Youth* (Wiley, 1949), chs. 9, 12, 15, 16.

girls had withdrawn from school, 41 per cent of the upper-lower- and 89 per cent of the lower-lower-class boys and girls had dropped out of school without graduation.   Many of these children leave school a year or two before the legal age for the state and (because many have been disciplinary problems in school) are not forced to return.   Most of them have completed not more than the eighth grade.   School has not been a pleasant experience, for they have met many discriminations at the hands of upper-status students and teachers; at home they have been associated with parents, brothers, and sisters who did not complete high school and who value ability to earn money more than continued academic attainments. Thus at mid-adolescence many lower-class boys and girls find themselves out of school, working at low-paid temporary jobs, and eligible for the status and responsibilities of adulthood, although still living at home, whereas boys and girls of their own age but a higher social class are still regarded by parents, school, and legal authorities as children, to be supported by their parents, protected from hardships, and with their misdeeds condoned by school authorities and courts.   The types of work open to lower-class boys and girls are menial in nature; the boys work on farms or do unskilled factory work; the girls are employed as maids, waitresses, or petty clerks.   The work of both is monotonous, lacks prestige, and merits very low pay.   With no plans for future training, both boys and girls soon realize that they are in a rut.   They frequently change jobs and gradually acquire sufficient maturity to find steady employment.   By late adolescence the boys have found the general type of work they will continue to do, and by mid-adolescence the girls are ready to leave their jobs for marriage.

Because of this tendency to leave school and find work, the out-of-school lower-class adolescent assumes the role of an adult from one to five years earlier than do boys and girls who finish high school.   He is accepted as adult by the community and is expected to assume adult responsibilities.   The adolescents themselves are quite willing to be regarded as adults, but their emphasis is upon the freedom from adult control that they thus secure.

This early adult status of the lower-class boy and girl affects their dating and courtship roles.   Whereas adolescents of their age still attending school find much of their social life in school- or church-sponsored parties or in parties given by their families or private clubs, the lower-class youth spend most of their free time outside their homes with small cliques of their own age and sex composed of other nonschool youths, or in dating.   One of the first expenditures of the boy after he secures a job is for a broken-down automobile that can be repaired by himself and his pals.   In such a car two or three boys tour the town in the evening, stop here and there for a coke, a beer, or to play the pinball machine, or drive to a nearby town hoping to pick up some girl who is willing to ride with them, park, and pet.   The girls in Elmtown, even of lower-class status, are sufficiently protective of their status not to allow themselves to be picked up by boys who recognize them, although some may ride with boys from another town as pick-up dates.   Sometimes the boys visit a local prostitute if they have sufficient money; otherwise, the evening may end with destruction of highway signs in the rural area, more stops for coke or beer, or hanging around a skating rink or some other public place of amusement.   Both boys and girls hope to preserve a certain amount of anonymity about petting or casual sex relations, except from their pals. This desire accounts for the boys' picking up girls in another town, and the girls' allowing themselves to be picked up only by out-of-town boys. Thus, each group hopes to keep its reputation clean in the home town.

At other times, especially Saturday nights, lower-class boys and girls congregate in restaurants or taverns that cater to young people, the lower-class youths going to places that are considered not quite respectable by the middle- and upper-class groups.   Here boys and girls may meet without the formality of making prearranged dates.   They often come in cliques of their own sex, thus having security until maneuvers between boys' and girls' cliques result in pairing off.   The skating rink, certain motion-picture houses, and a few dance halls are also gathering places for the lower-class adolescents.   Gradually boys and girls pair off, sometimes after a preliminary fight between two boys for a girl—an attention that enhances the girl's ego—and around midnight the boys take the girls home, stopping in tavern or café, and delaying on the way home for petting or sex play.   This casual milling around and dating after an evening of skating, dancing, fighting, and drinking continues for several years before pair dating is established.

Sex is accepted more naturally by lower-class than by middle- and upper-class youth; the distinction is especially marked as between the girls of the different class levels.   Lower-class families are large, and their homes are small; sex activities of parents are less easily kept secret. The greater sex activity of unmarried older youths and extramarital activities of some married people also gradually become known to the adolescent group.   The assumption should not be made that sex is openly flaunted even in the lower lower class, for the mores against open talking about sex prevail, and children are punished by their parents for displaying too much knowledge.   Hence children learn to conceal their knowledge from their parents, although they talk of it freely in their own sex and age groups.   Control of sex tensions thus becomes a problem to lower-class boys and girls while they are still preadolescent, and by the time of adolescence they have experimented with masturbation and occasionally homosexual activities.   By the time dating begins, therefore, the lower-class youth has definitely developed sex tensions and is ready for experimentation with heterosexual sexual activities.   Also, girls have learned from older girls, and boys from their seniors, the techniques by which the sex game is played.   The procedure is for the boy to provide a car, and make a romantic or exciting occasion by driving around and providing food, candy, or some gift.   The girl, in accepting these favors, knows what is expected of her and must follow through with permitting the boy to have sex relations with her.   Both are then expected to maintain a discreet silence about the affair, for neither boy nor girl wants to have a bad reputation.   The boy may brag about having a "woman" but not mention any girl specifically; the girl must guard against being too easy with too many boys or men.   Although it is known that both boys and girls are experimenting with sex, if the procedure is carried out discreetly, it is not an obstacle to marriage.   It is accepted as natural for the girl to have sexual tensions and to desire this experience (as contrasted with upper-middle- and upper-class attitudes that boys but not girls have sexual desires).

A typical example is given in the discussion of Elmtown of a girl, Mary, who left high school in her sophomore year because she was criticized for dating older youths from neighboring towns.   She began to date a local boy and after some weeks had her first sex experience with him.   This affair continued for several months before a quarrel separated them.   Her next affair was with a boy of the next higher social class, followed by affairs with four other young men.   She avoided the designation of "common property" by not permitting sex intimacies until after the fourth date.[11]   At the age of 18 she married and settled down.   None of the

___

[11] Compare this statement with the middle-class restriction in the girl's code of no kiss until the third date.

young men with whom she had been intimate had talked about her.

Boys receive status by having sex experience and are expected to have their first experience with a girl by the time they leave school (not later than 16 years of age).

The casual dating and picking up of girls is followed by more regularized dating, which rapidly turns into "going steady," the equivalent of courtship in the lower-class group.   Dating absorbs three or four evenings a week, and parents and friends assume that the couple will soon marry, although no formal announcement is made by a party or through the newspaper (as occurs with middle- and upper-class engagements).   Since sexual experiences are already a part of the dating patterns of most boys and many girls, intercourse is accepted as a normal part of dating between engaged couples.   When the girl becomes pregnant, marriage is the next step, and usually occurs through the offices of a justice of the peace or perhaps a minister, but without a formal wedding. The couple normally secure a license, become married, and tell parents and friends afterward.   Typically the lower-class girl is in her middle or late teens at the time of marriage, and her husband in the early twenties.

ETHNIC DATING

No common pattern of dating or other heterosexual social contacts exists for ethnic groups, since the mores of each group are colored by the special cultural characteristics of the group.   If the ethnic group has lived in the United States for a number of years, the mores will show the effect of intercultural contact, even though the ethnic group still lives in a partially secluded community.   Thus the social folkways and mores of young people are a blend of American and foreign culture.   The following description therefore applies only to the Italian group.

The Italian slum in Eastern City is peopled by a lower-class peasant group, in which the parents represent the old-country culture.[12]   The free heterosexual social relationships found in the American group are unknown.   In other words, there is no dating and little courtship.   Contacts are of two types: those with "good" girls (virgins), which eventually will lead to marriage; and those with girls who permit sex relations, a

[12] Based upon a three-and-a-half year study of an Italian slum in an eastern city. —William Foote Whyte, "A Slum Sex Code," *American Journal of Sociology,* XLIX (July, 1943), 24–31.

situation without obligations.   The Italian peasant folkways and mores govern the social activities of the good girls.   As long as parental control remains intact, these girls are never alone with young men in unsupervised situations, unless they are going steady with implications of early marriage. The young man may call upon the good girl in her home; this procedure is interpreted by parents, relatives, and the girl herself to indicate that the boy is her suitor.   Until the boy is ready for this serious step, he therefore confines himself to contacts outside the home, such as club dances, picnics, parties in some girl's home, or evenings at bowling alleys.   To these affairs, girls come in groups and men separately in groups.   Each man may choose his partner for a dance or other activity, at the end of which he returns her to her group of girl friends.   At the end of the evening, the girls leave as a group and go home unescorted by the men.   These affairs are a blend of Italian and American customs, with breaking away from the home on the part of the girl but an avoidance of pairing off between boys and girls.   If the girl is further emancipated from parental control, usually possible only for girls who are employed, she may meet a young man by appointment on some street corner, but not allow herself to be picked up; if she works outside the Italian district, she attains still greater freedom in contacts with non-Italians.   Usually, however, the girl does not seek pair dating because of parental disapproval and the implication that she may not be a virgin.   When the young man reaches the degree of maturity and economic competence that makes marriage possible, he selects his wife from the Italian group, for he desires a wife who will understand his ways, prepare the food that he is accustomed to, and accept the subordinate position of the Italian wife.

Although the social contacts of the respectable Italian girl are thus strictly limited, not so with the contacts of the boy and young man of equal social status.   The dictum is accepted that sexual relations are necessary for a boy's health and virility, and boys therefore early in adolescence establish contacts with another type of girl.   The girls who permit intimacy fall into three categories: one-man girls who for a period confine themselves to one man but without implication of permanency or marriage; promiscuous girls who submit to a man on casual acquaintance who has provided a social evening including food, drink, and a ride; and prostitutes with whom a purely business arrangement is made.   In the order given there are decreasing desirability of the women, decreasing responsibility on the part of the man in case of discovery or pregnancy, and decreasing degree of ego-satisfaction to the man.   These girls often come from outside the district, for the boys—theoretically at least—pride themselves upon not destroying the virginity of girls of their own social group (from among whom they will later select a wife).   The boys also prefer beautiful girls, particularly blondes, and if possible someone of a social class above their own.   They do not maintain continued contacts with one girl, for they wish to avoid falling in love or arousing an assumption of marriage on the part of the girl.

This description shows clearly the different motivations in the two situations.   For marriage, in-group solidarity and personal security are uppermost.   The young man wants some girl known to his family and friends, familiar with the group customs, and compliant to the mores. He wants exclusive possession of the girl with no hint of allegiance with some other man.   He may then feel socially and personally secure.   In the sexual contacts he seeks adventure with someone beyond his social group, freedom from obligations, and prestige among other boys through attainment of a desired type of companion, as well as sexual experience.

The control of the contacts between young men and nonvirgins is governed by well-developed folkways and mores that have grown out of the situation over a period of time and are accepted by men and girls alike, and, also, tacitly by good girls and parents, although not with approval. The boys accept the responsibility of not molesting a virgin of their own ethnic group, of conforming to the group mores where marriage is concerned, and of accepting limited degrees of responsibility for paternity among one-man girls.   These are peer mores, growing out of the activities of the boys and accepted by them and enforced by disapproval of the group itself.

SOCIETAL INTEGRATION OF DATING

As often happens when changed social conditions call forth a new activity, such as dating, the new activity creates problems.

If mixed recreation and dating are advantageous as preparation for marriage, what of the high school boys and girls and the college men and women who do not participate?   Are their reasons based on personal preference or on some inadequacy in the system?   Out of 2,163 tenth and twelfth grade pupils in 10 western Pennsylvania high schools, 1,370 (63 per cent) gave reasons for not attending dances.   Table 18 sum-

TABLE 18

Reasons Why High School Pupils Do Not Attend Dances *

	Boys	Girls
Lack of knowledge of social usages		
I do not know how to dance	74%	39%
I would only sit or stand around and not really have a good time	36	30
Feel inferior, inadequate, do not belong	6	18
Lack of proper clothes, equipment, for dances		
I felt that my clothing was not good enough	8	12
I did not have the money	25	18
Boys: I could not take a girl because I had no good way of getting her there and back	36	7
Lack of dating partner		
Only those who are paired off with a member of the opposite sex really have a good time	16	26
Girls: I did not have a special boy friend to escort me		42
Boys: I did not have a special girl that I wished to take	40	
Boys: I lack the nerve to ask a girl	25	
Disapproval		
I do not approve of dancing	11	6
Parents object to my dancing	6	10
I would be out late at night and my parents disapprove of that	11	21
NUMBER OF CASES	694	676

* Based on table in P. W. Hutson and D. R. Kover, "Some Problems of Senior High School Pupils in Their Social Recreation," *Educational Administration and Supervision,* 28 (1942), 503–510.   A number of miscellaneous reasons were given, applying in each case to less than 4 per cent.   Since pupils could indicate more than one reason, the total exceeds 100 per cent.

marizes the reasons.   Apparently dancing belongs to the socially sophisticated, the financially well-heeled, and the boys and girls already well advanced in dating.   The students who do not go to dances perhaps date at other levels or enter into other types of mixed activities.   Nevertheless, the emphasis on popularity and social rituals tends to exclude some students.

Other studies show that among both high school and college students are many for whom dating is an occasional event and a few who do not date at all.   Figure 33 presents the various dating patterns for urban, suburban, and rural high school students.   Among a sample of Minnesota college students, 45 per cent of the men and 34 per cent of the women participated little or not at all in formal social activities.[13]   Two thirds of the men and more than half of the women felt that they had inadequate opportunities to meet members of the opposite sex.   The men felt that their failure to meet women was most often because of lack of money and time, or they met the "wrong kind" of women.   Lack of social contacts and lack of time were the reasons given by women.

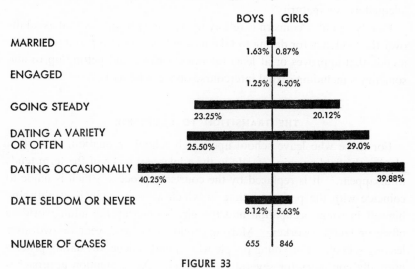

FIGURE 33

Dating among High School Youths

Occasional dating is most typical of the Michigan and Georgia youths whose dating experiences are combined in this figure; a small percentage do not date at all.   (Source: M. J. Williams, "Personal Education Needs," *Social Forces,* 27 [1948–49], 280.)

Dating, then, appears to be poorly integrated into the activities of high school and college students.   Unaided, many students are not able to manage the time, expense, and social training needed for successful dating.

The theoretical justification for dating is that it enables young people to meet those of the opposite sex and adjust their attitudes and activities to each other.   However, the area of adjustment that dating encompasses is confined to recreation; cooperative work between boys and girls on serious projects is neglected.   Can heterosexual relations on a recrea-

[13] Kirkpatrick and Caplow, *op. cit.,* p. 117.

tional level alone prepare the adolescent for adult heterosexual cooperation in such endeavors as managing a home or rearing children?

Another questionable phase of dating is the way in which adolescents
have been permitted—in fact, given an open field—to create a little exclusive social world of their own that tends to separate them from, rather
than integrate them into, the adult world and mature societal activities.
Might not participation in mixed groups of all ages prepare them more
adequately for maturity?

Finally, genuine concern is felt by many young people as well as adults
over the tendency for dating to take its cue from courtship and to include
a code that approves or at least tolerates necking and petting up to and
sometimes including sexual intercourse on a casual basis.[14]

THE TRANSITION TO COURTSHIP

For those who leave school upon high school graduation, or earlier,
playing the field or going steady in the adolescent sense of the term tends
to disappear.   It is replaced by the courtship process, which is made to
coincide with the period of time in which a young man is establishing
himself in some occupation and the girl is entering the adult world as
office or factory worker.   Marriage follows within a year or two after
leaving school.   For young people who attend college, the dating process
normally continues for several more years.   As graduation approaches
and college students face entrance into the adult world, courtship tends
to replace dating, just as it does at a younger age for those who do not
continue beyond grade or high school.

A young woman at a large Midwestern coeducational university described the progression from dating to courtship as follows:

College is heaven.   You've met so many wonderful kids and now you're
really on your own.   The date bureau has arranged loads of blind dates for
you and there's never a dull moment.   Freshman dates are just about like
high school dates, for you go to shows or mixers and then back to the student union for a coke and with the customary goodnight kiss you are off to
bed and another day.   After you've met a few fellows you are sure to be
invited to a beer party that some fraternity is giving.   To these you wear
your old clothes and sit around a fire singing college songs of all sorts and
drinking a little beer.   A few people spend the time necking, but they are
far from the majority.

[14] For a further discussion of premarital sex relations, see Chapter 14.

When you are a sophomore and move into your sorority house, dating usually becomes a little more serious.   Maybe this is because you are living now with older girls rather than just freshmen like yourself, but probably it is because you have a place where you can bring a date to neck.   Although dating is more serious and necking more prolonged, it is done in a crowd, and although some parents are shocked when they walk into a sorority house in the last fifteen minutes before the doors are locked, it is really very harmless.

Life and dating continue at about the same pace until you take that "dream of a man's" pin.   Even then the intensity of your necking varies little, but you begin to make serious plans for the future.

QUESTIONS

1. What seems to you to be the most important function of dating?
2. What is meant by the "rating and dating" complex?
3. How does the peer-group code control dating?   How is this code related to adult mores on sexual behavior?
4. Why does love-making play so prominent a part in adolescent dating?
5. How does dating differ from other pair-relationships?
6. What are the advantages to the boy and girl of going steady?   Is going steady a step toward maturity or does it hinder mature development?
7. In what ways are middle- and lower-class dating customs an outgrowth of the general class cultures?
8. Would it be advisable to give more adult guidance to dating?   If you think so, how could such guidance be given?

BIBLIOGRAPHY

Ehrmann, Winston W., *Premarital Dating Behavior* (Dryden, 1952).

Farnham, Marynia F., *The Adolescent* (Harper, 1951), ch. 8.

Hollingshead, August B., *Elmtown's Youth* (Wiley, 1949), chs. 9, 12, 15, and 16.

Horrocks, John E., *The Psychology of Adolescence, Behavior and Development* (Houghton Mifflin, 1951), ch. 6.

Lowrie, S. H., "Dating, a Neglected Field of Study," *Marriage and Family Living,* 10 (1948), 90–91, 95.

———, "Dating Theories and Student Responses," *American Sociological Review,* 16 (1951), 334–340.

Williams, M. J., "Personal and Family Problems of High School Youths and Their Bearing upon Family Education Needs," *Social Forces,* 27 (1948–49), 279–285.

Waller, W., "The Rating and Dating Complex," *American Sociological Review,* 2 (1937), 727–734.

13

Courtship and Engagement

At some point in the dating process the quality of the relationship changes. Outwardly, the same social rituals may be observed; but subjectively the dating couple find their attitudes toward each other changing. They wish to date only each other and begin to discuss, first tentatively and then seriously, the possibility of marriage. This period of dating that looks to a continued association with each other is courtship; when the intention of the couple to marry is announced, engagement begins. Courtship, an honorable word in the past, is not used currently by young people to describe the transition from casual dating to engagement. Young people recognize that "going steady" has lost its old meaning as a folk synonym for courtship; they may ask if a certain couple are "in love" or "serious" about each other, thus signifying a step beyond going steady. The step beyond "seriousness" is engagement. Recognizing that courtship now has no definite beginning but develops from the earlier patterns of casual dating, we will use it to signify the more intensive dating that looks to the future more than to the present for its objectives.[1]

---

[1] In an interesting article, Samuel Harman Lowrie criticizes the limitation of the term *dating* to the casual and ego-centered dating of adolescence and the use of *courtship* for the relationship that the public assumes has commitments for a future marriage. In present usage, he says, dating covers all degrees of paired relationships, the couple alone knowing whether their intentions are noncommittal or serious. In contrast to all dating is engagement, when the couple announce commitments for the future.—"Dating Theories and Student Responses," *American Sociological Review,* 16 (1951), 334–340. Nevertheless, for purposes of analysis it is convenient to recognize stages in the dating process, the later stage here being called by the conventional term *courtship*.

COURTSHIP CONTRASTED WITH CASUAL DATING

Whereas dating is a social arrangement linked with immaturity, courtship is a process of establishing identification between two adults. When people, instead of marrying, continue casual dating through the twenties and thirties, they are prolonging an immature relationship into adult years. This statement is true whether the dating is with a variety of companions or with one person only. In contrast, young adolescents who enter courtship often are introducing an adult relationship into their lives before they are psychologically and socially ready for it.

Courtship is not simply a late stage of dating; it has distinctive qualities of its own. The chief difference is in the contrasting goals of dating—a social event repeated with different partners that is an end in itself—and courtship—personal and social adjustment between a man and a woman that will continue through marriage into family life. The total psychological and social patterns built up about dating and courtship are related to these opposed goals. So at variance are the motives and standards of conduct of the two relationships that completely different types of personality in the partners may be sought for the two relationships. Dating often is cited as a means of selection of the marital partner. Although the partner chosen for courtship may be one of the earlier dating partners, often a new alliance is made that moves quickly through the exploratory period of casual dating into serious attempt at adjustment on the marital level.

The greater intensification of emotional involvement and depth of attachment during courtship also distinguishes it from dating. The young man may like his dating partner; he may love her and tell her so, but his love is light and gay; he may admire her beauty or the style of her dress. When he begins to court, he begins to love deeply. He also begins to project his love into the future; he promises and is sure he will love forever and that there will never be another woman for him.

Moreover, courtship is a period of progressive intensification of commitments. Whereas dating is a time of deliberate avoidance of commitments to or responsibilities for the other one, courtship has an equally strong trend toward increasing responsibilities. Pledges are given and accepted and with them attendant obligations. The young man who asks a girl to marry him implicitly binds himself to fulfill the role of husband; the girl as fully accepts that role from him and by inference promises to fill a wifely role.   Although the full significance of this implied contract may not be in their minds in the fullness of their personal feeling of love, it is soon impressed upon them by family and friends and comes to them as they imagine themselves sharing married life.

Adequate courtship assumes the prior attainment of a mature personality, well integrated, self-reliant, able to accept responsibility, and with energies directed toward well-defined future goals.   Valid courtship can come only after the person has made a satisfactory heterosexual adjustment and has accepted his masculine or feminine role.

In terms of his previous experience, the person who is ready for courtship should have no major conflicts, especially none relating to love, sex, and marriage; should be free from dependence upon his parents or parent-substitutes; should have a foothold in some occupation, if a man, or in some combination of occupation and domesticity, if a woman (this foothold might be either actual employment or well-planned preparation for it); should have experience in making decisions and abiding by them; should have the capacity for and habit of accepting some responsibility for others, either personally or in community or national movements; and should have defined realistic goals for himself and made some progress toward reaching them.   These are the concrete ways in which, in our culture, the mature personality expresses itself.

MOTIVATIONS OF COURTSHIP

The motivations of courtship are biological, psychological, and social.

Biological

Biologically, young men and women have been prepared for sexual relations since early adolescence.   Some have secretly satisfied their drives outside of marriage; others have repressed the drive or diverted it into compensatory channels.   In our culture the desire for sex relations normally precedes the desire for children.   Sex is regarded more or less as an individual affair, children as a social responsibility.   With greater maturity comes the desire both for more complete sex satisfaction than is possible outside of marriage and for children.   This full expression of biological drives has awaited psychological and social readiness. Courtship provides the avenue through which young people pass with social approval to the culmination of sex experience in marriage.

Psychological

The chief psychological motive is the need to establish identification with another person. Children are reared in a small family where they identify themselves closely with their parents. In adolescence they identify partially with a number of people, finally achieving relative independence from anyone. Identification is a mutual process of conscious or unconscious (usually the latter) acceptance of the attitudes of another person, in return for which come love and approval. Through both innate needs and habit, love and approval on an intimate personal basis become necessary to the happiness of the person. Few people ever become so self-sufficient that they can happily dispense for long with a mutual love relation or approval of intimates. Therefore the period of relative independence of later adolescence is followed by a craving for a new identification.

This new relationship differs from the identification of childhood in that it is between persons of equal status who are in the same age period and usually have the same general degree of maturity, whereas the identification of childhood is one of dependence on the part of the child and dominance on the part of the parent. The identification of courtship also differs from that of the adolescent, who is searching for a new personal tie to replace that with the parents. He tries out first this person and then that, finding in many some congenial similarity to himself but in none complete satisfaction. Also, out of his partial dependence and insecurity he still seeks to cling to older persons, such as teachers or club leaders.

Courtship, as stated above, is between equals; more important, it is a gathering into one strand all the partial identifications and a linking of that strand to the personality of one other person. Early courtship is a mutual testing of the other's personality to discover to what extent it offers basis for identification. Because the aura of romantic love encompasses courtship, idealization obstructs a clear view of the other's personality. The loved one is conceived of as almost perfect. A false sense of identification easily gives an equally false security. Thus one of the chief motivations of courtship—to find an object for identification —may also create one of the dangers of courtship.

The lover seeks not only someone similar to himself, but also someone who complements his characteristics and who therefore can satisfy his needs. If he craves love, he seeks a motherly or fatherly companion; if he needs to give love and to protect, he seeks someone needing protection. The person lacking in self-confidence unconsciously is drawn to someone who is able to give him admiration and support. Even when characteristics are not markedly opposite, the complementary character of the relationship is present. Biologically, men and women complement each other in that neither can enjoy full sexual satisfaction without the presence and cooperation of the other. Socially, the roles of men and women are interdependent in that each performs certain functions for the comfort and well-being of the other. Although the masculine and feminine roles have lost much of their distinctiveness in the past 50 years, they are still different and complementary in many respects.

Another psychological motivation is the urge toward adulthood. In our society full entrance into the adult world often is achieved only with marriage. Married people tend to treat the unmarried—even those older than themselves—as unfinished products, as adolescents who have not savored the fully ripe fruit of adult life. Unmarried people are excluded from intimate gossip or information on sexual affairs; sometimes they are not paid as much salary as the married; they are discouraged— especially women—from establishing their own households. If they live with parents, these parents constantly refer to them as boys and girls or as children, regardless of their mature years, and assume that final decisions even on personal matters should be made by the parents. In many ways, the unmarried are made to feel immature and rejected by the adult world.

Social

Socially, courtship is motivated by the desire and opportunity to consolidate two previously separate social worlds—those of the man and the woman engaged in courtship—for the urge toward psychological identification extends to social contacts. If the man and woman have not previously moved in the same social group, each must become acquainted with the friends of the other. Some, perhaps many, of these friends will not be congenial to the new partner. A more or less conscious conflict may be waged between the two as each tries to preserve as many of his old friendships as possible. Sometimes the social groups may compete as each tries to retain its old member and capture the allegiance of the other. Gradually, some degree of unification of the two social worlds is achieved, partly by elimination of the least congenial and by acceptance of the more compatible friends. In other cases, many of the old friends of unmarried days are dropped and the couple affiliates with a new circle of married people. Such a new affiliation is easily accomplished when the couple move to a new city upon marriage.

Courtship also provides opportunity to dispose of many close pair-friendships that do not fit into the marital pattern of life. The young woman who has had an intimate friendship with another girl, with whom she shared secrets, perhaps living quarters, vacations, even such property as a car, finds that she must gradually detach herself from this friendship in order to build up a unified relationship with her fiance. Many ties and habits hold her close to her feminine friend, and sometimes the break is not made without an inner struggle on her part and competition between the friend and the fiance. Sometimes the friendships are with those of the other sex. These may be especially difficult to handle if the friendship has developed beyond the dating stage and commitments have been actually or tacitly made.

LENGTH OF COURTSHIP

The length of acquaintance, courtship, and engagement between couples has become the subject of serious study. We know that in our own frontier past many marriages rested on brief acquaintance, and that in other cultures, where marriages are arranged by the parents, bride and groom may not see each other until the wedding day. According to our present philosophy of marriage, however, young people must find congenial mates largely by their own efforts and often in a social situation where first acquaintance is sought because one is attracted by the other's personal appearance. The emphasis upon personal happiness necessitates that, after acquaintance is achieved, the couple shall have time to explore each other's personalities before marriage. How much time is needed for the matching of personalities and the beginning stages of adjustment to take place? What criterion can be used to judge the most advantageous length of acquaintance, courtship, and marriage?

The usual criterion for measuring the most advisable length of premarital association is a successful marriage. In other words, married couples are first classified as to success in marriage, and the degree of success is related to the length of acquaintance, courtship, and engagement that each couple had.   Numerous studies support each other in linking a successful marriage with a long period of premarital association.

Paul Popenoe, long a professional marriage counselor, compared the marriages of 374 persons who came for advice with a control aggregate of 436 marriages known to students at the University of Southern California (but not student marriages).[2]   Unsuccessful marriages were defined as those necessitating the aid of a marriage counselor.   Among the poorly adjusted couples the average (mean) length of acquaintance before betrothal was 20.15 months as compared with 28.30 months for the control group.   The mean length of betrothal for the unadjusted group was 7.51 months and for the control group 12.46 months.   The number of couples who married without any formal engagement was eight times as great among the unhappy couples as among those in the control group.   Clearly, brief acquaintance and short engagements tend to be associated with later maladjustment of sufficient severity to prompt at least one of the couple to apply to a counselor for advice.

A more detailed study of 526 cases was made by Burgess and Cottrell, sociologists, for three stages of intimacy: acquaintance, courtship, and engagement.[3]   The criterion of successful marriage used was marital adjustment as measured by a self-rating scale covering various items of agreement or disagreement, common interests and activities, demonstration of affection, confiding, and feeling of satisfaction and happiness. Long acquaintance, courtship, and engagement were associated with later good adjustment in marriage.   Persons married with an acquaintance of less than six months achieved good adjustment in only 22.4 per cent of the cases; with acquaintance of five or more years, 52.3 per cent had good adjustment.   The percentage with good adjustment increased with length of courtship: of those who courted under one year, about one third were well adjusted in marriage; in contrast, among those who courted three or more years, over half were well adjusted.   Long engagements likewise were associated with good adjustment in marriage: only 37 per cent of those not engaged at all and 25.7 per cent of those with engagements of less than three months adjusted well in marriage.   In contrast is the group engaged for two or more years, 62.6 per cent of whom were happily married.

[2] Paul Popenoe and D. W. Neptune, "Acquaintance and Betrothal," *Social Forces,* 16 (1937–1938), 552–555.

[3] E. W. Burgess and L. S. Cottrell, *Predicting Success or Failure in Marriage* (Prentice-Hall, 1939), pp. 406–407.

Terman, a psychologist, in a study published prior to that of Burgess and Cottrell found similar evidence of the relation of long engagement to marital success.[4]   For the criterion of success he used the person's own estimate of marital happiness.   For both husband and wife the highest mean score of marital happiness was found among those whose engagements had endured five or more years.

All three of the studies cited refer primarily to urban middle-class marriages.   Upper- and lower-class marriages and rural marriages have not been studied with respect to length of prior association.

Although these studies show that a higher percentage of successful marriages have grown out of long than short courtship, the correlation between length of courtship and degree of good marital adjustment is far from perfect.   Other factors besides length of courtship also operate.

The significance of length of courtship is not in the exact number of months, but in provision for sufficient time in which the psychological and sociological processes of courtship may come to summation.   The interaction by which these processes are carried on cannot take place in an evening or a month.   Identification involves changes in attitudes and habits of two people.   Sometimes, as in conversion, attitudes and habits change quickly; but usually changes are made slowly, a step at a time. The change is especially likely to be slow when previous attitudes and habits have to be broken down and replaced by new ones.

The courting couple do not build up the attitudes and habits of courtship from a blank background of nonheterosexual relations.   For 5 to 10 years they have assiduously practiced the arts of dating; these arts must be disposed of before the different arts of courtship and marital preparation may be learned.   Dating emphasized an attitude of non-responsibility that must be replaced by an attitude of responsibility; exploitation must be replaced by protectiveness; the date as an end in itself by long-term planning; the practice of "safety in numbers" or "playing the field" by willingness to accept an exclusive relationship with one person.   Many habits of dating must be reversed: saving instead of spending; earlier hours rather than late in order to be efficient for the next day's job; and learning the household arts (for the girl) in contrast to overconcentration on personal appearance.

Another circumstance in modern America that requires a lengthy court-

[4] L. M. Terman, *Psychological Factors in Marital Happiness* (McGraw-Hill, 1938), pp. 197–201.

ship if happy marriage is to result is the lack of long friendship on a casual level or of acquaintance between the families of the interested couple.   On the college campus or in the office or factory of a city, men and women meet as individuals rather than as bearers of family, class, and ethnic culture.   A romantic interest or an infatuation may easily develop between two people of diverse attitudes and cultural background, who may even be drawn to each other because of their personal differences or because one forms a striking contrast to the customary social group of the other.   Under these circumstances, the process of social identification is especially slow.   The lower-class boy who has pushed his way into the middle-class milieu of the typical college only slowly can adapt himself to the expectations and folkways of the middle-class girl, and the girl in turn will require time in which to revise her estimates of what she expects from a husband to make allowances for the deficiencies of her husband as viewed by middle-class standards.   Even when the two are from the same social class, often neither has seen the other in a familial situation.   The young man has no way of knowing what the girl's response is to a sinkful of dirty dishes, nor does the girl know the man's attitude about shaving on a Sunday at home.   Love unfolds before the pair are familiar with each other's personalities and backgrounds. Time is the safeguard that prevents a transition from early dating to marriage without the needed courtship processes.

A long courtship is not always easy to attain, however.   Graduation from college, migration of young people from rural areas to cities or from one region to another, and military service are some of the types of mobility that tear young people apart before the courtship process has run its course.   Faced with separation and knowing from their dating experience of the past how tenuous a pair relationship may become when one or both are faced with a new social situation and the need for immediate social contacts, the courting couple terminate their courtship with a brief engagement followed by marriage.   Sometimes public engagement is omitted entirely and the first announcement of intention to marry comes with the marriage itself.   The mere fact that marriage vows have been given does not nullify the necessity for the courtship process to complete itself.   It then continues into the marital state, complicating the adjustment to marriage.   If the process is blocked, the husband and wife must go through the public legal procedure of divorce to withdraw from their responsibilities.   Prior to marriage, failure of the two to adjust may terminate the relationship.   Withdrawal at this point, however, is a private and individual act.   Property settlements, alimony, possible custody of children, and the public exposure of quarrels are avoided.

SELECTION OF MATE

Personal selection of the mate is part of the philosophy of American marriage.   Nevertheless, selection is narrowed down to a relatively limited group within which the personal choice may be made.   Some of the limitations have already been discussed in Chapters 9 and 10, and will only be mentioned here.

Cultural restrictions

Marriage within one's own race is the restriction most rigorously enforced both by law and by the mores.   When no law exists, it is true that persons of different races may marry, but so strong is the approval of marriage within the race and so severe the social penalties for outmarriage that few individuals feel the urge to marry into another race.

Religion sets the next limitation.   The majority of people marry within their own religious faith.   Although no law regulates marriage with reference to religion, the sanction of the church may be withheld from the one marrying into another religion, and especially so when the adherent of the other religion refuses to make concessions to the marriage pattern of the church.   Thus the Catholic whose marriage to a non-Catholic has not been sanctified by the Catholic Church is regarded as not married but as "living in sin."   The orthodox Jew who marries outside his faith is officially declared to be dead.

A third limitation is the boundary of the ethnic culture.   So long as families hold to the foreign culture of their youth or their ancestors, they circumscribe their children's social contacts by the ethnic culture, and the tendency is strong for marriages to occur within the ethnic group.

Less strong, but nevertheless a factor, is the inclusive nature of the social class.   The tendency of people to marry others of the same occupational status and the same degree of education is essentially the tendency to marry within the social class to which the person belongs.

Finally, marriages take place on the basis of personal contacts.   Those resulting from arrangement between families for young people who are not personally acquainted or through correspondence or "lonely heart" bureaus are very rare.   Among nonmobile groups the selection is limited to a narrow geographical area.   Among such mobile groups as college students, migratory workers, or men and women in military service the permanent residences of those who marry may be far apart; but for a time at least they have been placed in personal contact with each other.

With reference to cultural characteristics, therefore, in the majority of marriages husband and wife have very similar cultural heritages, values, and associations.   This natural sorting out of mates on a cultural basis is referred to as cultural homogamy (like-marriages), assortative mating, or cultural endogamy.   The tendency to marry within the same residential area is referred to as residential propinquity.   The out-marriages that sometimes occur across these barriers are in the minority, generally are disapproved by both cultural groups, and frequently create problems of personal adjustment and in family and community relationships.[5]

In addition to cultural homogamy, various fortuitous factors over which the individual has little control also affect mate selection.

Legal restrictions

Laws do not prescribe personal choices, but they proscribe marriages between certain groups or types of individuals.   Laws with reference to race have already been discussed: certain states forbid some types of racial intermarriages.[6]   The laws are not uniform as between states, and within one state certain races may be permitted to intermarry, while others are forbidden the privilege.

Age of marriage is also controlled by law.   The most frequent minimum age for marriage with the parents' consent is 18 years for males and 16 for females: 30 states set 18 for males and 27 states specify 16 for females; moreover, these two minimum ages are usually found in combination in the state laws.   Age 16 for males and 14 for females is another favored combination: 11 states set age 16 for males and 9 approve 14 for females.   In 4 states (Idaho, Mississippi, New Jersey, and Washington), the old common-law ages of 14 for boys and 12 for girls still prevail as the minimum ages.   Table 19 gives the ages for each state.

Most marriages, however, do not occur until long after the minimum

---

[5] For a somewhat different theoretical discussion of approved and forbidden marriages, see Robert K. Merton, "Intermarriage and the Social Structure: Fact and Theory," *Psychiatry*, 4 (August, 1941), 361–374.

[6] See pages 242–249.

age. The median age for first marriages, based on 1940 Census data, is 24.3 years for men and 21.6 for women.[7] White men marry about a year and a half later than nonwhites, and white women two years later than nonwhites. The northeastern states have a higher median age than any other region, with Massachusetts and New York having the highest medians in the nation for men, 26.2 years, and Massachusetts and Rhode Island the highest for women, 23.5 and 23.1, respectively. The South has the lowest median ages, for whites as well as Negroes, with Arkansas having the lowest median for men (23.0 years) and Oklahoma for women (20.0 years).

Socially interpreted, the legal minimum age for marriage is probably more closely related to the age at which schooling stops and earning begins than to any other factor. Only the common-law ages approximate biological maturity. The minimum marital ages all tend to be below the age for voting or for inheritance of property. In terms of the processes leading to marriage, the minimum legal age approximates the period when dating becomes well established, with engagement following several years later and marriage about six years after the initial dating. In Table 19 the median ages are placed in juxtaposition to the legal minimum ages to show the lack of close relationship. Only in a minority of cases does the young couple find the legal age a hindrance to marriage.

Mate selection is also subject to other legal regulations. The laws of all states prohibit marriage between those of close relationship—parent and child, sister and brother, aunt and nephew, uncle and niece, grandparent and grandchild; and marriage of first cousins is forbidden in about two thirds of the states. In addition to these blood relationships, some relationships based on marriage also are regarded in many states as a bar to marriage, the most common prohibition being that stepparent and stepchild may not marry. The marriages between blood relatives involve questions of inheritance as well as moral aversion to family endogamy. The marriage of stepparent and stepchild would not raise any question of heredity but arouses deep-seated aversions to incest, which are not limited to the strictly biological family. The insane and the feeble-minded in most states are forbidden to marry. In most states, too, premarital physical tests single out those with syphilis, who are not issued marriage licenses until the disease has been cured and a negative test is returned.

[7] *Population—Special Reports, Age at First Marriage,* Series P-45, No. 7 (Bureau of the Census, May 28, 1945), p. 1.

TABLE 19

Legal Age of Marriage and Median Age of First Marriage

State	Legal age of marriage, January 1, 1948 *				Median age of marriage †			
	With consent of parents		Without consent of parents		White		Nonwhite	
	Males	Females	Males	Females	Males	Females	Males	Females
The Northeastern states								
Maine	16	16	21	18	24.1	22.1		
New Hampshire	14	13	20	18	24.7	22.4		
Vermont	16	14	21	18	24.9	21.8		
Massachusetts	18	16	21	18	26.2	23.5		
Rhode Island	18	16	21	21	26.0	23.1		
Connecticut	16	16	21	21	26.0	22.8		
New York	16	14	21	18	26.2	22.5		
New Jersey **	14	12	21	18	26.1	22.3		
Pennsylvania	16	16	21	21	25.1	21.9		
The North Central states								
Ohio	18	16	21	21	24.3	21.8		
Indiana	18	16	21	18	23.6	21.2		
Illinois	18	16	21	18	24.9	22.0		
Michigan	18	16	21	18	24.2	21.8		
Wisconsin	18	15	21	18	25.1	22.6		
Minnesota	18	15	21	18	25.4	23.0		
Iowa	16	14	21	18	24.1	21.9		
Missouri	15	15	21	18	23.8	21.3		
North Dakota	18	15	21	18	25.7	22.4		
South Dakota	18	15	21	18	25.1	22.3		
Nebraska	18	16	21	21	24.6	21.9		
Kansas	18	16	21	18	24.1	21.4		
The West								
Montana	18	16	21	18	24.5	21.7		
Idaho **	14	12	18	18	23.5	21.2		
Wyoming	18	16	21	21	24.3	21.4		
Colorado	18	18	21	18	23.7	21.4		
New Mexico	18	16	21	18	23.4	20.4		
Arizona	18	16	21	18	23.5	21.0		
Utah	16	14	21	18	23.6	21.6		
Nevada	18	16	21	18	23.7	21.6		
Washington **	14	12	21	18	24.5	21.8		
Oregon	18	15	21	18	24.1	21.8		
California	18	16	21	18	24.1	21.9		

TABLE 19 (Continued)

Legal Age of Marriage and Median Age of First Marriage

State	Legal age of marriage, January 1, 1948 *				Median age of marriage †			
	With consent of parents		Without consent of parents		White		Nonwhite	
	Males	Females	Males	Females	Males	Females	Males	Females
The South								
Delaware	18	16	21	18	24.4	21.6	24.8	20.2
Maryland	18	16	21	18	24.2	22.0	23.7	20.9
District of Columbia	18	16	21	18	25.2	23.0	23.2	20.9
Virginia	18	16	21	21	24.1	21.6	24.0	20.7
West Virginia	18	16	21	21	23.7	21.1	23.4	19.4
North Carolina	16	16	18	18	23.2	21.2	23.4	20.3
South Carolina	18	14	18	18	23.2	21.1	22.1	19.7
Georgia	17	14	21	21	23.3	20.8	22.3	19.3
Florida	18	16	21	21	23.5	21.3	22.7	19.0
Kentucky	16	14	21	21	23.3	20.9	23.2	20.8
Tennessee	16	16	21	21	23.2	20.8	23.0	19.7
Alabama	17	14	21	18	23.1	20.6	22.6	19.6
Mississippi **	14	12	21	18	23.2	21.0	21.8	19.4
Arkansas	18	16	21	18	23.0	20.2	22.2	19.1
Louisiana	18	16	21	21	23.5	20.9	22.5	19.4
Oklahoma	18	15	21	18	23.1	20.0	23.6	19.3
Texas	16	14	21	18	23.6	20.5	22.7	19.2

* Sara Louise Buchanan, *The Legal Status of Women in the United States of America as of January 1, 1948,* Bulletin of the Women's Bureau, No. 157—United States Summary (revised), U. S. Department of Labor (Government Printing Office, 1951), pp. 60–61.

** The common law ages of 14 for males and 12 for females apply in the absence of specific laws.

† *Population—Special Reports, Age at First Marriage,* Series P-45, No. 7 (Bureau of the Census, May 28, 1945), p. 3. The median age of first marriage for women is based upon a sample for all women ever married, 45–64 years old; medians for males are estimated from complete count of male population by age and marital status, for 1940.

All these laws place further restrictions on the group from which a mate may be selected. Unlike the social prohibitions, all of which emphasize endogamy or marriage within the cultural group, some of the laws establish exogamy or forbid marriages within or between certain groups or types of individuals.

Sex ratio

The number of males per 100 females, called the sex ratio, may be a disturbing factor in mate selection. In 1950 for every 100 females in the United States there were 98.1 males; the sex ratio therefore was 98.1.[8] Since 1910 the sex ratio has been declining owing to reduced immigration. The European immigration included large numbers of young men who helped to maintain an excess of males for many decades. The sex ratio for 1950 is also disturbed slightly by the exclusion from the Census of men in service who were overseas on April 1, 1950, the date of the Census.

The overall sex ratio does not throw much light upon the marriage possibilities because the same ratio does not prevail for all age groups or in all communities. For some age groups and in some areas the sex ratio is more favorable for marriage than in other groups or areas. In general, the situation is favorable for marriage for whichever sex is in the minority, other factors being equal. Women, being more passive than men in initiating proposals of marriage, are more dependent upon a favorable sex ratio than are men. When men are abundant, they compete for wives and marry many women who under other conditions might not have been selected for wives; with an abundance of women, men may be so selective that marginally attractive women remain unmarried.

In any comparison of the sex ratios for different age groups, it is advisable to allow for the fact that men usually marry women a few years younger than themselves. Ratios have therefore been computed between men in one five-year age period and women in the next younger period, thus showing, for example, the number of men aged 20–24 per 100 women aged 15–19. Figure 34 shows that for the United States as a whole, the staggered sex ratio is approximately 100 for women aged 15–19 and 20–24, but only 93 for women aged 25–29. Out of every 100 women aged 25–29, seven would find no mate in the next older group of men.

The natural sex ratio in different sections of the United States has been seriously disturbed by internal migration.[9] Figures 34 and 35 give the

[8] *1950 Census of Population, Preliminary Reports, General Characteristics of the Population of the United States: April 1, 1950,* Series PC-7, No. 1 (Bureau of the Census, February 25, 1951), p. 6.
[9] See pages 74–77.

staggered sex ratios for urban and rural areas and for different regions. An excess of one sex indicates poor marriage possibilities for that sex but many marriage opportunities for the minority sex.

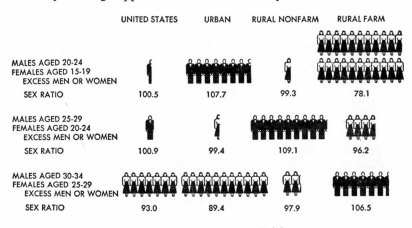

	UNITED STATES	URBAN	RURAL NONFARM	RURAL FARM

MALES AGED 20-24
FEMALES AGED 15-19
EXCESS MEN OR WOMEN
SEX RATIO   100.5   107.7   99.3   78.1

MALES AGED 25-29
FEMALES AGED 20-24
EXCESS MEN OR WOMEN
SEX RATIO   100.9   99.4   109.1   96.2

MALES AGED 30-34
FEMALES AGED 25-29
EXCESS MEN OR WOMEN
SEX RATIO   93.0   89.4   97.9   106.5

Each figure represents one man or woman.

FIGURE 34

Sex Ratios for Staggered Age Groups

The sex ratios are shown for men of a given age period and women in the next lower age period, to correspond to the age differential in most marriages. The symbols represent the excess number of men or women in each situation who will find no mates available in their areas. For the youngest age group, the city is most favorable for women, the rural farm areas for men. For the second age group, rural nonfarm communities are most favorable for women and farming areas for men. For the oldest age group, the farming communities are most favorable for women and the cities for men. The inequalities in numbers of men and women are closely related to internal migration (see Chapter 3). (Source: *1950 Census of Population, Preliminary Reports, General Characteristics of the Population of the United States: April 1, 1950,* Series PC-7, No. 1 [Bureau of the Census, February 25, 1951], pp. 6–7. NOTE: In Census terminology urban refers to all communities of 2,500 or over and includes densely settled fringe areas around larger cities.)

The conception of the ideal mate

Although ideal concepts of a spouse held by the unmarried young person may not be fully realized in marriage, nevertheless they function to screen out dating or courtship partners who run too far afoul of the ideal. The customary way of determining the ideal traits that young men and women desire in a mate has been to ask groups of young people —usually college students—to check on a long list of traits those desired in a mate or to rank the traits in order of desirability. This method has some limitations, inasmuch as it suggests possible ideal traits to the student that he might not include if he made his own list. Nevertheless, the studies are interesting in that they throw light on traits thought important in the spouse by college students, who are primarily middle class.[10]

Some of the traits commonly checked originate in the traditional roles of husband and wife. One such role is the dominant status of the husband in the family. Both men and women, according to 628 University of Wisconsin students, feel that the husband should be older than the wife: men desire on the average wives 2.3 years younger than themselves, women husbands 3.4 years older than they are. The actual age differential in marriage of 2.7 years, therefore, is no accident but a result of attitudes of long standing related to the superior status of the husband. Related to the same traditional role of the husband is the unwillingness of most women to marry a man with less intelligence and education than their own, whereas most men find a wife with less intelligence and education acceptable. Among New York students only 18 per cent of the women, but 56 per cent of the men, would marry a person with less intelligence than their own. Although almost none of this group wished a spouse with less education, the women were heavily in favor of husbands with more education, whereas the men would be content to have wives with the same education as their own. The sex differentials in these three items—age, intelligence, and amount of education—all point in one direction: the majority of men expect to have and most women desire to give the man the higher status in marriage. Interestingly, the men, who stand to lose by a shift in status, are more willing to accept equality than are the women, who seem reluctant to accept an equal status with men.

Traditional roles are also reflected in other desired traits. Man the good provider appears in the high rating given to "good financial pros-

---

[10] The discussion is based on the following three studies: Harold T. Christensen, *Marriage Analysis* (Ronald, 1950), p. 256, reporting responses of Purdue University students; Reuben Hill, "Campus Values in Mate Selection," *Journal of Home Economics,* 37 (1945), 554–558, for University of Wisconsin students; and Mirra Komarovsky, "What Do Young People Want in a Marriage Partner?" *Journal of Social Hygiene,* 32 (1946), 440–444, for students in a New York City college.

pect" and "ambition and industriousness" by women at both Wisconsin and Purdue.   Woman the homemaker is sought by Purdue men, and the good cook and housekeeper by Wisconsin men.

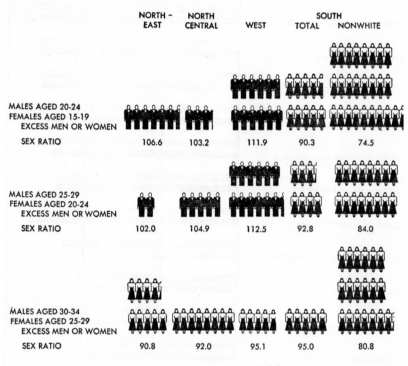

Each figure represents one man or woman.

FIGURE 35

Sex Ratios for Staggered Age Groups by Regions

The northeast, north central, and Western regions are most favorable for the marriage of women under 25, since each has an excess of men in the next older age group.   They are unfavorable for women aged 25–29, however. The South is unfavorable for women at all three age periods, but is favorable for a high marriage rate among men.   (Source: *1950 Census of Population, Preliminary Reports General Characteristics of the Population, By Regions: April 1, 1950,* Series PC-7, No. 3 [Bureau of the Census, April 30, 1951], pp. 8–9.)

Women are more concerned than men with social status.   Among the New York students, 92 per cent of the men but only 84 per cent of the women would marry a person of lower economic status than their own.

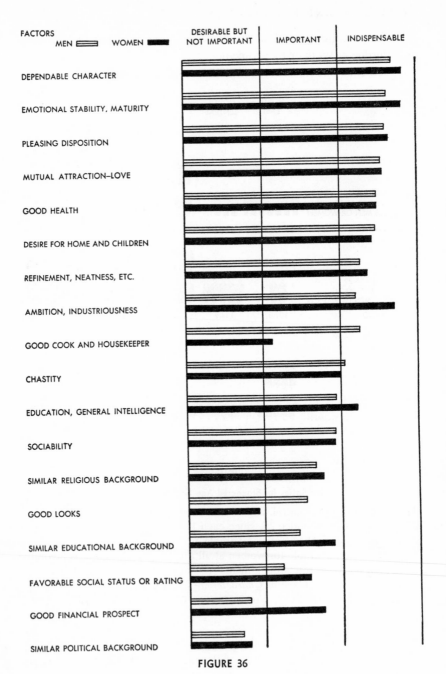

FIGURE 36

Traits Most Desired in the Spouse by College Students

348

Wisconsin and Purdue women ranked favorable social status of the spouse higher than the men rated this item.

Of great importance to both men and women are the personal qualities of the spouse (dependability, maturity, a pleasing disposition, affection, good grooming, and the like). Wisconsin, Purdue, and New York students gave their highest ratings to personal qualities, placing them in importance above the traits reflecting traditional roles. This ranking shows the trend away from the institutional family, with its utilitarian and differentiated roles for husband and wife, toward the family as an intimate primary group whose chief significance is derived from personal interrelationships.

Both men and women include as indispensable an expansion of the mate relationship into the family circle. Both Wisconsin and Purdue students rank the desire for a home and children, or family-mindedness, considerably higher than chastity in the spouse.

Generalizing from these studies, one may say that the college man of today desires a wife who has an attractive and dependable personality, who is healthy, well groomed, and affectionate, whose intelligence and education preferably are not greater than his own, who is several years younger, and who is a good homemaker. The college woman prefers a husband who is dependable and mature, in love with her, well groomed and mannered, whose intelligence and education preferably are greater than her own, who is more than three years older, and whose financial prospects are good and probably will be improved through his ambition and industriousness.

←The average ratings of traits by University of Wisconsin students shown on facing page are similar to ratings given in other colleges. Personal qualities are of great importance, whereas similarities of religion, education, and political beliefs are not regarded as important. The emphasis on personal qualities is in keeping with the present view that the function of marriage is primarily to give personal happiness. Other studies show, however, that similarity of social background is an important balance wheel in creating and maintaining marital adjustment. To secure the information for this chart, students were given a list of 18 traits and asked to rate them 3 if they were considered indispensable, 2 if important but not indispensable, 1 if desirable but not very important, and 0 if irrelevant or unimportant. The category into which the average rating placed each trait is shown in the chart. (Source: Reuben Hill, "Campus Values in Mate Selection," *Journal of Home Economics,* 37 [1945], 557.)

Personality needs in mate selection

Approaching the subject of mate selection from a somewhat different point of view, Strauss has tried to discover the extent to which felt personality needs have influenced the choice of husband or wife. He secured his data by asking 200 women and 173 men, engaged or recently married, to check their major needs on a long list of personality and emotional needs.[11] Other questions were also asked, and later in the questionnaire the same list was again presented with the request to check the needs that were filled by the mate, according to four degrees of satisfaction: very much, considerably, a little, or not at all. A comparison of the items checked as felt needs with those checked as being filled by the spouse made it possible to determine the extent to which each person secured satisfaction for his personal needs through his spouse. Eighteen per cent had from 90–100 per cent of their needs "very much" filled by their mates. Thus, approximately one fifth of the group had found in their mates almost perfect complements to their own personalities. Fifty-four per cent had from 61 to 89 per cent of their needs filled "very much," showing that more than half of the group had found a high percentage of response to their needs from their mates. Only 28 per cent had less than 61 per cent of their needs filled to a high degree by their chosen mates.

Among personality needs are included the following:

Affection and response
Acceptance and approval
Attention and affection
Trust and sympathy
Security and response
Needs derived from a critical emotional experience in early adulthood

Relating personality needs to ideal traits as factors in mate selection, we may conclude that from among those who possessed the ideal traits each person would tend to select the one who also met personal needs. Since the selection assumes that each of the pair finds in the other both ideal traits and qualities that will satisfy his personality needs, a fine degree of matching must occur. In some respects the matching is to find like

[11] A. Strauss, "Personality Needs and Marital Choice," *Social Forces,* 25 (1947), 332–335.

characteristics in each other (the mutual desire for a mate with a dependable and pleasing character); in others, to find complementary traits (the good provider–good cook combination); or to pair a given personality need (need for security) with the ability to fulfill that need (strong and protective personality). With these great and numerous personality demands now made of marriage—far more exacting than earlier conventional role-demands of the institutional family—there is no need to question either the desirability of a long period of acquaintance or the frequency with which friendships form and fade before marriage is accomplished.

Influence of parents

Although we have spoken repeatedly of the independence of young people in choosing friends, establishing dating codes, and selecting a mate, nevertheless parents have not been entirely eliminated from the process; in fact, it may be that parents exert more influence in courtship than in dating. Courtship is an old process, the ways of which are known to the parents; therefore a design exists that may be passed on to son or daughter, whereas dating as a new activity is still in the stage of having a pattern of behavior established. Also, courtship is pointed toward marriage, one of the most significant social transitions that a person makes. Parents, therefore, may regard dating with ease or only slight trepidation, but may feel justified in trying to influence the selection of a mate or even to break up a seemingly unsuitable courtship.

At one time in the middle and upper classes the parents had a definite role to play in the courtship of their children and especially their daughters. The young man was not regarded as a suitor until he had asked the girl's father whether he could court his daughter with marriage as the objective or, after courting was under way, whether he could have her hand in marriage. The father was then in a position to approve the courtship or to send the young man away. Except in selected groups, this custom has died out. When the father insists on maintaining this role, embarrassing situations may arise because of the emergence of new customs, as the following incidents illustrate.

I became engaged to a young man from Iowa while I was attending college in the Middle West. During vacation Jim visited me at my home in a suburb of Philadelphia. My parents liked him very much and approved of the match but were inhibited from saying anything about our engagement to our friends or announcing it because Jim did not realize that father expected him to ask for my hand.   Finally I had to tell Jim what was expected of him; in the Middle West people had laughed when anyone spoke of a young man asking the girl's father for her hand.

Father insisted that Bob ask him for my hand because he had had to ask my grandfather for mother's hand.   Bob thought I was old enough to decide for myself whether I would marry him and for many months refused to ask father.   Meanwhile I wore his ring, grandmother gave us a house which we began to redecorate, and mother and I made plans for the wedding.   But until I finally persuaded Bob to speak to father, he would not recognize that Bob and I were more than friends.

Parental influence now is directed usually at the daughter rather than her suitor, while sons also are subjected to attempted parental guidance. Among 136 young married people who were given extensive interviews, half of the men and over two thirds of the women said their fathers tried to influence them in their choice of a mate.[12]   Four fifths of the men and almost all women claimed that the mother had exerted some kind of direct influence.   Thus the mother-daughter relationship is the one most often involved, then the mother-son, third the father-daughter, and finally the father-son.

The type of influence is related to the personality of the parent, the family role of the parent, and the parent-child interrelationship.   The few disinterested parents are overshadowed by the many more parents who attempt to influence choice of close friends and courtship by verbal expressions of opinion, ridicule, expressions of disapproval or approval, or discussion of marriage plans.   In one fifth of Bates' cases the parents interfered directly, either because they thought the match unsuitable or for some personal reason objected to the child's marrying.   Parents accustomed to play a heavy authoritarian role fell into this group.

Young people may openly rebel against their parents by elopement or a secret marriage.   Others evade the issue by going away to college or moving to another city to work.

These devices remove the young person from the parent's direct influence.   But in a more subtle way, the son or daughter is prevented from escaping the parent's influence.   Attitudes ingrained since childhood cannot help but play a part in mate selection; the model of the parent's own marriage is always in the young person's mind as something

[12] Alan Bates, "Parental Roles in Courtship," *Social Forces,* 20 (1942), 483–486.

to be imitated or avoided; and many of the personality needs of young adults stem from the parent-child relationship.   The child whose needs are adequately met by one parent, whether father or mother, tends unconsciously to select a mate with some of the same qualities that the parent had, for in so doing he assures himself of continued satisfaction of his personality needs.   When both parents have contributed to the child's needs, the mate may have traits found in both parents.   This matching of mate to parents is not deliberate but is simply the natural result of an attempt to continue a satisfactory mode of life.[13]

Availability of marriageable partners

All of the restrictions of laws, mores, population distribution, personal ideals, and family pressures reduce the number of people in any community who are defined as marriageable from the point of view of a given group.   Figure 37 shows the ever-narrowing circle from which the choice must be made.   When marriageable partners are not available, three possible solutions exist.

1. Those not able to find partners within the prescribed classifications remain unmarried.   Thus, on the West Coast there are many unmarried male Chinese and Filipinos because of the abnormally high sex ratio; there simply are not enough women within their own or legally marriageable racial groups for all men to marry.   Another example is the situation in Yankee City, described by Warner; more upper-class young men than women move from Yankee City to other cities, leaving stranded a number of upper-class women who are forbidden by their class mores to marry into a lower class: they therefore become lifelong spinsters. Women college graduates have a high rate of spinsters because of their desire for a man of equal or greater education, and the typical man's desire for a wife with equal or less education.   Some college women therefore fail to find men whom they define as marriageable and who would regard them as marriageable.[14]

---

[13] Several studies throw some light on this question, but the data are not conclusive partly because few cases were studied and partly because resemblances are not clear-cut.—Anselm Strauss, "The Influence of Parent-Images upon Marital Choice," *American Sociological Review*, 11 (October, 1946), 554–559; Anselm Strauss, "The Ideal and the Chosen Mate," *American Journal of Sociology*, 52 (November, 1946), 204–208.

[14] Out of every 10 women college graduates aged 45 and over, 6 are or have been married, as compared to 9 married out of 10 in the general population.—F. L. Babcock, *The U. S. College Graduate* (Macmillan, 1941), p. 62.

2. Some of those unable to find partners within the approved classifications cross the barriers and marry into forbidden classifications. For
example, college students who fail to make a selection while in college

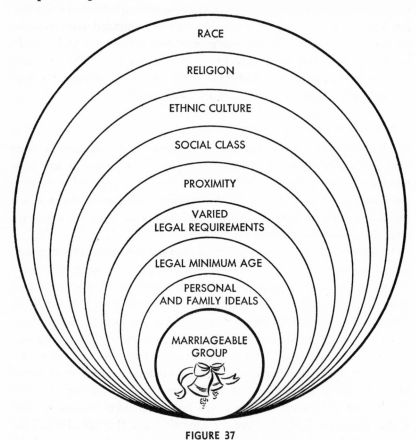

FIGURE 37

Restrictions on Free Choice of a Mate

The group from which choice of a mate usually is made is limited by strict
mores, laws, availability of members of the opposite sex, and personal preferences. For any one person, the marriageable group is small.

may later find themselves working in small towns where other college
graduates are not available. The small-town woman schoolteacher may
find herself in this position. Often, then, she marries someone of lower
educational level, who on his part is willing to have a wife of higher edu-

cational level than himself. This combination is contrary to the usual matching of educational levels.

The marriage of Catholics with non-Catholics and Jews with non-Jews has been found to be higher in communities where the Catholic or the Jewish population is small.[15] Some interracial marriages can be accounted for on the same basis, where an excess of one sex of a given race is able to marry into another race.[16]

In marriages that cross homogamous barriers, the pressure toward marriage outweighs the social disapproval. Some satisfactions of marriage are sacrificed in order to achieve other satisfactions.

3. The third possibility is an alliance without legal marriage. Relieved of the necessity for marriage license or ceremony, the couple may hide their relationship and thus avoid social disapproval. Partial satisfaction is gained, partial responsibility is assumed. In the United States such nonmarital sex alliances are condemned. In France, on the other hand, a male student, not yet in the marriage market because of his economic dependency, may make a semipermanent liaison with a girl of lower social class until such time as he becomes financially marriageable. The transient contacts with prostitutes also fall into this classification of giving partial satisfaction when marriageable partners are not available. Immigrants from groups with unbalanced sex ratios and older unmarried men often resort to prostitutes.

THE DATING-ENGAGEMENT SEQUENCE

On the basis of the preceding discussion, it is now possible to view dating, courtship, and engagement as parts of a continuous process that, once started, tends to proceed to summation in marriage. The entire dating-engagement sequence includes the steps of mixed-group activities (predating), casual or intermittent dating, "playing the field" in regular dating, "going steady," courtship, and engagement. As young people pass through this process, some aspects of it increase in intensity, others decrease.

1. Maturity. Mixed-group activities begin at about age 12, and engagement anywhere from 17 to 22, depending upon the social class of

[15] See pages 249–255.
[16] See pages 242–249.

participants.   The change in age roughly indicates increase in maturity
and independence, both in decision-making and economically.

2. Parental concern.   Parents are eager to launch their children into
mixed activities and dating.   Their concern for placing their children
in the right social groups and supervising their conduct is high at the
beginning of the dating period, declines as their children gain in ability
to manage their own social affairs, but wells up again with courtship and
the imminence of marriage.   A conflict therefore may exist between the
increasing maturity of son or daughter and the increased drive of the
parents to guide or control the courtship.

3. Number of partners.   Number of dating partners decreases throughout the process, from many at the beginning to one at the end.   Moreover, this change is generally approved by both adults and young people.
In the early stages many partners are regarded as a safeguard against
too early emotional involvement and also as a way of enabling the boy or
girl to formulate his attitudes regarding the type of partner he eventually
wants in marriage.   Failure to decrease the partners to one during courtship and engagement is an offense against the mores and a threat to the
future marriage.

4. Degree of mutual responsibility.   Carefree lack of responsibility
or responsibility only for each date as it comes is the hallmark of the
early date.   Increasing responsibility reaches a climax in engagement
when each feels deeply obligated to provide for the happiness and welfare of the other.

5. Degree of emotional involvement.   A transition from a very low
degree of emotional attachment in the early stages of dating to a high
degree in engagement is the normal process.   The young casual dater
likes the partner for superficial social qualities; the engaged person gives
love and receives love in return.   Mutual dependence for response therefore becomes part of the relationship.   When one participant in the
engagement exceeds the other in emotional involvement or when one
ceases to love the other, the engagement is threatened.

6. Degree of ego involvement.   Interest in one's own status and the
admiration or envy of others because of the high rating of the dating partner declines.   Ego involvement is never entirely lost; it seems relatively
less important as courtship and engagement progress because it is satisfied in part by identification with the partner, and enhancement of the
partner's status becomes a roundabout way of enhancing one's own status.

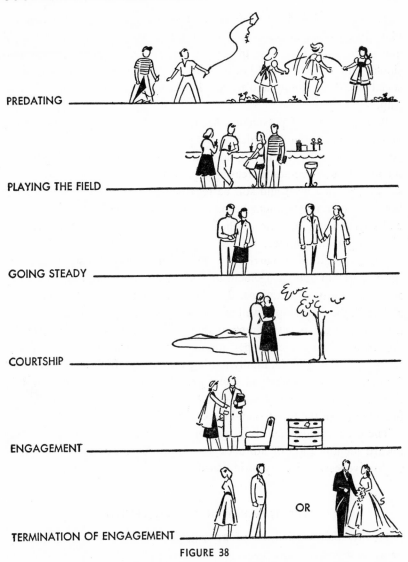

PREDATING

PLAYING THE FIELD

GOING STEADY

COURTSHIP

ENGAGEMENT

TERMINATION OF ENGAGEMENT

OR

FIGURE 38

The Dating-Engagement Sequence

7. Degree of identification. The dating couple have little if any identification. For a time a few interests may coincide, but deeper psychological merging is lacking. Identification increases with the dating-engagement sequence until the two partners seem as one in interests, likes, dislikes, and the ability to find mutual satisfactions in each other.

8. Degree of social assimilation. In dating young people are more likely to cross social-class, religious, and racial lines than in engagement and marriage. Typically, the engaged couple come from a somewhat similar cultural and social background and tend to pull their immediate social worlds of family and friends into a jointly shared social relationship.

9. Importance of personality needs. As the young person detaches himself from his family, which in the past has satisfied many personality needs, and narrows his dating down to one person, the matching of personality needs becomes increasingly important. The casual date might satisfy only one need and still be regarded as a valuable dating partner because other needs might be met through other contacts. Courtship and engagement, because of their exclusiveness, place heavy responsibilities upon the partner.

10. Expectation of marriage. Dating is regarded as a social relationship; courtship and engagement are oriented toward marriage. Family and community expectations, therefore, are that a marriage will occur; and, once the courtship is well advanced or the engagement made known, a social process is set in motion that reinforces the personal expectation of marriage. Newspaper announcement, an announcement party, "showers" for the bride, family parties, inquiries of friends as to the date for the wedding all serve as social pressures on the engaged couple to marry. A broken engagement therefore is not wholly a personal matter but an affair of the families and the community.

The general movement is away from individualism and independence, toward identification of attitudes, integration of social patterns, mutual responsiveness, and unity of interests and goals.

THE TERMINATION OF ENGAGEMENTS

Ideally, the termination of an engagement is marriage. Actually, many engagements are broken. Only recently has the frequency of broken engagements been realized. Among 1,000 engaged couples who participated in a study, 23.8 per cent of the men and 35.8 per cent of the women had broken one or more previous engagements, and 14.9 per cent later broke the engagement that existed when the study was started.[17]

[17] Ernest W. Burgess and Harvey J. Locke, *The Family* (American Book, 1945), p. 390.

Broken engagements as well as the adjustment that follows are now an important part of the marital process.

Engagements are broken primarily for three reasons. First, something may interfere with the progress of the dating-engagement sequence. The intrusive element may be the objection of parents, separation over a long period of time, illness of one partner, pressure from some institution, such as the church in an interreligious marriage, or some other factor not directly involved in the process itself. Second, the broken engagement may result from the inability of one or both of the partners to move from step to step through the sequence. The immature girl or boy may be able to enter the courtship phase but not accept the responsibilities of engagement; the philanderer may not be able to narrow his interests to one person as the conventional courtship demands. Third, although both may be able to follow through the entire sequence, they may not be well mated to each other and therefore find decreasing rather than increasing satisfaction in the sequence as it develops.

Sometimes more than one hazard appears in a courtship. For example, the immaturity of one partner (number two above) may be associated with interference of that partner's parents who try to direct the courtship (number one above). Or the person who has need for continued personal attention may not find this need met in the partner because of a long-continued separation (numbers three and one).

Although the final break may seem to come abruptly, usually it is the end of a disintegrating series of events. At some point the unifying effect of the dating-engagement sequence is counterbalanced by the disintegrating effect of the breaking-up process. Thereafter disintegration outweighs unification until the engagement is broken.

Because of the degree of personal involvement of one or both partners, personal disorganization often accompanies the broken engagement. Personality needs must be satisfied through other channels; emotional reactions, such as resentment, loneliness, jealousy, or hostility, must be dissipated; new social contacts must be established. Each person must become emotionally detached and individualized again.

The several aspects of broken engagements are illustrated through personal accounts.[18] The bracketed statements call attention to different phases of the dating-engagement and the disintegration sequences.

---

[18] These cases have been selected from a short series collected by the author. The writers were asked to put their accounts in the third person, even though, as in most cases, they referred to personal experiences.

Curt, newly inducted into the army, first met Violet at an Army camp service center dance where she and her mother were visiting her brother. Curt was invited to spend the week end at Violet's home in the city. Curt at this time was 19 and had just come from his home in a small Kansas town of 2,000 inhabitants; he had never before been away from home for any great length of time. Curt was soon spending as many week ends as possible with Violet. [Violet—and her family—satisfy Curt's need for companionship and inclusion in a family.]

Violet and Curt soon found themselves in love with each other. Violet was attracted as much if not more to the uniform than to Curt himself, although she did not realize this consciously. Curt found life in the city exciting. Violet, who was 17, was not only beautiful but an exciting girl to Curt, for she sang in a dance band. He readily adapted his week ends to Violet's manner of doing the town. Although Curt's parents had been opposed to dancing, drinking, smoking, and card-playing, and Curt previously had conformed to their expectations, now he found that he and Violet could live life to its fullest, so he thought, in a mad whirl of night clubs, drinking, love-making, and dancing. For both of them it was a wonderful romance. [At this point, the sequence is still in the dating stage. Although the two are narrowing their interests to each other, the main emphasis is upon the excitement that each receives. Violet is flattered to have a man in uniform at her side, and Curt's ego is enhanced by the attention of a city girl who knows her way around in night life. The influence of Curt's parents is present but inhibited by Curt for the time being. Although no mention is made of Violet's parents, one may assume that they were not opposed to Violet's way of spending her week ends, and their unvoiced approval may have helped Curt to indulge in activities disapproved by his parents.]

After three months of frequent week ends in the city, Violet and Curt mutually decided that they would become engaged. Curt's basic training was finished and it would soon be time for him to go overseas. [The engagement is occurring while the couple are still in the dating stage and before identification and unity have occurred.] The main reason that the couple were not married was that Curt knew the consternation the marriage would create in his family; he felt he might be better able to face the issue when he returned from the Army. [Indirect family influence is evident. Also, Curt is probably grasping for security in binding Violet to him before he goes into a new and dangerous experience.]

Curt left for the European theatre of operations two weeks after he became engaged. For Violet life continued in much the same manner as before, except that Curt was not with her to share the fast life that dance-band work afforded her. There was a frequent exchange of letters. However, it proved increasingly difficult for Curt to write Violet because her letters were filled with trivial events, while he felt there was a greater job to be done. Curt was in the front lines for months at a time. He was wounded during his second year abroad and returned to the States, prematurely old and broken-spirited. [The separation has given Curt new experiences and developed new needs—to take a responsible part in public affairs. He is still familiar with Violet's life, since she continued in the old round of activities; but she no longer shares his experiences or memories and cannot fill his new needs.]

Upon his release from the Army, Curt headed directly for Violet. When he met her he could scarcely believe his eyes for she was no longer a girl but a grown woman. In fact, she was an inch taller than Curt, which placed him at a disadvantage. It was difficult for them to find anything to talk about. After having seen death and destruction at its worst, Curt found Violet's trivial talk constantly irritating. He wondered why she couldn't come down to earth and see the more basic values of life rather than jabbering about the latest swing tune to be on the hit-parade. [They no longer meet each other's needs, but are held together by the formality of engagement and the thought of marriage, which has become habitual over the months.]

Curt wanted to get married but also he wanted to settle in a primarily rural section of the country. Violet could not think of giving up her present life and going off to live in the country with "a bunch of square farm characters." However, it was agreed that Violet would visit Curt's family in Kansas. Her visit was an unhappy experience for everyone. Their way of life was strictly nowhere as far as Violet was concerned, and the fact that she smoked and drank created ill-will toward her on the part of Curt's folks. [The differences in values between Curt and Violet now become sharply defined, and it becomes more evident than before that, although each is ready for and wants marriage, they are not well mated with each other. The family influence becomes overt and is directed against Violet, whereas previously the influence had rested solely in Curt's early training and his foreboding of how his parents would react to Violet.]

Curt discovered that during his absence, Violet had been going out with a sailor. Although Violet insisted the affair was purely platonic, Curt became suspicious. [Violet has violated the convention of concentration of attention upon one person during an engagement. A long separation tends to re-establish a dating situation, the conventions of which conflict with the conventions of engagement: freedom to play the field as against pair dating only between the engaged couple, which is made impossible by long separations.]

Soon after Violet returned home, she sent her ring to Curt and the engagement was at an end.

In summary, the factors involved fall under headings one and three. Factor one, intrusive elements, is apparent in the separation that forced an early engagement and prevented the romance from progressing to the identification and unity typical of an engagement, and in the influence of Curt's parents. Factor three is illustrated by the ability of Violet to meet the needs of a young, homesick rural boy lonely for affection and excited by the bright lights of the city, and by Curt's ability to meet the need of Violet, a young girl in a sophisticated environment of night clubs, for a personable escort.   Later, after Curt's war experience, they are no longer well matched, and the sequence is blocked by their lack of responsiveness to each other's needs.

Although the engagement ended when Violet returned the ring, Curt and Violet still faced the problem of adjusting to nonengagement and conceiving of themselves as detached from each other.   The account continues:

For Violet the adjustment after the broken engagement was not difficult, for there had been no great emotional involvement.   She resumed her vocal activities in the field of dance work, and in a few months became engaged to a dance musician whom she later married.   [Sharing a common field of interests, activities, and values, Violet and the musician probably meet each other's needs better than Violet and Curt could have done.]

Curt, in his search for something stable which might give purpose and meaning to his life, took up the study of agriculture under the G. I. Bill.   He did not date any of the home-town girls or girls at college for some months. He also spent much time in taverns, to his parents' dismay, trying to drown his sorrows.   [Curt's efforts at adjustment to the broken engagement and also to civilian life occurred simultaneously, and were of a type both to orient him toward a normal civilian and occupational life, and to induce personal demoralization.]

After some months, Curt began to date a girl in his home town who influenced him to stop his excessive drinking.   A few months later, the two became engaged.   [In this girl, with the same background and system of values, who found good qualities in Curt, he is able to find appreciation and fulfillment of personal needs.   His desire for his home town and the rural way of life perhaps indicate a need for security that he could not satisfy in a large city.]

The case that follows illustrates all three factors in broken engagements.

At 17, Bob was spending his summer vacation at home before returning to complete his senior year at prep school, where he had been sent because of family tensions.   His mother, from her strong sense of devotion and love, had almost overwhelmed her son with direction and affection.   Bob reacted by being stubborn, aggressive, and what his mother termed "wild."

Bob met Laura at a party.   Laura was 21 and a junior in college, but since Bob had always dated girls older than himself, they found the difference in age no bar and began dating regularly.   Laura was easy-going, sweet, and sincere.   She always like to help people and usually had gone with men who leaned on her for emotional help and understanding. [At this point Bob and Laura meet each other's needs: Bob for a mother-substitute who reassures him but does not dominate as his own mother does; Laura for someone upon whom she can lavish devotion and help. We do not know the origin of this need of Laura's.]

The two had many interests in common and got along well from the start; both were athletic, intelligent, and gregarious. Their families had similar educations and the same northern European cultural heritage. Both families were upper middle class. [These similarities helped them to build up mutual activities. They have essentially the same social-class and cultural values, which contribute to identification.]

Bob and Laura corresponded throughout the next school year and attended social functions at each other's schools. By the time Laura was graduated from college and Bob from prep school in June, they were thinking of marriage. After a second summer of tennis, swimming, dancing, and making mutual friends, they became unofficially engaged. Although Bob's family thought he was too young for marriage, they approved the choice, as did Laura's family also. [The family influence, especially on Bob's side, becomes a major factor in the engagement.]

They planned to be married the following summer. Bob was looking forward to a good companionship with Laura and a life that was calmer and less filled with emotional tension than his had been. He felt also that his marriage would free him from his mother's control, since his mother was fond of Laura, who, for her part, understood Bob's immaturity and his desire to be a nonconformist and accepted him and had great belief in his future. [Their needs are essentially the same as the previous summer—Bob for a gentler mother than his own and Laura for someone immature to help and mold.]

During Bob's freshman year at college, he and Laura became officially engaged, with Bob's family buying the engagement ring. They planned to be married the following summer. But by the end of the school year, Bob began to fear the prospect of marriage. Laura was no longer as excellent a companion for him as she had been. While Bob was becoming more intellectually curious, Laura remained conservative and complacent. Perhaps the main cause of the difficulty was that Bob began to fear marriage itself, feared responsibility, feared failing, and all the more so because he felt himself falling out of love with Laura. [Opposed factors are evident here. The pressure of Bob's family toward marriage and Laura's unquestioning acceptance of the marriage are opposed to Bob's increasing maturity and decreasing need for someone upon whom to lean. At the same time, he finds himself unready for marriage, fearing the responsibilities. Engagement brought him security, marriage threatens insecurity.]

That summer Bob started dating other girls, although he was still engaged. [Violation of engagement convention of dating only the partner is indicative of Bob's unreadiness for exclusive pair-relationship.] Laura knew of his dating but accepted it and thought everything would iron itself out when they were married. [Laura is the permissive parent.] Bob became restless, never going to bed until five or six o'clock in the morning and having his sleep interrupted by nightmares. He didn't want to make any plans for the wedding and wanted to push it entirely out of his mind, as a child would. He postponed one tentative wedding date, and became angry at Laura's family who were unwilling to spend much money on the wedding and reception. [Bob is still too immature and too much dominated by his mother to face the issue squarely and attempts childlike evasions, at the same time that his conflicts find an outlet in neurotic reactions.]

Bob's mother bought Laura a wedding dress and fur coat and arranged for the two to take a honeymoon trip to South America. [Heavy family pressure.]

Bob's restlessness increased as the postponed wedding date approached. Finally his parents realized his intense unhappiness and helped him postpone the date again by saying he was too young to get married as he had three more years of college. Bob used this reason to break off the wedding plans. [Bob's continued dependence on his parents makes it impossible for him to postpone the wedding without their approval.] Laura and Bob discussed the whole situation and Laura came to the realization that Bob did not love her. Laura was very understanding. [The forgiving parent.] Laura and Bob broke their engagement entirely following a quarrel between their parents over the postponed wedding.

After a period of several months, Laura and Bob began to date again although not exclusively. Laura hoped to restore the old relationship, and Bob tried to fall in love with her again. He felt guilty about her unhappiness and thought that he could never fall in love with another girl until Laura was happily married. Whenever he started to go with another girl seriously, he feared she would break off their relationship, as he had done with Laura, as retribution for the pain he had caused Laura.

Factor one, intrusive elements, is found in Bob's college experience, which gives him added maturity and changes his personal needs. Factor two is clear in Bob's inability to carry the relationship beyond the steady-dating stage into a true courtship situation; in time he rebelled against steady dating. Factor three is evident for Laura, who was ready for marriage. Bob at first found security in Laura's love but later found her unable to meet his newly awakened and more mature needs. He found decreasing satisfaction in the relationship. Up to the time the account was written he had not fully freed himself from emotional guilt feelings.

Since one engagement may follow another, the attempt of young people to find partners with whom the dating-engagement sequence may reach a climax in marriage is repeated until couple after couple are well matched and the sequence can go to completion.   A broken engagement is not a sign of a permanently broken heart or cause for lasting despair. Rather, it signifies the necessity for more careful selection of a partner.

LOVE AND SEX

Love and sex, often confused in popular thought as being identical, are both extremely important in the dating-engagement sequence.   In the next two chapters they are separately defined and discussed.

QUESTIONS

1. Contrast the motivations of dating and courtship.

2. How does the identification of courtship differ from parent-child identification?

3. Why is a fairly long period of courtship more closely associated with happiness in marriage than a short courtship?

4. What legal limitations are there to mate selection?   Are these restrictions justified?

5. What personal qualities do college men and women desire in a spouse? Do these qualities seem to you to be closely related to stability of marriage? To personal happiness?

6. How does parental influence affect courtship and mate selection?

7. Discuss the points in the dating-engagement sequence where the process may break down.

8. Analyze a case of broken engagement according to the dating-engagement sequence.

BIBLIOGRAPHY

Courtship

Bates, A., "Parental Roles in Courtship," *Social Forces,* 20 (1942), 483–486.

Cuber, J. F., "Changing Courtship and Marriage Customs," *The Annals* of the American Academy of Political and Social Science, 229 (1943), 30–38.

Kirkpatrick, C., and Caplow, T., "Emotional Trends in the Courtship Experiences of College Students as Expressed by Graphs with Some Observations on Methodological Implications," *American Sociological Review,* 10 (1945), 619–626.

Taylor, D. L., "Courtship as a Social Institution in the United States, 1930–1945," *Social Forces,* 25 (1946), 65–69.

Winch, R. F., "Courtship in College Women," *American Journal of Sociology,* 55 (1949), 269–278.

Winch, R. F., "Interrelations between Certain Social Background and Parent-Son Factors in a Study of Courtship among College Men," *American Sociological Review,* 11 (1946), 333–341.

———, "Primary Factors in a Study of Courtship," *American Sociological Review,* 12 (1947), 658–666.

———, "The Relation between Courtship Behavior and Attitudes towards Parents among College Men," *American Sociological Review,* 8 (1943), 164–175.

Mate selection

Burgess, E. W., and Wallin, Paul, "Homogamy in Social Characteristics," *American Journal of Sociology,* 49 (1943), 109–124.

Hollingshead, A. B., "Class and Kinship in a Middle Western Community," *American Sociological Review,* 14 (1949), 469–475.

Sexual Behavior

S exual behavior, both overt and attitudinal, is difficult to analyze because it stems from three origins rather than one: natural physiological processes common to all normal human beings; social norms that set
up a web of definitions, restrictions, and approved areas of freedom of
sex behavior; and psychological reactions of the individual as he works
out the expression of his physiological sex drives within the social norms.
No one of the processes taken alone can be accepted as the fundamental
one about which sexual behavior should center or which should control
sexual behavior.

PHYSIOLOGICAL PROCESSES

Although sex as a physiological process comes to maturity during the
period immediately following puberty, a certain amount of restricted
sexual expression is possible from infancy on and often occurs.   Accidental or intentional stimulation of an infant's external sex organs produces
pleasurable reactions in the child.   Although such practices are not common, in a few primitive societies adults play with small children in this
way,[1] and we find occasional records of sex stimulation and reaction of infants in our own society.[2]   Surveys of childhood sex practices of adults as
well as case records of social agencies and child guidance clinics unveil a
picture of widespread masturbation in early as well as later childhood in
the United States.   Nor are such activities confined to recent years when

[1] Clellan S. Ford and Frank A. Beach, *Patterns of Sexual Behavior* (Harper,
1951), pp. 188–192.
[2] A. C. Kinsey, W. B. Pomeroy, and C. E. Martin, *Sexual Behavior in the Human
Male* (Saunders, 1948), p. 177.

there is less criticism of masturbation than formerly; nor to boys, usually thought of as indulging more widely than girls in this type of sex expression. The survey of women (most of them college-trained) made by Katherine Bement Davis in the 1920's contains admissions by 39 per cent that they had masturbated at some time—with half of the number beginning the practice before the age of eleven.[3]   For the average woman this period of childhood occurred in the 1890's—a period when females of all ages were assumed to have little sexuality and when masturbation was believed to imply degeneracy.

It is not until after puberty, however, that sexual maturity is achieved, when the pituitary glands, ovaries, and testes create and secrete the necessary hormones.   The internal and external sex structures develop, as well as secondary sex characteristics, such as body hair, the beard of the boy, and the breasts of the girl.   The sex glands begin to produce mature germ cells: ova (eggs) in the case of the female and sperm in the male. With the completion of this development during adolescence, full sexual intercourse with the probability of conception becomes possible.   Internal physiological pressures and tensions tend to build up, especially in the male, creating discomfort until relieved.   Although the sex drive is very powerful and at least in some persons very insistent, it is also very flexible.   It is more flexible than the need for food, liquid, rest, or sleep, the denial of which after a certain period of time will result in death. Even lifelong denial of sex expression does not result in death; in fact, denial in time brings its own relief through certain safety valves provided by nature.   Nevertheless, the natural and expected outcome of the sex drive is intercourse between two persons of opposite sex.   Here again, however, we find a wide degree of latitude among different societies and among individuals in any one society as to the age when intercourse begins, how frequently it occurs once started, techniques of intercourse, and the exact pairing off of male with female.   The physiological drive does not include a definite pattern of sexual behavior.

SOCIAL NORMS

The flexible aspects of sex are brought under the control of social norms in all human societies, primitive and civilized alike.   Except in

[3] *Factors in the Sex Life of Two Thousand Two Hundred Women* (Harper, 1929), p. 158.

extreme cases, such as celibate religious groups, the norms strike some kind of balance between expression of sexual drives and the equally important need of each society to function smoothly and adequately in providing for all needs of its members. Sexual behavior, therefore, is nowhere allowed free and untrammeled expression in accordance with the impulses or even the considered judgment of individuals; it is integrated into the entire societal pattern of behavior. So important is it to maintain this integration that severe penalties are attached to violations of the sexual norms.

Norms that preserve family life

Although societies differ in the details of their norms, certain restrictions of sexual behavior are common to all known societies. These regulations for the most part support the integrity of family life, which anthropologists, whose knowledge ranges round the world, regard as the most significant social unit. The common supporting regulations of sex are as follows: [4]

1. Incest is universally forbidden, by even the most backward peoples. Moreover, the incest taboo extends beyond parents and children to include other, although not universally the same, relatives. Examples of incest sometimes cited for the Ptolemies of Egypt and the Incas of Peru do not pertain to the people as a whole but only to limited groups of high prestige where maintenance of status took precedence over other factors. The incest taboo is regarded as contributing to the integrity of the family by preventing sexual jealousy and rivalry and to the cohesiveness of the community by binding families into a whole through intermarriage.

2. All societies contain recognizable family groups consisting of a man, a woman, and children. These groups may form an independent family or be part of an extended or kinship family; nevertheless, this small-family unit is recognized. In some societies multiple husbands or wives may be acquired with social approval but usually are found in only a minority of families.

[4] George Peter Murdock, "A Comparative Anthropological Approach," in symposium on "Sexual Behavior: How Shall We Define and Motivate What is Acceptable," *Journal of Social Hygiene*, 36 (1950), 133–138; Margaret Mead, "The Sex Life of the Unmarried Adult in Primitive Society," in Ira S. Wile, editor, *Sex Life of the Unmarried Adult* (Garden City Publishing Co., 1940, reprinted from 1934), pp. 53–74; Ford and Beach, *op. cit.*, pp. 112–113.

3. Marriage between a man and woman is the legitimate way to found a family. Some ritual or definite form of behavior signifies the change of status from unmarried to married. It may be the simple giving of a gift and change of residence of some Eskimo groups or the elaborate church ritual of the upper-class American marriage, but it is recognized by the society where it occurs as the entrance upon family life with the assumption of new responsibilities and functions.

4. In general, societies disapprove of illegitimate birth. Even permissive societies give greater approval to legitimate births. With few exceptions it is generally conceded that the family is the primary agency for the physical care and the training or education of young children and that every child has the right to have socially recognized parents to assume his care. In primitive societies, as in ours, the pregnant girl usually marries or conceals the birth of the child, which is then adopted; in occasional societies she disposes of it by death immediately after birth.

5. Marriage provides the most highly approved regular outlet for sexual expression for those of marriageable age. In a survey of 205 societies, chosen as a world-wide sample, Murdock found only five, or 2 per cent, that condoned adultery. A more detailed statement, based on 139 societies, by Ford and Beach classifies 39 per cent as approving of some type of extramarital sex relations; but only seven permitted complete freedom to the individual, corresponding to adultery. In the other societies the extramarital sex relations were strictly limited and served other functions than free sexual expression. One example is the wife-lending of the Chuckchee of Siberia, whereby a married man traveling to a distant community makes arrangements with some man in that community to share his wife, in exchange extending the same hospitality to his host when he visits his community. Another occasion of release from strict marital fidelity may be during some ceremony when men and women are expected to have sexual relations without regard to marital ties, perhaps as a magical means of insuring fertility of crops.

The societies that are marginal or that seem to have some highly individualistic patterns are few indeed, and no society exists that does not maintain strict sexual taboos and regulations that bring sexual activities within a framework of general societal organization and especially of adequate family functioning.

Within this general framework many variations exist, but each pattern is regulated by the social norms of the particular society where it prevails. Variations occur in the following kinds of behavior, among others:

Minimum age of marriage, often differing for men and women

Form of marriage

Monogamy, or one husband and one wife

Polygyny, or one husband and several wives

Polyandry, or one wife and several husbands (found in only a few groups, such as the Todas of India and the Marquesans of the Polynesian Islands)

Group from which mate may be selected

Exogamous choices or selection of a mate from a different clan than one's own

Endogamous, or selection of a mate from one's own clan

Selection of auxiliary wives from among the sisters of the first wife

Assignment of initiative in choice of mate to the man or the woman

Degree to which parents or other older family members control the selection of the mate

Degree of permanence of the marriage and method of terminating the marriage if permitted

Rituals of puberty, marriage, and birth

Techniques of sexual intercourse

Family organization

Patriarchal in varying degrees

Matriarchal in varying degrees

Equalitarian

Premarital sex norms

The sweeping statement is often made by laymen that primitive people permit freedom of sex relations before marriage. Actually, primitive societies come within the same range of premarital sex norms as civilized people, varying from very restrictive to very permissive, with the restrictive societies being in the minority. Ford and Beach classify primitive societies into three types.[5]

Restrictive societies not only hold virginity, especially for prepubescent girls, as of high value, but take positive measures to enforce the restriction of sexual relations.

Semirestrictive societies are those with formal restrictions that are not strictly enforced so long as violations remain more or less secretive.

[5] Ford and Beach, *op. cit.*, pp. 180–192.

Permissive societies permit sex play among children and young un-married people as natural and normal; there are no moral implications. In some instances parents encourage it as contributory to successful mar-riage. The permissive attitude sometimes relates only to one sex or to certain age periods.

The early age of marriage of girls in many primitive societies actually reduces the period of time when sex play is allowed to a short period terminating in selection of a husband. The low number of pregnancies among unmarried girls reported from primitive societies tends to support the idea that sex relations are not unbridled. In other words, in per-missive societies, sex takes its place as one phase of normal behavior to be integrated into activities of work, play, religion, and all other facets of life; it does not constitute a continuous orgy.

Civilized societies can also be placed in this threefold classification. Sweden, for instance, would fall into the semirestrictive class. The Swedish Population Commission, in its *Report on the Sexual Question,* places highest official approval on sex within marriage; realistically ac-cepts the fact that in a situation where marriages are long delayed for economic reasons, premarital sex relations are practiced; does not con-demn premarital intercourse when the couple are bound together by affection; but severely condemns promiscuity and prostitution.[6] Russia, after the revolution of 1917 and until 1944, was a permissive society. Sex relations and marriage were private affairs, illegitimacy carried no stigma, and divorce could be had upon application. Even so, certain limitations were set. The father was responsible for the support of all children whether or not they were born in wedlock. Also disapproval attached to promiscuity although not to semipermanent sexual unions. New laws passed in 1944 placed greater obligations on marriage and restrictions on divorce. Unmarried mothers, however, were given greater official recognition with government allowances for each child. Russia thus moved toward the semirestrictive regulation of sex.

The United States in the past was legally and religiously a restrictive society. An unofficial exception was made for unmarried young men, whose casual sexual exploits were condoned. That the United States has been moving toward a semirestrictive society is supported by data from several studies that show a marked increase in frequency of pre-marital intercourse in the United States for persons born after 1909 in

[6] Alva Myrdal, *Nation and Family* (Harper, 1941), pp. 195–196.

comparison with the frequency for persons born prior to 1890. Terman, reporting on couples married at the time of the study, found that 86.4 per cent of husbands born after 1909 as compared with 49.4 per cent of those born before 1890 admitted premarital intercourse; 68.3 per cent of the younger wives but only 13.5 per cent of the older wives reported premarital intercourse.[7] Another study, reporting on very happily married couples, showed that 71.4 per cent of men born after 1909 as compared with 52.9 per cent of men born before 1890 had had premarital intercourse; among happily married women the corresponding percentages were 22.7 and 4.5.[8] Divorced men and women likewise showed an increase in premarital intercourse from the early period to the later one. The trend toward a semirestrictive pattern of sex behavior is further shown by the increase of intercourse with the future mate among the younger age group when compared with the older. This trend is indicative of acceptance of nonvirginity of the bride. Much of the earlier male premarital experience apparently was with prostitutes, whereas prospective wives were expected to be virgins.

The semirestrictive nature of American attitudes toward premarital sex experience is shown also by the widespread reluctance of police to arrest persons who engage in either premarital or extramarital intercourse. Prostitution, rape, or notoriously open nonmarital sex exploits may lead to arrest; when voluntary and noncommercial sexual activities are carried on with circumspection, arrests are rarely made even though the activities may be known. As one writer states, laws intended to control or eliminate fornication (intercourse of the unmarried) or adultery (extramarital intercourse) are "in a state of suspended animation."[9]

Traditional attitudes, laws, and publicly stated mores condemn premarital sex relations; but actual behavior shows an increase in incidence over the years, with penalties not enforced or lightly applied, so long as public notoriety is avoided. The trend is toward semirestrictive control.

[7] L. M. Terman, et al., Psychological Factors in Marital Happiness (McGraw-Hill), p. 321.

[8] Harvey J. Locke, Predicting Adjustment in Marriage: A Comparison of a Divorced and a Happily Married Group (Holt, 1951), pp. 136–137. Locke suggests that the incidence of premarital sex relations may actually be somewhat higher, especially for women, as he discovered a tendency toward concealment of this information; he also believes that more older people may have indulged than reported the experience, but were inhibited about admitting it.

[9] Morris Ploscowe, Sex and the Law (Prentice-Hall, 1951), p. 157; ch. 5 gives a detailed discussion of laws regarding premarital and extramarital sex relations and their nonenforcement.

DEFINITION OF SEX IN THE UNITED STATES

The increase in premarital intercourse and the accompanying leniency of attitude have their counterpart in the radical redefinition of sex that that has been under way for at least 30 years. It may seem that this is an unduly long period for a change of attitude that is not yet generally accepted. It must be remembered, however, that in this country for many years sex had not only important social connotations but moral ones as well. Also, regardless of the deviations and violations that always existed, a fairly united front was presented by adults, leaders and laymen alike, on the meaning of sex and the relation of sex behavior to social welfare. Finally, even after a break had been made in the older definition and younger people became vocal in their efforts to find a new meaning, older people reared under the earlier, uniformly accepted conception protested and criticized. It is small wonder then that the attitudinal change has been slow and is still not firmly grounded or universally accepted. A brief review of the stages of change will give a perspective for understanding the present, somewhat confused, attitudes.

The heritage of attitudes

Puritanism identified sex with the baser qualities of human nature. Sufficiently realistic to recognize that sex must have some outlet for both physical and social reasons, the Puritan leaders sought to confine sex within the boundaries of family life, where its chief function was defined in terms of reproduction. Sex outside of marriage was sinful, and heavy penalties were applied not only to actual sexual misconduct but to such behavior as kissing in public.

Rules were sternly enforced both by the church in its marked disapproval and legally. Many of the older laws supporting the Puritan attitude have been repealed or are no longer enforced; but others remain, with great inconsistency in enforcement. In many localities little effort is made to enforce laws against adultery unless the relationship becomes a public scandal or someone makes a specific protest. Nevertheless, the Puritan attitude toward sex as sinful is still accepted in some religious groups and is widely influential in the attitude toward nonmarital sex behavior.

In the South contrasting attitudes developed as a reaction to the dominance of a two-class society widely separated in prestige: slaveowners backed by the wealth of plantations, and slaves. To women of his own social class the Southern planter was extremely chivalrous, after as before marriage. Although the Southern lady might flirt in a restrained though provocative manner, any direct sexual approach before marriage was unthinkable to the gentleman. Sex after marriage was thought of as a function of the marital relationship and for the production of children to carry on the heritage of the family. At the same time, a more simple type of sex relation was possible and often obtained between the white planter and some comely slave girl. The planter, who already owned and provided for the girl, seems not to have regarded such a relationship as a violation of his code of conduct with women of his own class. Nor did he assume any special responsibility for any child that might result from the liaison, who psychologically as well as socially became identified with the Negro mother.

As the West was opened for settlement, the migrant carried with him his attitudes, Southern or Northern as the case might be. Much is made in popular literature and Western motion pictures of the wild free life of the frontier, with bars and brothels as the most prominent institutions and debauchery occupying most of the time. Actually, to the extent that such a phase existed, it was a transitory one during the opening of areas that offered great and quick wealth and prior to the establishment of settled community life. The permanent settlement of the West was accomplished by families, and the economic and social development through cool-headed leaders. The wide-open town was pushed into the background and in time was represented only by small restricted areas in the larger cities. The familism of settlement was tinged, however, with greater individualism than had been true for many years in the more settled communities of the East. The necessity under frontier hardships for each member of the family to carry his share of the load tended to equalize the status of men and women, and at the same time to break down some of the refinements and niceties of sex relations and sex control. A dearth of churches and courts of law prevented the imposing of severe penalties for violations of the sexual code of the East. Sex became a more natural function, and people solved their sexual relationships on a practical basis, according as nearly as possible with the older code but much less restrictive in nature. Common-law marriages frequently occurred; or a young couple, with full approval of their families and neighbors, set up housekeeping and perhaps produced their first child before a legal marriage could be performed by the minister whose circuit brought him to them only at widely spaced intervals of time.   Unmarried men sent East for girls they had known as neighbors to come to the West and marry them there without the protective solicitude of parents.   Matrimonial agencies sprang up to fill the need; the Caroline Fry Marriage Association and the Bloomer Marriage Association acted as go-betweens and arranged marriages.   Occasionally a group of girls would be sent West by some enterprising agent, there to take their chances at finding a suitable husband among the young men eagerly awaiting the arrival of the group.   In this freer life where young people made their own decisions, the old restrictions on sex tended to fade to a dim replica of the original stern Puritanical code.   Nevertheless, sex was still related closely to marriage and children, and deviations from the code were regarded as violations rather than as individual rights, with, however, social condoning and willingness to forget and overlook the digression.[10]

Meanwhile, in the East another development started that was destined to spread rapidly westward—the Industrial Revolution and the growth of large cities.   With this development came not only the crowding of many people with different cultural backgrounds and hence different conceptions of sex into close proximity to each other, but the freeing of women from economic dependence upon their fathers and husbands.

The feminists, who organized as early as 1848, in their battle for equality with men attacked the social order on many fronts: economic, educational, political, legal, and sexual.   In all these areas they demanded the same rights, privileges, and opportunities as men.   The struggle for sexual equality for many years did not approach sex directly but was reflected indirectly in such things as the controversy over the growing tolerance for divorce; the reaction against marriage by some leading feminists as a lowering of their status as human beings; and the development of the birth-control movement to free women from excessive childbearing.   The early feminist attitude toward sex, therefore, was in the nature of a protest against male control of the sexual situation before and after marriage.   The feminists were not personally seeking greater freedom of sex expression.   Sex restrictions applying to women, however, were a symbol of their bondage and like the other symbols must be abolished.

[10] Arthur Charles Cole, *The Irrepressible Conflict, 1850–1865* (Macmillan, 1934), p. 468.

Finally, consideration must be given to a recurrence of strictness follow-ing the Civil War. Wars typically disturb human relationships and de-stroy many of the controls of settled community life. After the Civil War a reaction to this freedom as well as the freedom of the preceding pioneer period found expression in the activities of Anthony Comstock and others who became either genuinely concerned or panicky over the sexual freedom of the period. For example, prior to and immediately following the Civil War divorce had been easier to obtain than at earlier periods and indeed in many states easier than at present. A number of states (at least seven) included in their divorce laws an "omnibus clause" that made it possible for the judge to grant a divorce not only for causes specified in the law but for any other cause that the judge might think justified a divorce. But in the five years following the close of the Civil War such clauses were repealed and other states repealed the clause soon after.[11] In pre–Civil War decades great latitude appeared in the types of advertisements appearing in newspapers and in other material sent through the mail. Newspapers carried advertisements of abortionists, pills guaranteed to induce miscarriages, and contraceptives, and thinly veiled notices of houses of prostitution.[12] Laws passed soon after the Civil War helped to eliminate such advertisements.

By the beginning of the twentieth century the heritage of sex definitions had become a tangle of conflicting attitudes and practices. Sex had the following definitions: a sin unless encompassed in marriage; an individual though secretive physical right outside of marriage; a privilege of men but not of women; a symbol of oppression; a means of producing children. The conflict came to an issue during and following World War I. Ex-travagant demands for freedom were placed in debate against demands for a return to more restrictive social norms and sterner measures of control; unlike the post–Civil War period when older social norms were reasserted, the post–World War I period fell to the newer trends.

The debate of the 1920's

The tendency in the 1920's was to remove sex from its social context and regard it as a unique phase of life, a thing apart of great value in and

[11] James H. Barnett, *Divorce and the American Divorce Novel, 1858–1937, A Study in Literary Reflections of Social Influences* (University of Pennsylvania, 1939), pp. 18–19.

[12] Carl Russell Fish, *The Rise of the Common Man, 1840–1850* (Macmillan, 1927), pp. 152–155; Morris L. Ernst, "Changing Laws and Changing Attitudes," in Wile, *op. cit.*, pp. 212–232.

of itself.   The physical pleasure of sex to the individual was emphasized. This attitude contrasted with earlier approved concepts in which sex was a means to an end, gaining its value through its relationship to the family and reproduction.   So far as sex existed apart from marriage it had been a thing of low value, debased, and unclean.   The new definition gave it meaning wherever found, as an individual right and pleasure but not as a social value.   Thus, the old concept that called for control and repression of sex began to yield to the new concept that opened the way for greater freedom.

In the 1920's repression of all types, and especially sex repression, was proclaimed a danger to the personality by causing emotional conflicts, psychoanalytic theories being cited in support of these declarations.   Actually, much of the appeal to psychoanalytic theory was merely rationalization for the fearful breaking of the dam that had restricted the freedom of women on many fronts.   For it was women, previously more restrained in their thinking and activities than men, who were especially active in tossing aside old social controls.   This tendency was expressed in their hard-won right to vote, their reluctance to give up war jobs, their great desire for careers, their refusal to accept the long skirts and long hair that had been symbols of femininity, and their grasping after masculine prerogatives, such as smoking and freedom for premarital sex experiences. Many types of behavior in the 1920's assumed unusual significance simply as symbols of freedom.   Smoking, bobbed hair, and the nonmarital sex relations were all symbols of this nature, and often one had no deeper significance than the others.   Many young women bobbed their hair, learned to smoke, and established a sex alliance with neither love nor marriage in order to demonstrate to themselves more than to others that they had freed themselves of old restraints.   They represented the "new woman," free, independent, and self-reliant.   They set the stage for a growing trend toward premarital sex relations between men and women of the same social class that has replaced the earlier pattern of men from one class associating sexually with women of a lower class, while those of their own class remained virgins until marriage.[13]

The 1920's did not give any new social evaluation to sex, and the physical evaluation was not universally accepted.   The reaction of community

[13] For an excellent discussion by an anthropologist versed in psychology that presents the conflicts of the 1920's, see E. Sapir, "Observations on the Sex Problem in America," *American Journal of Psychiatry,* 8 (1928), 519–534.   See also Goodwin Watson, *Youth After Conflict* (Association Press, 1947).

leaders and other adults was one of shock and protest. Dire results were predicted for the individual, the family, and society in general as a result of the new individual and physical conception of sex, the matching of woman's behavior to man's, and the increase of premarital sex relations. The trend toward greater freedom also did not extend into the period beyond marriage, except for small radical groups who either sought to delay or altogether avoid marriage as too restrictive, or who visualized sex on two levels, one in the family for the production of children, another outside the family equally open to husband and wife for individual experimentation and pleasure.[14] The chief change was a desire for freedom from old restraints, without too much thought of whether this freedom had any deeper implications, either for personality or for the family.

The great debate of the 1920's made one positive contribution: it made sex a subject of conversation among respectable people. Whereas previously sex had been almost exclusively the subject of smutty jokes in male groups and of secretive whispering among women, it then could be discussed openly and seriously in print and in mixed groups. This greater freedom of communication brought men's and women's points of view into juxtaposition and contributed to formulation of a jointly held point of view regarding the meaning of sex.

The fling of the 1920's was primarily one of youth. In time, greater maturity, marriage, children, and the depression of the 1930's had a sobering effect upon youth. But the experiments of the 1920's paved the way for a new attempt to define sex in social-psychological rather than physical or moralistic terms.

Present evaluation of sex

During the 1940's a discernible trend toward a new evaluation of sex became clear, differing from the older mutually exclusive definitions of sex as sin (moralistic); as the release of physical tension (physiological); or as reproductive (biological). The new evaluation includes elements of the physiological and biological concepts but emphasizes mainly a third, new attitude toward sex as a mutually enriching experience between two people for whom sex is a symbol of love. The point of view is well stated in many recent books.

Luther E. Woodward, an experienced minister and social worker,

---

[14] This point of view is expressed by Bertrand Russell, *Marriage and Morals* (Liveright, 1929).

speaking as Consultant on Community Services of the New York State Mental Hygiene Commission, in 1950 made the following statement:

. . . sexual behavior to be minimally acceptable, from the mental hygiene viewpoint, must satisfy both the demands of the partners' biological organisms for release and pleasure, and the demands of the personality for meaning and worth. To be maximally acceptable, sexual behavior must satisfy the demands of their personalities for a continuing, mutually satisfying, meaningful and enriching relationship. Only so can the dual need of human beings for integration and for fellowship be met through sexual activity.[15]

Symonds, a psychologist, recognizes the separateness of sex as a physical drive and love as an emotional relationship, but emphasizes the value to the participants of the confluence of sex and love.

. . . love must not be confused with sexual expression. There may be love of food and adventure in just as real and passionate a sense as the love which accompanies sex. On the other hand, sex must not be thought of too narrowly as the relief of physical tension. Indeed, most writers on sex would insist that the forepleasure and the personal relationship are important factors in the consummation of sexual pleasure. In this sense, sexual love involves a confluence of two separate streams of expression and feeling, one purely physical, the other, emotional based on human relationships. As these two come together, they result in a more profound and exalted experience than any other expression of love. . . . Sex is one form of joint sharing and activity through which love may be expressed. Indeed, it is the most complete union and sharing of which men and women are capable. It represents the highest degree of intimacy; but it has been emphasized time and again that sex must not be thought of in its narrow physical aspects but in the whole circle of relationships, experiences, and responsibilities which accompany it.[16]

Not only sexual intercourse between male and female but other types of sexual expression are being reviewed for redefinition. Until recently in our society, the only acceptable mode of expression was through intercourse. Recently masturbation has slowly come to be recognized as a harmless activity in moderation. The older stories of insanity and impotency resulting from masturbation, which created deep anxieties on

[15] "Viewpoint of the Mental Hygienist" in symposium on "Sexual Behavior: How Shall We Define and Motivate What is Acceptable?" Reprinted with the permission of the American Social Hygiene Association from the *Journal of Social Hygiene,* 36, No. 4 (copyright 1950), 139.

[16] Percival M. Symonds, *The Dynamics of Human Adjustment* (D. Appleton–Century, 1946), pp. 548–549. Used by permission of Appleton-Century-Crofts, Inc.

the part of children and adolescents, have now been discarded in books of advice to youth. The redefinition of masturbation has not reached the point of actual advocacy, but the attitude toward it by adults now tends to be permissive and tolerant. It is thought of now either as a normal activity of adolescents, especially of boys, that they learn by experimentation or from other boys, or as symptomatic of a stage of self-centered interest that adolescents go through between childhood when sex expression is at a minimum and the more outgoing sexual interests of the mature person.

The third—and a less frequent—mode of sex expression is homosexualism, or attraction and mutual sexual stimulation between members of the same sex. Homosexualism is regarded as a form of perversion indicative of some biological or mental abnormality. Only among very limited groups is it accepted as an alternative to other types of sex expression. Because of its limited expression and its very loose connection with marriage and family life (in fact, a confirmed homosexual would probably not contract marriage), it does not require extended discussion.

PREMARITAL SEX RELATIONS

Concurrently with the changing definitions of sex has gone a controversy over the relation of intercourse to marriage. During the nineteenth century the moral standard was complete virginity of both man and woman at the time of marriage, combined with complete fidelity between the two as long as both were alive. In the few instances where a divorce occurred, the social expectation was that there would be no remarriage. Lifelong monogamy—one man paired with one woman—was the ideal. Although there was never complete conformity to this ideal, the nonconformity fell into a rather restricted pattern. Premarital sex relations of men of all social classes were disapproved but condoned or at least tolerated. Men did not lose their social status so long as they were reasonably moderate and discreet in their behavior. Middle- and upper-class women entertained little thought of sex without marriage, and either pretended to be or actually were ignorant of the depredations of men of their class. The very occasional girl who was known to have fallen from grace or who had an illegitimate child was disgraced, as was her family also. The sexual partners of the middle- and upper-class men were women of the lower classes who had become professional prostitutes. These women never came into contact, physical or social, with the women of the middle and upper class, and their contacts with the men were on a physical or casual personal level, for they did not live in the same social worlds. It should be recalled that this state of affairs was linked with the definition of sex as primarily for reproduction within marriage, and that these nonmarital contacts were regarded as a concession to man's baser nature.

As definitions have changed to include the concept of sex as natural, pleasurable, and contributory to the personality, and as women have been conceded to have a sexual nature similar to men's, the above attitudes and conduct patterns have also changed. As has already been stated, the United States has moved from a restrictive to a semirestrictive society. A semirestrictive society is divided and lacking in agreement between stated norms and actual behavior, as is evidenced by the conflicting attitudes of scientists, other adult leaders, and young people themselves.

Conflicting attitudes of scientists and other adult leaders

Among mature adults who are in a position to exert leadership, two trends of thought appear.

1. Certain leaders believe that in the near future premarital intercourse will be universally practiced and accepted as normal, in other words, that the United States will become a thoroughly permissive society.

This attitude, long an undercover one, has come into overt utterance primarily since the publication in 1948 of the Kinsey report, which revealed more completely than any previous study the extent of premarital sex relations among men and boys.[17] Other, smaller reports support Kinsey's findings and also disclose a somewhat lesser degree of premarital sex activity among girls and young women than among men. The position taken by certain leaders does not distinguish between men and women but assumes the inevitability of premarital intercourse for both and quite largely between those of equivalent social-class status. The position was explicitly stated in 1950 by George Peter Murdock, an anthropologist, at a conference on "Sexual Behavior: How Shall We Define and Motivate

---

[17] Kinsey, et al., op. cit. This study analyzes the sexual activity of 5,300 white males living chiefly in the northeastern part of the United States. It is to be followed by a companion volume on the sex behavior of females. Written for scientists, the book took the public by storm and forced popular recognition of what professional people had long known from more limited studies, that premarital sex behavior is widespread especially among males and that the social norms are in the process of flux and revision.

What is Acceptable?" [18]   Dr. Murdock stated it as his opinion that premarital sex relations are here to stay, inasmuch as the older moral sanctions against them have weakened and the fears of pregnancy and venereal infection are lessened by contraceptives and prophylactics.   Left without guidance, the process would complete itself in about three generations, he felt, after which the practice would be general and would meet social approval.   He did not, however, approve of the present situation in which young people have premarital sex relations under the threat of social penalties if discovered.   Convinced that it would be useless to attempt to reinstate previous social controls, he suggested that the transition be expedited by social guidance under the hand of ministers.   The establishment of new social norms permitting premarital sex relations would, he felt, accomplish five purposes:

(a) Relieve young people of their present sense of guilt over premarital sex relations.

(b) Provide with approval for sexual expression during late adolescence when the sexual urge is strong but when marriage is still economically impossible.

(c) Enable adolescents to establish heterosexual intercourse rather than the deviant sex behavior now sometimes used, thus making later adjustment in marriage less complicated.

(d) Relieve sex frustration and thus place marriage on a different basis than primarily to satisfy such frustrations; other relationships in marriage would receive more attention with greater chance of successful marital adjustment.

(e) Voluntary control by young people themselves for the sake of future well-being.

2. But many others do not agree with Murdock and deny approval to premarital sex relations, even though recognizing their existence.   Premarital intercourse is not presented as a sin or moral lapse but as detrimental to personality development and lacking in social responsibility. Complete acceptance of this point of view would return the United States

---

[18] *Op. cit.,* p. 137.   An earlier prediction of acceptance of the practice as universal in the United States was made in 1938 by Terman, who stated that on the basis of a prediction from the increasing rate of premarital sex relations in the past, virginity at marriage would be almost unknown for men born after 1930 and women born after 1940, and that by 1950–1955 premarital intercourse with the prospective spouse would be universal.—Terman, *et al., op. cit.,* p. 321.

to the status of a restrictive society, but with new values supporting the restrictions.

The case for restriction is well developed by F. Alexander Magoun, Associate Professor of Human Relations of the Massachusetts Institute of Technology.[19]   Admitting the increased frequency of premarital intercourse, he discusses various types of premarital sex relations as well as the commonly recognized dichotomy of necking and petting.   Prostitution is designated the ultimate degradation of the sex relation, since it involves close bodily contact without closeness of thought or emotion. Promiscuity is condemned as a pretense at love that in reality is a gratification of selfish desires; love, however, involves mutual respect and satisfaction of emotional needs through mutual efforts.   Unhappy marriage is predicted for the youth who is habitually promiscuous.   Necking or light love-making is condoned, providing both parties to it understand that it is intended to be without deep emotional significance.   Petting or the fondling of erogenous zones is in reality the preliminary to intercourse and should be understood as such by both man and woman; Magoun does not advocate carrying it to the point of intercourse, however, and calls it "mutual arousal followed by mutual frustration."   Magoun, by implication, condemns all forms of premarital intercourse.

Writing of sexual experiments prior to marriage in the postadolescent group, two sociologists, husband and wife, state:

There is the possibility that the experimenting before marriage will be disappointing because of the conditions under which such experimentation must take place.   The couple may conclude they are not well matched whereas, if they had waited until they could start their sex life under the more ideal condition of marriage they would find the experience mutually successful.   The problems that are basic in difficult sex adjustments after marriage are not biological but psychological; and the psychic elements in sex adjustment require time and patience if a happy and permanently good sex adjustment is to be achieved.   Those who are experimenting before marriage are not building a relationship which meets the emotional and psychic needs of both.   Premarital intercourse must of necessity be chiefly on the physical level, characterized by selfishness rather than mutuality.   If it is between a couple who later marry each other, there is a strong possibility that their ability to achieve psychic union as well as physical after marriage will be limited by the fact that their relationship has been fixed at a physical level before marriage.[20]

[19] *Love and Marriage* (Harper, 1948), pp. 4–5, 103 ff.
[20] Judson T. and Mary G. Landis, *Building a Successful Marriage* (Copyright,

In terms of successful marriage, one of the most unfortunate effects of pre-marital experimentation on the part of the man is that such experience constitutes a type of education and fixes a set of habit patterns almost all of which will have to be unlearned or discarded if he is to be successful in marriage later. The major if not the total emphasis of the premarital experiences is self-centered sex gratification; physical techniques are developed which simply emphasize the one goal, satisfaction, or release from a physical pressure. There is neither awareness of the need for, nor desirability for the presence of, sympathy and identification with a loved personality as one of the satisfying essentials of sexual union. The more premarital experience a man has had the more fixed will become the pattern of sex expression. After marriage it will be exceedingly difficult for him even to realize the need for a wider and more inclusive emphasis. Since his conception of marital consummation will be exclusively physical, if the physical response of his wife is not exactly according to his premarital pattern he is disillusioned and inclined to seek physical response elsewhere, thus destroying the possibility of the physical and psychic identification which is one of the permanently satisfying aspects of successful marriage.[21]

To the extent that these standards of behavior are supported by psychological theories that premarital sex relations are conducive to stunted personality development, the standards are in conformity with the currently growing definition of sex itself and lay the basis for an integrated philosophy of sex applicable both to premarital and marital sex relations, and to both men and women. Earlier conceptions of sex tended to place men in one class and women in another with widely different sexual impulses and needs, and to place premarital and marital sex relations in separate moral categories.

Diverse attitudes and experiences of college students

Important to this discussion of premarital sex relations are the opinions and the experience of young people themselves. Over the years a number of studies have been made of college students, usually by means of questionnaires. Some of the more recent studies, summarized in Table 20, suggest the continued lack of unity of thought and behavior even among a somewhat homogeneous class of people. From these and other studies we may draw the following conclusions:

College men seem about equally divided between those with attitudes of approval and of disapproval toward premarital sex relations; they are

1948, by Prentice-Hall, Inc., New York), pp. 122–123. Reprinted by permission of the publisher.
[21] *Ibid.*, p. 129.

TABLE 20

Premarital Sex Intercourse among College Students

Study	Number of replies		Approval of pre-marital intercourse by		Had premarital intercourse	
	Male	Female	Males (%)	Females (%)	Males (%)	Females (%)
1. Premarital intercourse in long engagements: *	106	111				
Approved for the woman			53	22		
Approved for the man			53	23		
2. Premarital intercourse approved: **	73	100				
For both men and women			15.1	6.0		
For men only			23.3	11.0		
Between engaged persons only			11.0	6.0		
3. Premarital intercourse reported by unmarried males, mean age 21.3 years †	95				50.5	
4. Premarital intercourse reported by unmarried males mean age 19.4 years ††	111				45.0	
5. Premarital intercourse by age 21 for males with 13 or more years of education ‡	1,980				49.1	
6. Premarital intercourse reported by undergraduate and graduate students ‡‡	285	325			31.6	9.1

* John F. Cuber and Betty Pell, "A Method for Studying Moral Judgments Relating to the Family," *American Journal of Sociology,* 47 (1941), 21. A later study with a different group of college students shows fewer men but more women approving of intercourse during long engagements. A. H. Jones, "A Method for Studying Moral Judgments—Further Considerations," *American Journal of Sociology,* 48 (1943), 496.

** Lemo D. Rockwood and Mary E. N. Ford, *Youth, Marriage and Parenthood* (Wiley, 1945), p. 40. This study also summarizes the findings of a number of earlier studies, pp. 246–249.

also about equally divided between those who have and have not had premarital sex relations. Among college women, approximately one fourth approve of premarital intercourse, but only about one eleventh have had this experience.

The background from which students come as well as their vocational interests is related to their attitudes and experience. Students from farms and villages are less likely to approve of premarital sex relations than are city youth.[22] Also, rural men aged 21–25 at the college level slightly less often have premarital intercourse than do urban youth; the percentages for the two groups are 47 and 55 respectively.[23]

Religious affiliation is also associated with disapproval and a greater tendency to refrain from premarital sex relations than is shown by non-religious persons.[24] As between the major religions, approximately three fourths of Catholics were opposed to premarital sex relations, two thirds of Protestants, and one half of Jews.[25]

[22] Lemo D. Rockwood and Mary E. N. Ford, *Youth, Marriage and Parenthood* (Wiley, 1945), p. 43.

[23] Kinsey, *et al., op. cit.,* p. 455. A study of selectees of World War II ranging in education from the first grade to college failed to show similar differences; 79 per cent of city selectees and 80 per cent of rural selectees had had premarital intercourse. The men came from New York City, upper New York State, and Baltimore, and ranged in age from 21 to 27 years. This older heterogeneous group therefore has a higher percentage with sex experience and reveals no rural-urban differences.—L. B. Hohman and B. Schaffner, "The Sex Lives of Unmarried Men," *American Journal of Sociology,* 52 (1947), 504.

[24] A. L. Porterfield and H. E. Salley, "Current Folkways of Sexual Behavior," *American Journal of Sociology,* 52 (November, 1946), 212; Kinsey, *et al., op. cit.,* pp. 477–479.

[25] A. H. Jones, "Sex, Educational and Religious Influences on Moral Judgments Relative to the Family," *American Sociological Review,* 8 (1943), 410, 411. The disapproval referred to sex relations during a long engagement. The respondents

---

† R. T. Ross, "Measure of the Sex Behavior of College Males Compared with Kinsey's Results," *Journal of Abnormal and Social Psychology,* 45 (1950), 754.

†† F. W. Finger, "Sex Beliefs and Practices among Male College Students," *Journal of Abnormal and Social Psychology,* 42 (1947), 57–67.

‡ A. C. Kinsey, W. B. Pomeroy, and C. E. Martin, *Sexual Behavior in the Human Male* (Saunders, 1948), p. 550. The sample includes males both older and younger than 21 years who reported premarital intercourse before the age of 21. The other studies referred to in the table give the responses of specific groups of students in college at the time of giving the information.

‡‡ A. L. Porterfield and H. Ellison Salley, "Current Folkways of Sexual Behavior," *American Journal of Sociology,* 52 (1946), 211. The percentage for males is lowered by the inclusion of 148 ministerial students (51.9 per cent of the total) who had a low percentage with premarital intercourse. The percentages with experience for three groups of male students are as follows: ministerial, 19.6; students in the V-12 Navy program, 60.0; other male students, 32.5.

Men and women differ in their attitudes toward sex.   As the first two studies in Table 20 show, men are more lenient in their attitudes, not only for themselves but for women.   According to the first study, more than twice as many men as women thought premarital intercourse during a long engagement was right for both men and women.   The second study shows that men twice as often as women approved premarital sex relations for both men and women, for men only, and between engaged persons.

These studies show the lack of uniformity of thought and activity among college students.   Since college-trained people supposedly set the social standards, we may conclude that social standards regarding sex are in a state of flux.   The indecision on standards is still more evident from some studies that permit the student to register that he is "uncertain" about his attitudes on sexual questions.[26]   From 3 to 28 per cent indicated uncertainty on different questions in two studies.

Sex attitudes and experience in the lower social class

Most college students have been reared in middle- or upper-class homes.   Youth in lower-middle- and lower-class strata who do not attend college are not usually subjected to attitude questionaires.   Other types of studies show, however, that these youth tend to accept sex as a natural rather than moralistic phenomenon and enter into sex activities at a much earlier age and with greater frequency than do the middle-class college group.   By the time they had reached age 14, Kinsey's subjects, classified into three educational levels, had had intercourse in the following proportions:

Grades 0–8	28.0 per cent
Grades 9–12	33.4 per cent
Grades 13 and over	6.0 per cent [27]

consisted of 482 regular college students and 417 students enrolled in an adult education course in psychology.   In contrast to these findings are the results of the study of a mixed and slightly older group of World War II selectees, among whom Catholics with foreign-born fathers had 86 per cent with premarital intercourse, Catholics with native-born fathers, 74 per cent; Protestants, 71 and 73 per cent, respectively; Jews, 85 and 78 per cent.—Hohman and Schaffner, *op. cit.*, p. 504.

26 Cuber and Pell, *op. cit.*, p. 21; A. H. Jones, "A Method for Studying Moral Judgments—Further Considerations," *American Journal of Sociology*, 48 (1943), 496.

27 Kinsey, *et al.*, *op. cit.*, pp. 550, 349–351.   A study of 4,164 white selectees of World War II, aged 21–27, also showed that a higher percentage of the poorly educated than of the college-trained had had premarital intercourse.   The percentages of nonvirgins were as follows: grades 1–8, 88 per cent; grades 9–12, 81 per cent; college-trained, 68 per cent.—Hohman and Schaffner, *op. cit.*, p. 503.

By age 21, the corresponding percentages were 83.6, 76.7, and 49.1 for premarital intercourse. Frequency of premarital intercourse is low among college-trained men (only about 15 per cent of those with experience have weekly intercourse), whereas among men who had only some degree of grade school education premarital intercourse occurred with great frequency. The difference is not biological but cultural. The desire is probably as keen at both social levels, but cultural standards tend to uphold virginity of women and to a lesser degree of men at the upper-class levels; hence many techniques of love-making (petting) have been developed in the middle- and upper-class groups as substitutes for intercourse. The lower class looks askance at these techniques and accepts intercourse as natural. It is probable that the transition of middle- and upper-class men from lower-class girls to girls of their own social class as partners-in-love has encouraged love-making as a substitute for intercourse. Heavy love-making gives a high degree of sexual stimulation and satisfaction but permits the girl to remain technically a virgin and also to avoid the possibility of pregnancy. The lower class, man and woman alike, moves more directly to intercourse.

Although, in the lower classes, the attitudes toward premarital sex expression are more permissive than in the middle and upper classes, some conflict is indicated by the secrecy and discretion of sex activities. Both girls and young men may seek sexual satisfaction but not within their intimate social groups. Search for a sexual partner in some other community is common. The description of the sex code of an Italian slum given in Chapter 12 indicates that the girls protect themselves from sex relations with the men they hope to marry and that these same men respect their virginity but seek relationships with girls from a different cultural stratum, who are for them unmarriageable. Likewise, the study of young people in Elmtown, a small Midwestern community, points out that young men of the lower class avoid sex relations with lower-class girls of their own community (who are for them marriageable) and seek such contacts with the lower-class girls in some other community.[28] Meanwhile, the girls of their own community may well be granting sex favors to youths of another community, or to men of a higher social class whom they have no expectation of marrying.

If we generalize about casual sex relations, we might say that they tend to be carried on between members of classes who regard each other as

[28] A. B. Hollingshead, *Elmtown's Youth* (Wiley, 1949), pp. 418–426.

unmarriagable. The middle-class youth finds such a girl in the lower class or the casual acquaintance of his own class; the lower-class youth finds such a companion in his own class but in another community; the Italian finds a sexual partner in another ethnic group. Each tends to respect the chastity of girls he regards as marriageable. In some lower-class groups this respect is maintained only by shutting one's eyes to the probability that the girl actually has had sex relations with someone from another community. In middle- and upper-class groups, intercourse during courtship may be rationalized as a justifiable expression of love and preparatory training for marriage. The norm, however, still is avoidance of premarital intercourse between members of marriageable groups.

EVALUATION OF TRENDS

When attitudes and behavior are in a state of flux, it is difficult to assess the results of any particular pattern of standards or conduct, and especially so when public disapproval dictates secrecy for emerging ways that contradict the traditional codes.

It should be recognized that no widespread social disaster results from premarital sex relations; in some measure they have been carried on for many generations by people who on the whole did not become personally maladjusted or fail in marital adjustment. However, a few studies and impressions from reading many case studies and life histories justify some suggestions as to the possible results of premarital sex behavior for individuals in whose social world it is disapproved.

1. The conditions under which premarital sex relations now occur engender anxiety. Fear of discovery, and the possibility of arrest, with consequent family disapproval and loss of good name create temporary fears and at times prolonged anxiety. For the girl there is the added fear of pregnancy unless careful precautions are observed. She also faces the future problem of whether her lack of virginity will interfere with marriage, or, if her relations are with her fiance, whether he may fail to carry the relationship to the point of marriage.

2. If the act is in contradiction to earlier attitudes regarding chastity, mental conflict may develop with a sense of guilt and shame and a feeling that self-respect or the family good name has been violated.

3. The act may be associated with deceit if the couple finds it necessary to use assumed names or to lie regarding marriage.

4. The physical conditions may contribute to the attitude that the relation is shameful.   The back seat of a car, the side of a country road, or a motel room rented for an hour by the young man while the girl hides her face from the attendant gives an unsavory connotation to the event.

5. The experience tends to be personally segmental and unintegrated into the total personality pattern.   It may be contrary to ideas of honor, honesty, or morality instilled in childhood and therefore may be relegated to a sort of airtight compartment.   It is brought into open consciousness, talked about, or a repetition planned for, only under conditions unrelated to the usual round of life or with certain companions who will maintain the secrecy.

6. Premarital sex relations tend to be socially segmental also.   They cannot be discussed with family, close friends, the fiance or fiancée, or later with husband or wife.   When they occur between lovers they may later become a barrier and lead to the breakdown of the relationship. Only a rather sophisticated couple, somewhat withdrawn from the mores, are able long to defend their relationship.   Even in lower-class groups, where sex is regarded as a natural function to be used and enjoyed, secrecy surrounds the activity.

Many of these points are illustrated by a study of the "couple trade" at tourist camps or motels in the fringe area of Dallas, Texas, whose patrons are largely residents of Dallas.[29]   So lucrative is the renting of cabins to couples who wish to use them for only an hour or two for sexual relations that many camps refuse to rent to tourists over the week end. The tourist would pay one fee and remain all night; the couple pays the same fee and leaves in a short time, after which the cabin is straightened up and rented again to another couple.   The average turnover for Saturday nights was 1.5 in a sample of camps.   For a given camp the turnover may be much higher: in one camp 20 cabins accommodated 45 couples in one night; in another, one cabin was rented 11 times in one Saturday. The camps cater to the wishes of the couples.   Lights are dim to prevent identification of the couple by the clerk and porter; a side door to the cabin permits the couple to enter directly from the car which is parked at the side of the cabin; noise and disturbances are avoided.   Everything possible is done to provide secrecy and to avoid attracting public or police attention.   When couples were traced by their car numbers and registra-

[29] E. L. Hooker, "The Urban Tourist Camp," *Studies in Sociology,* I (Summer, 1936), 12–18.

tions, it was found that the drivers of the cars (usually the men) came from middle- and upper-class areas of Dallas with very few from the disorganized slum areas.   The conclusion is that these couples are indulging in behavior not tolerated in their communities and therefore necessitating secrecy.   One camp over a ten-week period was patronized by 254 couples of whom 109 lived in the city of Dallas; of this group only 7 gave their correct names and addresses.   Often one person came repeatedly to a camp, each time with a different partner.   The study does not indicate whether these patrons were married or unmarried, but the emphasis on youthfulness of the couples indicates a high proportion of the unmarried.   This study makes clear the segmental character, secrecy, and deceit involved in an activity carried on contrary to the social norms.

Premarital sex relations also have implications for the maintenance of society as a whole.

1. The group upon which youth depends for approval of premarital sex relations is the peer group of adolescents or youth, who form a small and to some extent exclusive social world of their own.   When a group within the total society follows a pattern of conduct and sets up standards that run counter to the standards of the more inclusive society, social integration is threatened until either the behavior and standards of the minority group are brought into conformity with the standards or norms of the larger group, or the large-group norms are brought into conformity with the minority-group behavior.   To the extent that the larger community simply reasserts its position without reasonable attempt at adjustment of one of the two types just suggested, it tends to force the smaller group into secretive behavior.   The situation that we now have with many adolescents and youth running counter in both attitudes and behavior to the larger-group norms tends to be socially disintegrative.   It would be more so, of course, if youth did not accept many of the other generally accepted sexual norms, such as monogamy, marriage as the ultimate goal, and legitimacy of birth.

2. Another occasional and highly condemned result of premarital intercourse is the birth of an illegitimate child.   Allied to the problem of illegitimacy are induced abortions for the specific purpose of terminating the pregnancy.   Because such abortions are illegal, they are concealed, and therefore no accurate records are available of the number of such abortions or the proportion that occur to unmarried women.   There are three social losses caused by abortions: destruction of an unknown

number of human beings; a high death rate for the mothers; and a high incidence of resulting pathologic conditions that often cause sterility. The last result is especially probable among unmarried women, since they often resort to quacks, whereas the married woman who has a spontaneous or therapeutic abortion secures the services of a competent physician. One series of 1,200 abortions showed that the abortion resulted in sterility among 33.0 per cent of the unmarried women as compared with 14.5 per cent of the married.[30]

Finally, premarital sex relations may be considered in relation to good marital adjustment. We know very little about this relationship because of the secrecy surrounding the experience. One study of marital adjustment shows a slightly higher frequency of good adjustment among couples who had not had premarital intercourse, a slightly lower frequency for those who had experienced intercourse only with the future spouse, and a still lower frequency of good adjustment for those who had been more casual in their relationship.[31] According to another study, a larger percentage of divorced than of happily married men reported premarital intercourse; few women, either divorced or happily married, reported premarital intercourse and the difference between the percentage for the two groups of women was not significant.[32] From both studies, we conclude that many couples who had had premarital intercourse were well adjusted in marriage, and that some who had been virgins at marriage did not make good adjustments. We are not sure of the exact process that takes place when premarital intercourse and poor adjustment are associated with each other. Quotations already given on pages 384–385 suggest possible attitudes developing from premarital intercourse that may adversely affect marital adjustment. There is also another possibility: some personality traits that cause the unmarried person to turn to sex relations may also later cause marital maladjustment. For example, the girl who, against her better judgment, permits herself to be persuaded

---

[30] The International List of Causes of Death defines an abortion as the termination of a uterine pregnancy prior to seven lunar months of gestation, whether the child is born dead or alive. An abortion may occur spontaneously, or be induced for therapeutic purposes or in the deliberate attempt to avoid the birth of a child, which is a criminal offense for both the mother and the abortionist.—*The Abortion Problem,* Proceedings of the Conference Held under the Auspices of the National Committee on Maternal Health, Inc., at the New York Academy of Medicine, June 19th and 20th, 1942 (Williams and Wilkins, 1944), pp. 2, 39, 43, 55–57.

[31] Terman, *op. cit.,* ch. 12.

[32] Locke, *op. cit.,* p. 133.

by the ardent youth to enter into sex relations may be generally lacking in independence and self-reliance; or the young man who enters into sexual exploits to prove his masculinity may continue to exhibit traits of immaturity.   Indecisiveness and immaturity would interfere with good marital adjustment regardless of whether or not there had been premarital sex experience.   In determining whether premarital sex relations hinder good marital adjustment, one should know other facts besides the mere incidence of such experience.   For example, how frequently and under what conditions did the experience occur: was it an adolescent adventure in response to curiosity; an unpremeditated emotional episode; a regular pattern of visitation to prostitutes; or a part of casual or serious love-making between those of the same social class?   In other words, what meaning did the experience have for the persons involved?   Had the pattern of freedom and variety of contacts become habitual and therefore likely to be carried over into marriage where limitation of intercourse to the spouse is part of the mores?

MARITAL AND EXTRAMARITAL SEX RELATIONS

Unlike premarital intercourse, sex within the confines of marriage is not a segmental experience either psychologically or socially.   It occurs with full public approval with a socially acceptable partner.   Therefore it is integrated into the personalities of the man and woman and receives the full support of community mores.   As a part of the general pattern of married life, it is discussed in Chapter 16, "Marital Adjustment."

Extramarital sex relations, like premarital, are concealed and segmental.   Since these are usually related to the adjustment of husband and wife, they are also discussed in Chapter 16.

QUESTIONS

1. In most societies what is the function of social regulation of sex activities?

2. In the United States, what function or functions do sex regulations serve?

3. Attempt to prove or disprove the statement that the United States is moving toward a semirestrictive position with reference to premarital sex relations.   In the future, is the United States likely to become a permissive society?

4. What conflicting definitions of sex are still current in the United States? How would you account for the confusion?

5. Comment on Murdock's stand on premarital sex relations, either critically or favorably.

6. Compare Landis' point of view on premarital sex relations with Murdock's. Which seems to you more sound?

7. Why have "necking" and "petting" become highly developed in middle-class groups?

8. What are some of the adverse psychological and sociological results of premarital sex relations? Are there compensating advantages?

BIBLIOGRAPHY

The statistical report on sexual behavior of boys and men published by A. C. Kinsey and his associates in 1948 called forth many criticisms of method, differences of opinion with Kinsey's interpretation of his data, and expansions of the whole theme of sex in human society. Listed below are, first, the report, and then some of the articles and books that followed the publication.

Kinsey, Alfred C., Pomeroy, W. B., and Martin, C. E., *Sexual Behavior in the Human Male* (Saunders, 1948).

Burlingame, C. C., book review of *Sexual Behavior in the Human Male, American Journal of Psychiatry,* 104 (1948), 811–812.

Deutsch, Albert, editor, *Sex Habits of American Men: A Symposium on the Kinsey Report* (Prentice-Hall, 1948).

Hobbs, A. H., and Lambert, M. A., "An Evaluation of *Sexual Behavior in the Human Male," American Journal of Psychiatry,* 104 (1948), 758–764.

Hoch, Paul H., and Zubin, Joseph, editors, *Psychosexual Development in Health and Disease* (Grune and Stratton, 1949).

"Sexual Behavior: How Shall We Define and Motivate What Is Acceptable," a symposium, *Journal of Social Hygiene,* 36 (1950), 139–145.

Trilling, L., "Sex and Science: The Kinsey Report," *Bulletin of the Menninger Clinic,* 13 (1949), 109–118.

Wallin, P., "An Appraisal of Some Methodological Aspects of the Kinsey Report," *American Sociological Review,* 14 (1949), 197–210.

Sexual behavior and attitudes and social control

Davis, Katharine Bement, *Factors in the Sex Life of 2,200 Women* (Harper, 1929).

Dickinson, Robert L., and Beam, Lura, *A Thousand Marriages: A Medical Study of Sex Adjustment* (2nd printing, Williams and Wilkins, 1949).

Ford, Clellan S., and Beach, Frank A., *Patterns of Sexual Behavior* (Harper, 1951).

Harper, R. A., *et al.*, "Premarital Sex Relations: The Facts and the Counselor's Role in Relation to the Facts," *Marriage and Family Living,* 14 (1952), 229–238.

Mead, Margaret, *Male and Female: A Study of the Sexes in a Changing World* (Morrow, 1949).

Ploscowe, Morris, *Sex and the Law* (Prentice-Hall, 1951).

Sapir, E., "Observations on the Sex Problem in America," *American Journal of Psychiatry,* 8 (1928), 519–534.

Seward, Georgene, *Sex and the Social Order* (McGraw-Hill, 1946).

Wile, Ira S., editor, *Sex Life of the Unmarried Adult* (Vanguard, 1934).

15

Love and Marriage

In our culture love is regarded as the primary motive for marriage. As a rule people do not consider marriage unless they are "in love" with each other. They do not say simply that they love each other; to be "in love" is not the same thing as to love. Love itself is a sentiment that may be lifelong; it is one of many attitudes that a person holds and that for many hours of the day—many days perhaps—may remain latent and still be expressed overtly when the proper stimulus appears. The person who is "in love" is dominated by his sentiment, which tends to obscure other attitudes and to be expressed overtly in words, facial expression, and bodily posture, whether or not the appropriate stimulus is present. On occasions when it cannot be openly expressed it suffuses mental life, and daydreams replace rational thought. The person deeply in love often dreams in sleep of the loved one. Love with this pervasive, trancelike quality is what is meant by being "in love." So closely linked in popular thinking are marriage and being in love that as soon as two young people feel the excitable reaction that they identify as love, they begin to think of marriage. Adolescents of 15 or 16, whose families have marked them for college and who therefore are far from a marriageable age, may nevertheless play with the thought of marriage. Their conversation swings from the fearful idea of an immediate elopement to the more serious prospect of an engagement of five or six years. Sometimes adolescents do marry at the peak of their in-loveness, and only later become aware that marriage is not the climax to being in love but is the beginning of a new way of everyday living.

Marriage for any other reason than being in love is popularly regarded as reprehensible. The institutional marriages officially uniting two families, which have a wider usage and older history than love-marriages, are scorned as distasteful and cold.   The marriage of convenience, marriage of two old people, or marriage of a young woman and an older protective man are all open to criticism as not meeting the test of two people who are in love.   "Love and love alone" is the popular conception of the proper basis for marriage.

Chapter 13 pointed out many other controlling factors in marriage—similarities of race, religion, social and ethnic affiliation, proximity, and the search for complementary personality traits.   Within this matrix of similarity love most often grows.   Nevertheless, in a large minority of marriages similarities are disregarded.   In other marriages within the homogeneous groups, personalities are not well matched.   Students of marital processes and marriage counselors alike advocate a long period of friendship and engagement before marriage.   During such a period the couple have an opportunity to outlive the initial stage of being in love and to discover whether a deeper affection binds them together.

The complexities of love, the confusion between being in love and loving, the tendency to mistake sexual attraction for love, and the place of love in marriage all merit discussion.

THE DEVELOPMENT OF LOVE

Definition of love

The verb to love is loosely used to indicate almost any pleasurable feeling, regardless of the object or stimulus that has aroused it.   People often say they love a sunset, a certain kind of food, a new dress, a special type of dancing, an attractive person newly met, or the whole human race. These same people also love, but in a different way, their close friends, parents, siblings, children, husband or wife.   In this chapter love is limited to the interpersonal bond that unites people.

Love may be defined as a pleasurable or joyous feeling aroused by some stimulus.   The capacity for love is innate.   Young babies coo, gurgle, and smile when they are fondled and cuddled.   The child has the innate capacity to react in a certain way when pleased.   The fondling provides the stimulus for the pleasurable reaction.

Origin of love

The baby's first reactions of pleasure are in response to physical satisfactions. The baby cries when he is hungry, wet, cold, or in pain. He smiles, coos, and cuddles when he is fed, dry, warm, fondled gently. His pleasure at first is in response to stimuli provided by his own physical sensations.

Soon, however, the child's feelings of pleasure are associated not only with his comfortable physical sensations but also with the person who induces those sensations. The child associates his mother or nurse with his physical pleasure, and, after many repetitions of the association, exhibits for the mother or nurse the same pleasurable reactions that originally were called out by his physical sensations alone. As other people come into the baby's social world, he will come to love them also, if they provide pleasure. By a further linking of associations, the little child may show love responses to all women who resemble the mother.

Soon the child responds to other influences than physical care and comfort. If the person whom he loves as the giver of physical comforts (the mother usually) praises him, he comes to value that also. Even before the child can understand the words, he will respond to the caressing and approving tone of the mother. This response is reinforced when the mother catches up the baby and fondles him as she praises. Thus early love grows out of physical comfort but is soon extended to those who praise and approve. It includes dependence upon the person who provides these satisfying experiences. Since the mother also loves the baby and is pleased by his smile and caresses, the relationship becomes mutual.[1]

Love objects

The baby's first responses of love are general and diffuse; they are not directed toward the person who arouses them. Soon, however, the loving adult seeks a personal response from the child, who is encouraged and urged to hug and kiss the mother, to pat the mother's cheek, and to become active in cuddling. Thus the child learns the appropriate responses to the sensation of love—the ways in which he may express love. These responses, learned from the mother, are used throughout life to express love of many types and many degrees of intensity with many different people.

[1] For a general discussion of love by a psychologist see Percival M. Symonds, *The Dynamics of Human Adjustment* (D. Appleton–Century, 1946), pp. 520–565.

The child's responses to the mother are given as a sort of reward to the mother for her care and approval.   The child's interest in love relationships is primarily directed inward toward his own satisfactions and gratification of his needs and drives.   He feels the need to be loved before he feels the need to give love.   This narcissistic or self-centered love is characteristic of the young child, reaching a climax at about age three to five.

During childhood, the child's love begins to turn outward, first to members of the family, then to friends.   The process is one of mutual satisfaction.   The child finds that if he likes or loves another and expresses his preference, that person will respond with love reactions to him.   Thus the person whom the child hugs, kisses, smiles upon, approves of, will in turn hug, kiss, smile at, and approve of him.   The child learns that giving love secures love in return.

Children vary in the degree to which they direct their love outward from themselves.   In general, the child who is amply loved and thus made to feel wanted, secure, and worth while in his own family, will exhibit these attitudes in his relations with others.   He has been worthy of being loved; he projects this feeling on those around him and unconsciously assumes that they too are worthy of being loved.

On the other hand, the child who has been denied parental love feels insecure and unworthy.   In his later extrafamily contacts he will not only carry over his feeling of unworthiness but will project that attitude upon others and assume that they too are unworthy.   Such a person has neither learned the techniques of expressing love toward others nor experienced the satisfactions to be secured from the love of others.   He tends, therefore, to seek satisfactions within himself.   Sometimes these satisfactions are on a physical level; sometimes in fantasy he imagines himself to be lovable and beloved, as he has witnessed these reactions in those around him.

The succession of new love objects that a child acquires tends to correspond to the social contacts that he has and his own maturing personality.   Thus it is almost inevitable that the first love objects of the child are the parents, and especially the mother who cares for him.   Siblings and other members of the family or household follow.   When the child's contacts expand beyond the family, friends of his own age are included within the circle of his love.   Since children are encouraged in direct and subtle ways to play with those of their own sex, boys tend to form close ties with other boys, and girls with other girls. At adolescence, heterosexual social contacts are encouraged and love turns in this direction. After marriage and the birth of children, love is also directed toward children of either sex.

NONSEXUAL AND SEXUAL LOVE

Nonsexual love

Love and sex are sometimes erroneously assumed to be identical. One of the earliest expressions of pleasure (love) that the child exhibits comes from physical fondling. Certain portions of the body, either by nature or learning, are especially associated with pleasant physical sensations. They include the genital areas, breasts, and lips. Many other parts of the body also are responsive to stroking or gentle tickling. In our culture, the genital areas and breasts are associated with the idea of sex, and it is contrary to the mores to stimulate or permit the child to manipulate these portions of his own body. It is permissible to stimulate pleasurable sensations in the child through other types of tactile contacts, as by kissing, patting, and stroking almost any other part of the child's body. Most people do not associate this fondling of the child with sex stimulation, so long as they avoid the forbidden areas. The child himself knows nothing of sex as heterosexual intercourse, and even if he manipulates his own sex organs places the resulting sensations in the same category as other pleasant physical sensations.

Nonsexual physical contacts are common in infancy, tend to disappear during childhood, and to reappear in a new setting during adolescence. In infancy, the contacts most often are between child and parents; in childhood, playmates are discouraged from ardent physical contacts and parents tend to decrease their fondling. Thus there is a period of freedom from physical contacts but not of freedom from loving. During this period the child expands his love objects to include many outside the family. Expressions of love are symbolic; smiles, verbal expressions, secrets emphasizing an exclusive relationship, letters, poems, Valentines, and gifts replace physical fondling. In adolescence, physical contacts again appear, this time between boys and girls, but often unrelated to any feeling of love.

Loving—even when expressed through physical fondling—therefore is not synonymous with sex. It occurs in relationships where sex is forbidden, and it neither carries sexual connotations nor arouses sexual desires on the part of participants.   All elements of erotic interest between family members other than husband and wife are sternly repressed if they appear.   Tenderness is the keynote of love between parents and children, and between brothers and sisters.   It also characterizes friendships, and the associations in other primary groups, such as religious brotherhoods. In a more general expression, nonsexual love becomes altruism, or the desire to aid and protect others.

Sexual love

Sex, in its simplest terms, is an instinctive biological drive, whose aim is to dissipate a physical tension.   The motive of sex is selfish, the release of one's own tensions.   The sexual object is merely a means to an end. At this level, sex is often spoken of as carnal, low, animalistic, and its expression usually is kept secretive.   Because of the definition of sex as unworthy, some justification must be found for it.   A social justification through the birth of children formerly was the highest motivation for sex, strictly limited to marriage.   Now, with a more personal definition of marriage, sex has found a new justification—as the expression of love. Although love and sex are now closely related and the deepest experiences of love and sex may occur between the same pair, they are not identical simply because they coincide.

Sexual love may be defined as intimate love between a man and woman who find sex as a means of expression for their love.   When two people love each other, they tend to identify themselves with each other.   Part of this identification is on a psychological level; that is, they probe each other's thoughts and feelings and seek similarities and develop new common attitudes.   They like to do things together and especially to build up activities shared by themselves alone.   When a man and woman love each other, shared sex experience becomes a symbol of their identification. Our culture requires privacy and secrecy for sex relations.   It also approves only of sex relations between one pair over a period of time.   Intercourse therefore becomes the ultimate in exclusive shared experiences and an almost ideal symbol of identification sought by those who love each other.

Although physical expressions of love have been at a minimum during childhood, the pattern of caressing and kissing lies in the memory and experience of each person.   It is to be expected, therefore, that heterosex-

ual love will use the old means of expression.   The early tentative expression of liking or love between boy and girl is a duplication of the methods
used in their families.   With growing intimacy and the arousal of physical
sexual feelings, these familial expressions seem inadequate and new and
more intimate techniques are sought to express their growing need of
identification and expression of love.   New patterns are easily found,
although rarely through the family.   Motion pictures, certain illustrated
magazines, pictures in advertisements, fiction, books on the art of love,
popular songs, and the accounts of slightly older young people supply by
example or description additional techniques.   Eventually, the physical
contacts that began as a duplication of early family expression will cul-
minate in intercourse.   Thus the sex act may become an expression of
love between man and woman, just as the stroking of the baby was an expression of love between mother and child.

INFATUATION

As the child comes into adolescence, his rather diffuse love for family
is overshadowed by a concentration of feeling directed toward a person of
the opposite sex.   At first this feeling is not worthy of the name of love,
for it is of a type that enhances the ego; only with maturity of personality
does mature love also come to full flower.   Nevertheless, these first brief
stirrings of feeling for the opposite sex cannot be dismissed as unimportant.   They are a step in the development of love, paralleling the
early dating stage when ego-satisfaction outweighs other considerations.

Brief heady attractions between two people are called infatuations
if they occur between those of opposite sex, and crushes when between
members of the same sex.   Both are especially typical of adolescents or
older persons of immature personality.   Infatuations build up rapidly,
sometimes upon the basis of a single contact.   They are like a balloon
that is blown to maximum tension and then either explodes from its own
inner tension or slowly loses air and shrivels to a saggy piece of rubber.

Infatuation is in part a result of the situation in which the adolescent
finds himself.   After years of partial or complete separation from the
other sex he suddenly finds himself urged to participate in mixed activities.   As pointed out in Chapter 12, he looks to the next older age group
for a model for his new relationship and finds love.   He feels that he too
should be in love, and an artificially stimulated emotion is developed to

fill the void.   The infatuation may have its inception from a particularly romantic dance, moonlight boat ride, or other occasion that is out of keeping with everyday experiences.   It is fed by what the adolescent has read or heard of romantic love.   He runs through the overt pattern of love—the flattery, the tender words, the caress—and interprets his inner response to his own behavior as love.

The infatuation grows from a superficial attraction and tends to be unrelated to the total personality, although for a time it seems to absorb all the attention of the adolescent.   It caters primarily to the boy's or girl's feeling of self-importance; at last he is experiencing this thing called love. He wishes to savor it to the full, and therefore other considerations and obligations are disregarded while he gives himself over to full appreciation of his new feelings.

When the infatuation begins with a particularly romantic situation, the infatuated person associates the thrill of the situation with the person who shared it.   He builds up a fantasy-conception of the other's personality, based upon the few characteristics that stood out in the moments of romance.   Sometimes the infatuation is still more remote from reality and may be completely one-sided; in fact, the object of the feeling may not know that he has been singled out for attention.   With young adolescents or those without adequate heterosexual social contacts, the infatuation may be entirely in the realm of fantasy.   The girl may become infatuated with a movie star, collecting photographs of him in romantic poses, seeing all pictures in which he stars, sometimes repeatedly, and daydreaming about romantic situations in which she and the star figure.

We may perhaps say that adolescent infatuation results from the need of the boy or girl to experience a personal relationship with one of the opposite sex before the personality is ready for mature love.   Among older persons other motives appear.   Monotony or boredom may lead to a craving for adventure or thrill without responsibility or permanence. A person with a more fundamental love relationship that has become routinized may be susceptible to the momentary attraction of a spectacular personality.   Sometimes lack of a satisfactory love object leads a person to seize upon a chance relationship with someone who attracts him, whipping it rapidly up to a froth that resembles but is not identical with lasting affection.   Infatuation thrives also in a situation in which the person finds himself freed from the usual routines of his life or when he is detached from his usual friends or family.   The short-lived romance of the summer vacation, the lake excursion, the ocean trip, or even the college year are typical of such situations. Infatuation therefore is an imitation of love, often mistaken by the young person but rarely by the older one for enduring love.

Sustaining an infatuation is difficult. When it is unreciprocated, it tends to fade out and to be replaced by other interests. When it is mutual, it continues for a longer time, but it is never permanent. In the mutual infatuation, each builds up an idealized conception of the other person. On dates each must live up to the imagined conception held by the other and each responds to that imagined personality. It is difficult to live in this unreal world or to find a succession of romantic situations that foster the imagined concepts. Consequently, the infatuation tends to break down rapidly. The person is forced in time to realize that the object of the infatuation does not meet the imagined conception; he has faults, loses his temper, is obstinate, has headaches or indigestion, is not always immaculately clothed, or fails to maintain a scintillating conversation. The contrast with the imagined person is too great to be bridged, and the person may react violently to the object of the infatuation. He may despise, shun, hate him as ardently as he previously was attracted. These feelings often are really toward himself for his foolish overevaluation of the person, but are redirected toward the other person in order to save the infatuated one's feelings of pride and self-respect.

Even when there has not been extreme overidealization, the infatuation tends to break down with better acquaintance. It was formed on the basis of one segment of the personality, the meeting of one need—that for excitement, for example. But each person has many needs and the person who seemed so perfectly to meet one need under particularly propitious circumstances may not meet other needs as they arise. The good companion for an exciting round of dancing and dining may fail completely when the person needs sympathy or encouragement or a loyal working partner for some project.

When a relationship that began with infatuation continues, it usually changes in character. The fantasy-conception is replaced by one of more realistic nature inclusive of ordinary human faults. And the object of the infatuation is able to meet many (rather than one) needs of the person. The emotional level also changes and declines in intensity. Less is expected of the object. Thus the object of the infatuation may come to be classified as a friend rather than the ideal or perfect person and may take his place among other friends, each of whom meets certain needs of the person and from no one of whom everything is expected.

ROMANTIC LOVE

Romantic love is a highly personalized form of love in which love outweighs more practical considerations. One "falls into" romantic love and thereafter one is "in love." Because of the generally excitable quality of romantic love, it has often been confused with infatuation. It resembles infatuation in that it involves fantasy and idealization of the love object. It differs, however, in being more inclusive of the whole personality and more readily adjusted to the realities of marriage. Because of the confusion of romantic love and infatuation, romantic love has been repudiated by many as not having a genuine place in courtship and marriage. More recently, the concept of romantic love has been reexamined and found worthy to be one (but not the only) ingredient of happy and satisfying marriage.

Romance and romantic love have received bad names from their use in popular songs, fiction, and motion pictures. The fast-moving story that begins with a chance acquaintance on the beach or at a dance, moves rapidly into love-making, and ends with marriage after an interval of a few days really concerns infatuation more than romantic love. Attitudes of infatuation, not love of any kind, are expressed in such phrases as "soul mate," "the one and only," "I've waited for you all my life," "I can't live without you," and other statements that emphasize the egocentric reactions of the one in love. These presentations, entitled romance, are now part of the cultural heritage of all young people who attend movies, read popular magazines, or listen to the radio. They encourage infatuations, misnamed love.

Historical development

The historical connotations of romantic love also are somewhat different from its more recent meaning. Extolled in songs, poetry, and stories and described in social histories, early romantic love had a special meaning that grew out of restrictive social contacts.

Romantic or courtly love first appeared in Western civilization in the twelfth century, to define a relationship not previously provided for in social institutions. Institutional marriage did not provide for fulfillment of personal desires or for any contact of men and women outside of marriage. Through courtly love a young knight might dedicate himself to a married woman of high status, idealizing her and receiving recognition for his deeds of bravery. The relationship was impersonal and unrelated to sex, which was regarded as carnal, whereas courtly love was idealistic and spiritual. Much later, in Europe and again against the background of institutional marriages, romantic love was used as the justification for extramarital sexual alliances based on personal preferences. In many societies the correct marriage, arranged between two families, was supplemented by unofficial heterosexual relationships in which the couple paired off because of personal attraction. The women might be of the same social class as the men, married or unmarried, or of a lower class. In each case they provided for personal emotional needs, whereas marriage fulfilled social and family obligations.

Only more recently, and primarily in the United States, has initial entrance to marriage been through the gateway of romantic love. The combination of romantic love and marriage involves an attempt to coordinate love, sex, and marriage into one unit of experience between one man and one woman. In the European social situations in which romantic love developed, marriage and sex relations were contained within an official relationship, whereas romantic love (and sometimes sex) with another partner remained outside of marriage on an individualistic basis. Marriage was the public and responsible relationship, romantic love the private and nonresponsible one. Marriage was permanent and stable, a means of conserving property and rearing children to continue the family name; romantic love lasted only so long as the personal preference for each other was fervid. Marriage and romantic love were, in fact, opposed to each other, serving different needs of people. The attempt to bring two such contradictory relationships into coincidence between two people involves tremendous difficulties.

If the traditional values of marriage are to be conserved, then something of romance must be sacrificed for stability and the needs of children. If romance rules, then partners may be changed time after time as one romantic episode gives way to another. Since our culture does not approve of such episodes outside of marriage, romance involves marriage and implies, at the end of the romance, divorce and remarriage. The epitome of romantic marriages is found among some of the much-publicized couples in Hollywood, where one marriage follows another in rapid succes-

sion, with the new romance highly developed before the previous marriage
has been dissolved.   With fewer changes of partners and less publicity,
the same procedure marks many other marriages.

Romantic love in the United States

Although romantic love has had a long history in Europe, its growth
in the United States is not an attempt to reproduce a European pattern of
culture.   Rather, it developed out of special situations, an important one
being the breakdown of family control as segments of families—and
especially young people—migrated about the country, seeking land, work,
and adventure.   In the young world of the frontier, strength, ingenuity,
and courage were highly valued; family connections were of less importance.   People were judged more by personal traits than by family ties.
Young people learned to think and act independently of their families.
The combination of independence and high evaluation of personal traits
placed selection of a mate on a personal basis and helped lay the foundation for the full development of romantic love.

The rise of the middle class was another factor; unhampered by upper-
class ideals of continuity of family lines through arranged marriage, the
middle class was more free to follow individual preferences in courtship;
at the same time, middle-class mores forbade the culmination of romantic
love in sex relations outside of marriage.   Individual choice and romantic
love might thrive, but they must find their fulfillment in marriage.

In the cities another influence pulled in the same direction.   The Industrial Revolution drew people, and especially women, away from their
narrow field of activities within the walls of the home and under the supervision of parents.   Women learned to be independent not only economically but in their thinking about problems and in their attitude toward
themselves.   They played a role unrelated to the family and conceived of
themselves not solely as members of the family but as individuals.   As
individuals, they were entitled to free choice of mates, and since they were
able to support themselves they could take the time to judge each suitor
and reject those who seemed personally undesirable.

The variety of occupations that gradually opened to women called forth
different combinations of personality traits.   Whereas the one role previously open to women had tended to develop uniformity of personality,
the new situation gave birth to distinctive personalities.   Men might
choose now not between one good potential housewife and another, but

among the housewife type, the brisk businesswoman, the cooperative social worker, the precise schoolteacher, and many other types.

Laborsaving machinery in the city and on the farm and the movement
of much labor from the home to the factory have provided a previously
unheard-of amount of leisure.   Whereas courting at one time had to be
sandwiched in between long days of work in shop or fields, with perhaps a
little more leisure on Sunday (there was no two- or three-day week end),
now the evening may start at four in the afternoon and the week end may
last from Friday afternoon to Monday morning.   Time now invites young
people to spend many hours together.

To fill these vacant hours commercial recreation provides varied activities, many calculated to increase the personal interest between the
sexes.   Public dance halls, night clubs, and privately sponsored dances
make it possible for a young couple to dance every night in the week.
Often they go alone and do not meet anyone they know.   They form a
small, although perhaps temporary, primary group, gaining privacy from
their status as strangers to all others.   Attention is concentrated on each
other and the soft lights, music, and embrace of the dance make this attention romantic in nature.   Thus even a blind date may have romantic
elements.   Motion pictures are another type of commercial recreation
that, by their content, stimulate romantic interests.   By identification with
the actor of the same sex, boy and girl thrill to the romance of the picture.
Sitting shoulder to shoulder, hand in hand—or actually embracing—the
young couple in imagination feel themselves to be undergoing with each
other the exciting love scenes of the picture.

With the great increase in independence of young people, and their
freedom to leave home and support themselves elsewhere, has necessarily
gone a decline in patriarchal authority.   Familial control is much less intense than in early generations and more indirect.   Social pressures
emanate from the family, especially toward young people who still live
at home, but direct commands or prohibitions rarely exist.   Each young
person is free to follow his romantic interests.

Qualities of romantic love

Romantic love in its pure form is the idealization of the emotion and
sentiment of love itself.   The person—or couple—enters a state in which
the supreme motivating factor in his life is a feeling of devotion to another
person and, of equal or greater importance, the personal satisfaction he

receives from his devotion and the response to it.   Although one person may fall in love with another who does not reciprocate, usually the process is mutual or it dies out.   Thus, being in love is not something that occurs to one person, but involves two people and the interaction between them.

This interaction is exclusive to the two people.   Whereas friends may wish to carry out their activities with congenial companions, the romantic couple seek privacy where a chain of stimulus and response may go on exclusively between them.   Since privacy makes secrecy possible, the feeling of exclusiveness is further enhanced.   The privacy and secrecy make identification easy, and the two build up a feeling of oneness and of separateness from the world.   They create and exist in a little world of their own, furnished with their shared memories.

Sexual impulses are involved inasmuch as romantic love normally occurs only between a man and a woman.   They are usually inhibited, however, so far as direct expression is concerned.   Secondary contacts, as holding hands, nonpassionate kisses, and close dancing, give a certain degree of pleasant stimulation to each.   Especially in the young and inexperienced lovers, these may not be identified as sexual in origin. Romantic love is thought to be pure and to verge on the spiritual; therefore, romantic lovers find it difficult to accept in the loved one—or in themselves—an interest in physical sexual pleasures.

Idealization of the loved one is a distinguishing feature of romantic love.   Although all love relations involve a loss of objectivity, romantic love becomes to some degree divorced from reality.   Each member of the relationship exhibits only a part of his personality, the part that responds to the expectations of the other.   If the young man has whispered to the girl that she is beautiful, she will thereafter take special care in dressing and arranging her hair, when she is to be with him, although at other times she is inclined to be careless about her personal grooming.   If the girl has told the young man that he is thoughtful and considerate, he will go to extreme measures to think up and carry out special little pleasures for her, although in other relationships he may be inconsiderate or may impose upon others.   When only a few special attributes of the personality are exposed, it is easy for the other person to build up an idealized conception of the lover.   The imagined conception of the other's personality is based upon a few desirable phases of personality rather than upon the entire personality, good and bad.   Because a few characteristics are unusually pleasing, it is assumed that the entire personality of the other is on the same plane.

The process of idealization is made easier, also, by the fact that romantic contacts take place under a rather standardized set of circumstances. The lovers withdraw to themselves. Therefore neither sees the other in ordinary work or friendly contacts with others, where less ideal traits may appear. Nor do they see each other performing the ordinary tasks of the day or their reactions to these duties. Rather, romantic love develops in an atmosphere of dim lights, moonlight, romantic songs, soft music, love stories on the screen, dancing, and personal conversation. Here there are no frustrations, no competition, no external crises.

Romantic love places a low value on such conditions as wealth or social position or success in the real world. Concentration is on personal characteristics. Thus, the upper-class girl may have a romantic affair with a boy of the lower class if the boy has certain characteristics of strength or virility that appeal to her. Or the son of wealth and culture may fall romantically in love with a girl of limited background if she has beauty and grace. Practical considerations are disregarded. The upper-class boy or girl may risk or accept disinheritance and social ostracism rather than give up the loved one.

Functions of romantic love

Although romantic love is of cultural origin, it serves certain psychological as well as social functions.

The long period between the beginning of adolescence and the acceptable social age for marriage has already been discussed. With the encouragement given to heterosexual social contacts, some device was bound to arise to channel the personal interests of young people for each other during this period. Infatuations, merging into more permanent romantic associations with more maturity, supply this need. Stimulating, thrilling, but not necessarily taken too seriously even by those involved, romance fills the dating period and becomes a halfway station to marriage; a way to sublimate gross sexual desires.

Psychologically, romantic love serves several purposes. It has some of the elements of a flight from reality—an escape from the prosaic working world, where one is appraised by his qualities and given status through competition, into a dream world where the idealized attitude of the partner gives one the illusion of perfection in himself.   The activities of romance certainly are in contrast to the orderly and often monotonous activities of the day.

Love of any type gives security and a sense of being important to someone, cared for, and protected.   Romantic love makes this feeling possible on short notice.   Also it removes the sense of loneliness that the detached young person may feel and provides not only incoming love but an object upon whom to expend love.   It may contribute to the lover's own sense of importance; he may hold a mediocre position in business but be a great success as a romantic lover in the eyes of the girl who is his dating partner.

At times romantic love may become the cloak that hides sexual relations.   Young people, especially, who have been taught that premarital sex relations are immoral, require a rationalization to assuage their sense of guilt.   The creed of romantic love, which places love above all other considerations, becomes their justification.   In fact, it is easily possible for young people to mistake sexual excitement for love, although one is physical in origin, the other attitudinal.   The girl, in particular, may make such an error, inasmuch as her early sexual reactions are more diffuse than the man's.   Because of her training she is also more likely to need a strong rationalization to overcome her inhibitions.   The man, responding to her demand for love-making, speaks the words of love and caresses her.   If intercourse is the final result, that too is interpreted as love, although the pair may be only superficially attracted to each other.

Outcome of romantic love

Romantic love, with its exclusiveness, its extreme idealization, its disregard for practical considerations, is an unstable relationship in spite of its intensity.   The spiraling process must eventually reach a limit; the couple must sometime bring their twosome into relationship with other people and groups; comparison of the idealized person with others follows; practical arrangements break into the situation.   Although the pattern of romantic love is fairly clear, there is more variation in the outcome.

1. The affair may fall apart of its own weight.   The very intensity of the relationship may be fatiguing.   It is not easy for boy or girl always to meet the ideal conception of the other—always to be beautiful, well-dressed, sweet-tempered, sympathetic.   Other interests intrude, and each may desire the companionship of other friends of both sexes.   Practical demands of work, family duties, or studying for examinations may inter-

fere with the concentration of time and activities upon each other.   Sometimes the relationship can be brought down to a lower emotional level and maintained on a more realistic basis.   But often the process simply brings disillusionment and disappointment, and the lovers fall out of love as rapidly as they fell into love.   The very short-lived romantic affairs verge into infatuations and leave only a momentary sadness when they end. Those of longer duration, which have aroused anticipations of continued love or have involved the prospect of marriage, may leave bitterness and deep disappointment when they are no longer tenable.

2. The romantic affair may always have been tempered by contact with reality.   The young man may always have been able to admit to himself that the girl had a harsh laugh but considered this amply offset by her kindness and sympathy.   Therefore his idealization does not carry him completely away from reality but involves merely an underevaluation of her unpleasant qualities and an overevaluation of her good qualities.   Romantic interludes of the two alone may have alternated with group contacts, a situation that has two results.   The two do not center all their interest in each other and thus expose themselves to complete disappointment if the other fails to meet all needs.   Also, each is able to observe the other in relation to other people in a variety of situations and thus make a more realistic evaluation of the other's personality than is possible under exclusive relationships.

With the tempered romance, progression may take place into the combination of romantic and companionship interests that make permanent conjugal love possible.   The relationship may then continue into marriage with a change of emphasis in the quality of the love relationship.

3. The highly keyed romantic love may continue into marriage without conversion to conjugal love, a situation that almost inevitably leads to conflict.   The realities of married life are incompatible with the idealized conceptions of undiluted romantic love.

LOVE IN MARRIAGE

Romantic love has frequently been attacked as an unstable basis for marriage.   It has been said that its overidealization breaks down under the impact of daily living, and that it is a fundamental cause of conflict and divorce.   On the other hand, this point of view has been contested. It has been pointed out that with the loss of practical reasons for marrying and the high expectation of finding in marriage great happiness and relief from all frustrating experiences love is perhaps the only bond strong enough to hold a couple together.   If we assume the need for love on a personal basis, confining that love to marriage has strengthened marriage at a time when other marital functions are very weak.[2]

It has also been pointed out that too much emphasis has been placed on cultural similarities as the basis for a stable marriage.   Individualism and a chance for personality growth are now also part of our ideal of marriage.[3]   They require freedom of choice of mates and an appreciation of the spouse's needs and abilities on the part of each partner to the marriage.   Romantic love provides for personal selection of the mate and evaluation of each other's needs and potentialities.

Mature love

The love that functions well in marriage, however, is not the extreme type of romantic love.   It is less demanding, less exclusive, and more tolerant.   This love has been dubbed conjugal love by some writers.[4]   It may also be called mature love.

Mature, or conjugal, love is compatible with the realities of marriage and later of family life inclusive of children.   Thus it is a type of love that makes it possible for the wife to accept her husband as still lovable when his chin is covered with a stubble of beard, when he is dirty and sweaty from a bout with the lawnmower or car, when he is cross because of some frustrating office experience, and when he is filled with anxiety over an unsettled business deal.   It is also the type of love that makes it possible for the husband to love his wife in spite of stringy hair, the nausea of pregnancy, the occasional poorly prepared meal, the sharp-tongued retort caused by anxiety or disappointment.   And it is the type of love that holds husband and wife together and to their children when the baby cries throughout the evening or demands food or other care in the middle of the night; when parents must refuse enticing invitations in order to remain at home with young children; when the purchase of a new car must be delayed in order to straighten a youngster's teeth.   These are the situa-

---

[2] The historical development of romantic love as well as an appraisal of its present function is given in Hugo G. Beigel, "Romantic Love," *American Sociological Review,* 16 (1951), 332–334.

[3] William L. Kolb, "Sociologically Established Family Norms and Democratic Values," *Social Forces,* 26 (1948), 451–456.

[4] Evelyn Millis Duvall and Reuben Hill, *When You Marry* (Heath, 1945), pp. 170–171.

tions that romantic love has not prepared the young couple to manipulate successfully.

Romantic love remains in mature conjugal love but is strongly supplemented by other attitudes and types of interaction. There is still a strong element of idealization: each believes he has the best spouse in the world, or at least the best one for him; shortcomings are generously overlooked, and desirable traits are valued and praised.

The romantic ideal of exclusiveness remains so far as sexual love of another adult of the opposite sex is concerned, inclusive of physical contacts and sexual relations. But jealousy of contacts with those of one's own sex or of the married couple with other couples is eliminated. It must be recognized that this ideal is not always achieved in marriage. One or the other may supplement marital relationship with an extramarital affair on either a physical or romantic basis; or one or the other or both may find they are no longer in love with the spouse, and a divorce follows.

Sexual impulses, present but inhibited before marriage, now find free expression. This situation in itself changes the quality of the love between the two, in that it removes a need to divert sexual interest into other channels or to seek expression in secondary ways or by subterfuge. The freedom to make love reduces the need for secret meetings or for love songs, dancing under soft lights, or presents of flowers. Such symbols of love tend to be attached only to special sentimental occasions, such as anniversaries, birthdays, or holidays, which formerly were the occasions for especially romantic episodes.

Replacing some of the romantic love and supplementing what remains is the growth of a new relationship that usually has its inception before marriage during the period of serious courtship and engagement. The new love is directed not toward the emotional responses and self-satisfactions of romantic love but toward the building of a mutual pattern of life, not limited to the present but extending into the indefinite future. Personality traits that are conducive to joint living gain in value, such as dependability, self-reliance, cooperativeness, sympathy, and unselfishness. The shift in emphasis is symbolized by the girl's willingness to forego expensive dates in favor of a growing bank account and the man's interest in the girl's ability to make a home. Glamorous dates provided by the young man and beauty and grace on the part of the girl are no longer sufficient. The emotions of this new relationship are less highly keyed than those of romantic love.   They are expressed by such words as companionship, partnership, mutual helpfulness, sympathy, tenderness.

Mature love takes more account of reality, such as poverty or moderate income, the difficulties of adjusting differences in religious beliefs or social-class standing, differences or conflicts in moral standards, even such small items as differences in tastes for food, types of houses, hours for arising and going to bed.   It is recognized that these and similar differences cannot be glossed over but will influence the daily interaction and mode of living of the couple.

Mature marital love provides many of the satisfactions that come from romantic love, but usually in a more permanent fashion.   Security is part of the picture in that each feels both beloved and able to express his own love.   The very fact of being loved and chosen for marriage increases the self-esteem of each, and therefore often self-reliance and ability.   Protectiveness is mutual; there is always someone to lean upon for a short space of time.

In some ways mature conjugal love at its best is a correlation of several types of love: the narcissistic love of the child and the adolescent, in that each partner receives a glow of satisfaction from having been selected for love; nonsexual outgoing tender love that seeks to benefit the love object; sexual love; and romantic love.

Importance of love in present-day marriage

Love of some type is extremely important in present-day marriage. Many of the practical reasons for marriage have been removed by outside agencies that have taken over necessary functions formerly performed in the family.   The personal relationship undoubtedly is the chief bond that holds husband and wife together.   Not only have utilitarian functions disappeared, but the former stabilizing effects of supporting institutions, such as the church and primary community, have declined and new controls have been slow in developing.   The one strong remaining bond is the personal relationship.

QUESTIONS

1. List as many popular uses as you can of the verb, to love.
2. Discuss the relationship between the child's innate capacity to love and the social development of this capacity.

3. Are sex and love necessarily found together? Why does popular thought in America tend to associate them with each other?

4. Discuss the statement that infatuations are typical of adolescents or older persons of immature personality.

5. What is the difference between the present conception of romantic love in the United States and its historical connotation in Europe?

6. Why is romantic love not an adequate basis for an enduring relationship?

7. How can romantic love be integrated into a stable marital relationship?

BIBLIOGRAPHY

Biegel, H. G., "Romantic Love," *American Sociological Review,* 16 (1951), 326–334.

Dell, Floyd, *Love in the Machine Age: A Psychological Study of the Transition from Patriarchal Society* (Farrar and Rinehart, 1930).

Reik, Theodor A., *A Psychologist Looks at Love* (Farrar and Rinehart, 1944).

Rougemont, Denis de, *Love in the Western World* (Harcourt, Brace, 1940).

Symonds, Percival M., *The Dynamics of Human Adjustment* (Appleton-Century, 1946), pp. 520–565.

16

Marital Adjustment

As the dating-engagement sequence moves to its logical conclusion, couple after couple change their status from single to married. Women begin to make the transition in the late teens and push rapidly into marriage in the early twenties; by the late twenties the process is almost as complete as it will ever be (Figure 39). The process for men is similar, but begins in the twenties. The concentration of marriages in the early adult years has been typical of the United States for many years past, with a tendency for the median age of marriage to decline. In 1949, half of all men who had ever been married entered their first marriage by the time they were 22.7 years of age; and half of the women ever married, by age 20.3 years.[1] One may fairly say that adjustment to marriage is the most important project of the girl in her late teens and early twenties and second only to vocational placement for the young man in early and mid-twenties.

THE NATURE OF MARITAL ADJUSTMENT

Adjustment may be briefly defined as the process whereby people work out the satisfaction of their needs in all areas—physical, psychological, and social. Since deviation from cultural norms brings great disapproval, it is scarcely necessary to add that the process goes on within the range of freedom of personal behavior allowed by the social norms. Marital adjustment falls within this definition but has several special aspects because of the nature of marriage in our culture.

[1] Paul C. Glick and Emanuel Landau, "Age as a Factor in Marriage," *American Sociological Review,* 15 (1950), 517.

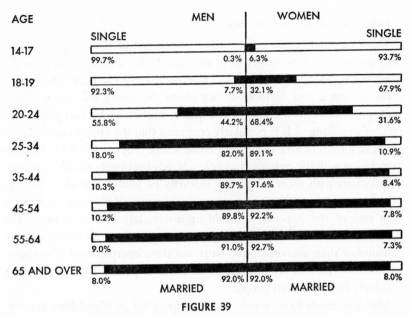

AGE	MEN		WOMEN	
	SINGLE			SINGLE
14-17	99.7%	0.3%	6.3%	93.7%
18-19	92.3%	7.7%	32.1%	67.9%
20-24	55.8%	44.2%	68.4%	31.6%
25-34	18.0%	82.0%	89.1%	10.9%
35-44	10.3%	89.7%	91.6%	8.4%
45-54	10.2%	89.8%	92.2%	7.8%
55-64	9.0%	91.0%	92.7%	7.3%
65 AND OVER	8.0%	92.0%	92.0%	8.0%
	MARRIED		MARRIED	

FIGURE 39

Single and Married Persons at Different Ages, 1950

After age 35 there is little change in the percentage of people who are married. Marriages that occur after this age often unite those who previously have been married but have been widowed or divorced. In this chart the married include widowed and divorced in order to show the contrast between the single and those who have at some time been married. The proportion of people who are married now is greater than at earlier periods. The percentage of married males aged 15 and over increased from 58 in 1890 to 67 in 1940; of males aged 14 and over in 1948 a record 72 per cent were married. For women the percentages were 68 in 1890, 74 in 1940, and 79 in 1948. The change in the minimum age from 15 in the earlier reports to 14 in 1948 tends to lower the percentage since few people are married by age 14. (Source for figure: *Current Population Reports, Population Characteristics, Marital Status and Household Characteristics: March, 1950,* Series P-20, No. 33 [Bureau of the Census, February 12, 1951], p. 10. Source for percentages married at different periods: *Statistical Abstract of the United States, 1950* [Bureau of the Census, 1950], p. 21; *Current Population Reports, Population Characteristics, Marital Status, Number of Times Married, and Duration of Present Marital Status: April, 1948,* Series P-20, No. 23 [Bureau of the Census, March 4, 1949], p. 1.)

Exclusiveness of marital relationship

Marriage tends to be an exclusive association of two people. If the man and woman who marry have not already freed themselves from dependence upon their parents, they are expected to do it forthwith. Many jokes are made and cartoons drawn about the young wife who, after a spat, goes home to mother; or the young husband who still prefers his mother's cooking. It is popularly conceded that the young married couple have a right to an independent home where they are cut off from close association with the parents of either. Needs previously satisfied through associations with those of greater maturity or younger or older siblings of the same or opposite sex now are to be satisfied through association with one of the opposite sex and approximately the same age. The couple are expected to finance their marriage, make their own decisions, consolidate their social life, and work out their interpersonal adjustment. In no other human relationship is so much expected from two young, relatively inexperienced people.

Marriage tends to be a pair relationship so far as friendships are concerned. The husband is not expected to meet his emotional or social needs through association with other women, nor the wife with other men. Each may continue to have friends of the same sex, but friends of the opposite sex must be shared with the spouse; they must be family friends rather than individual friends. Thus, most emotional and many social needs must be satisfied through one person, a limitation not imposed by the mores prior to engagement and marriage.

The husband has one outlet that many women do not have—his occupation. But occupational relationships are expected to be impersonal. They may satisfy needs for productive or creative activity and contribute to status and personal prestige; but wifely jealousy and public disapproval are quickly aroused if the husband becomes emotionally attached to any female fellow worker. The wife also has a special outlet, shared with the husband, but more especially her own, through her close relationship with her children. Her satisfactions here are affectional in nature and supplement her relationship with her husband, which is also affectional.

Even when there are children, the ideals of American marriage place allegiance between husband and wife on a higher level than parent-child attachments. It can truly be said that the deepest emotional satisfactions as well as social, financial, and household matters belong to the married couple as an exclusive pair.

Reciprocal relationship

The exclusive nature of marriage gains significance when it is realized that husband and wife must be so nicely matched that each receives this maximum satisfaction for personal needs from the other. Not only does each receive satisfaction, but each must be able to give satisfaction to the other. People scorn the henpecked husband who gives but does not receive, and pity the browbeaten wife who serves her husband without affection or respect from him. Our present ideal of marriage is democratic and equalitarian; both husband and wife are entitled to a rich personal life; neither is expected to be resigned and self-sacrificing to the exclusion of compensating satisfactions from the other.

The democratic nature of the relationship also calls for mutual compromise and tolerance of any differences in attitudes or habits. Neither is expected to have a position of status or dominance so far superior to the other that one would make all the concessions to reach harmony and agreement and the other none.

Dynamic quality of marital adjustment

Modes of interaction between husband and wife that yield mutual satisfaction tend to become habitual and predictable. Each learns to respect the deeply held convictions of the other; and each learns the little signs of restlessness and dissatisfaction that call for minor modifications of conduct. Each learns the personal happiness to be achieved by making the other happy and gaining the other's approval. Nevertheless, the relationship rarely becomes static. Both external changes that affect the marriage and personality changes require constant adjustment in the pattern of interaction.

The external changes may lie within the family itself, such as the birth of a child that necessitates a new marital relationship. Adjustment of the husband to a new job, or removal of the family to a new community of different type from the old may have its counterpart in a new pattern of marital relationships. As the husband achieves new occupational responsibilities much of his time and interests, previously wife-centered, may separate him from his wife. The wife must adjust to this situation.

Migration from a rural to an urban environment, previously discussed in detail, may involve a major reorganization of husband-wife relationships and roles. The frequent separation of the young pair when the husband is called into military service creates its own peculiar problems of curtailed interaction.

Personality also may change with the passage of time. ·The older dictum that the personality pattern is set by the time a child is four or five years of age is only partially true in a constantly changing social scene. New experiences destroy earlier personality formation, arouse new needs, and stimulate the mind to new interests and goals. Many couples who seemed well adjusted at one stage have found themselves at odds after one has fought in the front lines of a war, or attended college, or when both have attended colleges but of different types.[2] If marital adjustment is to survive personality changes, it must continue to be dynamic and to match change in one spouse with change in the other.

Personality changes are stimulated also by our present-day concept that marriage and family life should leave the door open for personality development not only of children but of husband and wife. Sometimes husband and wife are able to maintain their identity of interests and goals and to change in unison. But it also often happens that one becomes fixed at a certain stage of development while the other changes. Then the reciprocal quality of giving and receiving satisfaction for needs is threatened.

Marital adjustment therefore calls not only for matching of personal qualities at the time of marriage but for a dynamic process of interaction to strengthen and maintain the relationship.

TIME REQUIRED FOR INITIAL ADJUSTMENT

The process of mutual adjustment, begun in courtship, becomes intensified with marriage. The young husband and wife do not always spontaneously find themselves well adjusted in marriage. A study of middle-class couples shows that only slightly more than half of the husbands and wives felt that adjustment had been satisfactory from the beginning in matters of sex and in spending the family income. For six areas of married life, Figure 40 gives the percentage of husbands and wives who

---

[2] See the cases on pages 360–364 for examples of personality change and subsequent maladjustment that led to broken engagements.

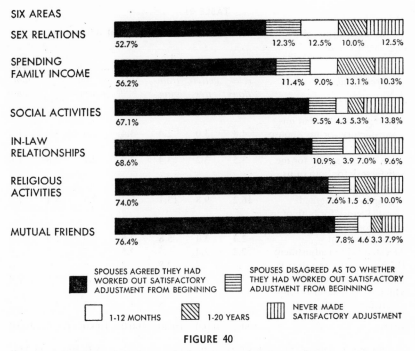

SIX AREAS

SEX RELATIONS
52.7%   12.3%   12.5%   10.0%   12.5%

SPENDING
FAMILY INCOME
56.2%   11.4%   9.0%   13.1%   10.3%

SOCIAL ACTIVITIES
67.1%   9.5%   4.3   5.3%   13.8%

IN-LAW
RELATIONSHIPS
68.6%   10.9%   3.9   7.0%   9.6%

RELIGIOUS
ACTIVITIES
74.0%   7.6%   1.5   6.9   10.0%

MUTUAL FRIENDS
76.4%   7.8%   4.6   3.3   7.9%

SPOUSES AGREED THEY HAD WORKED OUT SATISFACTORY ADJUSTMENT FROM BEGINNING

SPOUSES DISAGREED AS TO WHETHER THEY HAD WORKED OUT SATISFACTORY ADJUSTMENT FROM BEGINNING

1-12 MONTHS   1-20 YEARS   NEVER MADE SATISFACTORY ADJUSTMENT

FIGURE 40

Length of Time after Marriage Required for Adjustment

In six important areas of marital adjustment, husbands and wives, answering as individuals, stated the length of time required for satisfactory adjustment. Although in the majority of cases husband and wife agreed on the length of time, in some instances there was disagreement, the extent of which is shown only with reference to immediate adjustment after marriage. Sexual adjustment, often regarded as the key to happy marriage, had the highest percentage of disagreement and most often was reached only after months or even years of marriage. The subjects of this study were 409 couples with an average married life of 20 years without divorce or separation. For the most part the couples were middle class, with income and education above the average for the total population. (Source: Judson T. Landis, "Length of Time Required to Achieve Adjustment in Marriage," *American Sociological Review*, 11 [1946], 668.)

thought agreement was immediate and the percentage who specified different lengths of time required for delayed adjustment. In each area some believed that adjustment had not been reached even after many years of marriage. For these unsatisfied individuals, Table 21 gives detailed responses.

TABLE 21

Percentages of 409 Couples Reporting Degrees of Marital Adjustment *

Present adjustment	Sex rela-tions	Social activi-ties	Child train-ing	Reli-gion	Spend-ing the income	In-law rela-tion-ships	Mu-tual friends
Satisfactory for me but un-satisfactory for my spouse	4.8	3.0	2.4	3.4	2.6	3.0	1.5
Satisfactory for my spouse but unsatisfactory for me	3.5	3.2	3.4	2.6	2.7	2.6	1.6
Satisfactory for both of us							
Spouses agreed	63.1	72.1	70.7	75.8	77.0	76.5	82.1
Spouses disagreed	16.2	9.8	13.1	8.3	7.5	8.4	7.1
Unsatisfactory for both of us but working toward a bet-ter adjustment	2.4	3.4	5.8	2.6	6.0	1.9	3.0
At a standstill in adjustment	2.2	2.4	.5	2.5	1.2	.7	.9
Have many quarrels over it	.9	.7	2.8	.2	.6	.2	.6
Never discuss the subject	3.9	2.1	.7	3.2	.7	3.0	2.0
Think we will never reach a satisfactory adjustment	3.0	3.3	.6	1.4	1.7	3.7	1.2
TOTALS	100.0	100.0	100.0	100.0	100.0	100.0	100.0

* Judson T. Landis, "Length of Time Required to Achieve Adjustment in Marriage," *American Sociological Review,* 11 (1946), 671.

One may question how important to husband and wife is agreement in these areas. Each individual provided an estimate of his happiness in marriage. In spite of the large percentage of disagreements, 48.0 per cent said their marriages had been very happy; 34.6 per cent, happy; 16.4 per cent, average; and only 0.8 per cent, unhappy or very unhappy. Marked happiness was more frequent among those who made early adjustments, whereas average happiness characterized those who were still unadjusted. When lack of adjustment in several, rather than one, areas is compared with the happiness rating, the association between merely average happiness and unadjustment in several areas is striking, as Figure 41 shows. The early achievement of marital adjustment, therefore, is important not only for the happiness of bride and groom but for continued happiness throughout marriage.

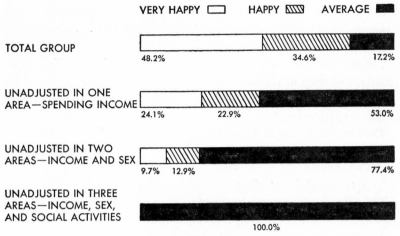

FIGURE 41

Association of Unadjustment and Degree of Happiness

Failure to adjust reduces the degree of happiness. All husbands and wives who felt that there was unadjustment in the three most difficult areas—spending income, sex, and social activities—were no more than average in happiness, and some were contemplating divorce. It should be noted that few husbands or wives, regardless of amount of adjustment, rated themselves as unhappy—less than 1 per cent of the total. (Source: Judson T. Landis, "Length of Time Required to Achieve Adjustment in Marriage," *American Sociological Review*, 11 [1946], 675.)

HAZARDS IN INTERPERSONAL ADJUSTMENT

In interpersonal adjustment, three hazards may interfere with a good working relationship: immaturity; neurotic traits; and incompatibility of husband and wife.

Immaturity

In Chapter 11 certain traits of the mature personality important for marital adjustment were discussed: integration of divergent attitudes and desires; narrowing of heterosexual interests to one person in conformity with our mores; self-reliance; and capacity for outgoing friendship. The same chapter also emphasized the necessity for the adolescent to free himself from childlike dependence upon his parents and to accept the adult masculine or feminine role. Failure of husband or wife to reach maturity before marriage places a heavy burden upon the spouse, who often must carry responsibilities for both that normally are equally shared. Examples of situations arising from immaturity are suggested here, garnered from case studies and observation.

The husband who secretly dates girls and the wife who flirts outrageously with men to reassure themselves—he of his virility, she of her youthfulness. Although married, they have not outgrown their adolescent dating attitudes.

The individual who seeks in the spouse a replica of a parent who has indulged and "spoiled" him and who expects the spouse to duplicate the parent's behavior.

Irresponsibility in spending.

The wife who expects her husband to leave his work for trivial reasons, such as to stay with her during a thunderstorm.

The husband who resents the attention his wife gives the new baby.

There is some evidence that girls are more likely than boys to come to adulthood with their attachment to their parents relatively unbroken.[3] The differential training of boys and girls encourages boys to become emancipated from their parents and permits them to have privacy in personal affairs, whereas girls are kept under the protective dominance of the parents. At marriage the girl finds it difficult to adjust to the greater independence expected of a wife. In some instances she may adjust by assuming a dependent relationship to her husband, but the trend of the times is toward greater equality between husband and wife. The wife therefore suffers from the loss of her close attachment to her parents, and the husband resents the attachment, feeling that his wife's loyalty should be turned toward him.

When, as occasionally happens, the husband is the one who has been unable to detach himself from his parents, the tension is still more acute, since traditionally the husband has been independent whether or not his wife was, and a parent-dominated husband therefore runs counter to the social norms. An extreme attachment may lead to situations such as the following:

The mother disapproved of marriage for her sons and daughters, especially for the eldest son, who bought her many luxuries. When the second son married, he established his home near that of his parents. Each evening he

[3] Mirra Komarovsky, "Functional Analysis of Sex Roles," *American Sociological Review,* 15 (1950), 508–516.

visited his mother and often would lie on the bed and cry, saying he wanted to remain there and sleep in his old bed. The mother would comfort him and tell his wife to go on home, saying that her son would be all right in a few weeks. After a few months the son's wife left him, and he returned to his mother's home. Later she was reconciled with her husband, who succeeded in detaching himself to some extent from his mother. After ten years of marriage the son still drove twelve miles every other evening to see his mother. When the eldest son was in his thirties he married, against the wishes of his mother. The mother accompanied him and his wife on their honeymoon, during the course of which she made personal purchases amounting to some $150, which the son, as usual, paid. Upon their return home the mother wished to dictate the policies of her son's home, a procedure that his wife resented. As friction grew, the son sided with his mother. When the marriage was only two months old, the son was having lunch with his mother every day and spending several nights a week at his old home. Soon the son had agreed to help his mother buy a home. At this point the wife decided that her husband's attachment to his mother was so much greater than his attachment to her that harmony would never be possible; she therefore left her husband and secured a divorce.[4]

Neurotic traits

Neurotic traits are symptoms of unresolved conflicts and unrelieved frustrations, which reveal themselves in exaggerated emotional reactions, fears, anxieties, compulsions, and symbolisms. Examples are the wife who dissolves into tears at the slightest opposition, who has unusual fears of pregnancy and childbirth, or who collects small china objects (symbols of babies) instead of having children; the husband who persistently refuses to allow his wife to work because he fears others will think he cannot support her; the parent who becomes unduly anxious and protective of adolescent children because of his own unresolved adolescent anxieties and guilt feelings, particularly with reference to sex; the husband's angry avoidance of household tasks because in his youth his mother forced him to do "girls' work"; the husband who periodically deserts his wife when some crisis arises; the wife who uses ill health or picks around at her food as a way of getting attention. It is impossible to list all the various ways in which neurotic attitudes show themselves.

Such neurotic reactions are related to happiness and adjustment in marriage. Terman, on the basis of a study of 792 couples, came to the conclusion that some people come to adulthood and enter marriage al-

[4] Unpublished record.

ready predisposed to happiness or unhappiness.[5] Terman did not attempt to distinguish between temperamental traits that might be innate and traits developed through early social experiences. The following summary points up the differences in traits between the happily and unhappily married women and men, according to Terman's study:

UNHAPPILY MARRIED WOMEN

Unhappy wives are subject to emotional ups and downs, feeling now exultant, now sad without apparent reason. They worry needlessly and useless thoughts run through their heads.

Lacking in self-confidence, they are overly sensitive to criticism or any seeming domination by others. They are timid and easily discouraged.

Unable to do exacting and painstaking work, they are unsteady and even flighty in work, unmethodical, and wasteful.

They tend to be egotistic.

To escape from their unhappiness they join numerous societies, seek romance, daydream, and visit fortune-tellers; they often adopt radical attitudes on religion, politics, and moral conventions.

HAPPILY MARRIED WOMEN

Happy wives are serene, optimistic, and untroubled by extreme emotional reactions.

They are steady workers.

They are kindly, cooperative, and interested in others, especially in those who need help, such as children and old people.

They seek conventional outlets through family excursions, educational movies, or personal correspondence.

UNHAPPILY MARRIED MEN

Unhappy husbands are inclined to be gloomy, ill at ease, and sensitive to group opinions. In compensation, they tend to withdraw from situations that would test their ability and try to dominate those to whom they feel superior. Given to day-

HAPPILY MARRIED MEN

They are even tempered and stable, cooperative, and kindly in attitude toward their inferiors. Socially, they tend to be unself-conscious and are able to function in group relationships with initiative and responsibility. They tend to be conservative,

[5] L. M. Terman, *et al., Psychological Factors in Marital Happiness* (McGraw-Hill, 1938), chs. 6 and 7.

dreams and fantasies, in imagination they play a superior role. They tend to be sporadic in work habits and lacking in thriftiness. More than the happy husbands, they express various radical attitudes.

cautious, and thrifty, and uphold prevailing conventions.

Terman's study indicates that the mature and personally well-adjusted individual tends to find happiness in marriage more often than the moody, insecure, and unintegrated one. Terman tends to assume that these characteristics existed before marriage; it might also be true, however, that the marriage relationship itself had produced or accentuated some of the reactions. Another study shows the association between neurotic traits and happiness in marriage without an attempt to decide whether the traits contributed to or were produced by marital unadjustment.[6] For 1,152 married individuals, low but positive correlations were found between self-estimates of marital happiness and the following traits: even-tempered +.30; usually in good spirits +.35; self-confident about own abilities +.27. Conversely, negative correlations were found between marital happiness and the following reactions: often feel lonesome even when with others —.31; often feel miserable —.31; bothered by useless thoughts —.30; and experience periods of loneliness —.47.

Incompatible personalities

Incompatibility is not related to any one type of personality or complex of traits. The word simply means that two persons do not find each other congenial, do not agree on fundamental issues in marriage, or do not meet each other's personality needs. Both may be individually mature and personally adjusted, but as a pair they are not well matched.

Congeniality is based upon common interests, enjoyable shared activities, and harmonious daily interaction. Happiness in marriage has a high correlation with agreement between husband and wife. Landis' study (discussed on page 425) demonstrated this fact and also that the earlier agreement was reached, the more likely was the marriage to be happy. Burgess and Cottrell also found high correlations between happiness and agreement on the following activities: handling finances, recre-

[6] E. W. Burgess and L. S. Cottrell, Jr., *Predicting Success or Failure in Marriage* (Prentice-Hall, 1939), p. 56. The coefficients are tetrachoric coefficients of correlation; happiness was stated in five degrees running from very happy to very unhappy.

ation, friends, dealing with in-laws, engaging in outside interests together, and leisure-time preferences.[7]   In certain other areas, agreement was of less importance for happiness; agreement on caring for the baby and in matters of conventionality was only moderately correlated with degree of happiness, and agreement on religious matters and table manners was of still less importance.   All of these areas of interaction, however, had some correlation with happiness.   When disagreements exist in more than one area, the chance of happiness is reduced.   Many agreements make for happiness, many disagreements for unhappiness.

Incompatibility may also relate to more fundamental values in marriage.   Children, now regarded as a matter of choice, constitute such a value.   The meaning of sex to each partner and the desire of the wife for paid employment are other areas in which issues may exist that are difficult to adjust.   When husband and wife disagree, each may feel justified in his position; nevertheless tension and discontent may result.

Finally, husband and wife may fail to meet each other's personal needs. Our doctrine of happiness as the chief value of marriage places immense importance on the meeting of personal needs.   Chapter 13, "Courtship and Engagement," discussed qualities that young people desire in their mates and needs that they hope to have fulfilled through the mate.   When the spouse fails to meet these expectations, dissatisfaction is present.

In general, the failure to find congeniality does not indicate personal maladjustment of husband or wife so much as a failure of the two to dovetail their interests, values, and needs.   It is conceivable that, unhappy together, the poorly matched pair might each find happiness if mated with someone who more nearly agreed with him and met his needs.

SEXUAL ADJUSTMENT

Sexual relations have been heralded by some writers as the keystone to marital happiness and are popularly thought to make or break the marriage.   It is natural that such an attitude should arise, since sex is a special ingredient of marriage that differentiates it from other social relationships.   Also, as Landis' study showed, sexual adjustment in marriage is of slow growth and therefore often a source of tension.   We know also that young people are poorly informed on sexual matters and that fears and anxieties related to an unwanted pregnancy sometimes inhibit

[7] *Op. cit.,* pp. 50–51, 53, 72.

full sexual expression.   Nevertheless, after the initial adjustment is made, sex becomes part of the total complex of interaction that constitutes married life.   Lack of adjustment in other activities and interrelationships may be as fatal to the marriage as sexual maladjustment.   It is true, however, that sexual adjustment is a very sensitive indicator of general adjustment, and dissatisfaction or conflict over sex relations may be symptomatic of other tensions.   Good sexual adjustment requires as a background a sympathetic and cooperative relationship.   Tension over handling of finances, quarrels about recreation or religion—in fact, conflict of any type—carries over into the more intimate relationships.   Sexual adjustment therefore may be studied in its primary aspects in terms of biological drives and attitudes directed toward sex; and as a secondary reaction to adjustment in other areas.

Primary adjustment

Basically, intercourse rests upon normal organic structure and ability to function.   In a limited number of cases sexual adjustment is prevented or made difficult because of some organic factor, such as structural malformation, disease, or temporary illness.   These conditions are rare and if severe often prevent marriage.

The strength of the sexual drive differs among individuals, although it is not always clear whether the difference has a biological base or is related to attitudes toward sex.   Whatever the origin, it is a factor in frequency of intercourse and in the sense of personal satisfaction secured. On the biological side, sexual drive decreases with age.   Kinsey's report on marital intercourse of married males, covering 3,342 cases, shows a regular decrease in mean frequency of intercourse per week from 3.75 for married males aged 16 to 20, to 0.83 per week for ages 56–60.[8]   Although there is no comparable extensive study for women, it is generally known that women also lose some of their responsiveness to intercourse with middle and old age.   If the drives of husband and wife parallel each other in decline, and if other aspects of their relationship remain warm and vital, there is no maladjustment.   But if there is a wide age difference or if one partner to the marriage for some reason suffers a premature decline in sexual drive, dissatisfaction may result.

Among married people happiness in marriage is associated to some

[8] A. C. Kinsey, W. B. Pomeroy, and C. E. Martin, *Sexual Behavior in the Human Male* (Saunders, 1948), p. 252.

extent with frequency of intercourse but more closely with mutual satisfaction. Frequency of intercourse in relation to marital happiness was studied by Terman for marriages in which the husband was between 30 and 40 years old.[9] Typically, their wives would be a few years younger. Marital happiness was measured by scores based on a series of questions; the mean happiness score for all husbands was 68 and for all wives 69. When husbands were classified according to the frequency of intercourse per month, those with no intercourse during the month had mean happiness scores of 44.8, well below the mean for the entire group; happiness scores increased with frequency of intercourse to a high mean score of 70.9 for husbands with 7 to 10 sexual episodes per month. Among their wives, mean happiness scores ranged from 42.5 for those with no intercourse during the month to 74.0 for those with 10 or more episodes per month.

Inasmuch as the mean happiness scores for those with frequent intercourse were not very much higher than the means for the 'entire group, Terman carried his investigation further in the attempt to find out why the mean scores were not higher. Using only 239 couples with intercourse of seven or more times per month, Terman discovered that the mean scores were pulled down by 36 husbands and 32 wives who had low happiness scores combined with high frequency of intercourse. These cases did not fit into the general pattern of association of frequent intercourse with high happiness scores. Terman concludes that biological urges and habit were factors in frequency of intercourse that sometimes were more important than congeniality of husband and wife. He suggests also that in some cases frequent intercourse may continue regardless of unhappiness. The satisfaction of physical drives may come to be the one satisfying means of communion between husband and wife; or one mate, feeling that marriage is becoming stale, may deliberately use sexual allure as a means of reviving interest. We may conclude, therefore, that in a general way frequency of intercourse is related to happiness, but that in some instances urgency of drives or persistence of habit overrides congeniality.

The above findings indicate that a more subtle approach to sexual adjustment than frequency of intercourse is needed. Terman throws some light on the relation of sexual satisfaction to happiness. By comparing frequency of intercourse with desire for intercourse, he identified three

[9] *Op. cit.,* pp. 267–355.

groups: those who desired intercourse more frequently than they had it, indicating sexual hunger; those for whom intercourse and desire coincided in frequency, leading to optimum satisfaction; and those for whom actual frequency of intercourse exceeded the desire for it, showing sexual satiety. When these measures of sexual satisfaction were related to marital happiness, two interesting relationships appeared. First, marital happiness of both husband and wife was associated with optimum satisfaction and decreased with either sexual hunger or satiety. Second, even though one spouse secured optimum satisfaction, if the mate suffered from either hunger or satiety, the happiness of the spouse with optimum satisfaction decreased. Sexual relations thus appear as a mutual experience, related to happiness in the degree to which they give satisfaction to both husband and wife. Neither frequency nor individual satisfaction, but mutual satisfaction is of most importance to marital happiness. Thus, if either husband or wife has a strong sexual drive and the other a weak drive, complete happiness may be difficult to achieve.

Primary sexual adjustment is related to attitudes as well as to biological drives. It seems probable that attitudes toward sex are more favorable for adjustment at present than in the past. Although sex education is still meager and faulty, the trend is toward more complete information for both women and men and toward acceptance of intercourse for both as a natural and constructive experience. Nevertheless, for some couples ignorance and inhibitive attitudes are a deterrent to easy adjustment. Women more commonly than men are inhibited by attitudes. The sex training of girls is still more repressive and restrictive than is that of boys; and, though it is often intended to apply only to premarital sex relations, attitudes once firmly established often carry over into marriage. The inhibitions and habits of adolescence may prevent the freedom of mind and action necessary for full sexual satisfaction. Feelings of aversion and guilt may cling to the young married woman. Fear of pregnancy may also inhibit her, although this attitude has decreased with the use of contraceptives.

A topic of current discussion is frigidity, by which is meant inability of the woman to have an orgasm or localized physical reaction to intercourse. Frigidity does not imply that she cannot have intercourse, but merely that she does not have an acute physical reaction. Many women have been happily married and have produced children without experiencing an orgasm. In fact, some married women do not even know that such an experience is possible.　Many elderly women, taught in their youth that sex was a duty rather than a pleasure, did not expect and probably would have felt depraved had they experienced an orgasm.　In extreme cases of frigidity the woman may wish to avoid intercourse itself, but as currently used the term does not apply to aversion to sex so much as to inability to respond fully.　As women have learned more about sex in the past two decades, they have come to expect a full physical reaction parallel to that of their husbands.　Orgasm has become a symbol of full satisfaction; the wife who does not experience it feels deprived of her rights.　Anxiety and intense effort to achieve it only add to the difficulty.　The feeling of frustration may carry over to the husband.　He may be accused openly or by implication of failing to bring his wife to a climax, and to the accusation he may respond by anger or a feeling of guilt.　The many popular books on premarital training emphasize the importance of the husband in aiding his wife to full satisfaction.[10]　This great concern with frigidity and lack of orgasm therefore is not limited to the wife's feeling of deprivation but may become a contentious subject leading to lack of satisfaction (and therefore diminution of happiness) for both husband wife.

A variety of other attitudes that interfere with full sexual adjustment are discussed in the many studies on marital adjustment.　Burgess and Cottrell provide information based on intensive case studies of 49 couples.[11]　One difficulty was a general lack of interest in sex.　When the individual's memory was pressed backward to summon early sexual experiences or attitudes, it was found that a common cause was the teaching during childhood that sex is sinful, wrong, or "dirty."　Even when the young husband or wife might have consciously covered this attitude with a conception of sex as normal, the earlier inhibition operated to prevent interest in sex relations.　In other cases the early sexual interests had been centered upon someone with whom sexual relations are forbidden (as the girl who was deeply attached to brother or father).　Repressed because of a feeling of guilt, they still operated to prevent good sexual adjustment with the spouse, who perhaps had unconsciously been selected because of a resemblance to the earlier love object.　In still other cases the interests of the person had become so thoroughly centered upon him-

[10] For example, see Morris Fishbein and E. W. Burgess, editors, *Successful Marriage* (Doubleday, 1948), pp. 200–201, for a statement by Dr. Thurman B. Rice of the Indiana University School of Medicine.

[11] *Op. cit.,* pp. 218–243.

self that he did not find it possible to give the high degree of cooperation required in mutually satisfactory intercourse.   Writing of both frigidity and impotence (the inability of the husband to have intercourse), Dr. Karl A. Menninger relates these conditions to subconscious fears, subconscious love of someone other than the spouse, or unconscious hate of the parent of the opposite sex that is projected upon the spouse.[12]   These forbidden emotions of which the person is unaware because they have been repressed are more important in controlling sexual behavior than rational or conscious attitudes.

Sexual adjustment in relation to adjustment in other areas

Sexual adjustment tends to be affected by the degree of adjustment in other phases of the husband-wife relationship.   Husbands and wives, generally happy in their marriage, are able to overlook some deficiencies of drive or attitude and to adjust satisfactorily in their sexual relationships. A pattern of satisfactory sexual relations that has been established during a period of general agreement and congeniality may, however, be destroyed if other tensions arise.   Bitterness, anger, and disappointments affect this most intimate relationship.   A mechanical carrying through of intercourse without active cooperation or evident enjoyment on the part of one will lessen or prevent satisfaction for the other.   Sometimes the situation becomes still less personal, and sex is used as a technique of control.   Either husband or wife can refuse to participate or can carry out the act in such a way that the other's satisfaction is lessened, or his ego feelings are attacked.   The wife, for example, can use sex as a weapon: she can simulate orgasm to give her husband a feeling of achievement, or withhold any overt indication of pleasure in order to dominate or humiliate him.[13]   In these situations, the crux of the problem is not in sex adjustment but in collateral interaction.

Extramarital sex relations

Marital infidelity is highly censured in American society.   The monogamous ideal and the demand for legitimacy of children are both attacked by extramarital sex relations.   The growing tolerance toward premarital intercourse does not extend to condoning of nonmarital sex relations by married people.   All states recognize adultery as a cause for

---

[12] "Impotence and Frigidity," *Bulletin, Menninger Clinic* (1937), pp. 251–260.
[13] A. H. Maslow, "Self Esteem (Dominance-Feeling) and Sexuality in Women," *Journal of Social Psychology,* 16 (1942), 281.

divorce and all but five provide criminal penalties for two persons living in adultery.[14]

Nevertheless, Kinsey is able to report that from 27 to 37 per cent of married men studied by him at each five-year age period admitted having had extramarital intercourse at some time or other during their married lives.[15]   Since feelings of guilt and fear of scandal undoubtedly caused some men to cover up their activities, Kinsey believes that these percentages are too low and that probably half of all married men at some time have intercourse with women other than their wives.   A higher percentage of lower-class men (as judged by educational level) have extramarital relations than higher-class (college-trained) men.   The difference is especially marked in the earlier age periods.   Lower-level males, married in the late teens, admit extramarital relations in 45 per cent of the cases, as compared with 15 to 20 per cent in the corresponding group of college-trained men.   Kinsey accounts for this situation by a carry-over of habits from the premarital period, when lower-class males freely indulge in sex relations, whereas higher-level males more often restrict their activities to love-making without intercourse.   In middle age, however, the situation is somewhat different.   By age 50, only 19 per cent of lower-level males, but about 27 per cent of higher-level males, have extramarital sex relations.   Frequency also changes with age and in a different pattern for lower- and higher-level males.   For lower-level males extramarital intercourse decreases in frequency from an average of about once per week to once in two weeks between late teens and middle age; higher-level males increase from an average of once in two or three weeks at early adulthood to approximately once per week at middle age. The frequencies are based only on married men practicing extramarital sex relations.   Kinsey does not suggest an explanation for the different trends with age.

Extramarital sex relations rarely are a regular part of sex life, integrated into the total pattern.   Kinsey reports that for most males at all social-class levels nonmarital intercourse is sporadic and often incidental to special situations, as a trip away from home or a summer vacation.   The typical sequence is a number of experiences with one woman, a long interval of abstinence, and then perhaps an experience with another woman.

[14] Morris Ploscowe, *Sex and the Law* (Prentice-Hall, 1951), p. 145.
[15] *Op. cit.*, pp. 585 ff.

Long-continued relations with one woman are the exception. The partner is a prostitute in 8 to 15 per cent of the instances. By far the majority of experiences are with nonprostitutes, who may range from chance pickups to married or unmarried women of the man's own social class. Social deterrents to extramarital sex relations are rural residence, religious affiliation, and higher-class status.

Comparable data for women are not available. Fragmentary reports and the greater condemnation of nonmarital sex relations for women indicate that fewer wives than husbands have illicit sex relations. Prostitutes and pickups who serve many men would account for a difference in number of husbands and wives reporting sex satisfaction outside of marriage.

Interpretation of extramarital sex relations is much more difficult than a mere chronicling of incidence and frequency of experience. The secrecy that surrounds the experience is a tremendous obstacle to adequate study. Here and there, however, appear fragmentary explanations, usually based on cases that have come to the attention of marriage counselors or psychiatrists. They are offered here as suggestions rather than as conclusive diagnoses of the situation.

One explanation that has been advanced is that the biological drive is so strong and demands such variety of contact that a single partner is inadequate. The marital sex relationship may be satisfactory and marriage itself may be highly valued as the setting for security, children, and permanency, but limitation of all sexual activities to one person may be seriously frustrating.[16] Before marriage, it is freely recognized, interest centers first on one person, then on another; with marriage permanent fixation on one person is expected. But actually, it is contended, many people cannot adapt themselves to strict monogamy. They desire a variety of contacts. Divorce and remarriage is not the solution, for soon another change would be desired. Moreover, the person wants other values to be found in marriage. The solution, though it must be carried out furtively, is marriage plus extramarital sex relations.

An extremely simple biological explanation that attempts to account for differences in extramarital relations of men and women is offered

[16] This point of view is advanced by C. C. Bowman, "Cultural Idealogy and Heterosexual Reality: A Preface to Sociological Research," *American Sociological Review*, 14 (1949), 627–629.

by Kinsey,[17] who states that the male is easily aroused sexually by a variety of stimuli provided by conversations, pictures, advertisements, or memories. The average female, on the contrary, is rarely aroused except by actual tactile stimulations, such as love-making. The male in his ordinary round of life is therefore constantly aroused sexually, whereas the female usually is aroused only under special conditions of physical contact.

The sociologist is more inclined to look for explanations in the different social norms for men and women that permit men a limited area of freedom that is denied to women; or in social-class folkways and mores whereby sex is interpreted as a natural activity in the lower classes but as a moral issue in the higher classes; or, finally, in differences in ethnic culture that permit or restrain extramarital sex relations.

The psychologists and psychiatrists offer still other interpretations, related to personality problems of the individual or psychological maladjustment between husband and wife. One writer states that the emotionally immature man, among other types of infantile behavior, follows "patterns of compulsive sexual promiscuity (the so-called 'Don Juan Complex') in an effort to compensate for latent feelings of masculine inadequacy." [18] Maslow would take promiscuous sex relations out of the field of sex satisfactions altogether and interpret them as motivated by a desire for reassurance of continued attractiveness, the thrill of novelty, unconscious hostility for the spouse, and often the desire to conquer the opposite sex by "collecting scalps." [19] Such activities are especially likely to indicate insecure persons, who, while pursuing thrill and reassurance outside of marriage, enjoy a comfortable sexual relationship with the spouse.

Summing up psychological explanations, Seward states that extramarital sexual interests, whether they remain in fantasy or are carried out, should be regarded as symptoms rather than causes of marital maladjustment.[20] Some psychiatrists interested in marital adjustment urge that when extramarital relations of one spouse are discovered by the other, the discoverer should not immediately take offense or interpret the action as a personal affront; rather the entire marital relationship as well as the per-

[17] *Op. cit.,* p. 589.
[18] Judd Marmor, "Psychological Trends in American Family Relationships," *Marriage and Family Living,* 13 (1951), 146.
[19] *Op. cit.,* p. 279.
[20] Georgene H. Seward, *Sex in the Social Order* (McGraw-Hill, 1946), p. 204.

sonality make-up of the digressing partner should be subjected to expert study.[21]   The behavior, although it violates marital mores, may be symptomatic of situations that can be adjusted.

SOCIAL AND CULTURAL FACTORS IN MARITAL ADJUSTMENT

Although initial sexual adjustment occurs more slowly than adjustment in other areas of interaction, and certain phases of sexual relationships have been shown to be related to marital happiness, other factors show a closer relationship to happiness than does sex.   Terman found that the happiness of the parents of husband and wife and the couple's own childhood happiness were more closely related to marital happiness than was sexual adjustment.   In fact, when the husband and wife were otherwise happy and congenial, they were tolerant of sexual shortcomings in their mates.

The relative closeness of association of sexual versus social factors to marital adjustment was not studied by Burgess and Cottrell.[22]   They found, however, that many aspects of the family backgrounds of husband and wife were important to marital adjustment as judged by the couple's marital adjustment scale (based on agreements and closeness of personal relationships).   The following may be listed as making for good adjustment:

Rural childhood residence of husband and wife

Close attachment to both parents

Lack of conflict with both parents

Parents' marriage regarded as happy or very happy

Three or more siblings

The type of parental family implied is the traditional rural family with a sufficient number of members to make a communal primary group; it is also a family with good adjustment between the parents and between parents and children.   It may be assumed that such a childhood background makes three contributions to the marital adjustment of the children: it provides an expectation of happy adjustment; it teaches the techniques of tolerance, compromise, and cooperation; and it develops well-adjusted personalities in the children.   Children from families that lack one or more of these characteristics are not, of course, doomed to

[21] John Levy and Ruth Munroe, *The Happy Family* (Knopf, 1938).
[22] *Op. cit.*, 375–384.

marital failure; but their chances of good adjustment are a little less certain.

In view of the extended discussion of cultural homogamy already given in Chapters 9 and 10, it seems unnecessary to say more than that, in general, similarity of race, ethnic culture, and religious affiliation prevents many potential conflicts and gives unity to family ideals and expectations.

SOCIAL ROLES IN MARITAL ADJUSTMENT

The roles of men and women in the United States have been changing over a long period of time, in an unplanned and often haphazard fashion. The result is confusion, which will continue until roles are better defined, new definitions more widely accepted, and a higher degree of coordination achieved.   So far as marital adjustment is concerned, the problem falls into three divisions: the role of the wife; the role of the husband; and coordination of the two roles.

The role of the wife

At present four theories of the rightful role of women are championed by different groups.

1. Woman, by her psychobiological nature, is basically feminine and finds her happiness and the fulfillment of her natural needs in the wifely role.   That there are biological differences between men and women relating to sexual organs and functions, to secondary sex characteristics, and to the production of children is unquestioned.   Are there also psychological concomitants?   Two women psychiatrists have been especially outspoken in asserting that women have an innate psychological need to be dependent, protected, and made to feel secure; they therefore want and need husbands who dominate (but do not abuse) them.[23]   Women also are somewhat self-contained and narcissistic; they need to be loved.   At the same time they are passive, willing to leave the initiative with men and to secure ego satisfaction through identification with their husbands. They are noncompetitive and tolerant.   These qualities fit women for wifehood and motherhood.   When, therefore, women try to emulate

[23] The point of view is discussed by Helene Deutsch in *Psychology of Women,* Vol. II, *Motherhood* (Grune and Stratton, 1945), especially ch. 5. Marynia F. Farnham is an exponent of the same point of view. See Ferdinand Lundberg and Marynia F. Farnham, *Modern Woman: The Lost Sex* (Harper, 1947); Marynia F. Farnham, "Battles Lost and Won," *The Annals* of the American Academy of Political and Social Science, 251 (1947), 113–119.

men, when they enter the man's competitive world, they are going against their natural needs and capacities and as a result are bitterly frustrated. The feminist movement with its demand for equality is assailed as detrimental to women.

2. Another conception of the role of the wife emphasizes her function as mother and the importance of this role to her children. Not the psychobiological needs of woman but the psychosocial needs of children are basic in this approach. With the small number of children in the family at the present time, the mother spends not more than two or three years in the biological "making" and nourishment of children. The development of their personalities requires many years, however, and the mother is conceived as central in this process until the children reach adolescence. During the 1920's and early 1930's, child psychologists and counselors, following the lead of John B. Watson, were fearful of too close a relationship between mother and child. Strict schedules, enforced early independence of the child, and an unemotional relationship between mother and child were advocated. During this period the mother could delegate the care of the child to nursemaid or day nursery with an easy conscience, secure in the belief that if he received good physical care and had freedom of activities within a strict schedule he was being adequately trained. Now, psychological research and concepts tend to show that the young child needs love, mothering, dependence upon the mother, and considerable freedom as to schedules. The role of the mother is thus given increased importance and more status because of the approval of psychologists.[24]

3. A third approach focuses attention upon the increased leisure and the shifting functions in the life of the typical wife. Laborsaving devices and the small number of children to be cared for provide leisure; the maturing of the youngest child while the mother is still in early middle age is the basis of shifting functions. The wife and mother therefore no longer has a fixed role throughout her married life. At each stage of married life it is advisable for her to look ahead to the next stage and prepare for a new role. Her role as the mother of preschool children differs from her role as the mother of adolescents. When the adolescents have left the home, the mother role is lost and other roles emerge. What

[24] J. McV. Hunt, editor, *Personality and the Behavior Disorders* (Ronald, 1944), I, ch. 3; II, chs. 20, 21. An interesting popular presentation of changing attitudes toward the mother role is found in Robert Coughlan, "How to Survive Parenthood," *Life,* 28 (June 26, 1950), 112–126.

the mother does with the leisure provided her while children are growing up and with the greater leisure of middle age may vary.   She may narrow her life by not making compensations for the lost functions, or she may resume earlier activities laid aside for the mother role or find completely new ones.   Not necessarily employment but community activities are urged upon the mother to fill out her life while children are young and to become her chief interest after they leave home.

4. Finally, there are those who insist that women should enter fully into political and economic life.   The most outspoken do not merely argue for the right of women to make a place for themselves in these traditionally masculine fields, but state it as an obligation of women that they must thrust themselves into these and similar fields.   They support their position by two assertions: women are stunting their personalities by restricting their activities to husband, home, children, and volunteer community activities; and public life under man's domination has developed many defects that women might help to correct.[25]   Femininity, far from being an innate psychobiological characteristic of women, has been forced on them by men who wish to keep women in a subordinate role.   "Real women," said Pearl S. Buck, do not want this "false femininity."   They want to use their brains, solve problems, take their place in the world.   In a less emotional but equally positive statement, Georgene H. Seward offers the following solution to the problem of woman's role:

In the writer's opinion, the solution consists not in sending women back to the home, but rather in a planned economy which would make it not only possible but *necessary* for all citizens, male or female, single or married, to contribute productively on an equal basis, and to share equally in the returns for their labor.[26]

These four conceptions of woman's basic role are in conflict at many points.   The psychobiological role and the role of women in public and economic life are in direct opposition in their basic philosophy and theory.   Each denies the validity of the other.   The maternal role, thought of as socially defined, does not wholly deny the psychobiological conception but at the same time permits an overlap with the role of woman in the wider community, provided that during the early years of childhood the

[25] Pearl S. Buck, *Of Men and Women* (John Day, 1941).
[26] "Cultural Conflicts and the Feminine Role," *Journal of Social Psychology,* 22 (1945), 192.

needs of children are placed first. It is interesting that the most out-spoken advocates of roles identical with those of men do not mention the birth or care of children; they do not suggest any way to provide for children and certainly seem unaware of the importance now given by child psychologists to the role of the mother.

The first three conceptions are capable of coordination with the traditional roles of men. They set aside distinctive functions for women, and they emphasize affection and cooperation. The fourth role places women in a competitive situation with men; in fact, some women writers who urge this role reveal great antagonism toward men and try to "whip up" their readers to attack men and force them to recognize the equal abilities of women.

Education of women for what role?

These formulations of possible roles are not idle mouthings. They appear not only in scientific journals and books but in popular writings. They have created factions among college administrators and faculty as to the proper education for women. One group urges greater emphasis upon human relations, the family, child psychology, and domestic arts and skills.[27] Their opponents emphasize that there is no difference in mental capacity of men and women and few differences in special abilities; all are to be citizens; all need a sound liberal arts education; and—the crucial point—women as well as men have vocational and professional roles to play.[28] Granting that most college women wish to and will marry, they nevertheless are opposed to loading the college curriculum with practical courses in child care and domestic skills. These, they believe, can be gained in short courses after college is ended.

The advocates of identical education for men and women have been attacked on the ground that education is no longer limited to basic liberal arts but in most institutions includes definite vocational courses, which are studied by women students as well as men. Even though they plan to

---

[27] A spokesman for this point of view is President Lynn White, Jr., of Mills College. See *Educating our Daughters, A Challenge to the Colleges* (Harper, 1950).

[28] In one eastern woman's college with high academic ideals, the great majority of students looked forward to marriage and motherhood as their chosen future; 60 per cent of the group did not wish to continue in jobs after they had children; 30 per cent hoped to resume work after their children were grown; only 10 per cent planned to combine wifehood, motherhood, and career throughout.—Mirra Komarovsky, "What Should Colleges Teach Women?" *Harper's Magazine*, 199 (November, 1949), 33–37.

marry, women then acquire an interest in some vocation, develop the aggressive and competitive attitudes that make the successful worker, and regard paid employment as of higher status than the domestic roles.   Later, caught in a web of homemaking and child care, they suffer from frustration because they lack opportunity to use their vocational skills; they may feel that they were educated for something better than cooking and baby tending; and they may become antagonistic toward their husbands who seem to be living richer and fuller lives.   The homemaking roles should be upgraded in public opinion and their importance to husband and children recognized, it is contended, through a new emphasis in college education.

Finally, one sociologist long interested in the problem of conflicting roles for women, carries the argument one step further and urges more education in human relations and child psychology for men as well as women—for potential fathers as well as potential mothers.[29]

Certain it is that a number of incompatible roles are spread before the young woman for her choice, each supported by reputable thinkers, scientists, and educationists.   It is equally certain that under present conditions of small family size, the role of motherhood is a temporary one and often, in hours consumed, a part-time one.   It is also true that the husband often has difficulty in carrying the full burden of support at the level of living desired by the lower- and upper-middle-class family.   At lower educational levels than college, less is heard about rights of women and frustration or expression of desires; but the conflict of roles is there also.   Families are larger and the necessity for the wife to work at least part of the time is more urgent.   The wife in the lower-class family must adjust to competing roles more often than the wife in the middle-class family; but she is less vocal in her reactions.

The young woman herself, with expectations of different groups impinging upon her, does not have a clear-cut line of action before her, and often is inconsistent in her thinking upon the subject.   A study of sophomore college women brings out many inconsistencies.[30]   These girls leaned toward the nondomestic roles in stating that they desired to share equally with men in education, professional preparation, working conditions, community activities, social contacts, and freedom of conduct; within the home, they desired equality with their husbands in such mat-

[29] Komarovsky, op. cit.
[30] Seward, Journal of Social Psychology, 22 (1945), 177–194.

ters as jurisdiction over family property, and solution of family problems even when it involved contributing to the support of children after a divorce. At the same time, they desired elements of the traditional feminine role. They desired marriage not alone for love but also for social and marital security; they did not feel free to propose marriage and had no desire to retain their maiden names; they wished their husbands to support them and did not wish to continue to work after the birth of a child. They also did not approve of community facilities that would relieve them of routine household labor—cooking, housecleaning, laundering, or child care—and thus free them for employment. Not all girls, of course, responded in the same way. Some were more completely domestic-minded, others leaned toward the equalitarian position. In exploring possible differences between the two groups, Seward found that the type of home from which the girl came was an important factor: girls from broken homes or whose mothers had not followed a feminine role were more inclined toward the equalitarian point of view than girls from unbroken homes in which the mother had followed a domestic role, with the father in an authoritarian position.

Seward and other investigators believe that the confusion in roles for young women makes for mental conflicts and prevents good adjustment to either role after marriage.[31]

The role of the husband

The role of the husband has not been made the subject for research as has the role of the wife, nor are many articles written attempting to define his role. There is general acceptance that his primary familial function is to work as steadily as possible after appropriate preparation; to marry and give love, kindness, practical care, and material support to his family. He is condemned if he does not work or if he neglects, refuses to support, abuses, or deserts his wife and children. He may choose between one vocation and another; but he is not faced, as the woman is, with choice between fundamentally different and opposed roles. He may hold simul-

[31] Mirra Komarovsky, "Cultural Contradictions and Sex Roles," *American Journal of Sociology,* 52 (1946), 184–190. Another sociologist using the same questionnaire that Komarovsky used concluded that the girl did not suffer from mental conflict, but would be in a conflict position if she married a man who expected her to play a role opposed to the one she preferred—for instance, if a career-minded girl married a man who desired a feminine wife.—Paul Wallin, "Cultural Contradictions and Sex Roles: A Repeat Study," *American Sociological Review,* 15 (1950), 288–293.

taneously a familial and a vocational role. The continuance of his roles rests, however, upon coordination with the role of his wife. The generally accepted masculine role, as outlined above, assumes that the wife will play the daily domestic role of homemaker and child rearer. To the extent that this role is changed for the wife, the husband's role is disturbed and a new correlation of roles is demanded.

Men at one time were more closely associated with the home. In the preindustrial economy of the early nineteenth century a man often had his professional office or his shop in one wing of his home or in a small detached building. Even those men whose work took them to a central business district often were able to have three meals at home. The great number of farmers also were closely associated with their families. Although the father did not take the same responsibility for the children and work within the home as the mother did, nevertheless the hours spent together, the opportunities for informal participation, the ability of the children to be near their father at work, all tended to make the father a more influential member of the family than at present. When the development of factories and the decreased need for rural man power drew men into cities and factories, they had to make an adjustment to new relationships. Since this adjustment was made a century ago, we are not now aware of whatever difficulties may have arisen. It seems probable, however, that the transfer from home to factory was made with much less difficulty than the present shift in the case of women. For one thing, the man was accustomed to spending most of his hours in producing goods; he followed this production into a new setting. Also, he had never had the care of the young children and, since his wife remained in the home to assume many of his responsibilities toward the older children, he could transfer to her his family duties with a feeling of confidence and without a sense of guilt. Man's problems of adjustment to industrial society have tended to center around relationships within his place of work or between industry and government. Woman's have tended to focus on the competition for interest and attention between job and family.

The husband's role is inherited from the patriarchal, although for many years it has been but a thin shadow of the truly patriarchal. It has been regarded as of higher status and greater prestige than the role of the wife. Officially the husband is always classified as the head of the family if he is present in it, and he is legally charged with support of the family. In the past he had many legal prerogatives that gave him superior authority, but one by one these have been shorn from him until husband and wife (man and woman) now have legal equality in such things as property rights, business responsibilities, and right to vote. As the husband has lost status, the wife has gained it. Moreover, outside the family women have gained a firm foothold; employed women compete with men, challenging their right to jobs and to higher pay. Although many men are willing to accept a position of equality with women, others attempt to keep a position of superiority. The tendency to marry women who are slightly younger, the willingness to marry those of less intelligence, and the aversion to women with more education, already discussed, give men a slightly superior status in the family. The most severe threat to their status, however, is employment of the wife, since the possession of money gives power in many areas. Employment of the wife, by consuming her time and energy, also threatens the birth and welfare of children, who are prized by men. At the same time, it places the wife in a position where she may request or demand that her husband take over some of the necessary domestic duties that in the eyes of many men symbolize inferior status or recall to them their childhood days when they were forced by their mothers into household tasks sadly lacking in masculine prestige. In many ways, therefore, men have not adjusted themselves to sharing their status with their wives. The greatest difficulty is encountered, of course, when men and women with diametrically opposed conceptions of the wifely role marry—when the husband who would like a wife to carry some of the burden of responsibility or share fully in vocational and public activities marries a girl who wishes to be protected and supported; or when the patriarchally minded man marries the career-bent woman.

Coordination of husband and wife roles

The importance of compatibility between the roles of husband and wife has been recognized for some time. A systematic analysis of the old and new roles of women as they affect the relationships between husband and wife, made by Kirkpatrick some 15 years ago, is still of great value.[32] He says that three roles are now open to the married woman, each of which carries its own privileges and obligations. If the obligations are not met by the wife and the privileges are not granted by husband and children, conflict and disorganization threaten.

[32] Clifford Kirkpatrick, "Ethical Inconsistencies in Marriage," *International Journal of Ethics,* 46 (1935–36), 444–460.

The first role discussed is the wife-and-mother role, which entitles the woman to the privileges of economic security, including alimony in case of divorce, respect of the husband and children in her capacity as wife and mother, a certain amount of domestic authority, the loyalty of the husband, and the gratitude of the children. The obligations are bearing and rearing children, making a home including the actual tasks of house-keeping, subordination economically to the interests of the husband, financial dependence upon him, and a limited range of outside interests and activities. This centralization of interests and activities in the home marks the wife-and-mother role as the traditional one of the married woman.

A second role is the companion role, which carries the privileges of sharing the pleasures of the husband, receiving a romantic emotional response, being admired, being allowed funds for dress and recreation, and having leisure for educational and social activities. The obligations are to maintain beauty, entertain the husband, make social contacts that are advantageous to him, and be an object of pride for him. This role has been called parasitic by less considerate writers, since the wife is more or less of an ornament in her husband's household, and a luxury inasmuch as she produces very little either in money or services. Since the role depends upon a rather ample income, it affects relatively few wives.

The third role, that of the partner, implies that the wife works and is economically independent; she has equal authority with her husband in finances and performs only her fair share of domestic services; she has equal social and moral liberty with her husband. The role obligates her to contribute to the support of the home and children, in proportion to her income; to refuse alimony in case of divorce except for the support of children; to ask no special privileges and make no appeal to chivalry on the basis of being a woman. This role is the one advocated by Buck and Seward, already discussed.

In any one of the three situations, harmony would prevail if husband and wife agreed upon the role that each would play and if each then played the role consistently. Sometimes, however, roles are not well coordinated. The husband, let us say, has a preconception of what his role in the family should be; he comes into marriage with an expectation that he will have a certain status, perform certain functions, and receive certain responses from his wife. He may find that he is unable to meet these expectations; his role as he actually lives it out may be very different from his preconceived idea. A discrepancy that may amount only to slight irritation or may reach the proportions of a definite mental and emotional conflict then exists for him. His wife, likewise, may find herself unable to fulfill her expectations and play the role she had idealized beforehand as the one for her to play after marriage. She, too, may experience tension or inner conflict. Since one factor in the failure to reach role expectations usually is the failure of the spouse to play the supporting role, resentment and antagonism may be directed against the spouse.

In other situations, role conflict arises because external circumstances prevent the playing out of an anticipated role. Death or prolonged illness of the husband, his inability to find employment, or his induction into the armed services may create a situation in which it is impossible for the wife to play a wifely role; she may then be forced to assume a more aggressive wage-earning role, the headship of the family and position of authority. If, on the other hand, the wife has established a satisfactory career for herself, the serious illness of a child may force her to abandon it for the maternal role. The husband likewise may find himself confronted with external circumstances that prevent his playing his preferred role. The demands of his business may necessitate his absence from home for long periods of time or absorb so much time and energy that his family is neglected as less important. In each situation the person whose role is initially disturbed must adjust to a new role, and in response to this change the spouse must also adapt himself to a new role if coordination is to be maintained.

Even when the essential roles are agreed upon between husband and wife, one or the other may not be desirous of playing the chosen role consistently. Kirkpatrick points out that the wife may wish to claim the privileges of one role but not the obligations; for instance, if she works she may wish to retain the money for her own use instead of contributing proportionately to the family needs.[33] Or she may wish to play the wife-and-mother role but neglect the care of the children or evade household duties. On the other hand, the husband may expect his wife to accept the obligations of two roles, perhaps to work and at the same time carry full responsibility for household management, which the husband should share. Kirkpatrick concluded that women tend to seize the privileges of several roles, whereas their husbands emphasize the obligations of their wives' roles.

[33] *Op. cit.*

The adjustment of roles is important to the marital satisfaction of husband and wife, according to a study of 50 married couples in the student-body of a Midwestern university. In private interviews husbands and wives gave information regarding the degree to which they had been able to carry out their own role-expectations and the degree to which the spouse played the role anticipated from him or her. When number of role conflicts was related to estimates of their own happiness given by husbands and wives, Table 22 resulted. As conflicts increase, happiness declines.

TABLE 22

Comparison of Happiness Ratings and Average Number of Conflicts *

Happiness rating		Average number of conflicts for total sample of men and women
High	10	1.02
	9	2.15
	8	4.4
	7	8.5
	6	8.8
	5	11.5
Low	4	19.0

* Robert S. Ort, "A Study of Role-Conflicts as Related to Happiness in Marriage," *Journal of Abnormal and Social Psychology*, 45 (1950), 691–699.

Employment of women as an illustration of changing roles

Employment of women affords a concrete example of changing roles, which are still in the process of adjustment. In the past 50 years, not only has employment of women increased, but the age and marital status of employed women have changed. In 1900 working women were primarily girls and young adults: 47 per cent of all women workers were under 25 years of age; in 1950 only 26 per cent were under 25.[34] The opposite trend is found for middle-aged women: in 1900 only 17 per cent of women workers were aged 45 and over; in 1950, 30 per cent. This change in age suggests that 50 years ago women workers were primarily unmarried girls or young married women working before the birth of the first child, whereas now more mature women form a heavy proportion of women workers.

[34] *Women as Workers, A Statistical Guide* (Women's Bureau, U. S. Department of Labor, 1950), pp. 4 ff.

It is not surprising, therefore, to find that in 1949 50.9 per cent of women workers were married and an additional 16.0 per cent widowed or divorced, whereas in 1910 only 24.3 per cent were married, and 14.7 per cent widowed or divorced. The percentage of single women declined from 61.0 per cent in 1910 to 33.1 per cent in 1949.[35]

Over a fifth of the women employed in 1949 had children under 18 years of age, and of this group one third had children under 6 years of age.[36] Most of these mothers were living with their husbands; only a small proportion were widows or divorced women with children.

Almost half of all employed women are clerical workers or factory operatives; a fifth are service workers or domestics; about 16 per cent are in the professions or managerial positions; the remainder are scattered in a number of occupations.[37] One would judge from this distribution that a minority are college-trained women, who may be torn between theoretical conceptions of what their role should be. Many women work because of necessity to supplement the husband's income or because they wish to maintain or improve their standards of living; during the war patriotism added another motive. A personal account by one mother of two young teen-age daughters listed the following as motives for working: decrease of financial worry, more money for educational and recreational activities for the children and for food, clothing, and household items; a better car; increased stimulating contacts for herself, which she thought made her a better mother; new friends and interesting experiences.[38]

How do these working mothers adjust their family and employment roles? Mrs. Meek, just cited, made these adjustments in her family: hiring someone to stay with her children during school vacations; buying ready-made clothing instead of sewing for herself and her daughters; buying hot lunches for the entire family instead of having lunch at home; buying foods for dinner that were quickly and easily prepared; and doing housework in the evenings at the sacrifice of time spent with the children. She adjusted her job to her family to the extent of staying home when the

[35] Chart entitled "Marital Status of Women in the Labor Force, 1910–1949," published by the Women's Bureau, U. S. Department of Labor.

[36] *Women as Workers, A Statistical Guide*, p. 10.

[37] "Major Occupations of Women, April, 1951," *Facts on Women Workers* (Women's Bureau, U. S. Department of Labor, May 31, 1951), p. 3.

[38] Hazel G. Meek, "There's Frosting on Our Cake, But—," *Public Welfare in Indiana*, 60 (February, 1950), 6.

children were ill or when stormy weather prevented the school bus from running that carried her children from their rural home to school. She also worried about the welfare of her children during the interval before they went to school and after they returned in the afternoon when she was not home.

Another study of women in war work in the early 1940's shows how women attempt to straddle the two roles of homemaker and paid worker.[39] Half of the married women reported that they managed their homes and did the major part of the work. They got breakfast, put up lunches, made beds, marketed, prepared the evening meal, laundered, cleaned house, and mended. Evenings and Saturdays were also utilized for housework. Sunday remained for extra tasks, rest, and recreation. The other half had help from some other family member, a few being relieved of all responsibility by some relative. A third of the married or widowed women had children under 14 years of age, few of whom were cared for in day nurseries or by paid "sitters." The most frequent source of care was some relative, and school-aged children often were left to their own devices. Sometimes the husband worked on one shift and the wife on another, each taking a turn at supervising the children.

Unfortunately, these accounts do not describe adjustment between husband and wife. They suggest that working wives attempt to carry the full or a heavy proportion of the domestic role as well as the role of the employed worker. What they cannot do tends to be left undone, even when this means neglect of the children.

Many employed women are of the lower class; it will be recalled that in lower-class families both husband and wife accept the fact that often the wife must work to provide necessities. In middle-class families the wife often works in order to improve the standard of living; perhaps the husband, who may feel his position threatened, is at least partially mollified by the extra security and higher standard of living provided by the additional income. A study of a small group of professional families, in some of which the wife was employed, showed no significant differences in scores on marital adjustment scales as between employed or unemployed wives, or between husbands of the two classes of wives.[40]

[39] *Women's Wartime Hours of Work, the Effect on Their Factory Performance and Home Life,* Bulletin No. 208 (Women's Bureau, U. S. Department of Labor, 1947), pp. 4–5.

[40] H. J. Locke and Muriel Mackeprang, "Marital Adjustment and the Employed Wife," *American Journal of Sociology,* 54 (1949), 536–538.

The results of this study cannot be applied, however, to other occupational groups, for it has been shown that professional men are more tolerant than any other occupational group regarding women's employment.   In an opinion poll made in 1945, samples of men from different occupations were asked, "Do you think woman's place should be in the home, or do you think women should be free to take jobs outside the home if they want them?" [41]   Fifty-one per cent of professional men thought women should be free to work outside the home.   For small-business men the percentage was 44; large-business men, 39; and for white-collar, skilled, semiskilled, and unskilled from 22 to 30 per cent. The low percentage of unskilled laborers who thought women should be free to work raises interesting speculations in view of the attitude, shown by other studies, that they accept as necessary the employment of their wives and daughters.

PREDICTION OF MARITAL ADJUSTMENT

Adjustment has been discussed in terms of interaction between husband and wife as they work out a satisfactory companionship that meets the essential needs of each.   Hazards to adjustment have been pointed out, some of which existed prior to marriage, others of which became apparent in the early years of marriage.   With the discovery of factors that were either favorable or unfavorable to adjustment came the possibility of constructing marriage prediction scales.   Like any other type of prediction, marital prediction scales forecast the future (type of future marital adjustment) from facts known in the present (prior to or in the early years of marriage).

Possibilities and limitations of prediction scales

To the extent that prediction scales are reliable, they make it possible for a couple to foresee the probability of good or poor marital adjustment. They do not, however, make possible exact prediction for the individual couple.   The couple would know that among all people tested who made the same scores that they did, a given percentage had achieved good ad-

[41] Richard Centers, "Attitude and Belief in Relation to Occupational Stratification," *Journal of Social Psychology*, 27 (1948), 159–185. The study was carried out through the Office of Public Opinion Research of the Psychology Department, Princeton University, using a representative cross section of the adult white male population.

justment, a given percentage fair, and a given percentage poor.   They would therefore know the chances out of 100 that they would have good, fair, or poor adjustment, but they would not know which adjustment group they would actually fall into as their marriage progressed.   The prediction scale might therefore prove more frustrating than satisfying, since they might learn that they had 75 chances out of 100 for good adjustment, 20 chances for fair, and 5 chances for poor.   Fear of the possibility of future poor adjustment might become a disturbing factor and actually might impede the adjustment process.[42]

The prediction scales so far produced distinguish between levels of future marital adjustment only at the extremes.   For instance, the high predictive scores usually show a high percentage with good adjustment and few cases of fair or poor adjustment; the low predictive scores show a high percentage of fair or poor adjustments with few instances of good adjustment.   But the moderate predictive scores are distributed about evenly between those with good, fair, and poor adjustment so that prediction is not possible.   The person or couple would not even have the satisfaction of knowing that the probabilities were very high (or very low) for good adjustment.

Predictive scales have value, however, within the limitations just stated. The couple with high probability of success in marriage may become more aware of their few difficulties and work to eliminate them and thus assure themselves of success.   Likewise, the couple with low probability of success may review their situation, decide to wait for a longer period and try to work out adjustments before marriage, break off the engagement entirely, or seek the help of a marriage counselor.   The prediction scales also often help a couple locate the source of tensions and disagreements so that they may concentrate upon adjusting them.

Prediction scales are useful not only for the couple involved but for the marriage counselor.   The counselor may use them to screen cases, thus isolating those most in need of assistance.   By giving a comparison of the individual case with a larger number of cases, the scales also reduce

---

[42] Criticisms of marriage prediction scales in general as well as of the techniques used in constructing the earlier scales are contained in Albert Ellis, "The Value of Marriage Prediction Tests," *American Sociological Review,* 13 (1948), 710–718; evaluations of prediction tests are given in Ernest W. Burgess, "The Value and Limitations of Marriage Prediction Tests," and Clifford R. Adams, "Evaluating Marriage Prediction Tests" and discussion of the two articles, *Marriage and Family Living,* 12 (1950), 54–58.

the subjectivity of the counselor in analyzing cases. They also help the counselor to isolate areas of tension. It has also been emphasized, however, that predictive scales are not a substitute for personal interviewing; they do not go below the level of consciousness into hidden attitudinal or emotional factors of which the person himself is unaware; and they are subject to the possibility of evasive replies by the person.

It must be conceded, therefore, that although marital prediction scales have added to our knowledge of what factors are associated with good and poor adjustment and make possible a limited type of prediction, they are not exact in prediction for an individual couple and at most identify trouble areas that must be worked over alone or with the aid of specialists if the probability of good adjustment is to be increased.

With these precautionary statements, three types of prediction scales are briefly reviewed.

Prediction from premarital factors

The Burgess-Cottrell study used as the criterion of marital adjustment a scale based on agreements between husband and wife, confidential relationships, feeling of satisfaction with the marriage, and presence or absence of neurotic traits. The details of the scale are listed below:

Extent of agreement or disagreement between husband and wife on:

Handling family finances	Demonstration of affection
Recreation	Friends
Religion	Intimate relations
Caring for the baby	Philosophy of life
Table manners	Ways of dealing with in-laws
Conventionality	

Method of settling disagreements, whether by one giving in to the other or by mutual give and take

Degree to which husband and wife engage in outside interests together

Agreement or disagreement as to how leisure time should be spent

Frequency of kissing

Degree to which husband and wife confide in each other

Whether husband and wife would marry each other if they had their lives to live over

Kinds and number of things about the marriage that are annoying or dissatisfying

Things done by the spouse that are disliked

The following general attitudes and reactions:

Whether the person often feels lonesome, even when with other people

Whether the person is even-tempered

Whether the person often feels "just miserable"

Whether useless thoughts keep coming into the person's mind

Whether the person usually is in good spirits

Whether the person experiences periods of loneliness

Whether the person is usually self-confident [43]

This marital adjustment scale was administered to 526 married couples who then could be classified into groups with very low, low, high, and very high scores on adjustment. Through experimentation with a long questionnaire given to the same couples, Burgess and Cottrell identified 24 items for men and 20 for women, present prior to marriage, that distinguished poorly adjusted from well-adjusted couples.[44] These items were given weights that might be added into a total score. The questionnaire could then be given to unmarried persons and their scores compared with the scores of the married group; it would be assumed that their future marital adjustment would have the same degree of success as the adjustment of the married couples who made the same scores on the questionnaire. The questionnaire thus became a scale for prediction of marital adjustment as measured by the marital adjustment scale.[45]

Table 23 shows the relationship between predictive and adjustment scores. Since the relationship is expressed in percentages the table serves as a table of probability. At the highest level of prediction scores, 80 per cent had very high adjustment scores; it might be assumed, therefore, that the chances were 80 out of 100 that persons who, prior to marriage, made prediction scores of 700–779 would make a very good marital adjustment. At the low end of the prediction scores, 75 per cent had very low adjustment scores; it might be assumed that persons making low scores before marriage could look forward to three chances out of

[43] Burgess and Cottrell, op. cit., pp. 64–65.

[44] Ibid., pp. 275–283. A revision of the prediction scale is given in Ernest W. Burgess and Harvey J. Locke, The Family (American Book Company, 1945), pp. 760–771.

[45] It is important to note that prediction is only in terms of the criterion of successful marriage that is used. The Burgess-Cottrell marital adjustment scale emphasizes agreements, congeniality, and evenly balanced personality. Their prediction scale therefore predicts attainment of this type of marriage relationship.

TABLE 23

Relation between the Prediction Scores and Marital Adjustment Scores *

Premarital prediction score	Marital adjustment score				No. of cases
	Very low	Low	High	Very high	
700–779	0.0%	10.0%	10.0%	80.0%	10
620–699	1.5	12.1	25.8	60.6	66
540–619	5.8	21.9	29.2	43.1	137
460–539	27.6	29.4	25.9	17.1	170
380–459	39.8	31.1	15.1	14.0	93
300–379	57.2	25.7	11.4	5.7	35
220–299	75.0	25.0	0.0	0.0	8
TOTAL					519

* Ernest W. Burgess and Leonard S. Cottrell, Jr., *Predicting Success or Failure in Marriage* (Copyright 1939 by Prentice-Hall, Inc., New York), p. 284. Reprinted by permission of the authors and publisher.

four of making a poor marital adjustment. The middle range of scores, especially those between 380 and 539, have almost no predictive value.

Prediction of adjustment in marriage from adjustment in engagement

Continuing his studies of adjustment prediction, Burgess in collaboration with Wallin carried out a long-term project whereby engaged couples were given an engagement adjustment test and, after some years of marriage, a marital adjustment test. The engagement adjustment test was adapted from the Burgess-Cottrell marriage adjustment test, the items of which have already been listed.[46] For 505 couples tested before marriage and again after three years of married life, the correlation coefficient between engagement adjustment scores and marital adjustment scores was .43 ± .04 for men and .41 ± .04 for women. These coefficients are not high, although they show a definite correlation between the scores on the two tests. The research team were of the opinion that with the addition of scores based on background scales and personality tests the correlation would be increased.

During the course of the study 123 couples out of 1,000 broke their

[46] Ernest W. Burgess and Paul Wallin, "Predicting Adjustment in Marriage from Adjustment in Engagement," *American Journal of Sociology,* 49 (1944), 324–330; a complete report of the study will appear in Ernest W. Burgess and Paul Wallin, *Engagement and Marriage,* announced for publication in 1953 by Lippincott.

engagements.   The average engagement adjustment scores for men and women who broke their engagements were lower than the averages for those who continued their engagements (146.4 and 153.1, respectively, for men and 144.2 and 153.2 for women).   From data given by Burgess and Wallin, Table 24 was constructed to show the distribution into

TABLE 24

Relation of Engagement Adjustment Scores to Broken and Unbroken Engagements *

Adjust-ment score	Men			Women		
	Broken engage-ments	Unbroken engage-ments	No. of cases	Broken engage-ments	Unbroken engage-ments	No. of cases
180–189	5.6%	94.4%	36	7.2%	92.8%	28
170–179	8.8	91.2	136	6.2	93.8	145
160–169	10.6	89.4	199	7.9	92.1	202
150–159	13.2	86.8	227	13.7	86.3	220
140–149	8.9	91.1	180	11.7	88.3	188
130–139	13.5	86.5	96	17.6	82.4	91
120–129	19.0	81.0	58	13.0	87.0	54
110–119	25.0	75.0	40	30.2	69.8	43
100–109	31.6	68.4	19	14.3	85.7	14
90–99	22.2	77.8	9	40.0	60.0	15
NO. OF CASES	123	877	1,000	123	877	1,000

* Based on Ernest W. Burgess and Paul Wallin, "Predicting Adjustment in Marriage from Adjustment in Engagement," *American Journal of Sociology,* 49 (1944), 329.

broken and unbroken engagements for different levels of the engagement adjustment scores. Although in general the percentage of broken engagements increases with decline in adjustment scores, the progression is not regular.   The small number of cases at some score levels may account for some of the irregularity.   Also, there is always the possibility that with a longer period of time, more couples with low scores would break their engagements rather than marry.

Prediction with divorce as the criterion of failure

Another attempt at prediction of adjustment is based on a comparison of happily married with divorced couples from the same community.[47]

[47] Harvey J. Locke, *Predicting Adjustment in Marriage: A Comparison of a Divorced and a Happily Married Group* (Holt, 1951).

A modified form of the familiar Burgess-Cottrell marital adjustment scale was used together with an extensive questionnaire on background data. The adjustment scale differentiated clearly between the happily married and the divorced, as Table 25 shows. The marital prediction scale, based on the background questionnaire contains 141 items and covers both premarital items and facts related to the marriage.[48] Al-

TABLE 25

Marital Adjustment Scores for Happily Married and Divorced Couples *

Score (Per cent of total possible score)	Happily married (Per cent)	Divorced (Per cent)
95–99	14.8	—
90–94	34.2	—
85–89	23.5	—
80–84	14.3	3.3
75–79	8.2	5.8
70–74	3.0	15.6
65–69	2.0	26.6
60–64	—	22.7
55–59	—	18.8
50–54	—	6.5
45–49	—	0.7
	100.0	100.0

* Harvey J. Locke, *Predicting Adjustment in Marriage: A Comparison of a Divorced and a Happily Married Group* (Holt, 1951), p. 54.

though Locke demonstrates that each item differentiates between the happily married and the divorced and gives weights for scoring the prediction scale, he does not give the range of scores for the happily married and the divorced and hence makes it impossible at present to state what the probability of divorce or happiness would be for anyone making a given score on the scale.

PREDICTIVE FACTORS

Although predictive scales are still in an experimental stage, they offer hope for future guidance and at present distinguish many premarital and marital factors associated with failure in marital adjustment. Table 26 gives a general statement of factors found to be associated with good

[48] *Ibid.*, pp. 319–337.

TABLE 26

Factors Predictive of Good Marital Adjustment *

Factor	Terman **	Burgess and Cottrell †	Locke ††
Family background			
Happiness of childhood	Above average		Above average
Happiness of parents	Happy	Happy	Happy
Attachment to parents	Equally close to father and mother	Close	No relationship
Discipline	Firm, not harsh	—	Mild, has own way
Conflict with parents	None	None or little	None or little
Institutional contacts			
Sunday school attendance	—	Beyond age 18	Husband beyond age 10 Wife beyond age 14
Church affiliation	—	Regular and frequent	Regular and frequent
Education	Beyond high school	College graduation or more	Beyond high school
Employment husband	—	Steady	Steady
Employment wife	—	Steady	No relation to wife's employment after marriage
Membership in organizations	—	Three or more	—
Social contacts			
Friends before marriage	Husband had large number of women friends	Husband and wife had at least several of each sex	Husband and wife had at least several of each sex
Sociability	Sociable	Sociable	Sociable
Relation of husband and wife to each other before marriage			
Acquaintance	Well acquainted	Two or more years	Wife over two years
Courtship	—	Three or more years	—
Engagement	Husband six or more months Wife three or more months	Nine or more months	One year or more

460

TABLE 26 (Continued)

Factors Predictive of Good Marital Adjustment

Factor	Terman **	Burgess and Cottrell †	Locke ††
Affection toward mate before marriage	—	—	Very great
"Petting"	Never	No relationship	—
Premarital sex	Husband none or future spouse only	—	Husband none; neither suspects the other
Conflict between the two	None	None	None or very little
Similarity of family backgrounds	—	Similar	—
Conditions of marriage			
Parental approval	—	Both parents approved	Both parents approved
Age at marriage	Wife 20 or more	Husband 22–30 Wife 19 or more	Husband 24–29 Wife 21–29
Married by whom	—	Priest, minister, or rabbi	Priest or minister
Place of marriage	—	Parsonage or church	At home
Conditions after marriage			
Enjoyment of common activities	—	—	Church, radio, reading, sports, music
Attitude toward sex	Satisfactory to both	—	Satisfactory to both
Attitude toward children	—	Both desire	Both desire
Economic status	Comfortable	Comfortable	Comfortable
Personality type	Adaptable	—	Adaptable, affectionate, takes responsibility

* In general only factors found significant in two studies are included, unless they seem of special importance or are part of a series of factors.

** Lewis M. Terman, *et al., Psychological Factors in Marital Happiness* (McGraw-Hill, 1938).

† Ernest W. Burgess and Leonard S. Cottrell, Jr., *Predicting Success or Failure in Marriage* (Prentice-Hall, 1939).

†† Harvey J. Locke, *Predicting Adjustment in Marriage: A Comparison of a Divorced and a Happily Married Group* (Holt, 1951).

adjustment in studies by Burgess and Cottrell and by Locke, already described, and in a study by Terman that was carried out parallel in time with the Burgess-Cottrell study and used a modification of the Burgess-Cottrell marital adjustment scale as the criterion for successful marriage. In the first part of this chapter and in earlier chapters most of these factors have been discussed in terms of interaction between men and women and the significance of the factors for good adjustment.   Clearly marital adjustment does not rest upon any one background factor or facet of personal relationship, but upon the integrated pattern of two people's personalities and the degree of mutual companionship and satisfaction of needs that they achieve.

QUESTIONS

1. How does the pair-relationship of marriage differ from other pair-relationships, such as parent-child, employer-employee, or friend-friend?

2. How are Landis' findings on the length of time required for adjustment in marriage related (1) to our present mode of mate selection and (2) to the expectation of supreme personal happiness in marriage?

3. What can immature or neurotic persons do to increase their chances of happiness in marriage?

4. What are the most significant factors in good sexual adjustment?

5. Contrast the attitudes toward extramarital sex relations with the attitudes toward premarital sex.   How would you account for the difference? If premarital sex gains more social approval, will extramarital sex relations increase in frequency and gain in approval?

6. How can the married woman handle the conflicting roles that are open to her?

7. Are men "behind the times" in their attitudes toward the roles of married women?

8. What are the possibilities and the limitations of prediction scales for marital adjustment?

9. If a young unmarried man or woman makes a low or middle score on a predictive scale, what course should he or she follow?

BIBLIOGRAPHY

Marital adjustment

Bossard, James H. S., editor, *Toward Family Stability, The Annals* of the American Academy of Political and Social Science, 272 (1950).

————, and Boll, Eleanor S., *Ritual in Family Living* (University of Pennsylvania Press, 1950).

Clark, Le Mon, *Emotional Adjustment in Marriage* (St. Louis: C. V. Mosby Co., 1937).

Fishbein, Morris, and Burgess, E. W., editors, *Successful Marriage: An Authoritative Guide to Problems Related to Marriage from the Beginning of Sexual Attraction to Matrimony and the Successful Rearing of a Family* (Doubleday, 1947).

Hollis, Florence, *Women in Marital Conflict* (Family Service Association of America, 192 Lexington Ave., New York 16, 1949).

Mowrer, Harriet R., *Personality Adjustment and Domestic Discord* (American Book, 1935).

Social roles, especially the contradictory roles of women

Buck, Pearl S., *Of Men and Women* (Day, 1941).

Foster, Robert G., and Wilson, P. P., *Women after College* (Columbia University Press, 1942).

Gruenberg, Sidonie M., and Krech, Hilda S., *The Many Lives of Modern Woman* (Doubleday, 1952).

Seward, G. H., "Cultural Conflict and the Feminine Role," *Journal of Social Psychology,* 22 (1945), 177–194.

Warren, R. L., "Social Disorganization and the Interrelationship of Cultural Roles," *American Sociological Review,* 14 (1949), 83–87.

Young, Louise M., editor, *Women's Opportunities and Responsibilities, The Annals* of the American Academy of Political and Social Science, 251 (1947).

Prediction

Burgess, E. W., and Cottrell, L. S., Jr., *Predicting Success or Failure in Marriage* (Prentice-Hall, 1939).

———, and Wallin, Paul, *Engagement and Marriage* (Lippincott, to be published in 1953).

Locke, Harvey J., *Predicting Adjustment in Marriage: A Comparison of a Divorced and a Happily Married Group* (Holt, 1951).

Terman, Lewis M., *et al., Psychological Factors in Marital Happiness* (McGraw-Hill, 1938).

17

Marital Disintegration and New Adjustment

When husband and wife fail to find happiness in marriage or when some circumstance destroys their marital adjustment, a process of marital disintegration may replace the adjustment process. If disintegration runs its course, the marriage eventually will be terminated as a functional relationship. Although the psychological and social disunity is not necessarily followed by physical separation of husband and wife, separation often follows disintegration. When the separation is made final by a divorce, the marriage has ended as a contractual relationship and the couple are free to remarry.

THE DISINTEGRATION PROCESS

Although husband and wife may not be completely happy, the marriage continues to function so long as each looks to the other for the satisfaction of some fundamental needs and there is a workable degree of unity in daily patterns and future goals. In some marriages, however, estrangement enters, and husband and wife begin to deviate from the mutual-interaction process. They enter a process of disintegration that tends to be the reverse of the adjustment process. Identification is gradually lost and roles become highly individuated and uncoordinated. The two partners no longer look to each other for satisfactions and happiness; they no longer consistently try to achieve better adjustment. As they turn away from each other, they begin to seek satisfactions outside the marriage. They may resort to other people—relatives, children, casual associates—for those functions usually performed in conjunction with the spouse. Or they may become personally disorganized or neurotic, seeking fulfillment of needs through fantasy, escape through illness or occasionally suicide, solution of fears through extreme anxieties, bolstering of the ego through suspicion or braggadocio.   They may evidence both the rejection of marriage and personality disorganization.   One spouse may exhibit one set of reactions, the other a different pattern. Such estrangement, such denial of the marriage as a mutual relationship and a source of satisfactions, is the beginning of disintegration.

Since even in poorly adjusted marriages some progress usually has been made toward identification and unity, the reverse process typically creates emotional conflict in each individual.   Some of the more obvious indications of this conflict are quarrels followed by reconciliation; temporary separations, sometimes made under the guise of visits to friends or relatives; or applications for divorce that are withdrawn and refiled. Gradually, however, the reconciliations become less frequent, the alienation deeper, the estrangement more open and complete.

Illustrations of the disintegration process are contained in the cases that follow.   They are arranged according to the degree of identification that had been attained before the disintegration process began.[1]

Sometimes marriages occur with little or no sense of unity and identification between the pair, to be followed by early divorce.   Forced marriages into which one or both enter unwillingly often are of this type. The first case describes a forced marriage following discovery that the girl was pregnant.   Although the couple had been dating for some time, the relationship had not progressed to the courtship stage.   The girl, but not the man, was emotionally involved; this one-sided relationship had not produced identification.   It can scarcely be said, therefore, that a process of disintegration occurred.   Nevertheless, the girl at least had to adjust to the termination of her social relationship with the man which followed the divorce.

Jane, the middle child among five siblings, came from a lower-class family. Her father drank constantly so that the family was on relief most of the time. When Jane was 14 her father was accidentally killed.   His death was a great shock to the family, as he had received their affection despite his shortcomings.   Two of Jane's sisters were married, following pregnancy, a circumstance that did not disturb the family.   At the age of 16 Jane fell in love with a Mexican boy several years her senior.   He was from a large farm family and was upwardly mobile: intelligent, nicely dressed, a good dancer and athlete, and popular in school.   Jane took the initiative and eventually

[1] Unpublished cases.

succeeded in securing dates with Manuel. Soon after his graduation the two eloped and were married, as Jane was pregnant. It was agreed that Jane would remain in another town because of the gossip, while Manuel returned home. But Jane become homesick and returned, hoping for a reconciliation with Manuel. He refused to live with her and persuaded her to file suit for divorce.

In the following case, also, marital adjustment was not accomplished before the process of disintegration began. In this case divorce is very similar functionally to a broken engagement that occurs when a couple find themselves unable to identify with each other and unify their lives socially. Jim and Martha found that continued identification with their parents interfered with marital identification and unity. Their brief courtship also prevented development of premarital identification or the making of future plans with reference to parental relationships.

Jim and Martha grew up in a small mining community in the South, where they attended the same school and church and belonged to the same social groups. Martha's family was closely united, with all members of the family rallying around the protection and care of an invalid mother. Jim also belonged to a strongly unified family organized on a patriarchal basis with a strict but benevolent father. Jim and Martha began to date while in high school and by their senior year were in the courtship process. The relationship was broken, however, and each began to date with others. A few months after graduation Martha moved with her parents to a distant city. Jim found work in his home town. His role in the family was abruptly changed when his father died suddenly and he became the head of the family at the age of 19 charged with the support of his mother and a younger brother and sister.

Subsequently Jim and Martha began to correspond and the following summer Martha returned to the small town to visit her relatives. She and Jim passed rapidly through a renewal of dating and courtship and were married within three months. Martha remained in the small town, with Jim and his family. Martha soon began to worry about her invalid mother in the distant city. She wanted her husband to move to the city, where she insisted he could earn enough to support them and also to send money home to his mother. Jim suggested that Martha should visit her mother but then return to him. He felt that as head of the family he should decide where they would live. He also was just as reluctant to leave his mother as Martha was to be separated from her mother. There were many bitter arguments. Friends contributed conflicting advice. Finally Martha decided to return to her parents, a move that hurt Jim deeply.

Efforts at reconciliation followed, with Jim making a long visit to Martha but still refusing to move to the city. Martha suggested divorce as the solution, a proposal that Jim at first refused to consider. After an interval of time, however, he agreed and the couple were divorced.

In the case that follows husband and wife had widely different conceptions of marriage. Although the courtship lasted almost two years, they had not visualized the adjustment problems that would arise. In the face of objections from the wife's parents, the two were married without a planned wedding. The first two paragraphs of the case describe the differences in family backgrounds.

Mack had been reared in an orphanage and therefore lacked childhood experience in a normal family situation. He had attended only grade school, but work experience and reading had made him an interesting and competent person. In his twenties he married; he and his wife had two children, and were divorced. Four years after the divorce he met Edith. At this time his children were being cared for by relatives. He was a traveling man, accustomed to hotel life and touch-and-go contacts with groups that drank and spent money loosely; he ran bills with little feeling of obligation about paying them promptly. He was not habituated to family life nor to a responsible father role. There are no available details about the first marriage and divorce.

Edith was reared in a family consisting of the parents and four children. They lived in a single house with a large yard. The family was well unified, sharing in work and recreation. There was no extravagance in spending; money was carefully used, and savings went into family projects. Edith had long earned her spending money. Unpaid bills and the use of money for drinking were unknown to the family pattern of living. Edith had had some college training as a librarian and was interested in education. She was 12 years younger than Mack.

[Although the couple made an effort to coordinate their roles, they were not successful, and their roles continued to be highly individualized.]

At the time of their marriage Edith did not fully appreciate the effect that different family experiences might have on their marriage. She expected to have children; she expected Mack to save his money and buy a home. Mack attempted to adjust to her ideas. He secured work in the city where Edith lived, and the two moved into an apartment; a year and a half later, at Edith's insistence, they moved into a house and took Mack's two children. Edith and the children liked each other, and their relationship was friendly and compatible. Mack, however, was not able to adjust to Edith's conception of marriage. He had never supported his children regularly and now found them an unwelcome financial burden. He did not like Edith's nondrinking friends. He could not confine himself to the neat pattern of family life idealized and expected by Edith.

[This couple were unable to reach agreement in many areas; they did not achieve full psychological identification nor develop common goals. They did not have a common social world, since neither liked the other's friends. With this unstable basis for marriage, disintegration came suddenly and completely, climaxing a growing realization that neither one was happy.]

The crisis came about two years after the marriage when Mack announced that he had invited a large group of his friends to the house for a party the following evening. Edith protested that she could not prepare for them on such short notice. In the quarrel that followed, Mack struck Edith several times. The following day he did not bring his friends. Edith wanted to "make up," and Mack threatened to strike her again. She then told him she was leaving, and he drove her to her parents' home.

[Edith turned to her parents for satisfaction of some of her needs—for sympathy and bolstering of her ego. The vacillation of attitude typical of many persons considering a divorce is also evident.]

Edith immediately determined to get a divorce, but in the months that followed Mack made many efforts to see her and effect a reconciliation. He promised to meet her conditions for marriage. Edith refused to see him, fearing that she would then return to him and the unhappy situation. She had difficulty freeing herself from a feeling of responsibility toward him (when he was old, who would take care of him?) and toward his children. Her family and friends were sympathetic and finally she broke her identification sufficiently to file suit for divorce.

The following case shows the mounting tensions through a dozen years of marriage, although at the outset the marriage had many of the elements that are predictive of good adjustment. Husband and wife were increasingly unable to satisfy their personal needs in each other: sexual adjustment was poor, and the husband could not give his wife the social status that she craved. Nevertheless, a number of years passed before divorce was mentioned. The couple did not proceed quickly to divorce but attempted time after time to come to some adjustment. Gradually, however, they deviated further and further from a common life together and found less and less satisfaction in their marriage. Divorce came as the final step in a long process of disintegration.

Both husband and wife had grown up on farms in stable families without any record of divorce; both had some college education and had business positions, with the wife giving up her position at marriage and the husband continuing his education until he became a Certified Public Accountant. By the end of the second year the marriage was a failure, in the opinion of the couple; nevertheless, it continued because of family and social pressures.

Sexual adjustment was poor. The wife lacked knowledge, and the husband at the beginning of the marriage failed to understand her difficulties and made the situation worse.

Another basic difficulty was the feeling of social insecurity and inferiority on the part of the wife.   Consequently she wished to live at a level beyond the income of an accountant.   Money became a point of severe tension.   Although the husband was advancing in his profession and felt that his income was as high as could be expected, his wife criticized and blamed him.   A personal conflict situation developed.   The wife implied that her husband was a failure; at the same time she seemed to feel inferior to him and found many opportunities in public to assert dominance over him, to his embarrassment. Her sharp tongue cut deeply; she seemed unable to relax and take life calmly.

In time the wife began to use the threat of divorce, which the husband wished to avoid, as a means of getting her own way.   The husband more and more avoided conflicts by yielding to her wishes.   Rather than solving the situation, this procedure caused more tensions in the wife.

After nine years of marriage a child was unexpectedly born to the couple. As they had earlier wanted a child but had given up hope of having one, the prospect of the baby and its presence gave a new point of adjustment.   But the basic tensions were still present, and soon the wife was turning her resentment and desire to dominate upon the child.   The husband tried to defend the child and conflicts became more frequent and tense than ever.   The husband finally made the decision that a divorce was the only solution.   The wife agreed although she vacillated in her attitude when faced with the actuality of the situation.   A separation of a year followed without reconciliation, after which the divorce was secured.

CHARACTERISTICS OF DIVORCED COUPLES

Marital unadjustment

The preceding discussion shows two tendencies: for marital disintegration to end in divorce; and for the disintegration to coincide with marital unadjustment.   Formal tests show the relationship between divorce and unadjustment, according to a comparison of scores for divorced and nondivorced couples secured by the use of the Burgess-Cottrell marital adjustment scale.[2]   The divorced couples, answering the test in terms of their broken marriages, had mean scores that compared with the mean scores for the nondivorced group as follows: divorced men 110.7, undivorced men 167.3; divorced women 106.8, nondivorced women 165.6.[3] In another comparison the divorced were contrasted with very happily married couples in the same community.   Members of both groups were given a test similar to the Burgess-Cottrell but with some additional questions.   Seventy-five per cent of the happily married people scored higher

[2] Described on pages 455–456.
[3] Harvey J. Locke, *Predicting Adjustment in Marriage: A Comparison of a Divorced and a Happily Married Group* (Holt, 1951), p. 53.

on the test (better adjustment) than any of the divorced; 75 per cent of the divorced scored lower than any of the happily married; and 25 per cent had overlapping scores.[4]   Interviews revealed that divorced people with scores that overlapped on the scores of the happily married had some areas of adjustment, but that some one conflict or crisis prevented continued acceptance of the marriage and the divorce followed.   The point at issue most often was adultery or paying too much attention to another person than the spouse, and in-law trouble was the second most frequent conflict.   It should be noted that the last comparison between happily married and divorced takes only the extreme groups, and omits the moderately happy or moderately disorganized.

For many couples unadjustment leads into disintegration in the early years of marriage.   In 1949, for example, 37.4 per cent of divorces were granted to couples married less than five years, with the peak number in the third year of marriage.[5]   This year is typical of the usual situation, as Figure 42 shows.   Except for two brief periods in the 1930's, for every year between 1922 and 1948 the divorce rate has been highest for couples married less than five years.   The longer the marriage endures, the lower is the probability of disintegration.

Premarital conditions

As stated in Chapter 16, "Marital Adjustment," certain childhood relationships and early social contacts as well as length of engagement are related to marital adjustment.   Locke's comparison of happily married and divorced couples living in the same community shows that some of the factors associated with unadjustment are also related to divorce. The happily married more often than the divorced had happy childhoods with limited conflict with their parents, and their parents' marriages more often were happy and free from divorce.[6]

Selection of the mate for love, to have a home, on the basis of common interests, to satisfy sex desires, and to have children were more often associated with happiness than with divorce.   Happily married women also more often than divorced women had an economic (security) motive. Approval of the choice of a mate by the parents also made for happiness.

[4] *Ibid.*, pp. 54–56.
[5] *Vital Statistics, Special Reports, Statistics on Divorces and Annulments, Specified States: 1949*, Vol. 36, No. 7 (Federal Security Agency, August 3, 1951), pp. 105–108; the report covers 70,256 divorces granted in ten states.
[6] Locke, *op. cit.*, ch. 6.

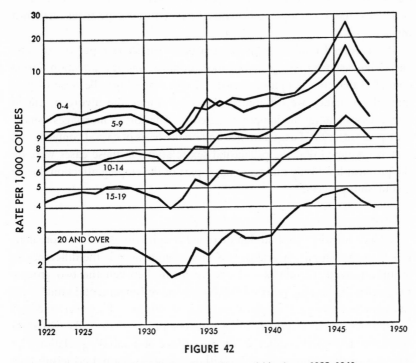

FIGURE 42

Divorce Rate per 1,000 Couples by Years of Marriage, 1922–1948

Most divorces occur early in marriage. The rate for those married less than 5 years consistently is about four to six times the rate for those married 20 or more years. For example, in 1948 the maximum rate was 26 per 1,000 couples in the third year of marriage as compared with a rate of 4 for those married 20 years. One would surmise that during the first one or two years of marriage the romantic aura carries the couple through their difficulties or that they recognize the need for time to adjust. By the third or fourth years, the most crucial tensions have mounted and patience has worn thin. Divorces in later years have several possible explanations: tensions may have been slow in accumulating to the breaking point; couples may wait until their children are adolescent or older before terminating an unhappy marriage; or new tensions or crises may have arisen to disturb a previously satisfactory marriage. (Source: Paul H. Jacobson, "Differentials in Divorce by Duration of Marriage and Size of Family," *American Sociological Review*, 15 [1950], 238.)

On the other hand, the divorced men, more often than the happy, married to escape loneliness, and divorced women to escape from their own families.[7]

The divorced tended to know each other for shorter periods of time and to have shorter engagements, more conflict, and less affection during courtship than the happily married. Forced marriages because of premarital pregnancy were found in 41 cases among the divorced, but in only 3 cases among the happily married.[8] The forced marriages usually took place after brief acquaintance and on the basis of casual contacts. It may be assumed that the premarital sex relations in these cases were on the physical level only and were not a part of developing affection during a courtship process.

Personality

It is not surprising to find that divorced couples disagreed on more matters than the happily married.[9] Of more significance is the difference in attitude toward difficulties and disagreements between the two groups. In general the happily married exhibited a more fundamental attachment to each other and greater security in their marriage. They were inclined to be tolerant, to overlook disagreements rather than make issues of them, and to regard conflicts as on the surface of an abiding relationship. The divorced had met difficulties with anger and personal criticism; they tended to separate temporarily when difficulties arose rather than to regard them as problems to be solved by mutual effort. Thus there was a basic difference in the conception of marriage held by the two groups.

This difference in conception of marriage is shown in part by the reasons for marrying and the difference in length of engagement. It is also evident in the degree of individualism found in the divorced couples and the higher development of companionship and democracy among the happily married.[10] A free interpretation of Locke's findings would characterize the divorced as more ego-centered and rigid, the happily married as more out-going and adaptable.

[7] *Ibid.*, 97–100, 123.
[8] *Ibid.*, pp. 86–97.
[9] *Ibid.*, pp. 81–84.
[10] *Ibid.*, pp. 75–76, ch. 12.

Children

Children are popularly regarded as a deterrent to divorce.   It is true that the rate of divorce among childless couples is almost double that among couples with children (Figure 43); but we cannot be sure that the absence or presence of children is the deciding factor.   It is probable that fundamental problems or attitudes contribute to both the childlessness and the divorce.   Also, some of the childlessness is accounted for by the large number of divorces that occur early in marriage, before there has

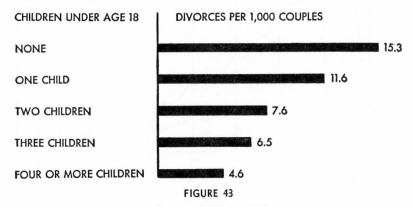

FIGURE 43

Divorce Rates and Number of Children

Not only do couples with children have lower divorce rates, but with each succeeding child the rate declines.   Probably, however, children are not always a direct deterrent to divorce.   Couples that do not adjust often seek a divorce during the early years of marriage, before a child has been born or when at most there are only one or two children.   Those who adjust remain married and in time have a number of children.   (Source: Paul H. Jacobson, "Differentials in Divorce by Duration of Marriage and Size of Family," *American Sociological Review,* 15 [1950], 242.)

been sufficient lapse of time for the birth of a child.   As couples often are estranged or separated for some time before the divorce suit is filed or the decree granted, the divorce secured in the second or third year of marriage may follow a separation of some months or a year or more; in the short space of time that the couple lived together no child was born.

Couples who work out an adjustment that survives the first few years of marriage generally have children.   Later, if some disturbance occurs that makes the marriage intolerable, a divorce may be secured.   For these later divorces, the rates for childless couples and couples with children show less and less variation with the duration of marriage and eventually become identical (Figure 44).

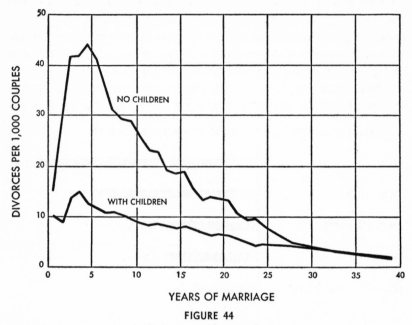

YEARS OF MARRIAGE

FIGURE 44

Divorce Rates for Childless Couples and Couples with Children under 18 by Duration of the Marriage, 1948

This graph suggests that children and marital adjustment are found in the same families; it also suggests that childless families that do not disintegrate during the early years of marriage have a good chance of survival. (Source: Paul H. Jacobson, "Differentials in Divorce by Duration of Marriage and Size of Family," *American Sociological Review,* 15 [1950], 243.)

SOCIAL SITUATIONS AND DIVORCE

From material presented in earlier chapters we know that the pattern of family life varies from one social situation to another. We recognize differences between rural and urban families; lower-, middle-, and upper-class families; and families with different religious affiliations. Each social situation creates its distinctive hardships and tensions, and, to the extent that it represents cultural differences, has specific attitudes toward divorce. Therefore from one social situation to another, the proportion of family unadjustment, disintegration, and divorce may vary.

Urbanism

We usually assume that family disorganization and divorce are more often experienced by urban than rural families.   Table 27 shows that as far as status of the population at any one period is concerned, a higher percentage of urban than of rural people are divorced.   The table does not indicate, however, the relative divorce rates.   People divorced in

TABLE 27

Marital Status of the Civilian Population, 14 Years of Age and Over, 1948 *

Marital status	Urban (2,500 and over)	Rural nonfarm	Rural farm
Males			
Single	26.9%	24.9%	33.0%
Married	66.8	70.0	61.8
Widowed	4.0	3.7	3.8
Divorced	2.3	1.4	1.6
Females			
Single	22.2	17.1	21.5
Married	61.8	70.3	68.2
Widowed	13.4	10.6	9.4
Divorced	2.6	2.0	0.9

* *Current Population Reports, Population Characteristics, Marital Status, Number of Times Married, and Duration of Present Marital Status: April, 1948,* Series P-20, No. 23 (Bureau of the Census, March 4, 1949), p. 10.   Comparable information based on the 1950 census groups widowed and divorced together in the preliminary reports.

rural communities may move to cities and thereafter be included by the Census in the urban population.   Also, many divorced people remarry and thus return to the status of married.

Urban and rural communities must be compared according to the rate of divorces granted.   To date, such comparisons have used counties as the basic units, classified according to the largest city within each county. Rates are computed as number of divorces per 1,000 of the total population in each county.[11]   The rural rates are probably understatements, since the rural total population includes a larger proportion of children than does the urban population.   Actually, the results of the studies are inconclusive.   Individual rural counties have higher rates than urban

[11] The crudity of the method is a result of the type of information found in published reports.

counties within the same state.   When counties within a state are grouped according to the size of the largest city within each county, variations in rates are evident between the groups.   In Iowa, for instance, counties without any towns as large as 2,500 population had the lowest divorce rates, 1.3 in 1947.[12]   The rates increased regularly with urbanness of the counties until a rate of 4 was reached for counties with one or more cities of 25,000.   These figures support the thesis that the divorce rate is higher in urban than in rural communities.   A Missouri study, however, shows a different pattern of rates.[13]   For 1947, 33 rural counties with no city of 2,500 population had a divorce rate of 2.2 per 1,000 population; 7 counties with cities of 10,000 or more had a rate of 7.5; St. Louis County (containing the city of St. Louis), however, had a rate of only 5.7.   A similar county study for Illinois showed great irregularity of rates, with the lowest rate (1.8) in the most rural counties having no cities of 2,500 population, and the highest rate (4.5) in counties with cities of between 2,500 and 25,000.[14]   Counties with larger cities had rates that fell between these extremes.   Cook County, containing the city of Chicago, had a rate of only 2.8.

These results indicate the need for more exact studies of divorce rates in urban and rural areas, which will take account of other factors than the size of population units.   Suggested factors are ethnic and religious backgrounds, racial composition, educational and economic status, and mobility.

Religion

Several studies indicate that when husband and wife both belong to the same religious faith, the divorce rate is lower than among mixed marriages or those in which husband and wife have no religious affiliation. Table 28 gives the result of three studies.   Caution must be used in interpreting the tables.   In all three studies the data were gathered from

---

[12] Kenneth L. Cannon, "Marriage and Divorce in Iowa, 1940–47," *Marriage and Family Living*, 9 (1947), 81–83, 98; since Cannon presented his data solely by graphs, the rates cited here are approximations only.

[13] "Missouri Marriage and Divorce Statistics, 1940–1947," *Journal of the Missouri Bar*, 4 (March, 1948), 38–39.

[14] Computed from population for 1950 and divorces for 1949. *1950 Census of Population, Preliminary Counts, Population of Illinois, by Counties: April 1, 1950*, Series PC-2, No. 40 (Bureau of the Census, September 11, 1950); *Vital Statistics, Special Reports, Statistics on Divorces and Annulments, Specified States: 1949*, Vol. 36, No. 7 (Federal Security Agency, August 3, 1951), pp. 111–112.

adolescents or young adults regarding the religion and marital status of their parents.   The parents therefore were middle-aged and represent the trends of a past generation rather than of recently married couples.   The presence of children is also a deterring factor in divorce.   Within these limitations of the groups studied, the three studies show a striking similarity.   The fact that most of the Spokane rates are higher than the Maryland or Michigan rates probably reflects a regional difference, since the total divorce rate for Washington is higher than for the other two states.[15]

TABLE 28

Marriages Ending in Divorce or Separation by Religion

	Spokane study *	Maryland study **	Michigan study †
No affiliation	23.9%	16.7%	17.9%
Mixed (intermarriages)	17.4	15.2	13.8
Both Protestant	10.1 ††	6.8	6.0
Both Jewish	—	4.6	5.2
Both Catholic	3.8	6.4	4.4
NUMBER OF CASES	5,490	13,528	4,108

* H. Ashley Weeks, "Differential Divorce Rates by Occupation," *Social Forces*, 21 (1943), 334–337.   The data were collected from public and parochial secondary school pupils and refer to their parents.   Results might be different for an unselected sample of the population which would include childless couples.

** Howard M. Bell, *Youth Tell Their Story* (American Council on Education, 1938), p. 21.   These figures are based on information regarding their parents given by 13,528 young people in Maryland.

† Judson T. Landis, "Marriages of Mixed and Non-Mixed Religious Faith," *American Sociological Review*, 14 (1949), p. 403.   Based on data given by students at Michigan State College regarding their parents.   The classification of mixed includes a number of categories, such as one parent no religion and the other Protestant or Catholic, and one parent changed religion at the time or after the marriage to correspond to the religion of the other, as well as straight intermarriages between those of different faiths.   For the detailed classification, see Table 15, p. 254.

†† All non-Catholic.

Several explanations may be suggested for the differences in rates. Religious groups differ in their pronounced attitude toward divorce.   The Catholic Church refuses to recognize divorce at all, although under certain conditions separations are sanctioned.   The Jewish faith emphasizes the

[15] For 1948, the last year for which rates are available for the three states, the divorce rate per 1,000 population in Washington was 3.5, Maryland, 2.6, and Michigan, 2.6.   In general the divorce rates are higher in the Western states than in the East, South, or Middle West.   *Vital Statistics, Special Reports, Summary of Marriage and Divorce Statistics, United States: 1949,* Vol. 36, No. 2 (Federal Security Agency, June 5, 1951), p. 23.

unity of the family. Protestant denominations differ: some strongly oppose divorce and forbid their ministers to perform the marriage ceremony for divorced persons; others are more lenient in attitude and practice. People reared in a particular religious faith tend to accept the attitudes of that faith; when divorce is forbidden or strongly disapproved, they tend to find other ways than divorce for settlement of marital problems. Frequently the church functions also as a counseling agency, the confessional of the Catholic Church and the modern pattern of family counseling of many Protestant groups holding the door open for troubled husbands and wives to find advice and solace. In addition, Catholics, Protestants, and Jews all maintain social-service agencies, whose staff members are trained not only in methods of social casework but in the religious doctrines of the faith. Thus religious institutions both set social norms that in general are opposed to divorce and offer help to those with marital difficulties.

Social class

Although divorce has not been studied directly according to social-class divisions, certain data are suggestive. Descriptive material shows that aggressiveness is common in lower-class families, and also that crises occur with greater frequency.[16] The assumption that there is greater dissatisfaction is borne out by a study of 845 middle- and lower-class married people. Figure 45 shows the percentage distribution of husbands and wives in four social-class divisions according to good, fair, or poor marital adjustment. Good adjustment decreases and poor adjust-

TABLE 29

Marriages Classified by Occupation That Ended in Divorce, Spokane *

Professional men	6.80%
Proprietors	8.39
Clerical workers	10.39
Skilled workers	11.60
Semiskilled workers	13.38
Unskilled workers	7.33
Unemployed	10.48

* H. Ashley Weeks, "Differential Divorce Rates by Occupation," *Social Forces,* 21 (1943), 336. The data pertain to the parents of pupils in public and private secondary schools.

[16] Chapters 5, 6, and 7.

ment increases as social status declines.   These data suggest that divorce rates also may vary according to social class.

Table 29 indirectly throws light on divorce and social class.   Among families of secondary school pupils in Spokane, the divorce rate varied greatly from one occupational group to another.   Occupations known to be heavily represented in the upper and upper middle classes had low divorce rates; at the other extreme of the occupational scale, the unskilled workers had equally low rates.   Clerical, skilled, and semiskilled workers

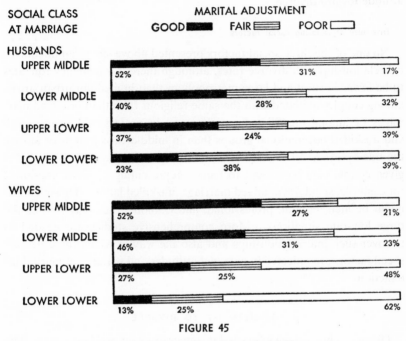

FIGURE 45

Marital Adjustment According to Social Class

According to the Burgess-Cottrell scale of marital adjustment, higher percentages of middle-class than of lower-class people achieve good adjustment. (Source: Julius Roth and Robert F. Peck, "Social Class and Social Mobility Factors Related to Marital Adjustment," *American Sociological Review*, 16 [1951], 479.)

had rates decidedly higher.   With the exception of the unskilled group, the increasing rates with decrease in social or occupational status might be explained in terms of increasing economic hardships, less class expectation of family stability, and a greater tendency to express dissatisfaction overtly through divorce.   The unskilled might avoid divorce because of the expense involved, although logically such an explanation would be expected to apply also to the unemployed, who have a high divorce rate. From other studies it is known that lower-class husbands often resort to desertion without the formality of a divorce to solve or escape from family difficulties; the desertion rate is not known for the Spokane group.   The lower-class Spokane group had a low percentage of Catholics, thus eliminating an explanation of the low divorce rate as a result of the Catholic attitude toward divorce.

Difficulty of isolating social factors

No one of the three social factors presented above shows an unequivocal relationship with divorce rates, although there is a tendency for rates to be lower in rural and large metropolitan than in medium urban areas; among couples affiliated with the same religious faith than in mixed marriages or among unaffiliated couples; and in professional, managerial, and unskilled occupational groups than in middle-class groups or among the unemployed.   The effect of any one factor is decreased because a given couple may be subject to factors representing opposed pressures; for example, small town, mixed marriage, unskilled labor.   Or the couple might be metropolitan, professional, and Catholic, thus representing the three low-rate situations.   More comprehensive studies are needed to uncover such interrelationships and also the way in which these general social factors are reflected in personal attitudes and patterns of marital interaction.

ADJUSTMENT TO DIVORCE

Divorce is but a stage in marital disintegration and readjustment.   The divorce marks the end of the marriage legally, defines obligations and relationships in a formal way, but leaves untouched the postdivorce adjustment of each individual.   This adjustment covers a number of phases: resolving residual emotions and attitudes toward the marriage and the ex-spouse; readjusting one's conception of oneself; rearranging personal habits, including finances and sexual satisfactions; and readjusting social life.[17]

[17] Not many studies have been made of adjustment to divorce. Willard Waller in *The Old Love for the New: Divorce and Readjustment* (Liveright, 1930) analyzed 33 cases; such a limited number of cases obviously leads to illustrative types of

Sometimes, when a long period of time intervenes between a definite separation and the granting of a divorce, many of the above processes may take place prior to the divorce itself. Divorce in such cases may be secured not to terminate the marriage, which in reality was terminated at the time of the separation, but perhaps in order to settle property or to define legal relationships to children. Usually, however, the readjustment follows the divorce.

Residual emotions and attitudes

Although the attitude toward the ex-spouse may be neutral, often it is not. In Goode's interview study of over 400 urban divorced mothers, half of the women stated they felt indifferent toward their former husbands.[18] One out of ten expressed strong affection; one out of four wished the husband to be punished. Another one out of four admitted a willingness to remarry the husband under certain circumstances. The interviews indicated, however, that many of those expressing indifference really had considerable emotional content in their attitudes but were giving a conventional reply, since the divorced person is expected to be indifferent to the former mate.

The divorced person may not have wanted the divorce and hence may still love the absent one. In other cases, the difficulties of personal and social adjustment may make the marriage in memory seem preferable to the later period. The marriage may be idealized; only the pleasurable aspects of periods of harmony may be remembered at such times.

The hostile and punitive attitude may have a realistic basis in mistreatment. But it may also be a defensive reaction, to protect the person

adjustment rather than to a comprehensive analysis. William J. Goode has made a study of adjustment to divorce of 425 women, divorced from six months to two years, between ages 20 and 38 at the time of the divorce, and with children. The cases represent divorces granted in the Michigan Circuit Court in Detroit during certain months in 1946, 1947, and 1948. The study has been reported by David G. Wittels in the *Saturday Evening Post,* which helped finance the study, under the title "The *Post* Reports on Divorce," 222 (January 21, 1950), 20–21, 98–100, 102–103: (January 28, 1950), 22–23, 82, 84, 86, 88–89; (February 4, 1950), 34–35, 42, 46, 48, 52; (February 11, 1950), 32–33, 93–94, 98, 100; (February 18, 1950), 28, 135–138. The *Post* report is popular and descriptive and does not purport to give a sociological analysis. The analysis in this section rests only slightly on the above reports. Other fragmentary reports and published and unpublished cases have contributed to it.

[18] William J. Goode, "Problems in Postdivorce Adjustment," *American Sociological Review,* 14 (1949), p. 400. Goode does not state the attitude of the remaining 15 per cent of the women.

from admission of partial responsibility for the divorce and a consequent feeling of guilt and failure.

The emotions felt and their overt manifestations do not fall into the same pattern in all cases. Goode states that repeated questions about sleep, forgetfulness, increased smoking or drinking, lessened efficiency or energy, lonesomeness, and so on, failed to reveal a definite pattern.[19] He believes that a more comprehensive study might uncover subpatterns of reactions, perhaps along social-class lines. He also believes that the emotional disturbance is not entirely due to the breakdown of the marriage itself, but that at least part is related to the conflict between the divorced person's inner problems of adjustment to a nonmarried state and the social expectation that he should be indifferent and show little affection for the divorced spouse.

These residual emotions impede adjustment to the divorced state and if not dissipated may hinder adjustment in a later marriage.

Readjusting conception of self

An early reaction to divorce seems to be the tendency to place all the responsibility for it on the other person. Each spouse, whether he has demanded the divorce, acceded to the other's demand or entered into a mutual agreement, feels the necessity to justify his action. This compulsion grows out of our attitude toward marriage and divorce. Regardless of the long-term upward trend in divorces, the social norm is still permanency of marriage. Any deviation must be explained and justified. When the couple belong to a religious group that strongly condemns divorce, personal defense is still more necessary because divorce is defined not merely as a social violation but as the flaunting of a moral law. In addition to fear or dislike of social condemnation, the person has a feeling of personal failure. The practice in our society of permitting young people to select their own mates and arrange for their own marriages places the responsibility for success or failure upon them personally. The young man who was elated over winning the most beautiful girl in his community and the girl who received a proposal from the most promising young man must now admit their errors in judgment. Also, marriage is regarded as a personal relationship in which each meets the needs of the other, as well as finding satisfaction for his own needs. Divorce signifies a failure, not only to find satisfaction, but to give satisfaction.

[19] *Ibid.,* p. 400

The divorced person therefore often has his sense of personal adequacy, his self-assurance, his belief in himself, shattered by the experience.

Marion divorced Harold after he had had several "affairs" with other women and finally wished to marry a woman with whom he had secretly been living intermittently. Marion, who knew of his affairs, had previously offered to divorce him, but he had always assured her that the current affair was ended and that he did not want to be divorced. When the divorce was finally secured at Harold's request, Marion's first reaction was "numb frigidity like that of bereavement." As this feeling wore off she felt a keen sense of personal failure. She also felt disgraced as she was a devoted member of a church that condemned divorce; she felt that she had violated her moral standards. She found comfort in her friends and eventually began to date but asserted that she would never remarry. After five years' time, her feelings of failure and disgrace had changed very little. She learned to counteract a tendency to idealize her marriage by deliberately recalling its drawbacks. Some compensation for her feeling of failure resulted from her increased emotional serenity and the financial security of her job.[20]

Writing ten years after her divorce, a woman of 35 states:

At first, I was sure the divorce did not affect me, and I felt I would remarry and be happy, because I was sure I just made a bad decision and everything was wrong about our marriage. However, I now look backward and I can see that it has affected my attitude toward other men, my feeling of being able to decide to remarry. For many years I was sure that it was not my fault and that there was nothing wrong with me. I have just in the last few years started to analyze my own attitudes, opinion, expectations and behavior and realize they had a great deal to do with the marriage.[21]

Feelings of being "let down," unwanted, insecure, and a personal failure are mentioned by others who have described their reactions after a divorce.

Rearranging personal life

Marriage is both a personal relationship and a way of life. Even when a couple are in conflict and declare they no longer love each other, many joint patterns of behavior are continued. The wife may still manage the household and prepare the food that both eat; the husband may still pay the bills and depend upon his wife to attend to such personal needs as clean clothing and mending. Both may meet social obligations in the midst of estrangement. Sex relations, the most intimate part of marriage,

[20] Unpublished record.
[21] Unpublished record.

often are discontinued early in the conflict period; but in other cases the couple continue sex relations through habit, to meet mutual needs, or as part of the vacillation between harmony and conflict that often characterizes the marriage prior to a divorce. All these functions and relationships are disturbed and perhaps completely destroyed by separation and divorce; they also have many emotional connotations.

When there are children who remain with the mother, and she is able to retain the family home, her adjustment in daily habits is less severe than is the adjustment of the husband who leaves or of the wife who finds it impossible or undesirable to maintain a house. Many women and some men retreat to their parents' home, where they may find solace in their parents' sympathy and may resume a filial relationship:

Jim's mother and friends were very sympathetic. Through conversation they made him feel that maybe the divorce was the best thing after all. They reasoned that he was the man and his wife should live where he provided the place for them.[22]

Other women change their place and mode of living, seemingly seeking to destroy the old pattern of daily life.

Janet, who never talked about her divorce even to intimate friends, used her share of the property settlement to buy a small house about five miles from her former home. She systematically sorted out all of her husband's possessions and left them in their old home, owned by her former husband. She burned all his letters to her and destroyed wedding mementos. She left all his photographs except one, and returned her wedding ring.[23]

Other men and women move away from the community and reconstruct life in a new social setting.

A financial adjustment usually is part of the divorce situation. Joint property is divided, sometimes with bitterness and a feeling of unfairness. Alimony may be allowed by the judge, although it is a less common practice than formerly for the wife to ask for or receive alimony. Alimony was a way of providing security for the divorced wife at a time when married women could not hold property and were completely dependent upon their husbands financially;[24] in an earlier period also they were less able to support themselves. At present there is less justification for

---

[22] See page 466 for statement of this divorce.
[23] Unpublished record.
[24] Robert W. Kelso, "The Changing Social Setting of Alimony Law," *Law and Contemporary Problems,* 6 (1939), 186–196.

alimony except in special cases, and alimony thus becomes a psychological weapon or the focusing point for the conflict.[25]   The man may resist, feeling resentful at the prospect of supporting an able-bodied woman to whom he is no longer married.   He may object to the loss of purchasing power involved and especially so if he wishes to remarry.   On the other hand, alimony relieves some men of a sense of guilt.   They may feel that ample payment of alimony (and support of children) relieves them of all other responsibilities.   The wife may use alimony as a punitive measure and insist upon financial payments as a way of maintaining power over her divorced husband.   Other women, compelled to accept alimony because they have no means of self-support, may be humiliated by the situation.   When the wife does not receive alimony, she becomes either dependent upon relatives or self-supporting.   The middle-aged woman who has never been gainfully employed or who has lost her skills may either bitterly resent the necessity for self-support or find in it a new purpose and objective in her life.

Intimate and sexual relationships are difficult to adjust.   The adult who has become accustomed to a close affectional and sexual union in marriage often finds single life irritating and frustrating.   Regression to the family life in the parental family may partially solve the problem for some; concentration of affection on children for others.   Dating and an overemphasis on social life is another solution tried by many, especially women.   Men, more than women, may frankly cultivate sexual relations on a casual basis.   Whirlwind love affairs, sometimes ending in marriage, are another effort at compensation.   These affairs also have other meanings; they restore assurance to the divorced woman of her attractiveness and to the man of his masculine virility.   They also offer public proof that the divorced person is indifferent, unhurt, and immune to the emotional ravages of the experience, although actually months or years may be required to repair the damage.

Edith [whose earlier history is given on pages 467–468] began to date as soon as her divorce was granted.   All her friends encouraged her to have a good time and introduced her to eligible men.   Eight months after the divorce she became engaged, but broke the engagement after two weeks.   She has continued to date many men, sometimes falling quickly in love with a man who in some way resembled the ex-husband, but later finding they were incompatible.

[25] Catherine Groves Peele, "Social and Psychological Effects of the Availability and the Granting of Alimony on the Spouses," *Law and Contemporary Problems*, 6 (1939), 283–292.

Readjustment of social life may be difficult. Although there is greater leniency of attitude toward divorced persons than formerly, in some communities or toward members of some professions disapproval is still strong. Teachers and ministers are especially likely to be stigmatized if divorced. Sometimes the curiosity, sympathy, or facetiousness of friends is as trying as disapproval. Mutual friends of the couple are placed in a peculiar predicament: shall they "take sides," shall they retain both friendships but try to keep the two apart at social affairs by inviting first one and then the other, or shall they drop both? It seems probable that few divorced couples are really comfortable if invited to the same social function, although a high degree of sophistication may make it possible for the two to continue their old joint social contacts. If friends invite only one of the couple, the question arises of a partner. The divorced person himself may seek to withdraw from old joint associates, sometimes going to the extent of moving to another community. Others, however, rush into social life as an escape from loneliness and as proof that the divorce has not hurt them, that they are not failures, have not lost attractiveness, and so on.

REMARRIAGE

Although the divorce experience may leave permanent scars or make lasting changes in attitude, it does not necessarily signify an end to married life for either partner.

Remarriage of the divorced

The rate of remarriage of divorced persons is high. A survey by the Bureau of the Census in 1948 leads to the conclusion that three fourths of all persons securing a divorce during the preceding five years had remarried; for those who had obtained a divorce 5 to 14 years prior to the survey, approximately 85 per cent had remarried.[26] The rate of remarriage for divorced persons is higher than the rate for widowed persons, and indeed higher than for single persons. For example, in 1940, it is estimated that three fifths of all remarried persons had previously been divorced, and two fifths widowed.[27] The difference becomes more sig-

[26] Paul C. Glick, "First Marriages and Remarriages," *American Sociological Review*, 14 (1949), 730. These estimates are based on a cross-section sample survey made by the Census Bureau and other official data.

[27] Paul C. Glick and Emanuel Landau, "Age as a Factor in Marriage," *American Sociological Review*, 15 (1950), 521.

nificant when one realizes that deaths cause the dissolution of many more marriages than do divorces. In 1940 slightly less than one third of marriage dissolutions were caused by divorces.[28] The high tendency of divorced persons to remarry is shown by estimates of the probability of marriage by divorced, widowed, and single women and men. One study estimates that at age 30, the divorced woman has 94 chances for subsequent marriage during her lifetime, the widow 60 chances and the unmarried woman 48 chances in 100.[29] For the man aged 30, the chances in 100 of subsequent marriage are 96, 92, and 67 for divorced, widowed, and single, respectively. A study of Massachusetts indicates that only in the late teens and twenties does the single person have a higher marriage rate than the divorced (Table 30).

TABLE 30

Ages of Persons Marrying, According to Previous Conjugal Condition, for Massachusetts, 1937 *

Age	Number	Previous conjugal condition		
		Single	Widowed	Divorced
Grooms				
Under 20		2.7%	0.0%	0.0%
20–29		72.6	4.6	16.0
30–39		20.7	19.4	45.3
40–49		3.2	28.8	26.5
50 and over		0.8	47.2	12.2
TOTALS	33,652	100.0	100.0	100.0
Brides				
Under 20		16.6	0	0.5
20–29		70.0	9.1	34.5
30–39		11.5	23.4	40.7
40–49		1.6	33.4	17.1
50 and over		0.3	34.1	7.2
TOTALS	33,652	100.0	100.0	100.0

* J. H. S. Bossard, "Previous Conjugal Condition," *Social Forces*, 18 (1939–1940), 244.

[28] Paul H. Jacobson, "Total Marital Dissolutions in the United States: Relative Importance of Mortality and Divorce," p. 8, reprinted from *Studies in Population* (Princeton University Press, 1949).

[29] Metropolitan Life Insurance Company, "The Chances of Remarriage for the Widowed and Divorced," *Statistical Bulletin*, 26 (May, 1945), 1–3.

Table 31 shows a further breakdown of remarriages of divorced persons in New York according to the interval of time between the divorce and the remarriage.   More than one fourth of the remarriages of both divorced men and divorced women occurred the same year in which the divorces were secured.

TABLE 31

Year of Divorce in Relation to Remarriage, New York State, 1922, 1929, 1936 *

	No. of cases	Year that divorce was obtained in relation to remarriage				
		Same year	One year previous	Two years previous	Three or four years previous	Five or more years previous
Groom	3,886	29.3%	19.0%	9.6%	13.4%	28.7%
Bride	4,564	29.3	21.5	10.4	12.2	26.6

* J. H. S. Bossard, "Previous Conjugal Condition," *Social Forces* 18 (1939–1940), 246.

Adjustment of remarried persons

In popular thought—and contrary to the high rate of remarriage—the divorced person is often regarded as a poor marital risk.   Although no thorough systematic survey has been made of remarriage after divorce, the results of a limited study suggest that remarriage may be quite happy. Table 32 shows the distribution of small groups of once-married and

TABLE 32

Marital Adjustment of Remarried Divorced Persons and Those Married Only Once *

	Scores on Burgess-Cottrell marital adjustment test			
	20–120 Poor	120–159 Fair	160–194 Good	Mean score
Married only once	10.9%	39.1%	50.0%	151
Remarried after divorce	17.0	38.3	44.7	149
Women married only once				151
Remarried women				157
Men married only once				159
Remarried men				138

* Harvey J. Locke, *Predicting Adjustment in Marriage: A Comparison of a Divorced and a Happily Married Group* (Holt, 1951), based on pp. 306–309.   This table is based upon 47 remarried persons and 64 persons married only once.   Although these two small aggregates do not represent a random sample, they are fairly well matched as to religion, education, income, and nativity.   The only comparisons that are significant are between the men married only once and the remarried men, and between remarried men and remarried women.

remarried according to scores on the Burgess-Cottrell marital adjustment scale.   The proportions with poor, fair, and good adjustment in the two groups are almost identical.   When once-married and remarried women are compared by mean scores, the difference in scores is statistically insignificant.   Men, however, differ.   The once-married have a much higher mean score than the remarried.   Those whose second marriage failed and led to a second divorce are, of course, not included.   The study does not throw light on factors leading to adjustment in the second marriage in comparison with factors in the marriage that failed; nor why women but not men seem to adjust as well in a second marriage as in a first marriage.   Suggestions only may be given.

Whether or not the remarriage is happy depends upon several things. If the original marriage dissolved because of personality difficulties, another marriage might also be unsuccessful, unless personality readjustment had been achieved during the interval between the two marriages. If, however, the original spouses were simply mismated, a second marriage with better selection of the mate might lead to happiness and permanence.   The degree and type of adjustment to the divorce is also important.   Resentment toward the first spouse may be projected upon the second.   Or if the divorced person retains a latent love for the divorced mate, he may be unable to make an adequate adjustment to the second.   Marriages because of loneliness, to prove that one is not a failure, or for financial reasons are probably not good risks, as we know that such reasons for first marriages are associated with unhappiness and instability.   If, however, the divorced person has rid himself of all or most emotional reactions to the divorced spouse, has revived his own feeling of adequacy, makes an appropriate selection of a new mate, and can progress through a normal courtship and marital adjustment process, the second marriage may well be happy and stable.

LEGAL TERMINATION OF MARRIAGE

The discussion so far has emphasized psychological and social elements of marital disintegration.   If the couple wish to make the dissolution of their marriage permanent and to relieve themselves of some of their obligations, they may secure a legal separation, a divorce, or—under certain circumstances—an annulment.   Divorce is the most common method used.

Divorce is a legal decree that sets aside the contract of marriage. Although the decree may be granted by a judge after hearings lasting no more than a few minutes, divorce usually has other connotations to the couple than the mere termination of a legal contract. The very decision to make an irrevocable end to the marriage and thereby to risk the social disapproval that is often directed toward the divorced may create insecurity. The necessity on the part of the one filing the suit of accusing the partner of some form of misconduct in order to come within the framework of the law may offend the sensitive or the fair-minded. Financial arrangements may be necessary but distasteful. Finally, the divorce precipitates the many phases of adjustment already described.

Divorce

Divorce relieves husband and wife of such privileges as sexual access or occupation of a common domicile and frees each for remarriage. However, certain obligations may be continued. By the terms of the individual divorce the husband may be required to continue financial support of his wife through alimony. When there are minor children, one parent, usually the wife, receives custody of the children for whose care she is then responsible; the father usually is required to contribute to the support of the children.

The philosophy underlying divorce is that one party to the marriage has violated the marriage contract, whereas the other party is innocent. The innocent party, as plaintiff, may bring suit for divorce and must prove by evidence and witnesses that the spouse, who is the defendent, is guilty. The plaintiff must not admit in court any share of responsibility for the situation, and any agreement between husband and wife to end the marriage must be concealed. Now that divorce is recognized as the end result of a process of interaction and often is desired by both husband and wife, the court procedure is a farce. Nevertheless, until the laws are changed, the farce must be played out to the end. Each state has passed legislation listing with considerable detail the violations of the marriage contract for which a divorce will be granted. New York has the most limited provision: divorce may be secured only upon proof of adultery. South Carolina, which until 1948 did not provide for any divorce, now allows divorce for adultery, desertion, physical cruelty, and drunkenness. Other states have varying causes. Table 33 lists the causes and the number of states granting divorce for each cause. Divorce laws also sometimes make fine distinctions between grounds for husband and wife; specify the length of time of desertion, drinking habit, or insanity; and the length of time (if any) that must elapse before marriage to another person. Length of time that the person must reside in the state before filing suit for divorce is also specified, a period that ranges from six weeks in Idaho and Nevada to five years in Massachusetts. Only an inspection of the laws of each state can make all the distinctions clear. This brief summary of laws is sufficient, however, to indicate the variety of grounds for divorce and the great specificity of misconduct that the plaintiff must prove. What actually happens, of course, is a fitting of the individual case into the legal requirements. A person may establish residence in a state requiring only a few weeks for the specific purpose of securing a divorce and then leave the state; an agreed-upon separation may be converted into desertion; or fraudulent testimony may be given to prove adultery that never occurred.

Various reforms have been proposed. One is a federal divorce law, which would make the procedure uniform for all states and thus prevent people from establishing residence and securing a divorce in one state that could not be secured in the state of real residence. Another is the substitution of social-worker procedures for the present legal ones, or their use as a supplementation to them. The report of the American Bar Association Committee to the Legal Section of the National Conference on Family Life, which met in Washington, D. C., in May of 1948, advocated the use of diagnosis and therapy by trained personnel to attempt a reconciliation rather than the present practice of granting quick divorces.[30]

Annulment

An annulment is also a legally recognized type of separation that terminates marriage, but it differs from divorce in being justified by conditions existent before or at the time of marriage that invalidate the marriage itself, whereas divorce is granted for events that occur after the wedding. For example, a marriage may take place under conditions where the consent of one party is not clearly obtained: one of the pair

[30] Sara Louise Buchanan, *The Legal Status of Women in the United States of America as of January 1, 1948, Summary for All States Combined,* Women's Bureau Bulletin No. 157 (Government Printing Office, 1951), pp. 71–72.

TABLE 33

Legal Grounds for Divorce *

Cause	Number of states prescribing each ground for divorce
1. Conduct violating the sanctity of the marriage relation	
a. Adultery	49
b. Gross misbehavior inconsistent with the marriage relation	1
c. Husband only: wife's undisclosed pregnancy at marriage by another man	14
d. Husband only: wife's unchaste conduct, though adultery not proved	1
e. Husband only: wife a prostitute before marriage, undisclosed	1
2. Violent or gross conduct menacing life, health or happiness	
a. Cruelty, variously defined	43
b. Attempt on or menacing other spouse's life	16
c. Intolerable indignities	15
3. Conduct showing willful or negligent disregard of marital obligations	
a. Desertion	40
b. Abandonment	
Either spouse	15
Wife only	3
c. Voluntary separation over extended period, either spouse	16
d. Nonsupport	
Either spouse	2
Wife only	21
e. Willful or gross neglect of duty	
Either spouse	8
Wife only	3
4. Incapacity to fulfill marital obligations	
a. Impotency, either spouse	33
b. Drink habit, either spouse	41
c. Narcotic drug habit	
Either spouse	7
Wife only	1
d. Mental incapacity, either spouse	27
e. Temperamental incapacity, either spouse	2
5. Civil "death"	
a. Criminal status, either spouse	42
b. Prolonged absence without word of whereabouts, either spouse	4

TABLE 33 (Continued)

Legal Grounds for Divorce *

Cause	Number of states prescribing each ground for divorce
6. Defective marriage	
a. Incapacity to give valid consent	
Nonage or mental incompetence, either spouse	3
Fraud or force to obtain consent, either spouse	10
b. Legal hindrances	
Existing valid marriage, either spouse	12
Prohibited degree of kinship between parties, either spouse	4
Legally void or voidable marriage, either spouse	2

* Buchanan, Sara Louise, *The Legal Status of Women in the United States of America, as of January 1, 1948, Summary for All States Combined,* Women's Bureau Bulletin No. 157 (Government Printing Office, 1951), pp. 65–69.   Causes for South Carolina have been added to the tabulation in this publication.

may be feeble-minded or insane and not capable of realizing what he is doing; one may be intoxicated; one may be forced at gun point or through fear to enter into a marriage.   Falsification of age by those under the legal age for marriage may be grounds for an annulment.   Fraud may be involved when one person suffers from some condition that prevents full consumation of the marriage, as concealment of known sterility, of venereal disease, or pregnancy by another person.   Annulments are also granted in cases of bigamy or failure to secure a divorce from a previous marriage.

Unlike divorce, which recognizes a legal marriage that is dissolved only from the date of the divorce, an annulment makes a marriage void and in effect declares that it never legally existed.[31]   Annulment therefore does not provide for continuation or settlement of property rights acquired through marriage, for alimony, or for legitimacy or support of children.   Since this situation often works a hardship on an innocent wife or child (who by an annulment becomes illegitimate), some states provide safeguards.   New York, for example, permits alimony to be granted to the wife in an annulment suit and provides for the support of children.   Other states include some of the usual causes for an annulment under causes for divorce and handle the dissolution of the marriage as a divorce, thus safeguarding the interests of the wife and children.

[31] *Ibid.,* pp. 63–64.

Legal separations

Although many people separate informally, the law in 24 states recognizes legal separations.[32]   A legal separation is a partial divorce. Neither husband nor wife may demand the privilege of living with the other; at the same time neither is free to remarry.

Voluntary nature of marriage termination

If the marriage is legal in the first instance, termination comes only at the voluntary action of one or both partners.   No condition makes a divorce mandatory.   Divorce therefore is a legal procedure to be used at the discretion of one spouse to end the marriage.   Although the legal provision is that the innocent or offended spouse shall bring the divorce suit, as a matter of custom the wife usually acts as plaintiff and brings the suit.   This procedure saves her from the ignominy of being officially labeled as a failure in marriage and officially throws the blame on her husband.   It also opens the way for her as the innocent parent to receive custody of her children and support from her husband, as the offending member of the marriage.   Often the legal cause of divorce is only remotely or perhaps not at all related to the real factors in the marital maladjustment.   The real reasons for maladjustment may be subtle ones involving frustrations, immaturity, or personal dissatisfactions not recognized by the law.   Or the reason may be included in the divorce law but be of such a nature that the couple do not wish to reveal it.   Hence the classification of causes of divorce based on court records does not help in an analysis of underlying causes of maladjustment; it simply reveals the legal causes most often selected for the suit of divorce.

In one respect, therefore, divorce is a ritual of conformity to laws by which dissatisfied couples terminate a marriage that has already ended for one or both as a psychological and social relationship.

Number of marital separations

From 1944 through 1948, 400,000 or more divorces occurred each year, reaching a peak in 1946 with 610,000 divorces in one year.   Since 1948 the number has dropped slightly below 400,000 per year.   These figures are estimates for the United States, based on actual known figures

[32] *Ibid.*, p. 65.

for part of the states.[33]   Annulments are negligible.   Reports from 17 states recording 95,521 divorces included only 1,183 annulments, or a number equivalent to 1.2 per cent of the divorces.[34]   Legal separations as distinct from divorces are not reported, and of course there are no general figures for the rate of informal separations that occur per year.

Divorce rates are usually stated in one of three ways: the number of divorces per 1,000 of the total population; as the ratio of divorces granted in a given year to the number of marriages contracted in that year; and as the number of divorces per 1,000 married females 15 years of age and over.   In 1949, the last year for which all three rates are available, divorces were equivalent to 2.7 per 1,000 of the total population of all ages.   Since each divorce involves two persons, twice 2.7, or 5.4, persons per 1,000 of the population were granted divorces in that year.   The divorces of 1949 equalled 25.1 per cent of the marriages of that year. This statement does not mean that the divorces were granted to the same couples who were married in 1949, as many of the couples had been married much longer.   It does mean, however, that for every four marriages that began in that year, one marriage was dissolved.   Divorces granted in 1949 affected 10.8 per cent of married women aged 15 years and over (and a somewhat similar per cent of married men); married women did not include widows or women living in a state of divorce at the time but only legally married women, who constitute the group susceptible to divorce.[35]

The above figures represent the record for one year.   Among the population at any one time are not only the divorced of that year but also the divorced of many years previous.   The remarriage rate for divorced people is very high, however, so that the number living in a state of divorce at any one time is much lower than the total number who at some time have been divorced.   In 1950, among all males aged 14 and

[33] *Vital Statistics, Special Reports, Provisional Marriage and Divorce Statistics, United States: 1948*, Vol. 31, No. 16 (Federal Security Agency, November 4, 1949), p. 229 and *News Release* (Federal Security Agency, Public Health Service, National Office of Statistics, April 23, 1951), p. 2.

[34] *Vital Statistics, Special Reports, Statistics on Divorces and Annulments, Specified States: 1949*, Vol. 36, No. 7 (Federal Security Agency, August 3, 1951), pp. 99–102.

[35] These rates are from *Vital Statistics, Special Reports, Summary of Marriage and Divorce Statistics, United States: 1949*, Vol. 36, No. 2 (Federal Security Agency, June 5, 1951), pp. 14, 24, 25.

over, only 1.6 per cent were divorced; and among females, 2.2 per cent. The number of divorced in 1950 in round numbers was two million.[36] An equal number of people were living separated from their spouses. It is difficult, however, to determine how many of these marriages were genuinely disintegrated as a result of maladjustment, for the classification included not only broken families (many awaiting divorce), but also husbands and wives separated by reasons of employment, service in the armed forces, migration of one spouse while the other remained in another area, and confinement in an institution.

Trends in divorce

The divorce rate in the United States has shown a long-term upward trend, with a temporary decline during the 1930 depression.   In the late 1940's the rates also declined from the abnormally high rate reached in 1946.   In the early 1950's the rates have tended to become stable and a slow upward trend may again be anticipated.   As many functions that formerly held couples together have passed to other agencies, as individualism has increased, as mobility and urbanism have lessened familial and neighborhood pressures, the provocations for divorce have increased and the sentiment against it has weakened.

NEED FOR SOCIAL REDEFINITION OF DIVORCE

The traditional attitude toward divorce as a violation of sacred obligations or moral laws has prevented the development of procedures other than the strictly legal ones to carry husband and wife through the experience.   Society has condemned and ignored; it has not sympathized and helped.   There is no uniform collective attitude toward divorce or the divorced person.   Family and friends do not know what their reaction should be to a divorce; the divorced person does not know how he should feel toward his own action or toward the ex-spouse.   Some of the emotional disturbance attending a divorce is generated by this undefined situation and the conflict between the traditional opinion that marriage is inviolable and the actual fact that many people are breaking their marriages. In the course of time social ideals for marriage and actual behavior will no doubt merge, or at least approach identity.   But at present the divorced

[36] *Current Population Reports, Population Characteristics, Marital Status and Household Characteristics: March, 1950,* Series P-20, No. 33 (Bureau of the Census, February 12, 1951), p. 10.

are running against the main current of opinion or form a small independent stream of their own within the total social body.

In view of the high percentage of marriages that end in divorce during periods of social crisis (war, for instance) and the long-term upward trend in the divorce rate, there is need to redefine divorce as a valid method of ending an unsatisfactory marriage rather than as a catastrophe because of personal failure and broken vows.   Nevertheless, even with such a redefinition, which would relieve many personal conflicts, divorce would continue to be traumatic to husband, wife, and children through the breaking of personal ties and family disorganization.   As a matter of social policy and personal happiness, care in mate selection and efforts at marital adjustment would still be paramount.   But when, as often happens in a mobile urban society, the very basis of the marriage itself prevents adjustment, divorce should be considered as a solution.   Goode, on the basis of his study of Detroit divorced women, suggests that marriage counselors (and others, it might be added) accept the fact that at present "many marriages are formed by incompatible individuals capable of happy marriages to others and the fact that a great proportion of marriages will end in divorce in any event." [37]   He suggests, further, that in many cases the energy and effort of counselors to persuade a couple to continue their marriage in the face of insurmountable obstacles really condemn the couple to prolonged misery and maladjustment.   It would be better, he believes, to advise such couples to divorce before the husband and wife become so emotionally dependent upon each other that the divorce will be a traumatic experience.

With a more accepting and less punitive attitude toward divorce, collective public opinion could exert a greater degree of control than at present when all divorces tend to be condemned or—the other extreme —divorce is regarded as a purely personal matter to be secured at the whim of husband or wife.   New policies could be developed to help people determine the conditions under which divorce would be socially justified and at the same time personally beneficial.   The way would then be opened for the formulation and natural growth of folkways and rituals to aid divorced people in their adjustment, just as, at present, we have accepted ways of helping people to adjust to severe illness or a death in the family.

[37] William J. Goode, "Education for Divorce," *Marriage and Family Living*, 9 (1947), 36.

QUESTIONS

1. What are the marks of marital disintegration? What is the logical end result?

2. At what period of marriage does the divorce rate reach its peak? Relate this period to the length of time required for marital adjustment (preceding chapter).

3. How do the divorced and the nondivorced groups differ? Which differentiating features could be eliminated or controlled in the interest of greater marital stability?

4. Are children a deterrent to divorce?

5. In what ways may religion affect the divorce rate?

6. What do you think is the most difficult aspect of adjustment to divorce?

7. How can you account for the high remarriage rate of people who have been divorced? Why is their rate higher than that of the widowed?

8. Discuss the philosophy and method involved in obtaining a legal decree of divorce. Are they in harmony with present-day attitudes toward divorce?

9. Suggest valid plans for (1) reducing the number of divorces and (2) bringing divorce procedures into line with present attitudes toward the function of marriage.

BIBLIOGRAPHY

Trends in occurrence and in attitudes toward divorce

Barnett, J. H., *Divorce and the American Divorce Novel, 1858–1937, A Study in Literary Reflections of Social Influence,* dissertation in Sociology for the Ph.D. degree (University of Pennsylvania, 1939).

Koster, D. N., *The Theme of Divorce in American Drama, 1871–1939,* dissertation for the Ph.D. degree (University of Pennsylvania, 1942).

Legal aspects of divorce

Alimony, entire issue, *Law and Contemporary Problems,* 6, No. 2 (1939).

Migratory Divorce, entire issue, *Law and Contemporary Problems,* 2, No. 3 (1935).

Ploscowe, Morris, *Sex and the Law* (Prentice-Hall, 1951), chs. 2 and 3.

Adjustment problems

Goode, W. J., "Problems in Postdivorce Adjustment," *American Sociological Review,* 14 (1949), 394–401.

Popenoe, P., "Remarriage of Divorcees to Each Other," *American Sociological Review,* 3 (1938), 695–699.

Waller, Willard, *The Old Love and the New: Divorce and Readjustment* (Liveright, 1930).

18

Parents of Children

Most young people marry with the expectation of having children. The many polls that have been made during the 1930's and 1940's as a rule show a low percentage of high school and college students who do not wish any children after marriage, and a tendency to regard three or four children as the ideal number. For example, the median number of children desired by a group of University of Wisconsin men was 3.28, by women, 3.50; Cornell University men 3.3, women 3.6; and Michigan State College, men and women combined 3.5. Figure 46 shows a typical distribution of the ideal number of children desired. When the number desired is compared with the number of siblings in the subject's own family, the desired family of the future is smaller than the actual family of the past generation. Nevertheless, on the whole young people are family-minded at the time of marriage.[1]

NUMBER OF CHILDREN

Desire for children does not mean that children will necessarily follow. Some men and women are incapable of having children because of sterility; marriage may be followed by widowhood or divorce before children are born, and unless there is a second marriage the person normally remains childless regardless of desire for children; also family conflict,

[1] Reuben Hill, "Campus Values in Mate Selection," *Journal of Home Economics,* 37 (1945), 556, for 600 University of Wisconsin students; Lemo D. Rockwood and Mary E. N. Ford, *Youth, Marriage, and Parenthood* (Wiley, 1945), p. 135 for 190 men and 174 women students at Cornell University; and Judson T. and Mary G. Landis, *Building a Successful Marriage* (Prentice-Hall, 1948), pp. 368–369, for 2,000 students at Michigan State College.

unforeseen poverty, adverse conditions, or illness may cause a couple to change their minds after marriage. Among native white women ever married and with families completed by 1940, one in six remained child-less.[2] The percentage of college graduates who remained childless (24.5) is far above the percentage of recent college students who desire

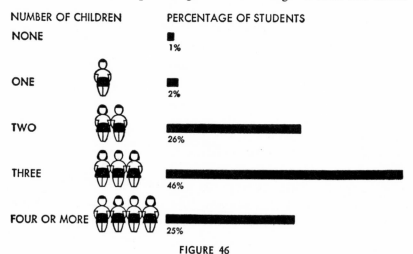

NUMBER OF CHILDREN   PERCENTAGE OF STUDENTS

NONE   1%

ONE   2%

TWO   26%

THREE   46%

FOUR OR MORE   25%

FIGURE 46

Number of Children Desired by 2,000 College Students

The distribution yields a median of 3.5 children. If no students desired more than 4 children, the average number would be 2.9, a figure well above the average of 1.8 children born to white women who were college graduates and who had completed families in 1940. It is not possible to know whether the more recent graduates will have more or fewer children than those from an earlier period. (Source: Judson T. and Mary G. Landis, *Building a Successful Marriage* [Prentice-Hall, 1948], pp. 368–369.)

childlessness (about 1 per cent). One must either assume that interest in children has changed between 1910 and the 1940's or that college graduates are unable to fulfill their desires for children.

Among women of completed fertility in 1940, no educational group has as high a percentage of childlessness or as few children per mother as college graduates (Figure 47). In fact, the lower the educational level the fewer are the childless women and the higher is the number of

[2] *Statistical Abstract of the United States, 1950* (Bureau of the Census, 1950), p. 28; the figure is based on childlessness among native white women ever mar-ried, reporting on children ever born, for women of completed fertility aged 45–54 years in 1940.

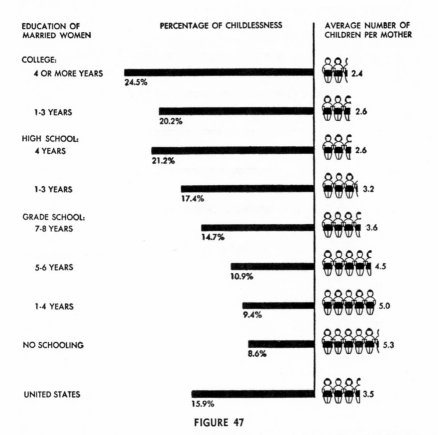

EDUCATION OF MARRIED WOMEN	PERCENTAGE OF CHILDLESSNESS	AVERAGE NUMBER OF CHILDREN PER MOTHER
COLLEGE: 4 OR MORE YEARS	24.5%	2.4
1-3 YEARS	20.2%	2.6
HIGH SCHOOL: 4 YEARS	21.2%	2.6
1-3 YEARS	17.4%	3.2
GRADE SCHOOL: 7-8 YEARS	14.7%	3.6
5-6 YEARS	10.9%	4.5
1-4 YEARS	9.4%	5.0
NO SCHOOLING	8.6%	5.3
UNITED STATES	15.9%	3.5

FIGURE 47

Childlessness and Average Number of Children According to Educational Level of Married Women

High school graduates and college trained women make the poorest showing with reference to children. More than a fifth of the married women at these educational levels do not experience motherhood, and those who do have children average less than three. The chart is based on a special Census study covering native white women of completed fertility in 1940, aged 45–54, who had ever been married and who reported on all children ever born. (Source: *Statistical Abstract of the Untied States, 1950* [Bureau of the Census, 1950], p. 28, and *The American Family, a Factual Background* [Government Printing Office. 1949], p. 48.)

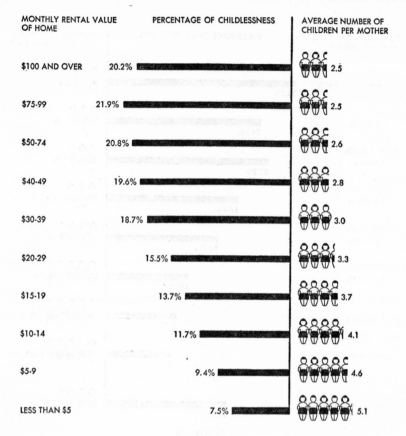

MONTHLY RENTAL VALUE
OF HOME

PERCENTAGE OF CHILDLESSNESS

AVERAGE NUMBER OF
CHILDREN PER MOTHER

$100 AND OVER   20.2%   2.5

$75-99   21.9%   2.5

$50-74   20.8%   2.6

$40-49   19.6%   2.8

$30-39   18.7%   3.0

$20-29   15.5%   3.3

$15-19   13.7%   3.7

$10-14   11.7%   4.1

$5-9   9.4%   4.6

LESS THAN $5   7.5%   5.1

FIGURE 48

Childlessness and Average Number of Children According to Monthly Rental Value of
the Home

The lower the economic status, as judged by rental, the more complete is the
experience of parenthood. The data are limited to native white women of
completed fertility in 1940, aged 45–54, who had ever been married and
who reported on all children ever born. (Source: *Statistical Abstract of the
United States, 1950* [Bureau of the Census, 1950], p. 28, and *The American
Family, a Factual Background* [Government Printing Office, 1949], p. 48.)

children per mother. Since, in general, amount of education is associated
with income, it is not surprising to learn (Figure 48) that degree of childlessness and average number of children vary also with economic status
as measured by monthly rental value of the home. There is less childlessness and a higher average number of children in low-rental than in middle-

rental groups.   The high-rental women, however, do not show any
marked deviation from the middle-rental women.

Several explanations may be suggested for the tendency for low educational and low economic groups to outstrip the more favored groups
in birth rate.   It has been noted in earlier chapters that lower-class families accept children as a natural and normal consequence of marriage,

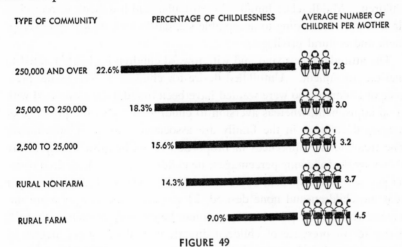

TYPE OF COMMUNITY	PERCENTAGE OF CHILDLESSNESS	AVERAGE NUMBER OF CHILDREN PER MOTHER
250,000 AND OVER	22.6%	2.8
25,000 TO 250,000	18.3%	3.0
2,500 TO 25,000	15.6%	3.2
RURAL NONFARM	14.3%	3.7
RURAL FARM	9.0%	4.5

FIGURE 49

Childlessness and Average Number of Children According to Type of Community

In the city children are an economic handicap.   On farms, although children
are now less useful than when hand labor prevailed, farm families continue to
be large.   Many of the large families are in the low-income rural areas of
the South, from which many migrants are now moving to the Northern and
Western industrial cities.   The chart pertains only to native white women of
completed fertility in 1940, aged 45–54, who had ever been married and who
reported on all children ever born.   (Source: *Statistical Abstract of the
United States, 1950* [Bureau of the Census, 1950], p. 28; and *The American
Family, a Factual Background* [Government Printing Office, 1949], p. 48.)

whereas the middle- or upper-class couple tend to plan the size of their
family.   Low-income groups in cities have a high proportion of families with recent European origin, often affiliated with the Catholic
Church, which values large families.   Also, many of these same families
came from rural areas and, as with American rural families, accept
children as the natural result of marriage.   It is true, too, that as education increases, the range of interests broadens and the desire for children
often competes with other interests or with a desired standard of living.

Childlessness and average number of children vary also with size of community (Figure 49). The percentage of childlessness in large cities is two and one half times that of farming communities and the average number of children is one third less. The urban-rural differences are in part related to the same factors that create the differences between educational and economic levels, and in part to the inhospitality of cities to children. Middle-class families in particular find it difficult to rear children in cities according to acceptable standards for personality development and cultural privileges.

The attitude of husband and wife toward children is closely related to marital adjustment. Unfulfilled desire for children as well as the presence of children who were wanted have been found to be associated with good adjustment, whereas aversion to children and also the presence of unwanted children in the family are associated with poor adjustment. The tremendous differences in proportion of well-adjusted couples are shown by the following percentages: no children but couple desired them, 64 per cent well adjusted; one or two children who were desired, 47 per cent; no children and none desired, 21 per cent; and one or more unwanted children 11 per cent.[3] It cannot be claimed, of course, that the desire for or presence of children directly caused the stated degree of adjustment. It is probable that people who desire children have a conception of the family as a stable interacting group, whereas those who do not desire children may be highly individualistic or too immature to desire parenthood—both characteristics that would make good marital adjustment difficult.

MARITAL ADJUSTMENT AND CHILDREN

Children begin to affect marital adjustment long before they are born. With the rational attitude now held by many toward children as a matter of personal choice of the parents, each couple may, if they wish, decide in advance how many children they will have and at what intervals. Inability to follow the plan then becomes a factor in adjustment, since more or fewer children than desired or children born at the wrong intervals are likely to disturb other parts of the couple's plan for marriage. Adjustment to disturbance of the plan may be as acute a problem as adjustment

[3] E. W. Burgess and L. S. Cottrell, *Predicting Success or Failure in Marriage* (Prentice-Hall, 1939), p. 414.

to the baby itself, and indeed may affect the attitudes of the parents toward the child.

Planning of families

It has already been stated that college students desire three to four children.   Cornell University students in 1940–1941 preferred not to have a child during the first year of marriage, and fully a third wished to wait until the third, fourth, or fifth year (Figure 50.)   Such a waiting period would require the use of contraceptives or limited intercourse,

YEAR OF MARRIAGE

FIGURE 50

Time Interval Desired between Marriage and Birth of First Child, Cornell University Students

The figure shows the percentage distribution of preferred year for birth of first child.   More men (17.4 per cent) than women (4.0 per cent) wanted a child during the first year of marriage.   More Catholics (22.9 per cent) than Jews or Protestants (9.7 per cent) favored the first year.   More town-reared (31.8 per cent) than farm-reared (17.3 per cent) preferred to wait until the third year or longer before having the first child.   Almost twice as many engaged persons (47.8 per cent) as those not engaged (27.2 per cent) specified the third year or later.   Students justified the delay by saying they would need a year or more to become adjusted; they also wished to continue their good times for a while after marriage before settling down to the responsibilities of parenthood.   (Source: Lemo D. Rockwood and Mary E. N. Ford, *Youth, Marriage and Parenthood* [Wiley, 1945], p. 634.)

since normally the first child arrives approximately 13 months after marriage and subsequent children at intervals of 20 to 26 months.[4]

The pros and cons of the first year versus a later year for the first baby are interestingly stated in a popular article by Dr. David R. Mace, Visiting Professor of Human Relations at Drew University.[5]   The com-

[4] Regina Stix and Frank W. Notestein, *Controlled Fertility* (Williams and Wilkins, 1940); H. T. Christensen, "The Time-Interval between Marriage of Parents and the Birth of their First Child in Utah County, Utah," *American Journal of Sociology,* 44 (1939), 518–525.

[5] "Should You Have a Baby the First Year?" *Woman's Home Companion,* 76 (December, 1949), 38, 93.

mon arguments for postponing the first baby are given as follows by Dr. Mace, with his criticisms of them, for he favors the first baby during the first year of marriage:

1. Preparation of a "good home" for the child. Dr. Mace points out that most homes today are far more comfortable than homes in the past and that this argument places too much emphasis on material comforts that after all are not essential.

2. Emotional adjustment of husband and wife. Unless the couple have rushed into marriage, part of this adjustment has occurred during courtship. Completion of the adjustment and the pleasure of cooperative activity is enhanced rather than hindered by the joint production of a child. Moreover, if the couple adjust to pair-marriage alone and habits become fixed, inclusion of a baby in the family becomes difficult. Better to shape the family to children in the first instance, Dr. Mace contends.

3. Sexual adjustment of husband and wife. The importance of sexual adjustment is not underestimated, but Dr. Mace raises the question whether pregnancy interferes with the working out of good adjustment. Contraceptives and fear of pregnancy may delay adjustment, whereas full acceptance of the implications of marriage and intercourse—willingness to have a baby—may set the stage for more rapid and complete adjustment.

A study of 212 married couples at Michigan State College throws some light on the relation of the first pregnancy to sexual adjustment.[6] Sixty-three per cent of the pregnancies occurred before the end of the first year of marriage, 23 per cent in the second or third year, and 14 per cent later. Fifty-eight per cent of husbands and wives reported that the pregnancy had had no effect upon their sexual adjustment; for the most part these couples had a good adjustment prior to pregnancy. Seventeen per cent of the wives and 19 per cent of the husbands believed the pregnancy had improved adjustment; most of these people had had poor adjustment prior to pregnancy. Twenty-five per cent of the wives and 23 per cent of the husbands felt that the effect of pregnancy had been unfavorable; in these cases adjustment had been good before the pregnancy, but had decreased largely because of the fatigue of the wife from care of the baby or be-

[6] Judson T. Landis, Thomas Poffenberger, and Shirley Poffenberger, "The Effects of First Pregnancy upon the Sexual Adjustment of 212 Couples," *American Sociological Review*, 15 (1950), 766–772.

cause she felt less desire than at an earlier period.   In approximately three fourths of the cases, therefore, sexual adjustment either was not disturbed or was improved by the first pregnancy.

When a couple have rigid ideas as to spacing the births of children and fail to accomplish their purpose, a general readjustment of plans and attitudes often is in order.   Spacing usually is secured by the use of contraceptive devices, in the effectiveness of which young married couples sometimes place inordinate faith.   Actually, failure of contraceptives sometimes is very great.   Among the 212 Michigan couples, 38 per cent had tried but failed to avoid pregnancy by contraceptive methods.   Physicians estimate that birth-control methods, intelligently applied, are effective in about 85 per cent of the cases.[7]   When husband and wife fail to control conception, they face two problems: first, they must accept the prospect of parenthood before they are ready for it; and, second, they must change other plans to which they had given priority over the birth of the child.   The situation is often frustrating, with the arousal of resentment and hostility.   The resentment may be immediately released either in general ill-temper or in accusations against each other as the cause of the failure.   Sometimes the hostility is directed against the child, even before birth; sometimes abortion is attempted or accomplished. In other cases either the husband or the wife does not feel free to express hostility openly and represses it; nevertheless, it is very likely to show itself later, either by subtle rejection of the child, animosity toward the spouse, or overindulgence of the child in an unrecognized attempt to compensate for the repressed rejection.   Fortunately, the hostility often is short-lived and is dissipated before the birth of the child.   In these cases the husband and wife are sufficiently flexible to rearrange their plans to include the child as a functioning member of the family.   Prolonged hostility probably is more likely to occur when husband and wife do not wish children at all; and temporary resentment when children are wanted but at a later date, so that rearrangement of plans is necessary but not the overcoming of a general aversion to children.

Change in husband-wife relationship

With pregnancy, and more especially after the birth of the child, both husband and wife have dual familial roles; to the husband role is added

---

[7] Morris Fishbein and Ernest W. Burgess, editors, *Successful Marriage* (Doubleday, 1948), p. 89, statement by Robert L. Dickinson, M.D.

the father role, and to the wife role is added the mother role.   The marital roles and the parental roles may be difficult to adjust; husband and wife whose roles were harmoniously coordinated before pregnancy may find their relationship seriously disturbed.

Often during the early period of marriage the role of the young wife resembles that of the "companion" as described in Chapter 16—the wife whose dominant activity is to look well and accompany her husband on pleasurable jaunts.   With the birth of a baby the wife begins to shift to the mother role, which calls for a corresponding change in the role of the husband.   The actual changes made may involve such things as the way evenings and week ends are spent, the wife being no longer free to accompany her husband to club, movie, or dance in the evening or to dash off at short notice on a week-end trip.   Sometimes both husband and wife remain home and develop family activities; sometimes the husband spends certain evenings away from home with men friends, and on other evenings cares for the baby while his wife meets her women friends. Occasionally the husband attempts to substitute some woman friend for his wife as a companion in recreation; but this violates the middle-class mores and may lead to serious conflict between husband and wife.

When the wife has followed the partnership role,[8] as developed by Kirkpatrick and advocated by many women interested in equality of women with men,[9] children are fitted into the marital pattern with still greater difficulty.   The wife who has trained herself for a definite business or profession receives much of her feeling of worth and self-esteem from following her chosen occupation.   Accustomed to participating in the stimulating rush of vocational activity, where she pits her abilities against those of competitors or cooperators, she feels let down when her social world is restricted to the home and her activities and mental stimulation to the physical demands and limited capacities of a small child.   The dilemma of the wife who may choose between the feminine and the equalitarian role has already been discussed in Chapter 16.   With a baby the dilemma becomes more acute, for there is a strong social feeling that the mother should herself care for her child.   In the middle-class neighborhood whispered comment of an unfavorable nature is directed toward the young mother who turns the care of her child over to a relative or maid while she continues to work.   The child may be well

[8] See pages 447–449.
[9] See page 442.

cared for, but in the folk belief there is an almost superstitious faith in the value of personal ministrations of the mother.   Often the mother herself shares this belief, while at the same time she continues to regard herself as an individual, entitled to the freedom of the childless wife.   Thus she may feel thwarted if she remains at home to care for her child, or guilty if she arranges otherwise for care and continues her outside activities.

The husband in the partnership marriage must also make adjustments. For one thing, if his wife stops working, their joint income may be cut in half.   The entire burden of support of the family is suddenly thrown upon him, at a time when medical care and the addition of a third member greatly increase expenses.   If the standard of living has been based upon the joint income, it is often necessary to reduce it—to sell the car, move to a less expensive apartment, or postpone buying a television set. The husband may value his fatherhood more than material assets and regard the exchange of income for a baby as worth while.   If he does not, he may resent the baby or the necessity of his wife's not working.

The husband may also find it difficult to adjust himself to the change in his wife's interests.   Instead of talking about the problems and successes of her job she now relates the latest achievements of the baby. If she is trying to carry on her job after the birth of the baby, she may be harassed and overburdened with the two tasks and have little time or attention for him.

As Dr. Mace pointed out in discussing the merits of having the first baby soon after marriage, the longer the delay, the more firmly fixed in pair-family life the husband and wife become.   Increasing difficulty is experienced in breaking up the habits and interests based upon interaction between two adults in order to meet the demands of a helpless child.

Fortunately, there are many compensating factors to these difficulties when they arise.   For one thing, all the evidence that we have indicates a great interest in parenthood and children, even among college women who are the ones most likely to suffer from conflicting ideas of roles.   The baby is anticipated with pleasure as a rounding out of the marriage rather than as an intrusion into a perfect relationship.   The couple feel pride that they have produced a new life.   They are regarded with new respect by their parents and with envy by their unmarried or childless friends.   As one 21-year-old girl said wistfully, "Just think of it!   All

my old schoolmates are having babies and I am not even married."
There is therefore a great deal of ego satisfaction in the birth of a child.

The baby also provides a new source of emotional satisfaction. The
helplessness of the baby calls out tenderness upon the part of the parents,
and as the child responds to their care with smiles and cuddling, they
feel repaid for the demands that child care makes upon them. Since the
baby is a joint product, their own feeling of attachment to and identification with each other usually increases.

PARENT-CHILD ADJUSTMENT

The conception of the approved parental role is now in the process of
change. The idea that parents should teach their children explicit obedience to rules laid down by the parents is yielding to the idea that each
child has a unique personality that he should be allowed to develop with
some freedom. It is also conceded that under present conditions of mobility and complex urban conditions rules cannot be made that will fit
all situations and last through a lifetime; therefore children should be
helped to become mature and well adjusted; they should be taught to
examine the situations in which they find themselves and make rational
decisions. Under the newer conceptions the functions of parents are
much more difficult to discharge than when parents assumed an authoritarian position and laid down rigid rules for their children to follow. The
parents must understand both the world in which they live and at least
the elements of child psychology; they must themselves be well organized
personally.

As is true in any period of shifting values, the old holds over while
the new is developing. Evelyn Duvall, in exploring current conceptions
of motherhood, has termed the old conception the traditional; the new,
the developmental.[10]

Traditional conception of motherhood

Basing her analysis upon a study of 433 mothers in Chicago, Duvall
found that certain mothers have a rather rigid disciplinary conception
of their role. The traditional "good mother" does the following things:

[10] Evelyn Millis Duvall, "Conceptions of Parenthood," *American Journal of
Sociology*, 52 (1946), 193–203.

1. "Keeps house." (Washes, cooks, cleans, mends, sews, manages household.)

2. "Takes care of child physically." (Keeps child healthy; guards child's safety; feeds, clothes and bathes child; sees that child rests.)

3. "Trains child to regularity." (Establishes regular habits, provides schedule, sees to regular hours for important functions.)

4. "Disciplines." (Corrects child, reprimands, punishes, scolds, demands obedience, rewards good behavior, is firm, is consistent, keeps promises.)

5. "Makes the child good." (Teaches obedience, instructs in morals, builds character, prays for, sees to religious education.)

Since roles develop in interaction, the good mother must be matched by a good child. Under the traditional conception, mothers said that good children had the following characteristics:

1. "Keeps clean and neat." (Is orderly, is clean, keeps self neat.)

2. "Obeys and respects adults." (Minds parents, no back talk, respects adults.)

3. "Pleases adults." (Has good character traits, is honest, truthful, polite, kind, fair, courteous at all times.)

4. "Respects property." (Takes care of his things, is not destructive, hangs up his clothes.)

5. "Is religious." (Goes to Sunday School, loves God, prays, follows Jesus.)

6. "Works well." (Studies, goes to school, is reliable, takes responsibilities, is dependable in his work.)

7. "Fits into the family program." (Has an interest in his home, does his share, runs errands willingly, helps out at home.)

The traditional mothers were most frequently found among white mothers in the lower social classes, Negroes of all classes,[11] and experienced mothers (defined as those whose first children were over five years of age). Middle- and upper-class mothers and those with children under five years of age tended to reject the traditional roles for themselves and their children.

[11] Middle- and upper-class Negroes often impose strict discipline upon their children in their desire to escape from the easy-going ways of the lower class.

Developmental conception of motherhood

The "good mother" in Duvall's study according to the developmental conception has the following relationship to her children:

1. "Trains for self-reliance and citizenship." (Trains for self-help, encourages independence, teaches how to be a good citizen, how to adjust to life, teaches concentration.)

2. "Sees to emotional well-being." (Keeps child happy and contented, makes a happy home, makes child welcome, helps child feel secure, helps child overcome fears.)

3. "Helps child develop socially." (Provides toys and companions, plays with child, supervises child's play.)

4. "Provides for child's mental growth." (Gives educational opportunities, provides stimulation to learn, reads to child, tells stories, guides reading, sends child to school.)

5. "Guides with understanding." (Sees child's point of view, gears life to child's level, answers questions freely and frankly, gives child freedom to grow, interprets, offers positive suggestions.)

6. "Relates self lovingly to child." (Shows love and affection, enjoys child, spends time with child, shares with child, is interested in what child does and tells, listens.)

7. "Is a calm, cheerful, growing person one's self." (Has more outside interests, is calm and gentle, has a sense of humor, laughs, smiles, gets enough recreation.)

The good child, in the developmental conception, is described as follows by mothers with this point of view:

1. "Is healthy and well." (Eats and sleeps well, grows a good body, has good habits.)

2. "Shares and co-operates with others." (Gets along with people, likes others, is developing socially, tries to help, plays with other children.)

3. "Is happy and contented." (Keeps in good humor, is a cheerful child, is happy, is emotionally well adjusted.)

4. "Loves and confides in parents." (Responds with affection, loves his parents, has confidence in his parents, trusts and confides in them.)

5. "Is eager to learn." (Shows initiative, asks questions, accepts help, expresses himself, likes to learn.)

6. "Grows as a person."   (Progresses in his ability to handle himself and different situations, enjoys growing up.)

Developmental mothers and children clustered in the upper social classes and were more frequently found among white than Negro mothers in the group studied.   Mothers of young children also more frequently were developmental in attitude than those with children over five years of age.

The developmental conception is an interesting corollary of the emphasis of child psychologists and preschool teachers upon the individuality of children and the need to give them loving guidance in personality development.[12]   The conception is not universally held, however.   It is most common among groups whose educational background has given them access to newer findings relating to child psychology and who have freedom for participation in child-study courses.   Lower-class mothers follow the old patterns that have come down from the past rather than experiment with new patterns that impose greater responsibility upon them.

The change in attitude with age of children is interpreted by Duvall to mean that in all probability when children leave the home and make wider contacts in the community they begin to escape from parental influence.   In their anxiety about their children's behavior parents then begin to impose the more rigid and authoritarian controls of the past and tend to give up the developmental methods with their greater permissiveness of irregular behavior.

The father

Few studies have been made and little has been written about the role of the father.   The mother's role is initially rooted in her inescapable biological relationship to her baby.   The father's role is more completely social in nature.   The traditional conception of parenthood placed the daily care of the child in the hands of the mother; the father fulfilled his role by supporting his family and providing overall protection and authority.   Urban conditions have removed many of the father's earlier functions and placed them in the hands of public or social agencies.   The growing status of the mother and her frequent contributions to income

[12] For additional discussion of parent-child relationships see Chapter 11 and portions of Chapters 5, 6, and 7 dealing with children in different social classes.

have further robbed the father role of unique significance.   Finally, the long hours away from home, especially of many suburban fathers, have placed added responsibility upon the mother.   The phrases "absentee father" and "matricentric suburban family" have been coined to point up the fragile relationship of the father to his children.   The implications are that the father has tended to withdraw from active interaction in the family but that so far as he functions it is still in an authoritarian role.

The concept of personality development for mature psychological adulthood as the objective of child training is not compatible with absenteeism. The need of both boys and girls for an adult male model has been emphasized by child psychologists; without such a model it is all but impossible for either boy or girl to develop an adequate conception of the husband and father roles.   The boy does not know what is expected of him; the girl does not know the masculine role to which she must adjust her own role.   The rearing of boys almost exclusively by women (the mother and female school teachers) has been attacked repeatedly, and men of today are accused of being both feminine and immature as a result of too exclusive an association with their mothers.[13]

The authoritarian paternal role is incompatible with the role played by the mother who is interested in the personality development of her children.   When the authoritarian role functioned adequately in the family, the mother as well as the children accepted the father in this capacity.   The mother held the father up to the children as the final authority and disciplinarian, and she attempted to carry out his expectations with reference to the children.   In many lower-class and ethnic families this relationship still holds; but when the middle-class mother, after studying child psychology in college or in child-study groups, adopts a nonauthoritarian philosophy and techniques of child training that the father does not have, parental unity is threatened.   The parents may differ openly regarding the treatment of the baby and older children; or the father may withdraw from family interaction, justifying his passive attitude by the statement that, after all, the children are "in the mother's department."

To discourage absenteeism and reduce potential conflict between husband and wife, some agencies that typically sponsor mother study groups have added father study groups or groups open to both parents.

[13] See page 269 for an elaboration of this point and references.

THE INADEQUATE PARENT

Immaturity and neuroticism, which have been discussed with reference to marital adjustment, also affect the relation of parent to child.   The files of child-guidance clinics, family-welfare agencies, child-placing organizations, and other agencies dealing with children are filled with records in which the basic family difficulty is the immature or unstable parent.   In other families in which the situation has not become serious enough to warrant professional treatment, the same difficulties arise in milder form. Since the mother is usually more closely associated with the child than the father, it is usually more serious for the child when the mother is not well adjusted.

In many cases the mother's inability to play an adult maternal role goes back to her own childhood, to the failure of her parents to love her enough, give her security, or provide her with an adequate model of motherhood.   The following brief summaries of actual cases indicate the relation between the mother's childhood treatment and her attitude toward her children.[14]

Mrs. H., the mother of four children, rejected them.   She insisted upon working, although the father's income was sufficient for their needs.   Responsibility for preparing lunch for the younger children and supervising their behavior was placed upon Walter, the oldest boy, aged twelve.   If the children misbehaved, the mother punished Walter.   The mother threatened repeatedly to leave home.   She had violent temper tantrums, during which she threw dishes, and beat Walter.   Although she treated all the children as though they were unwanted, most of her animosity was directed against the oldest boy.   The father was interested in his children and tried to compensate for their mother's mistreatment.   However, he feared to assert himself against his wife as he thought she might leave, taking the children with her.   He also feared the wrath of his wife when it was directed against himself.   The mother came from a home in which her parents were divorced and her mother had not wanted her.   She retained a bitter feeling against her mother and blamed her for not providing her with treatment for a disfiguring eye defect. As a result of his treatment at home, Walter openly said his mother did not love him.   He was unable to make friends among other boys and his behavior was unpredictable.   He was aggressive toward other boys and courted their aggressions, then cried when they turned upon him.   Tests and interviews showed that he was emotionally immature and hostile.   His sex identification was poor and he was not sure whether he wanted to be a boy or a girl (perhaps the result of his father's attempts to be both mother and

[14] Unpublished records.

father to his children). He was afraid his mother would leave his father and that he would have to go with the mother. His attacks on other boys were interpreted as attempts to prove that he did not care whether or not anyone liked him, while underneath he was very insecure and lonely.

Mrs. W. was reared in a family that was very formal and rigid. Her parents displayed little warmth toward each other or toward her. Her closest confidant was a boy cousin some years older than herself. In adolescence her steady boy friend was a plodding country boy as conventional and unromantic as her parents. She broke her relationship with him to marry, after short acquaintance, a young man with a more gay temperament. Her husband did not support the family regularly and rather openly carried on illicit affairs with other women, even during the times when she was in the hospital following childbirth. While her two children were very young, Mrs. W. divorced her husband. She readily found work for she was a steady and reliable worker and with the aid of a social agency placed her children in a foster family, where she regularly paid for their care. In the area of work and financial responsibility, Mrs. W. was stable and mature. But her personal relationship to her children reflected the failure of her parental home to give her adequate concepts of the mother role. Her visits with her children were very emotional; she brought them many presents, ignored the foster parents, turned the children's routine upside down, and cried over the children. The children, consequently were in a state of turmoil after each visit. Mrs. W. was especially upset when she learned that the children were addressing the foster mother as "Mom." She felt that she was being superseded; at the same time she refused to consider accepting Aid to Dependent Children and remaining at home with them. It finally became necessary to place the children in an institution where their relationship with the adults was less personal; Mrs. W. then did not feel that her role was threatened. Although Mrs. W. was emotionally attached to her children and financially responsible for them, she was not able to accept a maternal role. She could not allow them to be dependent upon her, but at the same time she needed them emotionally and was unable to permit them to become dependent upon the foster mother.

The basis of much parental immaturity lies in poor relationships of the parents, as children, with their parents. An unfortunate consequence is that they usually are unable to pass on to their children adequate concepts of parenthood and mature personalities. The process is repeated generation after generation.

PARENTHOOD IN THE DIVORCED FAMILY

When a married couple with children are divorced, the relationship of parents to children changes drastically.[15]

Number of children of divorced parents

Data collected for the period 1922–1932 and again for 1948 show that approximately two fifths of all divorces involve children, with the proportion of divorces affecting children rising from 38 to 42 per cent from the 1920's to 1948.[16] The number of children per divorce with children was 1.8 under age 18 in 1922–1932 and 1.8 under age 21 in 1948. In the latter year, 313,000 children under the age of 21 had their family life disturbed by the divorce of their parents.[17] The total number of children of divorced parents is much larger, of course, since the number accumulates from year to year. In 1940, Davis estimated that 1,533,000 children under age 18 had divorced parents.[18] Many of these children were very young when their parents were divorced; in 1948, 28 per cent of children of divorce had parents who were married between five and nine years.

Loss of parental roles

When both parents are at home, they share in responsibilities for the children and tend to work out coordinated mother and father roles. With divorce, the coordination of roles is lost. Usually the children are placed in the custody of the "innocent party" by the trial judge. Since the wife usually brings the suit for divorce, she therefore is assumed to be the "innocent" party and obtains custody of the children. When the husband brings the suit and charges his wife with misconduct or a violation of the marriage contract, the children may be awarded to him. In occasional cases the children are awarded to a third party. Usually all the children in the family are kept together. The customary arrangement, however, is for the mother to have the custody of the children, with the

[15] For a general discussion of divorce, see Chapter 17.

[16] Kingsley Davis, "Sociological and Statistical Analysis," *Law and Contemporary Problems*, 10 (1944), 713; Paul H. Jacobson, "Differentials in Divorce by Duration of Marriage and Size of Family," *American Sociological Review*, 15 (1950), 239.

[17] Annulments, which account for only a small percentage of marriage dissolutions, are included in this figure.

[18] Davis, *op. cit.*, p. 714.

father having certain privileges of visiting them or having them live with him or visit him.   One arrangement is for the children to live with the mother during the school year, spending vacations with the father. Usually the father is required by the court to pay a certain amount for the support of the children and sometimes alimony to his former wife. Therefore in daily life during all or the greater part of the year, the children have daily association with their mother, whereas their contacts with the father become intermittent, although he continues to play one part of his traditional role—that of contributing to the support of the children.   By this arrangement the child experiences discontinuity of family life, a situation that is both criticized and defended by social workers and judges.   One judge lists the advantages as follows: [19]

1. The child retains contacts with both parents and has the love and advice of both; both are in a position to protect the child's future welfare.

2. The child has the opportunity to experience two homes; this arrangement is especially advantageous in states in which at a certain age the child may choose the parent with whom he will thereafter live.

3. The father is more willing to help his children if he knows them.

Others concerned with the welfare of children have stated the disadvantages as follows:

1. If the child is shifted about, he must adjust to two domestic situations and perhaps to two stepparents, if both own parents have remarried; there is great risk of discontinuity of emotional and intellectual development.

2. The child becomes a means of comunication between the divorced parents.   Each may express his resentment toward the other through his treatment of the child, remarks about the other parent, and so on; the child not only carries the comments back and forth but is affected by them.[20]

3. The child may be used by one parent to punish the other.   He may be urged to make exorbitant demands when he visits the other for toys, clothing, and the like; if the parent refuses the child may feel unloved by the parent.

4. As a result, the child may be torn in his loyalties between the parents: he may feel rejected by both; or he may detach himself from loyalty

[19] Carl A. Weinman, "The Trial Judge Awards Custody in Children of Divorced Parents," *Law and Contemporary Problems*, 10 (1944), 726.

[20] Davis, *op. cit.*, p. 700, 708, for points 1 and 2.

to either and play one off against the other. Although these situations may exist in the family with both parents present, they are more likely to arise in the divorced family.[21]

Even when the parent with whom the child is staying does not attempt to undermine the relationship to the other parent, the situation presents problems. Each child is in need of both a mother figure and a father figure to serve as models for emotional and social development. During the time when the mother has the children she must attempt to be both mother and father; when the children are with their father he must attempt the dual role. This duality is difficult at any time and especially so when it is played only at intervals and when the parent of the opposite sex has recently been playing both roles. For instance, the mother in her behavior toward the children, her comments, and her admiration of certain men may hold up one masculine role to the children, which is sadly shattered when they visit their father who presents an entirely different masculine type. If the mother has remarried, she has often chosen a second husband somewhat in contrast to the first; the children may then have serious conflicts in their attempts to accept both the stepfather and the father as part of their array of adult models. The reverse situation is true when the father attempts to be both father and mother or when he presents to the children a stepmother, who may be markedly different in personality from their own mother.

The mother often has a difficult time in that the support received from the father may not be sufficient for expenses or she may have refused alimony for herself. She then faces the necessity of working and providing substitute care for her children. If part of the original marital maladjustment was the mother's dislike of the domestic role, she may be happier and make a better adjustment to her children than before the divorce. But if the employment is disliked or constitutes a severe physical strain, resentment against her ex-husband may grow and be transmitted to the children.

The father may also face a financial problem, especially if he wishes to remarry and must support two households. He may become increasingly bitter against his first wife and perhaps against his children. Many fathers also suffer from their inability to maintain a close relationship with their children. Accounts by fathers give the hopeful attitude

[21] James S. Plant, "The Psychiatrist Views Children of Divorced Parents," *Law and Contemporary Problems*, 10 (1944), 815, for points 3 and 4.

with which they at first agreed to the mother's having custody of the children.   Each hoped and planned to play a father role in his week-end and vacation visits and to remain an influence in the development of his children.   But he found that the children's lives soon became organized around their mother, school life, and friends; the father was an outsider. His children were ill at ease with him, reluctant to give up social plans at home for the legally allowed visits, and over longer visits became homesick for their mothers and friends.   The harder the father tried to please his children, the wider the rift became; moreover, the mother often resented the gifts or special events provided by the father.   The children were momentarily impressed by the break in their routine and, the mother felt, unappreciative of the daily care that she provided.   A father who tried to discipline his children found that they were rebellious and no longer accepted him as a person in authority.   Even the most solicitous father found himself an outcast.[22]

THE STEPPARENT

The stepparent plays a difficult parental role.   We do not know how many men and women are stepparents, but it is a small proportion of all parents.   Thirteen per cent of married people have been married more than once; the percentage of married people who are stepparents would therefore be less than 13 per cent since some of the remarriages would not involve children.   Stepparent situations have been the subject of fairy tales and fiction, and they appear in the case reports of psychiatric clinics; but no thorough systematic study has yet appeared.[23]   Moreover, what little has been written tends to emphasize the predicament of the stepchild rather than the stepparent.   The present discussion therefore suggests some of the probable complications but is in no sense conclusive.

Although formally a man or woman becomes a stepparent with marriage to a spouse having children from a previous marriage, functionally the role is developed through interaction between husband and wife and between parents and children.

In the case of a first marriage on both sides, custom grants the couple

[22] Anonymous, "What I Want My Kids to Know," *Saturday Evening Post*, 222, (June 24, 1950), 25, 110–111.

[23] Although Professor William C. Smith of Linfield College has been collecting data on stepparents and stepchildren for a number of years, his publications on the subject are limited to a few articles.

an interlude of romance and privacy.   The honeymoon and a home of their own are part of the mores and support the idea that newly married people are entitled to establish their married life without interference from others.   But these ideas are not shared by children.   If their father or mother, newly married, goes honeymooning, sends the children to boarding school, or substitutes social affairs with the new spouse for earlier family activities, the children interpret the situation as neglect.   They feel left out, unloved, rejected; they withdraw or rebel, as their temperament may dictate.   The twice-married husband or wife must continue to be a parent at the same time that he or she is groom or bride.   The new spouse must immediately be willing and able to include the children in their pair relationship.   Thus, the relationship established between husband and wife affects the stepparent role.

The stepparent, however, cannot impose himself upon the child without the child's consent.   No matter how zealous and eager to perform his functions, he cannot do so unless he is accepted as a parent by the child.   Several conditions discussed below may cause the child to reject, rather than accept, the stepparent.

The age of the child when the stepparent comes into the family is a factor.   Very young children who do not remember their own parent tend to look upon the stepparent with the same confidence and love that they would have felt toward the natural parent.   Older children have more difficulty, since they often must break the bond of loyalty to the natural parent before accepting the stepparent.

When the remarriage follows the death of husband or wife, the image of the dead member may linger in the minds of both the surviving spouse and the child.   The spouse may expect the new mate to be a duplication of the past mate.   The child, however, may resent the stepparent and regard him as a usurper.   This attitude was displayed by the little girl of eight whose father had been dead for two years.   Her mother began to receive calls from a suitor who eventually proposed.   The girl, on each occasion when the man came to see her mother, brought out her father's picture, showed it to him and said, "See, this is my daddy."   The mother, partly swayed by the child's attitude, declined the proposal.   Had she married, it seems probable that the child would not have accepted the new husband as a father.

If there has been a divorce and both parents are still living, the child may find it impossible to accept the stepparent even as a friend, provided he sees and remains attached to his own parent.   The situation becomes still more confusing when both divorced parents have remarried and the child finds four parents competing for his love and loyalty.   When half-siblings and stepsiblings are added to the family, the child may be still more uncertain of his relationship to the various members of the family. The stepparent may easily differentiate between his own and his step-children, if he sees in the stepchild a rival for the spouse's affection.   The following account, written from the point of view of one of the children, is illustrative.

Mr. S. was left a widower with three young children.   When Alice was 9, Bob 7, and Jean 3 he married a woman who had been divorced and who brought with her into the family a son, John, aged 14, and a daughter, Betty, aged 7.   The S. children found their stepmother very different from their own mother—she seemed less motherly to them and they missed the long walks with their mother, the singing around the piano, and the play-time that she provided with their father.   A barrier seemed to come between them and their father, who suddenly had no time for them.   Mrs. S. was interested in social activities and often took her husband off to evening parties.   Only on week ends did the old spirit of family life come alive; then the family worked in the yard or did minor rebuilding jobs.   The stepmother tried to promote good relationships among the children by inviting in friends and having birth-day parties for all.   Friction between the S. children and their stepmother centered in her daughter, Betty.   Mrs. S. favored her own daughter, con-fided in her, babied her when sick, and shielded her from punishment.   The children thus became jealous of Betty.   At the same time, they encouraged her to get favors for them from her mother—permission to go to a movie or extra candy.   They were also envious of the gifts that Betty received from her father, whom she visited four times a year.   Betty thus had a radio, dolls, and clothes that the other children did not have.   Although at first Mr. S. and his second wife seemed happy together, quarrels spread from children to parents and after ten years they were divorced.[24]

The child may also reject the stepparent who seems to steal the love of his own parent.   The following description, written by the daughter, shows the complete exclusion of the stepfather from the girl's life.

My parents were divorced when I was two and thereafter I seldom saw my father.   I never felt any love for him and had not established any emo-tional ties to him.   For eight years mother and I lived alone.   Then mother remarried.   My stepfather seemed always like a complete stranger to me and sort of an intruder whom I disliked.   As the years passed I became in-different toward him and never considered him really part of my family.

[24] Unpublished record.

Family to me was just mother. There were a lot of factors that helped prevent our becoming adjusted. My stepfather was a forty-year-old bachelor who had lived alone; it was hard for him to adjust to a family way of life. He had been brought up in a European family where the man was the complete authority in the home. He tried to establish some authority in our home but my reaction was negative. He resented my taking orders only from my mother, and I resented his trying to become head of the household, since I had always had to abide only by my mother's wishes. There is little that we can do as a family; my parents go out a lot to avoid the bickering between me and my stepfather.[25]

UNMARRIED PARENTS

Although the social stigma placed upon the unmarried mother and her illegitimate child has softened in comparison with earlier attitudes, society is far from approving unwed parents. Many women who find themselves pregnant although unmarried resort to illegal abortions; others marry before the birth of the child, thus legitimatizing the child. It is not known how frequent these two alternatives to bearing an illegitimate child are.

Frequency of illegitimacy

Since 1944 more than 100,000 illegitimate babies have been born each year; in 1947, the estimated number was 131,900. Among live births, 3.7 per cent were illegitimate, with the percentage being much lower (1.8) for whites than for nonwhites (17.1 per cent). This is the record for one year. In the ten-year period 1938–1947, an estimated 657,200 illegitimate babies were born. Since in the ten-year period some mothers would have given birth to more illegitimate babies than one, the number of unmarried mothers involved is less than this figure. In 1947, unmarried mothers equalled only 1.2 per cent of unmarried women between the ages of 15 and 44; unmarried includes never married, widowed, and divorced.[26]

Characteristics of unmarried mothers

Most unmarried mothers are young; in 1947, 43.8 per cent were under 20 years of age and an additional 31.9 per cent were between 20 and 24

[25] Unpublished record.

[26] "Illegitimate Births, 1938–47," *Vital Statistics—Special Reports,* 33, 5 (Federal Security Agency, National Office of Vital Statistics, February 15, 1950), pp. 72, 73, and 84; the estimated total number includes an estimate for each state that does not require a statement of illegitimacy on the birth record.

years old.[27]   Typically, white mothers are slightly older than nonwhite mothers (Figure 51).   Some of the girls are below the legal age for marriage in their respective states.   For example, in the seven states where girls of 15 may be married with the parents' consent, from 0.5 to 3.3 per cent of unmarried mothers in 1947 were under 15 years of age.

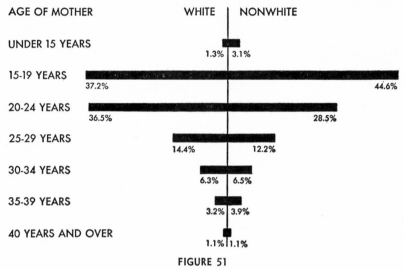

AGE OF MOTHER   WHITE | NONWHITE

UNDER 15 YEARS
                                          1.3% | 3.1%

15-19 YEARS
        37.2%   44.6%

20-24 YEARS
        36.5%   28.5%

25-29 YEARS
            14.4%   12.2%

30-34 YEARS
                6.3% | 6.5%

35-39 YEARS
                3.2% | 3.9%

40 YEARS AND OVER
                1.1% | 1.1%

FIGURE 51

Age of Unmarried Mothers

In 1947 the largest proportion of unmarried mothers fell into the five-year age period 15–19.   However, when illegitimate births are taken as a rate per 1,000 women of each age period, the 20–24 age group has the highest rate (18.7).   The peak rate has been with the group aged 20–24 for a long time; since 1938, however, the second highest rate has shifted from the 15–19 group to the 25–29 group.   (Source: "Illegitimate Births, 1938–47," *Vital Statistics—Special Reports,* 33, No. 5 [National Office of Vital Statistics, Federal Security Agency, February 15, 1950], pp. 75, 90.)

The youthfulness of many of the mothers points to another characteristic, their low educational level.   Special studies show that approximately three fourths of the unmarried mothers had not advanced beyond the eighth grade at a time (about 1930) when, for the country as a whole, approximately half of high-school-age boys and girls were in school.[28]

---

[27] *Ibid.,* p. 90, based on 98,677 illegitimate births from 34 states and the District of Columbia that record the fact of illegitimacy; 15 states no longer require this information on the birth certificate.

[28] D. F. Puttee and M. R. Colby, *The Illegitimate Child in Illinois* (University of Chicago Press, 1937), p. 100; A. M. Donahue, *Children of Illegitimate Birth Whose Mothers Have Kept Their Custody* (U. S. Department of Labor, Children's

The occupations of unmarried mothers correspond to their low educational level, one third to one half being in the domestic field and one tenth or more in factory work.[29]

The educational and occupational level indicates that many unmarried mothers are from the lower social class. It will be recalled that the attitude toward sex is much freer in the lower class than in the middle or upper class. Although illegitimate children are not approved, they are often accepted as members of the mother's parental family and the mother therefore feels less guilt and shame than does the middle-class girl who is made to feel that she has disgraced the family name. Especially among the untutored rural Negroes of the South, where sex relations begin in early adolescence, pregnancy carries little or no social stigma.[30] The young mother and her child remain with her parents, or the father of the baby may enter into a common-law marriage with her, giving protection and care at least for a period of time.

The minority of girls with high school or more education are probably middle class. If the trend continues toward premarital sex relations as part of middle-class dating or courtship, more illegitimate births may occur in the middle class. The middle-class girl is more likely to be the object of social discrimination than the lower-class girl, since middle-class mores emphasize marriage and the founding of a home as necessary prerequisites to the birth of a child.

Disposition of children

The experience of motherhood for many—perhaps most—unmarried mothers is chiefly on the biological side; few of them become mothers socially, for few are able to keep their children. Negro mothers in Southern rural areas are an exception, since they keep their babies with them in a family setting; but even here they often do not play the mother role. If the girl is young, her mother may rear the grandchild as her own child and the baby's mother may play the role of older sister. In cities, Negro families find the fatherless child an economic burden and assume the same attitude of rejection as whites.[31]

Bureau, 1928), p. 95; Ruth Reed, *The Illegitimate Family in New York City* (Columbia University Press, 1934), p. 132.

[29] Puttee and Colby, *op. cit.,* p. 98; Reed, *op. cit.,* p. 127.

[30] E. Franklin Frazier, *The Negro in the United States* (Macmillan, 1949), pp. 318–321.

[31] H. Hertz and S. W. Little, "Unmarried Negro Mothers in a Southern Urban Community; A Study of Attitudes toward Illegitimacy," *Social Forces,* 23 (1944), 73–79.

Unmarried mothers who come to the attention of social agencies are aided to make realistic plans for the care of their babies. These more often than not include adoption, since the girls are rarely able to make any other plan that will assure a secure home for the baby where it will be able to develop normally. Several studies show that approximately two thirds to three fourths of illegitimate children are placed with social agencies for care or future adoption.[32]

Motivations of the unmarried mother

Psychological analysis of cases shows that many unmarried mothers are not mature enough or sufficiently well adjusted to assume a responsible maternal role to their children; even if they kept their babies they could not function as mothers. Many come from broken homes or have had an unhappy relationship with their parents. No type of relationship predominates, however; some girls have never broken their dependence upon their mothers; others are resentful or antagonistic toward one or both parents. The girls, caught in the turmoil of their own unsolved problems, use sex relations and pregnancy to satisfy psychological needs that normally should have been satisfied in the relationship with their parents. Some girls present the baby to their mothers to express love; others to show hostility and defiance.[33]

The unmarried father

Little is heard of or known about the fathers of illegitimate children. The mother may refuse to reveal his name; she may not be sure who the father is if she has been at all promiscuous; or the father may disappear and become "lost" even when his name is known. The chief reason for attempting to locate the father is to establish paternity and exact medical costs or support for the child, either through court proceedings or voluntarily. Many girls or their families, however, prefer to shoulder the financial burden rather than have the attendant publicity.

The characteristics of known fathers differ from those of the mothers.

[32] Leontine R. Young, "Personality Patterns in Unmarried Mothers," *The Family* 26 (1945), 296–303; T. E. Sullenger and M. A. Nelson, *Problems of Illegitimacy in Nebraska* (Municipal University of Omaha, undated, multigraphed), p. 19.

[33] Young, *op. cit.;* Helene Deutsch, *The Psychology of Women, A Psychoanalytic Interpretation,* Vol. II, *Motherhood* (Grune and Stratton, 1945), ch. 10; Viola W. Bernard, "Psychodynamics of Unmarried Motherhood in Early Adolescence," *Nervous Child,* 4 (1944–45), 26–45.

They are older than unmarried mothers, few of them being under 20 years old.   The educational level is higher, with twice as many fathers as mothers having more than grade school education.[34]   These differences imply that unmarried fathers are of a higher social class than unmarried mothers, as well as more mature and experienced.   The man is likely to look upon the affair strictly in its sexual aspects and to feel little responsibility toward the child, although he may make some financial settlement at the time the child is born.

In analyzing the motivations and reactions of the unmarried father, Reider states that some men have unconscious needs to impregnate a woman, paralleling the unconscious needs found in some women.[35]   Unsure of their virility, they need proof not through sexual intercourse alone but through procreation.   Others, feeling themselves inferior, need proof of potency before they venture into marriage.   Some express their hostility toward women by causing women to become pregnant.   But for most men such neurotic tendencies are not dominant; they are engaged in sexual adventures, and the news of a pregnancy comes as a surprise and shock.   Shame and guilt are common reactions.

Reider feels that most men are willing to accept some financial responsibility, especially if pressure is put upon them during their first guilt reactions.   A study of 241 cases in which the mother kept the custody of the child showed, however, that only one third of the fathers contributed to the support of their children, either after court action, voluntarily, or by marrying the mother.   Many of them settled all responsibility by a flat payment of $50 to $500.[36]   It seems certain that a smaller percentage of fathers take responsibility when the child is adopted.   Thus the fathers evade a fundamental aspect of the father role.

Men evade the responsibility for a number of reasons: The child is a by-product of sexual experience—usually of a casual nature—and the man really does not feel personally responsible.   He may accept the custom of paying for illicit sexual adventures but not be ready to assume a larger payment or continuing support of a child.   He also wishes to avoid publicity.   He may believe that the child is not really his and rebel at the prospect of paying for another man's child.   Others try to escape

[34] Reed, *op. cit.,* pp. 115, 116.
[35] Norman Reider, "The Unmarried Father," *American Journal of Orthopsychiatry,* 18 (1948), 230–237.
[36] Donahue, *op. cit.,* pp. 24–25.

admission of paternity, because of shame, fear of being duped by the woman, or the feeling that they have been "suckers." [37]

The father therefore plays a parental role in still less degree than the mother. At best, he has a slight financial relationship with his baby, but does not assume the status of a father. He may not even be told by the mother that she is pregnant; he may deny the fact; he may admit the paternity but evade all responsibility except possible payments inadequate for the rearing of a child. Socially in relation to the child he does not function at all. Psychologically he probably has few paternal feelings.

Marriage following premarital conception

A halfway situation arises when the father and mother are married after pregnancy has progressed for some months. We have discussed the feeling of frustration and resentment that may accompany the unplanned-for and unwanted pregnancy after marriage. The pregnancy that occurs before marriage but where pressure is brought from some source (girl, her parents, social agencies) to effect a marriage may be much more frustrating, especially among middle-class people. Curtailment of high school or college education may force a complete change of life plans. The disapproval of parents usually is marked. Sometimes parents reject the couple completely, or they may exonerate their own child but refuse to have anything to do with the partner to the affair. At the present time when moral disapproval is less strong toward premarital sex relations than formerly, young friends of the couple may not condemn them for immorality but may ridicule them for having mismanaged their relationship or criticize them for failing to complete their education or establish a home before bringing a baby into the world. The lessened condemnation of premarital sex relations does not extend to the birth of a child before marriage. Young and old feel a strong sense of responsibility toward legitimacy of children.

Marriages to protect a pregnant woman or to "give the baby a name" have less chance of success than those based on mutual affection and congeniality. Even when the pregnancy occurs in the course of a courtship that might have led to marriage, the marriage has tensions because

[37] Maud Morlock, "Establishment of Paternity," *Proceedings of the National Conference of Social Work* (1940), 363–376; Margaret Marsh, "Common Attitudes toward the Unmarried Father," *Proceedings of the National Conference of Social Work* (1940), 377–387; Reider, *op. cit.*

individual ambitions may have to be sacrificed and the couple must face the disapproval of family and friends. Often the marriage is hurriedly carried through in a period of panic and fear of discovery of the pregnancy by others, without planning for the future. When there is little affection between the couple and the marriage is of the "shotgun" variety carried out under compulsion from parents or with threat of legal reprisals upon the man, the marriage has little chance of success.

THE ADEQUATE PARENT

The adequate parent is one who is personally mature and well adjusted. His relationship to the child is both warm and responsible. He recognizes the child's need for love and dependence, and he receives recompense for providing these needs through the child's response and the satisfaction of helping the child to develop. He does not expect to satisfy all his emotional or status needs through the child, however, and so does not burden the child by demanding from him the love that should come from the spouse or the ego satisfactions that an occupation or other accomplishments should afford.

Sometimes the parent functions under conditions that impair the relationship to the child, such as the death of one parent, divorce, or stepparenthood. These conditions need not be completely destructive, however. They call for more effort on the part of the parent and ability to accept added responsibilities.

QUESTIONS

1. How would you account for the difference between the number of children desired by college students and the number that college-trained adults actually have produced?

2. What are the advantages of trying to control the number and spacing of children? The hazards?

3. What change in roles of husband and wife is occasioned by the birth of the first child?

4. Are parental roles and individualism in marriage in harmony or in opposition?

5. In view of present urban conditions, does the developmental or the traditional conception of parenthood give more promise for well-adjusted children?

6. What does the child lose by having an absentee father?

7. How can divorced parents best contribute to their children's personality development?

8. Why do stepparents and children find it difficult to assume normal parent-child roles?

9. Do you approve of present attitudes and policies for the treatment of unmarried parents and illegitimate children?   If not, what changes would you suggest.

BIBLIOGRAPHY

Parenthood

Deutsch, Helene, *Psychology of Women, A Psychoanalytic Interpretation* (Grune and Stratton, 1945), Vol. II.

"Social and Psychological Factors Affecting Fertility," a series of research reports published in *Milbank Memorial Fund Quarterly,* covering such factors as planning for children, marital adjustment, socioeconomic status, religious affiliation, and feeling of economic security.   The first report appeared in Vol. 21 (1943) and the eleventh in Vol. 29 (1951).

Divorced parents

Children of Divorced Parents, entire issue, *Law and Contemporary Problems,* 10, No. 5 (1944).

Stepparents

Meriam, A. S., *The Stepfather in the Family* (University of Chicago Press, 1940).

Smith, W. C., "Remarriage and the Stepchild," in Fishbein, Morris and Burgess, E. W., editors, *Successful Marriage: An Authoritative Guide to Problems Related to Marriage from the Beginning of Sexual Attraction to Matrimony and the Successful Rearing of a Family* (Doubleday, 1947).

———, "The Stepchild," *American Sociological Review,* 10 (1945), 237–242.

———, "The Stepmother," *Sociology and Social Research,* 33 (1949), 342–347.

Unmarried parents

Bernard, V. W., "Psychodynamics of Unmarried Motherhood in Early Adolescence," *Nervous Child,* 4 (1944–45), 26–45.

Block, Babette, Oshlag, Sylvia, Scherz, Frances H., and Young, Leontine R., *Understanding the Psychology of the Unmarried Mother,* reprinted from *The Family* and *Journal of Social Casework,* 1945–1947 (Family Service Association of America, 122 East 22nd Street, New York 10).

Clothier, F., "Psychological Implications of Unmarried Motherhood," *American Journal of Orthopsychiatry*, 13 (1943), 531–549.

Davis, K., "Illegitimacy and the Social Structure," *American Journal of Sociology*, 45 (1939), 215–233.

———, "The Forms of Illegitimacy," *Social Forces*, 18 (1939), 77–89.

Futterman, S., and Livermore, J. B., "Putative Fathers," *Journal of Social Casework*, 28 (1947), 174–178.

Kasanin, J., and Handschin, S., "Psychodynamic Factors in Illegitimacy," *American Journal of Orthopsychiatry*, 11 (1941), 66–84.

Marsh, M., "Common Attitudes toward the Unmarried Father," *Proceedings of the National Conference of Social Work* (1940), 377–387.

Ploscowe, Morris, *Sex and the Law* (Prentice-Hall, 1951), ch. 4.

Reider, N., "The Unmarried Father," *American Journal of Orthopsychiatry*, 18 (1948), 230–237.

19

Adjustment to External Crises

The adjustment processes so far discussed have been limited to inter-action within the family. Outside pressures have been ignored. They are not absent from family life, however, and often create crises of great seriousness. Fluctuations of the economic cycle and military service are two recurring external threats to family adjustment and unity.

CRISES

A family crisis is any situation in which the family is not familiar with applicable mores and folkways. Habitual roles are inadequate; inter-action becomes confused; goals seem unattainable; and the family is unable to carry out its normal functions. To the individual family, al-most any event may be a crisis, if the family does not anticipate the event, has no patterns for adjustment, and lacks the resourcefulness and adapta-bility to invent new patterns of behavior and modification of roles to enable the family to function.

In contrast, when members of a family understand in advance how a given crisis will affect them and know how families in the past have best adjusted to the crisis, they are able to plan how to meet the crisis. They will know what their emotional reactions will probably be and that others have suffered the same reactions; they will know what changes in roles as well as in practical arrangements (such as finance or housing) will be needed; and they will learn the steps that lead to readjustment.

EFFECT OF SOCIAL CRISES ON MARRIAGE, BIRTH, AND DIVORCE RATES

The responsiveness of the family to social crises is clear from a study of trends in marriage, birth, and divorce rates.

Effect of depression

Figure 52 shows the fluctuations in marriage, birth, and divorce rates with major social crises.   The three rates dip during the depression years: marriages and divorces for 1930–1933, and births for a later period, 1933–1936.   It has been estimated that the decline in the marriage rate resulted in a loss of 788,000 marriages that normally would have occurred in the four years 1930–1933 (Figure 53).[1]   Counterbalancing to some extent the loss of new marriages were those preserved through the decline in the divorce rate.   By 1935 an estimated 171,000 divorces that normally would have occurred after 1930 had not been secured.[2]

Prior to the depression, the birth rate in the United States had been steadily declining.   There was an unusually sharp dip in the rate during the years of the depression, with an upswing in the following years.

Effect of war

The effect of war on marriage and related rates usually cannot be separated from the effect of prosperity resulting from the increased production of a war period.   During both World War I and World War II marriages increased during the early part of the war period, declined when the armed forces were in active service abroad, and increased at the end of the war, to be followed by a reversion to the normal trend. The upsurge was especially marked at the end of World War II, when the rate far exceeded any previous known rate; as a result, a higher proportion of the adult population is married at present than in at least the past 60 years.[3]

The high rates between 1940 and 1947, when there were three million more marriages than normal (Figure 52), cannot be accounted for solely

[1] *Population: The Wartime Marriage Surplus,* Series PM-1, No. 3 (Bureau of the Census, November 12, 1944), p. 2.

[2] Samuel A. Stouffer and L. M. Spencer, "Marriage and Divorce in Recent Years," *The Annals* of the American Academy of Political and Social Science, 188 (1936), p. 67.

[3] Paul C. Glick, "Family Life and Full Employment," *American Journal of Sociology,* 54 (1949), 521–522.

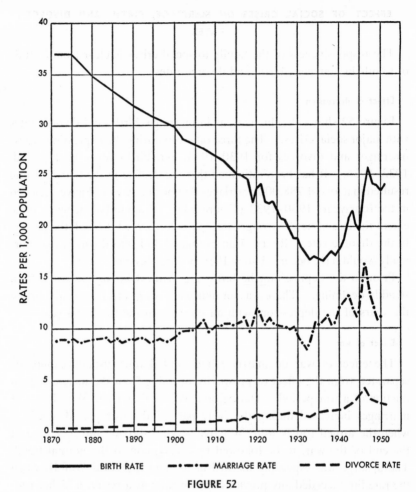

FIGURE 52

Marriage, Birth, and Divorce Rates, 1870–1951

The slowly changing long-term trends are in response to the growth of urbanism and industrialism; acute deviations in the trends are in response to unusual social situations—namely, World War I, which disturbed the rates in 1918–1921; the depression, 1930–1936; and World War II with the accompanying and subsequent period of prosperity, from 1941 on. (Constructed from Appendix A, columns I, II, and III.)

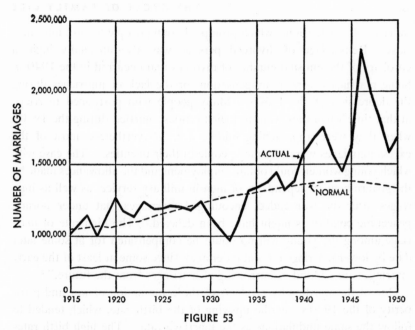

FIGURE 53

Anticipated Normal Number and Actual Number of Marriages, 1915–1950

The normal estimates represent the marriages that would have occurred in each year if the marriage rates had been the same as the average for the years 1920–1939. Although no single year in this period may have been "normal," the high and low rates tend to balance over this 20-year period. The actual numbers rarely correspond with the normal, inasmuch as they are largely determined by the proportion of eligible single persons and by the current economic situation. Specifically, the deviations in numbers are related to social situations as follows:

1917—early war and threat of separations

1918—war separations

1920—end of war and reunions

1921–1922—minor depression

1923–1929—prosperity

1930–1934—the great depression

1937—minor recovery

1938—economic recession

1941–1943—threat of early war separations, prosperity

1944—war separations

1945–1947—end of war and reunions

1948–1949—return toward normal in period of prosperity

1950—Korean disturbance

(Source: *Population, The Wartime Marriage Surplus,* Series PM-1, No. 3 [Bureau of the Census, November 12, 1944], pp. 1–3; *Vital Statistics, Special Reports, Summary of Marriage and Divorce Statistics, United States, 1949,* 36, No. 2 [Federal Security Agency, June 5, 1951] p. 24; *News Release* [Federal Security Agency, April 23, 1951], p. 1.)

in terms of war tensions, which prompted young people to rush into marriage. Remarriage of divorced persons was also unusually high, a corollary of the unusual number of divorces that occurred in the 1940's.[4] Some marriages were a compensation for the lack of marriages during the depression of the 1930's. Many people who postponed marriage at that time when they were in their twenties, married during the 1940's when they were approaching middle age. Nevertheless, most of the excess marriages were of young people in their twenties. The ease with which young women could obtain employment and the allowances made by the government to dependents of men in military service, as well as high wages after the war ended, encouraged marriages that under normal peacetime conditions might have been delayed. The high rate of marriage among the young will no doubt be compensated for at some later date by lower marriage rates at older ages, since some at least of the early marriages are "a kind of borrowing of marriages from the future." [5]

One of the startling by-products of the combination of war and prosperity of the 1940's was the upswing of the birth rate, which tended to follow the same undulations as the marriage rate. The high birth rates of the 1940's are not to be interpreted as a reversal of the long-term downward trend. As with marriages, the baby boom was a result of first births delayed from the depression-ridden 1930's and a borrowing from births that under other circumstances would have been delayed until the 1950's.[6]

Divorce rates also respond to the combination of war and prosperity (Figure 51). The long-term upward trend in divorce was accentuated just after World War I (1920–1921) and in much greater degree after World War II (1945–1947).

---

[4] Glick, *op. cit.*

[5] Glick, *op. cit.*, p. 522.

[6] P. K. Whelpton, "Cohort Analysis of Fertility," *American Sociological Review,* 14 (1949), pp. 735–749; T. J. Woofter, "Factors Sustaining the Birth Rate," *American Sociological Review,* 14 (1949), 357–366. The increased birth rate pertains to first and second births, but as yet there is no indication that third, fourth, and succeeding children will be born to these families. The high birth rate in the past resulted from the larger number of families with many children; families still have children, but they do not have so many. Until it can be demonstrated that the families who had one or two children in the 1940's continue to have children, no long-term increase in the birth rate can be assumed. In other words, it is not the total number of children born at any one time that determines the long-term trend but the number of children born per completed family.

THE DEPRESSION OF THE THIRTIES

Although the depression of the 1930's seems well in the background, there is no certainty that economic and governmental specialists can prevent a recurrence; also, many of the problems of depressions arise in miniature whenever there is prolonged unemployment, even on a local basis.   Industrial reconversion and the release of soldiers at the end of a war create unemployment, as does the constant replacement of workers by labor saving machinery.   On a smaller scale, the individual family in which the chief wage earner is unemployed—whatever the reason— suffers many of the same difficulties as the thousands of families face during a national depression.   The analysis of the effect of the Great Depression on family life therefore should not be ignored.   From studies made in the 1930's much can be learned that will reduce the crisis-effect of unemployment in the present or future.

Extent of unemployment

In its effect upon the family an economic depression may be thought of as a period of prolonged and widespread unemployment resulting from conditions in the general business situation over which the masses of wage earners and small proprietors have no control.   Such periods of unemployment tend to develop quickly, to be very acute for a few months or years, and then to be succeeded by periods of employment.   They occur at intervals of approximately five years.   In the 150 years from 1790 to 1940, there were at least 25 periods of economic depression; in the past 50 years there have been 15 periods, 8 classifiable as major depressions and 7 as minor depressions.   The average duration of depressions, exclusive of the last one, has been 18 months.[7]   The last depression, with some variations in severity, lasted throughout the 1930's.

Even in periods of prosperity a certain amount of unemployment exists. In 1929, various estimates placed the number of unemployed at three or four millions.[8]   At the depth of the depression, in 1932–1933, the number of unemployed rose to an estimated 14 to 16 million.   In percentages, the unemployment of 1929 amounted to about 6 per cent of the gainfully employed people, but in 1933 to about 33 per cent.   In

[7] From tables and charts cited in J. H. S. Bossard, *Social Change and Social Problems* (Harper, 1938), pp. 237–238.
[8] W. M. Leiserson, "A Balance Sheet of Benefits," *Survey Graphic,* 28 (1939), p. 218.

1935, the period of the maximum number of public assistance cases, eight million households received assistance. By 1937 the number had declined to five million, only to rise again in 1938–1939.[9] With increased employment during World War II, households on public assistance were reduced to a minimum.

Middle-class family the chief victim

The degree of deprivation caused by the depression differed among social classes. Families of low economic status, never financially secure, did not change their status materially. Many lower-class families, living precariously in normal times or fluctuating between self-support and relief, found increased security in their permanent reliance upon the relief agency. Well-to-do families slipped backward slightly but not so far as to suffer severe hardships. Socially and psychologically, the status-conscious middle-class family suffered most from the depression.

The following brief case summaries are of middle-class families that experienced great losses in the depression.[10]

The Linds had been comfortably self-supporting for years and never had a debt. When the father was no longer able to meet their needs and began to accumulate moderate debts (the interest on a $1,000 mortgage and $50 for milk), he worried excessively. It seemed impossible to him that he should not be able to meet his obligations. He cried at the relief office in telling of these debts; he walked the floor at night and felt "sort of desperate." At one period he drank, until his wife "put her foot down." Mrs. Lind likewise worried until she thought "the top of her head would come off with severe headaches." For two years the family struggled along, applying three times for relief before it was finally granted. They felt humiliated in asking for relief, but were desperate.

In the Garfinkel family, the father was described in 1928 as a quiet man, colorless, healthy, with no bad habits. He disliked to spend money but was generous with the mother. Each year he saved for periods of unemployment. The mother at this time was an emotional woman with little poise, given to loud, embarrassed laughter. The family seemed to be fairly happy except for the mother's tendency to over-protect her children. When the father's income was reduced from $40 to a few dollars a week, the relief agency helped intermittently whenever the income was less than $17 per

[9] *Trends in Public Assistance, 1933–1939,* Bureau Report No. 8 (Social Security Board, 1940), pp. 6–7.

[10] Ruth Shonle Cavan and Katherine H. Ranck, *The Family and the Depression,* (University of Chicago Press, 1938), pp. 60–61.

week. For a year or more the family lived with this uncertain status, neither on relief nor completely self-supporting. The father's reaction to his economic insecurity was to develop physical fears. Spots on his body burned; he had headaches; he feared cancer. He spent much time going from clinic to clinic, where no physical basis for his ailments could be found. The mother, her condition complicated by high blood pressure, developed a very excited state. At times her chief social interaction was excessive giggling. The relief agency finally assumed full responsibility; and when the father was placed on work relief, most of these difficulties in both father and mother disappeared.

First reactions

Usually, the first reaction to unemployment was the realistic attempt to find other work, at first of the accustomed type and later of any type.[11] The family attempted to maintain its economic independence through such practical measures as retrenchment of expenses, selling the car, borrowing upon insurance policies or from relatives and friends, or moving to a house with lower rent. Only gradually did the working members of the family come to an admission of inability to find work.

As the financial reserves were exhausted, the family was forced to face the loss of long-held desires and ambitions, the sweeping away of all sense of security for the future, and the sacrifice of the most highly valued symbols of social status. In many families sons who had been reared with the idea of college or professional training had to adjust themselves to a less ambitious goal and to take whatever kind of work they could secure. The parents themselves suffered an equal disappointment. Much of the restlessness and worry of the depression years did not relate to immediate needs but to the fear of losing savings and denial of long-time family plans. Often the family's emotional turmoil went through a long crescendo, reaching a climax when the savings were finally used up or the house irrevocably lost. After this climax the family was bitter or philosophical, quarrelsome or united, according to its habitual pattern of reaction to crises. But, whatever the immediate effect of such losses on the family, the turning point usually had been reached, and some form of adjustment to the new financial situation was possible.

Less dramatic than the use of all savings or the loss of investments, but also important for family relationships, was the curtailment of habitual expenditures. Summer vacations, club memberships, and even attend-

[11] Cavan and Ranck, *op. cit.*, chs. 5–6.

ance at motion pictures were given up.   As poverty increased, the family might be unable to pay for electricity, with the result that the family radio could not be used.   Young people especially felt the deprivation when the clothing budget had to be reduced.   Magazines and newspapers became luxuries.

. Most of these curtailments of expenditures had the indirect effect of reducing the contacts of the family with the community or with the world beyond the community.   Walking distance, rather than bus, streetcar, or automobile distance, circumscribed the social community.   Institutional contacts became fewer in number or perhaps shifted from those involving paid memberships to free ones in libraries and community houses.   As a corollary of reduced community contacts, intrafamily contacts increased and intensified.   The family spent its time at home because money was lacking for other types of activities.   Unemployed members were at home when formerly they would have been working.   Out-of-school children were at home because they could not find work.   The family often found itself cramped into smaller quarters than usual, often because they had moved to a smaller apartment or house to save rent, but sometimes because they had enough money to heat only one or two rooms of the house, into which the whole family must crowd and within which all activities must be carried on.   When the family was well integrated, this overcrowding seemed to create little ill-will; but when tension already existed, friction was common.

The tendency for segments of families to reunite during the depression was marked, as was also the willingness of some one member of the family to support the entire family after the father had lost his work. Sometimes the unmarried son or daughter was reabsorbed into the parental family, and sometimes the married son or daughter and their children became members of the household.   In other cases the parents moved in with a son or daughter.

Factors in adjustment

Family integration or unity was of great importance in carrying the family through the depression.[12]   When common interests, affection, and a sense of economic interdependence were present, the family had a strong bulwark against disorganization.   The omission of any of these elements from family life tended to weaken the stability of the family.   Other

[12] R. C. Angell, *The Family Encounters the Depression* (Scribner, 1936).

important elements of family unity were family objectives, such as plans for the children's education, buying a house; subordination of personal interests to the good of the family as a group; adherence to family ideals; and a capacity of the family to satisfy within the family circle the personal interests of its members, such as recreation, affection, and intellectual stimulation.[13]   Complementary roles of husband and wife also gave unity.   The unified or integrated family withstood the effects of the depression better than the family that was disorganized and lacking in unity at the beginning of the period of unemployment.

Previous habits of adaptability of the family also aided it to adjust to the depression.[14]   Three elements contributed to the necessary flexibility. A nonmaterialistic philosophy of life was important; this philosophy placed greater emphasis upon cultural values than upon material possessions.   Freedom from traditionalism also aided the family to accept new conditions.   Habits of responsibility also strengthened the family, in that each member was vitally interested in the welfare of the entire group.

Previous experiences in meeting crises set a precedent for adjustment to the depression.   The family pattern established before the depression tended to continue after unemployment, but in intensified form.[15]   Thus the family that had been able to adjust to earlier crises tended to adjust well to the depression, but the family that had not adjusted to prior crises, but instead had tended to disintegrate or fall back upon relatives or relief agencies, or in some other way had failed to revamp its customary ways to meet a crisis was unable to meet the depression in adequate fashion.

Thus the effect of a depression was not merely a matter of dollars and cents or even of loss of social status in the community; it was also closely related to the type of family organization that existed prior to the depression.   The integrated, adaptable family, with an adequate pattern of adjustment already developed, met the depression with less emotional turmoil and less loss of family strength than the family that was lacking in unity, that was rigid in family pattern, and that had an inadequate method of adjusting to changes.

Cutting across the change in social status of the family and the integration and adaptability of the family was a third factor—the change in personal roles within the family.[16]   The father's role was probably

[13] Cavan and Ranck, *op. cit.*, ch. 7.
[14] Angell, *op. cit.*
[15] Cavan and Ranck, *op. cit.*
[16] Cavan and Ranck, *op. cit.*, ch. 6; Angell, *op. cit.*

disturbed by the depression more than that of any other family member, for the loss of employment struck directly at the mainstay of his status— his position as financial supporter of his family.   The loss of club memberships, recreation, or the automobile due to the lack of money was of minor importance to many men as compared with the sense of not being able to fulfill their role as head of the family.   They became restless and unable to occupy themselves; some developed physical symptoms of illness although no real illness could be found by competent doctors; some resorted to drink in order to "feel like somebody" for a short time; some in time became resigned and sank into an early senility of helplessness.   A few maintained their role as head of the family even when on relief, taking over from their wives the management of the household, an arrangement that benefited the family if the wife was ill or incompetent.

The father's loss of status in the family was emphasized by the reaction of his wife toward him.   Especially in the early days of the depression, many wives did not understand that their husbands could not find work and accused them of trying to evade it.   Mothers feared for actual shelter and food for themselves and their children and nagged the fathers who had failed to provide for them.   If a son or daughter was working and had to provide the major amount of money for the support of the family, many mothers tended to turn to this son or daughter as the head of the family, to cater to his food tastes as they once had catered to the father's, and at every opportunity to express their gratitude.   The most disorganizing family situation was the one in which the chief earner (usually the father) suffered lowered status through loss of employment and income and had the experience of seeing some other (and often younger) member of the family step into his role.

Final adjustment to the depression

Some families, primarily those with latent or already active conflicts, disintegrated under the impact of the depression.   Others separated temporarily but reunited when some member found work.   Most families rode out the depression together.   Readjustment came with acceptance of new roles or re-establishment of old ones.   Often the roles were permanently modified.   Sons or daughters who found work when the father could not did not sink back to the dependent role when the father was re-employed.   The father's status remained a little lower and theirs considerably higher. Such a shift would normally occur as children matured and began to contribute financially to the family. The depression accentuated the shift and increased the respective rise and fall of statuses. Many older men were unable to find steady work even when employment increased in the late 1930's. Odd jobs or poorly paid work tided them over until they reached age 65 and could apply for Old Age Assistance. Interestingly enough some men on Old Age Assistance were re-employed after World War II began and in their old age again achieved the status of independent workers. Other families became so dependent upon social agencies that they resisted efforts made by these agencies to push them back into employment; their fears of insecurity had become permanent. The permanently dependent families were not necessarily maladjusted. The protection and sense of security afforded by Old Age Assistance or general relief agencies were sometimes the crutch that families needed to permit them to function without anxieties and fears. As suggested above, the families that made the best final adjustment were those with integration sufficient to enable the family to function as a unit but with adaptability to changed conditions and acceptance of changed roles and goals.

UNEMPLOYMENT

Unemployment during nondepression periods differs somewhat from depression unemployment because there is less sense of finality and futility. There is more possibility of pinning the unemployment down to specific causes that can be understood by the families involved. If these causes can be removed, there is reasonable assurance of re-employment. Nevertheless, families undergo many of the same stages of maladjustment and readjustment that featured the depression. They also have several other adjustments to make.

Technological changes that spread rapidly through an entire industry may outmode some special work skill. The unemployed person's problem then is not merely to find a new opening where he can use his skill; he may be forced either to learn some new skill or accept unskilled work. In the first case he goes through a period of insecurity typical of many learning situations; in the second he suffers a decline in status that affects his position in the family as well as among fellow workers. When the unemployed man finds it necessary to move his family to a different community, the family must make the adjustments already described for the migrant family in Chapter 3.[17]

The end of a war typically brings a period of unemployment. The conversion of industry from war to civilian production decreases the need for workers at least temporarily and perhaps permanently. It may also necessitate migration of workers, since war plants may close in one area and civilian production expand in another. Nor does the number of unemployed tell all the story. After World War II many women employed in war industries dropped out of the labor market to marry or return to their families, their places being taken by returned servicemen. A study of 3,600 war workers in the spring of 1945 before war's end and again in the winter of 1945–46 showed that 29 per cent of the women in war plants in the spring of 1945 had left the labor market by the following winter.[18] Returned veterans exceeded the number of women who withdrew. In October, 1946, 1,540,000 men were unemployed, more than a million above the number of unemployed men on V-J Day, some 14 months earlier; one half of the number were veterans.[19] In contrast, the number of unemployed women remained around 400,000 from the war period to 1946, with many of the unemployed women dropping out of the labor force. The peak of postwar unemployment was reached in March, 1946, when 2,710,000 were seeking jobs.

These periods of unemployment call for adjustments in the families or among the individuals affected: delay of marriage, curtailment of expenses, postponement of children, migrations. They weaken poorly adjusted families and call for adaptability in the well-integrated families. Industrial shifts occasioning unemployment are so commonplace that temporary unemployment has become one of the exigencies of modern life, to be anticipated and planned for. One type of preparation is the unemployment insurance provided by federal law that softens the blow of loss of income and prevents some of the feeling of panic. Full preparation will come, however, only when families realize that jobs are not

[17] For an analysis of adjustment problems when two plants shut down in 1929, see Ewan Clague, Walter J. Couper, and E. Wight Bakke, *After the Shutdown* (New Haven: Institute of Human Relations, Yale University, 1934).

[18] "Workers' Experiences During First Phase of Reconversion," *Monthly Labor Review,* 62 (May, 1946), 707.

[19] "Trends of Employment and Labor Turn-Over," *Monthly Labor Review,* 63 (December, 1946), 1019.

necessarily permanent but come and go with social and industrial changes.

Unemployment because of age or chronic illness, more common among the middle-aged and old than among the young, usually brings a permanent change in work status and family organization. The man, formerly with the position of highest status in the family, may find himself in a dependent role with permanently lowered status. His wife (usually younger than he) may be able to find employment when the man fails to find work because of age. She also often becomes the main support of the family when chronic illness strikes her husband. In other cases both man and wife become dependent upon their children, with a reversal of roles; or they become clients of a relief agency. The trials of readjustment that come to elderly people with loss of employment of the husband are more completely discussed in Chapter 20.

BOOMS AND PROSPERITY

Booms do not affect all parts of the country evenly; they bourgeon forth in selected spots where some new source of income or wealth has suddenly developed—a new factory site, a new source of natural resources, a newly irrigated area. The boom of the 1940's centered in certain industrial areas with expanded or entirely new plants and enormous orders for war materials. This centering of booms draws in people of all types from other, less promising areas. The effect of industrial mobility on the family has been discussed in Chapter 3.

An unusual increase in income itself may be a disturbing thing. Prosperity is not an attribute only of well-to-do or wealthy families. Any family with a rather sudden and unusual accretion of wealth beyond its usual standard of living feels prosperous. The way in which this extra margin—this "velvet"—is defined and used affects the family. Families with a well-established standard of living that already have a wide margin of safety in investments may make little change in their goals or mode of living. The stable middle-class family with modest security may define the added income as a means of improving security for old age or of increasing the amount of education of their children; they plow back the money into fortifying their position. Aggressively upwardly mobile families may use the money to push themselves into the next higher social-class stratum; they may buy a home in a neighborhood of higher status, invest in a different make of car, join clubs with high initiation fee and yearly dues, and otherwise attempt to identify themselves overtly with the higher class. The lower-class family that has always used up its income as it came in, often treats its new prosperity in the same way. Without trying to save for the future or climb the social scale, this family increases its comforts and pleasures. The small cottage may still huddle in a muddy yard on an unpaved street, but the soaring television antenna testifies to the immediate use of increased income for pleasures of the present. Middle-class people often criticize lower-class families for not saving for a rainy day, but saving for distant goals is not part of the philosophy of life nor the ingrained habits of the lower class as it is of the middle class.

Family roles are often disturbed by the higher incomes, especially when wife or adolescent son or daughter responds to the call for additional workers and earns perhaps as much as the father. Money typically gives status in the American family, and the husband, who won his status by hard work and a slow building up of skills over the years, now finds his position challenged by members of the family who, according to the American family pattern, should have slightly subordinate statuses. Thus, adolescents may defy the authority of the father or rebel completely, leave home, and set a new course without integration into either family or community pattern.

As in depression, prosperity also calls for good family organization, adaptability to new roles, and integration around family goals if the family is to retain its stability.

WAR AS A CRISIS

Although each war comes with a shock to the generation that must bear the brunt of it, war is not an uncommon phenomenon. The United States waged 13 wars between 1775 and 1946 and in 1950 engaged in activity in Korea not officially termed a war but with all the characteristics of a formally declared war—production of war materials; decline of civilian production; drafting, training, and exportation of men; fighting, injury, and death. Other men in military service, not engaged in fighting, are stationed in various parts of the world, often separated from their families. Military service entailing delays in marriage or separation of the husband from wife and children now seems so much a part of early married life that it can no longer be looked upon as an unexpected crisis but as an expected disturbance. A crisis that can be foreseen as inevitable takes on a different aspect from the totally unexpected crisis. A young couple who have a high degree of certainty regarding the future military service of the husband can anticipate the situation in imagination and make some preparation for it. They can learn how other engaged or married couples have handled the situation; they can frame their future plans to allow for the break in continuity; they can deliberately devise ways to maintain family unity and parental influence, if there are children, through a period of separation; they may even, no matter how harsh the prospect seems, face in advance the possibility of permanent injury to or death of the man.

World War II disturbed family functioning at several points, and it may be assumed that military service in the 1950's has similarly affected the family. The normal processes of courtship and engagement were interfered with or prevented altogether; newly married couples were separated within a few weeks or months and during their brief time together often were unable to establish a home; babies were born and spent the first few years of their lives in a one-parent family; long-established families were torn apart; men returned after long separations either to make their first marital adjustment or to resume their roles as husband and father; young women had to accept widowhood, normally the tragedy of the old.

Extent of war separations

The crux of the problem of war marriages was the prolonged separation of husband and wife. In February, 1944, 2,700,000 married women were separated from their husbands by the war, a number that accounted for 8 per cent of all married women and almost one third of married women aged 20-24.[20] In February, 1946, months after the end of the war, 1,240,000 married women were still separated from husbands in the armed forces.[21] Scarcely had families been re-established after World War II than the outbreak of trouble in Korea and the greatly expanded military program again tore families apart. Although many

[20] *Marital Status of the Civilian Population: February, 1944,* Series PS, No. 1 (Bureau of the Census, June 20, 1944).

[21] *Marital Status of the Civilian Population: February, 1946,* Series PS, No. 10 (Bureau of the Census, October 14, 1946).

of the separations in World War II and again in the 1950's affected established families, it seems probable that more of the separations applied to newly married couples.

The new marriage in wartime

Many marriages that occur in wartime or when military service is imminent do not differ from peacetime marriages: the couple have passed through a normal courtship period, made their plans, married, and entered into normal married life.   But in many others, marriage is followed within a few days, weeks, or months by separation of unknown length often with the danger of injury or death for the husband.   Sometimes the marriage has also been preceded by a long separation with the couple marrying during a short furlough.   We do not have percentages as to the types of war marriages, the length of courtship, or the number of months of separation.

Marriages, to be immediately followed by separation, perhaps of two or more years and with the possibility of injury to or death of the husband, violate many of our American principles of what constitutes a "good" marriage and one likely to succeed.   We believe that the first year or two of marriage are extremely important for working out good coordination between husband and wife.   American marriage has also been posited upon the belief that the husband should be able to support his wife and children, and that both husband and wife should have completed their basic education.   We assume that the husband has a job, that a place to live has been found and basic equipment bought, and that some secure plan has been made for children.

The war marriage is based upon a different set of assumptions.   There is a sense of urgency and immediacy about it.   There is not time to wait for education, jobs, a bank account, housebuilding or even apartment-finding, or for long-range planning.   In a certain number of weeks the man faces service; or a furlough is at hand and there may not soon be another.   The desire for marriage, identification, security, and sex fulfillment becomes more important than the long-range planning of a safe marriage in the traditional manner.   The philosophy of "marry in haste, repent at leisure" is replaced by other concepts that imply that certainty now is better than doubt about the future: "a bird in the hand" and "a half loaf" are also part of our folk philosophy of life.

Young people are divided between the two points of view.   Some draw back from the urgency of haste, others step forward to grasp the present. A study, too limited for generalizations, brings out some of the attitudes and also some rationalizations that no doubt conceal other motives. Small groups of college students, young unmarried business people, and women defense-plant workers checked answers to the question, "Do you approve or disapprove of war marriages in which the husband will be absent from his wife because of service in the armed forces?" [22] The reasons most frequently given for favoring war marriages support the philosophy of immediacy and relate to problems of the present: memories if nothing else; take happiness while you can, "rather be a widow than an old maid," and desire for a child. Those who favored delay were looking to future outcomes: fear of physical disability, limitation of social contacts after separation, difficulties of future marital adjustment, and fear that love would not last. The delaying group seemed motivated by fears and anxieties regarding the future. Those favoring war marriages looked to immediate needs and desires. In general, the subjects of this study favored war marriages (68 per cent), with women being more ready to accept them than men.

A young woman writes as follows of her personal dilemma in trying to solve the problem of whether to marry in the first glow of love or prudently to wait until her fiance returns from military service.

When the summer of 1950 began, Frank and I had known each other for a year. We were the best of friends, a sort of brother-sister relationship. We were together almost every week end at a summer cottage owned by his family. Any summer week end the cottage was filled with a riotous group of boys and girls; there was never any sitting in dark corners and making love. In the middle of the summer Frank asked me for a date and that first date led to many others. When the fighting started in Korea, Frank and I didn't realize it would affect us. By September we were reasonably serious about each other. When we held the final party of the season one of the boys, who was in a melancholy mood, said this might be the last time that all of us would ever be together again; with the situation in Korea who knew what would happen. When we heard him say this we all got lumps in our throats, especially Frank and me. From that time on the threat of war hung over us. By the time college opened we knew we wanted to marry. But our parents expected us to complete college and we too realized the importance of a college education. We did not have the finances to marry and continue in college. We have discussed the problem with our parents

[22] Florence G. Robbins, "Reasons for and Against War Marriages," *Sociology and Social Research,* 29 (1944–1945), 26–27.

and have decided not to marry until Frank is out of the service, if he has to go; but we plan to become officially engaged before he enters the service. Whether or not this is wise I don't know.   I feel that it is; I feel that it will be no trouble to wait for him and to deny myself the privilege of dating other fellows, and Frank feels the same way about dating other girls.   We think it best not to be married before he enters the service because war often changes a man's outlook on life and he might not love me when he is discharged, or he might be killed and never come home.   These are horrible thoughts to both of us, but we have decided there is no point in fooling ourselves.[23]

When the couple marry, faced with the imminent call of the husband to service, they are in a situation, very different from the conventional one, for which we have no established patterns of procedure.   The girl may never leave her parent's home; after a brief honeymoon she may continue in college and occupy her customary dormitory room; or she may follow her husband from camp to camp, living in a room, an apartment, a shack, or a trailer, depending upon available accommodations. When her husband is sent overseas, she must find a place for herself without him.   At this point some girls return to college or to the parents' home.   Two or three young women may rent an apartment together and find jobs.   They are legally married but lack the firsthand mutuality of marriage.   Whatever needs of love, security, or sex the marriage satisfied may now again be unmet.   This quasi-marriage [24] has little to give it stability.

Often the couple have married after an abbreviated courtship or perhaps only on the basis of casual dating.   The loneliness of the young man who is separated from family and friends in some training camp, his fears and uncertainties about the future, his need for someone to give immediate sympathy and love, may motivate him to marriage.   The girl may be carried away by the thrill of uniforms, the excitement of community dances held for servicemen, or the urge to follow the general pattern of other young people who are also marrying.   Such marriages have a less firm basis than the marriage of two who have progressed through courtship and have weighed the relative advantages of immediate marriage or waiting.

The attitude of the parents is important, especially for the girl who

[23] Unpublished record.

[24] This term is used by John F. Cuber, "Changing Courtship and Marriage Customs," *The Annals* of the American Academy of Political and Social Science, 229 (1943), 30–38.

remains at home or returns there after her husband leaves. Many parents disapprove of war marriages. When the girl has met and hastily married a young man while at college or working in some other city, the parents are suspicious of the man. Differences in religion or social class, overlooked by the young people in their desire for immediate marriage, may become issues of great importance argued over the weeks by parents and daughter.

Many girls are able to accept the separation, keeping interest and love alive through correspondence, and making the most of infrequent furloughs. Others tend to slip back into the premarital pattern that a few weeks of marriage were insufficient to change. They become daughters again, controlled by their parents, rather than wives working out plans with their husbands. They may also resume old friendships with men not in the service, or respond to the friendly approaches of new men. Since the mores prohibit dating by married women, they may see these men secretly. The friendship that began on a platonic basis to tide over the lonely evenings and make social life possible may easily become an entangled sexual affair filling needs aroused by the girl's marriage and denied by the absence of her husband; or the girl may find herself more in love with the man whom she sees frequently than with the absent husband whose image may grow dim in the course of time.

If a baby is born, complications are multiplied. The wife must fulfill two roles to the child; in time she must try to give the child some concept of his father although her own knowledge of him is limited. Housing arrangements are a much greater problem with a child than without one. If the wife is with her parents they may easily either resent the child or tend to absorb him.[25]

The unfocused, rootless life of the young wife whose husband is in the service is pointedly described by a young woman who speaks of the "helpless, anxious, lonesome feeling" that pervaded the years of separation:

In 1940 there was the threat of war. All talk was of war. I had been going with George for nearly four years. We had delayed marriage until

[25] The following articles discuss some of the problems of the war bride: Gladys Gaylord, "Marriage Counseling in Wartime," *The Annals* of the American Academy of Political and Social Science, 229 (1943), 39–45; Evelyn Millis Duvall, "Marriage in War Time," *Marriage and Family Living*, 4 (1942), 73–76; Evelyn Millis Duvall, "Loneliness and the Serviceman's Wife," *Marriage and Family Living*, 7 (1945), 77–81.

he could finish his education, which he did in the spring of 1940. I wished to spend some time with my family before I was married and went to visit them. Soon men were being drafted rapidly and the war news was alarming. Some of our relatives thought we should marry and others were opposed. We were married and settled into a four-room apartment, with new furniture and a new car. All went well for some time but the war pressure became too heavy. Many of our friends had already gone. We could make no future plans at all, for George expected to be called at any time. Finally, in 1943 he decided to enlist so that he might be able to choose the branch of service he desired. We decided I should go with him, working wherever he was sent. However, just after he left, I discovered that I was pregnant and so had to make other plans. As we had not saved enough to last for long, I stored our furniture and moved to another city to be with my folks. George and I saw each other twice in the next eight months, when he was sent overseas. Our son was born after he left. We remained with my parents, where a sister and sister-in-law with her child also were living. There were no serious arguments but some tension among us. When little Tommy was three months old I returned to the city where we had lived and moved into an apartment, where I remained with the baby until he was a year old. I had felt sure that the war would be over soon. I did not work as I could not conceive of leaving the baby with anyone else. We passed the time with friends who were in the same situation. Many of them also had babies whom the fathers had not seen. I moved into an apartment with a serviceman's wife who had one child a little older than Tommy and was expecting another. The children were not happy together and I was running short of money. I again returned to my parents where we stayed for about eight months until August, 1945. I felt sure George would soon be home and as I wanted him to return to his own home I again moved to our home city. With each move, my mother helped me get settled.

George came home after an absence of more than two years; we were more or less like strangers. Many of my friends were people I had met after he left and were strangers to him. His experiences had been so different from mine that at first there was little to discuss. He could hardly imagine he had a two-year-old son and didn't know how to respond in any way to him. He would say that I had pampered and spoiled him, that strict discipline was what he needed. At first Tommy was jealous of the attention I gave George and vice versa; but in time they became fairly well adjusted to each other.[26]

This statement recounts the unsettled life of the young married woman whose husband is in the service; it also suggests some of the problems of readjustment upon his return. This young couple was fortunate in having had several years together before the separation. When the couple have been married only a brief period, they must begin after the return the

[26] Unpublished record.

process that normally takes place immediately after marriage.[27] This process includes the establishment of a mutually exclusive pair relationship with the withdrawal from family and friends upon whom the wife has depended during her husband's absence. Coordination of goals and activities starts anew. Sexual adjustment, perhaps not accomplished in the short period together, assumes central importance for many couples. Matching of personalities and meeting of needs may be extremely difficult, since each may have developed new attitudes and needs in the period of separation. Compatible social roles must be found. All this must take place between two who are almost strangers and who in addition may be parents of a child who has never seen his father.

Adjustment of the established family to war separation

Not only courting and newly married couples are affected by war, but established families also when husbands enlist or are called into service. The family organization is seriously disturbed, with the husband's role left vacant.

The immediate reaction to departure of the husband is shock, according to the findings of two studies. Among a random sample of 135 middle-class Iowa families, in poorly adjusted and well-adjusted marriages alike, the wife's first reaction was numbness and loneliness.[28] The exceptions were 15 wives (11 per cent) who welcomed the separation as a release from an intolerable marital situation or as an opportunity to think through an unsatisfactory relationship. Another report, of cases previously known to social agencies, also notes the depression of wives, sometimes neurotic in severity; other wives in this group, however, directed their emotions outward in hostility toward the draft boards.[29]

As wife and children accept the reality of the separation, a process of reorganization begins that is not, however, uniform for all families. Two general patterns of good adjustment and one of poor adjustment were found among the Iowa families.

1. Good adjustment to the separation based on good marital and family adjustment prior to the disturbance.[30] Before the husband left, the fam-

---

[27] See Chapter 16, "Marital Adjustment."
[28] Reuben Hill, *Families Under Stress, Adjustment to the Crises of War Separation and Reunion* (Harper, 1949), pp. 55–56.
[29] Florence Hollis, "Impact of War on Marriage Relationships," *Proceedings of the National Conference of Social Work* (1943), p. 112.
[30] Hill, *op. cit.*, pp. 75–79, 223–252.

ily reviewed finances, readjusted living arrangements, and otherwise made practical adjustments. During the separation the family temporarily redistributed the husband's functions among other members of the family. It seemed to make little difference how his functions were redistributed so long as someone assumed the responsibility for them. At the same time, the family included the husband in its daily life through correspondence that recorded daily events and asked for his advice. He thus remained a vital part of the family, although it had reorganized to function during his absence. Typically plans were made for the reunion that would come with his discharge. The husband's readiness to play an absentee but active role was also important. Some men seemed willing to give up the husband and father role and did not enter into correspondence about family affairs; others felt a new interest and responsibility while away.

2. Good adjustment to separation based on prior poor marital adjustment.[31] When the marriage had been unsatisfactory, husband and wife sometimes agreed upon the husband's enlisting as a temporary relief from tension and conflict. In other families, the wife was dissatisfied with the subordinate role of wife and mother and welcomed the chance to work, make her own decisions, and live an independent life; initial loneliness was followed by enjoyment of the new freedom. In these families the ranks were rather definitely closed against the husband; he was not kept in close touch with family affairs through correspondence— in fact, correspondence might almost cease. Reunion after the husband's discharge was not planned for and might be anticipated with dread. The wife might dislike the thought of giving up her new independence; or she might dread a renewal of earlier conflicts. Adjustment to the separation was made with more finality and exclusion of the husband than in cases of good adjustment where there was eagerness for a reunion. The good adjustment of this type applies to the wife and children as the family unit. The husband is barred, and his adjustment to the separation therefore is very poor, unless he also welcomes the release. Then he might make an individual adjustment to a nonfamily status and for his part also dread the reunion.

Hollis mentions another outcome of poor marital adjustment—wives who reported their husbands to the draft board for nonsupport so that

[31] Hill, *op. cit.*, pp. 76–77.

they would be drafted.[32]   These women were resentful of their husbands' neglect and sought to punish them.   They talked of the helpful discipline their husbands would receive in the service and overlooked the possibility of injury or death.   Rarely, however, did the experience in the service solve any problems.   Neither husband nor wife was changed sufficiently to overcome their earlier tensions.

3. Poor adjustment to separation.[33]   Sometimes the wife, unable to accept the reality of the separation, could not prepare herself for it either practically or in her thinking.   Nervous tension and emotional upsets then tended to continue through the period of separation to the point of personal disintegration.   In the Iowa study, two of the wives in this group had "nervous breakdowns," and in several cases the husband was finally given a dependency discharge to return to the family; others relied heavily on outside help.   It is not surprising that in some of these families the children became maladjusted.

These families were unable to reorganize themselves to absorb the functions of the absent father.   They were unable to pick up his responsibilities and redistribute his functions.   The family organization and routine therefore broke down, and needs were not satisfied.

The inability to adjust to the separation is closely related to the personality of the wife.[34]   Wives who became fixated in the "panic of surprise" were passive persons who expected gratifications at the hands of others.   Unresourceful and lacking in self-reliance, they had previously functioned only within the protection of the family.   Without this protective wrapping they were helpless, panic-stricken, and unable to accept the new situation, which they defined not so much in terms of the loss of the husband as in terms of denial of a right of protection that they had come to accept as their due.   Their desire was to return to the previous condition, and they tried to secure the release of their husbands, demanding that others drop all responsibilities to help them.   They were in sharp contrast to the adjustive group that, after the initial emotional disturbance, accepted the reality of the husband's absence and attempted to adjust to the separation.

Other factors than the type of prewar marital adjustment also con-

[32] Hollis, *op. cit.*, pp. 110–111.
[33] Hill, *op. cit.*, pp. 79–80.
[34] Frieda Romalis, "The Impact of War on Family Life, I, Reactions to Change and Crisis," *The Family*, 23 (1942), 219–224.

tributed to separation-adjustment. The family with rigid patterns or set ideas of how a family must function adjusted with more difficulty than the adaptable family that was accustomed to modify family customs to meet new needs or unusual situations.[35]   It will be recalled that flexibility also eased the adjustment of families caught in the depression.

The number and severity of hardships also affected adjustment.   These hardships included such things as the degree to which the wife missed her husband, readjustment of finances, difficulties of child discipline, undesired necessity of living with in-laws, housing problems, management of the home, illness of wife or child, the birth of a baby after the father left, difficulties of adjusting employment of the wife to home management when the wife began to work, lack of social life, and injury of husband or reports that he was missing.   The series of cases did not include any in which the husband was killed.

Extent of maladjustment to separation

Although the number of Iowa families is small, they give some indication of the proportion of families that failed to adjust to the war separation.[36]   The 135 families were distributed as follows: 71 families made good rapid adjustment and 34 good slow adjustment, a total of 105 families (78 per cent) that adjusted to separation.   This total includes both the families that continued to regard the husband as an important though absent member and those that excluded him and closed their ranks against him, the latter type being much in the minority.   Twenty-two families (16 per cent) made fair adjustment to separation and only 8 families (6 per cent) poor adjustment.

Adjustment of established familes to reunion

With return of the husband, a second adjustment was in order.   The family that contracted its circle and absorbed the husband's functions during his absence had to expand and find a place for him, or—as sometimes happens—exclude him permanently.

The most extensive analysis of adjustment to reunion is found in the study of 135 Iowa families.[37]   In most of these families the return of the

---

[35] Hill, *op. cit.*, pp. 56–72, 305–307.
[36] Hill, *op. cit.*, p. 298.
[37] *Ibid.*, pp. 85–97, 147–156, 235–236, 244, 252–258, 262–263, 264–311.

husband was anticipated with pleasure. It was not a crisis inasmuch as husband and wife could immediately reapply or attempt to reapply types of interaction and family organization that had existed prior to the separation. The reunion did create a period when readjustment was necessary, however, as the husband had to resume his familial roles and others had to relinquish them. If this simple retransfer of roles was not agreeable, then a general modification of roles was necessary in order to incorporate the husband again within the family circle as a functioning member. The family was never quite the same as when the husband left; children were older, and in some cases there was a new baby scarcely known to its father. New emotional ties had been developed; in 20 families children had grown so close to the mother or some relative that they resented the return of the father to the family circle.

Practical considerations also entered into the readjustment. Many families had moved into smaller quarters or were living with relatives when the husband returned and were unable to find larger quarters; the disappointment was especially sharp for families that in their correspondence had built up an ideal of the home they hoped to have after the husband returned. Inability of the returned husbands to find work that they liked created worries for seven families. Illness prevented six men from functioning in their old roles. These situations for the most part were regarded as passing problems.

More serious was the outcropping of old conflicts that had been dormant during the separation. Out of nine families so afflicted, five came to the conclusion that divorce was the only solution. The divorces did not result from the separation; they were a recognition that the separation had not solved conflicts of long standing.[38]

The type of adjustment to separation was not entirely predictive of the adjustment to reunion. Good adjustment to reunion was made by families that adjusted well to separation, with the husband always included through correspondence in day by day activities and in plans for the future; it was also made by families that were well integrated prior to the separation but so inflexible and rigid that they could not adjust to the absence of a member. Poor adjustment to reunion was made by families with poor adjustment prior to the separation and good adjustment during the separation; these were the families in which separation brought

[38] *Ibid.,* pp. 85–86.

relief from conflicts and tensions which reappeared as soon as the husband returned. Only one family was poorly adjusted at all times—before, during, and after separation.[39]

Certain factors of family life aided in adjustment to reunion. The adaptable and flexible family that met separation well also met reunion adequately. These families were able to modify roles under both conditions so that needs were always met although not necessarily always by the same persons. The adaptable family could take up the slack left by the husband's departure but could also open to include the husband upon his return. Integration of the family was also related to good reunion, but it was not a positive factor in adjustment to separation. Apparently high degree of integration made for a certain amount of rigidity. Good husband-wife adjustment (compatibility, meeting each other's needs, and so on) made both for good separation and good reunion relationships.

Type of family authority was also related to adjustment.[40] The truly democratic family in which parents and children made decisions adjusted well to reunion; there were, however, only 10 families of this type. The equalitarian family (husband and wife about equal in authority) adjusted well to separation or reunion but not necessarily to both. Modified matriarchal or modified patriarchal families tended to make good adjustments both to separation and reunion. The strongly matriarchal families made a good adjustment to separation, since the mother could exercise her authority, but not to reunion when the mother was called upon to curb her authority. The strongly patriarchal families made good adjustment in the reverse order—to reunion but not to separation.

The disabled veteran

When the husband was disabled in service, special problems of readjustment arose, in addition to the more general problems already discussed.[41] Important to adjustment is the type of marital relationship that husband and wife had before the husband entered the service. If the separation occurred soon after the marriage, both often built up an idealized anticipation of what their life would be like after the discharge

---

[39] *Ibid.*, pp. 86–94.

[40] *Ibid.*, pp. 223–226, 305–307.

[41] Wilma T. Donahue and Clark Tibbitts, editors, "The Disabled Veteran," *The Annals* of the American Academy of Political and Social Science, 239 (May, 1945).

of the husband.   Serious disability often shattered this ideal, leading to
a permanent sense of frustration and dissatisfaction.   The marriage of
longer duration with good marital adjustment was better able to withstand
the shock of disability.   For one thing, the couple had already tasted
many of the joys of a good marriage, developed sympathy and deep affection for each other, and merged their interests and goals.   They tended
to function as a unit, making whatever adjustments the disability necessitated.   One such marriage successfully survived two years of overseas
separation, during a part of which the wife did not know where her husband was and communication stopped entirely, followed by notification
of the severe physical illness of her husband.   The wife managed to
see him for a few minutes as he was landed on a stretcher and then followed him from hospital to hospital for another two years, encouraging
him, asking friends to write to and visit him, and otherwise helping him
before he left the hospital to re-establish normal contacts.   After his
release and return to civilian work, the wife made it a part of her daily
function to see that he was well protected to prevent a recurrence of his
illness.   This marriage was strengthened rather than weakened by the
disability.

Adjustment is especially difficult if the disability interferes with normal
sex relations.   The marriage may disintegrate completely; otherwise affection and mutual interests may replace sex as a binding factor in identification and adjustment.   If the couple have not already had children,
the disappointment adds to the problem.   The wife may secretly wish
to leave her husband or to have him as he was before his injury.   The
husband may feel inferior and insecure, fearful that he will lose his wife,
or that perhaps she will take a lover.

Psychoneuroticism creates special problems.   The husband appears
well and able to work, but actually may be unable to do so.   He may
become very sensitive to the situation, using his illness as a defense against
all hardships and throwing undue responsibility upon other members
of the family.   He may simply need reassurance and a sense of security
to enable him to resume a civilian role and find work.   In some cases,
however, he actually may be unable to function in normal social roles
or may be hospitalized.

Disability may necessitate a revised family organization.   The wife
may feel compelled to work for financial reasons or because she cannot
face the adjustment to her disabled husband.   The couple may not at-

tempt the struggle alone, but may live with the parents of husband or wife, in which case the added care that can be given by the parents may ease the situation in some ways.   On the other hand, the arrangement often leads to new problems.   Moved by their sympathy, parents may overprotect a disabled son, thus unwittingly encouraging him to return to a childish state of dependency.   Such a situation is almost certain to be detrimental to marital adjustment.

Many disabilities occur also in civilian life.   Husbands are injured at work, contract tuberculosis, or become psychotic.   Civilian injuries differ, however, in that they do not so often occur to newly married people, or after a long separation that has already shaken the marital adjustment.   Some of the complications of adjustment to marriage and war disability combined are suggested by the following account:

Ann met John, a handsome young officer, a few months before he expected to receive an honorable discharge.   They had a romantic whirl with much dancing and dining together.   He played on her sympathies, telling her he was alone in the world.   Within a month, and without introducing John to her parents, they were married.   Although Ann's parents welcomed John into their home after his discharge, there was considerable family tension. The parents felt hurt because they had not been told of the impending marriage; they also disapproved of John's religion.   As John found it difficult to find work, soon he and Ann moved to a larger city.   Within a short time, John showed marked psychoneurotic reactions, based on his war experiences. When he was hospitalized, Ann returned to her parents' home, where she soon gave birth to a baby girl.   John was allowed to visit his family so that he could see the baby.   Instead of returning to the hospital, he left for another city presumably to find work.   Then followed two years during which Ann did not see her husband, and heard from him only intermittently.   He was alternately in and out of hospitals, trying to find work, wandering over the country.   Meanwhile, Ann's parents urged her to get a divorce and plan permanently to make her home with them; they offered love and security to her and the baby.   Ann herself was torn between her parents' wishes and her own desire for and sense of responsibility toward John.[42]

The final adjustment

Studies and reports made in the late 1940's refer primarily to the early stages of readjustment after the husband has been in service.   What of the final adjustment?   We know that divorces reached a high peak in 1945 and that many were secured by couples married for only a few

[42] Unpublished record.

years—in other words, war marriages. It is not clear to what extent the war experiences and separation motivated the divorces. Ill-advised marriages based on short acquaintance and romantic excitement or on insecurities and fear of never having another chance to marry often end in divorce without the added handicap of long separations and different experiences. Also, as in the Iowa families, the war separation sometimes gave the maladjusted couples an opportunity to try life apart; finding separation more pleasant than marriage, they then decided not to resume marriage but to get a divorce.

The high divorce rate has caused many to overlook the fact that most marriages occurring during the war did not break up. Husband and wife were happy with their reunion: newly married couples set about the business of establishing a home and having children; established families picked up old goals or found new ones. One bit of evidence of good adjustment to marriage and life in general comes from the records of veterans who attended college under the G.I. Bill, which provided them with financial assistance. A report from the University of Wisconsin for the year 1945–46 shows that veterans, both men and women, exceeded nonveterans in grade-point averages.[43] Among the veterans' group, the highest grade-point average was made by married veterans with children, the next highest by married veterans without children, and the lowest by unmarried veterans.

A study of married veterans at the University of Utah throws some added light on their adjustment.[44] With an average length of acquaintance before marriage of 19.6 months and an average marriage of 3.3 years, 96 per cent of the husbands and 94 per cent of the wives classified themselves as happy or very happy. Their most serious problem was financial, with other problems following in this order in terms of frequency: emotional, child rearing, in-laws, and sex. Only 4 per cent found sexual adjustment a problem. One fifth of both husbands and wives of the small group studied said they had no serious problems. In these cases postwar adjustment included not only the usual personal adjustment but also adaptation of the family to a low-income, college situation. The families, 80 per cent of whom had one or two children, lived

[43] Svend Riemer, "Married Veterans Are Good Students," *Marriage and Family Living,* 9 (1947), 11.

[44] R. A. Skidmore, T. L. Smith, and D. L. Nye, "Characteristics of Married Veterans," *Marriage and Family Living,* 11 (1949), 102–104; a study of 50 veteran's families.

in one-, two-, or three-room apartments in a special housing center composed of units transferred from a Japanese relocation center and various government war housing projects. One fourth of the wives attended college along with their husbands. Housework and earning of money were shared by husband and wife. The husbands had an average age of 26.5 years and the wives 25.1, having been married, on the average, at about 23 and 22 years, respectively. These couples were, therefore, at a stage in the marital cycle when they would normally have established themselves economically and would have had their first children; under peacetime conditions education would have been completed. Thus, they were telescoping two stages—premarital education and early married life. That they were able to do so successfully according to both educational and familial standards indicates a high degree of adaptability, mutuality of goals, and resourcefulness.[45]

Children and war

When World War II began, child psychologists and social workers expressed concern for the effect that war would have on children. In England, when cities were first bombed, it was anticipated that children would develop shock similar to that experienced by front-line soldiers during World War I. In the United States, the general talk of war, the movies and radio programs on the subject, and the departure of the father for service were regarded as conducive to extreme fear and anxiety on the part of children.

Young children experienced the war primarily through their parents, and especially their mothers. The war as such, even bombing in England, had little reality for young children. What was real to them was the way in which their mothers reacted. Anna Freud from close observation and study of small children, concluded that children suffered little psychological shock and developed little fear even when they were in houses that were destroyed by bombs, provided their mothers remained

[45] During and at the end of World War II many publications appeared advising veterans upon adjustment to civilian life and interpreting the veteran to families and communities. A long list of such material is given in Evelyn Millis Duvall, "Soldier Come Home: An Annotated Bibliography," *Marriage and Family Living,* 7 (1945), 61–63, 72. References to family adjustment are scattered through the books and articles. Especially helpful for family adjustment are portions of Willard Waller, *The Veteran Comes Back* (Dryden Press, 1944); and George K. Pratt, *Soldier to Civilian, Problems of Readjustment* (Wittlesey House, 1944).

calm and undisturbed.[46]   Conversely, children whose mothers became panicky and developed undue anxiety over bombing were extremely fearful and nervous.   Hill's study of Iowa families also implies that children reflected the adjustment made by their mothers to the absence of the fathers.[47]

In many instances, fear or hatred seemingly aroused in children by the war originated from some frustration inherent in the social training of children.   The natural reaction of young children to thwarting is aggressiveness—hitting the person who restrains them, pulling hair, fighting other children, or in more generalized form willfully breaking toys or engaging in other destructive acts.   Older children are trained to inhibit such aggressive actions toward parents, siblings, or playmates, and often express resentment by the types of games they play.   The war provided an entirely new outlet for aggressiveness, through playing war games and by verbal expressions of hatred for the Nazis or Japanese, an expression that would have been curbed if expressed against parents, teachers, or playmates.   Likewise, the war provided a new outlet for underlying fears and anxieties that also arise in the socializing process.   As children begin to internalize the precepts of their parents (begin to develop a conscience), they suffer feelings of guilt when they disobey.   Often they fear punishment—if not by the parent, then from some other source. In peacetime children are afraid of kidnappers, vague imaginary animals in dark corners, the policeman, earthquakes, and cyclones.   In war, they are afraid of the enemy, of bombing, of invasion.   The war therefore did not create the fear but provided a means of expressing it.   Older children who could comprehend the meaning of war often had realistic fears and anxieties, just as adults had.[48]

Usually the entrance of the father into war was accepted by children with only temporary disturbance, offset by pride in the father and his uniform.   The child received some degree of satisfaction through his identification with the father, and apparently accepted his absence in much the same way that he accepted absence because of the father's normal occupation.   This attitude was related, as stated above, to the mother's reaction.

[46] Anna Freud and Dorothy T. Burlingham, *War and Children* (Medical War Books, 1943), pp. 32–35.

[47] Hill, *op. cit.,* pp. 78–79.

[48] For a discussion of the various types of anxiety felt by small children, see Freud and Burlingham, *op. cit.,* pp. 25–36.

When the child reacted severely to the father's absence, the chief motive was not fear for the father's safety, but insecurity because of the father's previous close relationship to the child. Usually such dependence of the child upon the father was coupled with some degree of rejection by the mother, either because the mother had been unable to accept a true mother role to her child or because she worked or perhaps began to work after the father left for service. The child then felt that he had been abandoned by both parents. If the child felt guilty because of resentment against his parents or because he had in the immediate past shown open hostility toward them, he sometimes interpreted their loss as a punishment and suffered still more.[49] A study of American children whose mothers were unable to cope with them or their behavior disorders and who requested social agency help shows three types of situations.[50]

In one group were children with serious behavior problems that arose after the father left. Their mothers sought to shift the responsibility for their care to the welfare agency. In each case it was found that prior to the father's entrance into service the family relationships had been incompatible or unorganized. The mother had a rejecting attitude toward her children, and the father had filled the gap in the children's lives by an unusually close relationship. The child turned to the father alone for satisfactions usually received from both mother and father. Consequently, when the father left the child was destitute of love and protection.

In the second group of cases, the mother was so immature that she could not function as the family head. Overly dependent upon their husbands, these women were lost without them, and wished to place their children in foster homes or institutions.[51]

The third type found by Igel included very young married women and young unmarried mothers who had not experienced stable family life and were not ready for the responsibilities of motherhood. They resented their babies and wished to shift their care to the welfare agency.

[49] For an excellent discussion of the child's relationship to his parents at different ages and the reactions to evacuation from London without the mother, see *ibid.*, pp. 39–88.

[50] Amelia Igel, "The Effect of War Separation on Father-Child Relations," *The Family*, 26 (1948), 3–9.

[51] Hill, *op. cit.*, pp. 68–69, 78–79, 224, also has a brief discussion of women unable to function without their husbands.

The reactions of children and the difficulties of mother-child relationships when the father left therefore were not directly related to the war, but arose because the absence of the father accentuated a previously inadequate family unit or a personality deficiency on the part of the mother.

When, often because of employment, mothers turned the care of their children over to others temporarily but planned to reclaim them when the husbands returned, they and the children faced special difficulties. At a time when the children had lost their daily association with their fathers and had to make associations with other adults to replace the fathers, they also found their close association with their mothers reduced. They were forced to find substitutes for their mothers as well as their fathers. The mothers had to try to find care for them that would meet not only their physical but their emotional needs. The mothers often were torn by anxiety and feelings of guilt, even though they rationalized their employment by citing financial needs or patriotic motives.

Children's adjustment was related to the type of care provided. With day care children alternated between the real and substitute mothers each day, whereas children in foster homes or institutions spent little time with their own mothers and usually were emotionally upset when the mothers came to visit. If a child adjusted so well in the new environment that he was unaffected by his mother's visits, she became more or less an outsider or stranger to him. Nevertheless, with the return of the father, the mother typically reclaimed the child, who then had to tear himself away from his substitute mother and build up a new relationship with his own parents. Fortunately, most mothers retained their children in their own homes even under stress of war separations, so that few children were subjected to these severe breaks in emotional relationships.[52]

The absentee husband

Most of the research on the family during wartime concerned the wife and children. The husband and father, while absent, had to adjust to the temporary loss of his family. The vast amount of research, primarily in the form of attitude probing, carried out during World War II did not touch specifically on family attitudes. It shows, however, that the married man was less completely absorbed in fighting, less attached to the

---

[52] Care of children of employed mothers during wartime is discussed by M. A. Golton, "Family Day Care: What It Means for the Parent," *Family,* 26 (1945), 54–57; E. Forncock, "To Work or Not to Work," *Family,* 23 (1943), 349–351.

army, more eager for discharge than the unmarried.[53]   The married man, more often than the unmarried, worried about becoming a combat casualty, worried about his family, and found that combat became more rather than less frightening the more he saw of it.[54]

For such differences in attitude, several explanations are offered. Stouffer points out the conflict between the obligations that married soldiers felt for their families and the war obligations imposed by society.[55] The one called for self-preservation and a return home as soon as feasible, the second called for freedom from personal obligations and willingness to face danger and perhaps death.   These conflicts in values faced the unmarried man who was in love and desirous of marrying as well as the married man, although to a less degree.   Military service involved a negation of the family obligations that a married man is expected to assume.   Men and their wives often rationalized the conflict by the statement that the armed forces were fighting to preserve American homes; thus the protective function of husbands was emphasized to the exclusion of other functions.

The transition from the family as a social unit to the army is a drastic one for all men, and especially for married men.   From daily association with wife and children the man moves into a community of men only, where he finds no counterpart for the exchange of sympathy and love to which he has been accustomed.   For some married men the change from family to service unit may have compensations.   If the man feels that he has discharged his family obligations through financial allotments, he may welcome the freedom from daily responsibilities and irritations; he may temporarily enjoy his return to bachelor freedom.[56]   Others, however, suffer from loneliness and homesickness.   The sexual deprivation of the married man is also a hardship.[57]   Organized agencies try to provide impersonal social contacts for servicemen with young women in the communities where they are stationed.   Other women, by individual approaches, seek contacts with the men.   In American mores, impersonal contacts are permissible for the married man but he is condemned both

[53] Samuel A. Stouffer, *et. al., Studies in Social Psychology in World War II,* Vol. I, *The American Soldier: Adjustment During Army Life* (Princeton University Press, 1949), pp. 106–130.

[54] *Ibid.,* Vol. II, *The American Soldier: Combat and Its Aftermath,* pp. 84–86.

[55] *Ibid.,* pp. 84–85.

[56] Reuben Hill, "The Returning Father and His Family," *Marriage and Family Living,* 7 (1945), 31–32.

[57] Cuber, *op. cit.*

by society and his family if he falls in love with another woman or has sexual relations with someone other than his wife. Under war conditions with enforced long separations from his wife, the serviceman faces one of two situations: to isolate himself almost entirely from contacts; or to further such contacts on a more or less intimate basis and risk the result. He may fall in love with another woman to the extent that he asks his wife for a divorce in order to marry her. Or he may run through a series of temporary sex experiences about which he may feel guilty or which he may rationalize on the basis that they meet a physical need but have nothing to do with his love for his wife. In either case, his actions are likely to call down upon him social condemnation and may engender deep feelings of guilt on his part, since normally he shares the attitudes of the civilian community. (The wives left behind sometimes go through the same processes with corresponding emotional reactions.)

With time, men adjust themselves to military life. They find new companionships and loyalties among the men with whom they serve. They achieve identification with the group to which they are assigned. For effective service, individuality must be lost, with each man becoming simply part of a larger unit. Military life therefore rather deliberately destroys privacy and individuality. The group must function as a group, under command of an officer. With loss of individuality comes a feeling of belonging to the group, a sense of security, and a growth of loyalty, which may partly compensate for some of the lost satisfactions normally derived from family life.[58]

The adjustments made to military life may seem to erect high barriers to readjustment to civilian life and to the family group.[59] Social agencies and clinics have such cases in their records, of men who no longer loved their wives or were reluctant again to shoulder the personal responsibilities of the head of a family. For the most part, however, underlying personality factors had not been erased by the war experience and emerged again to contribute to or detract from the marital adjustment.

The war widow

It is difficult to generalize about the effect that a death has upon the remaining members of the family. The role that the person played in the family (husband, wife, child), age of the person, conditions of death

[58] Pratt, *op. cit.*, pp. 35–41.
[59] *Ibid.*, ch. 8.

(sudden, after long illness, accidental, and so forth), degree of attachment to and dependence upon the person: all these are factors in the reaction of people to a death in the family. Few psychologists or sociologists have approached the study of bereavement in a scientific spirit, and little special attention has been given to adjustment of war widows.[60] This discussion of the war widow, therefore, is offered tentatively.

It should be recognized that not all wives whose husbands are in military service live in fear of death; only a small proportion of the armed forces are in the combat area, and of these not all are actually fighting at any one time. The problems of separation uncomplicated by fear of death are much more widespread than dread of widowhood. For those women whose husbands are in combat, however, the emotional strain may be severe.

When death is announced, it is a climax to preceding alternating hopes and fears. Sometimes, however, the announcement lacks finality; some women continue to believe that their husbands are alive—a belief supported by the occasional reappearance of a serviceman reported as dead, perhaps after several years or at the end of a war. Eliot cites two women who were sure they had identified men reported as dead in group pictures subsequently published in magazines and a father who had heard that shockingly crippled men sometimes asked to be reported as dead and to be placed in hospitals.[61]

For most, this disbelief is followed by a realization that the death has occurred. Letters from the husband no longer arrive, and letters addressed to him are returned. Chaplain or fellow servicemen write letters with details and eulogies; personal possessions are sent home. These services soften the shock but prolong the period of time when grief is sharp. The return of the body for burial months, or even a few years, later arouses a recrudescence of grief, but is comforting to relatives in that the deceased one is collected into the family circle of dead and given a funeral.

Often the widow and other relatives crave details of the death, either

---

[60] Thomas D. Eliot, who with his students has studied bereavement in general, has published several articles on war bereavements, but he is frank to say that his conclusions are tentative. See "—of the Shadow of Death," *The Annals* of the American Academy of Political and Social Science, 229 (September, 1943), 87–99; "War Bereavements and Their Recovery," *Marriage and Family Living*, 8 (1946), 1–5, 8.

[61] Eliot, "War Bereavements and Their Recovery," p. 1.

to assure themselves that death really occurred, or if possible to relieve fears regarding the man's suffering. If they can believe that he died quickly and in an heroic action, some of their feeling of shock and futility is erased.

A complicated set of rituals follows death in civilian life, including notification of relatives, comforting visits from minister and friends, arrival of flowers, burial arrangements with the undertaker, and planning for the funeral service. These details not only absorb time and attention but offer a means of expression of grief verbally and in action. They also make possible a showing of love, respect, and admiration for the dead person. Finally, they confirm the death and make it final. The dispersal of relatives after the funeral is a signal that everyday life begins again. The immediate family still misses the deceased member and still has a personal and family adjustment to make to his loss; nevertheless customary activities may be resumed with the assurance that everything possible was done for him before his death and proper respect shown to him afterward. For the war death that cannot be followed by a funeral, no substitute set of social rituals has as yet been developed. The memorial service is the nearest substitute; but since it customarily is held at a later date, it does not provide immediate outlet for dammed-up emotions.

The widow in a war marriage is in a peculiarly difficult position. Separated from her husband within a few weeks or months of the wedding, she has not yet participated in married life to the fullest. She has few memories to sustain her; she finds crashing about her all the ideals and hopes for the future. Her recovery may take longer than that of a woman longer married who in spite of her loss feels that she has experienced a satisfying, though perhaps a short, married life. Nevertheless, these widows also recover and often marry again after a fairly short interval. They are young, and their attitudes are oriented toward marriage. At the same time, having experienced little of married life they therefore have few actual habits or strong marital ties to break. They can perhaps the more readily adjust to a second marriage that is functionally for them the first fully established marriage, although not the first love relationship.

PREPARATION FOR ADJUSTMENT TO CRISES

Since each type of crisis places a different strain on family life, the same family resources do not function for good adjustment to all crises. However, some general aspects of family life that ease adjustment may be listed:

1. Acceptance of the fact that social crises—such as depressions, booms, and wars—occur over and over. They have happened in the past and at present we do not have devices to prevent their recurrence in the future. The American tendency to expect life always to be at the crest of the wave prevents admission that there is also a trough. This blinding of one's eyes to the probability of problems is one basic factor in lack of preparation.

2. Maturity of husband and wife. Overly dependent women could not adjust to their husbands' absence in military service; unstable or dependent men and women could not adapt themselves to the depression.

3. Good marital adjustment prior to the crisis, with well-defined goals, compatibility, and coordination of roles.

4. Integration of the family that enables it to function as a unit for the benefit of all rather than disintegrate into its disparate members.

5. Adaptability to material changes, modifications in patterns of living, and shifting of responsibilities. Adaptability also implies that when the crisis passes (the husband returns from war or is re-employed) roles may again be shifted to restore the husband to a functioning place in the family.

6. Recognition that the first reaction to a crisis is likely to be emotional and to entail some family disorganization. The emotional reaction is normal and should be allowed to express itself. Reorganization to provide for family needs in terms of the crisis follows.

7. Acceptance without shame of supportive aid from outside groups or agencies without which many families cannot meet social crises. Supportive aid can be given by the larger family group, social-work agencies, or such community institutions as the church, organized recreation, civic clubs, or social clubs.

QUESTIONS

1. Define a family crisis. Illustrate from your own experience or observation.

2. How do depressions affect rates of marriage, birth, and divorce? How does war affect these rates?

3. What factors hindered and what factors aided adjustment to the depression of the 1930's?

4. What findings from the study of the depression can be applied to normal unemployment to aid families to adjust?

5. When the young man faces overseas military service, is it better for an engaged couple to marry before he leaves or wait until his return?

6. Explain the different processes involved in good adjustment to war separation on the part of well-adjusted couples and poorly adjusted couples (Hill's study).

7. How can readjustment after the separation be facilitated?

8. How can families be prepared to meet crises without extreme disorganization?

BIBLIOGRAPHY

Depression and unemployment

Angell, Robert C., *The Family Encounters the Depression* (Scribner's, 1936).

Cavan, Ruth Shonle, and Ranck, Katherine H., *The Family and the Depression* (University of Chicago Press, 1936).

Clague, Ewan, Couper, Walter J., and Bakke, E. Wight, *After the Shutdown* (Institute of Human Relations, Yale University, 1934).

Ginsberg, Eli, and Associates, *The Unemployed* (Harper, 1943).

Komarovsky, Mirra, *The Unemployed Man and His Family* (Dryden, 1940).

Morgan, Winona L., *The Family Meets the Depression* (University of Minnesota Press, 1939).

War

Abrams, R. H., editor, *American Family in World War II, The Annals* of the American Academy of Political and Social Science, 229 (1943).

Bossard, J. H. S., and Boll, Eleanor S., editors, *Adolescence in Wartime, The Annals* of the American Academy of Political and Social Science, 236 (1944).

Donahue, Wilma T. and Tibbitts, Clark, editors, *The Disabled Veteran, The Annals* of the American Academy of Political and Social Science, 239 (1945).

Hill, Reuben, *Families Under Stress* (Harper, 1949).

Romalis, Frieda, Zitello, Adelaide K., and Zurfluh, Ruth, *The Impact of the War on Family Life*, reprinted from *The Family*, October, November, and December, 1942 (Family Welfare Association of America, 122 East 22nd Street, New York 10).

Webbink, Paul, editor, *Postwar Jobs for Veterans, The Annals* of the American Academy of Political and Social Science, 238 (1945).

20

The Later Years
of Married Life

W hen elderly people are asked which period of their lives they consider the happiest, the period most often chosen is that between 20 and 40 years of age—"when the children were young," "when we were most needed," "when our family was all around us." [1] A middle-aged grandmother of three young children said feelingly, "The hardest time for a woman is when her children have completed college and she realizes they no longer need her." With old age come further changes that affect the family: retirement of the husband; changes in physical capacity; and widow- or widowerhood. Gradually the social unit of the family decreases, first with the departure of adult children from the home and later with the death of husband or wife. With the death of the widow or the widower, the family ends socially, even though through physical heredity and cultural heritage it flows into succeeding generations. Before this final dissolution of the family—during middle and old age—numerous family readjustments are necessary to meet the changes suggested above.

[1] Ruth Shonle Cavan, *et al, Personal Adjustment in Old Age* (Science Research Associates, 1949), p. 197. It should be noted, however, that 52 per cent of the men and 41 per cent of the women were unable to specify any one period of their lives as happier than any other. Among those who placed one period above all others in happiness, 46 per cent of the men and 52 per cent of the women selected the years between 20 and 40 as happier than childhood, adolescence, middle age, or old age. These percentages are based on responses of 2,988 men and women aged 60 and over.

THE POSTPARENTAL COUPLE

The postparental couple are the husband and wife, usually referred to as middle-aged, in their forties and fifties. The significance of middle age is less physical than social and psychological. The most obvious change is the withdrawal of adolescent and young adult children from the family, leaving husband and wife as the family unit—hence the phrase, postparental couple.[2]

From family to couple

The social unit that began as a couple with marriage, then expanded with the birth of children into a group of both sexes and varied ages, in middle age contracts again to the couple. Generalizing from Census reports, Glick states that the average number of children in families with children in which the mother had reached the end of the reproductive period by 1940 is 3.1.[3] With the first born about one year after marriage, the others follow within the space of four and one half years. These years, near the beginning of marriage, are years of family expansion and role changes, when husband and wife are converted into father and mother, and the area of family interaction includes the children. The social group then usually remains intact until the children leave home. If marriage of the children is used as the final breaking of ties, the conversion of the family to the postparental couple takes place when the mother is between 45 and 50 years of age, the father a few years older.

Actually children begin to "leave" the family long before they marry. With the little child's first inclusion in a play group, he is opposing a social group to the family. It is not until adolescence, however, that peer groups become strong competitors of the family and are a serious threat to family unity. The boy or girl begins to emancipate himself from the family when he finds his deepest satisfactions among his peers

[2] Different authors have tried to devise terms to point up the significance of middle age for family relationships. "Launching stage" is used in Willard Waller, *The Family, a Dynamic Interpretation* (revised by Reuben Hill, Dryden, 1951), pp. 425–449, to refer to the efforts that parents make to launch their children into jobs, marriage, and adult independence. Hill has also used the phrase "empty nest," emphasizing the stage after children have left the home. "Postparental couple" suggests both the withdrawal of children and the reversion of the family to a couple.

[3] Paul C. Glick, "The Family Cycle," *American Sociological Review,* 12 (1947), 166–169. Glick's figures are for 1940, with comparative figures for 1890. Although some changes might have occurred since 1940, the general picture undoubtedly is the same. A comparable analysis for 1950 has not been made.

rather than with his parents.   Sometime during adolescence the child prefers attending the movies with his contemporaries instead of his parents, turns down the family picnic in favor of the peer-group bicycle hike, or protests vigorously over spending Christmas with out-of-town grandparents because it will mean the self-denial of a dance or tobogganing. The child is withdrawing from the family and entering autonomous social groups.   The initiative for withdrawal usually comes from the child, who is supported in his emancipation by his peers and by a general philosophy that adolescents must make a heterosexual adjustment and free themselves from the family.[4]   When adolescents enter college or begin to work and earn their own money, they withdraw further from the family group; even if they continue to live at home, they participate more and more in extrafamily groups.   The final symbol of emancipation is the marriage of the son or daughter, since in our culture each newly married couple is expected to establish an independent family.

A corollary of social withdrawal is psychological independence.   The dependent child who leaned heavily upon the parents for love and approval loses this need with increasing maturity.   Identification with the parents is replaced by identification with the peer group or some members of it and finally identification with the spouse.

Each step that the child takes away from the social boundaries of the family, each advance in independence, necessitates an adjustment on the part of the parents.   In part, the adjustment is social.   The mother, who for many years kept her late afternoon hours free from engagements in order to be at home when children came from school, finds herself in an empty house when adolescent children lengthen the school day by athletic practice, extracurricular activities, or "dates" at the drug store; when grown children have jobs that take them from home for the entire day or when they leave home for college, the leisure hours are greatly increased.   The father is less affected than the mother, since he customarily spent less time with the children when they were young.   But he also finds the house empty when adolescents rush from home early in the evening for football or basketball games or to study at a chum's home. As with any change in social groupings, the remnants of groups left after the withdrawal of some members must reorganize.   The older patterns of interaction are impossible; new ones develop.   The group thus re-

[4] For a discussion of this situation from the point of view of the adolescent, see Chapter 11.

forms on the basis of those who remain; or new members are introduced into the membership to replace the old. In the case of the family, husband and wife may increase their own areas of interaction, building up couple activities as family activities die out. Also, they may increase nonfamily contacts through closer association with friends who are in a similar stage of the family cycle. The mother especially feels the need for increased social contacts. Observation suggests that many middle-aged women fulfill this need through increased community service; boards and committees of community agencies are heavily loaded with middle-aged women whose daytime hours are free. When women are reviewed by agency heads and boards for possible volunteer service the presence or absence of children is an important factor; the woman whose children are adult or near-adult is the one invited to serve. There is also at present a strong movement of middle-aged women into paid employment. From incidental information, it seems possible to state also that some middle-aged women are returning to college to complete college courses abandoned in order to marry, or to secure additional training for some profession.

Employment of middle-aged wives

Many of these methods of replacing children with other activities and work are not measurable; that is, specific information is not available to measure the extent of the movement. Certain facts about the employment of older women are known, however. We know that in 1948, 19.4 per cent of all married women aged 45–64 who were living with their husbands were employed. This percentage had almost doubled since 1940, when 10.3 per cent of married women of the same age and marital group were employed. This increase outstripped that for either single women or the widowed and divorced. Single employed women aged 45–64 equalled 60.9 of all single women of the same age in 1940 and 61.6 per cent in 1948; employed women among widowed, divorced, and separated women aged 45–64 were 39.0 per cent of the total women in this age group in 1940 and 48.9 per cent in 1948.[5]

This increasing movement of older married women into paid employment gives promise of permanency. It is related to various social factors,

---

[5] *Current Population Reports, Labor Force, Marital and Family Characteristics of the Labor Force in the United States: April, 1948*, Series P-50, No. 11 (Bureau of the Census, December 23, 1948), p. 10.

perhaps the most important of which is the long-term decrease in the birthrate. The middle-aged woman of a generation ago was still playing the role of mother to her younger children, and perhaps grandmother to the offspring of her older children. Another factor in the increased number of middle-aged employed women is the increased length of life: there are more middle-aged women to work. A third factor is the shift of population from farm to city with increased opportunities for work. Since all three factors will probably continue, it seems a safe prediction that older married women will remain in the labor force and in fact increase in numbers and as a proportion of the total number of women working.

The significance of employment of older married women for the family should not be underestimated. It establishes a new life organization for the wife and a new interactional relationship with her husband. The obvious changes in her life routine have to do with the hours of arising, planning of employment and housework, change in type of wardrobe, more rigid hours of work, and so forth. Her social groups change from the mothers and unemployed wives with whom she formerly associated to other employed women of varied ages and work experience. Some are married women like herself whose children are grown; others are married or unmarried workers whose entire adult experience has been shaped to employment. In order to secure status among these new associates and with her employer, her scheme of values changes. Work skills, efficiency, punctuality, concentration, impersonality, control of emotions, ability to maintain smooth secondary relationships, and acceptance of regimentation replace the homemaking skills, permissiveness of conduct and emotional expression, personal relationships, and independence of work arrangements of family life. Competitiveness directed toward promotion replaces family cooperativeness, and individualism is sharpened, for each worker must look out for herself, whereas in the family unity gives protection and security. If the woman is a successful worker, her ego-satisfaction may be greater than that she secured as wife and mother, which often came indirectly through the success of husband or children. On the other hand, her affectional relationships are curtailed, and the impersonality of the work situation is in sharp contrast to the warm emotional relationship between mother and children. Until the adjustment to new values is made, the work group may seem cold and remote, interested only in her skills and not in her as a personality. Although one set of satisfactions cannot replace another (ego-satisfaction cannot replace emotional response), increase in one satisfaction can compensate for loss of another. Thus the employed woman may continue to regret the loss of her earlier affectional relationship with her young children, but be highly gratified at the increase in ego satisfaction.

Employment also has the advantage of giving the woman a future to which to look forward, a future of success in her job, financial compensation, and perhaps added security for old age. The middle-aged woman who does not find activities to compensate for the lost maternal functions tends to look backward, to long for and relive in fantasy the past when her children were small, and to feel that the future holds little for her. Her useful period is over, and life comes to be a matter of waiting without enthusiasm for the end.

The relationship between husband and wife also changes with employment of the middle-aged woman. Whereas formerly they filled paternal-maternal roles or the wife served as companion to her husband, in middle age they assume partnership roles.[6] Any role adjustment is difficult, not only for the person making the change but also for others affected by interrole relationships. The wife cannot drastically change her role without the husband's making corresponding changes in his role. The wife, upon employment, cannot become a partner unless the husband adjusts his role and a new interactional pattern is established. These role and interrole changes often cause temporary tension and even conflict. The wife has less time to care for her husband's personal needs and wishes —to prepare his favorite foods, to give the same care to his clothing, to act as hostess to friends or business associates, or to enter joint recreation. The husband may feel to some extent rejected, or that his wife's new job has become more important to her than he is. The fact that the wife is earning money regularly also affects the relationship. The increased family income may be welcomed, especially if the wife begins to work when children are in college or after the husband (usually older than his wife) has reached a standstill or has begun to decline in earning power. When additional income is not actually needed, it may nevertheless make possible the fulfillment of plans long delayed, such as purchase of a house or an extended vacation trip. Such partnership in income is an incentive to equal status of husband and wife in planning and decision

[6] See discussion of these roles on pages 447–450.

making.   However, this happy adjustment is not always made.   In general, in American families the husband holds a slight dominance over the wife as official head of the family and chief income producer.   Unless the husband is very secure in his feeling of personal adequacy he may resent his wife's financial contribution as an encroachment upon his rights.   Her earnings give her increased power and the ability to make independent decisions; his own power and authority relative to hers decrease.

The clinging parent

In contrast to women who expand their activities in new directions with maturity of their children are those who cling to the mother role when no dependent children remain to be mothered.   Fathers also sometimes resist giving up the role of protector and adult model to their children.   Such parents continue to direct, supervise, and make decisions for adolescent and older sons and daughters.   The role often becomes intensified and is overplayed as son or daughter ignores the parental directives or openly rebels.   Parents who play an outmoded parental role underestimate the abilities of their children to look out for themselves and hence are riddled by fears and insecurities.   They also see their only avenue for ego-satisfaction and status closing before them.   Hence, the departure of a child for college or the marriage of son or daughter is treated as a bereavement, with parents grieving for the loss of the child's dependency as they might grieve over the physical death of the child. Sometimes this actual physical withdrawal of the child from the family and his acceptance of new adult roles in other groups is not sufficient to turn the parent's activities into other channels.   There are parents who insist that a child attend college in the home town so that he may remain at home; or who move to a college town for the same reason.   Other parents cling closely to the son or daughter who has married, the extreme cases being those who accompany the young married couple on their honeymoon, who insist that they share the parental home, or who attempt to plan the lives of the young couple.   This attempted prolongation of the parental role has provoked many acrimonious in-law, and especially mother-in-law, jokes by which younger people unleash the hostility that they cannot express overtly in personal relationships.   In part, the jokes indicate immaturity on the part of the jokers, who are still struggling for independence from an older generation.   In part, however, they spring from the failure of parents to find other roles to replace the parental one. When the young married couple live with the parents of one, as did an unusually large proportion of people after World War II, tensions easily arise over the conflict between attempted dominance by the parents and the desire of the young couple for autonomy. Very maternal women find great happiness in the situation since it not only permits them to continue the maternal role to their own adult children but to add to their brood the son-in-law or daughter-in-law and in time grandchildren. Such women not uncommonly use the term "children" inclusively to refer to the young parents and the grandchildren as though all were in the same category of immaturity and degree of dependency.[7]

Other middle-aged people, less enwrapped in parental roles, see in the maturity of their children a threat to their own youthfulness. Some try directly to evade the issue by insisting that sons or daughters in the early or middle twenties are not ready for marriage. Others identify themselves with their children and attempt to become members of their children's social circle. They may attach themselves to their adolescent children's groups, outdoing the young people in use of current slang, vigorous dancing, or vivid dressing. The mother may habitually refer to her husband and sons as "the boys," while her husband calls her and her daughters "the girls," implying contemporary status to middle-aged and adolescent. The mother may take pride in the fact that she is "accepted" by her daughter's friends as "one of them." With marriage of the son or daughter, the parents may continue this identification. The unoccupied mother may follow her daughter through all the rituals of an elaborate wedding with enthusiasm equal to the daughter's own; if, as often happens under the pressure of war conditions or imminent military service, the daughter wishes to curtail the social and ceremonial aspects of the wedding, the mother feels cheated. Finally, grandchildren are regarded less as members of a third generation than as children of the grandparents.

[7] A deficiency of the English language is that there is no collective term to apply to the adult offspring. In one sense, *child* denotes a biological relationship; a man of 60 may rightfully be called the child of his 90-year-old mother. In another sense child refers to an immature and chronologically young person. Son or daughter may be used but does not indicate degree of maturity. There is no collective word that means sons and daughters of maturity in the sense that children refers to sons and daughters who are young. The invented word *sibling* emphasizes the relationship between children. A similar word is needed for adult offspring to express the relationship to their parents.

Emotional hindrances

Emotional conflicts of earlier years that have not been solved may emerge into consciousness or become aggravated at middle age.   Social insecurities or sexual tensions experienced by parents during their own adolescence, as well as guilt over early violation of sexual norms, may be reactivated.   Submerged during the full and active years when children were young and safe in the family circle, these tensions now are projected upon the children who are assumed to have the same problems, feel the same inferiorities, make the same mistakes as the parents.   Conversely, parents who have solved their earlier problems, who accept them as part of the progress toward maturity, are able to be more objective toward their children.   They view their children as individual entities rather than revivals of their own adolescent personalities.

Husbands and wives who have failed to make a good marital adjustment and have turned to their children for the love and encouragement that normally comes from the spouse also face a difficult adjustment with independence of the children.   Young children respond to the needs of their parents and find their own needs fulfilled in the close relationship. With maturity, however, they look elsewhere for emotional satisfactions, although the wrench to free themselves may be especially violent when the parent-child relationship has been extremely intimate.   The widowed, divorced, or estranged mother who has found in her son a replacement for her husband may fight with every weapon at her command the introduction of a daughter-in-law into the family.   The daughter-in-law is a rival for the son's affection and consideration, and according to our mores is entitled to a greater claim upon the man than his mother has. The father who is overly attached to his daughter may experience similar reactions toward his son-in-law.

Climacteric of the wife

Accidentally coincident in time with the departure of children are the biological changes of the climacteric, which create physical tensions and discomforts, and, of more importance to the family, psychological adjustments.   Among women, the most noticeable outward change is the menopause or cessation of menstruation, which usually occurs during the forties.   It is caused by changes in the sex glands and is accompanied by mild reactions, such as hot flushes (similar to severe blushing), digestive disturbances, languor, headaches, and digestive disturbances; it may also involve irritability, increased sensitivity to noise, emotional instability, and feelings of depression. These symptoms of slow glandular changes may extend over a period of five or six years.[8] Whether or not men also experience a climacteric in middle age is a matter of debate.[9]

The climacteric affects marriage and family life through its relation to reproduction, its effect on sex life, and its general interpretation as the end of youth.

With our present small families, most women have completed their reproductive period during their twenties or early thirties. The actual inability to conceive that comes with menopause therefore is felt more as a symbol of loss of youthfulness and vitality than because it deprives the woman of additional children. Most women in their forties have long since produced all the children they desire and would be aghast at the prospect of a new baby. A few, feeling keenly the withdrawal of adolescent children, may long for dependent children, but as a rule they wish they could be young again and retrace the past rather than launch themselves into a new cycle of parenthood.[10] Nevertheless, many women face the forties with a distinct feeling that an era has come to an end in their

[8] Nathan W. Shock in Oscar J. Kaplan, editor, *Mental Disorders in Later Life* (Stanford University Press, 1945), pp. 44–45; A. A. Werner, "Sex Behavior and Problems of the Climacteric," in Morris Fishbein and E. W. Burgess, editors, *Successful Marriage* (Doubleday, 1948), pp. 471–484.

[9] Shock says that cases of men with symptoms similar to those of women are rare and that the concept of a male climacteric is not generally accepted.—*loc. cit.* Another writer (Eugene Davidoff) in the same volume accepts the concept but states that difficulties of adjustment occur less frequently among men than women. Kaplan, *op. cit.*, pp. 187–188. Werner explicitly states that men experience a climacteric.—*loc. cit.*, pp. 480–484.

[10] On the other hand, Helene Deutsch states that some women rush to produce one or two late children before the menopause shuts off the highly valued ability to reproduce. She attributes these births to a "thrust of activity" that results from the threatened blow to the ego given by the imminence of the climacteric. In other women the thrust of activity carries them into outside activities where they seek to create in some other field than the production of children. The urge toward late motherhood and the entrance into outside activities are analyzed by Deutsch as a defense mechanism against personal decline. They represent resistance to middle age.—Helene Deutsch, *Psychology of Women, A Psychoanalytic Interpretation,* Vol. II, *Motherhood* (Grune and Stratton, 1945), pp. 457–459. The analysis in the preceding paragraphs of this chapter treats outside activities as compensations for maternal duties no longer possible, which, if successful, give status in a new area of activity. They are not directly related to the climacteric so much as to the withdrawal of children.

personal lives.   Although women do not gain status in our society through fertility beyond the production of two or three children,[11] they gain it by youthful appearance and vigor.   Changes in physical appearance, and reduced capacity of the sense organs, energy, speed, and coordination come gradually over the years; there is no sudden decline at the climacteric.   The mild physical symptoms of the menopause do, however, focus the woman's attention upon her body, and she often becomes fully aware for the first time that she no longer looks or acts as she did at the age of 20.

The woman's personal and family adjustments at the time of the menopause are important in determining her acceptance of it.   Some of her reactions that verge on the neurotic are perhaps more closely related to her personal adjustment and relation to husband and children than to the physical changes.   If her maturing children are withdrawing at this time, their rejection of her as a maternal figure may increase her anxieties and insecurities.   If her husband is nearing the peak of his occupational striving, he may seem to neglect her.   She may easily misinterpret these situations, viewing them not as growing out of external social relationships but as proof that her physical changes make her unattractive and unappealing.   Clinical experience of psychiatrists and controlled studies emphasize that women with marked reactions to the menopause are those with previous neurotic symptoms or maladjustments, which become exaggerated at this time but are not created by the physical changes themselves.[12]   This statement does not mean that the fears and insecurities are any the less real to the woman, but that their origin should be sought in personal adjustment and family relationships.

Sexual readjustment

At certain periods in life, sex comes to the fore as a personal and social problem.   We have already discovered that the little child's curiosity

---

[11] So firmly fixed in our collective attitudes is the norm of the small urban family that married couples with four, five, or more children are looked at askance; they may be pitied even though they ardently desired a large family, regarded as incompetent in their failure to use contraceptives, or ridiculed as being slightly animalistic in allowing nature to take its course.

[12] Franz Alexander, *Psychosomatic Medicine, Its Principles and Applications* (Norton, 1950), pp. 238–240; Norman Cameron in Kaplan, *op. cit.,* 143–184; M. H. Greenhill, "A Psychosomatic Evaluation of the Psychiatric and Endocrinological Factors in the Menopause," *Southern Medical Journal* (Birmingham), 39 (1946), 786–794.

about his body and its differences from those of the opposite sex are a matter of concern to his parents. Their repressive measures tend to drive the interest underground or at least into secretive practices during childhood. At adolescence, with the maturing of the sex organs and the great freedom of heterosexual social relationships, attitudes and practices toward sex are again reviewed and brought into a new framework of control orientated toward marriage and greater freedom of sexual activities within marriage. The restrictions and controls, it should be noted, are social in nature and only moderately related to biological changes. When men and women come into middle and old age they encounter new social attitudes toward sex, again of a disapproving and restrictive type. One writer attributes the restrictive attitude to "one ancient prejudice identifying sex with sin and another denying the right of sinning to elderly men and women." [13]   It seems likely that the attitude derives also from the identification of sex with childbearing and the belief that sex in older couples without the possibility of conception is licentious. Nowadays, of course, this attitude is not rational, for the use of contraceptives has divorced intercourse from conception for many families long before the menopause. In addition, there are erroneous folk beliefs of the absence of sexual capacity and desire in middle-aged and older persons. Although women are unable to bear children after the menopause, they do not lose their desire for sexual experiences. They are still able to participate in and derive satisfaction from sex relationships; in fact, being relieved of any fear of an undesired pregnancy, they may even enjoy the experience more freely than in earlier years.[14]

Whether or not men undergo physical changes in middle age similar to the climacteric in women, they usually lose neither the power to beget children nor the capacity for intercourse until some years later. There is, however, a decline in frequency of sexual activity and, one would infer, a decline in drive.[15]   Complete loss of potency does not follow a uniform pattern for all men: a few men become impotent during middle age; on the other hand, some men are able to father children in extreme old age. By age 65, 25 per cent of Kinsey's sample of males were impotent; but at age 80, 25 per cent were still able to have intercourse. Thus, the oc-

[13] Cameron, *loc. cit.,* p. 148.

[14] LeMon Clark, "Sex Life of the Middle Aged," *Marriage and Family Living,* 11 (1949), 58–60.

[15] A. C. Kinsey, A. B. Pomeroy, and C. E. Martin, *Sexual Behavior in the Human Male* (Saunders, 1948), pp. 226–259, 567–568.

currence of the male's impotency as measured by inability for intercourse may occur at any time over a long age range, in contrast to the concentration of the female climacteric within less than one decade of life.   It must be remembered, however, that women may continue to have and enjoy intercourse after the menopause into extreme old age.   There is therefore no sudden cessation of sexual activity at one age period for either men or women.   Moreover, as men become impotent, their power declines gradually and without a sudden break; adjustment to nonsexual life may therefore be made gradually.   Kinsey's data show such a gradual decline in total sexual activity for men, with a peak in the teens and long slow decline thereafter.   Marital intercourse shows a similar decline in frequency; from a peak of high frequency among married men of 16–20 (newly married) to infrequent occurrence in very old age.   The decline is regular with no sharp drops.

However, the pattern of intercourse for married men changes in middle age.   For each five-year age period, Kinsey found that from 27 to 37 per cent of married males had recourse to extramarital sources; the percentage declined only slightly with age.   These outside sources included both prostitutes and companions (Kinsey's term for all nonprostitutes providing extramarital experience for men).   Kinsey found that middle-aged and elderly married men secured a higher proportion of their total sexual intercourse with outside contacts, a lower proportion with their wives, than did younger married men; also that prostitutes were resorted to with increasing frequency in middle and old age, whereas younger men sought companions.   Any conclusions drawn from these findings are speculative, as Kinsey did not secure case histories by which to interpret his statistics.   Does the wife, burdened with the minor discomforts of the menopause and her emotional readjustments, thrust her husband aside at this time?   Does the husband, feeling neglected by his wife, and perhaps therefore doubting his own virility, attempt to prove his youthfulness by extramarital affairs?   It must be remembered, however, that this shift from wife to companion to prostitute characterizes only a minority of husbands.   If other husbands feel neglected, they find other means of solving their problem.

Adjustment of men

The social and psychological adjustment of middle-aged men is usually regarded as less acute than that of their wives.   Men have a dual set of satisfying relationships—family and vocation; the majority of women have only the family or at most family and fragmentary community contacts. Family and vocation are related to each other, in that family relationships may be an incentive to greater vocational effort or so disturbing that the man is unable to work at top capacity. Conversely, success or failure at work has repercussions upon family life, in terms of the standard of living and the respect in which the man is held by his wife and children. Nevertheless, the man usually has two outlets for personal satisfactions, whereas the woman has one. When children withdraw from the family, the father is less affected than the mother. Proud though he may be of his children, he is not so dependent upon them for status as is their mother. If his children are complete failures, he may feel his share in their failure less because he can turn to his work for success. Also, since he devotes less time than the mother to childbearing, he is less likely than she to attribute the shortcomings of children to personal failure as a good parent. (It should be noted that the woman who has consistently combined motherhood with a vocation may take a similar attitude toward her children, unless she shares the traditional attitude that the mother should devote her entire time to her children; then she may have an underlying feeling of insecurity and guilt even when her children meet every standard for success.) The middle-aged man's revaluation of himself is more likely to concern his vocational status than his status as a parent. Middle age is regarded as the "prime of life," the point when youthful drive is not yet noticeably diminished, experience is great, and the combination of the two carries the man to his peak of success. If he has reached success in middle life, he may relax later— even retire before old age—knowing that he has met social expectations. The man who has not found success easily, on the other hand, increases the pressure upon himself during middle age. He works under strain and tension and concentrates upon his business time and energy that previously had been divided between family and work. Many men during middle age are forced to realize that no matter how hard they try they cannot fulfill the American dream that "any boy can be President," or even that "home-town boy makes good." Younger men are promoted to positions above them. Only extreme lack of realism can prevent them from knowing that they have reached their maximum success and fallen short of what they once expected of themselves or what was expected of them by others. Their sense of failure and frustration may exhibit itself in irritability toward their wives, in irrational blame of their wives, or in depressions and withdrawal.   Some men may turn to or increase extramarital sexual affairs in the effort to prove to themselves that they are still young and virile.

Satisfactory readjustment

When husband and wife are in sympathetic communication with each other and understand that each has a problem of loss of status-giving activity, a feeling of uselessness, and especially for the wife a diminution of response-giving contacts, a closer relationship may develop.   Each may turn to the other, as in the first years of marriage, as the chief source of personal satisfactions.

The description that follows is of a family that made a successful progress through the middle years.

The Martins are a family in the middle years.   Their married son lives with his wife and little son some three hundred miles distant; their unmarried daughter is a secretary in a city a hundred miles away.   During the period when they were rearing their children, the Martins lived in a comfortable six-room frame house in a middle-class neighborhood.   Mrs. Martin, aided by her daughter, did all her housework, while Mr. Martin and his son made necessary repairs and usually redecorated their home, which they owned.   As a moderately successful engineer, Mr. Martin was able to send his son to the state university and his daughter to the local junior college. The focus of family life was their home; here they entertained friends and relatives, listened to the radio, helped the children with their school work, and gave occasional parties for the son or daughter.   The church provided their only organizational contact.   Because of her close contacts with her children and her dearth of outside activities, Mrs. Martin found it difficult to relinquish her children.   She wanted her son, who married immediately after his graduation, to postpone his marriage; and she tried in vain to persuade her daughter to find work in her home city so that she might remain at home. The father, however, maintained that both son and daughter must make their own decisions in these matters.   Slowly, the Martins adjusted to the middle years.   Persuaded by her daughter, who made frequent visits home, the mother began to patronize a beauty parlor and substituted gay hats and blouses for the more conservative ones she had previously worn; with the expense of child rearing ended, there was no longer the necessity for buying clothing that would outlast minor changes in style.   She also joined the Woman's Club for the first time and faithfully attended their weekly meetings; her interest was thus aroused in many new fields and her conversation widened from domestic affairs to include current events and cultural subjects.   In her middle years she thus seemed to become younger, both in appearance and outlook, than she had been during the time when she was absorbed in her children.   The frame house now seemed too large for husband and wife, and too full of memories of their children; moreover, the neighborhood was changing and the new neighbors were not congenial.   Mr. and Mrs. Martin therefore sold their home and bought a smaller house nearer the edge of the city.   Unhampered by the care of children, Mrs. Martin occasionally accompanies her husband on business trips and from time to time visits her son or daughter.

Although the middle years have brought greater freedom and a lessening of some responsibilities, they have also brought the shadow of future problems.   Mrs. Martin is beginning to feel the twinges of arthritis.   Moreover, for certain periods she assumes the care of her widowed mother, a woman in her eighties; this responsibility is shared with several sisters, for the mother prefers to make long visits with each daughter rather than to spend all her time in one place.   Mr. Martin, still capable and in fact at the peak of his productive period, nevertheless is beginning to feel his years.   Recently he declined a new and promising position in another city, for it seemed that the financial advantages of the new position would be a poor substitute for the security he felt in his present position, and that the cultural advantages of a larger city would not compensate for the strain of adjustment and the loss of old friends.[16]

Summing up the family situation of middle-aged people, we may regard it as a time of reappraisal and redirection for husband and wife. Physical changes, psychological independence of children, their withdrawal from the family as a social unit, and the vocational adjustments of the husband converge upon husband and wife during the forties or fifties.   Physical changes are less significant for the husband than for the wife; for her they have their greatest significance because of their psychological and social implications.   The impact of these forces upon husband and wife compels them to bring into consciousness previously half-denied facts of the mounting years and the maturity of children. Some men and women cannot face or accept these facts and look for some escape: identification with adolescents; clinging to the maternal or paternal role; neurotic reactions, especially on the part of the wife; seeking of extramarital sex relations, especially on the part of the husband. Other couples reorganize their lives, pulling their interpersonal relationships closer together, accepting a new status of equality with their mature children, and revising their roles to permit the wife to shift from a maternal to a partnership role with activities beyond the home.

The effects of middle-age changes on marriage and the family are

16 Unpublished report.

largely unknown.   Studies reported so far center on the sexual life of males, physical changes, and neurotic and psychotic reactions of the middle aged.   Adolescent-parental relationships are almost invariably stated from the point of view of the adolescent's personality development. The neglect of middle age as an area for serious psychological and sociological study is perhaps related to the recency of this period as a special stage in family life, which has been created by the increasing length of life that now carries men and women far into old age and the declining birthrate that liberates them from the care of children while they still have many years of vigorous life before them.

FAMILY LIFE OF THE OLD

At the present time, husband and wife have on the average a period of about a decade together after the marriage of their last child and before death removes one of them.   Glick gives the future situation for people married in 1940, which would probably be somewhat more favorable than for those married earlier and now at middle or old age.[17]   For those married in 1940, a median total married life of 39 years can be predicted, with the last child marrying after the parents have been married 28 years. The wife would then be 50 years old and her husband 53.   For 11 more years, until the wife was 61 and her husband 64, they could expect to live together.   Since the death rate is less favorable for men than for women, the husband usually is the first to die.   With his death occurring when the couple are in the early sixties, the widow would expect to live 13 more years to age 74.   When the wife is the first to die, her age would be 61 and the husband could anticipate 6 additional years to age 70.   In either case, the postparental period as a couple is followed by a post-marital period when the family shrinks to one person.   Thus the family in old age falls into three types: husband and wife couples; widows; and widowers.   Although these various ages that mark stages in marital life are medians—half of the men (and half of the women) would make the transition steps earlier and half later than the ages given above—they afford a general framework within which to discuss the old family.

---

[17] Glick, *op. cit.,* pp. 168–169.   Glick's figures are medians, which means that half of the people would be younger and half older than the age given in each case.

Marital status after age 65

The generalized picture of the change in status of the median couple may be supplemented by the actual marital distribution of persons aged 65 and over, as shown in Figure 54.   The most striking fact is that more than half of the women are widowed, as compared with less than one fourth of the men.   Widowhood begins early for women, during the

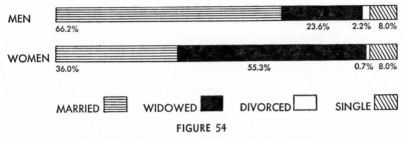

| MEN |
| 66.2%   23.6%   2.2% 8.0% |

| WOMEN |
| 36.0%   55.3%   0.7% 8.0% |

MARRIED   WIDOWED   DIVORCED   SINGLE

FIGURE 54

Marital Status of Persons Aged 65 and Over, 1950

Widowhood is the most common status for women after age 65.   The longer span of life of women as compared with men creates more widows than widowers.   In addition, more elderly widowers than widows remarry and thus reacquire the status of married.   (Source: *Current Population Reports, Population Characteristics, Marital Status and Household Characteristics: March, 1950,* Series P-20, No. 33 [Bureau of the Census, February 12, 1951], p. 10.)

period of middle age.   Among women aged 45–54, 12 per cent are widowed; among men of the same age only 3 per cent.   Among women aged 55–64, 26 per cent are widowed; among men, 7 per cent.   Figure 55 shows marital status by five-year age periods into extreme old age. Death decreases the total number of old people with each passing period, and increases the percentage of widows and widowers.   At all ages widows greatly exceed widowers.

The rate of remarriage in the United States is high.   It follows that many old people, classified as married, at one time were widowed or divorced and then remarried.   For all men aged 50 and over in 1948 who were classified as married, 80.3 per cent had been married more than once; for women, 86.1 per cent had ventured into marriage two or more times.   The ages above 50 are not broken down into a finer classification.[18]   Many of these remarriages had occurred when the couples

[18] *Current Population Reports, Population Characteristics, Marital Status, Number of Times Married, and Duration of Present Marital Status: April, 1948,* Series

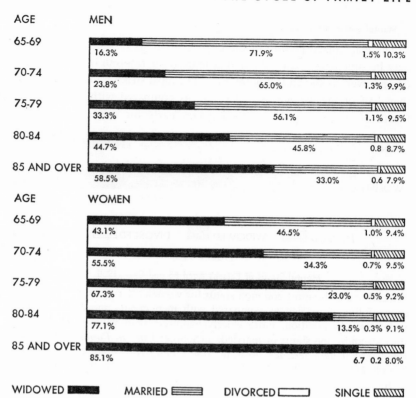

FIGURE 55

Marital Status of Persons Aged 65 and Over by Age, 1940

One of the most severe trials of old age is the loss of husband or wife. With each advancing decade, more and more men and women are left without this vital companionship. Women, especially, must anticipate widowhood in later life. (Source: Ruth Shonle Cavan, *et al., Personal Adjustment in Old Age* [Chicago: Science Research Associates, 1949], p. 43.)

were young and therefore had stood the test of time; others, however, took place during old age, thus projecting the old person into a new

---

P-20, No. 23 (Bureau of the Census, March 4, 1949), p. 21. These percentages should not be misinterpreted. Among all men aged 50 or over ever married, 7.7 per cent have been married once, 31.4 per cent married more than once, 55.0 per cent are widowed, and 5.9 per cent divorced. The corresponding percentages for all women ever married are: married once, 1.4; married more than once, 8.9; widowed 87.0; divorced 2.6. The percentages in the text compare only those married at the time of the Census report according to number of times married; widowed and divorced are omitted from the calculation.

marital situation with motives and potentialities that differ from those of the young marriage.

The married woman of 65 or over is much more likely than the man of similar age to be a member of an "old" marriage in which the spouse also is 65 or over (Figure 56). Almost 93 per cent of all married women of 65 or over have husbands who also are aged 65 or over, and none of the women were married to men under 45 years of age. Men, however, tend

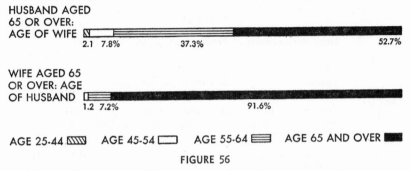

HUSBAND AGED
65 OR OVER:
AGE OF WIFE
2.1 7.8%   37.3%   52.7%

WIFE AGED 65
OR OVER: AGE
OF HUSBAND
1.2 7.2%   91.6%

AGE 25-44 ▨▨▨   AGE 45-54 ▭   AGE 55-64 ▤   AGE 65 AND OVER ▰

FIGURE 56

Age of Spouse of Husbands and Wives Aged 65 and Over, 1949

Many men past 65 have middle-aged or youthful wives, thus tending to continue into old age the type of married life typical of younger men. Elderly and old women tend to have husbands of their own age range. At least part of the explanation lies in the fact that a greater proportion of elderly widowers than widows remarry, and they seek young wives rather than women near their own ages. (Source: *Current Population Reports, Population Characteristics, Marital Status and Household Characteristics: April, 1949,* Series P-20, No. 26 [Bureau of the Census, January 27, 1950], p. 19.)

to marry younger women and even old men sometimes marry very young women. Only 52.7 per cent of men aged 65 and over are married to women in the same age range. A few are married to women still in their twenties.

From the difference in marital patterns of elderly men and women, it follows that family patterns also may differ. Old women are the parents of adult children only; but old men sometimes are the fathers of young children. A small minority of men, therefore, either experience fatherhood for the first time in their later years or, having reared one family and become widowers, remarry and sire a second family of children whose ages approximate those of their grandchildren by the children of their first marriages. These cases, few in number, often create tangled family relationships, with antagonism of the older children toward the new wife and resentment that the father has turned for affection to a second wife and young children rather than to his adult children and his young grandchildren. When wealth or property is at stake, relationships may become especially strained. The tensions may center about a conflict between adult children and new wife for control or inheritance of the wealth, which becomes a tangible symbol of the affection that is diverted from the adult children and their dead mother to the new wife and her children.

TABLE 34

Living Arrangements of Persons Aged 65 and Over, 1940 *

| Age and sex | Live outside private house- hold ** | Live in private household | | | | | | Total |
		Head of family	Wife of head	With chil- dren	With rela- tives	Lodger	Serv- ant	
Males								
65–69	4.1%	81.2%	—	5.5%	3.7%	5.0%	0.5%	100.0%
70–74	4.5	77.0	—	9.3	3.7	5.2	0.3	100.0
75 and over	5.7	65.1	—	18.9	4.3	5.8	0.2	100.0
Females								
65–69	2.7	30.1	41.3	15.0	6.3	3.3	1.3	100.0
70–74	3.4	34.5	29.7	21.0	6.7	3.8	0.9	100.0
75 and over	5.1	34.6	14.0	33.2	8.0	4.7	0.4	100.0

* Ruth Shonle Cavan, *et al., Personal Adjustment in Old Age* (Science Research Associates, 1949), p. 44, based on *Sixteenth Census, 1940,* Vol. 4, Part I: *Population,* p. 3. Interim reports for dates between 1940 and 1950 do not give comparable information; reports for the 1950 census when published undoubtedly will give similar detailed data.

** Those outside private households are in boarding or lodging houses, institutions, and hotels.

The pattern of the independent family established in youth at the time of marriage continues into old age. Table 34 shows that many men and women, though widowed, continue to maintain an independent household. The movement into the homes of children is slight, even at age 75 and over. Only a third of women of this age and less than one fifth of men live with children. Those who retreat to institutions are still fewer in number. This tendency of the widowed to maintain an independent existence, often in the homes formerly occupied by husband and

wife, using the same furniture, following the same daily routine, upholding the ideals and goals once held by both, and surrounded by marital
memories and symbols, justifies the use of the term postmarital family.

Adjustment and its interruptions

After adjustment to the climacteric and the withdrawal of children has
been completed, the middle-aged couple tend to settle into a quiet companionable relationship.   Many remain in the old family home; some
move from the house that accommodated four or five people into smaller
quarters.   With the release of pressure on their income they may make
their financial provisions for old age more secure, or take long-hoped-for
trips.   They often feel greater peace of mind than they had when children were small or adolescent; for better or worse their children are now
out of their hands.   With only themselves to consider they are better
able to adjust their activities to their greater need for quiet and rest,
slower rate of movement, and slowness in learning new skills or games.
A general slowing up of physical and mental capacities is characteristic
of old age.   It is easier for elderly people to accept these changes in
themselves when they are not in direct competition with their children
or other young people.

Once established, this relationship continues until some drastic change
forces another reappraisal and readjustment.   Three changes are sufficiently frequent to be regarded almost as normal for old age: unemployability or retirement; chronic illness, either physical or mental; and
widowhood.   Although one or more of these events may be anticipated
by every couple with a high degree of certainty, there is general avoidance
of facing them in advance.   Older people do not face them because of
the emotional stresses involved, young people because they are too emotionally affected when their parents suffer and also because the events
throw added responsibilities upon the young.   The three changes therefore strike as personal crises to old people, who are unprepared for them.
They also assume the nature of a chronic social disturbance, since society
has failed to develop, first, adequate attitudes and rituals to guide old
people through the disruption to their lives and, second, social measures,
such as financial aid, housing, or counseling, to give old people the support that they need at these times of change.

Until age 64 well over 90 per cent of all married men (including widowed and divorced) are employed. With age 65 begins a general withdrawal from employment that increases with each passing year. Few men over 75 are employed. For the entire group aged 65 and over, only 48 per cent are employed, or approximately half the percentage employed at all periods after ages 18–24.[19] For women a similar decline occurs. From employment of 25 to 30 per cent of women ever married between ages 18 and 64, the percentage drops to 6 for ages 65 and over. Some old people withdraw from work because they wish to; they have inherited or saved sufficient money to support themselves and their dependents throughout old age. Others are compelled to retire because of illness, physical decline, or their employer's policy of automatic retirement. Still others, let out of one job for whatever reason, try desperately to secure other work, but are considered unemployable and hence cannot find work: they gradually drift into the permanently unemployed although they never definitely retire. Although some people work past the age of 65, this age has come to be accepted as the dividing line between two groups—those who have a right to expect full employment and those for whom industry, business, and institutions employing professional staffs accept little or no obligation to provide employment. When an industry or institution has an automatic retirement age, 65 usually is the age specified. When an organization provides old-age pensions, usually the pensions cannot be secured before age 65. The governmental provisions for Old Age Assistance and Old Age and Survivors Insurance (usually called Social Security) set 65 as the age of eligibility. Age 65 is a social definition of old age, since it is evident that people do not suddenly and uniformly become incapable of work at any given age. Retirement or unemployability of the wage earners affects the family, and the most common period of personal and family adjustment to cessation of work begins when the wage earner reaches age 65.

Release from employment usually brings a decrease in income. Many old people have extremely low incomes, in relation both to their earlier status and their present needs. Table 35 gives an estimate of the numbers receiving certain means of support and the average monthly amounts

[19] *Current Population Reports, Population Characteristics, Characteristics of Single, Married, Widowed, and Divorced Persons in 1947,* Series P-20, No. 10 (Bureau of the Census), February 6, 1948, p. 24.

received from some of the chief sources. Some improvement in the financial status of future old people was instituted in the late 1940's and early 1950's through expansion of Old Age and Survivors Insurance to cover more occupations than previously, and through private pension plans established by many industries to supplement the amount received from Old Age and Survivors Insurance. With greatly lowered income, old people face downward social mobility. It will be recalled that the American open-class system and philosophy of equality of opportunity

TABLE 35

Sources and Amounts of Financial Support for People 65 and Over

Source of support	Number of old people	Percentage of old people	Average monthly amount, June, 1950
Old Age and Survivors Insurance *	2.1 million	17	Man— $26.80 Woman— 20.80 Couple— 41.90
Old Age Assistance *	2.8 million	24	Individual—$44
Government programs for railroad and government workers and aged veterans **	1.0 million	9	$36 to $100
Employment †	2.7 million	24	——
Other sources	3.0 million	26	——
TOTALS	11.6 million	100	

* *Annual Report of the Federal Security Agency, 1950* (Government Printing Office, 1951), pp. 21, 46, 53.

** *Ibid.*, p. 21, and Federal Security Agency, *Social Security Yearbook, 1945* (Government Printing Office, 1946), p. 15. The amounts are for 1945.

† *Current Population Reports, Population Characteristics, Characteristics of Single, Married, Widowed, and Divorced Persons in 1947*, Series P-20, No. 10 (Bureau of the Census, February 6, 1948), pp. 24–25.

and right of individual success encourages and sanctifies upward mobility. Many old people, fired by the American dream, succeeded in their younger years in making a slight upward climb, but clung only precariously to their new position; any decrease or cessation of income threatened a downward movement. With old age and substitution of a small pension or relief grant (Old Age Assistance) for regular wages or salary, the threat becomes a reality. All that was gained through years of struggle is lost, and the old couple taste the bitterness of personal defeat and failure. Some old people cannot face the reality of decline in status and insist upon maintaining the same establishment as when they had a regular and higher income through employment, reducing expenses by heating only one or two rooms, neglecting repairs, eating insufficient food and exercising the greatest care in expenditures for clothing and recreation. Other couples are forced to move to lower-status areas with cheaper rental, carrying with them the material symbols and the culture and attitudes of their past status. They hold themselves aloof from their new neighbors. When old friends visit them in their poverty, they are embarrassed and ashamed. If the friends try to help them, their pride is hurt; but if the friends ignore them, they are bitter and resentful. Sometimes the bitterness turns toward each other, and each blames the other for their plight: the wife accuses her husband of lack of ambition in his earlier days, the husband asserts that had his wife been less extravagant they would have more savings. With typical middle-class abhorrence of charity, they avoid as long as possible applying for relief, leaving rent unpaid and running up bills for groceries and clothing. When they finally become relief clients, they accuse the relief agency of unfairness and discrimination and dread the visits of the social worker who seems to pry into their personal affairs and whose visit may seem to announce to the neighbors that they receive relief. Their own frustration and its attendant hostility creates a hostile world in which they live. Since no one person is responsible for their situation, they direct their hostility indiscriminately toward many people and also feel that the world is hostile toward them. Mr. and Mrs. Barnes, both aged 69 and receiving Old Age Assistance, represent the hostile couple.

Mrs. Barnes had graduated from high school and taught school before her marriage. Mr. Barnes attended rural school for about seven years and after leaving farming had always done semiskilled work. Mrs. Barnes set the status for the family, which followed middle-class customs as far as possible. The family lived in various middle-class neighborhoods when the children were young; the girls had dancing lessons; and all the children were encouraged to complete high school. Mr. Barnes lost his job during the depression of the 1930's and was never able to re-establish himself permanently. During these hard years, Mrs. Barnes earned some money by sewing. They moved frequently, as the housing that they could afford was unsatisfactory. After age 60, they received local public relief as Mr. Barnes' health was very poor. It was not until they reached age 65 and became recipients of Old Age Assistance that Mrs. Barnes gave up the struggle to follow a middle-class pattern of life.

When, at the age of 69, they were interviewed in the course of a study of problems of old age, they lived in a two-room light-housekeeping apartment in a grand old mansion near the center of the city that had been converted into small apartments. The mansion had never been equipped with central heating; each unit had its own oil heater placed in the kitchen but presumably heating both rooms. Several families used the one bathroom, which Mrs. Barnes said was always dirty. Into their two small rooms, Mrs. Barnes had crowded massive pieces of upholstered furniture left from their better days. These material symbols of her earlier status were very precious to Mrs. Barnes.

Mr. Barnes, whose health was very poor, had an attitude of complete defeat: he waited for death. Mrs. Barnes, still with many activities and interests, was irritated and disappointed that they were forced to live in such poor quarters. She was rarely able to leave her husband alone and when she did go out was dependent upon a daughter to take her in her automobile. She expressed dislike for the other tenants of the building whom she regarded as of a lower class than herself; she was bitter toward the Old Age Assistance staff because of the small size of their grant. She was hurt by the neglect of two of her four children who did not come to see her very often. Some of her irritation was also directed toward her husband who was unable to fulfill his role as the financial supporter of the family.[20]

To other old people the dependency of old age brings added security. Many lower-class families with small and often irregular incomes have a precarious existence. Able to meet routine expenses, they often resort to relief agencies when a financial crisis arises from temporary unemployment or illness of husband or wife tends to increase with age. The years between 55 and 65 may be uncertain ones. Age 65 brings the right to apply for Old Age Assistance; and, small though the grants are, they at least give stability of income and also an agency staff upon which to lean for advice and personal encouragement. Since these families are already lower class, they do not suffer from downward social mobility or a sense of defeat when they accept relief. Tom and Mary Brown illustrate this group.

Equipped only with grade school education, Mr. Brown had worked steadily as a factory operative in an industry that did not provide pensions for retirement. He and his wife, who was three years his senior, reared their children whom they saw safely married, and found most of their extrafamily contacts through the church. They were never able to buy a home or save much for the future. They typically lived in an old house, unequipped with central heating. Unemployability came early to Mr. Brown because of

[20] For a more complete description of this family, see Cavan, et. al., op. cit., pp. 68–71. Other cases of old people and a general discussion of adjustment illustrated by cases are found on pp. 62–90.

heart trouble. In his late fifties he began to have long periods of serious illness. Their small savings were soon exhausted. Because of his long and steady work record, his employer always considered him as ill rather than unemployed so that when he was able to work he was always given work to do. Many hospital and medical expenses were covered by group insurance through the plant. Nevertheless, as the illness brought longer and longer periods of unemployment, the family applied for and secured assistance from the township relief office. Eventually they were able to move into a public housing project where they had three well-ventilated rooms equipped with an electric refrigerator, their own furnace located in a convenient utility room, and a modern bathroom. Mrs. Brown said this was the nicest home she had ever had, and with lower rent than they had paid previously. When Mr. Brown was 62 years old, his condition became such that he was told by a physician that he could not work again and his employer released him permanently. He and his wife were therefore forced to face a situation that they had been approaching for many years but always with the hope that something could be done to improve Mr. Brown's health. They faced their financial problems realistically, knowing that there would be no more income from wages. Soon after the physician's statement of unemployability, Mrs. Brown became 65 and immediately applied for Old Age Assistance which gave her a small but regular income. The township relief office supplemented the amount to cover Mr. Brown's expenses until he should be 65 when he also will become a recipient of Old Age Assistance.[21] According to an established policy, the rent on the housing unit was decreased as soon as Mrs. Brown was accepted for Old Age Assistance. The housing project in which they live reduces the rent for Old Age Assistance recipients to the amount allowed for rent in the official budget for recipients. Mrs. Brown felt therefore that their financial position was more secure than it had been for some years past. While the financial security eased her anxieties in one direction, it did not relieve her or her husband of great fears aroused by the knowledge that he was chronically ill.[22]

Couples who have enough for comfortable living from inheritance, savings, or pensions may be free of the anxieties of financial insecurity or downward social mobility. Often, however, they face another problem —the complete leisure that suddenly confronts the husband at the time of retirement. Women seem to make the adjustment to leisure more

[21] Old Age Assistance is a grant given to old people on the basis of need. The money is supplied in part by the federal government and in part by the state. The amount varies from state to state, depending upon the size of the state's contribution. In the state in which the Browns live the maximum monthly grant per person is $71. Many people receive less, if their expenses are decreased by ability to prepare their own food or if they have small amounts of income from other sources, the average amount being between $50 and $60 per month. Additional amounts are granted for medical and hospital expenses.

[22] Unpublished report.

readily than men. Employed women often are happy to return to the role of homemaker or to assume it for the first time. One widow who retired at the age of 70, after many years of employment during which she had struggled to pay for and maintain a home, said the day of retirement was the happiest of her life; she could again give her full time to her home. Unemployed wives gradually adjust their work to declining strength and never fully retire. For the husband, however, the transition from full employment to full leisure often comes overnight. His focus of activity shifts from office or factory to his home. In the home his wife reigns supreme; if he is to find a function there it must be under her direction with a further decrease in status to add to the one already suffered in his transition from employed to unemployed. Moreover, a new role and new habits must be created; the skills and work habits of his job are not those needed in homemaking. He must learn new skills and find a new role; to permit him to function, his wife must modify her role. If the husband is willing to adopt a homemaking role, a happy partnership may grow, as his wife may welcome another pair of hands to supplement her own. The case that follows illustrates a happy adaptation of old skills to the home.

John and Martha Dilley owned their home where they had lived happily through the years when Mr. Dilley worked steadily as a mechanic for a large industry. Mrs. Dilley enjoyed her role as housewife and her husband carried out his early farm-boy interests through a vegetable garden and chicken raising for their own use. Their savings and Mr. Dilley's pension made them financially secure for old age. Since Mr. Dilley's employer automatically retired all employees at age 65, they had planned accordingly. Soon after his retirement they sold their home and all furniture, and moved to California where they previously had enjoyed a short vacation. They soon found that they missed their home and their friends; Mr. Dilley had nothing with which to fill his time; the regional ways of life differed from their accustomed Middle West habits. After a few months they returned to their home town. The only house they could find to buy was a run-down frame building near the business district, which seemed a poor substitute for their earlier modern home on the edge of town. The condition of the house was a challenge to Mr. Dilley, who immediately began to repair and remodel it. In a leisurely manner he went about his work, doing only as much in one day as he felt like doing, but gradually making a more comfortable home out of the house and increasing its value. The work lasted over a period of years, until physical ailments made work less attractive to him. His wife, meanwhile, had renewed her contacts with friends and church groups and in time found the central location of their home more convenient from the point of view of transportation than the old home on the edge of the city. Thus after a period of restlessness and wanderlust both Mr. and Mrs. Dilley made a good adjustment to his retirement.[23]

Chronic illness

Illness may come to any family.   The illness of a child or young adult is likely to be acute and to have a definite beginning, short duration, and a definite end in recovery or death.   It is a crisis to be met by the strong rallying of family resources.   The illness of the old tends to come slowly and insidiously, to be debilitating with ever-increasing handicaps, and to last long.   It becomes a part of the daily and yearly pattern of life, not only of the afflicted person but of other members of the family who must adjust themselves to the presence and care of a chronic invalid.   If there is a crisis it is at the point of some sudden change of condition, as the stroke that brings paralysis to the person who for years has suffered from high blood pressure; or the fall and broken hip that is suffered by an old person who has tottered up and down stairs with increasing difficulty; or the wandering from home and inability to recall the way back of the oldster with slowly failing memory.   The crisis may bring home to the old person that he is old; it also brings a realization on the part of others that the old person is no longer capable of functioning independently.

The chronically ill person has needs not felt by the well.   In addition to physical care, he also needs someone upon whom to lean for a sense of security and protection.   His role changes from that of a self-reliant person to the childlike role of the invalid.   Consequently the roles of others in the family change in adjustment to his new role and new needs. Since men tend to die at earlier ages than women, a common situation finds the elderly wife with an invalid husband from five to ten years older than herself.   The man has the difficult problem of changing his conception of himself from self-sufficient to dependent and of accepting his wife in the dominant role.   His functions shrink, his world contracts.   In contrast, the role of the wife expands to encompass functions relinquished by her husband.   She may not only be overburdened by the double duties but may have to learn many new skills and acquire knowledge formerly confined to the husband's role.   If the husband's illness involves his mental capacities, she may find it advisable to be appointed his guardian and to take charge of all financial affairs.   She may find this situation

[23] Unpublished report.

either a strain or a challenge as she struggles to understand a new field. At the same time that she is expanding her role she finds the fulfillment of many old needs denied her by her husband's illness, ranging all the way from his performance of heavy household tasks through recreation to satisfaction of affectional and perhaps sexual needs. When, perhaps after years of invalidism, the husband dies, the wife frequently feels a sense of great relief. One woman, happily married, in her seventies had nursed her husband through an illness of some four years' duration, during which he became progressively more and more helpless physically. She learned to manage all the household tasks, community contacts, and financial affairs. She gradually adjusted herself to the contraction of social activities and to the heartache of seeing her husband suffer. At his death she could not cry; she could not wish him to live longer. Having learned to handle all the practical problems alone, she continued to live in their large home, gradually expanding her social life to give additional satisfactions.

When the wife is invalid, the situation is to some extent reversed. The husband expands his functions to include those of housekeeper and nurse; the wife is compelled to see an inexpert male fumble with cooking, cleaning, and the serving of meals. Often, however, if the wife becomes a chronic invalid it is after the death of her husband and the adjustment is between the invalid and her adult children who then find themselves in the unaccustomed role of dominance over their parent, a reversal of their childhood years when they were dependent upon the mother for physical care and love. This parent-child adjustment often is more difficult than that between invalid and spouse. The old person may resent her dependence upon the son or daughter and the assumption of authority by her offspring. Old resentments and tensions may emerge from some long-hidden place in the subconscious to complicate the relationship. Middle-aged Mrs. Hall could not give her widowed mother the care that she needed nor include her within her own family circle because of hostility based upon her mother's rejection of her as a child. So long as Mrs. Hall's father was alive and the two family units remained separate, friendly relationships were maintained. But when, as a widow in failing health, the mother turned to her daughter, anticipating protective care, the daughter could not respond. All the old resentment of her childhood came forth and she visited upon her mother the same rejection that the mother had imposed upon her when she was a child. Maturity and understanding on the part of both mother and adult child are necessary to facilitate the reversal of roles when the adult child must assume authority and make decisions for the aged and the ailing parent.

The postmarital family

The postmarital family consists of the widow or widower. As has already been suggested, when widow- or widowerhood follows a long and trying illness on the part of the spouse, many adjustments have already been made to the postmarital role.   When a reciprocal companionship has been maintained until the time of death, however, the change from marital to widowed status may create almost insurmountable hardships.   Instead of the gradual adjustment possible with chronic illness, adjustment must be made abruptly to the absence of the deceased spouse. The companionship between a retired man and his wife may be closer than at earlier periods of their lives: their decrease in outside activities has increased their dependence upon each other, and often their social world has narrowed to the home and each other.   When death removes one, the other feels that half of himself has suddenly been cut away.   A younger person in similar circumstances tends to widen his activities, to seek new contacts and new interests, and, in time, to marry again.   The old person often lacks the energy and flexibility for such broadening of activities and the assumption of new community roles.   For many, life remains a stunted existence until death releases them also.   One old woman whose companionship with her husband had been very close because of their childlessness, regarded her widowhood as a period of waiting until, in her firm belief, death would reunite them.   "In the course of nature, the time will not be long until I go also," she said complacently.

Some old widows and widowers remarry, but the number of oldsters who do not remarry is very great.   Since women outlive men, the sex ratio is very unbalanced in later years, and any program to encourage remarriage would fail because of the great excess of old women.   The convention whereby women marry those of their own age or older inhibits many elderly widows from marrying men younger than themselves. Widowers are less handicapped, since they find an excess of women their own age and also may approach those younger than themselves.   But a new marriage means the breaking up of old habits of life, adjusting to a new personality, and the comparison of the new spouse with the memory of the deceased.   Moreover, public opinion tends to be opposed to the marriage of the old, for there is little understanding on the part of younger people of the affectional and social needs of the old.   For these reasons most widows and widowers tend to accept their half-lives, which may last over a long period of time.

When widow and widowers do not continue to live independently in their own households (as many of them do, according to Table 34), the most typical move is into the home of an adult married son or daughter. Approximately a third of all old women—most of them widows—live with children.   A movement that is less prevalent but still requires drastic change in living habits is into an institution or old people's home.

The old parent in the family

The assumption often is made that in the past it was a common practice for the old parent, without income or widowed, to become a member of the family of an adult child.   Although this may have been a fairly common practice in a day when Old Age Assistance and various forms of public and private pensions did not exist, it would be a mistake to envision every family as including a grandparent or two.   For one thing, the life expectancy was much less than at present; a much smaller proportion of the population lived into the seventies and eighties, and the span of time between the end of independent adulthood and death was shorter.   Also, the birthrate was higher so that each old parent had a number of children to whom to turn in necessity.   If the old parent lived with one adult child, the siblings of that child were relieved of his care; or all children shared in financial support or in rotating care of the parent. Now, one or two adults may be responsible for several elderly parents; in fact, two only children married to each other might find themselves with four elderly parents anticipating personal care.   The burden of care therefore tends to be concentrated upon fewer people and for a longer period of time than in the past.

Conflicting values in present-day culture prevent development of a clear-cut line of action for adult children to follow.   Deeply rooted in our culture is the attitude of the independent and self-sufficient family that takes care of its members.   In some states this attitude is reinforced by laws to compel children to support dependent parents.   When the family has split into segments according to the generations, each segment may cling to a different interpretation of the attitude.   The old couple may cling to their right of independence while their children suffer from a feeling of guilt over not caring for their needy or ailing parents. The public relief now provided for the old through Old Age Assistance arouses conflicting emotional reactions in old and young. The old may seize it as a means of maintaining their independence but at the same time suffer a feeling of degradation because the relief violates the old value of family self-sufficiency. Therefore a system of rationalization has developed to cushion the acceptance of relief. The grants customarily are called pensions instead of assistance or relief; old people rationalize that they have worked hard all their lives and paid taxes and are therefore entitled to public support. Nevertheless, they often try to conceal the fact that they are recipients of relief. Their children also battle with conflicting values. On the one hand, they share with their parents the attitude that the family should be self-sufficient and that they should aid their parents; on the other, relief for the parents will release them from this burden, and they therefore also rationalize acceptance of relief by their parents. Other values also compete with the value of care of parents. The education and personality development of children now has high value and is interpreted to include not only long years of schooling and dependency of children but such additional costly programs as dancing and music lessons and summer camps. Children therefore compete with old parents for the resources of the intermediate generation. Added to this situation is the further value of the right of adults to fulfill their individual needs and interests through such activities as continued education, travel, or a career for the wife, all of which either call for expenditure of money or, by taking the wife away from the home, make personal care of old parents an impossibility. These competing values tend to fall into a hierarchy in which care of the old parents has less rank than child training or adult personality fulfillment on individual lines. Nevertheless, the hierarchy is neither so well established or so widely accepted that the adult child is freed from feelings of uneasiness and guilt if he does not in some way provide for the care of his old parents.

With these diverse and conflicting values, automatic acceptance by children of responsibility for the care of aged parents cannot be assumed. To a high degree each case stands alone, and an individual decision must be made by parents and children. This decision rests in part upon the traditional values of the group (religious, ethnic, rural, or urban) and in part upon personal factors of the relationship between parents and

children.   A study based upon the attitudes of high school and under-
graduate and graduate college students shows a slightly greater tendency
for Catholics than Protestants to believe that children should support
their aged parents.[24]   Those of rural birth also were somewhat more
inclined to accept this responsibility than those of urban birth.   The
differences in response to bluntly stated questions of support, however,

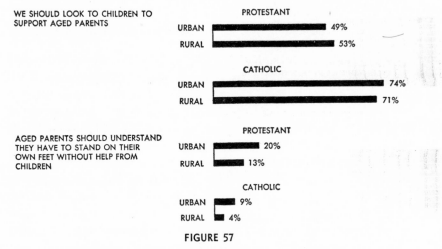

FIGURE 57

Attitudes of Students toward Obligation to Support Parents

The percentages of students who agree with the first statement show little
rural-urban difference but a much stronger sense of obligation on the part of
Catholics than of Protestants.   Agreement with the second statement indicates aversion to supporting parents; rural students show less aversion than
urban students and Catholics less than Protestants.   (Source: Robert M.
Dinkel, "Attitudes of Children toward Supporting Aged Parents," *American
Sociological Review,* 9 [1944], 376.)

are much greater between the religious groups than between rural and
urban groups, as Figure 57 shows.   Among neither Protestants nor
Catholics, however, is there widespread rejection of parents.   The traditional values based upon family solidarity are only part of the situation.
Questions concerning the type of hardship that care of the parents in the
children's own homes would entail show that the greater the hardship the
less children felt that they had an obligation to take their parents into
their homes.   Figure 58 shows the decreasing percentage of young people

[24] Robert M. Dinkel, "Attitudes of Children toward Supporting Aged Parents,"
American Sociological Review, 9 (1944), 370–379.

who would feel obligated to give a home to their parents as the hardships involved become more serious. Although this study concerns the attitudes of high school and college students, not yet faced with the actual care of aged parents, it is probably a reflection of general social attitudes at the present time. The feeling of obligation based on traditional values

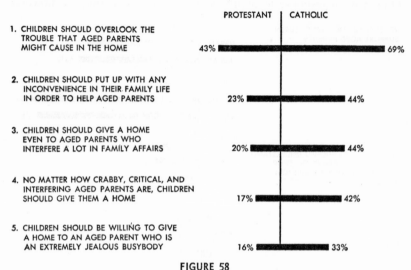

FIGURE 58

Attitudes of Students toward Support of Troublesome Parents

The graph shows the percentages of students agreeing with the statements, which are arranged in order of the increasing hardship that the parent would cause in the home. Although both Protestant and Catholic students feel a decline in obligation with increase in hardship, Catholics consistently feel more obligation than Protestants. The responses of students classified by residence (not shown here) follow the same pattern, with a slightly higher percentage of rural than urban students at each level indicating willingness to care for their parents. (Source: Robert M. Dinkel, "Attitudes of Children toward Supporting Aged Parents," *American Sociological Review*, 9 [1944], 377.)

is tempered by the degree to which aged parents would interfere with such other values as harmony in the home and the right of the family to order its own affairs.

When the old parent comes to live with an adult child and his family, the enlarged family is faced with four types of adjustment.

1. When the elderly parent and his adult child have the same cultural beliefs, one basis for sound adjustment is at hand. Often, however, they

adhere to different patterns, based upon different social experiences. The past 50 years have witnessed a marked growth of children away from their parents in cultural patterns. Examples are the migration of rural young people to cities and the assumption of urban attitudes and ways of living that may be wholly foreign to the rural parent who in later life may come to live with the urban son or daughter; the great increase in the number of young people completing high school or college as compared with the number of parents with similar education has created a wide difference between the generations in values and interests; the children of the foreign-born who surged into this country by the millions prior to 1915 follow an American pattern of culture that clashes with the remnants of foreign culture retained by their old parents. These and other cultural conflicts often are dismissed by saying that "times have changed" and the parents should adjust. It cannot be overlooked, however, that more than conflicting cultural patterns are involved. The parents have woven into their personal standards and ideals the values of their culture and have invested these values with moral and religious significance. It is impossible for them to witness opposed behavior in their children or grandchildren without feelings of shock, fear, and anxiety. When the children have also invested their attitudes and behavior with moral significance an impasse exists. Only deep understanding of the relation between culture and ideals and great tolerance can bring harmony.

2. Often the old person must break his social ties when he becomes a member of his child's family. Usually it is the old person who "breaks up" his home and moves into the household of a younger person. If the move is within one local community, he may be able to retain his friends, church membership, and social affiliations; he retains his social identity and the comfort of accustomed contacts. A move to another community may be almost disastrous. The social groups in which the old person normally is interested have elderly members who often form a closed group impenetrable by a new person. The burden of making new social contacts falls upon the newcomer at a time when self-assurance and desire for new experiences are overshadowed by the need for security and ready acceptance.

Few avenues are open to the old person to establish his status and his individuality in a new setting. In a community where he has lived for some years his status is established long before old age: he is known among friends and in his community as a steady worker, a church leader, a good parent, and so forth. He is an individual. As a member of his child's family in a new community he is all too likely to lose his individuality and be known only as Bob Brown's father or Judge Addison's aunt. He becomes a social nonentity. In his own mind, however, he thinks of himself in terms of his earlier status acquired by birth, marriage, or occupation; he resents the lack of regard of the new community for him.

3. On the more personal side is the necessity to break old identifications and try to build new ones. Some of these identifications are with the status of the family in the old community—old Mrs. Smith is the daughter of a pioneer family; some are with material symbols that may relate to community status or to the intimacies of family life. The nonmaterial symbols are lost. Often the material symbols also must be left behind since the fully furnished household of son or daughter rarely has room for cherished pieces of furniture or an appropriate setting for the display of beloved photographs, handwork, or old china.

New identifications are hard for the old person to make. There are no memories attached to the new household, and on the personal side often there seems to be no place in the family circle for the old person. The husband and wife and their children have an integrated pattern of family interaction that forms a closed circle. When a new member is added through the birth of a child, the situation is very different. The baby seems to be an extension of the parents' personalities into the future; it offers many opportunities for parental pride and feelings of accomplishment; it is small, loving, and appealing. The old person seems to demand as much or perhaps greater readjustment and sometimes physical care than a baby, but without compensating the caretaker in equal amount.

4. Individual personalities also must be adjusted to each other. If it is assumed that husband, wife, and children have found mutually acceptable ways to fulfill each other's needs, the readjustment becomes one of helping the elderly parent find need-satisfactions and of finding in the old person satisfactions for some of their own needs. The general shifting necessarily brings both sacrifice and richness of experience. The child may have to yield some of his mother's attention to his grandparent but in return will receive added love from the grandparent. The husband may find his old mother demanding attention from him formerly given to his wife, but she may also assume some care of the children and thus release his wife for more free time with him. As with all periods of

transition, the early period of readjustment may bring acute discomfort until a new network of interaction is woven.

These changes include adjustment of personal roles, with some possibilities of clashes. Although there are few studies on adjustment of roles in the three-generation family, personal accounts point to the adjustment between the old mother and her daughter or daughter-in-law as full of tension. The earlier role of the old mother as head of her home is in direct conflict with the corresponding role of the daughter or daughter-in-law as head of her home. The old mother may feel that her longer experience gives her precedence in making decisions and organizing the household; but the younger woman feels that her position as wife of the family head gives her the superior role. Another clash may occur between the old mother and her daughter-in-law for first place in her son's affections. The mother dwells on her long years of care of her son as a child and longs again to be first in his esteem. The young woman claims first place is due her as his wife. Only when such conflicts of roles have been adjusted so that each receives some satisfaction will the relationship become harmonious.

Grandparents

As with old parents, so also with grandparents—their status is not well defined. Older people often refer to grandchildren as the compensation for old age or state that grandchildren can be enjoyed without a feeling of responsibility for them such as they felt as parents toward their own children. Parents may regard the grandparents as something of a threat to their own status with their children and to modern methods of child rearing, a point of view also sometimes set forth by psychologists. Most of what has been written about grandparents points to the grandmother as a disturbing factor.

One writer emphasizes that the grandchild fulfills an emotional need of the grandmother at a time when she feels that her period of usefulness is ended.[25] Since the child divides his love between his grandmother and his mother, the grandmother feels insecure and struggles for the child's devotion by indulging his whims and belittling his mother. Another writer, however, interprets the excessive love of a grandmother for her grandchildren as originating in guilt feelings caused by early neglect of

[25] Hermann Vollmer, "The Grandmother: A Problem in Child-rearing," *American Journal of Orthopsychiatry*, 7 (1937), 378–382.

her own children.[26]   A third writer proclaims that "Grandmother made Johnny delinquent" [27] by arousing hostilities and aggressions in him.   Still another report covers 15 cases in which the grandmothers tended to dominate their daughters, whom they lived with or near, and to usurp the mother role with their grandchildren.[28]   As a consequence, the daughters felt inadequate and the grandmother-daughter relationship became a major factor in the behavior problems of the children.   These reports from the guidance clinic and the social worker's counseling room emphasize problem situations.

In a general statement that attempts to include all types of grandmothers, Helene Deutsch says that "there are as many types of grandmothers as there are individual types and characters of mothers." [29]   She continues with a discussion of three types of good grandmothers.   The first type of good grandmother is the woman who continues her motherhood through her grandchildren and thinks of the grandchildren simply as the youngest of her children.   They give her a new opportunity to play the mother role and a new emotional satisfaction.   The second type of grandmother has adjusted herself to the loss of the mother role when her children matured; through identification with her daughter or daughter-in-law, however, she experiences grandmotherhood as a "new edition" of her original role.   In order to avoid a hateful competition, she must be satisfied with a position of assistant mother and not attempt to impose her wishes or ideas of child training upon the child and his mother.   The third type of good grandmother has made her peace with age and no longer reaches backward for her past motherhood or outward for identification with her daughter or daughter-in-law.   She is tender and solicitous without seeking self-gratification in return.   Consequently her grandchildren love her dearly.   The only danger is that she may "spoil" her grandchildren by pampering them.   Deutsch continues with a brief statement that there are also "wicked grandmothers," who either do not want to be disturbed by their grandchildren or whose envy for their daughters or daughters-in-law causes them to try to intrude between children and their parents.

[26] E. G. Fried and K. Stern, "The Situation of the Aged within the Family," *American Journal of Orthopsychiatry,* 18 (1948), 31–54.

[27] G. A. Strauss, "Grandmother Made Johnny Delinquent," *American Journal of Orthopsychiatry,* 13 (1943), 343–347.

[28] B. Borden, "The Role of Grandparents in Children's Behavior Problems," *Smith College Studies in Social Work,* 17 (1946), 115–116.

[29] *Op. cit.,* pp. 483–486.

The role of the grandfather has not been explored, and it is evident that the relationship of both grandparents to their grandchildren merits more extensive study than it has had.

THE END OF THE CYCLE

Family life is a series of alternating periods of adjustment and unadjustment.   To each change within the family and to the impact of external changes, the husband, wife, and children must adjust.   When satisfactory adjustment has been reached, it tends to continue until another change calls for a new modification of attitude and behavior.   A minority of families live in a continuous state of tension or disintegrate.   Husbands and wives who obtain divorces as a way out of difficulties tend to remarry.   Thus, the majority of the adult population is married until the transition in old age into widow- or widowerhood; even then the patterns of living established in the family are continued.

Adjustments in the mid-1900's differ from those of our earlier rural economy.   Emphasis now is on interpersonal adjustments related to personal rather than utilitarian needs.   Hardships that solidified the earlier rural family in its effort to survive now frequently disorganize families, each member of whom may seek an individual solution of problems.   The qualities of a good husband or wife now place less stress on family background or property and more upon personal traits and compatibility than was true in the past.   Recognition is also given to the importance of likenesses of social background.

Families that best survive both internal strains and external crises are both well integrated and adaptable.   Held together by common bonds of affection and goals, they are nevertheless able to adjust roles and plans to changing conditions.

The need for adjusting continues into old age, with the final adjustment being to death itself, which closes the family cycle.

QUESTIONS

1. Why is it necessary for the middle-aged couple to modify their roles?
2. What would you regard as good and as poor adjustment of middle-aged parents to their children?
3. Why do women seem to find adjustment to middle age more difficult than men?

4. Report on a couple who have made a satisfactory adjustment to middle age. What seem to be the significant factors?

5. What changes in family organization follow the retirement of the husband?

6. What changes in marital roles are occasioned by chronic illness of husband or wife?

7. What are the attitudes of young people toward accepting an elderly parent into their household? Are these attitudes a logical sequence of our present conception of the function of marriage?

8. How can the elderly widow or widower best meet his psychological and social problems: by living alone; living with his children; or entering an institution? What are the advantages and disadvantages of each situation?

BIBLIOGRAPHY

Cavan, R. S., "Family Life and Family Substitutes in Old Age," *American Sociological Review,* 14 (1949), 71–83.

———, Burgess, E. W., Havighurst, R. J., and Goldhamer, Herbert, *Personal Adjustment in Old Age* (Chicago: Science Research Associates, 1949).

Donahue, Wilma, and Tibbitts, Clark, editors, *Planning the Older Years* (University of Michigan Press, 1950), ch. 2.

Fried, E. C., and Stern, K., "The Situation of the Aged within the Family," *American Journal of Orthopsychiatry,* 18 (1948), 31–54.

Kaplan, Oscar, editor, *Mental Disorders in Later Life* (Stanford University Press, 1945), chs. 7 and 8.

Lawton, George, editor, *New Goals for Old Age* (Columbia University Press, 1943), pp. 50–70.

Man and His Years, An Account of the First National Conference on Aging Sponsored by the Federal Security Agency (Raleigh, North Carolina: Health Publications Institute, 1951), ch. 8.

Strauss, G. A., "Grandmother Made Johnny Delinquent," *American Journal of Orthopsychiatry,* 13 (1943), 343–347.

Vollmer, N., "The Grandmother: A Problem in Child-Rearing," *American Journal of Orthopsychiatry,* 7 (1937), 378–382.

PART FOUR

Adjustment of Family
and Society

21

Integration of Society
and Family

This text opened with a discussion of incompatible and often conflicting values related to marriage and family life that create issues about which there are at present no uniform collective attitudes. These issues were analyzed as originating in two sets of social conditions: the transition from an agrarian to an urbanized culture; and the social mobility between social classes, subcultural groups (ethnic and religious), and races. This social analysis constituted Parts I and II of this book. In Part III, the orientation shifted to individual families and the interaction taking place within the family circle. The progress of family life was followed from the premarital activities of dating through marriage and into old age with its postmarital individual—the elderly widow or widower. In Part III it was constantly necessary to refer to the social setting in which interaction took place. Now, at the end of the book, the task remains of examining trends toward greater integration of the family into the social organization, and of increased integration within the family.

SOCIAL INTEGRATION AND DISINTEGRATION

In a strongly organized society, the various institutions tend to be well unified in two respects: they proclaim the same or mutually compatible social norms or values; and their functions dovetail together without undue overlapping and without leaving gaps in the services that people need.[1]

[1] For discussions of integration, see Ronald Freedman, Amos H. Hawley, Werner S. Landecker, and Horace M. Miner, *Principles of Sociology* (Holt, 1952), chs. 4, 5, and 13; Robin M. Williams, *American Society* (Knopf, 1951), chs. 11–14; Robert Cooley Angell, "The Moral Integration of American Cities," *American Journal of Sociology,* 57, Part 2 (July, 1951), especially pp. 115–122.

Integration as a static condition is easy to visualize in a stable and unchanging society.   Over years of time the values become coordinated, and the various functions are distributed among the institutions.   Moreover, functions and values are themselves integrated and support each other, and to a large extent are achieved by the institutions that subscribe to them.   The coordinated values and functions are passed on from one generation to another and are constantly reinforced through legends, rituals, and ceremonies.   When integration is viewed as a process through a period of time in a stable society, the institutions may be compared to so many regimented units, marching, halting, and wheeling in conformity with a master plan controlled by one system of values, with the movements of each unit synchronized with the movements of all other units.

In a changing society, however, the high degree of unity of values, the careful assignment of functions, and the synchronization of activities lack coordination.   Some institutions retain much of the past; others revamp themselves to fit new conditions and, finding themselves out of step with more conservative institutions, tend to become separated from the main societal body and to lose sight of the total value system of society, although they may be well organized within themselves.   In time, each institution may become a more or less autonomous unit within society, developing its own values and functions in relative independence from other institutions.   Under these conditions societal integration is replaced by conflict and confusion between institutions.   If this process—the development of independence by institutions—goes far enough, the society becomes generally disorganized.   More often, however, a process of reorganization accompanies the process of disintegration.   Although revised values may not be uniformly accepted throughout the society, a number of institutions will accept one set of social values or norms and bring their functions into conformity with each other.   Thus, reorganization will offset the effects of confusion and conflict.

Unless the society again becomes stable, complete integration of values, functions, and pace of activities among institutions cannot be expected. As long as there is change of any sort (entrance of new cultural groups, social or technical inventions, depression, and wars), changes in values and functions must also be anticipated.   One sociologist suggests that in a changing society stability of culture does not refer to a static condition but to "a dynamic process in which a delicately balanced system of values is maintained." [2]

In the light of this general statement about societal integration, let us look at the specific case of the family.

The family in the integration process

The family is one of the major social institutions. From a societal point of view the family is more than an intimate group whose members are seeking satisfaction of individual needs; traditionally it is an institution ranking with such more formal organizations as the church, the school, industry, or the political system. It supports basic values related not only to personal needs but to society in general, some of which are maintenance of the population, indoctrination of children in societal culture, personality development of children, provision of a common family living unit, and maintenance of health. In the past, the family fulfilled these and other functions.

The nine issues presented in Chapter 1 are evidence of the inability of the family to maintain old values and functions under present urbanized conditions. The factory system alone destroyed the ideal of the family as a patriarchal organization with the father maintaining his headship through close personal contacts, sometimes on an hourly basis, with his wife and children. It destroyed, also, much of the ability of the father to support his family through all exigencies and crises, launch his children into productive activities, and save for the old-age needs of his wife and himself. The great improvement in medical practice that has prolonged life into old age has also changed family ideals and functions. As more and more people live into an old age for which they are unable to prepare themselves financially, they become an increasing—in some cases insuperable—burden upon the few children that now constitute the urban family, or they are threatened with a long dependency upon relief agencies. The separation of family members into diversified activities tends to break down the characteristics of the family as a primary group that typically exerts control over individual conduct and helps to establish integrated personalities. In like manner other time-honored family values and functions were disturbed or destroyed by the development of modern urban institutions.

[2] Williams, *op. cit.*, p. 374.

The family seemed at odds with other institutions.   Unaided, it could neither uphold societal values nor perform expected traditional functions. The process of societal disintegration with reference to the family tended to come to a climax after World War I.   The increased employment of women and their break with the older restrictive moral codes, often viewed as a conflict between the sexes, in reality represented a movement toward conformity with the changed social conditions that had destroyed the older patriarchal family organization in which the husband and father had been able both to support and to give leadership to his family.   In the 1930's the depression brought into sharp focus the inability of the family to continue as an independent economic unit and, in fact, the inability of the local community to care for the family in distress.   At the same time the ease with which adolescents could escape from family supervision and control became apparent.   During the depression great numbers of boys and some girls became transients, wandering aimlessly back and forth across the country.   Neither family, school, industry, nor law could control these wandering groups.   In general, the urban family has found it difficult to cope with adolescents.   Although school laws and labor laws tend to prolong the economic dependence of the child on the family, many adolescents have found ways to circumvent the law.   The city child can falsify his age and secure work; he can evade the school attendance officer; he can, in the summer at least, sleep out in the "jungles" along railroad tracks or in vacant garages, houses, or stores.   Automobiles, owned or stolen, carry him beyond the eyes of his family and the gossipy interest of neighbors.   In many ways urban conditions prevent the family from meeting social expectations based on the older rural situation.

REINTEGRATION OF FAMILY AND SOCIETY

In the United States reintegration of the family with other institutions has begun to take place.   The process does not fall into a neat and precise system.   Outmoded relationships exist alongside new and modern attempts at coordination, and great areas in need of coordination are still untouched.   Governmental and various voluntary agencies overlap in their efforts.   Some attempts at integration occur on the purely local level, others at the hands of state agencies, while the federal government and national organizations attempt to draw the entire picture together into some form of unity. Little has been done to redefine values. Many new services are in the nature of stopgaps for emergencies and not part of an overall plan. Certain aspects of the family have received intensive attention, others, equally significant, very little. Nevertheless, in this general and seemingly unguided stirring of interest and activity, certain organized movements and trends can be discerned.

Values and norms

Three important movements have helped to crystallize new values. One of these, the feminist movement, has spent its force; another, the White House Conferences on children, has become a recurring phenomenon to re-evaluate children's needs and services at ten-year intervals; the third, the National Conference on Family Life, convened in 1948 for the first time.

The feminist movement, in its agitation for equality of women's status with men's, contributed to the transition from the patriarchal family to the present-day ideal of the partnership family in which husband and wife share equally in rights and responsibilities. Even the paternal family—which is still more characteristic than the partnership family—owes much to the feminist movement. The partnership and paternal families both give women high status, relative freedom in their choices of roles, and also increased responsibilities. These attributes of wives are now accepted as values of family life.

The feminist movement, after years of sporadic propaganda, was organized in 1848 at a Women's Rights Convention held in Seneca Falls, New York. In a "Declaration of Sentiments," it took its stand against disfranchisement of women, legal incapacity arising from marriage, unequal divorce laws, double standard of morals, occupational limitations, denial of educational opportunities, and subordination in church government.[3] Its major accomplishment is usually regarded as the Nineteenth Amendment, which, in 1920, granted women the right to vote. Other accomplishments of the movement for equality of women's opportunities with men have perhaps been more closely related to marriage and family life. One of these has been the trend toward state laws giving married women separate property rights, the same right of inheriting property when there is no will that the husband would have if the wife died, the right

[3] Bernhard J. Stern, "Women, Position in Society: Historical," *Encyclopedia of the Social Sciences,* (Macmillan Company, 1937), Vol. 15, pp. 442–450.

to contract their services and receive their earnings, and the same rights and liabilities as litigants that their husbands have. With reference to certain rights and responsibilities, some states still adhere to the common law, which typically gave the husband control over all property and made him liable for his wife's actions and for entire support of the family; nevertheless the trend has been toward equality of both rights and responsibilities for women where property, earnings, contracts, and liabilities are concerned.[4] Control of property and earnings gives not only an equal voice in family affairs but freedom of the married woman to carry out many of her personal interests and, in case of incompatibility or continued conflict, ability to support herself.

Over the years women have also gained entrance to colleges, universities, and many professional schools on an equal basis with men, although some specialized schools may limit the acceptance of women to a "quota." The exigencies of urban living and the effect of World War I accomplished another objective of the feminist movement—freedom for women to enter employment. Although it cannot be said that they have equal opportunities for all types of position, advancement, or earnings, nevertheless the way has been opened for women to use their own initiative regarding work. In many ways, therefore, the feminist movement helped to promote equality of men and women and to safeguard women as they moved from the home into the community. On the other hand, the feminist movement hindered marital adjustment in some respects. Since men had previously commanded political, educational, and economic opportunities, much of the struggle for equality was directed against men rather than against the institutions that excluded women. Many feminists became hostile in their attitudes toward men as persons, and bitter sex antagonism characterized the relationship between men and women. To the extent that this antagonism was carried over into marriage it tended to pit husband and wife against each other and to create opposition rather than cooperation.

Many of the objectives of the feminist movement have now been incorporated into the work of the Women's Bureau of the United States government. Organized in 1920 under the Department of Labor, the

---

[4] *Legal Status of the American Family* (Women's Bureau, 1950); Sara Louise Buchanan, *The Legal Status of Women in the United States of America as of January 1, 1948, Summary of All States Combined,* Women's Bureau Bulletin, No. 157 revised (U.S. Government Printing Office, 1951).

Women's Bureau acts as a clearing house for information on all matters that pertain to women workers.   It collects, analyzes, and publishes information on employment, legislation concerning women, problems of special groups, such as older women or Negro women, and the civil and political status of women.   Although it does not administer any laws, it supplies information and makes recommendations on proposed laws.[5] It might be called the watchdog of women's public rights.

The equality sought by the feminist movement, now incorporated in many laws and guarded by the Women's Bureau, has carried over into the family, where it is interpreted as a partnership between husband and wife. This partnership is a new value of the family that gives the wife many rights she did not have previously, but also gives her added responsibilities.

The second value-making movement is the series of White House Conferences on children.   The effect of these has been to establish the child as a personality in his own right rather than as an adjunct of the family for its use or pleasure; at the same time, the family has been held to be the central agency in the child's development.   The first White House Conference, on the Care of Dependent Children, convened in 1909 at the call of President Theodore Roosevelt.   It emphasized the need of each child for home life as the most important force in his life.   It was concluded that the child should not be deprived of his home except in cases of extreme unsuitability.   An immediate outcome was the establishment by states of systems of Mother's Aid, whereby certain classes of mothers deprived of a husband's support could receive financial aid to enable them to maintain a home for their children.   The movement for such aid culminated in the Aid to Dependent Children as part of the Social Security Act of 1935, whereby federal and state governments cooperate in granting aid for the maintenance of homes when the husband is dead or for certain reasons is unable to support his family.   Another result of the 1909 conference was the establishment of the Federal Children's Bureau in 1912 whose function is "to investigate and report upon all matters pertaining to the welfare of children and child life among all classes of our people."   Specifically, the Children's Bureau has been concerned with infant mortality, the birth rate, orphanages, juvenile courts, desertion,

---

[5] *The Women's Bureau, Its Purpose, Its Functions* (Women's Bureau), folder undated.

dangerous occupations, accidents to and diseases of children, employment of children, and legislation affecting children.[6]

The repetitive nature of the White House Conference keeps the cause of children constantly before the public and points out new needs at ten-year intervals.   The conference of 1919 was devoted to Child Welfare Standards.   The conference of 1930 on Child Health and Protection was preceded by extensive research, which was reported at the time of the conference.   The 1940 conference emphasized the position of children in a democracy, and that of 1950 stated that its purpose was "to consider how we can develop in children the mental, emotional, and spiritual quali-ties essential to individual happiness and to responsible citizenship, and what physical, economic, and social conditions are deemed necessary to this development."[7]   This conference differed from preceding ones in two respects: it received a Congressional grant of money, insufficient for the needs of the conference but conveying an official status beyond that of earlier conferences; and groups invited to prepare for and participate in the conferences included citizens' committees as well as the customary specialists and research workers.   A strong follow-up in community dis-cussions and action was urged.

These successive conferences keep alive the importance of children, reaffirm the value of the home to the child, and give the home supportive aid through revitalized agencies and new services.   Since the conferences are attended by professional and lay delegates from all parts of the United States, the findings of the conferences tend to filter back into local com-munities and to give some uniformity to the formation of values as well as service to children.

The third national movement important to the creation of new family values is in an incipient stage.   The feeling that a national conference on family life, called by the White House as are the children's conferences, would help to clear up confusion about the family was expressed in 1938 at the first annual meeting of the National Council on Family Relations.[8]

[6] A brief summary of the White House Conferences on children is given in Mar-garet B. Hodges, editor, *Social Work Year Book, 1949* (Russell Sage Foundation, 1949), pp. 100, 103.
[7] Kathryn Close, "Everybody's Business—the Young of the Nation," *Survey,* 86 (1950), 535–540.
[8] Evelyn Millis Duvall, "Organization of Social Forces to Promote Family Stabil-ity," *The Annals* of the American Academy of Political and Social Science, 272 (November, 1950), 83.

It was not until 1944, however, that practical action began at the annual meeting of the American Home Economics Association; four years later, in May, 1948, the conference was held in Washington, D.C. The implication is that future conferences may be held. The first conference enlisted specialists to prepare factual material on the family prior to the conference, and members of professional groups to prepare reports on ten action areas. Preliminary discussions were held by numerous organizations. The conference was well attended by varied representatives, was adequately reported in newspapers and journals, and produced later repercussions in conferences and activities on the part of organizations and local communities.

This first National Conference on Family Life avoided the task of formulating definite values, although values were stated or implied in many of the individual addresses. A preconference article by Lawrence K. Frank stressed the need for a national policy for the family.[9] Defining a policy as "a formulation of long term goals and purposes and of the values and aspirations by which those goals and purposes are not only defined but are to be translated into activities and practices," Frank urged integration of the many agencies and professions now offering services to the family. At other points in the article, however, he seems to assume that values to guide the family have been established and are well known, although he does not enumerate them. Charles S. Johnson, President of Fisk University, in an address at the conference stated that "Many of the old values have lost their sacredness with such swiftness and completeness that our first reaction is likely to be one of despair and even horror," but that "What we are viewing in terms of disintegration may well be studied as phases of a deep and far reaching recasting of the role of the family and the role of women in western culture." [10] He posits as the two most important functions of the family the satisfaction of affectional response needs and socialization of personality patterning. He does not press behind the functions to find values.

It is perhaps to be expected that in the first holding of a conference

[9] "A National Policy for the Family," *Marriage and Family Living,* 10 (1948), 1–4. Mr. Frank is Director of the Caroline Zachry Institute and at the time of his article was President of the National Council on Family Relations and very active in the National Conference on Family Life.

[10] "Disintegrating Factors in Family Life," *Marriage and Family Living,* 10 (1948), 53–55.

attended by diverse groups it would be inadvisable to attempt to formulate values; but it is equally to be hoped that if similar meetings occur in the future, values will begin to emerge from the joint discussions.

In addition to these organized movements concerned with redefining marital and family values are the public statements of people who have given special attention to trends in family life and emerging valuations. Since each person speaks only for himself, we cannot be sure how far consensus of opinion on values would go among these specialists.

A number of the specialists cite stability as a desirable value of family life. By stability, however, they do not mean automatic continuity of marriage until it is terminated by the death of one spouse. Goode, after a careful consideration of various goals involving stability, happiness, and child rearing, concludes that the most widely accepted goal now is "family stability based on happiness." [11] Another sociologist carries the concept of stability further to include sufficient resiliency within the family to enable it to come back to normality in time of crisis and to maintain inter-relationships that contribute to the emotional needs of the family members.[12] Stability is not conceived of as identical with continuity of the marriage; it is a special quality of marriage that enables individuals to achieve goals of their own while remaining married. It follows that when husband or wife no longer feels that the marriage contributes to his goals or happiness, divorce is the next step. Students of marriage now tend to take a middle ground on the subject of divorce: they do not condemn it; neither do they openly advocate it; rather, they recognize it as a logical conclusion to the conception of marriage whose highest value is the happiness or fulfillment of personal needs of husband and wife.[13] High valuation is thus not placed upon marriage permanence per se, but upon a marriage of sufficient value to husband and wife that they voluntarily continue the relationship.

Happiness and emotional needs are not narrowly conceived. More rounded statements speak of companionship, emotional security, personality development, and maximum expression of the personality. The

[11] William J. Goode, "Social Engineering and the Divorce Problem," *The Annals* of the American Academy of Political and Social Science, 272 (1950), 86–89. Volume 272 of *The Annals* is entitled "Toward Family Stability."

[12] Ray H. Abrams, "The Concept of Family Stability," *ibid.*, p. 7; Reuben Hill, "The American Family: Problem or Solution?" *American Journal of Sociology,* 53 (1947), 125–130.

[13] Adoph S. Tomars, "Human Relations in a Changing Society," Ethical Frontiers Pamphlets (New York Society for Ethical Culture, 1949), pp. 28–30.

family in its ideal form is less concerned with housekeeping and more with homemaking, less with material needs and more with personality needs, than formerly.[14]

The equalitarian or partnership aspect of marriage has already been discussed as a value that was furthered by the feminist movement. Present-day writers on trends in family values almost unanimously identify an equalitarian relationship as of high value. It is widely spoken of as democracy in family life and as of value to children as well as parents.

Also unanimously accepted (and already discussed) is the tremendous value placed upon the personality development of children, with the family designated as the place where wholesome personalities are most readily nurtured.

Beyond these four values or goals for marriage and the family—fulfillment of personality needs, stability based upon such fulfillment, equalitarian relationships, and fine personality development of children—it is difficult to discover trends of sufficient strength to indicate consensus of opinion. It should be noted, also, that these values have not as yet been accomplished in full; they are in the nature of future goals toward which families and family agencies may work.

At the same time that these new values are emerging, the spokesmen for other groups reaffirm traditional values. Perhaps the most articulate group is the Catholic Church, whose values relating to marriage and the family are very different from those emerging from present urbanized society. Believing in unchanging, sacred values, the Church conceives of matrimony as instituted by God and subject to sacred laws. Family life, based on stable, monogamous marriage, is of high value. Divorce is forbidden. Sex receives sanction as the natural means provided for production of children, who are of extreme importance to the Church and to their parents, but is condemned as an end in itself; therefore contraceptives, which interfere with the divine plan for children, are prohibited. Woman's basic function is to bear children and rear them in the Catholic faith. She therefore fulfills an important obligation and merits respect and reverence. Matched with the woman's role of mother and homemaker is the husband's role of provider and head of the family. Gainful

---

[14] Hill, *op. cit.;* R. J. Havighurst, "The American Family, Essential and Accidental Functions," *Vital Speeches,* 14 (1948), 565–568; E. W. Burgess, "The Family and Sociological Research," *Social Forces,* 24 (1947), 1–6.

employment for a woman is discouraged as being detrimental to her fundamental role for which nature and God designed her.   Family life and children are of high value and financially should take precedence over costly pleasures or efforts to raise the standard of living.[15]   Marriage and family life are thus closely linked with religious beliefs, and the Church sanctions, approves of, and supports marriages that conform to the values it upholds.   These values in many ways resemble those commonly held a century ago.   Whereas many non-Catholics have now come to regard marriage as a social institution and, consequently, as adaptable to changing social conditions, the Catholics, regarding marriage as in accordance with divine laws, view their family values as immutable.   Nevertheless, in the United States Catholics live under the same social conditions as non-Catholics.   Will the Catholic Church be able to hold its adherents to the officially stated values or will the pressure of social conditions bring a deviation in behavior from the stated values?

Transfer of family functions

Many family functions have been or are in the process of transfer to other institutions.   This transfer often is regarded as indicative of the break-down of the family.   On the contrary, the transfer relieves the family of burdens that it cannot shoulder in an urban environment and thus releases it for more complete fulfillment of functions that are still retained. The transfer of functions has been going on for a long time, as the result of two factors.   First, the growth of cities has made it impossible for families to perform many older functions.   Physical protection, safe drinking water, disposal of sewage and garbage, and protection from contagious diseases must be handled on a community basis, for the safety of all.   These services, having long since passed to community agencies, now are accepted as the normal duties of the community.   Second, the highly specialized nature of some services has forced their conversion from family to organizational functions.   Medical care, education, and recreation are examples; specialists trained in these and other fields bring their professional training to the service of many families.   As people become accustomed to an outside service, they accept it, and the next

[15] For a complete discussion, see Edgar Schmiedeler, *Christian Marriage, An Analysis of and Commentary on the Marriage Encyclical* (The Catholic Conference on Family Life, 1312 Massachusetts Avenue, N. W., Washington, D.C., 1946); a brief summary is given in R. P. Odenwald, "Psychiatric and Religious Aspects of Marriage Problems," *Marriage and Family Living,* 14 (1952), 7–13.

generation rarely questions the loss of the function by the family. It is usually when functions are in the process of transfer that anxiety and suspicion as to the effect on the family arises. Even those who benefit by the transfer sometimes question the advisability of the change.

The following functions were once handled by the family but are now the responsibility of other agencies.

Regulation of marriage and family relationships by an outside institution (church or state) extends many generations into the past and is no longer questioned, although in some lines of the cultural ancestry families handled these matters themselves. Laws now regulate procedures for a legal marriage, rights and obligations of husband and wife, obligations between parents and children, inheritance, and dissolution of marriages.

Protection from physical disaster is handled by such special agencies as the military service and police and fire departments.

Education is the function of an elaborate system of public schools. Significantly, when public schools first spread across the country and pressure was put upon families to send their children regularly to school, many parents objected. They felt that the state had no right to deprive them of the work of their children or to make the decision as to how much education their children should have. They regarded free public education as a detriment to family life.

Health protection is shared by the family with a number of agencies. Public health agencies provide for control of contagion and conformity to sanitary standards; schools have added physical education programs, medical inspections, and healthful lunches to their programs; both public and private hospitals of many types are ready to care for the ill; doctors with many specialists are ready to assume responsibility for diagnosis and treatment.

Other functions have more recently been assumed by nonfamily institutions or are still subject to controversy.

Recreation has spread far beyond the family and is being claimed by special organizations. Community agencies such as park boards, settlement houses, some churches, and schools sponsor organized recreational programs. Commercial recreation has also had a phenomenal development through motion pictures, sports, public dance halls, and similar institutions that cater to large numbers of people.

Personality development, still regarded as one of the most highly valued functions of the family, has also become the task of a number of other agencies.   Schools, churches, youth organizations, child-guidance clinics, and many social-work agencies are concerned with the personalities of children.

Economically, also, the family has not held all its old functions.   Not long in the past the family was regarded as fully able to care for its own economic needs and to provide for dependents both old and young.   Inasmuch as the transfer of economic functions away from the family is now in process, this area is full of controversy.   Two movements have developed, toward compulsory savings, and toward the assumption by employers of financial responsibilities toward their employees not only during periods when they are working but also during periods of unemployment and after retirement.   Old Age and Survivors Insurance (commonly called Social Security) is a system whereby employers and employees of certain classes of occupations pay specified amounts to the federal government, throughout the years of employment.   The employee is forced to save something, and the employer to augment it.   At age 65, regardless of whether or not the employee needs the money, he receives retirement payments.   Provision is also made for payments to dependents both before and after the wage earner's death.   Unemployment compensation also represents transfer of economic function from the family to the employer.   Employers pay to the federal government a certain percentage of their total payroll, from which unemployed persons are paid provided they are employable and unable to find work. Again, the question of need is not raised.   Earlier provisions for payments in case of industrial accidents also place support upon the employer. In addition to these legal provisions for support from employers over and above payment for work performed, other types of financial payments are made by employers.   In the past ten years many industries have established pension plans to supplement the amounts received from Old Age and Survivors Insurance, thus assuming almost complete responsibility for support of their employees until death, regardless of how long they may live after retirement.   This revolutionary movement whereby industry and business take over a responsibility traditionally the duty of the family has interesting implications not all of which are clearly delineated.   We do not know the full effect upon choice of an occupation, status of the husband, family thrift, or plans for retirement.

Many industries and business concerns are moving into other areas traditionally within the family circle.   They provide recreational rooms and organized sports programs, assist young people in occupational choices by giving vocational aptitude tests, and help their employees solve personal or family problems through professional counseling.

Two areas in which there is agitation for other institutions to assume greater functions are medical care and housing.

At present medical care is provided for those who can afford the specialized and often expensive services of physicians and hospitals and for the impoverished who are completely unable to pay. The middle group with moderate incomes often finds itself handicapped. A movement for some form of federal health insurance supported by payroll taxes has been started, but so far has not resulted in any action. The high wages of the 1940's and early 1950's have made the problem less acute than it was in the 1930's. In addition, 80 or more programs have been established for hospital insurance, whereby people may make small payments individually or through their place of work in a group insurance plan, that covers the basic cost of hospital care. Doctor's fees usually are not included.

The movement for federal public housing that began in 1933 with the construction of 21,800 units in 51 developments under the Public Works Administration had resulted by 1949 in the construction of, or projected plans for, 220,000 units; additional units have since been made possible. The projects are built and managed by a local housing authority but subsidized by the federal government; tenants are selected from applicants whose income does not exceed a prescribed amount, which varies with the number in the family. Later, if the income exceeds the maximum, the family is required to move, thus making way for another low-income family. Families in public housing projects are not "down and outers." They are primarily families with small children whose income is insufficient for them to buy or build a home and who are unable to find suitable housing for their children at rents they can afford to pay. Old people whose income is small also find a haven in public housing projects. Negroes, often discriminated against in the matter of housing, frequently apply and sometimes have entire projects set aside for their use. Since the end of World War II, veterans frequently are given preference over other applicants. The movement for public housing meets resistance from certain business interests that see a threat to their own profits or fear a general movement toward government ownership of business. Others regard it as a democratic procedure whereby the government is strengthening the family by making available comfortable and sanitary housing at feasible rents.

Both the formulation of new values and the absorption of earlier family functions by other institutions represent reintegration of the family and other institutions into a coordinated social organization. The reintegration is far from complete, but the lines of development that have been traced indicate the trend of change. As the transfer of some functions comes to be more universally accepted as a necessary adjustment to urbanism, families will be able to strengthen the performance of functions remaining to them.

AMELIORATION

Social incoordination often prevents individuals and families from meeting their needs adequately. The effects of social crises on families have been discussed, as well as the difficulties originating in migrations, social mobility, and impersonal urban living. Families often need special help in making adjustments and achieving or restoring integration among their members. One source of such help is the ameliorative agency, whose primary function is to step in with supportive aid or remedial training when a family is having difficulty with some phase of normal functioning. Its work is usually short-term, a prime objective being to restore the family to independence. Ameliorative agencies should not be confused with the various institutions that have permanently assumed functions previously performed by families. These institutions provide services, open to all people of a certain classification, that are no longer regarded as the obligation of the family, whereas ameliorative agencies aid families themselves to improve or restore performance of functions still regarded as belonging to the family.[16] Thus amelioration preserves or

[16] In distinguishing between functions assumed by other institutions, which therefore represent a reintegration of family and society, and functions that are merely ameliorative, the following criterion was used. If the function serves all families of a large class, regardless of special hardship, it is regarded as a normal function of the institution that performs the service, and therefore reintegrative. If the function serves only families suffering a special handicap that prevents them from performing a function still regarded as belonging to the family, it is ameliorative. For example, Old Age and Survivors Insurance, financed by employer and employee and administered by the government, is now a normal function of industry and government to give support in old age—formerly purely an individual or family obligation. Old Age Assistance, however, is ameliorative only, since it is granted only to old people who can prove that they are in financial need; it is an ameliorative service of the federal and state governments offered old people in hardship.

increases the integration of the individual family, but does not materially increase social integration.

Ameliorative agencies are included in the loose classifications of social agencies and counseling services. Not all social agencies, however, are ameliorative: most agencies that work with youth are not, for they offer programs open to all boys and girls; some counseling services—for example, premarital counseling services open to anyone who wishes to come for educational purposes as well as those with acute problems—are not classified as ameliorative. Ameliorative services cover many areas of family life, often paralleling the normal services and sometimes being administered by the same institutions that provide other services to all families.

Laws not only set up the framework for the family, but also afford amelioration in certain cases of hardship. They make divorce available for the marriage that has become intolerable; they make it possible to compel the husband to meet his age-old obligation of support of wife and children; they provide for care and treatment of unmanageable children.

Ameliorative laws often are administered through special courts established to aid the family in trouble. The juvenile court, first established in 1899, has jurisdiction over all juvenile offenders (except of the most serious type), rather than the criminal court. Acting on the theory that the child is a ward of the state, the juvenile court intervenes under special circumstances between parents and child, typically when the child is delinquent, dependent, or neglected. Although not all courts achieve the highest standards of treatment, the ideal is study of the child in all phases of his life, treatment of the difficulties, and a total future plan for him. The services of such a court are offered, not to all children, but to those who do not respond to the programs available to the masses of children, such as those of schools or recreational agencies. Juvenile courts have now been established by legislation in all states, and some 3,000 are in operation.[17] Among other courts created by various states to aid the family that is unable to solve its own problems is the domestic relations court, originated in 1910 in Buffalo with jurisdiction over all criminal activities relating to domestic affairs, including paternity cases. Nonsupport and desertion cases and sometimes divorce cases are handled in domestic relations courts, which number about 175 and are found in

[17] Margaret B. Hodges, editor, *Social Work Year Book, 1949* (Russell Sage, 1949), p. 270.

approximately one third of the states. Family courts (first established in Hamilton County, Ohio, in which Cincinnati is located, in 1944) are another development; they tend to combine the functions of the domestic relations court and the juvenile court.[18]

To aid the family in need of legal advice but without funds, Legal Aid Societies, financed by voluntary contributions, have been opened in many cities; Legal Aid Committees of local bar associations give a similar service.

Regardless of the general prosperity of the country, many families suffer poverty. Some types of poverty linked to the economic structure or to the aging of the human being are being brought under control by such previously discussed means as Old Age and Survivors Insurance, industrial pensions, and Unemployment Compensation. But there are still many families who cannot claim insurance or pensions as a result of normal employment during their employable years. People whose working days ended before these provisions went into effect, those who worked for occupations not included in the law, handicapped, chronically ill, and mothers of young children all fall outside the normal provisions for support during unemployment. For these groups various types of ameliorative aid are available, but only for the person who can prove that he is destitute. As an example, Old Age Assistance, which was established under the Social Security Act, affords a minimum amount of support for old people. Though jointly financed by the federal government and the states, this aid is provided under a plan devised by each state; hence, the amounts differ from one state to another. The average monthly payment in June, 1950, ranged from $20.49 in Alabama to $70.68 in California, with an average of $43.85 per month for all states.[19] Aid to Dependent Children, another provision of the Social Security Act, makes it possible for mothers and children to remain together when the mother is a widow or the children for other specified reasons are deprived of their father's support. Again, financial need must be proved. The establishment of Aid to Dependent Children was an important step in giving the destitute family a bulwark against disintegration. In the colonial period, local authorities placed destitute children in almshouses; this system was followed by placement of children in individual homes as indentured serv-

[18] *Ibid.*
[19] *Annual Report of the Federal Security Agency, 1950* (U.S. Government Printing Office, 1951), p. 92.

ants, a plan that later developed into foster-home placement. Later the belief grew that the best place for the child is in his own home and that it was for the benefit of the child to aid the mother and make it possible for her to keep her children with her. Mother's Aid on a state basis began in 1911 and was succeeded in 1935 by the federal and state sponsored program of Aid to Dependent Children.

The educational system, in addition to schools for all normal children, also has facilities for special classes of children—crippled, educable feeble-minded, hard of hearing and deaf, those with defective vision and the blind. Some cities have special schools for problem children. In addition, states support residential schools of many types, for feeble-minded, deaf, and blind. Some states have residential schools for mentally disturbed children, and all have some provision for training of delinquent boys and girls. These varied institutions relieve the family of heavy burdens in the special care and training of many types of children who are not able to benefit from the institutions provided for normal children.

When families cannot care for their own health problems, special agencies are ready to step in. Public hospitals, nursing homes, and infirmaries absorb both acutely ill and chronic invalids. Special hospitals care for the mentally afflicted. The family, struggling with its ill at home, may call upon the Visiting Nurses' Association.

Mental health has been of growing concern over the years, with concentration upon treatment in the early stages. There has been, therefore, a widespread growth of mental-health clinics, counseling centers, and child-guidance clinics to aid the family unable to solve adjustment problems of its members. Since 1900, when there were only four psychiatric clinics in the entire United States, the number grew to 688 in 1949, 285 of which were for children only. The movement was given great impetus by demonstration child-guidance clinics established in the 1920's by the National Committee for Mental Hygiene with aid from the Commonwealth Fund.[20]

Important as ameliorative agencies and services are to families undergoing hardship, they do not modify the underlying causes of the hardships and therefore cannot prevent a recurrence of the hardship or its appearance among other families. As the family becomes more and more integrated into urbanized society and other institutions assume functions

[20] Hodges, *op. cit.*, p. 320.

that the family cannot handle, some of the hardships may disappear and the corresponding ameliorative services may not be needed.   However, if our standards for health, education, recreation, and personality development continue to rise, conditions now thought of as normal may come to be defined as hardships, thus creating the demand for new ameliorative services.

MARRIAGE AND FAMILY EDUCATION AND COUNSELING

Another supportive movement is directed toward individuals, couples, or family units who are in need of assistance in marital or family adjustment.   One phase of this movement is preparatory and is planned for young people prior to marriage; another phase of the service is focused upon poorly adjusted husbands and wives; and a third upon general family problems including children.   In part, the movement is educational, planned to forestall trouble; in part, it is correctional, offering treatment to those already in difficulty.   The same agency often offers both educational and remedial services.

Educational programs

Although still in an experimental stage, family-life education at the secondary school level is spreading rapidly.[21]   It is designed to aid the student prior to or during his early courtship days to consider basic problems of adjustment and to direct his attention to some of the problems of the first years of marriage.   Therefore the course is keyed to the students' present and future needs, with emphasis upon practical, everyday problems, such as dating, courtship, mate selection, premarital standards of conduct, desirable masculine and feminine roles and relationships, sex education, and parent-child relationships.   Through reading, lectures by specialists, discussion, and personal counseling, the student is helped to understand his personal problems.

As often is true in new fields, the quality of aid given depends in large part upon the special preparation of the professional staff.   Many teach-

---

[21] Many articles on family-life education have appeared in *Marriage and Family Living:* see especially the following articles by Lester A. Kirkendall, "Principles Basic to Education for Marriage and Family Life in the High School," 11 (1949), 131–132, 135; with Esther Handwerk, "Preparation of Teachers for Education in Marriage and Family Living," 12 (1950), 7–8, 19; "Family Life Education in the High School: Looking Ahead," 13 (1951), 109–112.

ers, especially the typical unmarried woman teacher, are hesitant about embarking upon a family-life course; the teacher needs not only to know the facts about courtship, sex, and marriage, but to have a healthful attitude toward these facts and to have solved any emotional problems of her own.

Community support is also necessary.   In some communities, parents, ministers, newspaper editors, and other adults have misunderstood the nature of family-life courses; school administrators therefore often carry on a general educational program in the community prior to establishing the course, drawing the Parent-Teacher Association, ministers, and others into a sponsoring group.   Much community misunderstanding collects around the unit on sex education that is a part of most of the courses. This one unit may become so magnified in the public mind that other aspects of the course are forgotten; thus, in one community, after a period of community sponsorship, one parent induced a local newspaper to print a sensational story about the teaching of sex in the public schools. Only careful community work again established support of the course.

At the college level, courses on preparation for marriage have had enormous popularity since the first one was given for credit by Ernest R. Groves at Boston University in 1924.   Soon transferring to the University of North Carolina, Groves further developed this type of course. Equally outstanding with Groves as a leader in college courses preparatory to marriage, is Henry Bowman, whose course at Stephens College is well known.   The course covers "the differences and similarities between the sexes; why people marry; why some do not and the problems they face; courtship and engagement and the problems involved in the pre-marital associations of the sexes and the relationship of those problems to marriage; choice of marriage partner; the wedding; the adjustment of personalities in marriage—as individuals regardless of sex, as individuals of different sex, as individuals subject to certain social influences and facing certain problems that usually arise in marriage; the use of money; the use of leisure time; reproduction; marital failure and divorce." [22]   The appeal that preparation-for-marriage courses make to students is evident from the large enrollments: at Stephens College each year between 300 and 400 students enroll, approximately 50–60 per cent of the second-year

[22] Henry Bowman, "Marriage Education in a Junior College," *Marriage and Family Living,* 8 (1946), 36–37.   Bowman has written a text for his course, *Marriage for Moderns,* and developed a series of films to open discussion.

class of this junior college; [23] a noncredit course running for 12 to 14 weeks given by the University of California at Berkeley draws about 2,000 students per year; [24] at Michigan State College the course given by Judson T. Landis when he taught at that institution drew over 3,000 students per year, with the course being offered four times a year. [25] Individual counseling often accompanies the course and is regarded by some instructors as a necessary part of the program. The preparation-for-marriage course should not be confused with the systematic study of the family given in departments of sociology, which emphasizes social background of the family as well as interactional processes within the family. The preparation-for-marriage course usually has no prerequisites; it is a "service" course, open to all—or to all students of a certain class level—and designed to aid students in a wise selection of a mate and management of their own courtship and marital adjustment.

The movement for premarital courses has fanned out into the community with churches, Young Men's and Young Women's Christian Associations, community houses, and other agencies offering short popular courses for young men and women. Catholics have developed a special program of education for married life called Cana Conferences; either half days or entire days are devoted to the discussion of marriage and family problems under an expert leader. For these many courses, special outlines, pamphlets, and textbooks have been prepared, "translating" scientific findings into popular language. [26]

It is difficult to know to what extent these many courses prevent marital unadjustment; it would seem logical to assume that as they reach more

[23] *Ibid.*, p. 37.

[24] Noel Keys, "Youth and Marriage Today," *Marriage and Family Living,* 8 (1946), 41.

[25] Judson T. Landis, "An Evaluation of Marriage Education," *Marriage and Family Living,* 10 (1948), 81.

[26] Three of the many agencies with helpful pamphlets are: The National Council on Family Relations, 5757 South Drexel Boulevard, Chicago 37; The American Institute of Family Relations, 607 South Hill Street, Los Angeles; and The Association for Family Living, 209 South State Street, Chicago 4. The Catholic point of view is presented in material published by the Family Life Bureau, National Catholic Welfare Conference, 1312 Massachusetts Avenue, N.W., Washington 5, D.C. A few of the recent books adaptable to popular courses are: Harold T. Christensen, *Marriage Analysis: Foundations for Successful Family Life* (Ronald, 1950); Evelyn Millis Duvall, *Family Living* (Macmillan, 1950); Evelyn Millis Duvall and Reuben Hill, *When You Marry* (Association Press, 1945); Judson T. Landis and Mary G. Landis, *Building a Successful Marriage* (Prentice-Hall, 1948); John Levy and Ruth Munroe, *The Happy Family* (Knopf, 1940); and Paul Popenoe, *Marriage Is What You Make It* (Macmillan, 1950).

and more young people they will gradually establish new and less romantic standards of courtship and lead to a previewing before marriage of problems that may arise later. To the extent that they accomplish these ends, they should lead to better marital integration and greater happiness and stability of marriage.

A slightly different educational movement offers to parents study programs that center on problems of children. Parent-Teacher Associations, organized nationally through the National Congress of Parents and Teachers, sponsor mother-study groups. Many other organizations, such as the Child Study Association of America, which publishes *Child Study*, and the Michigan Child Study Association, sponsor programs for parent education. Through these study groups parents are kept in touch with some of the newer findings in child psychology. Although there is a certain risk that what they learn is too fragmentary to be of much assistance to them and may simply create insecurity in their relationships with their children, if the leadership is good and the contact long continued this danger is reduced.

Marital counseling

The first marriage counseling service is claimed by Drs. Abraham and Hannah Stone, who established such a service in New York City in 1929.[27] Fully developed counseling services are still few in number, among the best known being the American Institute of Family Relations in Los Angeles and the Marriage Council of Philadelphia. Counseling is carried on, however, in connection with many smaller agencies as well as by teachers and ministers. Attention is given to problems of both the unmarried and the married. The service is becoming professionalized with development of standards of training and national coordination through the American Association of Marriage Counselors.

The field of marriage counseling is defined as primarily educational—to give young people and husbands and wives knowledge and insight into differences of viewpoints relating to areas of married life. People come to counselors seeking factual information, help in making decisions affecting their marriage, clarification of cultural conflicts between husband and wife, and understanding of personal differences. Sometimes they come with individual problems of maladjustment, neuroses, or even psy-

---

[27] Abraham Stone, "Marriage Counseling Today and Tomorrow," *Marriage and Family Living*, 12 (1950), p. 39.

choses; these cases are not regarded as part of the legitimate clientele of the marriage counselor and are referred to a psychiatrist or mental-health clinic.   The training advocated for the counselor is broad and primarily in the biological, sociological, and psychological fields, with special emphasis upon human relations and marriage and family fields.   He needs to know when to refer his client to a specialist in some field as well as how to aid him to understand and manage his marital problems.[28]

Family casework agencies also deal with marital problems, and at times seem to compete with marital counseling centers.   Family casework originally was preoccupied with economic problems of the family.   When the Social Security Act removed many financial problems from the private casework agencies through the creation of large-scale public relief (Old Age Assistance, Aid to Dependent Children, Unemployment Compensation, and so on), the private agencies had to redefine their function. They retained the family-adjustment side of their work and began to develop it, several substituting "family consultation," "family service," or some similar phrasing for "charity" in their names.   They differ from the marital-counseling agency in that they usually handle all types of family problems, parent-child as well as marital, and of whatever origin except the purely financial.   Many who come to them have serious personality problems and require some degree of therapeutic treatment on an individual basis.   This treatment may be provided by the psychiatric caseworker who typically staffs the family agency, or it may be given by a psychiatrist.   The family agency clearly overlaps the marital-counseling service in some areas, but it gives more extensive service and is also equipped to handle some types of personality maladjustment.   Marital counseling is narrower and more highly specialized in its concentration upon marital adjustment of essentially normal people.[29]

Counseling by teachers of family and marriage courses in high schools and colleges has already been mentioned.   Ministers also are especially interested in the field of counseling.   Based upon a background of ministerial help to people with personal problems, marriage counseling is a new specialization rather than entrance into a new field.   Many seminaries now give some courses in counseling to aid the minister.   It has

---

[28] *Marriage and Family Living,* published by the National Council on Family Relations, has specialized in marital counseling.   See Vol. 12 (Spring, 1950).
[29] Margaret B. Bailey, "Social Casework Training for Marriage Counseling," *Marriage and Family Living,* 13 (1951), 166–168.   For the casework approach to family problems, see *Journal of Social Casework.*

been pointed out, however, that the minister is only secondarily a marital counselor and that his training may not be as thorough as that of the professional counselor.[30]   Many ministers limit their counseling to premarital conferences with couples who request the minister to perform their marriage ceremonies, whereas others are beginning to extend their services to poorly adjusted married couples as well.   In addition to the usual counseling approach, ministers are peculiarly well equipped to draw attention to moral and religious ideals in relation to marriage.[31]

Counseling is both educational and remedial, aiding both couples in doubt about some information or line of action and those who have encountered some obstacle.   Like courses of study, counseling is aimed at integration and stability of individual families.

Training of leaders

Counselors find their training primarily in the graduate courses of universities.   There is great need, however, for training leaders who cannot attend the universities and for coordinating and pointing up previous training in terms of marital and family problems.   The summer workshop has become a popular and effective answer to this need. Stimulated by the National Council on Family Relations, workshops are now held in many sections of the country each summer.   Teachers, ministers, social workers, and key community leaders meet for one to four weeks, to engage in concentrated discussion groups under the guidance of specialists.   The participants then return to their home communities to use their new knowledge in their work or in stimulating new groups in study of the family.   To prepare leaders for the Cana Conferences, Catholic University each summer holds a workshop for leaders.[32]

RESEARCH

Many movements toward better societal integration and ameliorative and educational services are based on trial-and-error attempts to stabilize or otherwise aid the family.   Movements are not always coordinated, and sometimes much money and effort are expended upon relatively

[30] Sylvanus M. Duvall, "The Minister as Marriage Counselor," *Marriage and Family Living*, 9 (1947), 63.

[31] Commission on Marriage and the Home, *Premarital Counseling, a Manual of Suggestions for Ministers* (Federal Council of the Churches of Christ in America, 1945).

[32] *Marriage and Family Living*, 13 (Winter, 1951), is a speical workshop issue.

minor problems or upon the attempt to cure symptoms instead of finding the underlying causes. Gradually, research is providing information and analyzing marital and family processes. Sound programs make use of research findings and eagerly await new publications.

Popular though marital and family research is at present, it is a new field, offering many opportunities for different types of investigation. The present trends in research are indicative of the varied approaches now being made by widely different professional groups.

Demographic studies show long- and short-term trends in family life and offer basic data for isolating problems for further research. The United States Census, other official statistical reports, and attendant professional analyses provide information on number and types of families, their characteristics, and their dissolution, as well as trends in marriage and divorce rates, age of marriage, birth rates, and death rates. With the greatly increased interest in family research in recent years, official reports are becoming more detailed and appear with greater frequency than formerly.

Child psychology and child development have long been a special field of research for psychologists. Few sociologists have studied either children or adolescents, except juvenile delinquents. Since psychologists tend to emphasize individual development, an opportunity is present for sociological (or, better, interdisciplinary) research that would study the social roles of children and family interaction. Studies of adolescents would be especially helpful, with reference to masculine and feminine roles and the folkways and mores of dating.

With Kinsey's study of sexual behavior of males, biology has made a contribution to our knowledge of behavior related to marriage. A parallel study of sex behavior of females is reported in process. The Kinsey report set off a series of interdisciplinary conferences and stimulated a flood of books and articles that examined Kinsey's data critically and— of more significance—re-examined the lack of coordination between sexual moral standards and actual practice. Since part of the present indirection of the family is due to the inadequacy of old values and ideals, more research is needed in other areas to bring traditional values and present conduct into juxtaposition with one another. Divorce is in need of such study.

Family life in other cultures than our own has long been a subject of interest to anthropologists. Earlier studies were limited to the more formal aspects of primitive families—kinship groupings, formal family organization, lines of descent, and the like. The writings of Margaret Mead introduced a new approach in which primitive people come to life as human beings with motivations, emotions, and patterns of personal interaction. The newer studies of other cultures make possible a re-examination of many of our concepts regarding the basic nature of human beings, processes of personality formation in the family, and forms of marital interaction.

Sociologists, also, have found the family a fertile field for research. The first studies, historical in nature, produced Goodsell's history of the European family and Calhoun's of the American colonial family. Recently the development of the American Negro family has been thoroughly studied by Frazier. Rural and urban families have also been subjected to study. These studies analyze the family as a cultural product, changing in response to new social conditions.

Another trend of research has concentrated attention upon personal interaction within the family and especially between the courting couple and husband and wife. Mate selection and prediction of adjustment have received special attention. Since only a beginning has been made, research continues in these areas with frequent new publications. Burgess has been a leader in this field.

Changing roles and adjustment of roles within the family constitute another field of interest, which recently has come to new attention with the many articles pro and con on the best type of education for women. The increasing number of employed women also is drawing attention to the question of roles. Research is badly needed in this area.

A strong beginning has been made in studying the reaction of families to social crises imposed from without, with economic depressions and war separations and reunions as the two fields for study. These great social crises afford a unique opportunity for study in an area where experiments cannot be set up or hardships deliberately imposed upon families.

Personal conflicts between husband and wife are only partially understood. The tendency to explain them in terms of overt tensions has given way to recognition that underlying psychological and sociological factors are involved.

Many areas of research call for a multiple approach; it is encouraging therefore to know that specialists in biology, psychology, and the social sciences are converging upon the same marital and family problems.

As research findings accumulate, it may be anticipated that more rational efforts will gradually be made to readjust intrafamily relationships and the mutual adjustment between the family and other institutions. The exact form of family that will emerge cannot be fully predicted, but present research indicates the need for a family that is flexible, with leeway for individual development; adjustable to external social conditions; keyed to mobility and social change; interdependent with other institutions, and ready to accept important though limited functions, such as meeting personal and sexual needs, giving emotional security, and rearing children for life in an industrialized, urban society.

QUESTIONS

1. How did the development of urban living threaten the integration of the family in the total society?

2. What new family values and norms are developing?   What three movements have been important in their development?

3. The loss of family functions to other institutions often is regarded as a sign of family disintegration.   Is it justifiable to regard the transfer of functions as a means of strengthening the family?

4. Distinguish between reintegrative transfer of functions and amelioration.

5. Why is amelioration necessary for the family?

6. Is it probable that education for marriage and family life will contribute to greater stability of marriage and more marital happiness?   Support your answer.

7. Would it be advisable to require all applicants for a divorce to consult a marriage counselor or similar specialist in personal and social adjustment?

BIBLIOGRAPHY

Supportive aid for the family

Andrews, F. E., "Family Allowances for America," *Proceedings of the National Conference of Social Work* (1942), 216–228.

Hodges, Margaret B., editor, *Social Work Year Book, 1951* (Russell Sage Foundation, 1951).

Legal Status of the American Family (Women's Bureau, United States Department of Labor, December, 1950).

Sellin, Thorsten, editor, *Toward Family Stability, The Annals* of the American Academy of Political and Social Science, 272 (1950).

State Laws to Protect Family Health, A Summary of State Legislation Requiring Premarital and Prenatal Examination for Venereal Disease, 1935–1949 (American Social Hygiene Association, 1790 Broadway, New York 19, 1949).

Education for marriage and family living

Family Life Education and the Sixteenth Annual Library Number, entire issue, *Journal of Social Hygiene,* 35, No. 6 (1949).

Marriage and Family Living constantly publishes articles in this area; see especially Vol. 8 (May, 1946), Vol. 11 (Spring, 1949), and Vol. 12 (Winter, 1950).

Counseling

Benz, Margaret C., *Family Counseling Service in a University Community,* Contributions to Education No. 800 (Teachers College, Columbia University, 1940).

Berkowitz, Sidney J., *et al., Diagnosis and Treatment of Marital Problems,* reprinted from *Journal of Social Casework,* 1947–1949 (Family Service Association of America, 192 Lexington Avenue, New York 16, 1949).

Cuber, John F., *Marriage Counseling Practice* (Appleton-Century-Crofts, 1947).

Goldstein, Sidney E., *Marriage and Family Counseling* (McGraw-Hill, 1945).

Gomberg, M. R., and Levinson, Frances T., editors, *Diagnosis and Process in Family Counseling* (Family Service Association of America, 192 Lexington Avenue, New York 16, 1951).

Marriage and Family Living constantly publishes articles on counseling; see Vol. 12 (Spring, 1950) and Vol. 13 (Spring, 1951).

Group psychotherapy for marital and family problems

Caplan, G., "Mental Hygiene Work with Expectant Mothers, A Group Psychotherapeutic Approach," *Mental Hygiene,* 35 (1951), 41–50.

Levine, L., and Brodsky, J., "Group Premarital Counseling," *Mental Hygiene,* 32 (1949), 577–587.

Lloyd, W., "Group Work with Mothers in a Child-Development Center," *Mental Hygiene,* 34 (1950), 620–640.

Stone, A., and Levine, L., "Group Therapy in Sexual Maladjustment," *American Journal of Psychiatry,* 107 (1950), 195–202.

APPENDIX A

Marriage, Birth, and Divorce Rates in the United States

I. Number of marriages per 1,000 estimated midyear population *
II. Number of births per 1,000 population †
III. Divorces per 1,000 population ‡
IV. Divorces per 100 marriages occurring in the same year ‡
V. Divorces per 1,000 married women, 15 years of age and over ‡

Year	I	II	III	IV	V
1867	9.6		0.3	2.8	—
1868	9.0		0.3	3.0	—
1869	8.9		0.3	3.1	—
1870	8.8	(1871–75	0.3	3.1	—
1871	8.8	37.0)	0.3	3.2	—
1872	9.0		0.3	3.3	—
1873	9.0		0.3	3.4	—
1874	8.7		0.3	3.6	—
1875	9.1	(1876–80	0.3	3.4	—
1876	8.8	34.9)	0.3	3.6	—
1877	8.7		0.3	3.8	—
1878	8.8		0.3	3.8	—
1879	8.9		0.3	4.0	—
1880	9.0	(1881–85	0.4	4.3	—
1881	9.0	33.2)	0.4	4.5	—
1882	9.2		0.4	4.5	—
1883	9.3		0.4	4.6	—
1884	8.8		0.4	4.7	—
1885	8.9	(1886–90	0.4	4.6	—
1886	9.2	31.9)	0.4	4.8	—

Year	I	II	III	IV	V
1887	8.7		0.5	5.4	—
1888	8.8		0.5	5.3	—
1889	9.1		0.5	5.6	—
1890	9.0	(1891–95	0.5	5.8	—
1891	9.2	30.8)	0.6	6.0	—
1892	9.2		0.6	6.1	—
1893	9.0		0.6	6.2	—
1894	8.6		0.6	6.6	—
1895	8.9	(1896–1900	0.6	6.5	—
1896	9.0	29.8)	0.6	6.7	—
1897	8.9		0.6	6.9	—
1898	8.8		0.7	7.4	—
1899	9.0		0.7	7.6	—
1900	9.3	—	0.7	7.9	4.0
1901	9.6	—	0.8	8.2	—
1902	9.8	28.8	0.8	7.9	—
1903	10.0	—	0.8	7.9	—
1904	9.9	—	0.8	8.1	—
1905	10.0	—	0.8	8.0	—
1906	10.5	—	0.8	8.1	—
1907	10.8	27.7	0.9	8.2	—
1908	9.7	—	0.9	9.0	—
1909	9.9	—	0.9	8.8	—
1910	10.3	—	0.9	8.8	4.7
1911	10.2	—	1.0	9.3	—
1912	10.5	26.4	1.0	9.3	—
1913	10.5	—	0.9	8.9	—
1914	10.3	—	1.0	9.0	—
1915	10.0	25.1	1.0	10.3	—
1916	10.6	25.0	1.1	10.6	—
1917	11.1	24.7	1.2	10.7	—
1918	9.7	24.6	1.1	11.6	—
1919	11.0	22.3	1.3	12.3	—
1920	12.0	23.7	1.6	13.4	8.0
1921	10.7	24.2	1.5	13.7	—
1922	10.3	22.3	1.4	13.1	—
1923	11.0	22.2	1.5	13.4	—
1924	10.4	22.4	1.5	14.4	—
1925	10.3	21.5	1.5	14.8	—
1926	10.2	20.7	1.6	15.4	—

Year	I	II	III	IV	V
1927	10.1	20.6	1.6	16.3	—
1928	9.8	19.8	1.7	16.9	—
1929	10.1	18.9	1.7	16.7	—
1930	9.2	18.9	1.6	17.4	7.5
1931	8.6	18.0	1.5	17.7	7.1
1932	7.9	17.4	1.3	16.7	6.1
1933	8.7	16.6	1.3	15.0	6.1
1934	10.3	17.1	1.6	15.7	7.5
1935	10.4	16.8	1.7	16.4	7.8
1936	10.7	16.7	1.8	17.2	8.3
1937	11.3	17.1	1.9	17.2	8.7
1938	10.3	17.6	1.9	18.3	8.4
1939	10.7	17.3	1.9	17.9	8.5
1940	12.1	17.9	2.0	16.5	8.7
1941	12.7	18.9	2.2	17.3	9.4
1942	13.2	20.9	2.4	18.1	10.1
1943	11.8	21.5	2.6	22.8	11.0
1944	11.0	20.2	2.9	27.5	12.1
1945	12.2	19.6	3.5	30.8	14.5
1946	16.4	23.3	4.3	26.8	17.8
1947	13.9	25.8	3.4	24.2	13.7
1948	12.4	24.2	2.8	22.4	11.3
1949	10.6	24.0	2.7	25.1	10.8
1950	11.0	23.5	2.5	23.1	—

* *Vital Statistics, Special Reports, Summary of Marriage and Divorce Statistics, United States, 1949,* Vol. 31, No. 2 (Federal Security Agency, June 5, 1951), p. 24; *News Release* (Federal Security Agency, April 23, 1951), p. 1. For 1917–1919 and 1940–1949, armed forces overseas are excluded.

† Rates for 1871–1935 from A. J. Lotka, "Modern Trends in the Birth Rate," *The Annals* of the American Academy of Political and Social Science, 188 (1936), 2–3; rates for 1936–1948 from *Statistical Abstract of the United States, 1950* (Bureau of the Census, 1950), p. 63; rates for 1949–1950 from "Annual Summary for 1950: United States, by States," *Monthly Vital Statistics Bulletin,* 13 (April 24, 1951), 1.

‡ *Vital Statistics, Special Reports, Summary of Marriage and Divorce Statistics, United States, 1949,* Vol. 36, No. 2 (Federal Security Agency, June 5, 1951), 14, 24, 25; *News Release* (Federal Security Agency, April 23, 1951), p. 2.

APPENDIX B

Suggestions for Term Papers and Research Projects

I. The Family in Other Cultures

In this text, the discussion of families in other cultures has been limited to adjustment problems of certain ethnic families in the United States. Study of families in their natural cultural setting reveals the great flexibility of the family.

A. Folk families. Folk societies are biologically and culturally homogeneous, more or less isolated from outside contacts, and exposed to few innovations that disturb the social organization. The folk family can be studied profitably with two problems in mind: (1) the coordination of the family with other groups and institutions: and (2) the goals and methods of socialization of children in comparison with our goals and methods. Folk societies include most undisturbed primitive communities and also unsophisticated rural groups, such as plantation Negroes in the South and residents of some isolated mountain communities in the United States.

B. The family in urbanized cultures. Certain European nations, as they have moved from rural to urban conditions, have experienced changing family values and functions. In some, the government has undertaken to regulate and support family life to a much greater degree than in the United States. A study of these societies shows some of the problems that arise in deliberate manipulation of a traditional group, such as the family, and also—on a practical level—some modern methods of supplementing the family in urban society. Russia, Sweden, and England have all attempted rational control of family life.

II. Deviant Family Types in the United States

In the pioneering period, more easily than at present, groups could withdraw from the settled portions of the country to experiment with new social forms. Three of these experiments involved family forms that deviated markedly from the standard family pattern: the Oneida Community, which experimented with group marriage; the Shakers, who tried to eliminate marriage altogether; and the Mormons, who successfully practiced polygyny at one period in their history. Although all three have passed into oblivion, their study reveals the possibilities for family organizations different from our own, and also the pressures exerted by the larger community when experimentation carries a subsociety too far from the main culture.

III. Repetitive Studies

One need in social science is to repeat studies that have been made, either to check the validity of the original study or to compare and contrast, if the second study differs in some way from the original. Many limited studies have been made that could be repeated by a student or group of students. Below are listed some published reports of studies that might be repeated. The student should be sure to use the same schedules, questionnaires, and methods of analysis as were used in the original, if he wishes to compare his results with those of the original.

Richard Centers, "Occupational Mobility of Urban Occupational Strata," *American Sociological Review,* 13 (1948), 197–203.

A. B. Hollingshead, "Cultural Factors in the Selection of Marriage Mates," *American Sociological Review,* 15 (1950), 619–627.

J. T. Landis, "Marriages of Mixed and Non-Mixed Religious Faiths," *American Sociological Review,* 14 (1949), 401–407.

Clifford Kirkpatrick and Theodore Caplow, "Courtship in a Group of Minnesota Students, *American Journal of Sociology,* 51 (1945), 114–126.

Kenneth L. Cannon, "Marriage and Divorce in Iowa, 1940–1947," *Marriage and Family Living,* 9 (1947), 81–82, 98.

IV. Application of Analyses Presented in the Text

At various places in the text family processes are analyzed in theoretical terms. A history of an individual family could be analyzed according to the theoretical concepts. This procedure would both check on the validity of the theory and give the student greater understanding of family processes.   Analyses that might be applied are as follows:

Patterns of migration (Chapter 4)
The process of upward mobility (Chapter 9)
The dating-engagement sequence (Chapter 13)
The disintegration process (Chapter 17)

V. Expansion of Topics Treated Briefly in the Text

Many subjects that are merely referred to in the text may be of special interest to some student.   Suggested topics are listed below:

Adoptions
Annulments
Conceptions of marriage held by major religious groups in the United States (such as Catholics, Jews, Protestants, and Mormons) or by religious groups in other countries (such as Mohammedan and Hindu)
Critical study of prediction of marital adjustment
Divorce laws by states (comparative study)
Family adjustment of displaced persons in the United States
Interracial marriages of men in military service in the Pacific
"Momism"
Oedipus complex
Planned parenthood, or rational spacing of children

VI. Practical Plans for the Solution of Problems

Students planning to enter or already engaged in such activities as teaching, social work, or governmental procedures often are interested in practical plans and programs.   Investigation of programs in this country or abroad is of value.   Some programs of interest are as follows:

Education for family living at the high school level
Group therapy for premarital and marital problems
Marriage counseling
Marriage courses in colleges
Psychodrama applied to marital problems
Public housing
Publicly subsidized medical care

Index